D0131002

CCSP IPS
Exam Certification Guide

Earl Carter

Cisco Press

800 East 96th Street
Indianapolis, Indiana 46240 USA

CCSP IPS Exam Certification Guide

Earl Carter

Published by:
Cisco Press
800 East 96th Street
Indianapolis, IN 46240 USA

Printed in the United States of America 1 2 3 4 5 6 7 8 9 0

First Printing September 2005

Library of Congress Cataloging-in-Publication Number: 2004113728

ISBN: 1-58720-146-1

Warning and Disclaimer

This book is designed to provide information about the CCSP IPS exam. Every effort has been made to make this book as complete and as accurate as possible, but no warranty or fitness is implied.

The information is provided on an "as is" basis. The author, Cisco Press, and Cisco Systems, Inc., shall have neither liability nor responsibility to any person or entity with respect to any loss or damages arising from the information contained in this book or from the use of the discs or programs that may accompany it.

The opinions expressed in this book belong to the author and are not necessarily those of Cisco Systems, Inc.

The Cisco Press self-study book series is as described, intended for self-study. It has not been designed for use in a classroom environment. Only Cisco Learning Partners displaying the following logos are authorized providers of Cisco curriculum. If you are using this book within the classroom of a training company that does not carry one of these logos, then you are not preparing with a Cisco trained and authorized provider. For information on Cisco Learning Partners please visit:www.cisco.com/go/authorizedtraining. To provide Cisco with any information about what you may believe is unauthorized use of Cisco trademarks or copyrighted training material, please visit: http://www.cisco.com/logo/infringement.html.

Feedback Information

At Cisco Press, our goal is to create in-depth technical books of the highest quality and value. Each book is crafted with care and precision, undergoing rigorous development that involves the unique expertise of members from the professional technical community.

Readers' feedback is a natural continuation of this process. If you have any comments regarding how we could improve the quality of this book, or otherwise alter it to better suit your needs, you can contact us through e-mail at feedback@ciscopress.com. Please make sure to include the book title and ISBN in your message.

We greatly appreciate your assistance.

Corporate and Government Sales

Cisco Press offers excellent discounts on this book when ordered in quantity for bulk purchases or special sales.

For more information, please contact: **U.S. Corporate and Government Sales** 1-800-382-3419 corpsales@pearsontechgroup.com

For sales outside the U.S. please contact: **International Sales** international@pearsoned.com

Trademark Acknowledgments

All terms mentioned in this book that are known to be trademarks or service marks have been appropriately capitalized. Cisco Press or Cisco Systems, Inc., cannot attest to the accuracy of this information. Use of a term in this book should not be regarded as affecting the validity of any trademark or service mark.

Publisher	John Wait
Editor-in-Chief	John Kane
Executive Editor	Brett Bartow
Cisco Representative	Anthony Wolfenden
Cisco Press Program Manager	Jeff Brady
Production Manager	Patrick Kanouse
Development Editor	Andrew Cupp
Technical Editors	Jerry Lathem, Shawn Merdinger, Marcus Sitzman
Team Coordinator	Tammi Barnett
Book and Cover Designer	Louisa Adair
Composition and Copy Editing	Interactive Composition Corporation
Indexer	WordWise Publishing

CISCO SYSTEMS

Corporate Headquarters
Cisco Systems, Inc.
170 West Tasman Drive
San Jose, CA 95134-1706
USA
http://www.cisco.com
Tel: 408 526-4000
800 553-NETS (6387)
Fax: 408 526-4100

European Headquarters
Cisco Systems Europe
11 Rue Camille Desmoulins
92782 Issy-les-Moulineaux
Cedex 9
France
http://www-europe.cisco.com
Tel: 33 1 58 04 60 00
Fax: 33 1 58 04 61 00

Americas Headquarters
Cisco Systems, Inc.
170 West Tasman Drive
San Jose, CA 95134-1706
USA
http://www.cisco.com
Tel: 408 526-7660
Fax: 408 527-0883

Asia Pacific Headquarters
Cisco Systems Australia, Pty., Ltd
Level 17, 99 Walker Street
North Sydney
NSW 2059 Australia
http://www.cisco.com
Tel: +61 2 8448 7100
Fax: +61 2 9957 4350

Cisco Systems has more than 200 offices in the following countries. Addresses, phone numbers, and fax numbers are listed on the Cisco Web site at www.cisco.com/go/offices

Argentina • Australia • Austria • Belgium • Brazil • Bulgaria • Canada • Chile • China • Colombia • Costa Rica • Croatia • Czech Republic • Denmark • Dubai, UAE • Finland • France • Germany • Greece • Hong Kong Hungary • India • Indonesia • Ireland • Israel • Italy • Japan • Korea • Luxembourg • Malaysia • Mexico The Netherlands • New Zealand • Norway • Peru • Philippines • Poland • Portugal • Puerto Rico • Romania Russia • Saudi Arabia • Scotland • Singapore • Slovakia • Slovenia • South Africa • Spain • Sweden Switzerland • Taiwan • Thailand • Turkey • Ukraine • United Kingdom • United States • Venezuela • Vietnam Zimbabwe

About the Author

Earl Carter has been working in the field of computer security for about ten years. He started learning about computer security while working at the Air Force Information Warfare Center. Earl's primary responsibility there was securing Air Force networks against cyber attacks. In 1998, he accepted a job with Cisco Systems to perform IDS research for NetRanger (currently Cisco IDS) and NetSonar (Cisco Secure Scanner). Earl spent approximately one year writing signatures for NetRanger and developing software modules for NetSonar. Currently, he is a member of the Security Technologies Assessment Team at Cisco. This team is part of the Consulting Engineering department. Earl's duties involve performing security evaluations on numerous Cisco products as well as consulting with other teams at Cisco to help enhance the security of Cisco products. He has examined various products, from the PIX Firewall to the Cisco CallManager. Presently, Earl holds a CCNA certification and is working on earning his CCIE certification with a security emphasis.

In his spare time, Earl is very active at church as a youth minister and lector. He also enjoys training in taekwondo, in which he currently holds a second-degree black belt and is working on becoming a certified American Taekwondo Association (ATA) instructor.

About the Technical Reviewers

Jerry Lathem has been working with computers for 25 years and in the field of computer security for 15 years. He worked for ten years with the U.S. Department of Defense as a research engineer, working on both information security and computer security. He joined the WheelGroup Corporation (later acquired by Cisco) early in its start-up phase. He has a wide variety of experience, including performing security assessments, developing both defensive and offensive software, and prototyping the first Cisco IDS module for the Catalyst switches. He is currently one of the lead developers for the sensing technology in the Cisco IPS product line.

Shawn Merdinger is an independent security researcher based in Austin, Texas. He previously worked for the Cisco Systems Security Technologies Assessment Team (STAT) where he performed security evaluations on Cisco products. Shawn holds a master's degree from the University of Texas at Austin where he focused on computer and network security.

Marcus Sitzman, CCIE No. 9004, is a network security engineer in the Advanced Services for Network Security team at Cisco Systems. He has more than eight years of experience in the networking field. Since joining Cisco in 2000, he has continued to focus on security technologies and products. He currently provides Cisco customers with security consulting services, including security posture assessments, security designs reviews, and security product implementations. He is a repeat technical speaker at the Cisco Networkers conventions as well as other security conferences.

Dedication

Without my loving family, I would not be where I am today. They are always support all of the projects that I undertake. Therefore, I dedicate this book to, my wife, Chris; my daughter, Ariel; and my son, Aidan. I would also like to dedicate this book to my parents, Tommy and Rosemary Carter, because if it were not for them, I would not be here today.

Acknowledgments

First, I want to say that many people helped me during the writing of this book (too many to list here). Everyone I have dealt with has been very supportive and cooperative. There are, however, several people who I think deserve special recognition.

I want to thank Jeanne Jackson (the Cisco IPS course developer) and everyone else who contributed to the course's development. The course material provided me with the foundation on which to develop this book. The technical editors, Marcus Sitzman, Shawn Merdinger, and Jerry Lathem supplied me with their excellent insight and greatly improved the accuracy and clarity of the text.

Finally, I want to thank Jesus Christ for gracing me with numerous gifts throughout my life, such as my understanding family members, who have helped me through the many long hours (and late nights) writing this book.

This Book Is Safari Enabled

The Safari® Enabled icon on the cover of your favorite technology book means the book is available through Safari Bookshelf. When you buy this book, you get free access to the online edition for 45 days.

Safari Bookshelf is an electronic reference library that lets you easily search thousands of technical books, find code samples, download chapters, and access technical information whenever and wherever you need it.

To gain 45-day Safari Enabled access to this book:

- Go to http://www.ciscopress.com/safarienabled
- Complete the brief registration form
- Enter the coupon code XSP0-VN3O-PYWG-ZHOW-HWLQ

If you have difficulty registering on Safari Bookshelf or accessing the online edition, please e-mail customer-service@safaribooksonline.com.

Contents at a Glance

Contents

Command Syntax Conventions

The conventions used to present command syntax in this book are the same conventions used in the IOS Command Reference. The Command Reference describes these conventions as follows:

- **Boldface** indicates commands and keywords that are entered literally as shown.
- *Italics* indicate arguments for which you supply actual values.
- Vertical bars (|) separate alternative, mutually exclusive elements.
- Square brackets [ ] indicate optional elements.
- Braces { } indicate a required choice.
- Braces within brackets [{ }] indicate a required choice within an optional element.

Foreword

CCSP IPS Exam Certification Guide is an excellent self-study resource for the CCSP IPS exam. Passing the exam validates the knowledge, skills, and understanding needed to design, install, and configure a Cisco Intrusion Prevention solution. It is one of several exams required to attain the CCSP certification.

Cisco Press Exam Certification Guide titles are designed to help educate, develop, and grow the community of Cisco networking professionals. The guides are filled with helpful features that allow you to master key concepts and assess your readiness for the certification exam. Developed in conjunction with the Cisco certifications team, Cisco Press books are the only self-study books authorized by Cisco Systems.

Most networking professionals use a variety of learning methods to gain necessary skills. Cisco Press self-study titles are a prime source of content for some individuals, and can also serve as an excellent supplement to other forms of learning. Training classes, whether delivered in a classroom or on the Internet, are a great way to quickly acquire new understanding. Hands-on practice is essential for anyone seeking to build, or hone, new skills. Authorized Cisco training classes, labs, and simulations are available exclusively from Cisco Learning Solutions Partners worldwide. Please visit www.cisco.com/go/training to learn more about Cisco Learning Solutions Partners.

I hope and expect that you'll find this guide to be an essential part of your exam preparation and a valuable addition to your personal library.

Don Field
Director, Certifications
Cisco Systems, Inc.
September, 2005

Introduction

This book explains every major aspect of the Cisco Intrusion Prevention System (IPS). The book uses the information provided in the Cisco IPS course as a foundation and provides a reference guide that explains the Cisco IPS suite of products. It also provides useful tools for preparing for the Cisco Certified Security Professional (CCSP) IPS exam.

CCSP Certification and the CCSP IPS Exam

The network security market is currently in a position where the demand for qualified engineers vastly outweighs the supply. For this reason, many engineers consider migrating from routing or networking over to network security. The CCSP certification offers an opportunity to display proficiency in the security area. Passing the CCSP IPS exam is one of the requirements for attaining CCSP certification.

Remember that network security is simply security applied to *networks*. This sounds like an obvious concept, but it is actually a very important one if you are pursuing your security certification. You must be very familiar with networking before you can begin to apply the security concepts. For example, the skills required to complete the CCNA will give you a solid foundation that you can expand into the network security field.

> **NOTE** The CCSP IPS exam is a computer-based exam with multiple-choice questions. The exam can be taken at any Thomson Prometric testing center (http://www.prometric.com/Default.htm) or Pearson VUE testing site (http://www.vue.com). You should check with Thomson Prometric or Pearson VUE for the exact length of the exam. The exam is constantly under review, so be sure to check the latest updates from Cisco at http://www.cisco.com/en/US/learning/le3/le2/le37/le54/learning_certification_type_home.html.

Tracking CCSP Status

You can track your certification progress by checking https://www.certmanager.net/~cisco_s/login.html. You will need to create an account the first time you log in to the site.

Cisco Security Specialists in the Real World

Cisco has one of the most recognized names on the Internet. Typically, you cannot go into a data center or server room without seeing some Cisco equipment. Cisco-certified security specialists are able to bring quite a bit of knowledge to the table because of their deep understanding of the relationship between networking and network security. This is why Cisco certifications carry such clout. Cisco certifications demonstrate to potential employers and contract holders a certain professionalism and the dedication required to complete a goal. Face it, if these certifications were easy to acquire, everyone would have them.

Cisco IPS Course

The Cisco IPS official training course provides an explanation of the Cisco intrusion prevention solution through classroom instruction and lab exercises. Since it is based on the Cisco IPS course, this book provides a detailed reference to help you prepare for the exam. You can learn more about the course at http://www.cisco.com/en/US/learning/index.html.

Audience for This Book

This book is a reference of the CCSP Intrusion Prevention System exam topics. It provides assessment and study tools to help you prepare for the exam. It incorporates information on Cisco products from the endpoint products all the way up to the enterprise products. It also makes an excellent reference for someone who must maintain and operate Cisco IPS.

Before reading the book, you should have completed the CCNA certification or have an equivalent level of knowledge. Strong user-level experience with the Microsoft Windows 2000 operating system and a basic understanding of the IOS user interface are important. Furthermore, you should have taken the Securing Cisco IOS Networks exam or have an equivalent level of knowledge.

A valid CCNA or CCIP certification is a prerequisite for CCSP certification.

Organization of This Book

The book is organized into five major parts, an answers appendix, and a CD-ROM. Each part explains an aspect of Cisco IPS and helps you prepare for the exam. The parts are divided into chapters and subjects, described in the following paragraphs.

Part I: Cisco IPS Overview

This section provides a good overview of intrusion prevention systems. If you are unfamiliar with intrusion prevention (or intrusion detection), this section of the book is an excellent place to begin. It introduces the basic concepts you need to understand as you read other sections in the book. If you are familiar with intrusion prevention, you can probably skim this section. The only chapter in this section is Chapter 1, "Cisco Intrusion Prevention System (IPS) Overview."

Part II: Cisco IPS Configuration

This section explains the tasks necessary to configure your Cisco IPS devices. The first step is initializing your sensor. Then you need to configure the basic operational parameters. Finally, you can tune your sensor and the Cisco IPS signatures to match your operating environment. Except for the initialization task, the configuration operations can be performed using either the sensor's command line interface (CLI) or the Cisco IPS Device Manager (IDM). The chapters in this section include the following:

- Chapter 2, "IPS Command-Line Interface"
- Chapter 3, "Cisco IPS Device Manager (IDM)"
- Chapter 4, "Basic Sensor Configuration"
- Chapter 5, "Basic Cisco IPS Signature Configuration"
- Chapter 6, "Cisco IPS Signature Engines"
- Chapter 7, "Advanced Signature Configuration"
- Chapter 8, "Sensor Tuning"

Part III: Cisco IPS Response Configuration

Correctly configuring the response that your Cisco IPS devices provide during and after detecting intrusive traffic is vital to protecting your network from attack. This section explains the various signature responses that you can use when protecting your network (including the inline options introduced in Cisco IPS 5.0). The only chapter in this section is Chapter 9, "Cisco IPS Response Configuration."

Part IV: Cisco IPS Event Monitoring

Effectively monitoring the alerts generated by your Cisco IPS devices is crucial to protecting your network from attack. The Cisco Security Monitor is the graphical tool you can use to monitor the events being generated by your various Cisco IPS devices. The section explains how to configure Security Monitor. The only chapter in this section is Chapter 10, "Alarm Monitoring and Management."

Part V: Cisco IPS Maintenance and Tuning

Regularly updating your intrusion protection system and troubleshooting problems is vital to maintaining a high level of security on your network. This section contains the following chapters that explain how to update your Cisco IDS software. The chapters also highlight some common troubleshooting, maintenance, and tuning techniques.

- Chapter 11, "Sensor Maintenance"
- Chapter 12, "Verifying System Configuration"
- Chapter 13, "Cisco IDS Module (IDSM)"
- Chapter 14, "Cisco IDS Network Module for Access Routers"
- Chapter 15, "Capturing Network Traffic"

Answers Appendix

The "Answers to the 'Do I Know This Already?' Quizzes and Q&A Questions" appendix provides the answers to the questions that appear in each chapter. This appendix is available in printable format from the main menu of the CD-ROM.

CD-ROM

The CD-ROM contains a database of questions to help you prepare for the actual CCSP IPS exam. You can take a simulated exam or focus on topic areas where you feel you need more practice. There is also an electronic copy of the book on the CD-ROM.

Using This Book to Prepare for the CCSP IPS Exam

This book covers the published topics of the CCSP IPS exam (see "CCSP IPS Exam Topics" in this introduction). The book focuses on familiarizing you with the exam topics and providing you assessment and preparation tools. There is also a wealth of explanatory text, configuration and output examples, figures, diagrams, notes, sidebars, and tables to help you master the exam topics. Each chapter begins with a "Do I Know This Already?" quiz made up of multiple choice questions to help you assess your knowledge of the topics presented in the chapter. After that, each chapter contains a "Foundation and Supplemental Topics" section with detailed information on the exam topics covered in that chapter. A "Foundation Summary" section follows. The "Foundation Summary" section contains chapter highlights in condensed format. This makes for excellent quick review and study the night before the exam. The "Foundation Summary" sections of each chapter are available in printable format from the main menu of the CD-ROM. Each chapter ends with a "Q&A" section of short-answer questions that are designed to highlight the major concepts in the chapter. The purpose of the review questions is to test your knowledge of the information through open-ended questions that require a detailed understanding of the material to answer correctly and completely. The answers to the review questions are included in the appendix.

The CD-ROM includes a database of sample exam questions that you can use to take a full practice exam or focus on a particular topic. When you view your results, note your areas of deficiency and follow up with extra study in those areas.

Preparing for an Exam

As with any Cisco certification exam, you should be thoroughly prepared before taking the CCSP IPS exam. There is no way to determine exactly what questions will be on the exam, so the best way to prepare is to have a good working knowledge of all subjects covered on the exam. As you will see, this book does a thorough job of presenting the topics on the exam and providing you with information and assessment tools for mastering them.

You should combine preparation resources, labs, and practice tests with a solid knowledge of the exam topics (see "CCSP IPS Exam Topics" in this introduction). This guide integrates several practice questions and assessment tools with a thorough description of the exam topics to help you better prepare. Of course, if possible you will want to get some hands-on time with an IPS sensor and Security Monitor. There is no substitute for experience, and it is much easier to understand the commands and concepts when you can see alerts generated in real time. For this reason, this book provides configuration and output examples, diagrams and figures, and tables in addition to explanatory text to help you master these topics.

Besides hands-on experience, Cisco.com provides a wealth of information on the Cisco IPS solution and all of the products that it interacts with. Remember, no single source can adequately prepare you for the CCSP IPS exam unless you already have extensive experience with Cisco products and a background in networking or network security. At a minimum, you will want to use this book in conjunction with resources at the "Technical Support & Documentation" page on Cisco.com (http://www.cisco.com/public/support/tac/home.shtml) to prepare for this exam.

Assessing Exam Readiness

After completing a number of certification exams, I have found that you cannot completely know if you are adequately prepared for the exam until you have completed about a third of the questions (during the actual exam). At that point, if you are not prepared, it is too late. Be sure that you prepare for the correct exam. This book covers material for the CCSP IPS exam. The best way to assess your current understanding of the material is to work through the "Do I Know This Already?" quizzes, the Q&A questions, and the CD-ROM practice questions with this book. Use your results to identify areas of deficiency. Then use this book and Cisco resources to improve in these areas. It is best to work your way through the entire book unless you can easily answer the questions for a particular topic. Even then, it is helpful to at least review the "Foundation Summary" section of a chapter before moving on.

CCSP IPS Exam Topics

Table I-1 contains a list of all of the CCSP IPS exam topics. The table indicates the chapter where each topic is covered, so you can use this as a reference when you want to study a particular topic.

Table I-1 *CCSP IPS Exam Topics by Chapter*

Topic	Chapter Where Topic Is Covered
Identify the Cisco IDS/IPS sensor platforms and describe their features.	
Identify the network sensor appliances that are currently available and describe their features.	1
Identify the interfaces and ports on the various sensor appliances.	1
Describe the Cisco NM-CIDS.	1, 14
Explain how the NM-CIDS works.	14

Table I-1 *CCSP IPS Exam Topics by Chapter (Continued)*

Topic	Chapter Where Topic Is Covered
List the tasks for configuring the NM-CIDS.	14
Describe the Cisco IDSM-2.	1,13
Describe the IDSM-2 features.	13
List tasks for configuring the IDSM-2.	13
Distinguish between the functions of the various IDSM-2 ports.	13
Explain the various intrusion detection technologies and evasive techniques.	
Define intrusion detection.	1
Define intrusion prevention.	1
Explain the difference between promiscuous and inline intrusion protection.	1
List the network devices involved in capturing traffic for intrusion detection analysis and explain when they are needed.	15
Explain the similarities and differences among the various intrusion detection technologies.	1
Explain the differences between Host IPS and Network IPS.	1
Describe Cisco IPS signatures, alarms, and actions.	5, 7, 9
Explain the difference between true and false and positive and negative alarms.	1
Explain the evasive techniques used by hackers and how Cisco IDS/IPS defeats those techniques.	8
Install and initialize a Cisco IDS/IPS sensor.	
Describe the considerations necessary for selection, placement, and deployment of a network intrusion prevention system.	1
Install a sensor appliance in the network.	2
Install an NM-CIDS in a Cisco router.	14
Install an IDSM-2 in a Cisco Catalyst 6500 switch.	13
Obtain management access to a sensor appliance.	2
Obtain management access to an NM-CIDS.	14
Obtain management access to an IDSM-2.	13

continues

Table I-1 *CCSP IPS Exam Topics by Chapter (Continued)*

Topic	Chapter Where Topic Is Covered
Describe the various CLI modes.	2
Navigate the sensor CLI.	2
Use the CLI to install the sensor software image.	2
Use the CLI to initialize the sensor.	2
Describe essential sensor settings and explain how they can be used to meet the requirements of a given security policy.	
Describe allowed hosts.	2, 4
Describe user accounts.	2
Describe interfaces and interface pairs.	3
Define traffic flow notification.	3, 4
Describe software bypass mode.	1
Use the IDM to perform essential sensor configuration and administrative tasks.	
Configure network settings.	2, 3
Configure allowed hosts.	4
Set the time.	4
Create and manage user accounts.	4
Configure interfaces and interface pairs.	4
Configure traffic flow notification.	4
Configure software bypass mode.	4
Use the IDM to configure SSL/TLS and SSH communications.	4
Monitor events.	10
Shut down and reboot the sensor.	11
Use the sensor CLI to perform essential configuration and administrative tasks.	
Perform a configuration backup.	11
Verify the configuration.	12
Use general troubleshooting commands.	12
Monitor events.	12

Table I-1 *CCSP IPS Exam Topics by Chapter (Continued)*

Topic	Chapter Where Topic Is Covered
Describe Cisco IDS/IPS signatures and alerts.	
Explain the Cisco IDS/IPS signature features.	1, 5, 7
Explain how signatures protect your network.	3, 5
Describe signature actions.	9
Explain how the sensor sends SNMP traps.	12
Describe signature engines and their purposes.	6
Describe the engine parameters that are common to all engines and explain how they are used.	6
Describe the engine-specific engine parameters and explain how they are used.	6
Describe IPS alerts.	5
Explain the fields in a Cisco IDS/IPS alert.	5
Explain how signatures can be tuned to work optimally in a specific environment.	7
Describe the use of custom signatures.	7
Use the IDM to configure signatures to meet the requirements of a given security policy.	
Enable and disable signatures.	5
Tune a signature to perform optimally in a given network, including configuring signature actions, common engine parameters, and engine-specific parameters.	7
Create custom signatures.	7
Configure the sensor to send SNMP traps to an SNMP management station.	12
Explain how to tune a Cisco IDS/IPS sensor so that it provides the most beneficial and efficient intrusion protection solution.	
Define sensor tuning.	8
Describe sensor tuning methods.	8
Describe the IP logging capabilities of the sensor.	8, 9

continues

Table I-1 *CCSP IPS Exam Topics by Chapter (Continued)*

Topic	Chapter Where Topic Is Covered
Explain IP fragment and TCP stream reassembly options.	8
Describe Event Action Rules.	8
Describe Meta events.	1, 7
Use the IDM to tune a Cisco IDS/IPS sensor so that it provides the most beneficial and efficient intrusion protection solution.	
Configure IP logging.	8
Configure IP fragment and TCP stream reassembly options.	8
Configure Event Action Rules.	8
Configure Meta events.	7
Explain how to maintain a Cisco IDS/IPS sensor appliance, the IDSM-2, and the NM-CIDS.	
Describe the sensor image types.	11
Describe sensor image file names.	11
Describe service pack updates.	11
Describe service pack file names.	11
Describe signature updates.	11
Describe signature update file names.	11
Describe maintenance tasks unique to the NM-CIDS.	14
Use the CLI and the IDM to maintain the Cisco IDS/IPS sensor appliance, the IDSM-2, and the NM-CIDS.	
Use the CLI to upgrade the sensor image.	11
Use the CLI to recover the sensor software image.	11
Use the IDM to install IDS signature updates and service packs.	11
Use the IDM to configure automatic updates.	11
Use the IDM to restore the sensor default configuration.	11
Use the IDM to reboot and shut down the sensor.	11
Use the IDM to update the sensor license.	11

Table I-1 *CCSP IPS Exam Topics by Chapter (Continued)*

Topic	Chapter Where Topic Is Covered
Monitor the health and welfare of the sensor.	
Describe sensor error and status events.	12
Describe the Cisco Product Evolution Program (PEP).	12
Display PEP information.	12
Use general CLI troubleshooting commands.	12
Use the IDM to run a diagnostics report.	12
Use the IDM to view sensor statistics.	12
Use the IDM to obtain system information.	12
Explain how SNMP can be used to monitor the sensor.	3
Configure the sensor for monitoring by SNMP.	12
Verify the status of the NM-CIDS.	14
Verify the status of the IDSM-2.	13
Describe the Cisco IDS/IPS architecture.	
List the Cisco IDS/IPS services and describe their functions.	1
Explain how the sensor communicates with external management and monitoring systems.	1
Describe Cisco IDS/IPS configuration file format.	1
Describe Cisco IDS/IPS event format.	1
Describe sensor management and monitoring options.	1, 2, 3
Explain the features, benefits, and system requirements of the IDM.	3
Explain blocking concepts.	
Describe the device management capability of the sensor and how it is used to perform blocking with a Cisco device.	3, 9
Design a Cisco IDS/IPS blocking solution.	3, 9
Use the IDM to configure blocking for a given scenario.	
Configure a sensor to use a Cisco device for blocking.	9
Configure a sensor to use a Master Blocking Sensor.	9

Part I: Cisco IPS Overview

This chapter covers the following subjects:

- Cisco Intrusion Prevention Solution
- Intrusion Prevention Overview
- Cisco Intrusion Prevention System Hardware
- Inline Mode Versus Promiscuous Mode
- Software Bypass
- Cisco Sensor Deployment
- Cisco Sensor Communications Protocols
- Cisco Sensor Software Architecture

CHAPTER 1

Cisco Intrusion Prevention System (IPS) Overview

The latest technology to protect your network is known as an Intrusion Prevention System (IPS). Unlike a traditional Intrusion Detection System (IDS), intrusion prevention technology enables you to stop intrusion traffic before it enters your network by placing the sensor as a forwarding device in the network. This chapter provides an overview of this technology and how you can use it to protect your network from attack.

IPSs are the latest addition to the set of tools available to secure your network. This chapter defines the characteristics of an IPS and explains the terminology associated with IPS products. Cisco security devices that support this functionality are also identified. If you are unfamiliar with Intrusion Prevention technology, reading this chapter is vital to understanding the terminology used throughout the rest of the book.

"Do I Know This Already?" Quiz

The purpose of the "Do I Know This Already?" quiz is to help you decide if you really need to read the entire chapter. If you already intend to read the entire chapter, you do not necessarily need to answer these questions now.

The 10-question quiz, derived from the major sections in the "Foundation and Supplemental Topics" portion of the chapter, helps you determine how to spend your limited study time.

Table 1-1 outlines the major topics discussed in this chapter and the corresponding "Do I Know This Already?" quiz questions.

Table 1-1 *"Do I Know This Already?" Foundation and Supplemental Topics Mapping*

Foundation or Supplemental Topic	Questions Covering This Topic
Intrusion Prevention Overview	1, 2
Cisco Intrusion Prevention System Hardware	3, 6
Inline Mode Versus Promiscuous Mode	5
Software Bypass	4

continues

Table 1-1 *"Do I Know This Already?" Foundation and Supplemental Topics Mapping (Continued)*

Foundation or Supplemental Topic	Questions Covering This Topic
Cisco Sensor Deployment	9, 10
Cisco Sensor Communications Protocols	7, 8
Cisco Sensor Architecture	-

CAUTION The goal of self-assessment is to gauge your mastery of the topics in this chapter. If you do not know the answer to a question or are only partially sure of the answer, you should mark this question wrong for purposes of the self-assessment. Giving yourself credit for an answer you correctly guess skews your self-assessment results and might provide you with a false sense of security.

1. What do you call a signature that does not fire after observing normal user traffic?
   a. False positive
   b. True negative
   c. False negative
   d. True positive
2. Which of the following is a valid risk rating?
   a. High
   b. Severe
   c. 80
   d. Critical
   e. Catastrophic
3. Which of the following sensors does not support inline mode?
   a. IDS 4215
   b. IDS 4255
   c. IDS 4240
   d. IDS Network Module
   e. IDS 4235

4. Which software bypass mode causes the sensor to stop passing traffic if the analysis engine stops running?

   a. Auto
   b. Off
   c. On
   d. Fail open
   e. None of these

5. In which processing mode does your sensor passively monitor network traffic as it looks for intrusive activity? How many interfaces does it require?

   a. Promiscuous, 1 interface
   b. Inline, 1 interface
   c. Promiscuous, 2 interfaces
   d. Inline, 2 interfaces

6. Which of the following appliance sensors is diskless so that it can provide greater reliability?

   a. IDS 4215
   b. IDS 4235
   c. IDS 4240
   d. IDS 4250
   e. IDS 4210

7. Which standard defines a product independent standard for communicating security device events?

   a. SDEE
   b. LDAP
   c. RDEP
   d. TLS
   e. IDIOM

8. Which communication protocol does your sensor use to communicate event messages to other Cisco IPS devices on the network?

   a. IDIOM
   b. SMTP
   c. RDEP
   d. SDEE
   e. None of these

9. What is the name of the boundary between your network and your business partner's network?

   a. Internet boundary

   b. Extranet boundary

   c. Intranet boundary

   d. Remote-access boundary

10. Which of the following are internal boundaries that separate network segments within a network?

   a. Intranet boundaries

   b. Internet boundaries

   c. Extranet boundaries

   d. Segment boundaries

   e. None of these

The answers to the "Do I Know This Already?" quiz are found in the appendix. After correcting your quiz, count the number of correct answers to determine your next objective:

- **8 or less overall score**—Read the entire chapter, including the "Foundation and Supplemental Topics," "Foundation Summary," and Q&A sections.
- **9 or 10 overall score**—If you want more review on these topics, skip to the "Foundation Summary" section of this chapter and then go to the Q&A section. Otherwise, move to the next chapter.

Foundation and Supplemental Topics

Cisco Intrusion Prevention Solution

Proactively protecting your network resources is the latest trend in security. Most Intrusion Detection Systems (IDS) passively monitor your network for signs of intrusive activity. When intrusive activity is detected, the IDS provides the capability to block further intrusive activity from the suspect host. This reactive approach does not prevent the initial attack traffic from reaching the targeted device. An Intrusion Prevention System (IPS), however, can proactively stop even the initial attack traffic. This chapter provides an overview of the Cisco IPS solution by focusing on the following topics:

- Intrusion Prevention Overview
- Cisco Intrusion Prevention System Hardware
- Inline Mode Versus Promiscuous Mode
- Software Bypass
- Cisco Sensor Deployment
- Cisco Sensor Communications Protocols

Intrusion Prevention Overview

Since intrusion prevention is a relatively new technology, it is helpful to review how it differs from a traditional IDS and to explain the terms commonly used in discussions on this subject. This review and explanation will be covered by the following topics:

- Intrusion-Prevention Terminology
- IPS/IDS Triggers
- IPS/IDS Monitoring Locations
- Cisco Hybrid IPS/IDS Solution
- Risk Rating
- Meta-Event Generator
- Inline Deep-Packet Inspection

Intrusion-Prevention Terminology

Table 1-2 describes the primary terms that are used to describe the functionality of the Cisco IPS solution.

Table 1-2 *Primary IPS Terminology*

Terminology	Description
Inline mode	Examining network traffic while having the ability to stop intrusive traffic from reaching the target system
Promiscuous mode	Passively examining network traffic for intrusive behavior
Signature engine	An engine that supports signatures that share common characteristics (such as same protocol)
Meta-Event Generator	The capability to define meta signatures based on multiple existing signatures
Atomic signature	A signature that triggers based on the contents of a single packet
Flow-based signature	A signature that triggers based on the information contained in a sequence of packets between two systems (such as the packets in a TCP connection)
Behavior-based signature	A signature that triggers when traffic deviates from regular user behavior
Anomaly-based signature	A signature that triggers when traffic exceeds a configured normal baseline
False negative	A situation in which a detection system fails to detect intrusive traffic although there is a signature designed to catch that activity
False positive	A situation in which normal user activity (instead of intrusive activity) triggers an alarm
True negative	A situation in which a signature does not fire during normal user traffic on the network
True positive	A situation in which a signature fires correctly when intrusive traffic for that signature is detected on the network (The signature correctly identifies an attack against the network.)
Deep-packet inspection	Decoding protocols and examining entire packets to allow for policy enforcement based on actual protocol traffic (not just a specific port number)
Event correlation	Associating multiple alarms or events with a single attack
Risk rating (RR)	A threat rating based on numerous factors besides just the attack severity

> **NOTE** Some systems refer to promiscuous mode as passive mode. Both of these terms refer to passively examining network traffic.

IPS/IDS Triggers

The purpose of any IPS/IDS is to detect when an intruder is attacking your network. Not every IDS/IPS, however, uses the same *triggering mechanisms* to generate intrusion alarms. There are three major triggering mechanisms used by current intrusion systems:

- Anomaly detection
- Misuse detection
- Protocol analysis

> **NOTE** *Triggering mechanisms* refer to the action that causes the IDS/IPS to generate an alarm. The triggering mechanism for a home burglar alarm could be a window breaking. A network IDS may trigger an alarm if it sees a packet to a certain port with specific data in it. A host-based IPS/IDS may generate an alarm if a certain system call is executed. Anything that can reliably signal an intrusion can be used as a triggering mechanism.

Anomaly Detection

Anomaly detection is also sometimes referred to as profile-based detection. With anomaly detection, you must build profiles that define what activity is considered normal. These profiles can be learned over a period of time or they can be modeled on historical behavior. After defining which traffic or activity is considered normal, then anything that deviates from this normal profile generates an alert (since it is abnormal).

The main advantage of anomaly detection is that the alarms generated are not based on signatures for specific known attacks. Instead, they are based on a profile that defines normal user activity. Therefore, an anomaly-based intrusion system can generate alarms for previously unpublished attacks, as long as the new attack deviates from normal user activity by a significant amount.

Misuse Detection

Misuse detection, also known as signature-based detection, looks for intrusive activity that matches specific signatures. These signatures are based on a set of rules that match typical patterns and exploits used by attackers to gain access to your network. Highly skilled network engineers research known attacks and vulnerabilities to develop the rules for each signature.

Some of the benefits of misuse detection are as follows:

- Signatures are based on known intrusive activity
- Attacks detected are well defined
- System is easy to understand
- Detects attacks immediately after installation

Protocol Analysis

The final triggering mechanism is a variation on misuse detection. Misuse detection is looking for a specific attack signature in your network traffic. With protocol analysis, the IPS/IDS analyzes the data stream based on the normal operation of a specific protocol. Therefore, the intrusion system is verifying the validity of the packets with respect to the protocol definition and then looking for specific patterns in the various fields of the protocol or a packet's payload. This in-depth analysis utilizes a protocol's Request for Comments (RFC) as a baseline and focuses on two major areas:

- Verifying validity of packet (based on protocol RFC)
- Checking the contents of payload

Using protocol analysis, not only must the attack traffic match a valid packet for the protocol in question, but it must also then contain known attack traffic in the payload or protocol fields of the packet.

IPS/IDS Monitoring Locations

Now that you have a basic understanding of the intrusive activity that can generate alarms from your intrusion system, it is time to examine where your IPS/IDS watches for this intrusive traffic. The major IPS/IDS monitoring locations are as follows:

- Host-Based
- Network-Based

Host-Based

Host-based intrusion systems check for malicious activity by checking information at the host or operating system level. These intrusion systems examine many aspects of your host, such as system calls, audit logs, error messages, and so on.

Since a host-based IPS/IDS examines traffic after it reaches the target of the attack (assuming the host is the target), it has first hand information on the success of the attack. With a network-based intrusion system, the alarms are generated on known intrusive activity, but only a host-based intrusion system can determine the actual success or failure of an attack.

Network-Based

A network-based intrusion system examines packets traversing the network to locate attacks against the network. The network-based IDS *sniffs* the network packets and compares the traffic against signatures for known intrusive activity. A network-based IPS actually checks network traffic for malicious activity while functioning as a Layer-2 forwarding device.

> **NOTE** To *sniff* network packets means to examine all of the packets that are traveling across the network. Normally, a host only examines packets that are addressed to it specifically, along with packets that are broadcast to all of the hosts on the network. To be capable of seeing all of the packets on the network, the IDS must place the network interface card (NIC) into promiscuous mode. While in promiscuous mode, the NIC examines all packets regardless of their destination address.

A network-based intrusion system (compared to a host-based solution) has the following benefits:

- Overall network perspective
- Does not have to run on every OS on the network.

By viewing traffic destined for multiple hosts, a sensor receives a network perspective in relation to the attacks against your network. If someone is scanning multiple hosts on your network, this information is readily apparent to the sensor.

Another advantage to a network-based intrusion system is that it does not have to run on every OS in the network. Instead, a network-based intrusion system relies on a limited number of sensor devices to capture network traffic. Managing these various sensor platforms is accomplished through a couple of management platforms. Based on specific performance requirements, you can choose different sensor platforms to provide complete coverage of your network. Furthermore, these sensing devices can easily be hardened to protect them from attack, since they serve a specific purpose on the network.

Cisco Hybrid IPS/IDS Solution

IDSs passively monitor network traffic for intrusive activity. When intrusive activity is detected, the sensor can reset TCP connections and block future traffic from the attacking system. The initial attack packet, however, will still reach the target system. In Cisco IPS version 5.0, this mode of operation is known as promiscuous mode. It requires only a single sensor interface to monitor each network location.

With intrusion prevention, your sensor functions as a layer 2 forwarding device on your network. In Cisco IPS version 5.0, this mode of operation is known as *inline mode* and requires allocating two sensor interfaces (known as an interface pair) at each monitoring point in your network. The major advantage of intrusion prevention is that network traffic is examined in line, enabling your sensor to drop all intrusive packets before they reach the target system, as well as resetting TCP connections and blocking future traffic from the attacking system.

Cisco IPS version 5.0 enables you to operate your sensors in both modes of operation simultaneously. For instance, if your sensor has four monitoring interfaces, your system can operate in the following configurations:

- 2 interface pairs (both inline)
- 1 interface pair, 2 promiscuous interfaces
- 4 promiscuous interfaces

Depending on your network topology, you may want to combine inline processing and promiscuous processing to create a hybrid security protection solution. Inline processing works well in situations in which all of the traffic being examined goes through a single location (such as the Internet entry point into your network). Promiscuous mode works better than inline mode in situations in which the number of paths makes inline processing prohibitive (such as when traffic is monitored between numerous hosts on a single subnet). In promiscuous mode, your system can monitor all of this host-to-host traffic by using a traffic capture mechanism such as a Switched Port Analyzer (SPAN), whereas inline mode requires a sensor between each host pair.

NOTE The Cisco hybrid IPS solution also includes a host-based component through the Cisco Security Agent (CSA) product. Discussion of this product is out of the scope of this book. For more information on CSA refer to the documentation at Cisco.com (http://www.cisco.com/en/US/products/sw/secursw/ps5057/index.html) or the Cisco Press book *Cisco Security Agent* (ISBN: 1-58705-205-9).

Risk Rating

One of the limiting factors associated with IDSs is false positive alarms. False positives generate more work for your security analysts and can reduce their confidence in the alarms that the intrusion system identifies. To reduce the probability of false positives, Cisco IPS version 5.0 calculates a risk rating (RR) for alerts from 0 to 100 (with 100 being the most severe). The RR is calculated according to not just the severity of the attack but also the following factors:

- Event severity
- Signature fidelity
- Asset value of target

Each of these factors is discussed in the following sections.

Event Severity

The event severity is also known as the attack severity or the alert severity. This value weights the RR based on the severity of a successful exploitation of the vulnerability. The event severity can be one of the following values (listed from most severe to least severe):

- High
- Medium
- Low
- Informational

Signature Fidelity

The signature fidelity weights the RR based on how well the signature might perform in the absence of specific knowledge of the target. This value is a numeric value between 0 and 100 (with 100 being the highest fidelity). Signatures that are based on very specific rules will have a higher signature fidelity value than signatures based on more generic rules. For instance, consider the two Cisco IPS 5.0 signatures shown in Table 1-3:

Table 1-3 *Sample Signature Fidelity Ratings*

Signature ID	SubSignature ID	Signature Name	Signature Fidelity
5406	0	Illegal MHTML URL	72
5406	1	Illegal MHTML URL	0

These signatures are designed to detect illegal MHTML URLs in a monitored connection. The signature with a SubSignature ID of 0 examines web traffic (to port 80), and the signature with a SubSignature ID of 1 examines e-mail traffic (to port 25). Assume that you treat the fidelity rating as a percentage indicating the likelihood that the signature detected the traffic that it is designed to identify (not a false positive).

Based solely on the signature fidelity, there is an approximately 72 percent likelihood that the traffic is not a false positive when the web signature triggers. The e-mail signature, on the other hand, has a fidelity rating of 0, indicating that without any target specific information the alarm is almost guaranteed to be a false positive.

NOTE MIME (Multipurpose Internet Mail Extension) encapsulation of aggregate documents such as HTML (MHTML) is an Internet standard (RFC 2557) that defines a mechanism to enable a protocol to retrieve a complete multiresource HTML multimedia document in a single transfer. Although originally developed for e-mail messages, MHTML can also be employed by protocols such as HTTP and FTP.

NOTE Signature fidelity is calculated by the signature author on a per-signature basis.

Asset Value of Target

The final weight, also known as the target-value rating, is based on the perceived value of the target. This value is user-configurable based on the IP address. You can assign one of the following values (listed in order, from lowest to highest priority) to a specific IP address or range of addresses:

- No value
- Low
- Medium
- High
- Mission critical

The assignment of values to systems is a subjective process. The important point is that the asset values enable you prioritize the devices on your network based on their perceived value. For instance, you may use the following classification model:

- Mission critical—Server systems
- High—Infrastructure systems
- Low—Desktop systems
- No value—Guest laptops

Meta-Event Generator

Suppose that you determine that a worm attack against your network will trigger five distinct signatures. Traditionally, to detect this worm, your security analyst must sift through all of the alarms detected by the IDS and then determine which of those individual events represent the worm attack.

With the Meta-Event Generator (MEG), you can perform this event correlation at the sensor level. Assume that a specific worm attack causes five distinct signatures to fire when it is launched against your network. If worm attacks are bombarding your network, then the number of alarms being generated is extensive (since each worm attack instance triggers multiples alarms). Using MEG, you can decrease the severity of the individual signatures that the worm triggers and use a meta-event to identify only instances of the worm attack.

Inline Deep-Packet Inspection

By definition, IDS and IPS solutions incorporate signatures that trigger based on information that is located throughout the packet. Inline deep-packet inspection refers to the ability to perform actual protocol analysis on network traffic. Many applications (including malicious programs) attempt to use open ports to pass information through access control lists on your network. Using inline deep-packet inspection enables you to enforce your security policy beyond basic port numbers. For instance, this functionality enables you to prevent attackers (and applications) from sending traffic to or from port 80 unless the traffic is legitimate HTTP traffic.

Cisco Intrusion Prevention System Hardware

Cisco provides a wide range of intrusion detection devices. Having multiple sensor platforms enables you to decide the best location within your network to monitor for intrusive activity. Cisco provides the following types of sensor platforms:

- Cisco IDS 4200 series network sensors
- Cisco IDSM-2 module for Catalyst 6500
- Cisco IDS network module for access routers
- Router sensor
- Firewall sensor

Cisco IDS 4200 Series Network Sensors

You must understand the features, connections, and interfaces on the different appliance models when installing these devices on your network. Knowing the bandwidth limitations will help you determine which appliance model matches your network environment. The following models will be examined in detail:

- IDS 4215
- IDS 4235
- IDS 4240*
- IDS 4250
- IDS 4250XL
- IDS 4255*

NOTE The sensors marked by * are the appliance sensors most recently added to the Cisco IPS solution. These sensors use flash memory for storage instead of a regular hard disk. Using flash memory is more reliable than using a hard disk since flash memory has no moving parts.

Cisco 4215 Appliance Sensor

The low-end sensor is the IDS 4215. Its capabilities are as follows:

- Performance—80 Mbps
- Monitoring interface—10/100BASE-TX
- Command and control interface—10/100BASE-TX
- Optional interface—4 10/100BASE-TX
- Performance upgrade—Not available

The features on the front of the IDS 4215 sensor are shown in Figure 1-1.

Figure 1-1 *IDS 4215 Front Panel*

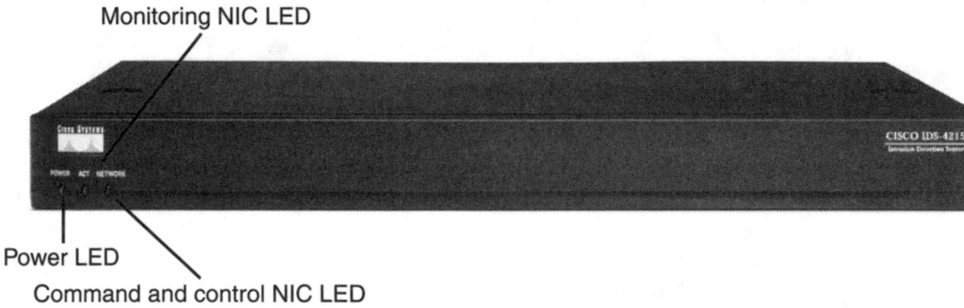

Most of the connections are located on the back of the IDS 4215, including the two Ethernet interfaces (see Figure 1-2). The command and control interface is on the right, whereas the monitoring interface is on the left. The monitoring interface is FastEthernet0/0.

Figure 1-2 *IDS 4215 Back Panel*

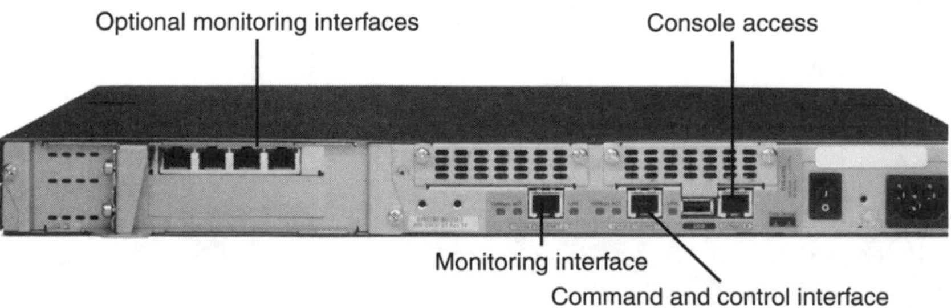

> **NOTE** When you use the optional four-port interface, the additional monitoring interfaces are (from left to right) FastEthernet1/0, FastEthernet1/1, FastEthernet1/2, and FastEthernet1/3.

The performance of the Cisco IDS 4215 sensor is based on the following factors:

- 800 new TCP connections per second
- 800 HTTP connections per second
- Average packet size of 445 bytes
- Presence of Cisco IDS software version 4.1 or greater

Cisco 4235 Appliance Sensor

The following are the technical specifications for the Cisco IDS 4235 sensor:

- Performance—250 Mbps
- Monitoring interface—10/100/1000BASE-TX
- Command and control interface—10/100/1000BASE-TX
- Optional interface—4 10/100BASE-TX
- Performance upgrade—Not available

The connections are on the back of the IDS 4235 (see Figure 1-3). The command and control interface is on the left (labeled 2), whereas the monitoring interface is on the right (labeled 1). The monitoring interface is FastEthernet0/0.

Figure 1-3 *IDS 4235 Back Panel*

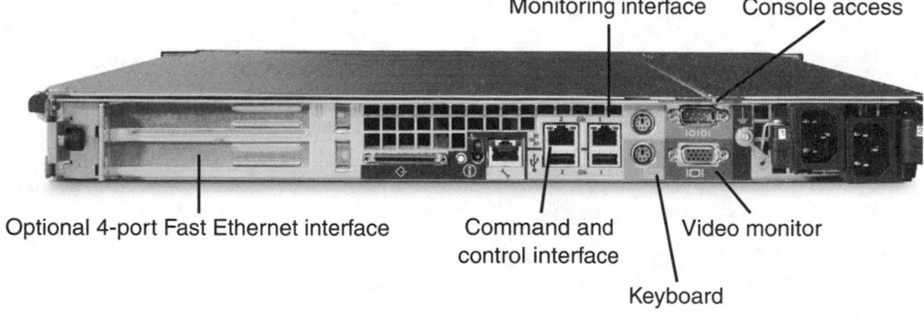

The performance of the Cisco IDS 4235 sensor is based on the following factors:

- 3000 new TCP connections per second
- 3000 HTTP connections per second

- Average packet size of 445 bytes
- Presence of Cisco IDS software version 4.1 or greater

Cisco 4240 Diskless Appliance Sensor

The following are the technical specifications for the Cisco IDS 4240 sensor:

- Performance—250 Mbps
- Monitoring interface—4 10/100/1000BASE-TX
- Command and control interface—10/100/1000BASE-TX
- Optional interface—4 10/100BASE-TX
- Performance upgrade—Not available

The connections are on the back of the IDS 4240 (see Figure 1-4). The command and control interface is on the left above the USB ports. The four monitoring interfaces are near the middle on the bottom (when interface 0 is on the right). The monitoring interfaces are GigabitEthernet0/0 and GigabitEthernet0/3.

Figure 1-4 *IDS 4240 Back Panel*

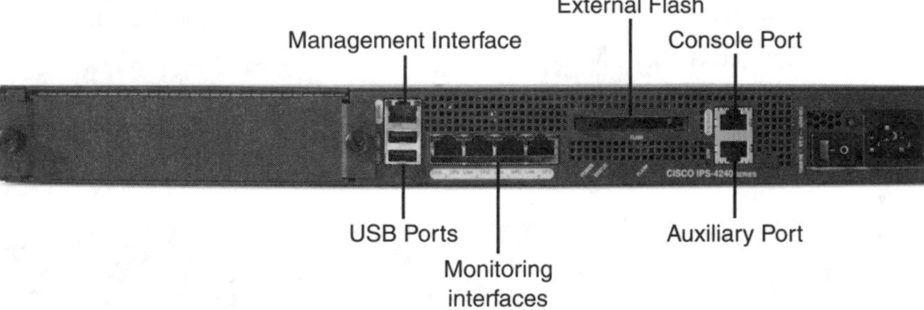

The performance of the Cisco IPS 4240 appliance is based on the following factors:

- 2500 new TCP connections per second
- 2500 HTTP connections per second
- Average packet size of 445 bytes
- Presence of Cisco IDS software version 4.1 or greater

Cisco 4250 Appliance Sensor

The following are the technical specifications for the Cisco IDS 4250 sensor:

- Performance—500 Mbps
- Monitoring interface—10/100/1000BASE-TX
- Command and control interface—10/100/1000BASE-TX
- Optional interface—1000BASE-SX (fiber) or 4 10/100BASE-TX
- Performance upgrade—Yes

The connections on the back of the IDS 4250 are identical to those on the IDS 4235 (see Figure 1-3). The command and control interface is on the left (labeled 2), whereas the monitoring interface is on the right (labeled 1). The monitoring interface is GigabitEthernet0/0.

The performance of the Cisco IDS 4250 sensor is based on the following factors:

- 5000 new TCP connections per second
- 5000 HTTP connections per second
- Average packet size of 445 bytes
- Presence of Cisco IDS software version 4.1 or greater

Cisco 4250XL Appliance Sensor

The following are the technical specifications for the Cisco IDS 4250XL sensor:

- Performance—1000 Mbps
- Monitoring interface—Dual 1000BASE-SX interface with MTRJ
- Command and control interface—10/100/1000BASE-TX
- Optional interface—1000BASE-SX (fiber)
- Performance upgrade—Not available

The connections located on the back of the IDS 4250XL are identical to those on the IDS 4235 and IDS 4250, with the exception of the IDS Accelerator (XL) Card (see Figure 1-5). The command and control interface (labeled 2) is the leftmost of the two built-in interfaces, whereas the TCP Reset interface (labeled 1) is the built-in interface on the far right. The monitoring interface is the IDS Accelerator Card ports. The monitoring interfaces are GigabitEthernet1/0 and GigabitEthernet1/1.

Figure 1-5 *IDS 4250XL Back Panel*

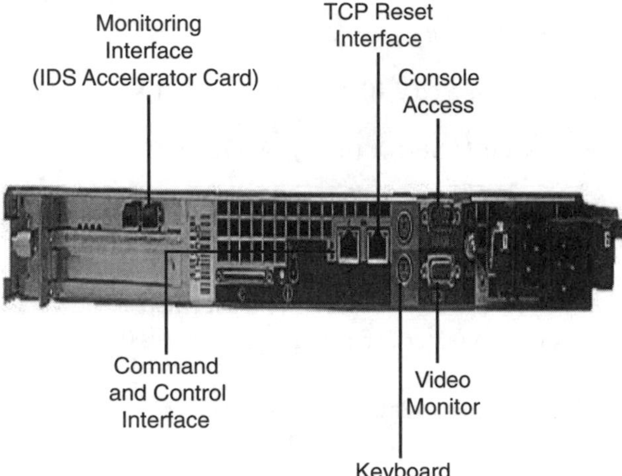

The performance of the Cisco IDS 4250XL sensor is based on the following factors:

- 5000 new TCP connections per second
- 5000 HTTP connections per second
- Average packet size of 595 bytes
- Presence of Cisco IDS software version 4.1 or greater

Cisco 4255 Diskless Appliance Sensor

The following are the technical specifications for the Cisco IDS 4255 sensor:

- Performance—600 Mbps
- Monitoring interface—4 10/100/1000BASE-TX
- Command and control interface—10/100/1000BASE-TX
- Optional interface—1000BASE-SX (fiber) or 4 10/100BASE-TX
- Performance upgrade—Yes

The connections on the back of the IDS 4255 are identical to those on the IDS 4240 (see Figure 1-4). The command and control interface is on the left, above the USB ports. The four monitoring interfaces are near the middle on the bottom (when interface 0 is on the right). The monitoring interfaces are GigabitEthernet0/0 and GigabitEthernet0/3.

The performance of the Cisco IPS 4255 appliance is based on the following factors:

- 6000 new TCP connections per second
- 6000 HTTP connections per second
- Average packet size of 445 bytes
- Presence of Cisco IDS software version 4.1 or greater

Cisco IDSM-2 for Catalyst 6500

The following are the technical specifications for the Cisco IDSM-2 (IDS Module 2) for Catalyst 6500:

- Performance—600 Mbps
- Built-in interfaces—2 10/100/1000BASE-TX
- Command and control interface—10/10 10/100BASE-TX
- Optional interface—Not available
- Performance upgrade—Not available

The performance of the Cisco IDSM-2 is based on the following factors:

- 4000 new TCP connections per second
- Average packet size of 450 bytes
- Presence of Cisco IDS software version 4.1 or greater

NOTE For more information on the IDSM-2 for Catalyst 6500, refer to Chapter 13, "Cisco IDS Module (IDSM)," in the section titled "IDSM-2 Technical Specifications."

Cisco IDS Network Module for Access Routers

The IDS network module for access routers deploys sensor functionality in low-end routers such as the Cisco 2600XM, 2691, 3660, and 3700 series routers. The following are the technical specifications for the Cisco IDS network module for access routers:

- Performance—Up to 45 Mbps
- Monitoring interface—Router internal bus
- Command and control interface—10/10 10/100BASE-TX

- Optional interface—Not available
- Performance upgrade—Not available

The performance of the IDS network module for access routers is based on the following factors:

- 500 new TCP connections per second
- 500 HTTP connections per second
- Average packet size of 445 bytes
- Presence of Cisco IDS software version 4.1 or greater

NOTE For more information on the network module, refer to Chapter 14, "Cisco IDS Network Module for Access Routers."

Router Sensor

The router sensor (Cisco IOS IDS) incorporates intrusion-detection functionality into the IOS software. Cisco IOS IDS can detect a limited subset of attacks that are detectable by the appliance sensor. The software and hardware requirements for Cisco IOS IDS are as follows:

- Cisco IOS software release 12.0(5)T or greater
- Cisco 830, 1700, 2600, 3600, 7100, 7200, or 7500 series routers

NOTE Beginning with Cisco IOS software release 12.3(T), Cisco IOS IDS uses the same signature engines that are available with the appliance sensors. Although with Cisco IOS IDS you cannot check for all of the signatures that can be checked with an appliance sensor (because of performance reasons), you can identify a limited set of signatures to check (choosing from virtually all of the signatures available on the appliance sensor). You can also create custom signatures that can be addressed in your specific network environment.

Firewall Sensor

The firewall sensor (PIX Firewall IDS) integrates IDS functionality into PIX Firewall software. A PIX Firewall IDS can detect only a fixed subset of attacks that are detectable by the appliance sensor. The software and hardware requirements for using PIX Firewall IDS are as follows:

- PIX Firewall software, version 5.2 or greater
- PIX models 501, 506E, 515E, 525, or 535

Inline Sensor Support

Beginning with version 5.0, Cisco sensor software supports attack prevention by operating in inline mode. The following Cisco IDS sensors support inline mode:

- IDS 4215
- IDS 4235
- IDS 4240
- IDS 4250
- IDS 4255
- IDSM-2

> **NOTE** Inline functionality is currently not supported on the network module.

Inline Mode Versus Promiscuous Mode

An Intrusion Detection System (IDS) passively monitors network traffic at multiple locations within your network by using IDS sensors. This monitoring is referred to as promiscuous mode because it involves placing a network interface into promiscuous mode and then examining all of the traffic through the interface. Promiscuous interfaces are virtually invisible on the network because they are associated with no IP address.

When intrusive activity is detected, the IDS can generate an alarm. The IDS can also usually be configured to take reactive measures such as the following:

- TCP connection reset
- IP blocking
- IP logging

> **NOTE** For detailed explanations of IDS signature responses, refer to Chapter 9, "Cisco IPS Response Configuration."

Although these reactive measures can prevent further intrusive activity, the initial intrusive traffic still reaches, and can compromise, the target system.

An Intrusion Prevention System (IPS) also monitors network traffic by using sensors at specific locations throughout your network. These sensors, however, can be configured to examine traffic in inline mode. In inline mode, a pair of sensor interfaces serves as a layer-2 gateway for network traffic. Normal network traffic packets are received on one interface and then transmitted to the other interface (simulating the network wire). The sensor, however, examines the packets received on either inline interface. If the examined traffic triggers signatures that are enabled on the sensor, the sensor can drop the packets instead of transmitting them through the outbound interface (if that is the action configured for the signature). Therefore, a sensor operating in inline mode can drop intrusive traffic before it reaches the target system.

Software Bypass

A sensor operating in inline mode can disrupt the operation of your network if the sensor's analysis engine stops operating for some reason (since it would no longer be passing network traffic). To prevent a disruption (caused by the sensor no longer passing network traffic), the Cisco IPS sensor software provides a bypass mechanism that kicks in when a failure or stoppage occurs. The bypass can be configured to operate in one of the following modes:

- Auto
- Off
- On

Auto Mode

In *Auto* mode (also known as *Fail Open* mode), a sensor running in inline mode will continue to forward traffic even if the sensor's analysis engine stops processing traffic. Although this traffic is not inspected by the sensor, the network is still operational. Auto mode is useful on networks in which continued operation of the network takes highest priority.

Off Mode

In *Off* mode (also known as *Fail Close* mode), a sensor running in inline mode will stop forwarding traffic if the sensor's analysis engine software fails or stops. Since the sensor stops forwarding traffic, none of the traffic is allowed to pass the sensor without inspection. Off mode is useful on networks in which the security of the network takes highest priority.

On Mode

In *On* mode, a sensor running in inline mode will always forward traffic without inspecting it. This mode is useful in debugging situations in which you want to configure the sensor to forward traffic without inspecting the traffic.

Cisco Sensor Deployment

Cisco IPS supports various sensor platforms. Each platform has varying capabilities and is designed to operate in a specific network environment. You need to consider the following factors when deciding where to place sensors on your network:

- Internet boundaries
- Extranet boundaries
- Intranet boundaries
- Remote access boundaries
- Servers and desktops

Figure 1-6 shows a sample network with IPS sensors monitoring key functional boundaries (Internet boundaries, extranet boundaries, remote access boundaries, and so on) in the network.

By carefully analyzing your network topology, you can identify the locations at which your Cisco IPS should monitor the traffic flow. Then you can determine which Cisco IPS sensor is appropriate for each monitoring location that you have identified (as well as if you want to monitor with promiscuous or inline mode).

Figure 1-6 *Deploying Sensors at Common Functional Boundaries*

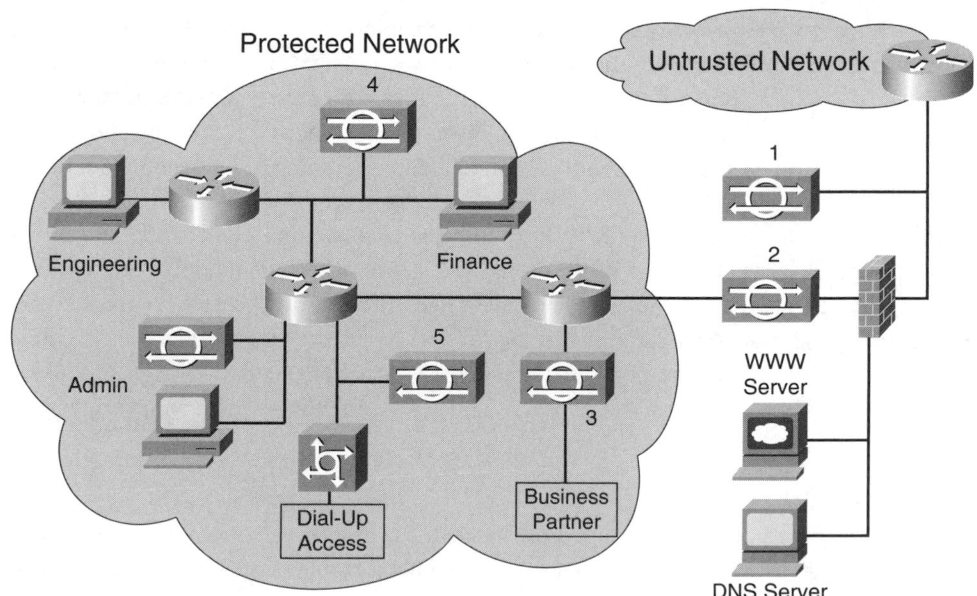

Internet Boundaries

Sensor 1 in Figure 1-6 monitors the perimeter of the network. All traffic traveling to and from the untrusted network is visible to this sensor. In most networks, perimeter protection refers to the link between your network and the Internet. Instead of monitoring the traffic outside the firewall, sensor 2 examines only the traffic that actually passes through the firewall. This can reduce the amount of traffic that the sensor must process. Sensor 2 also operates in inline mode so that it can prevent intrusive traffic from entering the network.

NOTE Be sure to locate all Internet connections to your network. Many times, administrators forget that remote sites contain Internet connections. Departments within your network may have their own Internet connection, separate from the corporate Internet connection. Any connection to the Internet needs to be properly monitored.

Extranet Boundaries

Sensor 3 in Figure 1-6 is another inline sensor. It is positioned so that it can monitor the traffic traversing the link between your network and your business partner's network. This extranet link is only as strong as the security applied to either of the networks that it connects. If either network has weak security, the other network becomes vulnerable as well. Therefore, extranet connections need to be monitored. Because the IPS sensor monitoring this boundary can detect attacks in either direction, you might consider sharing the expense of this sensor with your business partner.

Intranet Boundaries

Sensor 4 in Figure 1-6 monitors traffic between the engineering network and the finance network. This is an example of a sensor monitoring traffic between separate network segments within a larger network. Many times organizations use intranets to divide their network into functional areas, such as engineering, research, finance, and human resources. At other times, organizations drive the boundary definitions. Sometimes both of these classifications define intranet boundaries.

In this example, the engineering network is separated from the finance network (and the router that separates the other networks) by its own router. A firewall is also commonly used to increase security. In either situation, you can use a sensor to monitor the traffic between the networks and to verify that the security configuration (for the firewall or router) is defined correctly. Traffic that violates the security configuration generates alerts, which you can use as a signal to update the configuration of the firewall or router because it is enforcing the security policy.

Remote Access Boundaries

Sensor 5 in Figure 1-6 monitors traffic from the dialup access server. Do not assume that dialup lines are safe because a hacker could not determine the phone numbers of your dialup modems; war dialers are freely available on the Internet. Furthermore, many remote users use home computers that are continuously connected to the Internet through high-speed Internet connections. An attacker who compromises one of these home systems can easily penetrate your remote access server.

> **NOTE** A *war dialer* is a tool that dials a specified range of phone numbers, looking for modem connections. Attackers can start a war dialer on their computer and let it run for days to locate potential modem connections. Hackers can then connect to an identified modem phone number and can infiltrate networks whose connections have weak authentication mechanisms.

Servers and Desktops

With the current Cisco host-based sensors, you can deploy intrusion-prevention functionality on your servers and desktop systems. Each host-based sensor is actually a software agent that runs on the individual systems on your network, serving as a security barrier around each host. These agents provide a final layer of security that can help protect your network from attack.

Sensor Deployment Considerations

Deploying Cisco IPS on your network requires a well-thought-out design to maximize its effectiveness. Besides the basic sensor capabilities and placement, you must also consider the following design issues when deploying Cisco IDS on your network:

- Sensor placement
- Sensor management and monitoring options
- Number of sensors
- External sensor communications

Sensor Placement

When you place an IPS sensor in front of a firewall (on the Internet, or external, side of the firewall), you allow the IPS sensor to monitor all incoming and outgoing network traffic. However, when deployed in this manner, the IPS sensor does not detect internal network traffic (such as traffic between two internal hosts). An internal attacker taking advantage of vulnerabilities in internal network services would remain undetected by the external IPS sensor. Placing an IPS sensor (a monitoring or sniffing interface) behind a firewall shields the IPS sensor from any policy violations that the firewall rejects.

Sensor Management and Monitoring Options

Each of your Cisco IPS sensors monitors network traffic at a specific location in your network. You must also, however, be able to communicate with your sensors by using their command and control interface. This communication path enables you to configure and manage your sensors as well as to retrieve alarm events for monitoring and reporting. The Cisco IPS 5.0 communication protocol uses

Transport Layer Security (TLS) or Secure Sockets Layer (SSL) and Extensible Markup Language (XML) to provide a standardized interface between Cisco IPS devices. You have two options with respect to your sensor management:

- Out-of-band management network
- In-band management network

Number of Sensors

The number of sensors that you plan to deploy on your network will dictate how many management consoles you will need to also deploy to configure and manage your Cisco IPS Sensors. Each management solution is designed to effectively manage a specific number of sensors. The two management solutions for Cisco IPS version 5.0 are as follows:

- IDS Device Manager (IDM)
- IDS Management Center (IDS MC)

> **NOTE** IDS Management Center support for Cisco IPS version 5.0 sensors requires IDS MC release 3.0.

IDM enables you to configure a single sensor. This software is provided with Cisco IDS sensors that provide full IDS functionality. IDS MC, on the other hand, enables you to configure up to 300 sensors from one management system.

As the number of sensors deployed on your network increases the amount of work needed to monitor alerts, apply signature updates, and manage the sensors also increases. This increased workload may require a larger support staff than the workload that results from smaller sensor deployments.

External Sensor Communications

Traffic on the communication port between sensors and external systems must be allowed through firewalls to ensure functionality. Most of this communication passes through either TCP port 443 (TLS/SSL) or TCP port 22 (Secure Shell [SSH]).

Cisco Sensor Communications Protocols

Communication between your Cisco IPS sensors and other network devices involves the following protocols and standards:

- SSH
- TLS/SSL

- RDEP
- SDEE Standard

Secure Shell

SSH provides a protocol for secure access to remote devices by encrypting the communication session (refer to http://www.ietf.org/html.charters/secsh-charter.html for more information). SSH is the secure replacement for Telnet, since Telnet transmits its session information in an unencrypted form.

Transport Layer Security (TLS)/Secure Socket Layer (SSL)

The TLS/SSL protocol provides communication privacy (encryption) over the Internet, allowing client/server applications to communicate in a way that prevents eavesdropping, tampering, and message forgery. RFC 2246 details the TLS protocol.

Remote Data Exchange Protocol

Besides communicating between different applications or processes located on your sensor, your sensor must also communicate with your network's other Cisco IPS components, such as Security Monitor. RDEP handles all sensor communications to and from external systems. It uses HTTP and TLS/SSL to pass XML documents (over an encrypted session) between the sensor and external systems. XML files on the sensor control the configuration and operation of your sensor.

Each RDEP message consists of an HTTP header section followed by an optional entity, or message body. Event and transaction message entity bodies consist of XML documents. Your sensor configuration is stored in XML documents on your sensor, so processing XML information is built into the Cisco IPS software. The schema for the XML documents is specified by the Intrusion Detection Interaction and Operations Messages (IDIOM) specification. For more information on both RDEP and IDIOM, refer to the documentation provided at Cisco.com.

NOTE The IDIOM specification defines the content of XML documents that are communicated between Cisco Intrusion Prevention System (CIPS) devices using RDEP. By following the IDIOM and RDEP specifications, third-party applications can easily interact with the Cisco IDS.

RDEP is an application-level communications protocol that is used to exchange IDS events, IP log information, and sensor configuration information between your sensor and an external system.

RDEP communication comprises request and response messages. The following three classes of request messages are supported by RDEP:

- Event messages
- IP log messages
- Transaction messages

Event Messages

Event messages include IPS/IDS alerts, status, and error messages. Monitoring applications such as IEV and the Security Monitor use RDEP to retrieve these events from the sensor. Since the monitoring application is responsible for retrieving or pulling the events (such as alerts) from the sensor, it can request the events at a pace that it can handle.

Events on the sensor are stored in a 4 GB circular queue. Since this queue is large, your monitoring application can lose connectivity for a fairly long time without losing any alarms. Under normal conditions, the event store will take at least a couple of days to fill up. Nevertheless, your monitoring application must retrieve events from the sensor before the queue becomes full; otherwise, the sensor will start overwriting the unread events.

> **NOTE** The circular queue used by Cisco IPS is a 4 GB fixed length file. As events are added to the file, it gradually gets full. When the file is full, the sensor starts overwriting the events at the beginning of the file. This process is repeated indefinitely, enabling the sensor to maintain a fixed amount of storage for events.

IP Log Messages

You can configure signatures to log the packets coming from the attacking system after a signature fires. These packets are stored on your sensor and represent the actual packets coming from the attacking system. Via the IP log RDEP request messages, your external monitoring application can request copies of the IP log information stored on the sensor. This information can also be viewed via the sensor CLI.

Transaction Messages

The first two message types are used by external systems to retrieve information from your sensor. Your management software uses the transaction messages to configure and control the operation of your sensor. This is accomplished by sending XML information that the sensor uses to change the configuration on the sensor and alter its operational characteristics.

Security Device Event Exchange Standard

The SDEE Standard is a product-independent standard for communicating security device events (see http://www.icsalabs.com/html/communities/ids/sdee/index.shtml). Cisco has been leading the development of this standard that is being adopted by various IDS/IPS vendors. SDEE does not replace RDEP; rather, it enhances RDEP with extensibility features that are needed for communicating events generated by various types of security devices.

NOTE RDEP version 2 will specify that CIPS devices communicate events in accordance with the SDEE standard.

Cisco Sensor Software Architecture

Beginning with Cisco IDS 4.0, the entire communication infrastructure was rewritten. Therefore, the services running on the sensor were changed to match this new communication infrastructure. Figure 1-7 shows the Cisco sensor software architecture.

Figure 1-7 *Cisco Sensor Software Architecture*

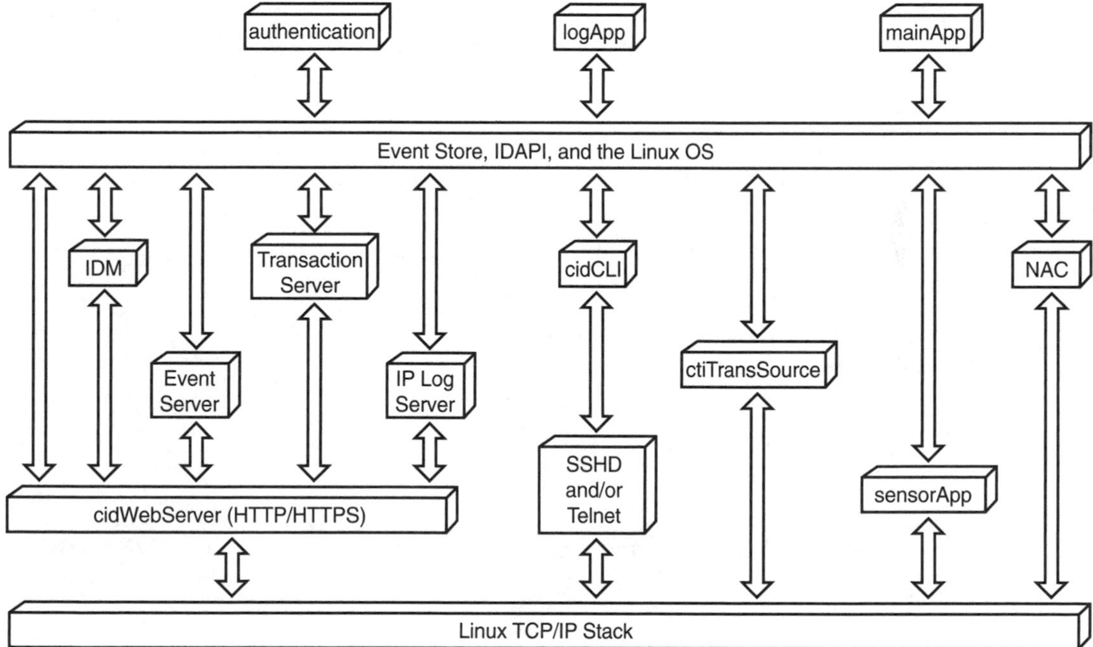

One of the main differences of the new architecture is that the sensor no longer pushes events to your monitoring system. Instead, beginning with Cisco IDS 4.0 your monitoring system pulls the events from the sensor as it is ready to process them. The Cisco sensor software architecture can be broken down into the following main interacting applications or processes:

- cidWebServer
- mainApp
- logApp

- authentication
- Network Access Controller (NAC)
- ctlTransSource
- sensorApp
- Event Store
- cidCLI

cidWebServer

The *cidWebServer* application is the sensor's web server interface that facilitates interaction between the sensor and other Cisco IPS components on your network. This web server is capable of both HTTP and HTTPS communication sessions. Instead of simply providing static web pages, however, the web server provides functionality via several servlets. These servlets perform most of the real work accomplished via the cidWebServer application. One of the main functions provided by the web server is a front-end for the IDM.

NOTE A *servlet* is a shared library that is loaded into the cidWebServer process at runtime.

The cidWebServer uses the following servlets to provide its functionality:

- IDM Servlet
- Event Server Servlet
- Transaction Server Servlet
- IP Log Server Servlet

NOTE All of the cidWebServer application's servlets communicate with the RDEP. RDEP serves as the sensor's external communication protocol.

IDM Servlet

The IDM Servlet provides the IDM web-based management interface. You can use this interface to configure your sensors one sensor at a time.

Event Server Servlet

The Event Server Servlet is responsible for serving events to external management applications, such as Security Monitor.

Transaction Server Servlet

Whenever an external management application needs to configure or control your sensor, it needs to initiate a control transaction with the sensor. The Transaction Server Servlet manages these control transactions.

IP Log Server Servlet

The IP Log Server Servlet enables external systems to assess IP log information from the sensor. Like alert events, IP log information is stored on your sensor until retrieved by an external application (such as Security Monitor).

mainApp

The mainApp process is the first application to be launched on the sensor. It is responsible for configuring the sensor's operating system configuration (such as the IP address). The mainApp also handles starting and stopping all of the other Cisco IPS applications.

logApp

Your sensor logs various application messages to log files on the sensor. The logApp application handles writing all of an application's log messages to the log files on the sensor. It is also responsible for the writing of an application's error messages to the event store.

authentication

The authentication process configures and manages user authentication on the sensor. User access to the sensor is based on the following three factors:

- Username
- Password
- Assigned role

When a user accesses the sensor, he must specify a valid username and password combination to gain authenticated access to the sensor. Then the authorization for the user is handled by the user role that is assigned to the specified username.

Network Access Controller (NAC)

Your sensors support the ability to block traffic from an attacking system. This blocking action is enabled by the sensor communicating with one of your network devices and updating an ACL to block the offending system (initiate a shun command on a PIX firewall). The sensor uses the NAC process to initiate IP blocking.

ctlTransSource

Sometimes one of your sensors needs to initiate a control transaction with another one of your sensors. This functionality is performed by the ctlTransSource application. Currently, ctlTransSource is used to enable the master blocking sensor functionality.

sensorApp

The sensorApp process performs the actual sensing functionality on the sensor. Initially, the sensorApp processes the signature and alarm channel configurations for the sensor. Then it generates alert events based on this configuration and the IP traffic that is traversing the sensor's monitoring interface. The sensorApp stores these events (like all other applications) in the Event Store.

Event Store

The Event Store is a large, shared, memory mapped file where all events are stored on your sensor. The Event Store holds the events on your sensor in a 4 GB circular queue until you retrieve those events using your monitoring software or the events get overwritten. By storing the events on the sensor, your alarms are not lost, even if your monitoring software losses network connectivity with your sensor for a short period of time. The sensorApp is the only application that will write alert events into the Event Store, but all other applications may write log, status, and error events into the Event Store.

cidCLI

The cidCLI process is the process initiated when a user logs into the sensor via either Telnet or SSH. A separate cidCLI process is started for each CLI user shell.

Foundation Summary

Table 1-4 shows the primary terms that are used to describe the functionality of the Cisco IPS solution.

Table 1-4 *Primary IPS Terminology*

Terminology	Description
Inline mode	Examining network traffic while having the ability to stop intrusive traffic from reaching the target system
Promiscuous mode	Passively examining network traffic for intrusive behavior
Signature engine	An engine that supports signatures that share common characteristics (such as the same protocol)
Meta-Event Generator	The capability to define meta signatures based on multiple existing signatures
Atomic signature	A signature that triggers based on the contents of a single packet
Flow-based signature	A signature that triggers based on the information contained in a sequence of packets between two systems (such as the packets in a TCP connection)
Behavior-based signature	A signature that triggers when traffic deviates from regular user behavior
Anomaly-based signature	A signature that triggers when traffic exceeds a configured normal baseline
False negative	A situation in which a detection system fails to detect intrusive traffic although there is a signature designed to catch that activity
False positive	A situation in which normal user activity (instead of intrusive activity) triggers an alarm
True negative	A situation in which a signature does not fire during normal user traffic on the network
True positive	A situation in which a signature fires correctly when intrusive traffic for that signature is detected on the network (The signature correctly identifies an attack launched against the network.)
Deep-packet inspection	Decoding protocols and examining entire packets to allow for policy enforcement based on actual protocol traffic (not just a specific port number).
Event correlation	Associating multiple alarms or events with a single attack.
Risk rating (RR)	A threat rating based on numerous factors besides just the attack severity

Cisco provides a hybrid solution that enables you to configure a sensor to operate in promiscuous and inline mode simultaneously.

To help limit false positives, Cisco IPS version 5.0 incorporates a risk rating for alerts. This risk rating is calculated based on the following parameters:

- Event severity
- Signature fidelity
- Asset value of target

For IP addresses on your network, you can assign one of the following asset values:

- Low
- Medium
- High
- Mission critical
- No value

Beginning with version 5.0, you can use the Meta-Event Generator (MEG) to create complex signatures that cause multiple regular signatures to trigger before the meta-event signature triggers.

Cisco IPS version 5.0 also enhances the ability of the sensor to perform deep-packet inspection on network traffic. This enables the sensor to enforce security policies beyond simple port numbers.

Cisco IPS version 5.0 supports the IDSM-2, the network module, and the following appliance sensors:

- IDS 4215
- IDS 4235
- IDS 4240*
- IDS 4250
- IDS 4250XL
- IDS 4255*

> **NOTE** The sensors marked by * are the newest appliance sensors in the Cisco IPS solution. These sensors are highly reliable because they use flash memory (which has no moving parts), not a regular hard disk, for storage.

Inline mode enables your sensor to act as a layer-2 forwarding device while inspecting network traffic, providing the ability to drop intrusive traffic before it reaches the target system. The following sensors support inline mode:

- IDS 4215
- IDS 4235
- IDS 4240
- IDS 4250
- IDS 4255
- IDSM-2

When your system is running in inline mode, you can configure one of the following software bypass modes:

- Auto
- Off
- On

When deploying sensors on your network, consider the following network boundaries:

- Internet boundaries
- Extranet boundaries
- Intranet boundaries
- Remote access boundaries
- Servers and desktops

You must also consider the following when deploying your sensors:

- Sensor placement
- Sensor management and monitoring options
- Number of sensors
- External sensor communications

Communication between your Cisco IPS sensors and other network devices involves the following protocols and standards:

- Secure Shell (SSH)
- Transport Layer Security (TLS)/Secure Sockets Layer (SSL)
- Remote Data Exchange Protocol (RDEP)
- Security Device Event Exchange (SDEE) Standard

The Cisco sensor software architecture can be broken down into the following main interacting applications or processes:

- cidWebServer
- mainApp
- logApp
- authentication
- NAC
- ctlTransSource
- sensorApp
- Event Store
- cidCLI

Q&A

You have two choices for review questions:

- The questions that follow pose a greater challenge than the exam questions, because these use an open-ended format. By reviewing now with this more difficult question format, you can better exercise your memory and prove your conceptual understanding of this chapter. The answers to these questions are found in the appendix.
- For more practice with exam-like question formats, use the exam engine on the CD-ROM.

1. What is a false positive?
2. What is a true positive?
3. If your sensor has only two monitoring interfaces, can you operate in promiscuous and inline modes simultaneously?
4. What factors are use to calculate the risk rating?
5. How is the asset value of a target configured?
6. Which appliance sensors support the inline mode of operation?
7. Which appliance sensors are diskless?
8. Which appliance sensor comes with dual 1 Gb monitoring interfaces?
9. What are the three modes that you can configure for software bypass when using inline mode?
10. If you want the sensor to fail close when operating in inline mode, what software bypass mode would you use?
11. What are the four network boundaries that you need to consider when deploying sensors on your network?
12. What factors (besides network boundaries) must you consider when deploying your sensors?
13. Which XML-based protocol does your sensor use to transfer event messages to other Cisco IPS devices?
14. Which standard provides a product-independent standard for communicating security device events?
15. What is a true negative?
16. What is the Meta-Event Generator (MEG)?
17. What is the main difference between intrusion detection and intrusion prevention?

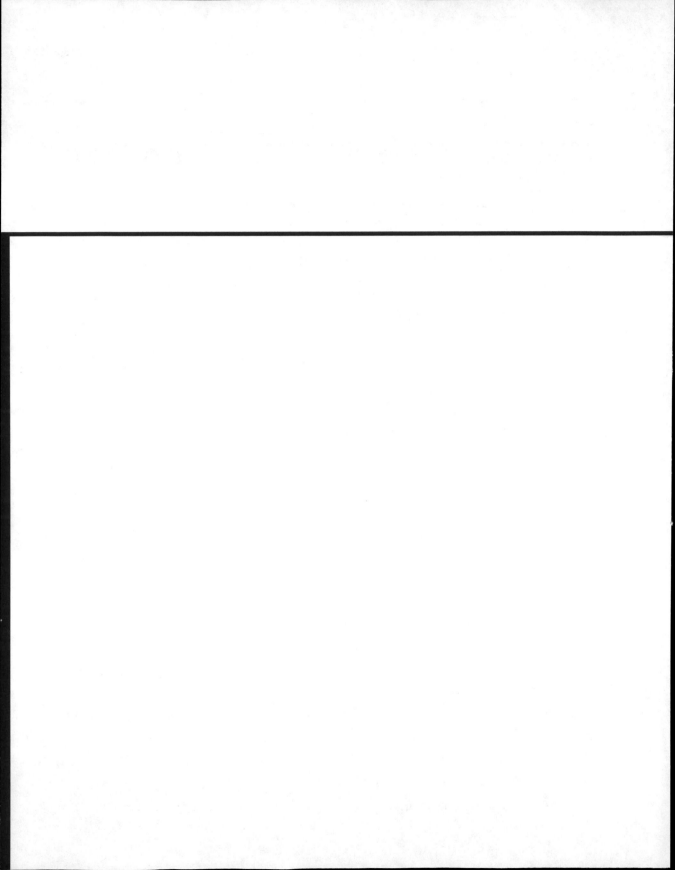

Part II: Cisco IPS Configuration

This chapter covers the following subjects:

- Sensor Installation
- Sensor Initialization
- IPS Command-Line Interface

CHAPTER 2

IPS Command-Line Interface

Each Cisco IPS sensor provides a robust command-line interface (CLI) that enables you to configure the operational characteristics of your sensor. This CLI operates in a way similar to the IOS CLI. You must understand this interface to appropriately install a sensor as well as to debug sensor problems.

"Do I Know This Already?" Quiz

The purpose of the "Do I Know This Already?" quiz is to help you decide if you really need to read the entire chapter. If you already intend to read the entire chapter, you do not necessarily need to answer these questions now.

The 10-question quiz, derived from the major sections in the "Foundation and Supplemental Topics" portion of the chapter, helps you determine how to spend your limited study time.

Table 2-1 outlines the major topics discussed in this chapter and the corresponding "Do I Know This Already?" quiz questions.

Table 2-1 *"Do I Know This Already?" Foundation and Supplemental Topics Mapping*

Foundation or Supplemental Topic	Questions Covering This Topic
Sensor Installation	1, 5, 10
Sensor Initialization	2, 6, 9
IPS CLI	3, 4, 7, 8

CAUTION The goal of self-assessment is to gauge your mastery of the topics in this chapter. If you do not know the answer to a question or are only partially sure of the answer, you should mark this question wrong for purposes of the self-assessment. Giving yourself credit for an answer you correctly guess skews your self-assessment results and might provide you with a false sense of security.

1. Which sensor CLI command should you use to update the sensor software from version 4.1 to 5.0 via the network?
   a. **migrate**
   b. **update**
   c. **upgrade**
   d. **copy**
   e. None of these
2. Which command should you use to initialize a new sensor that you install on your network?
   a. **setup**
   b. **initialize**
   c. **update**
   d. **configure**
   e. None of these
3. Which is the most privileged role that you can assign to a normal user account on the sensor?
   a. Root
   b. User
   c. Operator
   d. Administrator
   e. System
4. Which is the least privileged role that you can assign to a user account on the sensor?
   a. Basic
   b. User
   c. Operator
   d. Admin
   e. Viewer
5. What must you do before upgrading your sensor's software by using SCP?
   a. Add the Secure Shell (SSH) server's X.509 certificate to the sensor's authorized list.
   b. Add the SSH server key to the sensor's authorized list.
   c. Add the SSH key for the sensor to the SSH server.
   d. Add the sensor's X.509 certificate to the SSH server.
   e. Nothing.

6. Which of the following cannot be configured by using the **setup** command?
   a. Web server port
   b. Sensor time settings
   c. Sensor default gateway
   d. TCP port that Telnet uses
   e. Sensor access list entries

7. What should you type at the sensor CLI to get help?
   a. **help**
   b. **?**
   c. **show**
   d. Either **help** or **?**
   e. None of these

8. Which account is used by the Technical Assistance Center (TAC) to troubleshoot problems with your sensor?
   a. Administrator
   b. TAC
   c. Service
   d. Operator
   e. Support

9. Which of the following is true about the account configured with the Service role?
   a. It is a privileged sensor CLI account that TAC uses to troubleshoot sensor problems.
   b. It is an account made to enable end users to bypass the CLI.
   c. You can configure multiple accounts with the Service role.
   d. This account bypasses the sensor CLI.
   e. None of these.

10. Which sensors provide no keyboard or mouse ports? (Choose 2.)
   a. IDS 4210
   b. IDS 4240
   c. IDS 4235
   d. IDS 4215
   e. IDS 4250

The answers to the "Do I Know This Already?" quiz are found in the appendix. The suggested choices for your next step are as follows:

- **8 or less overall score**—Read the entire chapter, including the "Foundation and Supplemental Topics," "Foundation Summary," and Q&A sections.
- **9 or 10 overall score**—If you want more review on these topics, skip to the "Foundation Summary" section of this chapter. Then go to the Q&A section. Otherwise, move to the next chapter.

Foundation and Supplemental Topics

Sensor Installation

When installing your appliance sensor, the necessary steps vary depending on whether you are upgrading an appliance from a version 4.1 or configuring a brand new appliance. When configuring a brand new appliance, you need to initialize the sensor. If you are upgrading, however, your sensor has already been initialized. Therefore, you need to upgrade only the sensor software to Cisco IPS version 5.0. The two methods for upgrading the sensor software from version 4.1 to 5.0 are as follows:

- Installing 5.0 software via the network
- Installing 5.0 software from a CD

NOTE Installing a second hard-disk drive in a 4235 or 4250 sensor may render the sensor unable to recognize the **recover** command used for re-imaging the appliance. Spare hard-disk drives are meant to be replacements for the original hard-disk drives, not to be used along with the original hard-disk drive.

Installing 5.0 Software via the Network

Some appliance sensors have no CD-ROM drive. On these systems, you can't upgrade the software by using a CD. Instead, you must perform software upgrade across the network. These systems also require you to connect to the sensor via the serial port to access the sensor CLI since they have no keyboard or mouse ports.

The following appliance sensors are diskless and do not have CD-ROM drives:

- IDS 4215
- IDS 4240
- IDS 4255

To upgrade a diskless appliance sensor, you use the **upgrade** command (from the sensor's CLI) to install the 5.0 software. The syntax for the **upgrade** command is as follows:

```
upgrade source-url
```

You can retrieve the new software image through Secure Copy (SCP), FTP, HTTP, or Secure Hypertext Transfer Protocol (HTTPS). When specifying the *source-url* you can specify either the complete location or simply **scp:**, **ftp:**, **http:**, or **https:**, in which you will be prompted for the necessary fields. The prompts you see when using SCP are displayed in Example 2-1.

Example 2-1 *Prompts When Using SCP*

```
Sensor(config)# upgrade scp:
User: IDSuser
Server's IP Address: 10.89.139.100
Port[22]:
File Name: IDS50/IPS-K9-maj-5.0-0.15b-S91-0.15-.rpm.pkg
Password: ********
Warning: Executing this command will apply a major version upgrade to the
application partition. The system may be rebooted to complete the upgrade.
Continue with upgrade? : yes
```

> **NOTE** To use SCP to upgrade the sensor software, you must first add the Secure Shell (SSH) server public key (for the host where the new software is located) to the list of sensor's authorized SSH hosts. Do this by using the **ssh host-key** global configuration command (see the "Adding a Known SSH Host" section later in the chapter).

Installing 5.0 Software from a CD

On sensors that have a CD-ROM drive, you can install the 5.0 software by using the recovery CD, instead of installing through the network.

> **NOTE** Installing the 5.0 software via the recovery CD is not an upgrade of the existing 4.1 software. Therefore, the installation will remove your existing software (including all of your configuration information). You should save your configuration before performing the installation.

After powering on the appliance, insert the Cisco IDS 5.0(1) Upgrade/Recovery CD into the CD-ROM drive located in the front of the appliance. Example 2-2 displays the boot menu text that explains the two options you can use to install the 5.0 software.

Example 2-2 *Boot Menu*

```
                           Cisco IPS 5.0(1) Upgrade/Recovery CD!

- To recover the Cisco IPS 5.0(1) Application using a local keyboard/monitor,
   Type: k <ENTER>.
   (WARNING: ALL DATA ON DISK 1 WILL BE LOST)

- To recover the Cisco IPS 5.0(1) Application using a serial connection,
   Type: s <ENTER>, or just press <ENTER>.
   (WARNING: ALL DATA ON DISK 1 WILL BE LOST)

boot:
```

NOTE If you do not insert the CD into the drive quickly enough, the system may boot the normal image on the disk. If the system does not boot from the CD, then just leave the CD in the drive and reboot the system.

You can install either from a keyboard connected to the appliance or through a serial connection (via the console port). Your two options are as follows:

- **s** (for console port connection)
- **k** (for attached PS/2 keyboard)

After the installation is complete, you can continue with the sensor configuration. At this point, the sensor needs to be initialized just like a brand new appliance sensor.

Sensor Initialization

When you install a brand new appliance, you need to perform the following initial configuration tasks:

- Access the CLI
- Run the **setup** command
- Configure trusted hosts
- Create the Service account
- Manually set the system clock

Some other tasks you also may need to perform during initialization include the following:

- Change your password
- Add and remove users
- Add known SSH hosts

Accessing the CLI

To begin sensor initialization, access the CLI by using either an attached keyboard or a serial connection to the console port. The default account is *cisco,* with a password of *cisco*. You will be immediately prompted to change this default password. Your new password must have the following properties:

- Be at least six characters long
- Contain at least 5 different characters

> **NOTE** Selecting strong passwords helps ensure that an attacker cannot easily guess the passwords by using commonly available password cracking tools. The sensor performs some basic checks to strengthen the passwords you use, but you can also take your own precautions. Keep in mind the following when selecting a password:
>
> - Do not use only letters or only numbers.
> - Do not use recognizable words.
> - Do not use foreign words.
> - Do not use personal information.
> - Do not write down your password.
>
> Improve your password selection by observing the following practices:
>
> - Make the password at least eight characters long.
> - Mix uppercase and lowercase letters.
> - Mix letters and numbers.
> - Include special characters, such as & and $.
> - Pick a password that you can remember.

Besides accessing the CLI from the serial port (or directly attached keyboard and monitor), you can also connect to the CLI by using either Telnet or SSH. By default, the access lists on the sensor allow access only from systems on the class C subnet 10.1.9.0 (with the sensor being 10.1.9.201 and a default gateway being 10.1.9.1). To enable CLI access to the sensor from other systems, you will need to update the sensor's access control lists (through the **service host > network settings** sensor global configuration command). By default, access to the sensor through Telnet (TCP port 23) is disabled. SSH access (TCP port 22), however, is enabled.

Running the setup Command

Once you access the CLI by using the default account, you will see the Sensor# prompt. To configure the basic sensor parameters, run the **setup** command. This command enables you to configure the following sensor parameters:

- Host name
- IP address
- Netmask
- Default gateway
- Access list entries
- Telnet server status (default is disabled)
- Web server port (default 443)

- Time settings
- Promiscuous interfaces
- Inline interface pairs

When using the **setup** command, you will see output similar to that in Example 2-3.

Example 2-3 **setup** *Command Output*

```
Sensor# setup


    --- System Configuration Dialog ---

At any point you may enter a question mark '?' for help.
User ctrl-c to abort configuration dialog at any prompt.
Default settings are in square brackets '[]'.


Current Configuration:


service host
network-settings
host-ip 10.1.9.201/24,10.1.9.1
host-name Sensor
telnet-option disabled
access-list 10.1.9.0/24
ftp-timeout 300
login-banner-text
exit
time-zone-settings
offset -360
standard-time-zone-name GMT-06:00
exit
summertime-option disabled
ntp-option disabled
exit
service web-server
port 443
exit
service interface
physical-interfaces GigabitEthernet0/3
no description
admin-state disabled
duplex auto
speed 1000
alt-tcp-reset-interface none
exit
```

continues

Example 2-3 **setup** *Command Output (Continued)*

```
physical-interfaces GigabitEthernet0/2
no description
admin-state disabled
duplex auto
speed 1000
alt-tcp-reset-interface none
exit
physical-interfaces GigabitEthernet0/1
no description
admin-state disabled
duplex auto
speed 1000
alt-tcp-reset-interface none
exit
physical-interfaces GigabitEthernet0/0
no description
admin-state disabled
duplex auto
speed 1000
alt-tcp-reset-interface none
exit
exit
service analysis-engine
virtual-sensor vs0
description default virtual sensor
exit
exit

Current time: Mon Jan 31 09:54:44 2005


Setup Configuration last modified: Sun Jan 30 00:16:47 2005

Continue with configuration dialog?[yes]:
Enter host name[Sensor]: IDS4240
Enter IP interface[10.1.9.201/24,10.1.9.1]:10.40.10.100/24,10.40.10.1
Enter telnet-server status[disabled]:
Enter web-server port[443]:
Modify current access list?[no]: yes
Current access list entries:
  [1] 10.1.9.0/24
Delete:
Permit: 10.40.0.0/16
Permit:
Modify system clock settings?[no]:
Modify virtual sensor "vs0" configuration?[no]: yes
Current interface configuration
  Command control: Management0/0
```

Example 2-3 **setup** *Command Output (Continued)*

```
  Unused:
    GigabitEthernet0/3
    GigabitEthernet0/2
    GigabitEthernet0/0
    GigabitEthernet0/1
  Promiscuous:
  Inline:
    None
Delete Promiscuous interfaces?[no]:
Add Promiscuous interfaces?[no]:
Add Inline pairs?[no]: yes
Pair name: perimeter
Description[Created via setup by user cisco]: Perimeter protection sensor
Interface1[]: GigabitEthernet0/3
Interface2[]: GigabitEthernet0/2
Pair name:

The following configuration was entered.

service host
network-settings
host-ip 10.40.10.100/24,10.40.10.1
host-name Ids4240
telnet-option disabled
access-list 10.9.1.0/24
access-list 10.40.10.0/16
ftp-timeout 300
no login-banner-text
exit
time-zone-settings
offset -360
standard-time-zone-name GMT-06:00
exit
summertime-option disabled
ntp-option disabled
exit
service web-server
port 443
exit
service interface
physical-interfaces GigabitEthernet0/3
no description
admin-state enabled
duplex auto
speed 1000
alt-tcp-reset-interface none
exit
```

continues

Example 2-3 **setup** *Command Output (Continued)*

```
physical-interfaces GigabitEthernet0/2
no description
admin-state enabled
duplex auto
speed 1000
alt-tcp-reset-interface none
exit
physical-interfaces GigabitEthernet0/1
no description
admin-state disabled
duplex auto
speed 1000
alt-tcp-reset-interface none
exit
physical-interfaces GigabitEthernet0/0
no description
admin-state disabled
duplex auto
speed 1000
alt-tcp-reset-interface none
exit
inline-interfaces perimeter
description Perimeter protection sensor
interface1 GigabitEthernet0/3
interface2 GigabitEthernet0/2
exit
exit
service analysis-engine
virtual-sensor vs0
description default virtual sensor
logical-interface perimeter
exit
exit
[0] Go to the command prompt without saving this config.
[1] Return back to the setup without saving this config.
[2] Save this configuration and exit setup.

Enter your selection[2]:
```

NOTE You manage your sensor through the command and control interface. To allow your management systems to access the sensor, you must configure the appropriate network access list entries for appropriate management of IP addresses. In conjunction with using the **setup** command, these access list entries can be modified at any time by using the **service host > network-settings** CLI command.

After entering the information for the **setup** command, you receive the prompt shown at the end of Example 2-3.

Enter **2** (or just press **Enter**) to save the configuration. After the configuration is saved, you will see the following prompt to change the system time (unless you configured the sensor to use a Network Time Protocol server):

```
*06:33:33 UTC Thu Nov 18 2004
Modify system date and time?[no]:
```

If the time is incorrect, enter **yes** to change it. You may also be prompted to reboot the sensor with the following prompt:

```
Continue with reboot? [yes]:
```

Enter **no** to this prompt because you still need to configure a few more parameters. You can reboot the sensor later to make all of the changes take effect at the same time.

NOTE To reboot the sensor later, you can use the **reset** command from the Privileged Exec mode.

Creating the Service Account

You should create a Service account for the Cisco Technical Assistance Center (TAC) to use when troubleshooting problems with your IPS appliance. Unlike other user roles in which the same role can be assigned to multiple user accounts, you can assign the Service role to only one account on your IPS appliance.

To create a Service account, to perform the following steps in an Administrator account:

Step 1 Log in to CLI on the appliance.

Step 2 Enter Global Configuration mode by using the following command:

```
sensor# configure terminal
```

Step 3 Create the Service account (named serv_acct) by using the following **username** command:

```
sensor(config)# username serv_acct privilege service
```

Step 4 Enter a password for the Service account when prompted.

Step 5 Exit the Global Configuration mode by using the following command:

```
sensor(config)# exit
```

When you log in to the IPS appliance by using the Service account, you will receive the warning in Example 2-4.

Example 2-4 *Warning When You Use the Service Account to Log in to the IDS Appliance*

```
************************ WARNING ************************
UNAUTHORIZED ACCESS TO THIS NETWORK DEVICE IS PROHIBITED.
This account is intended to be used for support and
troubleshooting purposes only. Unauthorized modifications
are not supported and will require this device to be
re-imaged to guarantee proper operation.
*********************************************************
```

This serves as a reminder that the Service account is designed solely for troubleshooting your sensor's operation and for other support purposes. Adding or enabling additional services or applications will make the IPS appliance configuration unsupported.

Manually Setting the System Clock

Many network environments use automatic clock functionality, such as Network Time Protocol (NTP). These configurations automatically adjust the time on your devices based on a known time source. If you do not have such a mechanism, you may need to manually set the time on your IPS appliance.

> **NOTE** The IDS module obtains its time configuration from the Catalyst 6500 switch in which it is housed, so you should not need to set the time by using the **clock set** command.

Besides running **setup**, you can also manually set the time on your IPS sensor by using the **clock set** Privileged Exec command. The syntax for this command is as follows:

```
clock set hh:mm[:ss] month day year
```

The parameters for the **clock set** command are described in Table 2-2.

Table 2-2 ***clock set*** *Parameters*

Parameter	Description
hh:mm[:*ss*]	Current time in 24-hour format. Seconds are optional.
day	Numeric value indicating the current day of the month (such as 1–31).
month	Name of the current month (without any abbreviation), such as January or March.
year	The current four-digit year value (such as 2005).

Suppose that you want to set the current time on your IPS appliance to one o'clock in the afternoon on January 1, 2005. To accomplish this, you would use the following command after logging in to your appliance:

```
sensor# clock set 13:00 January 1 2005
sensor#
```

Changing your Password

All users on your IPS appliance can change their password. You can change your password through the CLI by using the **password** Global Configuration mode command.

> **NOTE** You can also change your account password through graphical management applications (such as IPS Device Manager).

The **password** command requires no parameters. To change your password, enter your old password and then enter your new password twice (to verify that you entered it correctly, since it is not displayed on the screen).

> **NOTE** Since the Service account bypasses the sensor CLI, you can change its password either by using an account with administrative privileges or by using the **passwd** command at the bash shell prompt.

Adding and Removing Users

In the Global Configuration mode, you can add new users to and remove existing users from your sensor. The **username** Global Configuration mode command enables you to add new users. To remove an existing user, simply insert the keyword **no** in front of the regular **username** command. The syntax for the **username** command is as follows:

```
username name [password password] [privilege administrator|operator|viewer|service]
```

The sequence of commands in Example 2-5 illustrates the process of adding to your sensor the user newuser with a privilege level of Operator.

Example 2-5 *Adding to Your Sensor the User newuser with a Privilege Level of Operator*

```
sensor# configure terminal
sensor(config)# username newuser privilege operator
Enter new login password: ******
Re-enter new login password: ******
sensor(config)# exit
sensor#
```

> **NOTE** From the Privileged Exec mode, you can confirm your user configuration changes by running the **show users all** command.

You will want to add accounts to support your network environment. At minimum, you need to create an account with Viewer privileges; you will need this to enable your monitoring application to access the sensor and retrieve alarm information.

NOTE You can also add and remove accounts through the graphical management applications (such as IPS Device Manager).

Adding a Known SSH Host

Your sensor maintains a list of validated SSH known hosts so that the sensor can verify the identity of the servers with which it communicates when it is operating as an SSH client. Adding an entry to the known SSH hosts list also enables you to do the following:

- Automatically or manually upgrade the sensor by using SCP
- Copy current configurations, backup configurations, and IP logs via SCP

The syntax for the **ssh host-key** command is as follows:

```
ssh host-key ip-address [key-modulus-length] [public-exponent] [public-modulus]
```

The parameters for the **ssh host-key** command are described in Table 2-3.

Table 2-3 **ssh host-key** *Parameters*

Parameter	Description
ip-address	IP address of the SSH server
key-modulus-length	(optional) American Standard Code for Information Interchange (ASCII) decimal integer in the range 511–2048
public-exponent	(optional) ASCII decimal integer in the range $3–2^{32}$
public-modulus	(optional) ASCII decimal integer, x, such that $(2^{\text{key-modulus-length}}) < x < (2^{\text{key-modulus-length + 1}})$

NOTE You will normally specify an IP address only for the **ssh host-key** global configuration command. The sensor will contact the server and retrieve the other information. These keys are also used for SSH servers that the sensor needs to connect to. You do not have to define keys for the clients that connect to the sensor itself. You can also view the currently configured SSH host keys by using the **show ssh host-keys** command.

The command sequence in Example 2-6 adds the SSH host key for 10.89.132.78 to the list of known SSH host keys.

Example 2-6 *Adding the SSH Host Key for 10.89.132.78 to the List of Known SSH Host Keys*

```
sensor(config)# configure terminal
sensor(config)# ssh host-key 10.89.132.78
MD5 fingerprint is BE:70:50:15:2C:13:97:5C:72:53:06:9C:DC:4D:A3:20
Bubble Babble is xepof-tudek-vycal-cynud-tolok-holek-zygaf-kuzak-syfot-tubec-paxox
Would you like to add this to the known hosts table for this host?[yes]: yes
sensor(config)# exit
sensor#
```

NOTE To increase security when adding a new SSH host key, you should manually verify the key value presented before you add the new SSH host-key entry. Not verifying the key can allow someone to impersonate the real server.

IPS CLI

Beginning with Cisco IDS version 4.0, the IDS appliance has an IOS-like CLI that you can use to configure your sensor. When initially configuring your IPS appliance, you will use the CLI to perform many of the configuration steps.

NOTE Although you can change most of the appliance's properties via the CLI, you will probably use the graphical user interfaces provided by IDS Device Manager and IDS Security Monitor to make most of the configuration changes to your appliance.

Using the Sensor CLI

You can configure essentially every property of your appliance through the CLI. Understanding the following CLI characteristics enables you to use the CLI more effectively:

- Prompts
- Help
- Tab completion
- Command recall
- Command case sensitivity
- Keywords

Each of these characteristics is described in the following sections.

Prompts

Prompts displayed by the CLI are not user changeable, but they do indicate the area of the CLI that you are currently operating in. For instance, the Global Configuration mode is indicated by the following prompt (with a sensor name of "Sensor"):

```
Sensor(config)#
```

For certain CLI commands, the system requires user input. When this happens, a prompt displays an option enclosed in square brackets (such as "[yes]"). To accept this default value, all you need to do is press **Enter**. Or you can override the default value by typing in another value.

Sometimes the information displayed in CLI exceeds the number of lines available on the screen. When this occurs, the appliance presents you with the *–more–* interactive prompt (indicating that more information is available). To display more of the information, you have the following two options:

- Display the next screen by press the space key.
- Display the next line by pressing **Enter**.

Sometimes you may want to abandon the current command line and start over with a blank one. You can abort the current command line by pressing either the **Ctrl-C** or **Ctrl-Q** keys.

To return to a previous command level, use the **exit** command.

Help

To get help on a command, use the **?** character. You can use the **?** character to obtain help in the following situations:

- After a complete command
- In the middle of a command

When using the help character after a complete command, you enter the command, then a space, and then the help character (**?**), as in Example 2-7.

Example 2-7 *Using the Help Character After a Complete Command*

```
Sensor# show ?
clock               Display system clock.
configuration       Display the current system configuration.
events              Display local event log contents.
history             Display commands entered in current menu.
interfaces          Display statistics and information about system interfaces.
inventory           Display PEP information.
privilege           Display current user access role.
```

Example 2-7 *Using the Help Character After a Complete Command (Continued)*

```
ssh                 Display Secure Shell information.
statistics          Display application statistics.
tech-support        Generate report of current system status.
tls                 Display tls certificate information.
users               Show all users currently logged into the system.
version             Display product version information.
Sensor#
```

Help will display all of the keywords or options that can be used with the partial command that you have already entered.

You can also enter an incomplete command or option and use the help character to display all of the commands or options that begin with the specified sequence of characters, as in Example 2-8.

Example 2-8 *Using the Help Character with an Incomplete Command*

```
Sensor(config)# service a?
alarm-channel-configuration authentication analysis-engine
Sensor(config)# service a
```

Tab Completion

Sometimes you may be unsure of the complete command to enter. After you type the beginning of a command, you can press the **Tab** key to have the system complete the command for you. If multiple commands match the command segment you typed, the system can't fill in the command; instead, it displays the commands that match your partial entry and then redisplays your partial command, as in Example 2-9.

Example 2-9 *Using the Tab Key*

```
IDS4240(config)# service a<tab>
alarm-channel-configuration  authentication
analysis-engine
IDS4240(config)# service a
```

Command Recall

To cycle through the commands you have entered during your CLI session, use the up and down arrow keys on your keyboard. When you reach the end of the list, you will see a blank prompt.

> **NOTE** Instead of the arrows keys, you can press **Ctrl-P** for the up arrow and **Ctrl-N** for the down arrow.

Command Case Sensitivity

The CLI is case insensitive. For example, **Configure** and **CONFigure** represent the same command. When the system echoes the commands that you enter, however, it reproduces the commands in the case you typed. Suppose that you type the following at the command line:

```
Sensor# CONF
```

Now if you press the **Tab** key to invoke command completion, the system displays the following:

```
Sensor# CONFigure
```

Keywords

When using the CLI, you will enter various commands to change the configuration of your appliance. You can also use the following two keywords when entering commands via CLI:

- **no**
- **default**

If you want to reverse the effect of a command, you simply precede the command with the **no** keyword. For example, the **access-list** command allows management access from a specific host or network; using the **no access-list** command removes the previously granted access.

Some commands (such as those associated with signature tuning) have a default value. To return a command to its default value, use the **default** keyword when entering the command.

For instance, when you configure the analysis-engine parameters (accessed via the **service analysis-engine** global configuration command) as in Example 2-10, the **default** command option enables you to set either the **global-parameters** or the **virtual-sensor** to its default settings.

Example 2-10 *Setting Default Values*

```
Ids4240(config-ana)# ?
default               Set the value back to the system default setting.
exit                  Exit service configuration mode.
global-parameters     Platform-wide configuration parameters.
no                    Remove an entry or selection setting.
show                  Display system settings and/or history information.
virtual-sensor        Map of virtual sensor definitions.
Ids4240(config-ana)# default ?
global-parameters     Platform-wide configuration parameters.
virtual-sensor        Reset virtual-sensorcontents back to default.
Ids4240(config-ana)# default
```

User Roles

Beginning with version 4.0, the IDS appliance incorporated multiple user roles. When you create an account, you must assign it a user role. This user role determines the privileges of the account, and consequently the operations that the user can perform. Your Cisco IPS version 5.0 appliances support the following four user roles:

- Administrator
- Operator
- Viewer
- Service

Each of these is discussed in the following sections.

Administrator

When you assign the Administrator role to an account, you enable the user of that account to perform every operation on the appliance that is available through the CLI. Some of the capabilities available to accounts with Administrator access are as follows:

- Add users and assign passwords
- Enable and disable interfaces
- Assign interfaces to an interface group
- Modify host allowed to access appliance
- Modify sensor address configuration
- Tune signatures
- Assign virtual sensor configuration
- Manage routers for IP blocking

Operator

The second-highest user role is the Operator role. Any accounts assigned the Operator role have unrestricted viewing capability to sensor information, along with the following functions:

- Modify their own password
- Tune signatures
- Manage routers for IP blocking

Viewer

The lowest-privileged user role is the Viewer role. When you assign the Viewer role to an account, you enable the user to view the configuration and event data on your appliance. The only appliance information that users with this role can change is their password.

NOTE Applications (such as the IDS Security Monitor) that you use to monitor your IPS appliance can operate with only Viewer-level access to the sensor. You can create an account with Viewer access by using the CLI and then configure your monitoring applications to use this account when retrieving information from your IPS appliance.

Service

The Service role enables you to create a special account that can access the native operating system (OS) command shell rather than the sensor's normal CLI interface. The purpose of this account is not to support configuration of the sensor, but instead to provide an enhanced troubleshooting capability. By default, your sensor does not have a service account. You must create a service account to enable TAC to use this account during troubleshooting.

The sensor allows you to assign the Service role to only one account on the sensor. When the Service account's password is set (or reset), the Linux root account's password is automatically synchronized to this new password. This enables the Service account user to use the **su** command to access root privileges on the sensor.

NOTE On UNIX systems, the most privileged account is named *root*. This account has virtually unlimited powers on the system. Gaining *root* access to a system enables an attacker to totally control the system. Similarly, the Service account has virtually unlimited powers on the sensor. Therefore, you need to protect access to the Service account.

CAUTION Making modifications to your sensor by using the Service account can make your sensor unsupported by the Cisco TAC. Cisco does not support adding any services or programs to your sensor, since doing so can impact the proper performance and functioning of the other IDS services. Furthermore, access to the Service account is recorded on the sensor.

CLI Command Modes

The CLI on your IPS appliance is organized into various modes. Each of these modes gives you access to a subset of the commands that are available on your IPS appliance. Numerous CLI modes such as the following are available on the IPS appliance:

- Privileged Exec
- Global Configuration

- Service web-server
- Service analysis-engine
- Service host
- Service network-access
- Service signature-definition

Each of these is described in the following sections.

Privileged Exec

The Privileged Exec mode is the initial mode that you enter upon logging in to the IDS appliance. You can recognize this mode because it is composed of simply the sensor name followed by the # character, such as in the following example (assuming a sensor name of IDS4250):

```
IPS4250#
```

Some of tasks that you can perform in the Privileged Exec mode are as follows:

- Initialize the sensor
- Manually set the time
- Reboot the sensor
- Enter Global Configuration mode
- Terminate the current login session
- Display system settings

Global Configuration

You need to enter the Global Configuration mode, as you do in IOS, to change the configuration parameters on your IPS appliance. You access the Global Configuration mode by entering the **configure terminal** command from the Privileged Exec mode. When you enter this mode, the prompt changes to the following:

```
IPS4250(config)#
```

Some of tasks that you can perform in the Global Configuration mode are as follows:

- Change the sensor's host name
- Create user accounts
- Configure SSH, Telnet, and Transport Layer Security (TLS) settings
- Re-image the application partition

- Upgrade and downgrade system software and images
- Enter service configuration modes

Service

The Service mode is a generic third-level command mode. It enables you to enter the configuration mode for the following services:

- analysis-engine
- authentication
- event-action-rules
- host
- interface
- logger
- network-access
- notification
- signature-definition
- ssh-known-hosts
- trusted-certificates
- web-server

Each of these is described in the following sections.

Service Analysis-Engine

The analysis-engine mode is a third-level service mode that enables you to perform various tasks such as the following:

- Create new virtual sensors
- Assign signature-definitions to virtual sensors
- Assign event-action-rules to virtual sensors
- Assign sensing-interfaces to virtual sensors

You can recognize this mode because the prompt changes to the following:

```
IDS4250(config-ana)#
```

Service Authentication

The authentication mode is a third-level service mode that enables you to configure the maximum failure attempts allowed before an account becomes disabled.

You can recognize this mode because the prompt changes to the following:

```
IPS4250(config-aut)#
```

This setting applies to all accounts on the system. By default, account lockout is not enabled. You need to be careful when enabling it, since you can potentially lock out your account that has administrative access.

Service Event-Action-Rules

The event-action-rules mode is a third-level service mode that enables you to perform various event-related tasks such as the following:

- Define target risk values
- Define event filters
- Configure system- and user-defined variables

You can recognize this mode because the prompt changes to the following:

```
IPS4240(config-rul)#
```

When entering this mode, you must specify the name of the instance configuration. Currently, the only instance allowed is *rules0.* In the future, however, you may be able to specify multiple configuration instances. Therefore, to access the event-action-rules mode, you use the following command:

```
IPS4240(config)# service event-action-rules rules0
IPS4240(config-url)#
```

NOTE The event-action-rules configuration replaces the alarm-channel-configuration that was available in Cisco IDS version 4.0.

Service Host

The host mode is a third-level service mode that enables you to perform various host-related tasks such as the following:

- Enter the network-settings configuration mode

- Enter the time-zone-settings configuration mode
- Enable use of an Network Time Protocol (NTP) server
- Display current settings

You can recognize this mode because the prompt changes to the following:

```
IPS4250(config-hos)#
```

The following two fourth-level configuration modes are accessible via the host mode:

- network-settings
- time-zone-settings

The network-settings mode enables you to configure numerous host-related items, such as the following:

- Configure a sensor's IP address
- Define a default gateway
- Define access lists
- Enable or disable the Telnet server

You can recognize the network-settings mode by the following command prompt:

```
IPS4250(config-hos-net)#
```

The time-zone-settings mode enables you to complete time-related tasks, such as the following:

- Configure the sensor's time zone
- Display current time configuration

You can recognize the time-zone-settings mode by the following command prompt:

```
IPS4250(config-hos-tim)#
```

Service Interface

The interface mode is a third-level service mode that enables you to perform the following tasks:

- Configure physical interfaces
- Configure inline interface pairs (for inline-capable devices)
- Configure interface notification parameters

You can recognize the interface mode by the following command prompt:

```
IPS4250(config-int)#
```

Service Logger

The logger mode is a third-level service mode that enables you to configure the debug levels for the sensor. You can recognize this mode because the prompt changes to the following:

```
IPS4250(config-log)#
```

Service Network-Access

The network-access mode is a third-level service mode that enables you to perform the following tasks:

- Configure settings for PIX firewalls controlled by the Network Access Controller (NAC) process
- Configure settings for routers controlled by the NAC process
- Display current NAC-related settings

You can recognize this mode because the prompt changes to the following:

```
IPS4250(config-net)#
```

You can also enter a general fourth-level command mode that enables you to define many of the sensor's IP-blocking (shun) settings, such as the following:

- Configure never-shun address
- Configure the master blocking sensor
- Enable Access Control List logging
- Display current shun-related settings

You can recognize this fourth-level mode because the prompt changes to the following:

```
IPS4250(config-net-gen)#
```

Service Notification

The notification mode is a third-level service mode that enables you to configure the Simple Network Management Protocol (SNMP) characteristics of the sensor, such as the following tasks:

- Define community names
- Define SNMP port
- Define SNMP trap characteristics

You can recognize this fourth-level mode because the prompt changes to the following:

```
IPS4250(config-not)#
```

Service Signature-Definition

The signature-definition mode is a third-level service mode that enables you to perform various signature-related tasks, such as the following:

- Define fragment reassembly parameters
- Define stream reassembly parameters
- Modify specific signature characteristics

You can recognize this fourth-level mode because the prompt changes to the following:

```
IPS4250(config-sig)#
```

When entering this mode, you must specify the name of the instance configuration. Currently, the only instance allowed is *sig0*. In the future, however, you may be able to specify multiple configuration instances. To access the signature-definition mode, use the following command:

```
IPS4240(config)# service signature-definition sig0
IPS4240(config-url)#
```

Service SSH-Known-Hosts

The ssh-known-hosts mode is a third-level service mode that enables you to perform various SSH-related tasks, such as the following:

- Define SSH keys for allowed hosts
- Remove SSH-allowed hosts

You can recognize this third-level mode because the prompt changes to the following:

```
IPS4250(config-ssh)#
```

Service Trusted-Certificates

The trusted-certificates mode is a third-level service mode that enables you to perform various TLS/SSL-related tasks, such as the following:

- Define X.509 host certificates for allowed hosts
- Remove X.509 host certificates

You can recognize this third-level mode because the prompt changes to the following:

```
IPS4250(config-tru)#
```

Service Web-Server

The web-server mode is a third-level service mode that enables you to perform the following tasks:

- Enable or disable secure Web access
- Define the port for secure Web access
- Define the server ID for secure Web access

You can recognize this third-level mode because the prompt changes to the following:

```
IPS4250(config-web)#
```

Administrative Tasks

The sensor command line enables you to perform numerous administrative tasks, such as the following:

- Display the current configuration
- Back up the current configuration
- Restore the current configuration
- Display events
- Reboot the sensor
- Display technical-support information
- Capture network packets

Some of these tasks will be covered in Chapter 12, "Verifying System Configuration." For detailed information on how to perform these administrative tasks, refer to the CLI documentation at Cisco.com (http://www.cisco.com/go/ids).

Configuration Tasks

The CLI provides you with a textual interface that enables you to configure essentially every facet of the sensor's configuration, such as the following:

- Configure system variables
- Configure event filters
- View signature engines

- Configure virtual sensor system variables
- Tune signature engines
- Generate IP logs

Configuring these tasks through the CLI, however, is not a simple task. Most people prefer to use a graphical interface, such as Cisco IPS Device Manager, to configure these parameters. Numerous chapters in this book explain how to configure these characteristics of your sensor by using the Cisco IPS Device Manager. For complete documentation on Cisco IDS version 5.0 CLI, refer to the documentation at Cisco.com (http://www.cisco.com/go/ids).

Foundation Summary

Installing network sensors correctly is an important component in protecting your network with Cisco Intrusion Prevention. Cisco provides appliance sensors that support a wide range of bandwidths and deployment locations.

You can upgrade your sensors from 4.1 to 5.0 by using one of the following two methods:

- Install 5.0 software via the network
- Install 5.0 software from a CD

NOTE For the diskless sensors (IDS 4215, IDS 4240, IDS 4255), you can install the 5.0 software only through the network since the sensors do not have a CD-ROM drive.

When installing a new sensor (or upgrading via the recovery CD), you need to perform some basic initialization steps to get the sensor running. The basic appliance initialization tasks are as follows:

- Run the **setup** command
- Configure trusted hosts
- Manually configure the time
- Create the Service account

The **setup** CLI command configures the following parameters:

- Sensor host name
- Sensor IP address
- Sensor netmask
- Access list entries
- Default gateway
- Telnet server status
- Web server port
- Time settings

Some other tasks that you may need to perform during initialization include the following:

- Change your password
- Add and remove users
- Add known SSH hosts

Beginning with Cisco IDS version 4.0, the appliance sensors have an extensive CLI that enables you to configure every aspect of your sensor's operation. Although the commands are different, using the CLI is very similar to using IOS. The CLI is divided into the multiple configuration modes, each of which provides a subset of the commands available to the user, such as the following:

- Privileged Exec
- Global Configuration
- Service web-server
- Service analysis-engine
- Service host
- Service network-access
- Service signature-definition

Although the CLI enables you to configure every aspect of the sensor, configuring certain aspects, such as signature tuning, are easier to do in the graphical interfaces (such as Cisco IPS Device Manager). When troubleshooting, however, you may use this configuration capability to identify a problem, or you may create custom configuration scripts that you use to adjust the operation of your sensor.

Q&A

You have two choices for review questions:

- The questions that follow give you a bigger challenge than the exam itself by using an open-ended question format. By reviewing now with this more difficult question format, you can exercise your memory better and prove your conceptual and factual knowledge of this chapter. The answers to these questions are found in the appendix.
- For more practice with exam-like question formats, use the exam engine on the CD-ROM.

1. What character do you use to obtain help via the appliance CLI, and what are the two ways you can use it to obtain help?
2. What command enables you to allow a host or all of the hosts on a network to connect to the sensor?
3. How many different user roles are available to assign to accounts on your sensor?
4. What is the most privileged user role that you can assign to a CLI user?
5. Which user role provides the user with the ability to examine the sensor's events and configuration but does not allow the user to change the configuration?
6. What parameters can you configure by using the **setup** CLI command?
7. What is the purpose of the Service user role?
8. What command do you use on the CLI to enter Global Configuration mode?
9. How many Service accounts can you have on your sensor?
10. What user role would you usually assign to the account that you use to enable your monitoring applications to retrieve information from your sensor?
11. What character do you use on the CLI to cause your sensor to automatically expand the rest of a command for you?
12. When a CLI command's output extends beyond a single screen, what character do you use to show the next screen of information?
13. When a CLI command's output extends beyond a single screen, what character do you use to see just the next line of output?
14. Which sensors cannot be upgraded with a recovery CD and why?
15. What are the transfer options available for upgrading appliance sensors through the network?
16. Before you can use SCP to retrieve a new image file or signature update, what must you do on the sensor?

This chapter covers the following subjects:

- Cisco IPS Device Manager
- System Requirements for IDM
- Navigating IDM
- Configuring Communication Parameters by Using IDM

CHAPTER 3

Cisco IPS Device Manager (IDM)

The Cisco IPS Device Manager (IDM) is a tool that enables you to configure and manage a single Cisco network sensor. This Java-based web tool provides you with a graphical interface to manipulate the operation of your sensor. Each IPS appliance running on your network has its own web server that provides access to the IDM application on the sensor.

Accurately configuring your Cisco IPS devices is vital to efficiently protecting your network. This chapter explains how to navigate the graphical configuration tool that comes with each sensor. Beginning with Cisco IPS version 5.0, the IDM interface has been completely revamped. Reviewing this chapter will provide you with information on how the new interface is structured. This information will be important for you to follow the configuration examples used throughout the rest of the book.

"Do I Know This Already?" Quiz

The purpose of the "Do I Know This Already?" quiz is to help you decide if you really need to read the entire chapter. If you already intend to read the entire chapter, you do not necessarily need to answer these questions now.

The 10-question quiz, derived from the major sections in the "Foundation and Supplemental Topics" portion of the chapter, helps you determine how to spend your limited study time.

Table 3-1 outlines the major topics discussed in this chapter and the "Do I Know This Already?" quiz questions that correspond to those topics.

Table 3-1 *"Do I Know This Already?" Foundation and Supplemental Topics Mapping*

Foundation or Supplemental Topic	Questions Covering This Topic
System Requirements for IDM	1, 4, 5
Navigating IDM	3, 6, 8, 10
Configuring Communication Parameters by using IDM	2, 7, 9

> **CAUTION** The goal of self-assessment is to gauge your mastery of the topics in this chapter. If you do not know the answer to a question or are only partially sure of the answer, you should mark this question wrong for purposes of the self-assessment. Giving yourself credit for an answer you correctly guess skews your self-assessment results and might provide you with a false sense of security.

1. Which version of Linux is supported for use with IDM?
   a. Red Hat
   b. Debian
   c. Slackware
   d. Mandrake
   e. SUSE
2. Which of the following is a configurable sensor communication parameter?
   a. Changing the TLS/SSL port
   b. Changing the Telnet port
   c. Changing SSH port
   d. Changing the TLS/SSL port and the Telnet port
   e. None of these
3. Which of the following is not a configuration category in IDM?
   a. Sensor Setup
   b. Analysis Engine
   c. SNMP
   d. IP Logging
   e. Event Action Rules
4. Which of the following Solaris versions is supported for use with IDM?
   a. Version 2.6
   b. Version 2.7
   c. Version 2.9
   d. Version 2.5

5. Which web browser is supported on Microsoft Windows 2000 for access to IDM?
   a. Opera 7.54u1
   b. Internet Explorer 5.5
   c. Netscape 7.1
   d. Netscape 6.0
   e. Firefox 1.0
6. Which of the following is not a monitoring category in IDM?
   a. Blocking
   b. Denied Attackers
   c. IP Logging
   d. Events
   e. Network Blocks
7. Which of the following is not a configurable sensor communication parameter?
   a. Telnet port
   b. TLS/SSL port
   c. Default route
   d. IP address
   e. Host name
8. Where are the configuration options on the IDM screen?
   a. The location of the options is configurable.
   b. The options are listed on the right side of the screen.
   c. The options are accessed via pull-down menus.
   d. The options are listed across the top of the screen.
   e. The options are listed on the left of the screen.
9. Where should you configure the sensor communication parameters?
   a. **Sensor Setup>Network**
   b. **Interface Configuration>Interfaces**
   c. **Sensor Setup>Allowed Hosts**
   d. **Analysis Engine>Virtual Sensor**
   e. **Analysis Engine>Global Variables**

10. Which Simple Network Management Protocol (SNMP) operations are supported by Cisco IPS version 5.0?

    a. Get only

    b. Set only

    c. Trap only

    d. Get, Set, and Trap

    e. SNMP is not supported

The answers to the "Do I Know This Already?" quiz are found in the appendix. The suggested choices for your next step are as follows:

- **8 or less overall score**—Read the entire chapter. This includes the "Foundation and Supplemental Topics," "Foundation Summary," and Q&A sections.
- **9 or 10 overall score**—If you want more review on these topics, skip to the "Foundation Summary" section and then go to the Q&A section. Otherwise, move to the next chapter.

Foundation and Supplemental Topics

Cisco IPS Device Manager

The Cisco IDM is a Java-based web interface that enables you to configure and manipulate the operation of your Cisco network sensors. Each IPS appliance running on your network has its own web server that provides access to the IDM application on the sensor. The web server uses Transport Layer Security (TLS) to encrypt the traffic to and from the sensor to prevent an attacker from viewing sensitive management traffic. The web server is also hardened to minimize an attacker's ability to disrupt or compromise its operation.

This chapter focuses on the following topics:

- System requirements for IDM
- Navigating IDM
- Configuring communication parameters by using IDM

System Requirements for IDM

Because the IDS Device Manager is a web-based application, the major system requirement is a web browser. Having sufficient memory and screen resolution also promotes effective operation of IDM. The recommended memory and screen resolution are as follows:

- 256 MB memory (minimum)
- 1024 x 768 resolution and 256 colors (minimum)

Cisco has identified system requirements based on the following three operating systems for use with IDM:

- Microsoft Windows
- Sun Solaris
- Red Hat Linux

The recommended configuration for using Windows is as follows:

- Microsoft Windows 2000 or Windows XP

- Internet Explorer 6.0 with Java Plug-in 1.4.1 or 1.4.2, or Netscape 7.1 with Java Plug-in 1.4.1 or 1.4.2
- Pentium III or equivalent, running at 450 MHz or higher

The recommended configuration for using Solaris is as follows:

- Sun Solaris 2.8 or 2.9
- Mozilla 1.7

The recommended configuration for using Red Hat is as follows:

- Red Hat Linux 9.0 or Red Hat Enterprise Linux WS version 3, running GNOME or KDE
- Mozilla 1.7

NOTE Although any web browser may work with IDM, Cisco supports only the browsers and system configurations mentioned here.

Navigating IDM

Starting with Cisco IPS version 5.0, the IDM interface has been completely restructured. The new graphical interface (see Figure 3-1) contains an icon bar with the following options:

- Configuration
- Monitoring
- Back
- Forward
- Refresh
- Help

Configuration

Configuring the operational characteristics of the sensor is the main functionality provided by IDM. By clicking on the **Configuration** icon (located on the top menu bar), you can display a list of configurable items down the left side of the screen (see Figure 3-1). These items are divided into the following operational categories:

- Sensor Setup
- Interface Configuration

- Analysis Engine
- Signature Definition
- Event Action Rules
- Blocking
- SNMP
- Auto Update

Figure 3-1 *Main IDM Screen*

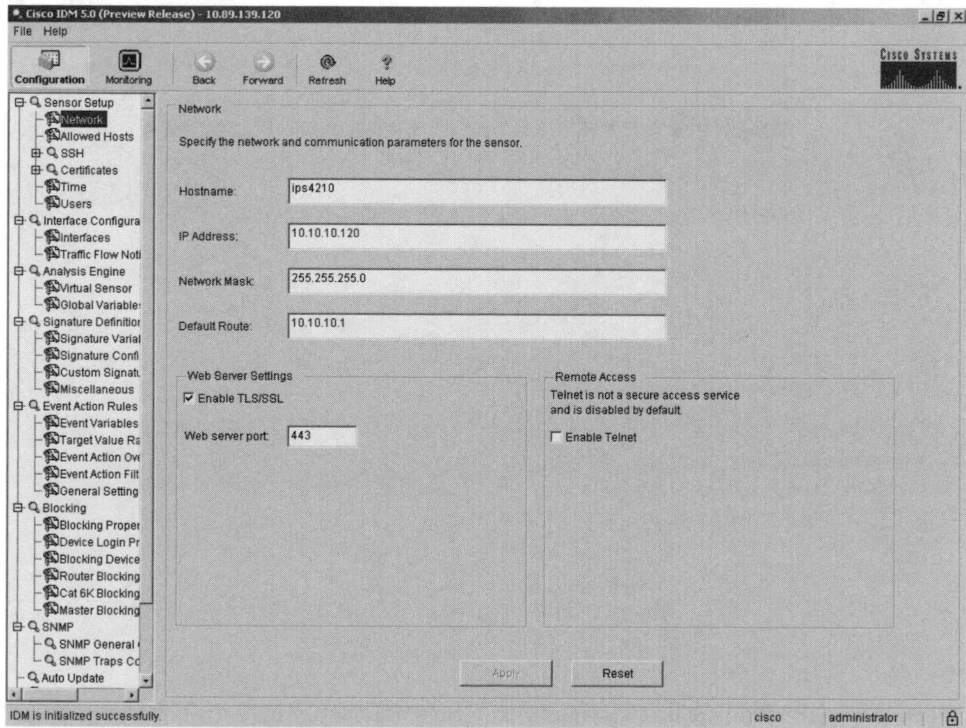

These operational categories are explained in the following sections.

> **NOTE** Most operational categories have multiple options. If the individual options (for a specific category) are not shown, click on the plus sign on the left of the category name. This will expand that category and show all of the next-level options. Clicking on the minus sign (to the left of a category name) collapses the individual options under the category name.

> **NOTE** The configuration options displayed vary depending on the privilege level of the user who logs in to IDM.

Clicking on one of the configuration options (shown on the left side of the IDM interface) displays the configuration information for that option in the main portion of the screen. For example, Figure 3-2 shows the configuration screen displayed when you select **Sensor Setup>Users**.

Figure 3-2 *Sensor Setup Users Screen*

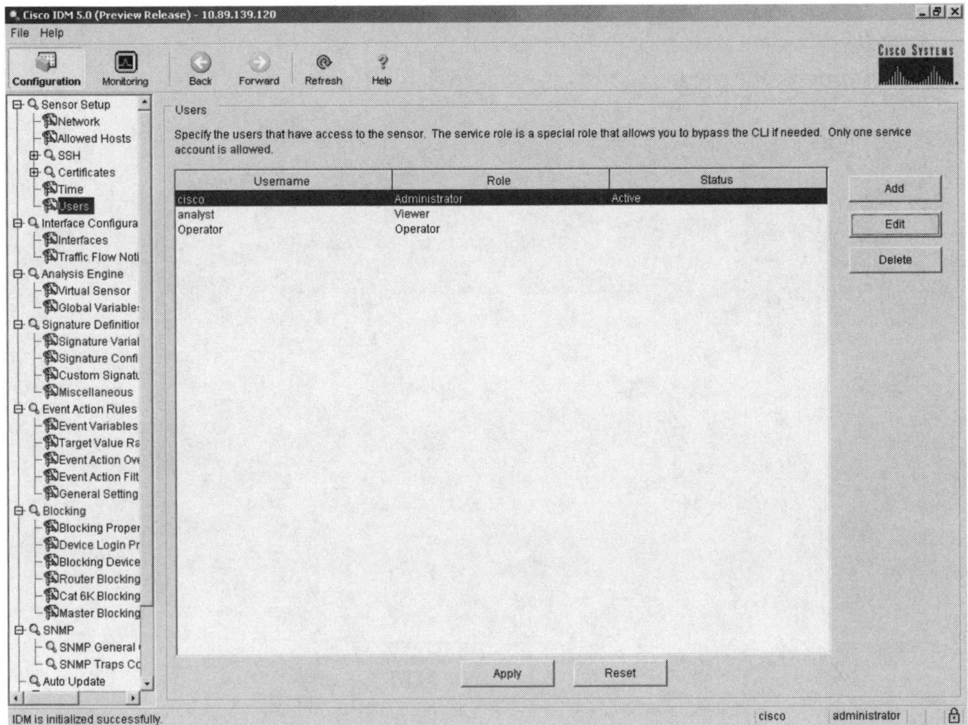

When you make changes to a configuration screen, the **Apply** icon is no longer grayed out. To save the changes, click on the **Apply** button at the bottom of the configuration screen. Clicking on the **Reset** button removes your changes (restoring the original configuration values).

> **NOTE** When you make changes to a configuration screen and then attempt to move to another configuration screen (without clicking on either the **Apply** icon or the **Reset** button), the popup window shown in Figure 3-3 appears. To save your changes, simply click on **Apply Changes**. To discard the changes, click on **Discard Changes**. Clicking on **Cancel** causes you to remain at the current configuration screen without applying changes or restoring them to their original values.

Figure 3-3 *Accept Changes Popup Window*

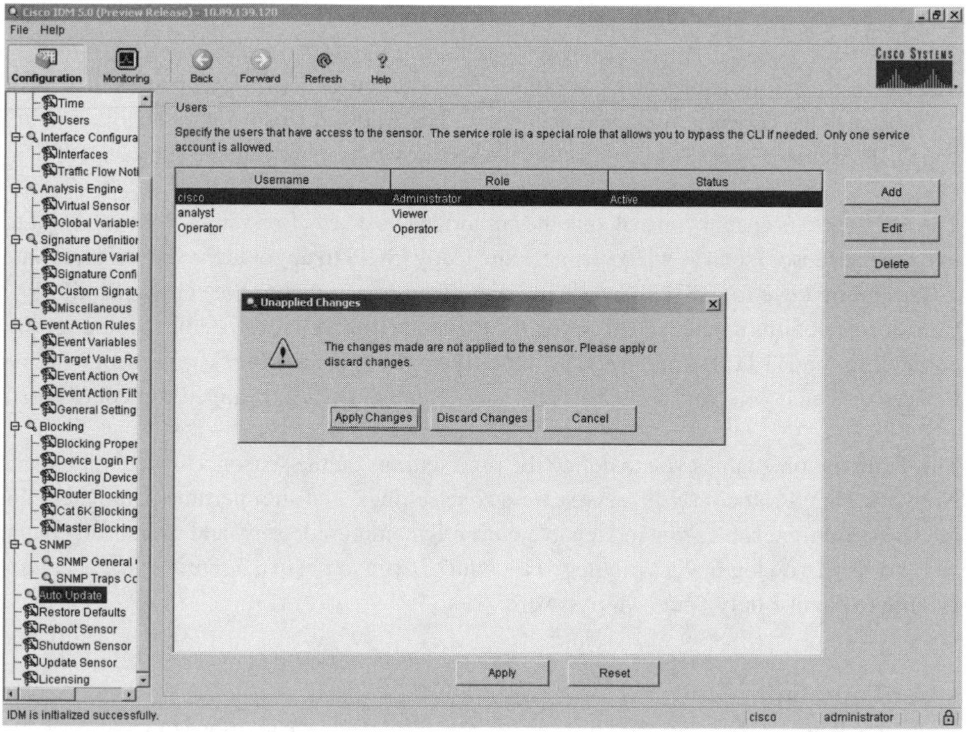

Sensor Setup

When configuring access to your sensor, you will use the options available in the Sensor Setup category. These include configuring the sensor's IP address, the users on the system, and the sensor's time parameters. Through the Sensor Setup options, you can also configure access to the sensor for Secure Shell (SSH) and secure web access (using HTTPS). The Sensor Setup category is divided into the following options:

- Network
- Allowed Hosts
- SSH>Authorized Keys
- SSH>Known Host Keys
- SSH>Sensor Key
- Certificates>Trusted Hosts
- Certificates>Server Certificate

- Time
- Users

The Network option enables you to configure the basic sensor network properties such as IP address, default gateway, network mask, and host name. The Allowed Hosts option enables you to define which IP addresses are allowed to access the sensor via its management interface.

The SSH options enable you to define the authorized host keys for systems that you want to connect to from the sensor (such as when using Secure Copy [SCP] to upgrade the sensor's software) as well as the public keys for SSH clients that are allowed to connect to the sensor. Similarly, the two Certificates options enable you to define the trusted certificates for systems that the sensor needs to connect to via HTTPS. This would commonly apply to master blocking sensors and other IPS devices to which your sensor connects by using Remote Data Exchange Protocol (RDEP).

The Time option enables you to define the time settings on the sensor. This includes specifying a Network Time Protocol (NTP) server, time zone settings, and summertime parameters. Finally, the Users option enables you to view the currently configured users, add users, and change users' passwords (if you log in via a privileged account). If you log in to a nonprivileged account, you will be able to change only your own password.

Interface Configuration

Each time your sensor is powered on; it automatically detects the interface modules that are installed in the sensor. The network interfaces enable your sensor to monitor network traffic, using either promiscuous or inline modes of operation. Before monitoring traffic, the interfaces need to be configured.

The command and control interface enables you to access your sensor. This interface is permanently mapped to a specific physical interface (depending on the model of the sensor).

The Interface Configuration category includes the following options:

- Interfaces
- Interface Pairs*
- Bypass*
- Traffic Flow Notifications

NOTE The selections marked with an asterisk (*) may not be shown if your sensor does not have enough interfaces to support inline mode. Inline mode requires at least two interfaces in addition to the command and control interface.

The Interfaces option enables you to configure basic interface properties, such as speed and whether the interface is enabled. The Interface Pairs option enables you to define pairs of interfaces that will be used for inline monitoring. When using inline mode, you may also need to use the Bypass option to configure the software bypass mode, which determines how network traffic is handled during operational disruptions in the sensor's inspection applications.

The Traffic Flow Notifications option enables you to configure the following parameters:

- Missed Packet Threshold
- Notification Interval
- Interface Idle Threshold

These parameters determine when event notifications are generated based on the flow of traffic across the sensor's interfaces. For more information on Traffic Flow Notifications, refer to Chapter 4, "Basic Sensor Configuration."

Analysis Engine

The analysis engine performs packet analysis and alert detection. It monitors traffic that flows through the specified interfaces and interface pairs.

The Analysis Engine category provides the following options:

- Virtual Sensor
- Global Variables

To use the any of the sensor's interfaces to analyze network traffic, you must assign it to a virtual sensor. The Virtual Sensor option enables you to assign or remove sensor interfaces from a virtual sensor.

> **NOTE** Currently, sensor software supports only a single virtual sensor (vs0). In the future, however, Cisco IPS sensors may support multiple virtual sensors. These virtual sensors would enable you to make one physical sensor appear to be multiple sensors, each with unique configuration settings. This concept is similar to that of virtual firewalls, where a single physical firewall can be configured (via software) to operate as multiple virtual firewalls that each have unique configuration parameters.

The Global Variables option enables you to configure the maximum number of IP log files that the sensor will support.

Signature Definition

Network intrusions are attacks and other misuses of network resources. A signature is a set of rules that a sensor uses to detect intrusive activity. As the sensor scans network traffic, it searches for matches to the signatures that it is configured to detect. When a match to a signature is found, the sensor takes the action that you have configured for that signature.

The Signature Definition category has the following options:

- Signature Variables
- Signature Configuration
- Custom Signature Wizard
- Miscellaneous

Using the Signature Variables option, you can configure signature variables that define ranges of IP addresses. You can then use these signature variables when defining signatures. When you change the value of the variable, the change is automatically replicated to all of the signatures where it is referenced. You can also change the predefined signature variable that determines which ports are examined during web analysis.

Using the Signature Configuration option, you can view the available signatures and their properties. You can enable and disable signatures as well as adding new signatures and editing the properties of existing signatures.

Using the Custom Signature Wizard option, you can create custom signatures by using a menu-driven interface that simplifies the creation process.

The Miscellaneous option enables you to configure specific global sensor parameters for the following aspects of the sensor's operation:

- Application policy settings
- Fragment reassembly settings
- Stream reassembly settings
- IP log settings

For more information on configuring these options, refer to Chapter 8, "Sensor Tuning."

Event Action Rules

Event action rules define how your sensor will process specific events when it detects them on the network. Event action rules define the following functionality on the sensor:

- Calculating the Risk Rating
- Adding event-action overrides

- Filtering event action
- Executing the resulting event action
- Summarizing and aggregating events
- Maintaining a list of denied attackers

The Event Action Rules category provides the following options:

- Event Variables
- Target Value Rating
- Event Action Overrides
- Event Action Filters
- General Settings

Using the Event Variables option, you can define variables that you use when defining event filters. These variables identify lists or ranges of IP address. By defining event variables (instead of using the actual addresses in the filters), you can more easily update IP addresses. Whenever you need to add or remove an address, you just change the event variable definition.

The Target Value Rating enables you to configure an asset rating for specific IP address ranges. The asset rating can be one of the following values:

- No value
- Low
- Medium
- High
- Mission critical

The Event Action Overrides option defines when actions are automatically assigned to events based on the value of the Risk Rating. You can assign an event action override for each of the actions that you can normally assign to a signature.

The Event Action Filters option enables you to define event action filters. These filters prevent (or filter) configured actions from being applied to specific events. Filters can be based on numerous factors such as IP address, signature ID, and Risk Rating.

The General Settings option enables you to define general settings that apply to event action rules. These include the following parameters, as well as the ability to enable and disable the meta-event generator and summarizer:

- Deny attacker duration
- Block action duration
- Maximum denied attackers

Blocking

One of the actions that you can configure your sensor to take when a signature triggers is to block traffic from the system that initiated the intrusive traffic. The two types of blocking actions that you can configure are as follows:

- Host block
- Connection block

When you configure a signature to block a connection, it blocks only traffic from the host that triggered the signature to the destination port, the protocol (such as TCP or UDP), and the destination IP address that triggered the signature. Therefore, the blocking decision is based on the following parameters:

- Source IP address
- Destination IP address
- Destination port
- Protocol

A host block, on the other hand, blocks all traffic from the attacking host regardless of the destination port, protocol, or destination IP address.

The Blocking category has the following configuration options:

- Blocking Properties
- Device Login Profiles
- Blocking Devices
- Router Blocking Device Interfaces

- Cat6k Blocking Device Interfaces
- Master Blocking Sensor

Using the Block Properties option, you can configure the basic blocking properties along with the IP addresses that the blocking devices should never block. The Device Login Profiles option defines the credentials necessary for the sensor to access the blocking devices that you add by using the Blocking Devices option. To block network traffic, the blocking device applies an access control list (ACL) to one of its interfaces. You configure which interface the blocking ACL will be applied to on routers by using the Router Blocking Device Interfaces option. Similarly, you configure which interface the blocking ACL will be applied to on Catalyst 6000 switches by using Cat6k Blocking Device Interfaces.

NOTE For Cisco PIX and ASA blocking devices, you do not need to configure a specific interface since each uses the device's **shun** command to block the traffic.

The Master Blocking Sensor option enables you define which sensors will serve as master blocking sensors. A master blocking sensor initiates IP blocking for another sensor, since only one sensor can initiate IP blocking on a specific blocking device.

Simple Network Management Protocol

Beginning with Cisco IPS version 5.0, sensor software supports Simple Network Management Protocol (SNMP) functionality (see RFC 1157, "Simple Network Management Protocol [SNMP]"). SNMP facilitates the exchange of management information between network devices, enabling network administrators to manage network performance as well as find and solve network problems. Using SNMP, management stations can efficiently monitor the health and status of many types of network devices, including switches, routers, and sensors.

NOTE SNMP is a simple protocol in which the network-management system issues a request, and managed devices return responses. This interaction is implemented by using one of the following four operations:

- Get—Retrieves information for a specific SNMP field
- GetNext—Retrieves the next SNMP field
- Set—Sets the value for a specific SNMP field
- Trap—Configures SNMP to generate a SNMP response when a certain event occurs

Besides polling for SNMP responses, your can configure your sensors to generate SNMP traps. In this situation, the management station does not poll the sensor for information. Instead, when a specific event occurs, the sensor sends an unsolicited message to the management system. SNMP traps are effective in environments where it is impractical to constantly poll every device on the network.

The SNMP category provides the following options:

- SNMP General Configuration
- SNMP Traps Configuration

SNMP Gets, Sets, and Traps are disabled by default. To use these features to manage your sensor, you need to enable them.

Auto Update

To maintain the latest software images on your sensors, you can configure your sensor to automatically load service pack and signature updates from a central FTP or SCP server. Selecting Auto Update displays the configuration values that your sensor will use to automatically update software.

NOTE Your sensor cannot automatically load service pack and signature updates from Cisco.com. You need to download them to your FTP or SCP server, from which your sensors can automatically retrieve them. Furthermore, if you need to downgrade the software (return to a previous software version) on your sensor, you can use the **downgrade** global configuration command via the sensor CLI.

NOTE FTP transmits login credentials in the clear (in other words, the traffic is not encrypted). Therefore, the FTP server should be on a separate management network since it will be a prime target for attack. At minimum, the user account used to retrieve sensor software images needs to have minimal privileges on the FTP server.

Monitoring

Besides helping you configure your sensor, IDM also provides the ability to monitor the status and operation of the sensor. The monitoring functionality is divided into the following options (see Figure 3-4):

- Denied Attackers
- Active Host Blocks
- Network Blocks
- IP Logging
- Events
- Support Information>Diagnostic Report

- Support Information>Statistics
- Support Information>System Information

> **NOTE** The monitoring options displayed vary depending on the privilege level of the user who logs in to IDM.

Figure 3-4 *IDM Monitoring Functionality*

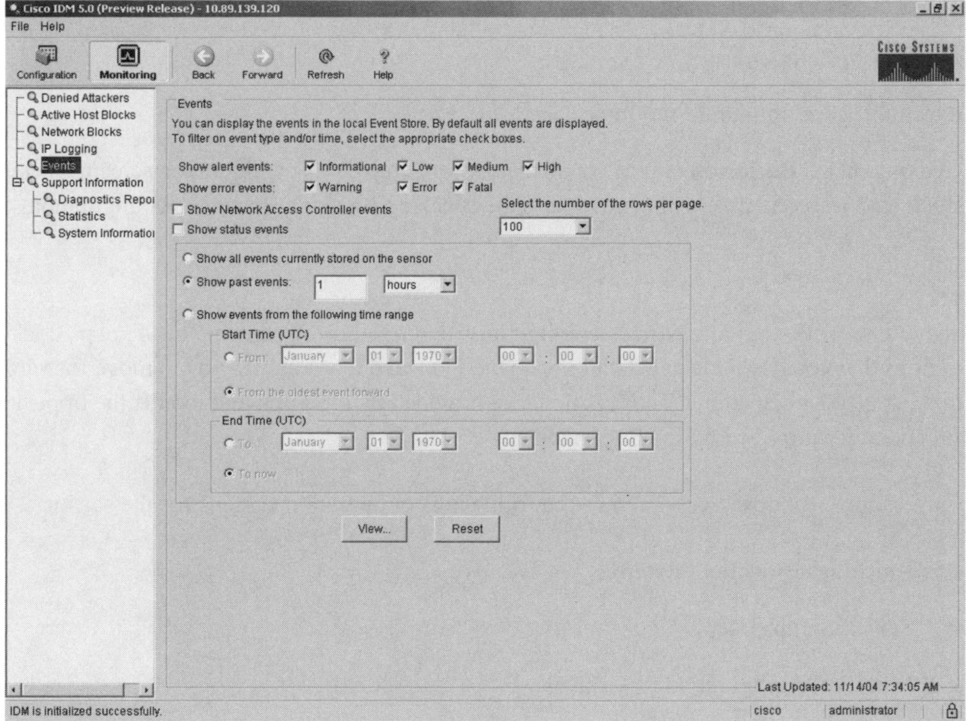

The Denied Attackers option enables you to view the IP addresses that are currently blocked by the sensor. The Active Host Blocks option enables you to manually block specific hosts for a specified duration. Similarly, the Network Blocks option enables you to manually establish a block for an entire network. Using the IP Logging option, you can manually log traffic from a specified host.

Using the Events option, you can view events generated by the sensor. Monitoring events provides a basic mechanism that you can use to examine the events that your sensor is generating.

The Support Information options provide information useful in debugging the operation of the sensor. Refer to Chapter 12, "Verifying System Configuration," for more information on debugging the operation of your sensor.

Back

As you move through the various configuration and monitoring screens, IDM keeps track of the options you have selected. Clicking on the **Back** icon enables you to return to one of previous configuration screens that you were modifying or viewing (the **Back** icon is similar to your browser's **Back** button). Each click on the **Back** icon takes you back one screen in the list of configuration screens that you have visited.

For instance, suppose that you view the following configuration screens for the sensor:

- Blocking > Blocking Properties
- Sensor Setup > Users
- Interface Configuration > Interfaces

Clicking on the **Back** icon returns you to the Sensor Setup Users configuration screen. Clicking on the **Back** icon a second time will return you to the Blocking Blocking Properties configuration screen.

Forward

As you move through the various configuration and monitoring screens, IDM keeps track of the options that you have selected. Clicking on the **Forward** icon enables you to move forward through this list of your selections. The functionality provided by the **Forward** icon is the opposite of the functionality provided by the **Back** icon.

For instance, suppose that you view the following configuration screens for the sensor:

- Blocking>Blocking Properties
- Sensor Setup>Users
- Interface Configuration>Interfaces

Clicking on the **Back** icon returns you to the Sensor Setup Users configuration screen. Clicking on the **Forward** icon returns you to the Interface Configuration>Interfaces configuration screen.

Refresh

Clicking on the **Refresh** icon causes the current screen to update based on the configuration information stored on the sensor. If you try to refresh without applying changes that you have made, you will be prompted to either save the changes or discard them.

Help

Clicking on the **Help** icon brings up context-sensitive help in a separate browser window. Suppose that you are configuring the blocking properties for the sensor (via Blocking Blocking Properties).

Clicking on the **Help** icon brings up Help information on configuring the blocking properties (see Figure 3-5).

Figure 3-5 *IDM Help Screen*

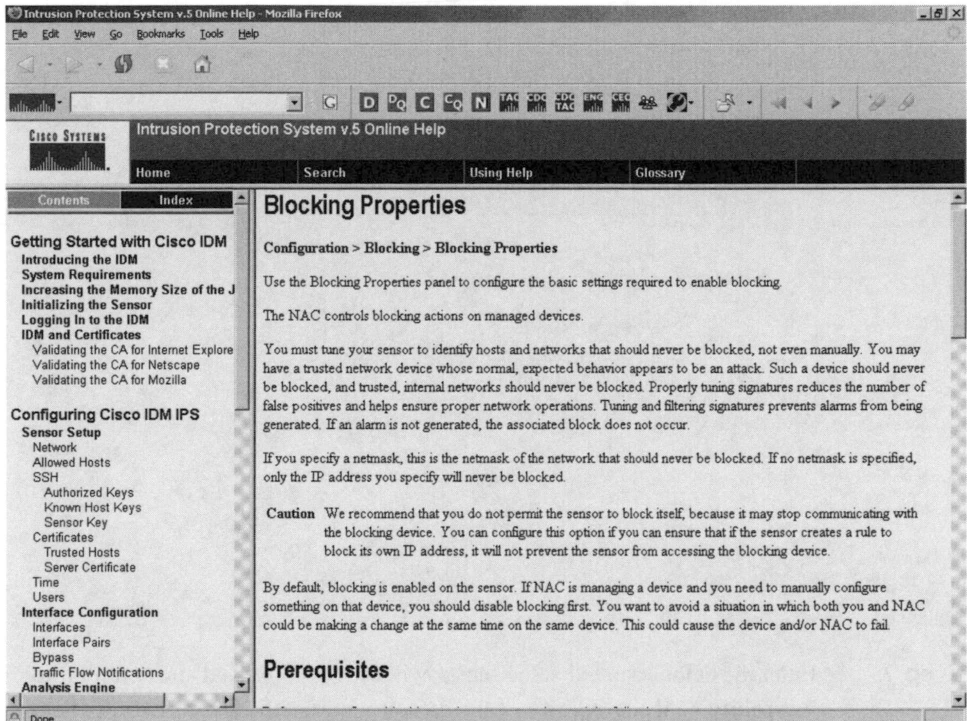

Configuring Communication Parameters Using IDM

To configure the sensor communication parameters on your sensor, perform the following steps:

Step 1 Click on the **Configuration** icon located on the top IDM menu bar.

Step 2 If the **Sensor Setup** category is not expanded, click on the plus sign to the left of **Sensor Setup**.

Step 3 Click on **Sensor Setup>Network**. This will display the sensor's current communication parameters (see Figure 3-6).

Step 4 Enter the host name to be used for the sensor in the **Hostname** field.

Step 5 Enter the IP address of the sensor in the **IP Address** field.

Step 6 Enter the network mask in the **Network Mask** field.

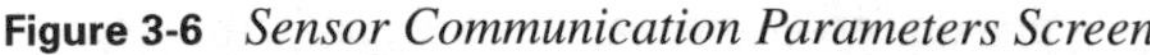

Figure 3-6 *Sensor Communication Parameters Screen*

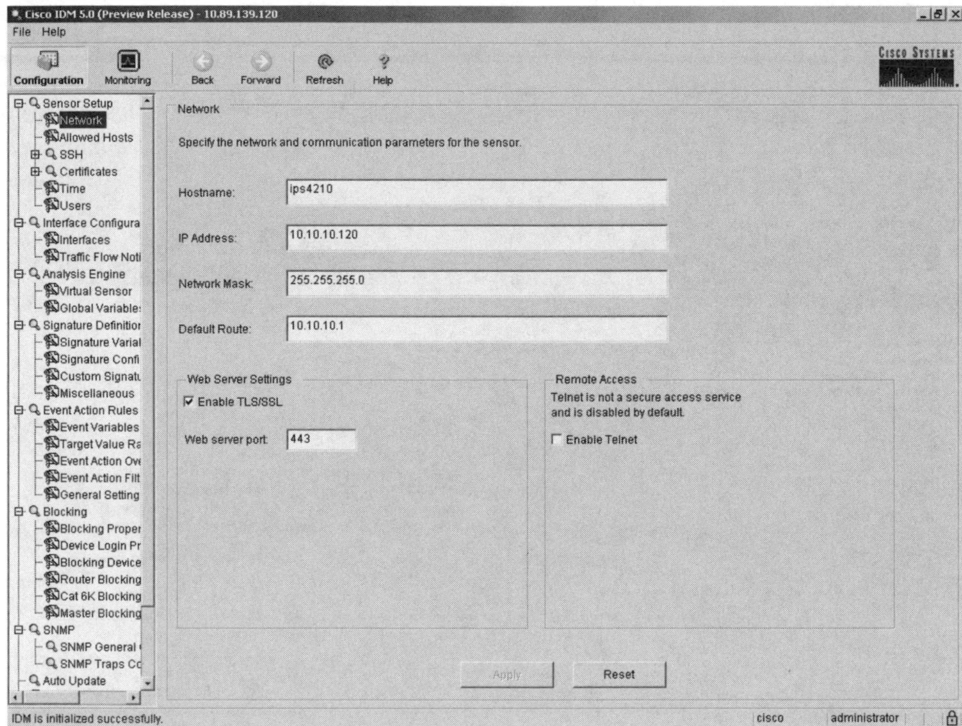

Step 7 Enter the default route that the sensor will use for command and control traffic by specifying the IP address of the default router in the **Default Route** field.

Step 8 To enable secure web access, click on the **Enable TLS/SSL** check box. You can also specify the port for secure web access by specifying a port number in the **Web server port** field (the default is 443).

> **NOTE** Many tools automatically target systems based on default ports (such as port 443 for TLS/SSL). Changing the web server port may make it more difficult for an attacker to directly attack your web server since doing so requires the attacker to scan the network first to determine the new port assigned to TLS/SSL.

Step 9 To enable Telnet access to the sensor, click on the **Enable Telnet** check box (the default is for Telnet access to be disabled because it is an insecure management protocol since it does not encrypt the traffic).

Step 10 Click on the **Apply** button to save the changes to the communication parameters.

Foundation Summary

The Cisco IPS Device Manager (IDM) provides a graphical interface that enables you to configure the operational characteristics of a single sensor on your network. IDM is a Java-based web application that should work with most web browsers.

The recommended memory and screen resolution are as follows:

- 256 MB memory (minimum)
- 1024 x 768 resolution and 256 colors (minimum)

Cisco has identified system requirements based on the following operating systems for use with IDM:

- Microsoft Windows 2000 and Windows XP
- Sun Solaris 2.8 and 2.9
- Red Hat Linux 9.0 and Red Hat Enterprise Linux WS version, 3 running GNOME or KDE

The functionality provided by IDM is divided into the following two categories:

- Configuration
- Monitoring

The configuration tasks are divided into the following categories:

- Sensor Setup
- Interface Configuration
- Analysis Engine
- Signature Definition
- Event Action Rules
- Blocking
- SNMP
- Auto Update

Each of these categories provides one or more configuration screens that control the operation of the sensor. The monitoring functionality is divided into the following categories:

- Denied Attackers
- Active Host Blocks
- Network Blocks
- IP Logging
- Events
- Support Information>Diagnostic Report
- Support Information>Statistics
- Support Information>System Information

The monitoring categories provide you with information about the current operation of the sensor.

IDM provides online help and also supports **Back** and **Forward** icons (as in a browser) to help you operate more efficiently while using IDM to configure your sensor.

Q&A

You have two choices for review questions:

- The questions that follow give you a bigger challenge than the exam itself by using an open-ended question format. By reviewing now with this more difficult question format, you can exercise your memory better and prove your conceptual and factual knowledge of this chapter. The answers to these questions are found in the appendix.
- For more practice with exam-like question formats, use the exam engine on the CD-ROM.

1. Which Windows operating systems are supported for accessing IDM?
2. What is the minimum amount of RAM that is recommended for systems to run IDM?
3. Which fields can you configure when you access the **Sensor Setup>Network** option?
4. What SNMP functionality is available for Cisco IPS version 5.0?
5. Which web browsers are supported for IDM use on systems running Windows operating systems?
6. Which web browser is supported for accessing IDM from both Solaris and Linux operating systems?
7. Is Telnet access to the sensor enabled by default?
8. What two blocking actions can you configure on the sensor?
9. What versions of Solaris are supported for access to IDM?
10. What is the purpose of the **Back** icon?
11. What are the main categories of configuration options available to a user with Administrator privileges?
12. Is SSH access to the sensor enabled by default?

This chapter covers the following subjects:

- Sensor Host Configuration Tasks
- Interface Configuration Tasks
- Analysis Engine Configuration Tasks

CHAPTER 4

Basic Sensor Configuration

For all Cisco IPS deployments, you need to perform certain basic sensor configuration tasks (such as defining the hosts allowed to connect to the sensor and creating new user accounts). Understanding how to perform basic sensor configuration tasks is vital to any successful Cisco IPS deployment.

You must correctly configure your sensors to protect your network. This chapter focuses on various basic sensor configuration tasks. Although you can configure your sensors via the command-line interface (CLI), the examples in the chapter use the Cisco IPS Device Manager (IDM) graphical user interface.

"Do I Know This Already?" Quiz

The purpose of the "Do I Know This Already?" quiz is to help you decide if you really need to read the entire chapter. If you already intend to read the entire chapter, you do not necessarily need to answer these questions now.

The 10-question quiz, derived from the major sections in the "Foundation and Supplemental Topics" portion of the chapter, helps you determine how to spend your limited study time.

Table 4-1 outlines the major topics discussed in this chapter and the "Do I Know This Already?" quiz questions that correspond to those topics.

Table 4-1 *"Do I Know This Already?" Foundation and Supplemental Topics Mapping*

Foundation or Supplemental Topic	Questions Covering This Topic
Sensor Host Configuration Tasks	1, 6, 7, 9
Interface Configuration Tasks	2, 3, 4, 8
Analysis Engine Configuration Tasks	5

CAUTION The goal of self-assessment is to gauge your mastery of the topics in this chapter. If you do not know the answer to a question or are only partially sure of the answer, you should mark this question wrong for purposes of the self-assessment. Giving yourself credit for an answer you correctly guess skews your self-assessment results and might provide you with a false sense of security.

1. Which of the following is a valid user role on the sensor?
   a. Operator
   b. Analyst
   c. Guest
   d. System
   e. Manager
2. Which of the following parameters cannot be configured when you are editing a monitoring interface via IDM?
   a. Interface Duplex
   b. Interface Speed
   c. Alternate TCP Reset Interface
   d. Interface Description
   e. Interface Name
3. When the inline software bypass is configured to Off, which of the following is true?
   a. Inline traffic continues to flow through the sensor if the analysis engine is stopped.
   b. Inline traffic stops flowing through the sensor if the analysis engine is stopped.
   c. Inline traffic is never inspected.
   d. Inline traffic stops flowing through the sensor if the analysis engine is running.
4. Which of the following is not a configurable traffic-flow notification parameter?
   a. Missed Packet Threshold
   b. Notification Interval
   c. Interface Idle Threshold
   d. Maximum Packet Threshold

5. Which of the following statements is true?

   a. You can assign promiscuous interfaces or inline interface pairs only to a virtual sensor but not both at the same time.

   b. You can assign both promiscuous interfaces and inline interface pairs to a virtual sensor, but only one can be enabled at a time.

   c. You can assign both promiscuous interfaces and inline interface pairs to a virtual sensor.

6. When defining your summertime configuration, which of the following is false?

   a. You can specify a time zone for the summertime configuration.

   b. You can specify only the hour (0 to 24) at which the time change will occur.

   c. You can specify exact dates (such as October 23) on which the time change will occur.

   d. You can specify a recurring date (such as first Sunday in October).

7. When making changes to the sensor's time configuration and clock setting, which of the following is true?

   a. Clicking on **Apply** saves your time configuration changes and updates the sensor's clock setting.

   b. Clicking on **Apply** save your time configuration changes, but then you must click on **Apply Time to Sensor** to save the changes to the sensor's clock setting.

   c. You must first click on **Apply Time to Sensor** to save the changes to the sensor's clock setting and then click on **Apply** to save the changes to the time configuration.

   d. The updates to the sensor's clock settings occur automatically, so you need to click only on **Apply** to save your configuration changes.

8. Which parameter specifies the interval over which the missed packet percentage is calculated for traffic flow notification?

   a. Notification Interval

   b. Missed Packet Threshold

   c. Missed Packet Interval

   d. Interface Idle Threshold

   e. Interface Interval

9. Which of the following is true?

   a. You can configure multiple keys for the Network Time Protocol (NTP) server.

   b. You can configure different time zones for the sensor as well as the summertime settings.

   c. You must choose a preconfigured time zone.

   d. The start time and the end time for your summertime settings must be the same.

10. Configuring inline processing on your sensor uses how many interfaces?

   a. 1

   b. 3

   c. 2

   d. Either 1 or 2

The answers to the "Do I Know This Already?" quiz are found in the appendix. The suggested choices for your next step are as follows:

- **8 or less overall score**—Read the entire chapter, including the "Foundation and Supplemental Topics," "Foundation Summary," and Q&A sections.
- **9 or 10 overall score**—If you want more review on these topics, skip to the "Foundation Summary" section and then go to the Q&A section. Otherwise, move to the next chapter.

Foundation and Supplemental Topics

Basic Sensor Configuration

In every Cisco IPS deployment, basic sensor configuration tasks enable you to effectively use your Cisco IPS to monitor and protect your network. This chapter focuses on the following configuration tasks:

- Sensor host configuration
- Interface configuration
- Analysis engine configuration

Sensor Host Configuration Tasks

Besides configuring the IPS functionality on your sensors, you also need to configure characteristics of the sensor itself, such as the following:

- Allowed hosts
- User accounts
- Time parameters
- Secure Shell (SSH) hosts

Configuring Allowed Hosts

During the initial sensor configuration using the **setup** CLI command, you define the basic sensor network parameters (such as IP address and default gateway) as well as change the list of hosts allowed to access the sensor. Only hosts that have been allowed via access list entries are allowed to manage your sensors. To configure the systems (via the IDM interface) that are allowed to access the sensor's command and control interface, perform the following steps:

Step 1 Access IDM by entering the following URL in your web browser: **https://**_sensor_ip_address_.

Step 2 Click on the **Configuration** icon to display the list of configuration tasks.

Step 3 If the items under the **Sensor Setup** category are not displayed, click on the plus sign to the left of **Sensor Setup**.

Step 4 Click on **Allowed Hosts** to access the Allowed Hosts configuration screen (see Figure 4-1). This screen displays the current list of allowed hosts.

Figure 4-1 *Allowed Hosts Configuration Screen*

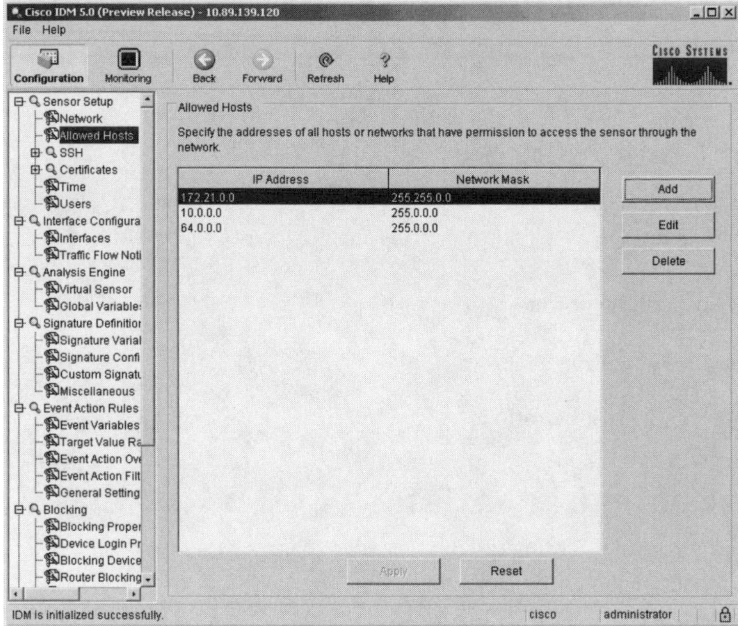

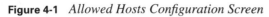

Step 5 To add a host or network to list of allowed hosts, click on **Add** to display the Add Allowed Host popup window (see Figure 4-2).

Figure 4-2 *Add Allowed Hosts Popup Window*

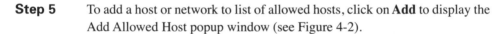

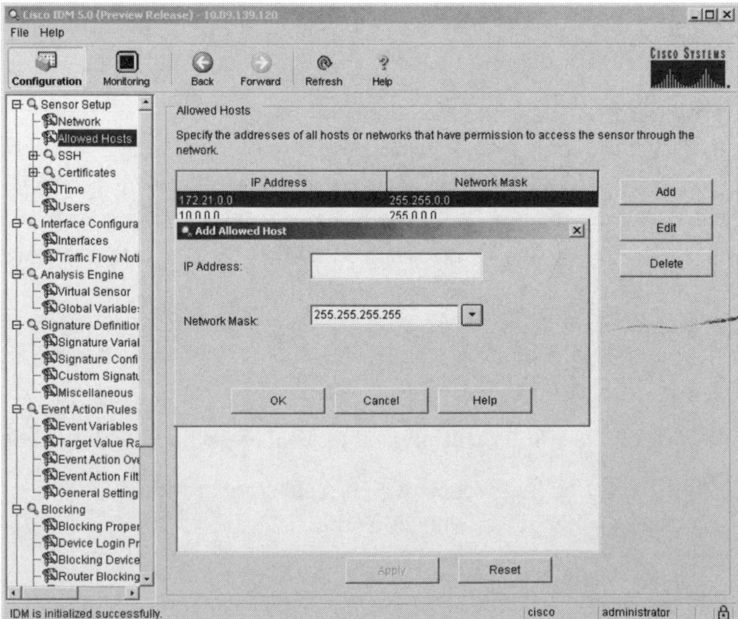

Step 6 Enter the IP address and network mask for the host or network you want to add to the Allowed Hosts list.

Step 7 Click on **OK** to add the new entry to the Allowed Hosts list (or click on **Cancel** to abort the addition).

Step 8 Click on **Apply** to apply the changes to the sensor's configuration.

NOTE Besides adding new entries to the Allowed Hosts list, you can also edit and delete existing entries by highlighting an entry and then clicking on either **Edit** or **Delete**. When removing access list entries, you can remove access for the system that is currently accessing the sensor via IDM. If you do this, you will no longer be able to access the sensor once you apply the changes (the sensor does not wait for the IDM session to end before the access changes are applied).

Configuring Sensor User Accounts

When accessing your sensor (via the web interface, the console port, Telnet, or SSH), you authenticate by using a username and password. The role of the user account that you use to access the sensor determines the operations that you are allowed to perform on the sensor. Each account is assigned one of the following roles (explained in detail in the "User Roles" section of Chapter 2, "IPS Command-Line Interface"):

- Administrator
- Operator
- Viewer
- Service

NOTE The Service role can be assigned to only one user account on your sensor. It is provided solely as an account that the Technical Assistance Center (TAC) uses to troubleshoot operational problems on your sensor.

To add a user account with Administrator privileges to your sensor using IDM perform the following steps:

Step 1 Access IDM by entering the following URL in your web browser: **https://***sensor_ip_address*.

Step 2 Click on the **Configuration** icon to display the list of configuration tasks.

Step 3 If the items under the **Sensor Setup** category are not displayed, click on the plus sign to the left of **Sensor Setup**.

Step 4 Click on **Users** to access the Users configuration screen (see Figure 4-3). This screen displays the current list of user accounts.

Figure 4-3 *Users Configuration Screen*

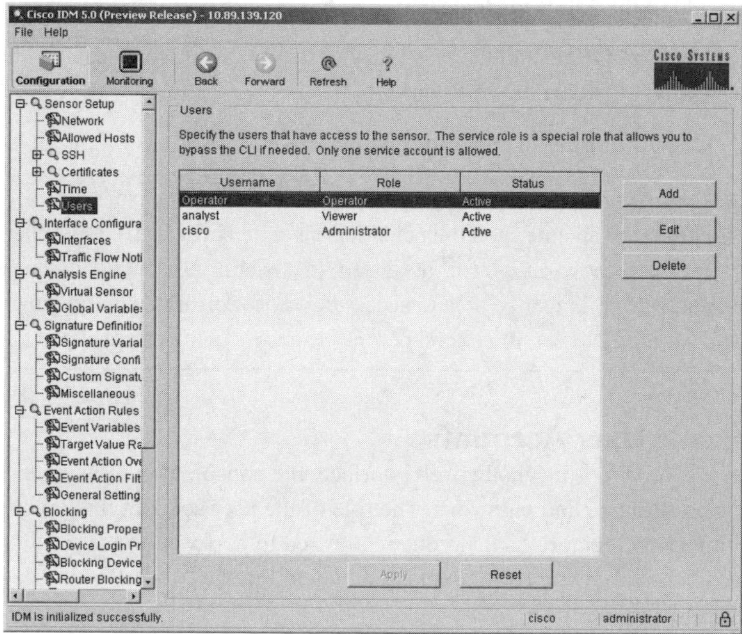

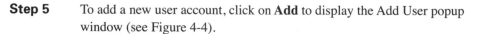

Step 5 To add a new user account, click on **Add** to display the Add User popup window (see Figure 4-4).

Figure 4-4 *Add User Popup Window*

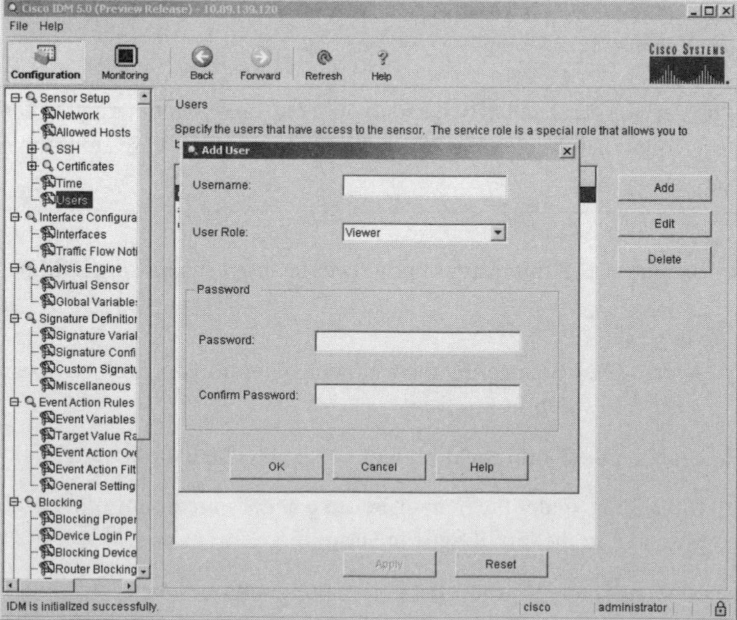

NOTE If your browser is configured to block popup windows, this will interfere with the operation of IDM since many operations (such as Add User configuration) are displayed in a popup window. Therefore, for IDM to operate correctly, you will need to enable popup windows for the sensor's IP address.

Step 6 Enter the name of the new account in the **Username** field.

Step 7 Specify the user role for the new account by using the **User Role** pull-down menu.

Step 8 Next, specify the password for the account in the **Password** field. You will need to re-enter the same password in the **Confirm Password** field.

NOTE Your password must be at least six characters long and contain at least five different characters. If your password is less than six characters long, you will see an Error popup window (see Figure 4-5), and you will not be able to add the new account. These are the minimum password requirements; passwords should also follow guidelines in your security policy for devices on your network.

Figure 4-5 *Password Error Popup Window*

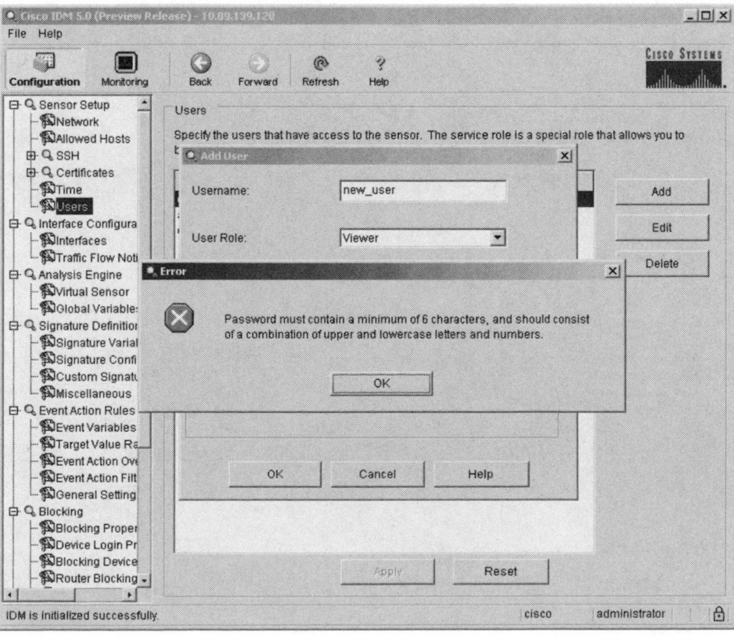

Step 9 Click on **OK** to add the new account (or click on **Cancel** to abort the addition).

Step 10 Click on **Apply** to apply the changes to the sensor's configuration.

Configuring the Sensor's Time Parameters

Maintaining the correct time on your sensors is important to help correlate events across multiple devices on your network. You can configure your sensor's time manually, or you can use a Network Time Protocol (NTP) server. When configuring time settings on your sensor, you can make the following major changes:

- Manually set the clock
- Configure the NTP server settings
- Configure the time zone
- Configure the summertime settings

All of the time settings are configured via the Time sensor configuration screen (see Figure 4-6).

Figure 4-6 *Time Configuration Screen*

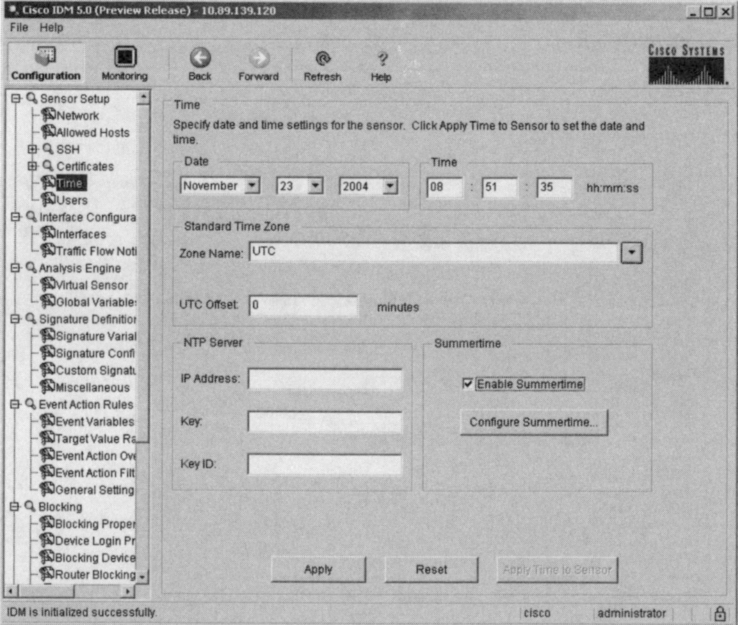

Manually Setting the Clock

To manually set the sensor's internal clock, you need to perform the following steps:

Step 1 Click on **Sensor Setup > Time** from the IDM configuration options to access the Time configuration screen.

Step 2 Change the information in either the **Date** or **Time** fields.

Step 3 Click on **Apply Time to Sensor** to propagate the time changes to the sensor.

NOTE If you make changes to both the actual time (setting the sensor's clock to a new time value) and the sensor's time configuration parameters (such as time zone and summertime settings), click on **Apply Time to Sensor** before you click on **Apply**. Failing to do so will cause you configuration changes to be saved, but your changes to the sensor's clock settings will be lost.

Configuring the NTP Server Settings

Instead of manually configuring the time on your sensor, you can synchronize the time on your network devices by using an NTP server. To configure your sensor to retrieve its time from an NTP server, perform the following steps:

Step 1 Click on **Sensor Setup > Time** from the IDM configuration options to access the Time configuration screen.

Step 2 Enter the IP address of the NTP server in the **IP Address** field.

Step 3 Enter the key to be used to access the NTP server in the **Key** field.

Step 4 Enter the identification number of the key in the **Key ID** field.

Step 5 Click on **Apply** to change the configuration on the sensor.

Configuring the Time Zone

Using time zones enables you to have the correct local time on your sensors yet easily correlate events from sensors across multiple geographic regions. To adjust a sensor's time based on the local time zone, you need to change the time zone of the sensor. Changing the time zone on the sensor involves the following steps:

Step 1 Click on **Sensor Setup > Time** from the IDM configuration options to access the Time configuration screen.

Step 2 Select the appropriate time zone from the pull-down menu for the **Zone Name** field.

NOTE When you select a preconfigured time zone, the **UTC Offset** field is automatically filled in with the correct value.

Step 3 Click on **Apply** to change the configuration on the sensor.

> **NOTE** Besides using the preconfigured time zone values, you can also configure a custom time zone by typing a name in the **Zone Name** field and specifying the appropriate **UTC Offset**.

Configuring the Summertime Settings

During the summer months, many regions change time to what is commonly called daylight savings time. Configuring the summertime settings involves setting a start date and an end date as well as defining what day and time the change is to occur. When defining the dates, you can use one of the following formats:

- Recurring
- Date

With Recurring format, you specify a date based on the three parameters shown in Table 4-2. Using the Date format, you specify only the month and day (such as "October 23").

Table 4-2 *Recurring Date Parameters*

Parameter	Valid Values
Month	January, February, March, April, May, June, July, August, September, October, November, December
Day of the week	Sunday, Monday, Tuesday, Wednesday, Thursday, Friday, Saturday
Week of the month	First, Second, Third, Fourth, Fifth, Last

You can configure your sensor to automatically change its time according to your summertime schedule by performing the following steps:

Step 1 On the IDM configuration options, click on **Sensor Setup > Time** to access the Time configuration screen.

Step 2 To enable your sensor to alter its time during the summer months, check the **Enable Summertime** check box.

Step 3 To configure the summertime parameters, click on the **Configure Summertime** button to access the Configure Summertime configuration screen (see Figure 4-7).

Figure 4-7 *Configure Summertime Configuration Screen*

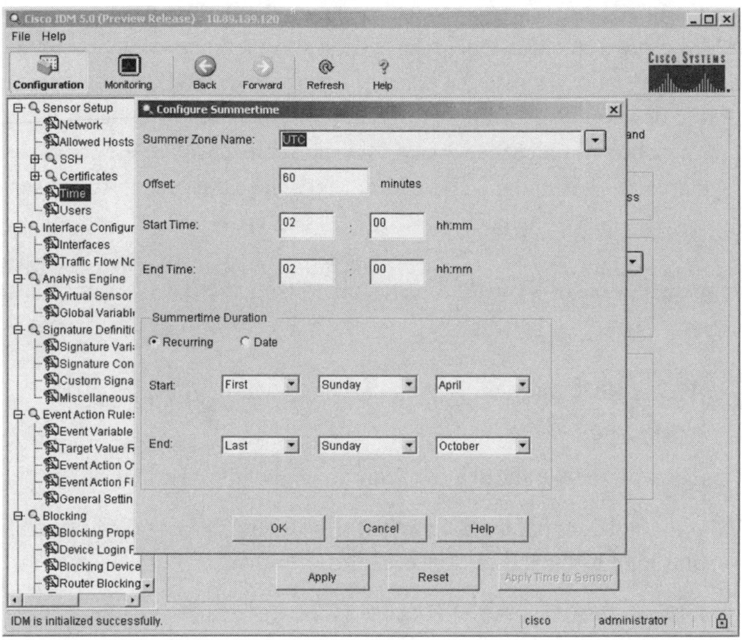

Step 4 Select the time zone by using the pull-down menu next to the **Summer Zone Name** field.

> **NOTE** Selecting the time zone in the **Summer Zone Name** field automatically fills in the **Offset** field.

Step 5 Enter the time at which the starting-day change takes place by entering a value in the **Start Time** field.

Step 6 Enter the time at which the ending-day change takes place by entering a value in the **End Time** field.

Step 7 If the time change is recurring, select the **Recurring** radio button. Otherwise, select the **Date** radio button to indicate that the time change occurs on a specific date.

Step 8 Using the pull-down menus, specify the date on which the time change starts.

Step 9 Using the pull-down menus, specify the date on which the time change ends.

Step 10 Click on **Apply** to change the configuration on the sensor.

Configuring SSH Hosts

When you use your sensors to perform blocking, they log in to your network infrastructure devices by using SSH. Before you can establish an SSH session from your sensor to another device, you must add the device's public key to the sensor's list of known SSH hosts. Presently, the IPS sensor's CLI is limited to defining SSH version 1 public keys (meaning that the target system the sensor is connecting to must be running SSH version 1). When connecting to the sensor using SSH, however, your client system can be running SSH version 1 or 2 since the sensor's SSH server can handle both versions.

To add systems to the sensor's known SSH host list (using the IDM graphical interface) perform the following steps:

Step 1 Access IDM by entering the following URL in your web browser: **https://**_sensor_ip_address_.

Step 2 Click on the **Configuration** icon to display the list of configuration tasks.

Step 3 If the items under the **Sensor Setup** category are not displayed, click on the plus sign to the left of **Sensor Setup**.

Step 4 If the items under the **SSH** category are not displayed, click on the plus sign to the left of **SSH**.

Step 5 Click on **Sensor Setup > SSH > Known Hosts** from the IDM configuration options to access the Known Hosts configuration screen (see Figure 4-8).

Figure 4-8 *SSH Known Hosts Configuration Screen*

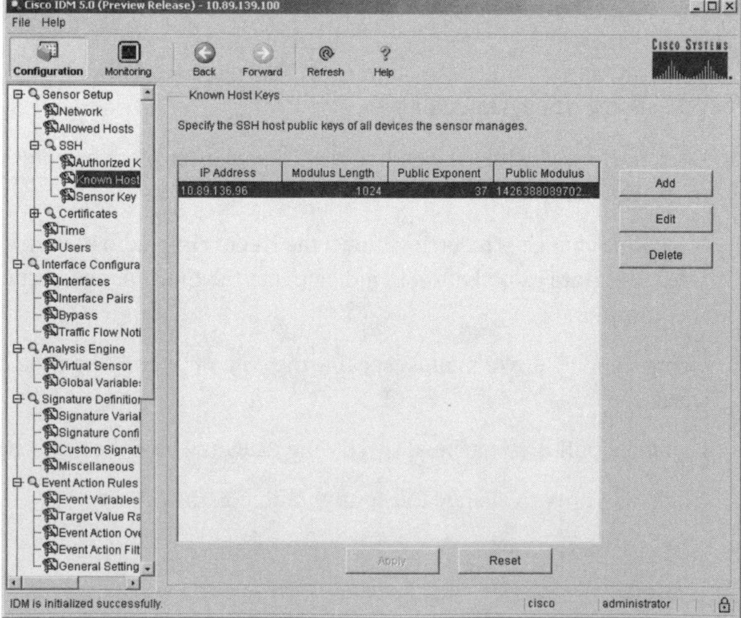

Step 6 Click on **Add** to access the Add Known Host Key popup window (see Figure 4-9).

Figure 4-9 *Add Known Host Key Window*

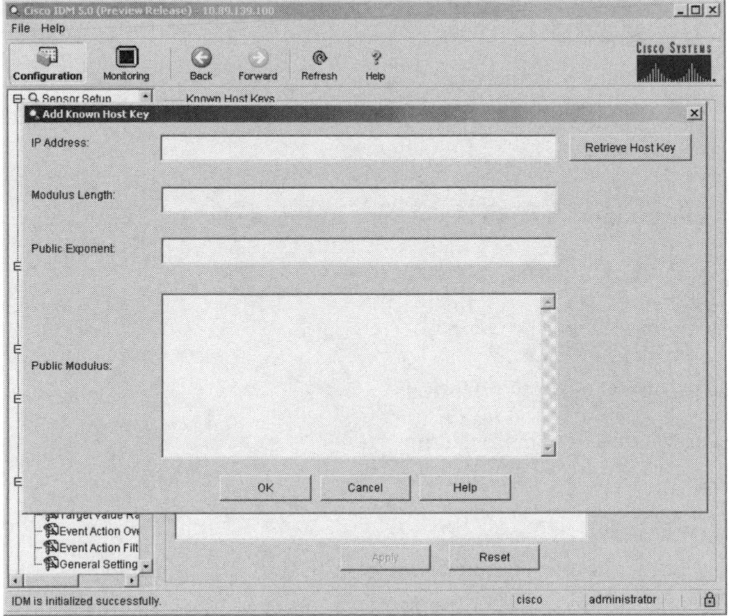

Step 7 Enter information for the fields listed in Table 4-3.

Table 4-3 *Known Host Key Parameters*

Parameter	**Description**
Modulus Length	ASCII decimal integer in the range 511 to 2048
Public Exponent	ASCII decimal integer in the range 3 to 2^{32}
Public Modulus	ASCII decimal integer, x, such that $(2^{key\text{-}modulus\text{-}length}) < x < (2^{(key\text{-}modulus\text{-}length + 1)})$

NOTE Instead of manually specifying the known host key parameters, you can retrieve this information after entering the IP address by clicking on **Retrieve Host Key**. This causes the sensor to connect to the device over the network by using SSH and querying the remote system for its unique host ID key. Although this mechanism is quick, for security reasons you should still manually verify that the key ID presented is the correct one for the remote system (to prevent a man-in-the-middle attack where a rogue system impersonates the remote system).

Step 8 Click on **OK** to save the new known host entry.

Step 9 Click on **Apply** to save the configuration information to the sensor.

> **NOTE** For information on configuring SSH known hosts by using the sensor's CLI, refer to Chapter 2.

Interface Configuration Tasks

Your IPS sensors protect your network by processing the traffic they receive on their monitoring interfaces. With Cisco IPS version 5.0, configuring the sensor's interfaces to process network traffic involves various tasks, such as the following:

- Enabling monitoring interfaces
- Editing monitoring interface parameters
- Configuring inline interface pairs
- Configuring inline software bypass
- Configuring traffic flow notifications

Enabling Monitoring Interfaces

By default, all of the monitoring interfaces on your sensor are disabled. Before you can use the interfaces for either promiscuous or inline processing, you must enable them. To enable monitoring interfaces on your sensor, perform the following steps:

Step 1 Access IDM by entering the following URL in your web browser: **https://**_sensor_ip_address_.

Step 2 Click on the **Configuration** icon to display the list of configuration tasks.

Step 3 If the items under the **Interface Configuration** category are not displayed, click on the plus sign to the left of **Interface Configuration**.

Step 4 Click on **Interfaces** to access the Interfaces configuration screen (see Figure 4-10). This screen displays the state of the interfaces on the sensor.

Step 5 Highlight an interface by clicking on an interface name.

Step 6 Click on **Enable** to enable the highlighted interface.

> **NOTE** You can click on **Select All** to highlight all of the interfaces, or you can hold the **CTRL** key while clicking on interfaces to select multiple interfaces. Then you can enable all of the highlighted interfaces by clicking on **Enable**.

Step 7 Click on **Apply** to save the configuration changes to the sensor.

Figure 4-10 *Interfaces Configuration Screen*

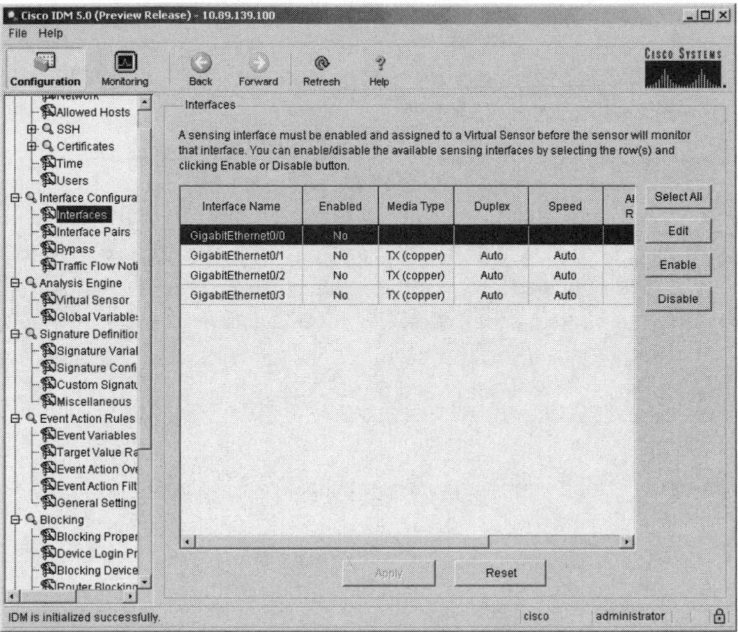

Editing Monitoring Interface Parameters

Besides enabling monitoring interfaces, you can also change the following characteristics for each interface:

- Interface description
- Interface speed
- Interface duplex
- Enabled status
- Alternate TCP Reset interface

The *interface description* is simply a textual description that you can use to describe the specific monitoring interface. The *interface speed* indicates the bandwidth that the interface is configured to support. The options available are as follows:

- 10 MB
- 100 MB
- 1 GB
- Auto (attempts to automatically calculate the correct interface speed)

The *interface duplex* indicates whether the interface is capable of transmitting and receiving data simultaneously (full duplex) or not simultaneously (half duplex). To use a monitoring interface to examine network traffic, you must *enable* the interface. The *alternate TCP-reset interface* enables you to specify an interface (different from the monitoring interface) that the sensor will use to transmit TCP reset traffic.

NOTE In certain sensor configurations (such as those using IDSM2), you cannot send TCP-reset traffic out the monitoring interface. If you want to use the TCP-reset functionality in these configurations, you need to send the TCP resets through the alternate TCP-reset interface. With the IDSM2, port 1 is dedicated to providing an interface to support sending TCP-reset traffic. You may also have to configure an alternate TCP-reset interface in certain configurations when your switch traffic capture mechanism (for promiscuous mode monitoring) does not allow the port receiving the captured traffic to also send traffic.

To edit the properties of an interface, perform the following steps:

Step 1 Access IDM by entering the following URL in your web browser: **https://** *sensor_ip_address*.

Step 2 Click on the **Configuration** icon to display the list of configuration tasks.

Step 3 If the items under the **Interface Configuration** category are not displayed, click on the plus sign to the left of **Interface Configuration**.

Step 4 Click on **Interfaces** to access the Interfaces configuration screen (see Figure 4-10). This screen displays the state of the interfaces on the sensor.

Step 5 Highlight an interface by clicking on its name.

Step 6 Click on **Edit** to edit the properties of the highlighted interface by using the Edit Interface popup window (see Figure 4-11).

Step 7 Enter the interface description in the **Description** field.

Step 8 To enable the interface, click on the **Yes** radio button across from **Enabled**. To disable the interface, click on the **No** radio button.

Step 9 Select the duplex for the interface by using the pull-down menu for the **Duplex** field. Your options are Auto, Full, and Half.

Step 10 Select the speed for the interface by using the pull-down menu for the **Speed** field.

Step 11 If you want to use an alternate interface for TCP resets, click on the **Use Alternate TCP Reset Interface** check box. Then specify the interface by using the pull-down menu across from **Select Interface**.

Figure 4-11 *Edit Interface Popup Window*

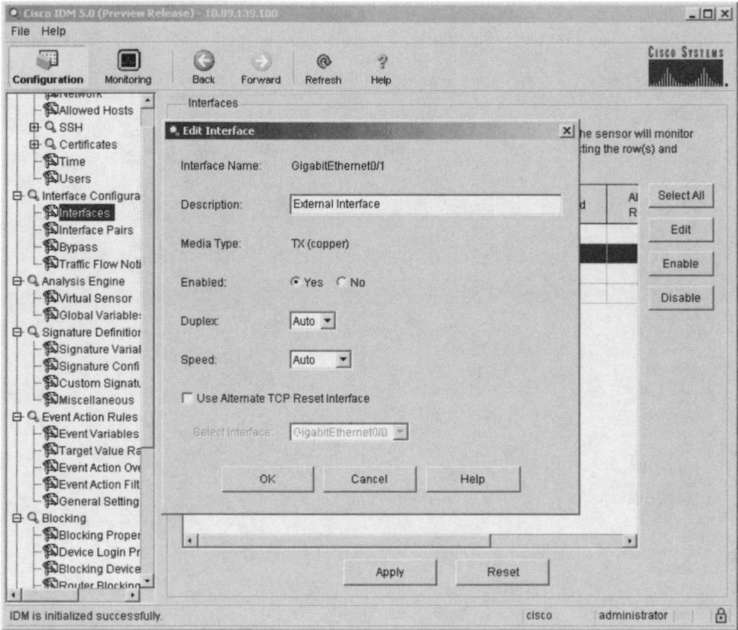

Step 12 Click on **OK** to save your changes.

Step 13 Click on **Apply** to save your changes to the sensor's configuration.

Configuring Inline Interface Pairs

When operating in inline mode, your sensor bridges the traffic between two distinct virtual LANs VLAN or network interfaces. To perform this bridging requires the use of two interfaces on the sensor. These two interfaces are known as an inline interface pair. To configure inline interface pairs, perform the following steps:

Step 1 Access IDM by entering the following URL in your web browser: **https://** *sensor_ip_address*.

Step 2 Click on the **Configuration** icon to display the list of configuration tasks.

Step 3 If the items under the **Interface Configuration** category are not displayed, click on the plus sign to the left of **Interface Configuration**.

Step 4 Click on **Interface Pairs** to access the Interface Pairs configuration screen (see Figure 4-12). This screen displays interface pairs configured on the sensor.

Figure 4-12 *Interface Pairs Configuration Screen*

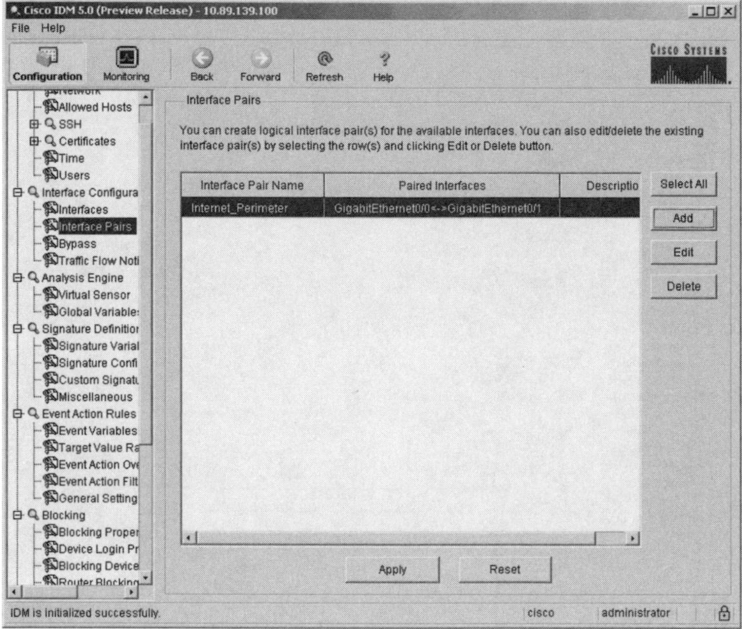

Step 5 Click on **Add** to access the Add Interface Pair popup window (see Figure 4-13).

Figure 4-13 *Add Interface Pair Popup Window*

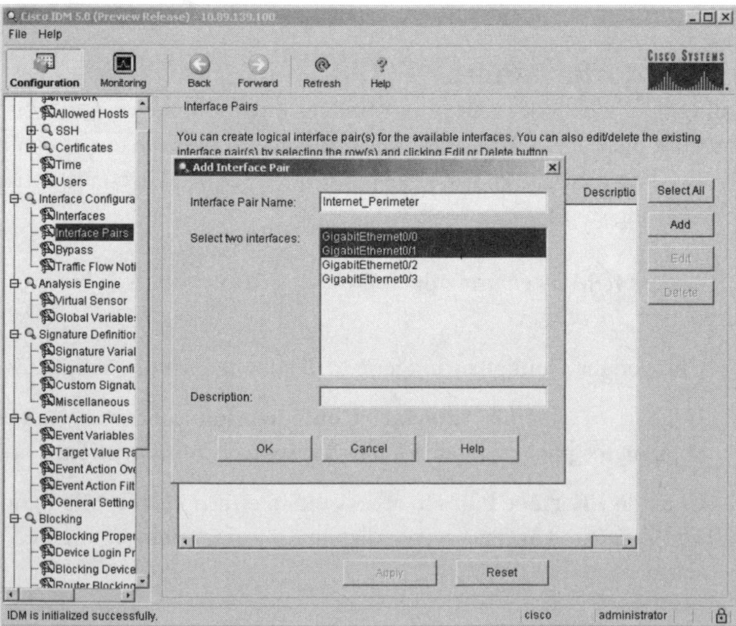

Step 6 Enter a name for the interface pair being added in the **Interface Pair Name** field.

Step 7 Highlight the two interfaces to be used in the interface pair.

Step 8 Click on **OK** to save the interface pair.

Step 9 Click on **Apply** to save the changes to the sensor's configuration.

Configuring Inline Software Bypass

When operating in inline mode, your sensor bridges the traffic between two devices or VLANs. Similar to a switch in your network, the sensor transfers traffic from one inline sensor interface to the other (after the packet has been inspected). If the sensor software fails or you update the software on your sensor, you need to decide how the sensor will pass traffic (for the inline processing interfaces) while the sensor is not operating. You can configure the sensor to use one of the following three software bypass options:

- Auto—Bypass inspection when analysis engine is stopped
- Off—Always inspect inline traffic
- On—Never inspect inline traffic

Auto bypass mode (the default mode) causes your sensor to automatically bypass inspection whenever the sensor's analysis engine is stopped. This will allow your network traffic to continue to travel through the sensor even if the sensor is not operating.

Configuring the bypass mode to Off forces your sensor to inspect network traffic. In this mode, if the analysis engine is stopped, network traffic will not be allowed to pass through the sensor. Therefore, while the analysis engine is stopped, the operation of your network will be impacted because the traffic flow through the sensor also stops.

The final bypass mode, On, configures your sensor to never inspect inline traffic. In this mode, the sensor is physically connected as a Layer 2 forwarding device, but the traffic is not inspected. In this mode, the sensor operates purely as a Layer 2 bridge. You should generally use this mode only when debugging problems with your network, because it removes the functionality provided by the sensor.

Configuring the bypass mode on your sensor involves the following steps:

Step 1 Access IDM by entering the following URL in your web browser: **https://** *sensor_ip_address*.

Step 2 Click on the **Configuration** icon to display the list of configuration tasks.

Step 3 If the items under the **Interface Configuration** category are not displayed, click on the plus sign to the left of **Interface Configuration**.

Step 4 Click on **Bypass** to access the Bypass configuration screen (see Figure 4-14). This screen displays the currently configured software bypass mode.

Figure 4-14 *Bypass Configuration Screen*

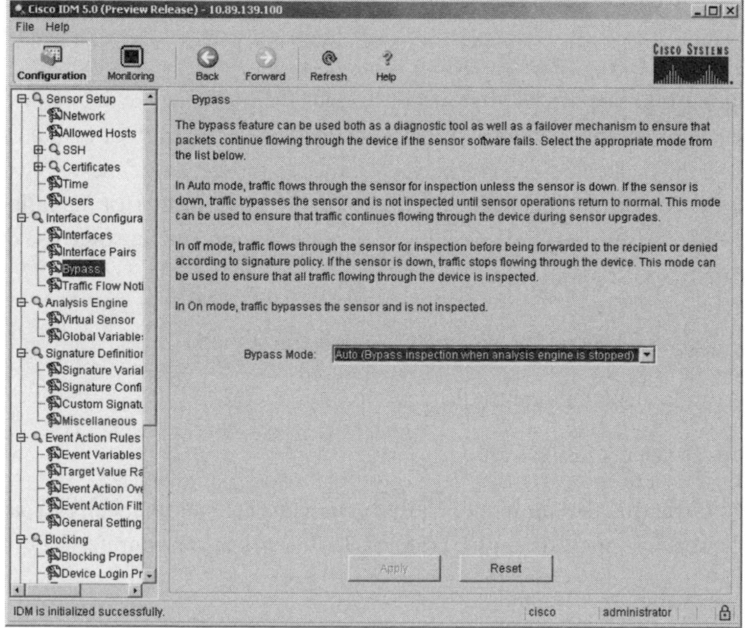

Step 5 Select the correct bypass mode by using the pull-down menu for the **Bypass Mode** field.

Step 6 Click on **Apply** to save the changes to the sensor's configuration.

Configuring Traffic Flow Notifications

You can configure your sensor to generate event messages when the traffic flow across an interface changes based on the following two traffic characteristics:

- Missed packets
- Idle time

Table 4-4 shows the parameters that you can configure with respect to traffic flow notifications.

Table 4-4 *Traffic Flow Notification Parameters*

Field	Description
Missed Packet Threshold	Specifies the percentage of packets that must be missed during the notification interval before a notification is generated
Notification Interval	Specifies the interval in seconds that the sensor uses for the missed packets percentage notification
Interface Idle Threshold	Specifies the number of seconds that an interface must be idle (and not receiving traffic) before a notification is generated

NOTE Each of the Cisco IPS sensors has a maximum amount of network traffic that it can analyze. For instance, the IDS 4240 can analyze a maximum of 250 Mbps of network traffic. The monitoring interfaces, however, can operate at 1 Gbps. Therefore, it is possible for the sensor to receive traffic faster than it can examine it. If a sensor interface is receiving packets that are not processed (in other words, the packets are getting dropped at the interface because they are arriving too quickly for the sensor to examine them), the number of packets that were not processed is recorded in the interface statistics. This information is used to calculate the Missed Packet Threshold. The Missed Packet Threshold notification enables you to determine how often and to what extent your network traffic is exceeding the capacity of the sensor that you are using to monitor the traffic. When it exceeds the capacity of your sensor, the traffic can enter your network without being examined by the sensor.

To configure the sensor's traffic flow notification parameters, perform the following steps:

Step 1 Access IDM by entering the following URL in your web browser: **https://** *sensor_ip_address*.

Step 2 Click on the **Configuration** icon to display the list of configuration tasks.

Step 3 If the items under the **Interface Configuration** category are not displayed, click on the plus sign to the left of **Interface Configuration**.

Step 4 Click on **Traffic Flow Notifications** to access the Traffic Flow Notifications configuration screen (see Figure 4-15). This screen displays the currently configured traffic flow notification settings.

Step 5 Enter the threshold for missed packets in the **Missed Packets Threshold** field.

Step 6 Enter the number of seconds used for the missed packet percentage threshold in the **Notification Interval** field.

Figure 4-15 *Traffic Flow Notifications Configuration Screen*

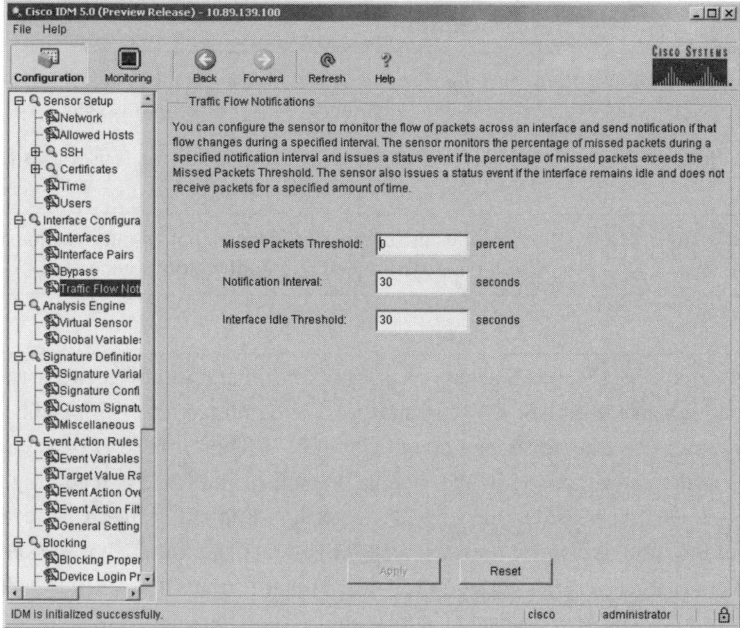

Step 7 Enter the allowed number of idle seconds in the **Interface Idle Threshold** field.

Step 8 Click on **Apply** to save the changes to the sensor's configuration.

Analysis Engine Configuration Tasks

After configuring the interfaces on your sensor, you must assign them to a virtual sensor before your sensor can use the interfaces to analyze network traffic. You can assign both promiscuous interfaces and inline interface pairs to the same virtual sensor. This capability enables you to have a sensor performing inline functionality at one location at the same time that it is passively monitoring another location in your network.

> **NOTE** Currently the sensor software supports only a single virtual sensor (vs0). In the future, however, Cisco IPS sensors may support multiple virtual sensors. These virtual sensors will enable you to make one physical sensor appear to be multiple sensors (each with unique configuration settings). This concept is similar to that of virtual firewalls, where a single physical firewall can be configured (via software) to operate as multiple virtual firewalls that each have unique configuration parameters.

> **NOTE** Passively monitoring network traffic refers to operating an interface in promiscuous mode. Using a traffic-capture mechanism (such as Switched Port Analyzer [SPAN] ports), you forward a copy of the network traffic to be analyzed to the specific sensor interface (operating in promiscuous mode). The sensor then examines all of the traffic. Since the traffic is being capture passively, however, the sensor can only react to the traffic, meaning that initial attack packets will still reach the destination system until the sensor initiates an IP-blocking action.

Assigning an interface to a virtual sensor involves the following steps:

Step 1 Access IDM by entering the following URL in your web browser: **https://***sensor_ip_address*.

Step 2 Click on the **Configuration** icon to display the list of configuration tasks.

Step 3 If the items under the **Analysis Engine** category are not displayed, click on the plus sign to the left of **Analysis Engine**.

Step 4 Click on **Virtual Sensor** to access the Virtual Sensor configuration screen (see Figure 4-16). This screen displays the currently assigned interfaces for the virtual sensor.

Figure 4-16 *Virtual Sensor Configuration Screen*

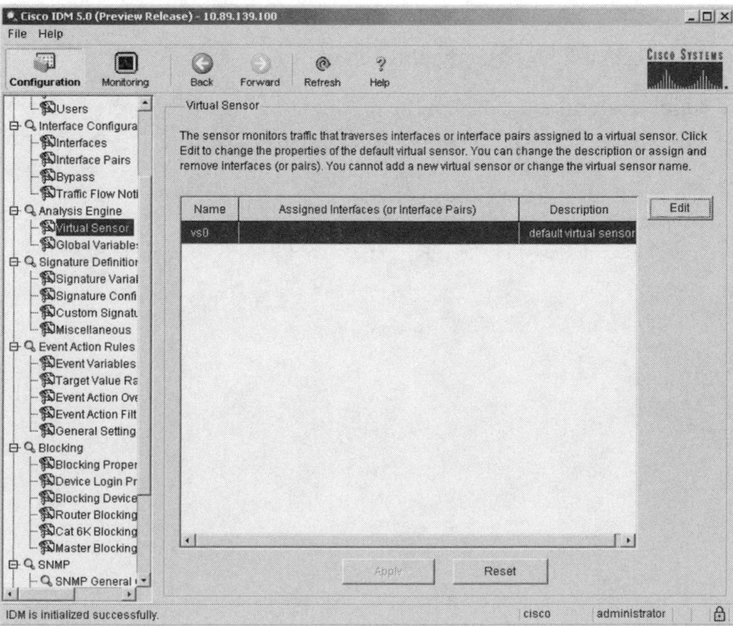

Step 5 Click on **Edit** to access the Edit Virtual Sensor popup window (see Figure 4-17).

Figure 4-17 *Edit Virtual Sensor Configuration Screen*

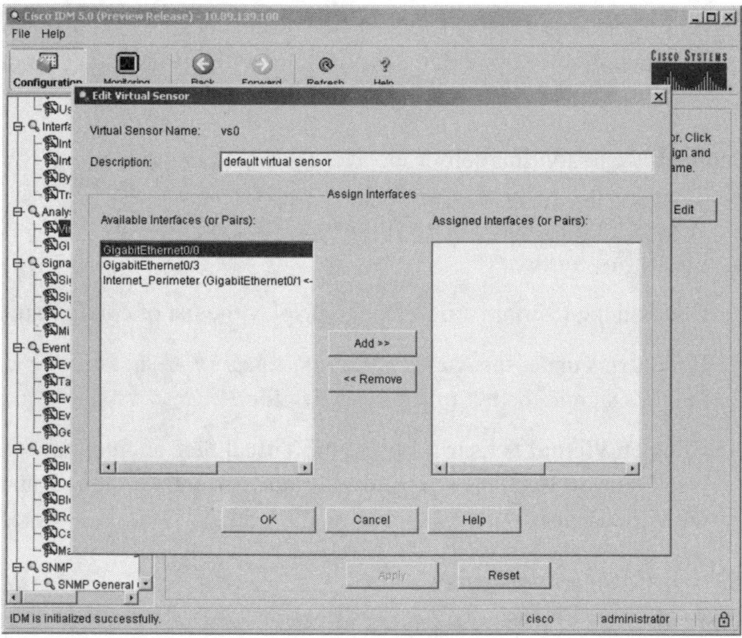

Step 6 Highlight an interface by clicking on it.

Step 7 Click on **Add>>** to assign the highlighted interface to the virtual sensor (or click on **<<Remove** to remove an already assigned interface).

Step 8 Click on **OK** to save the changes.

Step 9 Click on **Apply** to save the changes to the sensor's configuration.

Foundation Summary

In every Cisco IPS deployment, basic sensor configuration tasks enable you to effectively use your Cisco IPS to monitor and protect your network. This chapter focuses on the following topics:

- Sensor host configuration tasks
- Sensor interface configuration tasks
- Analysis engine configuration tasks

The basic sensor configuration tasks include the following:

- Configuring allowed hosts
- Configuring sensor user accounts
- Configuring the sensor's time parameters
- Configuring Secure Shell (SSH) hosts

The basic sensor interface configuration tasks include the following:

- Enabling monitoring interfaces
- Editing monitoring interface parameters
- Configuring inline interface pairs
- Configuring inline software bypass
- Configuring traffic flow notifications

When using inline processing, you can configure software bypass to operate in one of the following modes:

- Auto—Bypass inspection when analysis engine is stopped
- Off—Always inspect inline traffic
- On—Never inspect inline traffic

Configuring traffic flow notifications involves customizing the following parameters to your network environment:

- Missed Packet Threshold
- Notification Interval
- Interface Idle Threshold

After configuring the interfaces on you sensor, you must also assign them to a virtual sensor before your sensor can use the interfaces to analyze network traffic.

Q&A

You have two choices for review questions:

- The questions that follow give you a bigger challenge than the exam itself by using an open-ended question format. By reviewing now with this more difficult question format, you can exercise your memory better and prove your conceptual and factual knowledge of this chapter. The answers to these questions are found in the appendix.
- For more practice with exam-like question formats, use the exam engine on the CD-ROM.

1. What must you do before you can manage or configure your sensor across the network?
2. What roles can you assign to a user account on your sensor?
3. Which user role can be assigned to only a single user account?
4. What are the two ways that you can configure time on your sensor?
5. When configuring your summertime settings, what are the two date formats that you can use?
6. What fields should you use to specify recurring dates?
7. What must you do before your sensor can initiate blocking via your infrastructure devices?
8. When editing a monitoring interface's parameters by using IDM, what parameters can you alter?
9. What are the three options for configuring inline software bypass?
10. How does the Auto software bypass mode work?
11. What is the Missed Packet Threshold?
12. How does the Off software bypass mode work?
13. Can you configure inline interface pairs and promiscuous interfaces to the same virtual sensor?

This chapter covers the following subjects:

- Configuring Cisco IPS Signatures
- Signature Groups
- Alarm Summary Modes
- Basic Signature Configuration

CHAPTER 5

Basic Cisco IPS Signature Configuration

The heart of the Cisco IPS is the signatures that the sensor uses to identify intrusive traffic on your network. Viewing signatures by using signature groups enables you to efficiently configure the numerous Cisco IPS signatures to match your unique network configuration.

Your Cisco IPS sensors check network traffic against signatures of known intrusive traffic. It is important to understand how to locate the signatures available as well as to determine which signatures are most important in your unique network environment. This chapter explains how you can use IPS Device Manager (IDM) to view the different signatures by signature group and to enable the numerous signatures that are available. Advanced signature configuration operations, such as signature tuning and creating custom signatures, will be covered in Chapter 7, "Advanced Signature Configuration."

"Do I Know This Already?" Quiz

The purpose of the "Do I Know This Already?" quiz is to help you decide if you really need to read the entire chapter. If you already intend to read the entire chapter, you do not necessarily need to answer these questions now.

The 10-question quiz, derived from the major sections in the "Foundation and Supplemental Topics" portion of the chapter, helps you determine how to spend your limited study time.

Table 5-1 outlines the major topics discussed in this chapter and the "Do I Know This Already?" quiz questions that correspond to those topics.

Table 5-1 *"Do I Know This Already?" Foundation and Supplemental Topics Mapping*

Foundation or Supplemental Topic	Questions Covering This Topic
Signature Groups	1, 2, 6
Alarm Summary Modes	3, 4, 5
Basic Signature Configuration	7, 8, 9, 10

CAUTION The goal of self-assessment is to gauge your mastery of the topics in this chapter. If you do not know the answer to a question or are only partially sure of the answer, you should mark this question wrong for purposes of the self-assessment. Giving yourself credit for an answer you correctly guess skews your self-assessment results and might provide you with a false sense of security.

1. Which of the following is not a valid IDM signature group?
   a. Attack
   b. Operating System
   c. Service
   d. Signature Release
   e. Policy Violation
2. Which of the following is not a valid signature response option?
   a. Deny Victim Inline
   b. Deny Attacker Inline
   c. Produce Alert
   d. Request SNMP Trap
   e. Log Pair Packets
3. Which of the following is not a valid summary key?
   a. Attacker address
   b. Attacker address and victim port
   c. Victim address and attacker port
   d. Attacker and victim addresses
   e. Attacker and victim addresses and ports
4. Which of the following is not a valid alarm summary mode?
   a. Fire Once
   b. Summary
   c. Global Summary
   d. Fire All
   e. Fire Global

5. Which parameter determines when alarm summary mode takes effect?

   a. Global Summary Threshold
   b. Summary Threshold
   c. Choke Threshold
   d. Throttle Interval
   e. None of these

6. Which of the following is not a valid service signature group?

   a. DHCP
   b. General Service
   c. SOCKS
   d. ARP
   e. File Sharing

7. Which of the following is not a field on the Network Security Database (NSDB) signature information page for version 5.0?

   a. Description
   b. Benign Trigger(s)
   c. Recommended Signature Filter
   d. Related Threats
   e. Related Vulnerabilities

8. Which button activates a signature that has been disabled?

   a. Enable
   b. Activate
   c. Add
   d. No Disable
   e. None of these

9. Which button activates a signature that has been retired?

   a. Enable
   b. Activate
   c. Restore
   d. Add
   e. You cannot retire signatures

10. When you create a custom signature, which option starts with the settings for an existing signature?

    a. Add

    b. Duplicate

    c. Copy

    d. Clone

    e. Replicate

The answers to the "Do I Know This Already?" quiz are found in the appendix. The suggested choices for your next step are as follows:

- **8 or less overall score**—Read the entire chapter, including the "Foundation and Supplemental Topics," "Foundation Summary," and Q&A sections.
- **9 or 10 overall score**—If you want more review on these topics, skip to the "Foundation Summary" section and then go to the Q&A section. Otherwise, move to the next chapter.

Foundation and Supplemental Topics

Configuring Cisco IPS Signatures

Monitoring network traffic, identifying intrusive activity, and responding to network attacks is the core functionality provided by Cisco IPS. Cisco IPS provides numerous signatures that enable your sensors to determine which traffic on your network represents potential attacks or violates your security policy. To efficiently protect your network from attack, you should understand the numerous signatures that are provided and the actions they perform when intrusive activity is detected.

This chapter focuses on the following signature-related topics:

- Signature groups
- Alarm summary modes
- Basic signature configuration

Signature Groups

To facilitate configuring Cisco IPS signatures, you can view signatures based on the following groups:

- Attack
- L2/L3/L4 Protocol
- Operating System
- Signature Release
- Service
- Signature Identification
- Signature Name
- Signature Action
- Signature Engine

The following sections explain how to view the Cisco IPS signatures by using these different groups.

Displaying Signatures by Attack

Sometimes you want to view the signatures that fall into a specific attack category. To do this, go to the **Select By** field of the signature configuration screen and select **Attack** (see Figure 5-1).

Figure 5-1 *Viewing Signatures by Attack Type*

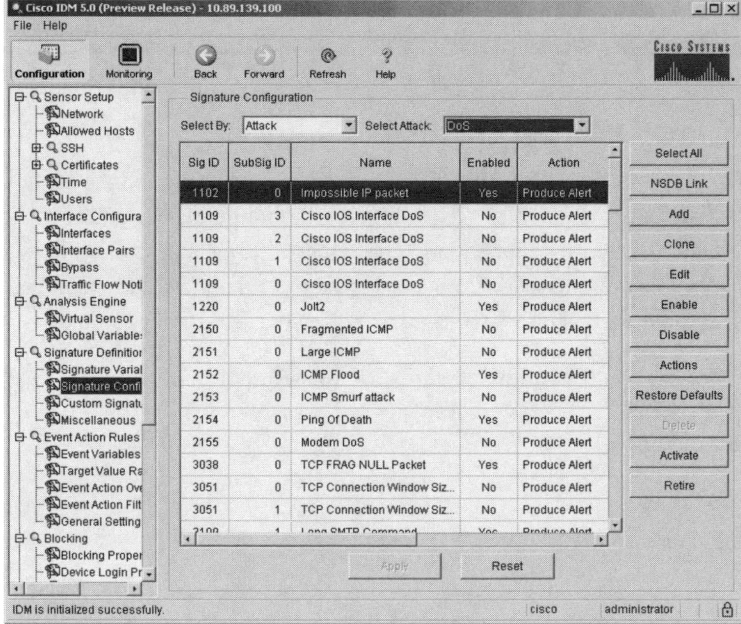

After selecting **Attack**, you can choose to view the signatures for any of the following attack categories:

- Adware/Spyware
- Code Execution
- Command Execution
- DDos
- DoS
- File Access
- General Attack
- IDS Evasion
- Informational
- Policy Violation
- Reconnaissance
- Viruses/Worms/Trojans

You select a specific attack category by using the pull-down menu for the **Select Attack** field.

Adware and spyware are programs that typically get installed on your system without your knowledge while you are normally accessing websites on the Internet. These programs surreptitiously monitor you actions and can impact the performance of your system. The signatures in the Adware/Spyware category identify traffic that indicates the operation of common spyware and adware applications on systems on your network.

Code Execution and Command Execution attacks are those in which an attacker attempts to either run code on a system on your network (such as through a buffer overflow attack) or use known system vulnerabilities to execute commands on a system.

Denial-of-service (DoS) attacks are those in which an attacker tries to disrupt the operation of devices on your network. Distributed denial-of-service (DDoS) attacks are those in which an attacker uses a large number of compromised systems to disrupt the operation of devices on your network. By using a large number of attacking systems (thus increasing the traffic volume), a DDoS is much more effective at disrupting the operation of your network.

In File Access attacks, an attacker attempts to retrieve files from systems on your network by using known system vulnerabilities. Most of these attacks exploit vulnerabilities associated with web servers, but they may also involve specific signatures for other protocols such Trivial File Transfer Protocol (TFTP) and Server Message Block (SMB) protocol.

The General attacks category includes attacks that do not logically fit into any of the more specific categories. These attacks range from detecting bad IP options to identifying traffic to ports associated with well-known back doors created by various attacks.

IDS Evasion signatures detect attacks that are specifically designed to evade intrusion-detection systems. The informational signatures represent traffic patterns that may represent a potential attack or just normal user activity. For instance, signatures in this category include those that detect both successful logins and login failures on numerous protocols. Informational signatures also include signatures that detect simple malformed packet signatures (such as invalidly specifying an incorrect length in a Simple Network Management Protocol [SNMP] request).

Policy Violation signatures detect traffic on your network that indicates that users are running applications that your security policy forbids. The applications that typically fall into this category include peer-to-peer software (such as Kazaa) as well as instant messenger software (such as Yahoo! Messenger).

The first step in attacking a network usually involves identifying the systems (or targets) on the network. Besides locating potential systems, an attacker also needs to identify network services running on those systems. Reconnaissance signatures detect network traffic that indicates someone is trying to map out systems or services on your network.

Viruses, worms, and Trojan horses exploit known vulnerabilities on systems in your network. The signatures in the Viruses/Worms/Trojans category detect known network traffic that is associated with systems infected by viruses and worms. The category also includes signatures that identify traffic associated with well-known Trojan horse programs (such as Back Orifice).

Displaying Signatures by L2/L3/L4 Protocol

The Open Systems Interconnection (OSI) model divides network stacks into the following layers (from lowest to highest):

- Physical Layer (Layer 1)
- Data Link Layer (Layer 2)
- Network Layer (Layer 3)
- Transport Layer (Layer 4)
- Session Layer (Layer 5)
- Presentation Layer (Layer 6)
- Application Layer (Layer 7)

The Data Link Layer (Layer 2) involves protocols that send frames on the physical hardware. An example protocol is the Address Resolution Protocol (ARP), which enables a system to associate an IP address with a specific Ethernet address. The Network Layer (Layer 3) handles the routing of IP packets based on the IP address in the packets. The most common Layer 3 protocol is the Internet Protocol (IP). The Transport Layer (Layer 4) enables systems to establish connections between each other to transfer information. The two common transport protocols are the Transmission Control Protocol (TCP) and the User Datagram Protocol (UDP).

Another way to view signatures is by the protocol that the signature is examining. To do this, go to the **Select By** field of the signature configuration screen and select **L2/L3/L4 Protocol** (see Figure 5-2).

After selecting **L2/L3/L4 Protocol**, you can choose to view the signatures based on any of the following options:

- ARP
- General ICMP
- General IP
- General Protocol
- General TCP
- General UDP
- ICMP Floods
- ICMP Host Sweeps
- ICMP Protocol Anomalies

Figure 5-2 *Viewing Signatures by L2/L3/L4 Protocol*

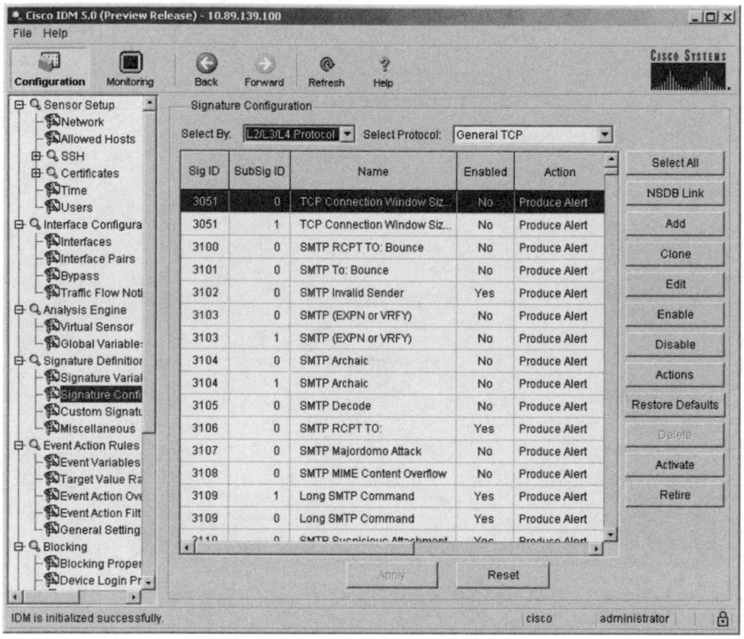

- IP Fragments
- TCP Anomalies
- TCP Floods
- TCP Hijacks
- TCP Host Sweeps
- TCP Port Sweeps
- TCP/UDP Combo Sweeps
- UDP Floods
- UDP Port Sweeps
- UDP Protocol Anomalies

You select the specific protocol by using the pull-down menu for the **Select Protocol** field.

Displaying Signatures by Operating System

Another way to view signatures is by the operating system (OS) that they apply to. To do this, you select **OS** in the **Select By** field of the signature configuration screen (see Figure 5-3).

Figure 5-3 *Viewing Signatures by Operating System*

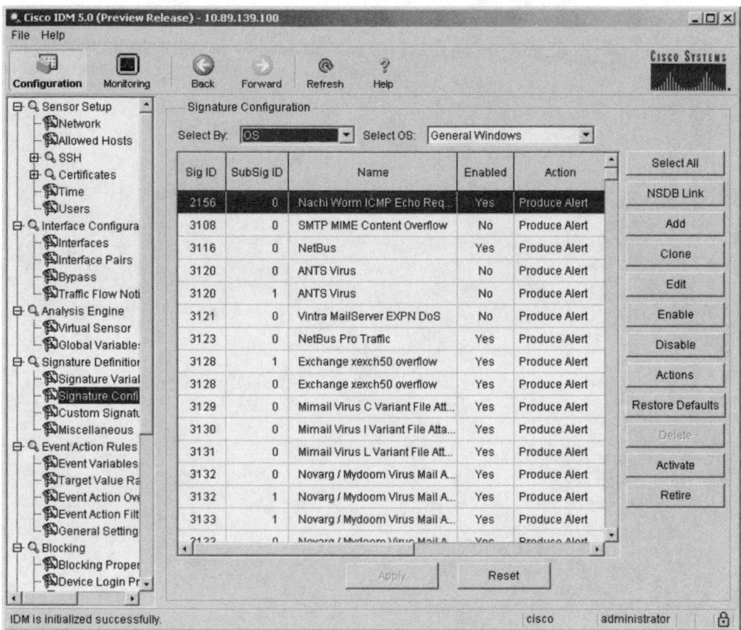

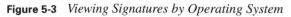

After selecting **OS**, you can choose to view the signatures for any of the following operating systems:

- AIX
- General Linux
- General OS
- General UNIX
- General Windows
- General Windows NT/2000/XP
- Gentoo L0inux
- HP-UX
- IOS
- IRIX
- MacOS
- Mandrake Linux
- Netware
- Red Hat Linux
- Solaris
- SuSE Linux
- WinNT

You select the specific operating system by using the pull-down menu for the **Select OS** field.

Displaying Signatures by Signature Release

Many times you may want to view signatures based on either the Cisco IPS software release or a specific Cisco IPS signature update. To do this, you select **Release** in the **Select By** field of the signature configuration screen (see Figure 5-4).

Figure 5-4 *Viewing Signatures by Signature Release*

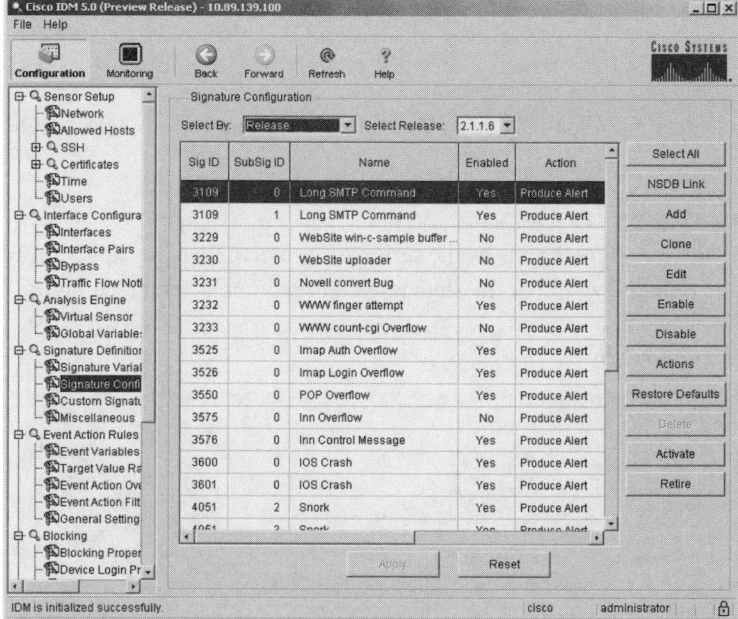

> **NOTE** Viewing signatures by signature release enables you to quickly see which new signatures were added by a specific signature release.

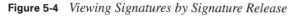

After selecting **Release**, you can choose to view the signatures for the various Cisco IPS software and signature releases. Some sample software and signature releases are as follows:

- 1.0
- 2.1.1
- 2.1.1.3
- 2.1.1.4
- 2.1.1.5

- 2.1.1.6
- S10
- S100
- S101
- S102
- S11

You select the specific release by using the pull-down menu for the **Select Release** field.

Displaying Signatures by Service

Another way to view signatures is by the service or protocol that they apply to. To do this, you select **Service** in the **Select By** field of the signature configuration screen (see Figure 5-5).

Figure 5-5 *Viewing Signatures by Service*

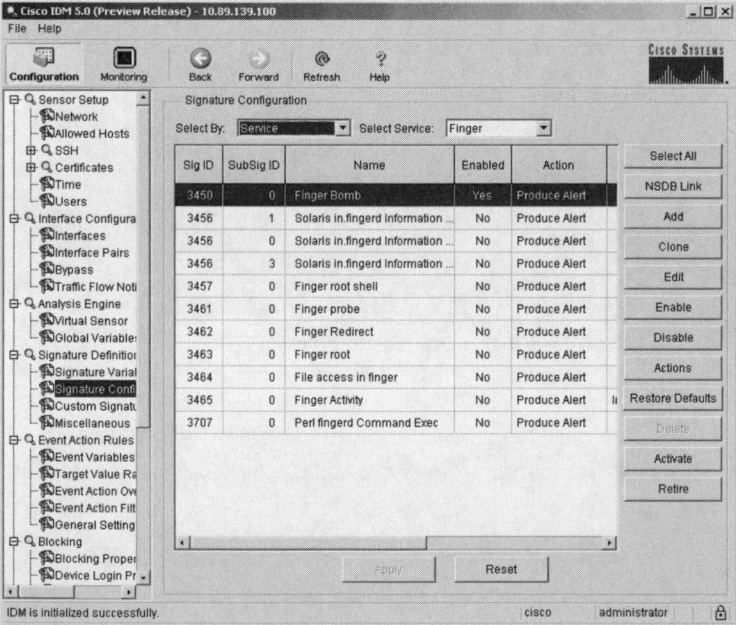

After selecting **Service**, you can choose to view the signatures for any of the services shown in Table 5-2. You select the specific service category by using the pull-down menu for the **Select Service** field.

Table 5-2 *Signature Service Options*

Service	Description
DHCP	Used to monitor Dynamic Host Configuration Protocol (DHCP) traffic (RFC 2131). DHCP enables systems to dynamically request an IP address for the local network.
DNS	Used to monitor Domain Name System (DNS) traffic. DNS provides the ability for a system, given the DNS (human-readable) name of the system, to request the IP address for a system.
FTP	Used to monitor FTP traffic. FTP is a TCP protocol that enables you to transfer files between two systems on the network.
File Sharing	Used to monitor peer-to-peer file sharing applications (such as Kazaa).
Finger	Used to monitor traffic from the Finger application. The Finger application enables a user to locate the users currently logged in to another UNIX system.
General Service	Used for signatures that do not fall into one of the more specific service categories.
HTTP	Used to monitor HTTP traffic (RFC 2616). HTTP enables a user to efficiently retrieve files from an HTTP server using a web browser.
HTTPS	Used to monitor HTTP Secure (HTTPS) traffic. The difference between HTTP and HTTPS is that HTTPS traffic is encrypted when traversing the network.
IMAP	Used to monitor Internet Message Access Protocol (IMAP) traffic (RFC 3501). IMAP can be used to retrieve mail messages from an e-mail server.
Ident	The signatures associated with the Ident service option involve signatures that monitor traffic for the Identification protocol specified by RFC 931, "Authentication Server."
LPR	Used to monitor traffic to the Line Printer (LPR) utility on UNIX and Linux systems.
MSRPC	Used to monitor Microsoft remote procedure call (MSRPC) traffic.
NetBIOS/SMB	Used to monitor Network Basic Input/Output System (NetBIOS) and Server Message Block (SMB) traffic. These protocols enable systems to perform operations such as sharing files and printers.
NNTP	Used to monitor Network News Transfer Protocol (NNTP) traffic (see RFC 977). NNTP is used to transfer news articles between servers and to enable the reading and posting of news articles.
NTP	Used to monitor Network Time Protocol (NTP) traffic (see RFC 1305). NTP enables systems to synchronize their clocks over the network.
POP	Used to monitor Post Office Protocol (POP) traffic (see RFC 1725). POP is one of the protocols by which users can retrieve mail messages from a mail server.

continues

Table 5-2 *Signature Service Options (Continued)*

Service	Description
R-Services	Used to monitor remote login (rlogin) traffic (see RFC 1258). The rlogin protocol allows users to remotely connect to a UNIX system that is more robust than Telnet.
RPC	Used to monitor remote-procedure call (RPC) traffic (see RFC 1831). RPC enables one system to execute procedures or applications remotely on another system across the network.
SMTP	Used to monitor Simple Mail Transfer Protocol (SMTP) traffic (see RFC 0821). SMTP enables the efficient and reliable transportation of mail between mail servers.
SNMP	Used to monitor Simple Network Management Protocol (SNMP) traffic (see RFC 1157). SNMP provides a protocol to manage devices on your network.
SOCKS	Used to monitor SOCKS traffic. SOCKS is a generic proxy protocol for TCP-based networking applications.
SQL	Used to monitor Structured Query Language (SQL) traffic. SQL is a computer language for accessing and manipulating database systems.
SSH	Used to monitor Secure Shell (SSH) traffic. SSH is a protocol that enables you to securely log in to a computer across the network and to execute commands on the remote system.
Telnet	Used to monitor Telnet traffic (see RFC 0854). Telnet provides a simple TCP communication protocol.
TFTP	Used monitor Trivial File Transfer Protocol (TFTP) traffic (see RFC 1350). TFTP provides a simple unauthenticated file transfer protocol.

Displaying Signatures by Signature Identification

When displaying signatures by signature identification, you select **Sig ID** in the **Select By** field of the signature configuration screen (see Figure 5-6). Next you specify a signature number (in the **Enter Sig ID** field) and then click on **Find**. This will search for the specific signature that you entered (see Figure 5-7).

Displaying Signatures by Signature Name

When displaying signatures by signature name, you select **Sig Name** in the **Select By** field of the signature configuration screen (see Figure 5-8).

Figure 5-6 *Viewing Signatures by Signature Identification*

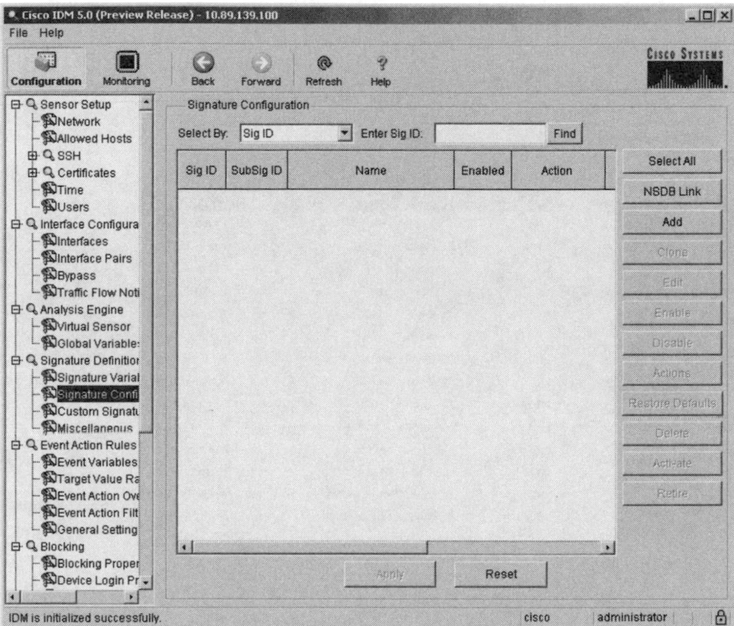

Figure 5-7 *Viewing Signatures with Sig ID 1200*

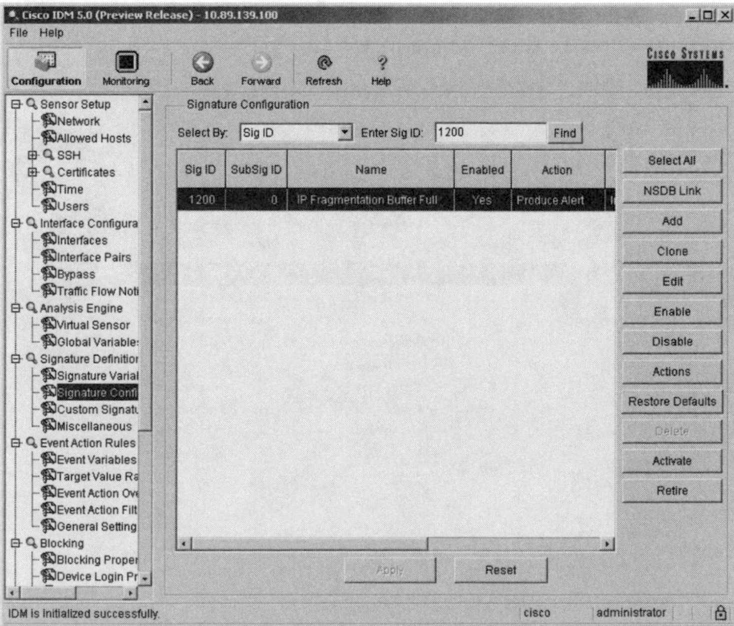

Figure 5-8 *Viewing Signatures by Signature Name*

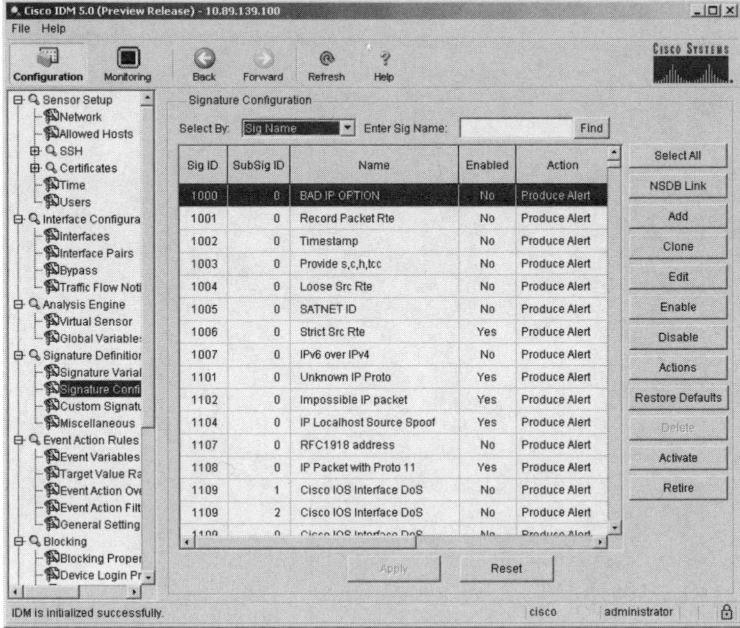

Next you specify a text string (in the **Enter Sig Name** field) and then click on **Find**. This will search for any signatures where the signature name contains the text string that you entered (see Figure 5-9).

Figure 5-9 *Viewing Signatures with "flood" in the Name*

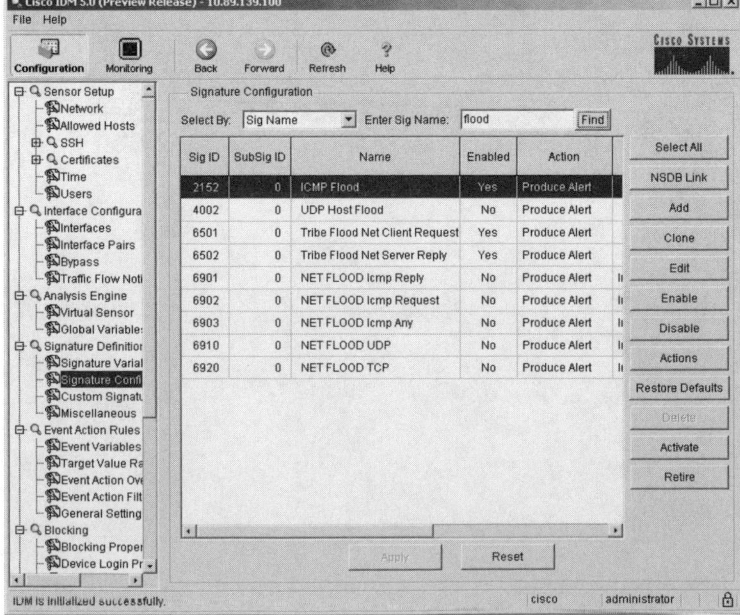

Displaying Signatures by Response Action

Displaying signatures by response action enables you to easily view which signatures are configured for a specific action. To view signatures by response action, you select **Action** in the **Select By** field of the signature configuration screen (see Figure 5-10).

Figure 5-10 *Viewing Signatures by Assigned Action*

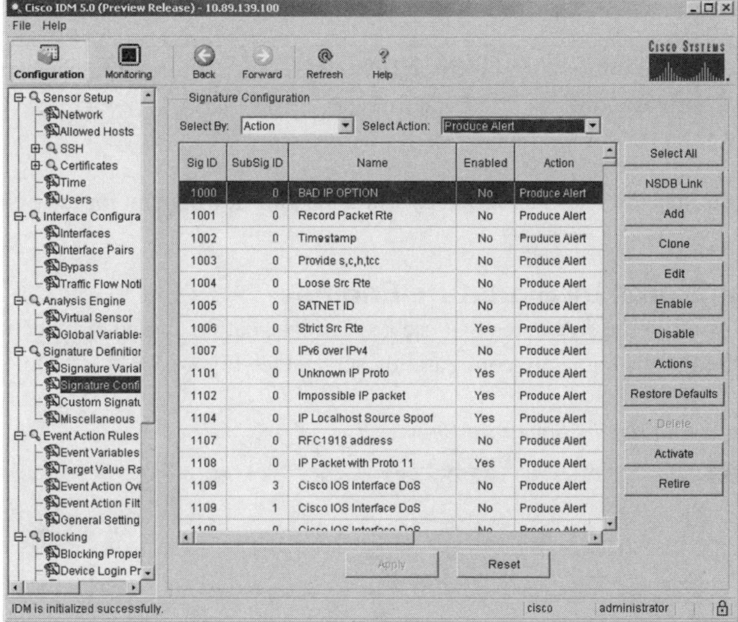

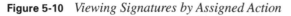

You can view the signatures for the following specific signature response actions:

- Deny Attacker Inline
- Deny Connection Inline
- Deny Packet Inline
- Log Attacker Packets
- Log Pair Packets
- Log Victim Packets
- Modify Packet Inline
- Produce Alert
- Produce Verbose Alert

- Request Block Connection
- Request Block Host
- Request SNMP Trap
- Reset TCP Connection

> **NOTE** For more information on Cisco IPS response actions, refer to Chapter 9, "Cisco IPS Response Configuration."

You select the specific response action by using the pull-down menu for the **Select Action** field.

Displaying Signatures by Signature Engine

You can view all of the signatures that use a specific signature engine by selecting **Engine** in the **Select By** field of the signature configuration screen (see Figure 5-11).

Figure 5-11 *Viewing Signatures by Signature Engine*

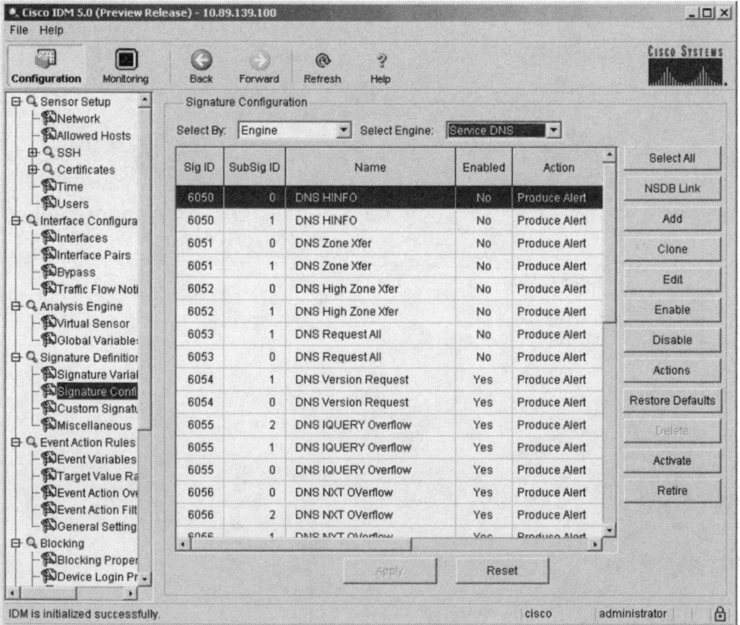

You can view signatures for the following signature engines:

- AIC FTP
- AIC HTTP
- Atomic ARP
- Atomic IP
- Flood Host
- Flood Net
- Meta
- Multi-String
- Normalizer
- Other
- Service DNS
- Service FTP
- Service Generic
- Service H225
- Service HTTP
- Service Ident
- Service MSRPC
- Service MSSQL
- Service NTP
- Service RPC
- Service SMB
- Service SNMP
- Service SSH
- State
- String ICMP
- String TCP
- String UDP
- Sweep
- Sweep Other TCP
- Trojan ICMP
- Trojan Bo2K
- Trojan Tfn22K
- Trojan UDP

You select the specific signature engine by using the pull-down menu for the **Select Engine** field.

> **NOTE** For more information on the various Cisco IPS signature engines, refer to Chapter 6, "Cisco IPS Signature Engines."

Alarm Summary Modes

Managing alarms efficiently is vital to the success of your Cisco IDS deployment. To enhance your ability to control the volume of alarms generated by your sensors, Cisco IDS supports several alarm modes. Each of the following alarm summary modes is designed to assist you in regulating the number of alarms generated by intrusive traffic in different situations:

- Fire Once
- Fire All
- Summarize
- Alarm Summarization
- Variable Alarm Summarization

The following sections explain the alarm summary modes in detail. To understand these alarm summary modes, however, you also need to understand the summary key. This parameter determines which alarms are considered duplicates. The summary key can be based on the source (attacker) and destination (victim) IP address as well as the source and destination port (for a given signature). The various alarming modes regulate the number of alarms generated, but you need to be able to determine which instances of an attack are considered duplicates of an alarm that has already been generated. The summary key can be one of the following values:

- Attacker address
- Attacker address and victim port
- Attacker and victim addresses
- Attacker and victim addresses and ports
- Victim address

For instance, assume that you have the alarms listed in Table 5-3.

Table 5-3 *Sample Alarm List*

Alarm	Source IP Address	Source Port	Destination IP Address	Destination Port
1	10.89.100.10	3201	10.90.10.100	25
2	10.89.100.10	3201	10.90.10.200	25
3	10.89.100.10	3201	10.90.10.100	25
4	10.91.10.100	2500	10.90.10.200	512
5	10.89.100.10	2300	10.90.15.100	25
6	10.89.100.10	100	10.90.10.100	80

Assuming that a specific signature is configured with the different values for the summary key, the following alarms would be considered duplicate alarms:

- Alarms 1, 2, 3, 5, and 6 for the summary key "attacker address"
- Alarms 1, 3 and 6 for the summary key "victim address"
- Alarms 1, 3, and 5 for the summary key "attacker address and victim port"
- Alarms 1 and 3 for the summary key "attacker and victim addresses and ports"
- Alarms 1, 3, and 6 for the summary key "attacker and victim addresses"

NOTE The different alarm modes determine duplicate alarms using only instances of the same signature in conjunction with the summary key information.

Fire Once

A signature configured with the Fire Once alarm summary mode will trigger a single alarm for a configured summary key value and then wait a predefined period of time (usually specified by the Summary Interval parameter) before triggering another duplicate alarm for the same signature.

For instance, assume the summary key value is set to "attacker address." If host A causes the signature to fire, then the same signature will not trigger from host A again until the time specified by the Summary Interval parameter has expired.

Fire All

A signature with the Fire All alarm summary mode triggers an alarm for all activity that matches the signature's characteristics. This is effectively the opposite of the Fire Once alarm summary mode and can generate a large number of alarms during an attack.

Alarm Summarization

Besides the basic alarm firing options, signatures can also take advantage of the following alarm fixed summarization modes:

- Summarize
- Global Summarize

Like Fire Once, these alarm summary modes limit the number of alarms generated and make it difficult for an attacker to consume resources on your sensor. With the summarization modes, however, you will also receive information on the number of times that the activity that matches a signature's characteristics was observed during a user-specified period of time.

When you use alarm summarization, the first instance of intrusive activity triggers a normal alarm. Other instances of the same activity (duplicate alarms) are counted until the end of the signature's summary interval. When the length of time specified by the Summary Interval parameter has elapsed, a summary alarm is sent, indicating the number of alarms that occurred during the time interval specified by the Summary Interval parameter.

Both summarization modes operate essentially the same way, except Global Summarize mode is based on a summary key, which consolidates alarms for all address and port combinations.

Variable Alarm Summarization

Setting the Summary Threshold or Global Summary Threshold parameters with the following alarm summary modes enables a signature to use variable alarm summarization:

- Fire All
- Summarize

When traffic causes the signature to trigger, the alarms are generated according to the initial Alarm Summary mode (see Figure 5-12). If the number of alarms for the signature exceeds the value configured for the Summary Threshold parameter (during a summary interval), the signature automatically switches to the next higher summary alarming mode (generating fewer alarms). If the number of alarms for the signature exceeds the Global Summary Threshold (during the same summary interval), the signature switches to Global Summarize (if not already at this level, since this is the maximum level of alarm consolidation). At the end of the summary interval, the signature reverts back to its configured alarming mode.

For instance, assume that you have a signature with the following values:

- Summary Threshold—10
- Summary Interval—5 seconds
- Global Summary Threshold—30
- Alarm Summary Mode—Fire All

Figure 5-12 *Automatic Alarm Summarization*

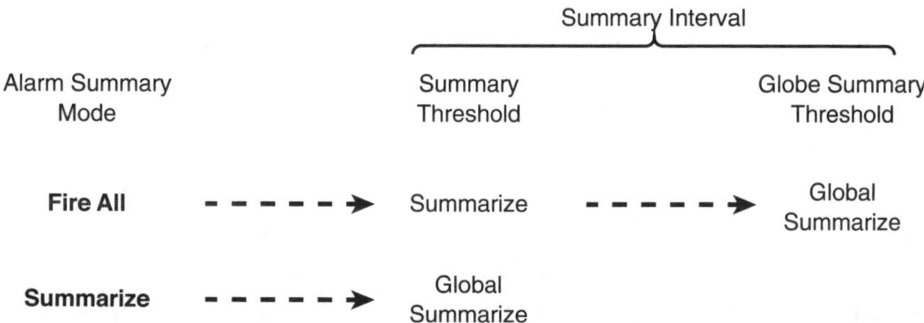

Initially, every time the signature is triggered an alarm is generated. Then if the number of alarms for the signature exceeds 10 (during a 5-second period), the signature automatically switches to Summarize mode. Finally, if the number of alarms exceeds 30 (during the same 5-second period), the signature automatically switches to Global Summarize mode. At the end of the Summary Interval (after 5 seconds), the signature reverts back to the Fire All alarm summary mode. After switching to one of the summarization modes, a summary alarm is generated at the end of the summary interval. The summary alarm indicates the number of alarms that were detected during the summarization period.

The variable alarming modes provide you with the flexibility of having signatures that trigger an alarm on every instance of a signature but then reduce the number of alarms generated when the alarms start to significantly impact the resources on the IDS. The reduction in alarms also improves the ability of the network security administrator to analyze the alarms being generated.

Basic Signature Configuration

After locating signatures by using signature groups, you can perform various configuration operations on signatures or groups of signatures. These configuration operations fall into the following categories:

- Viewing Network Security Database (NSDB) information
- Enabling signatures
- Creating new signatures
- Editing existing signatures
- Retiring signatures
- Defining signature responses

Besides understanding the basic signature configuration operations, it is helpful to understand the fields that an alert contains. Table 5-4 describes the major fields found in an alert.

Table 5-4 *Alert Fields*

Field	Description
Alert Type	Type of alert event generated. Valid types are Error, NAC, Status, or Alert.
Application Name	Application on the sensor that generated the alert.
Attacker Address	IP address of the system that originated the traffic.
Attacker Port	Source port on the system originating the traffic.
Block Requested	Indicates if the event generated an IP blocking response action.
Description	Name of the signature that triggered the alert.
Dropped Packet	Indicates if the traffic was dropped by an inline drop response action.
Event ID	Numerical identifier that the sensor assigned to the event.
Host ID	Name of the sensor on which the traffic was detected.

continues

Table 5-4 *Alert Fields (Continued)*

Field	Description
Interface	Sensor interface on which the traffic was detected.
IP Logged	Indicates that the event generated an IP Logging response action.
Interface Group	Name of the inline interface pair on which the traffic was detected.
Protocol	Protocol of the traffic that caused the signature to trigger.
Risk Rating	Risk Rating of the event associated with the alert.
Sensor UTC Time	Time that the event occurred.
Severity	Severity of the signature that caused the alert.
SigID	Numerical identifier of the signature that fired and caused the alert event.
Signature Version	Identifies the signature release when the signature was first incorporated into the sensor software.
SubSig ID	Identifies the sub-signature ID of the signature that caused the alert event.
Target Address	IP address of the system receiving the traffic.
Target Port	Destination port to which the traffic is sent.
TCP Reset	Indicates if the alert generated a TCP reset response action.
Trigger Packet	Actual packet that caused the signature to trigger. Only available if signature is configured to capture the trigger packet.
Vendor	Identifies the vendor who developed the signature.
VLAN	Virtual LAN (VLAN) on which the traffic was detected.

Viewing NSDB Information

The NSDB links to an online Cisco HTML-based encyclopedia of network vulnerability information (also known as the Cisco Secure Encyclopedia [CSEC]). CSEC was developed as a central "warehouse" of security knowledge to provide Cisco security professionals with an interactive database of security-vulnerability information. CSEC contains detailed information about security vulnerabilities such as countermeasures, affected systems and software, and Cisco Secure products that can help you test for vulnerabilities or detect when malicious users attempt to exploit your systems. The CSEC can be found at http://www.cisco.com/go/csec.

Signature Information

Each signature has an Exploit Signature page (located in the NSDB) that describes the characteristics of the signature. A typical NSDB Exploit Signature page contains numerous fields that provide information about the signature that triggered the alarm. The following three fields provide you with valuable information:

- Description
- Benign Trigger(s)
- Recommended Signature Filter

The Description field describes what type of network traffic the signature is looking for. The Benign Trigger(s) field identifies situations in which the signature may trigger on normal user traffic, thus generating a false positive. The final field, Recommended Signature Filter, identifies a recommended filter that you can apply to your monitoring application to reduce the chances that the signature will generate false positives. Figure 5-13 shows an NSDB Exploit Signature page for the Windows Shell External Handler signature.

Figure 5-13 *NSDB Exploit Signature Page*

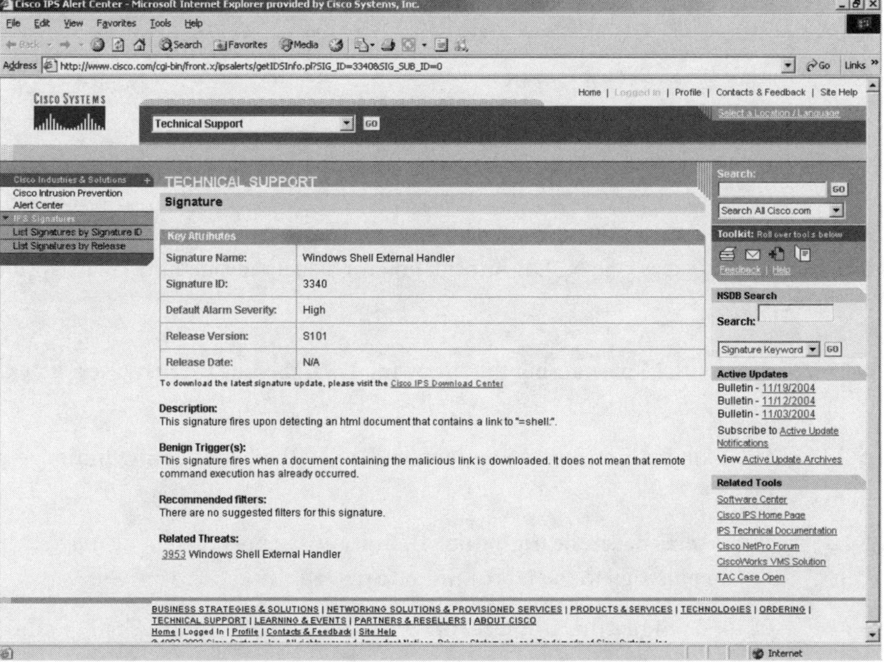

Related Threats Information

Each signature page provides a link (in the Related Threats field) to an NSDB Threats page that provides information on the threats associated with a given exploit. A typical NSDB Threats page (see Figure 5-14) provides information such as the threatened systems, known countermeasures, and consequences of the threat.

Figure 5-14 *NSDB Threats Page*

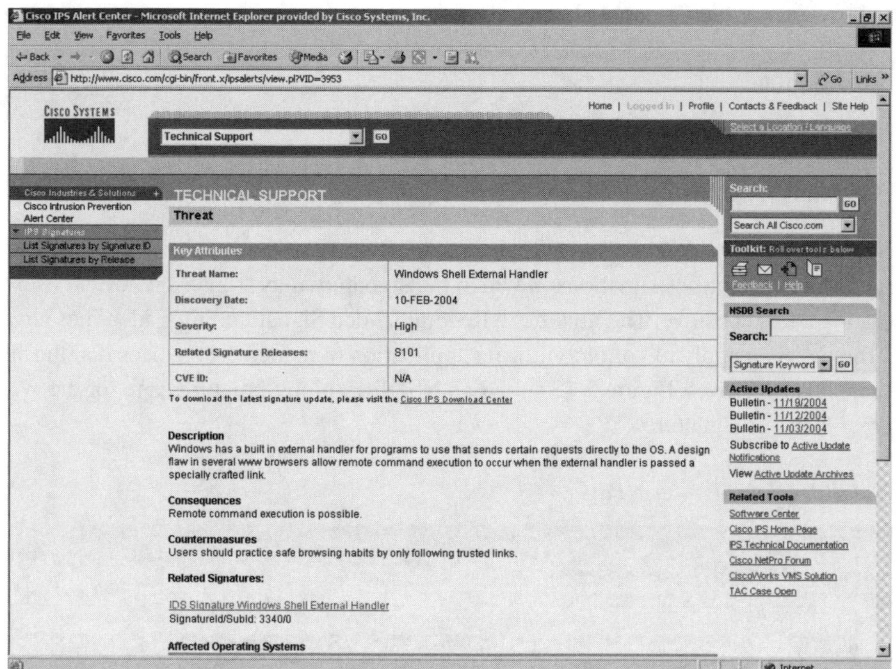

Viewing NSDB Information

From IDM, you can access the NSDB information for a specific signature by performing the following steps:

Step 1 Access IDM by entering the following URL in your web browser: **https://** *sensor_ip_address.*

Step 2 Click on the **Configuration** icon to display the list of configuration tasks.

Step 3 If the items under the **Signature Definition** category are not displayed, click on the plus sign to the left of **Signature Definition**.

Step 4 Click on **Signature Configuration** to access the Signature Configuration screen.

Step 5 Highlight the signature for which you want to see NSDB information by clicking on the name of the signature.

Step 6 Click on **NSDB Link** to access the NSDB information via Cisco.com. To access this information, you need to log in with a registered user account.

Step 7 After you log in, the NSDB signature page for the highlighted signature is displayed in a new browser window (see Figure 5-13).

Step 8 To view the threat information for the signature, simply click on the **Related Threats** link. This will display the threat information for the signature (see Figure 5-14).

Enabling Signatures

By default, not all signatures are enabled. Some are disabled because they are known to generate false positives unless you configure specific event filters for your network configuration. Occasionally, you may find that a signature that is enabled by default needs to be disabled because it generates false positives in your network configuration.

It is a simple task to enable or disable Cisco IPS signatures through the IDM interface. The following are the steps to enable a Cisco IPS signature:

Step 1 Access IDM by entering the following URL in your web browser: **https://** *sensor_ip_address*.

Step 2 Click on the **Configuration** icon to display the list of configuration tasks.

Step 3 If the items under the **Signature Definition** category are not displayed, click on the plus sign to the left of **Signature Definition**.

Step 4 Click on **Signature Configuration** to access the Signature Configuration screen.

Step 5 Highlight the signature(s) that you want to enable by clicking on the name of the signature.

> **NOTE** You can highlight multiple signatures by holding down the **Ctrl** key while clicking on signature names. You can also highlight a signature and hold down the **Shift** key while clicking on another signature name to highlight all of the signatures between the two selected signatures.

Step 6 Click on **Enable** to enable the highlighted signature(s).

Step 7 Click on **Apply** to save the configuration to the sensor.

> **NOTE** The process for disabling a signature is the same as that for enabling a signature, except that you click on **Disable** instead of **Enable**.

Creating New Signatures

Although Cisco IPS provides numerous signatures, you may want to create your own signatures in addition to these. When creating new signatures, you have the following two options:

- Add
- Clone

The difference between these two options is that cloning an existing signature enables you to construct a new signature that starts with the parameters of an existing signature. You can then customize the settings to match your requirements. Adding a signature fills in default values for more of the signature parameters and allows you to construct a signature to match your custom signature requirements. For more information on creating custom signatures, refer to Chapter 7.

Editing Existing Signatures

Along with creating your own custom signatures, you can tune existing signatures by changing the signature parameters to match your network requirements. For more information on tuning existing signatures, refer to Chapter 7.

> **NOTE** You can always restore a signature to its default settings by using the **Restore Defaults** option on the Signature Configuration screen.

Retiring Signatures

Cisco IPS provides a large number of signatures that cover numerous operating systems and applications. Not all of these signatures may be applicable to your environment. If you choose, you can retire a Cisco IPS signature. When you retire a signature, the signature is actually removed from the signature engine (thus removing any impact that the signature has on the performance of your sensor). The steps to retire a signature are as follows:

Step 1 Access IDM by entering the following URL in your web browser: **https://***sensor_ip_address*.

Step 2 Click on the **Configuration** icon to display the list of configuration tasks.

Step 3 If the items under the **Signature Definition** category are not displayed, click on the plus sign to the left of **Signature Definition**.

Step 4 Click on **Signature Configuration** to access the Signature Configuration screen.

Step 5 Highlight the signature for which you want to see the NSDB information by clicking on the name of the signature.

Step 6 Click on **Retire** to retire the highlighted signature(s).

Step 7 Click on **Apply** to save the configuration changes to the sensor.

NOTE If you decide to activate any signatures that you have retired, you can follow the steps for retiring a signature, but instead of clicking on **Retire**, you click on **Activate**. This will add the previously retired signature back into the signature engine. Rebuilding the signature engine, however, can be a time-consuming process.

Defining Signature Responses

You can configure each Cisco IPS to perform one or more of the following responses when a signature fires (see Figure 5-15):

- Deny Attacker Inline
- Deny Connection Inline
- Deny Packet Inline
- Log Attacker Packets
- Log Pair Packets
- Log Victim Packets
- Produce Alert
- Produce Verbose Alert
- Request Block Connection
- Request Block Host
- Request SNMP Trap
- Reset TCP Connection

Figure 5-15 *Signature Response Actions*

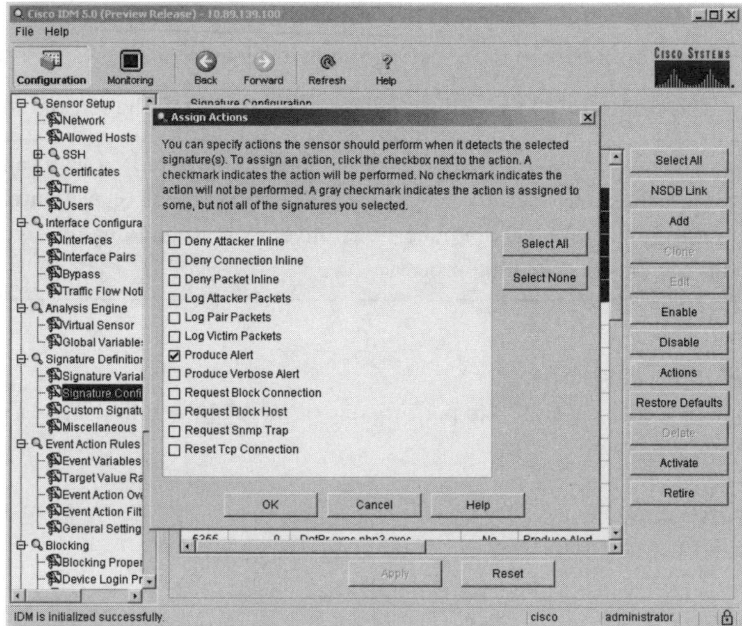

You can select one or more of these operations for each Cisco IPS signature. By clicking on the check box next to an action, you can toggle between selecting the operation and removing the operation. When a check mark is displayed next to an action, that action will be performed when the signature fires.

Foundation Summary

Basic signature configuration focuses on the following topics:

- Signature groups
- Alarm modes
- Basic signature configuration

Signature groups enable you to view Cisco IPS signatures more efficiently, based on the following categories:

- Attack
- L2/L3/L4 Protocol
- Operating System
- Signature Release
- Service
- Signature Identification
- Signature Name
- Signature Action
- Signature Engine

After locating signatures by using signature groups, you can then easily perform the following signature operations:

- Viewing Network Security Database (NSDB) information
- Enabling signatures
- Creating new signatures
- Editing existing signatures
- Retiring signatures
- Defining signature responses

When creating new signatures, you can start with an existing signature by using the Clone option, or you can create a signature from scratch by using the Add option.

Retiring signatures enables you to improve performance by removing unneeded signatures from the signature engines. The signatures can be easily activated if they are needed in the future.

You can configure one or more of the following signature responses (actions) to be performed when a signature is fired:

- Deny Attacker Inline
- Deny Connection Inline
- Deny Packet Inline
- Log Attacker Packets
- Log Pair Packets
- Log Victim Packets
- Produce Alert
- Produce Verbose Alert
- Request Block Connection
- Request Block Host
- Request SNMP Trap
- Reset TCP Connection

Q&A

You have two choices for review questions:

- The questions that follow give you a bigger challenge than the exam itself by using an open-ended question format. By reviewing now with this more difficult question format, you can exercise your memory better and prove your conceptual and factual knowledge of this chapter. The answers to these questions are found in the appendix.
- For more practice with exam-like question formats, use the exam engine on the CD-ROM.

1. In IDM, which signature groups can you use to view signatures?
2. In IDM, which types of attacks can you view signatures by?
3. In IDM, what field is searched when you display signatures by signature name?
4. What summary-key values can you specify for a signature?
5. What is the difference between Fire All and Fire Once alarm summary modes?
6. What is the difference between Summary and Global Summary alarm summary modes?
7. What does the Benign Trigger(s) field on the NSDB signature page provide?
8. What are the two methods (via IDM) that you can use to create new custom signatures?
9. Using IDM, how can you remove a signature from a signature engine?
10. What signature responses (actions) are unique to inline mode?
11. Which signature response (action) uses SNMP?
12. Besides using the **Select All** button, how can you select multiple signatures on the Signature Configuration screen?

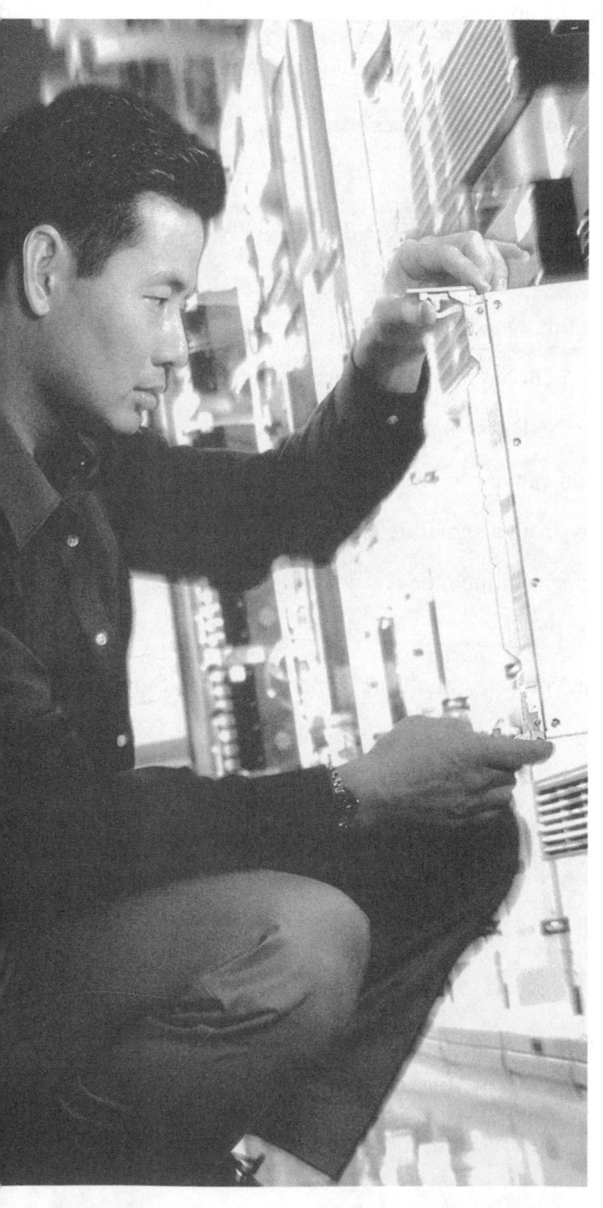

This chapter covers the following subjects:

- Cisco IPS Signatures
- Cisco IPS Signature Engines
- Application Inspection and Control (AIC) Signature Engines
- Atomic Signature Engines
- Flood Signature Engines
- Meta Signature Engine
- Normalizer Signature Engine
- Service Signature Engines
- State Signature Engine
- String Signature Engines
- Sweep Signature Engines
- Trojan Horse Signature Engines

CHAPTER 6

Cisco IPS Signature Engines

The heart of the Cisco IPS solution is the various signature engines that enable signature designers and customers to easily and efficiently develop IPS signatures that cover a wide range of protocols and applications. Each signature engine supports various parameters that are used to create signatures.

Cisco IPS supports numerous signature engines that are each designed to support signatures for a specific function, application, or protocol. The operation of the signature is regulated by specific parameters. Some parameters are unique to a specific signature engine, whereas other parameters are used by multiple engines. Understanding the Cisco IPS signature engines and their parameters is vital to tuning and customizing your Cisco IPS solution to your network environment.

"Do I Know This Already?" Quiz

The purpose of the "Do I Know This Already?" quiz is to help you decide if you really need to read the entire chapter. If you already intend to read the entire chapter, you do not necessarily need to answer these questions now.

The 10-question quiz, derived from the major sections in the "Foundation and Supplemental Topics" portion of the chapter, helps you determine how to spend your limited study time.

Table 6-1 outlines the major topics discussed in this chapter and the "Do I Know This Already?" quiz questions that correspond to those topics.

Table 6-1 *"Do I Know This Already?" Foundation and Supplemental Topics Mapping*

Foundation or Supplemental Topic	Questions Covering This Topic
Cisco IPS Signature Engines	-
Application Inspection and Control (AIC) Signature Engines	4, 7, 8
Atomic Signature Engines	1, 5
Flood Signature Engines	-

continues

Table 6-1 *"Do I Know This Already?" Foundation and Supplemental Topics Mapping (Continued)*

Foundation or Supplemental Topic	Questions Covering This Topic
Meta Signature Engine	2, 6
Normalizer Signature Engine	-
Service Signature Engines	9
State Signature Engine	10
String Signature Engines	-
Sweep Signature Engines	3
Trojan Horse Signature Engines	-

CAUTION The goal of self-assessment is to gauge your mastery of the topics in this chapter. If you do not know the answer to a question or are only partially sure of the answer, you should mark this question wrong for purposes of the self-assessment. Giving yourself credit for an answer you correctly guess skews your self-assessment results and might provide you with a false sense of security.

1. Which signature engine would you use to create a signature that searches for the pattern "Confidential" in a single packet?
   a. Atomic IP
   b. String TCP
   c. Meta
   d. AIC FTP
   e. Service Generic

2. Which signature engine would you use to create a signature that will trigger when the following three HTTP signatures occur: 3202, 3209, and 3217?
   a. AIC HTTP
   b. Service HTTP
   c. Normalizer
   d. Meta
   e. State

3. Which parameter do you configure when creating a TCP port sweep signature that you do not configure for a TCP host sweep signature?
   a. TCP Mask
   b. Port Range
   c. Unique
   d. Swap Attacker Victim
   e. Storage Key

4. Which signature engine can you use to create a signature that verifies that no application is using port 80 for any traffic except for HTTP?
   a. Service Generic
   b. Service HTTP
   c. AIC HTTP
   d. Normalizer
   e. State

5. Which parameter would you use to require a regex match to be at least 20 bytes when you are creating an Atomic TCP signature?
   a. Min Match Length
   b. Min Match Offset
   c. Max Match Offset
   d. Min Regex Size
   e. Exact Match Offset

6. What is in the Component Count field in a meta signatures?
   a. The number of component signatures in the meta signatures
   b. The number of times a meta signatures triggers
   c. The number of component signatures that have triggered for a meta signature
   d. The number of times a component signature must be detected for the component signature entry to match

7. Which of the following is not a valid signature type for the AIC HTTP signature engine?
   a. Max Outstanding Requests Overrun
   b. Request Methods
   c. Define Web Traffic Policy
   d. Content Types
   e. URL Link Pattern

8. Which of the following is not a valid option for the FTP Command parameter of the AIC FTP signature engine?
   a. **site**
   b. **anon**
   c. **retr**
   d. **pwd**
   e. **stor**

9. Which of the following fields is not a valid regex field for the Service HTTP signature engine?
   a. Uri Regex
   b. Arg Name Regex
   c. Arg Value Regex
   d. Header Regex
   e. Body Regex

10. Which of the following is not a state machine supported by the State signature engine?
   a. Cisco Login
   b. SMTP
   c. SNMP
   d. LPR Format String

The answers to the "Do I Know This Already?" quiz are found in the appendix. The suggested choices for your next step are as follows:

- **8 or less overall score**—Read the entire chapter. This includes the "Foundation and Supplemental Topics" and "Foundation Summary" sections and the Q&A section.
- **9 or 10 overall score**—If you want more review on these topics, skip to the "Foundation Summary" section and then go to the Q&A section. Otherwise, move to the next chapter.

Foundation and Supplemental Topics

Cisco IPS Signatures

To identify malicious activity, Cisco IPS monitors network traffic and generates alerts when traffic matching specific signatures is detected. A signature is basically a description of network traffic that attackers use while conducting network-based attacks. To support a wide range of signatures and enable users to develop their own custom signatures, Cisco IPS uses a set of signature engines that each examine network traffic for intrusive activity with similar characteristics. An example of these signature engines are the TCP-based string engines, which handle signatures that search for specific textual strings in TCP traffic. Signature engines parse a list of signature definitions and then search for traffic matching those signatures in the network traffic stream.

Since signature engines and signatures are the foundation of Cisco IPS, Cisco security engineers are continually researching and developing these components. The signature engines are designed to perform a wide range of functions, such as pattern matching, stateful pattern matching, protocol decoding, deep-packet inspection, and other heuristic methods. Furthermore, new signature engines are being added to efficiently support a larger range of signatures.

Cisco IPS Signature Engines

Cisco IPS monitors network traffic with a suite of signature engines. By spreading signature processing across distinct categories where all of the signatures for a category share similar characteristics, you can analyze network traffic more efficiently and add your own custom signatures more easily. The signature engines fall into the categories shown in Table 6-2.

Table 6-2 *Signature Engine Categories*

Engine Category	Usage
Application Inspection and Control (AIC)	Used to provide deep-packet inspection from Layer 4 through Layer 7
Atomic	Used for single-packet conditions
Flood	Used to detect denial-of-service (DoS) attempts
Meta	Used to create meta signatures based on multiple individual signatures
Normalizer	Used to normalize fragmented and TCP streams when in inline mode (cannot create custom signatures)
Service	Used when services at OSI Layers 5, 6, and 7 require protocol analysis
State	Used when stateful inspection is required

continues

Table 6-2 *Signature Engine Categories (Continued)*

Engine Category	Usage
String	Used for string pattern matching
Sweep	Used to detect network reconnaissance scans
Miscellaneous	Various assorted signature engines (such as Traffic ICMP and Trojan horse signature engines)

Understanding the capabilities of each of the signature engines is crucial to tuning built-in signatures and developing custom signatures that are unique to your network environment. This section will explain the various signature engines and highlight many of the parameters that you will need to use to both tune built-in signatures and develop custom signatures. Before examining the different engines, you should understand the parameters that you will use to define a signature.

Signature Parameters

To identify the traffic that a specific signature is looking for, you should define each signature by specifying a set of parameters. Some parameters are unique to a signature engine whereas other parameters are common to all signatures. All of the parameters are stored in configuration files for each signature engine to parse. Each parameter falls into one of the following groups:

- Basic signature fields
- Signature description fields
- Engine-specific fields
- Event counter fields
- Alert frequency fields
- Status fields

Along with the parameters that are common to every signature, each signature also has engine-specific parameters. These parameters enable the efficient creation of signatures without an unwanted number of extra and unnecessary parameters being tagged onto every signature that you create. Some of the major engine-specific parameters will be explained in the explanation of the signature engines themselves.

Application Inspection and Control Signature Engines

HTTP and FTP are protocols that commonly traverse firewalls on many networks. Because of this, many applications (and attackers) have started using these protocols to tunnel traffic (other than HTTP and FTP) through firewalls in an attempt to circumvent the security policies implemented on various networks. Cisco IPS version 5.0 enables you to conduct a more thorough analysis of HTTP and FTP through application policy enforcement. Currently, application policy enforcement is available through the signature engines listed in Table 6-3.

Table 6-3 *AIC Signature Engines*

Engine	Description
AIC FTP	Application layer-inspection signatures for FTP traffic
AIC HTTP	Application layer-inspection signatures for HTTP traffic

AIC FTP Signature Engine Parameters

Using the Application Inspection and Control (AIC) FTP signature engine involves configuring the parameters shown in Table 6-4.

Table 6-4 *AIC FTP Signature Engine Parameters*

Parameter Name	Values	Description
Signature Type	FTP Commands Unrecognized FTP Command	Identifies the type of FTP commands that the signature will detect
FTP Command	Help, Noop, Stat, Syst, User, abor, acct, allo, appe, cdup, cwd, dele, list, mkd, mode, nlst, pass, pasv, port, pwd, quit, rein, rest, retr, rmd, rnfr, rnto, site, smnt, stor, stou, stru, type	The FTP command that the signature will check for

Basically, AIC FTP signatures look for either specific or unrecognized FTP commands. You specify the signature type and then the command that the signature triggers on (if the signature type is FTP Commands).

AIC HTTP Signature Engine Parameters

Using the AIC HTTP signature engine involves configuring the parameters shown in Table 6-5.

Table 6-5 *AIC HTTP Signature Engine Parameters*

Parameter Name	Values	Description
Signature Type	Content Types Define Web Traffic Policy Max Outstanding Requests Overrun Msg Body Pattern Request Methods Transfer Encodings	Identifies the type of HTTP traffic that the signature will detect or analyze

When configuring an AIC HTTP signature, you first specify the signature type shown in Table 6-5. Then you configure the parameters unique to that type of signature. These unique parameters will be explained in detail in the following sections.

Content Types Parameters

When defining AIC HTTP signatures by using the Content Types signature type, you specify the content types that the signature will search for in the HTTP messages. The parameters for this AIC HTTP signature type are shown in Table 6-6.

Table 6-6 *Content Types Parameters*

Parameter Name	Values	Description
Content Type	*string*	A specified HTTP content type
Content Types	Define Content Type Define Recognized Content Types	Type of content type processing the signature will use
Content Type Details	Content Verification Length No Additional Details	Identifies the extra information to be specified for the content type
Content Type Verify	Yes No	Indicates whether the signature verifies the content type
Enforce Accept Content Types	Yes No	Identifies whether the signature verifies that the content type specified matches one of the types specified in the Accept field
Entry Key	*string*	Name of a specific recognized content type entry
Length	0–65535	Length of the content type
Name	*string*	Description name of the content type entry
Recognized Content Types	*Entry_Keys*	List of recognized content types composed of one or more entry keys
Regex String	*string*	(Optional) Specifies the regular expression that the signature will search for
Regex End Offset	0–65535	(Optional) Indicates the maximum number of bytes to be inspected during the search for the string match
Magic Number List	*Magic_Number_Keys*	A list of regex (regular expression) entries to search for

Define Web Traffic Policy Parameters

When defining a signature by using the Define Web Traffic Policy signature type, you are creating a signature that checks if the traffic is valid based on the HTTP RFC (RFC 2616). The only parameter for the signature type is Alarm on Non-HTTP Traffic. This parameter can be either Yes (default) or No. If you specify Yes, the signature will trigger whenever non-HTTP traffic is detected going to the specified ports.

Msg Body Pattern Parameters

When defining AIC HTTP signatures by using the Msg Body signature type, you specify a list of regex strings to search for in the HTTP messages. The parameters for this AIC HTTP signature type are shown in Table 6-7.

Table 6-7 *Msg Body Pattern Parameters*

Parameter Name	Values	Description
Entry Key	*string*	Name of a specific regex entry
Regex Pattern	*string*	(Optional) Specifies the regular expression that the signature will search for
Regex Min Match Length	0–65535	(Optional) Requires the string matched to be at least the specified minimum number of bytes
Regex End Offset	0–65535	(Optional) Indicates the maximum number of bytes to be inspected when looking for the string match
Regex List	*Entry_Keys*	A list of regex entries to search for
Regex List in Order	Yes No	If Yes, the signature must search for the regex entries in the order in which they are listed in the regex list

Basically, you configure a list of regex entries to search for in the body of the HTTP message. For each regex you can specify the minimum match length and number of bytes in the stream or packet to search for the pattern. Finally, you can also specify whether the regex strings need to be found in the order specified by using the Regex List in Order parameter.

Request Methods Parameters

When defining AIC HTTP signatures by using the Request Methods signature type, you specify a request method or a list of request methods to search for in the HTTP messages. The parameters for an AIC HTTP Request Method signature are shown in Table 6-8.

Table 6-8 *Request Methods Parameters*

Parameter Name	Values	Description
Request Method	*string*	A specified HTTP request method
Request Methods	Define Request Method Define Recognized Request Methods	Type of request method processing the signature will use
Define Request Method	*string*	Identifies a specified request method for the signature to use
Entry Key	*string*	Name of a specific recognized request method entry
Recognized Request Methods	*Entry_Keys*	List of recognized content types composed of one or more entry keys

Transfer Encodings Parameters

When defining AIC HTTP signatures by using the Transfer Encodings signature type, you specify a transfer encoding or a list of transfer encodings to search for in the HTTP messages. The parameters for this AIC HTTP signature type are shown in Table 6-9.

Table 6-9 *Transfer Encodings Parameters*

Parameter Name	Values	Description
Define Transfer Encoding	*string*	A specified HTTP transfer encoding method
Transfer Encodings	Chunked Transfer Encoding Error Define Transfer Encoding Recognized Transfer Encodings	Type of transfer encoding processing the signature will use
Content Type Details	Content Verification Length No Additional Details	Identifies the extra information to be specified for the content type
Transfer Encoding	*string*	The transfer encoding configured for a specific entry key
Entry Key	*string*	Name of a specific recognized transfer encoding entry
Recognized Transfer Encodings	*Entry_Keys*	List of recognized content types composed of one or more entry keys

Atomic Signature Engines

The two signature engines shown in Table 6-10 handle all of the atomic signatures. Each of these engines is designed to efficiently support signatures that trigger based on information in a single packet. Whenever a packet that matches a configured signature is detected, the appropriate signature engine triggers an alarm. The atomic engines are constructed to efficiently handle searching different types of traffic streams (such as ICMP, TCP, and UDP).

Table 6-10 *Atomic Signature Engines*

Engine	Description
Atomic ARP	ARP simple and cross-packet signatures
Atomic IP	Simple IP alarms based on various IP parameters (including TCP, UDP, and ICMP simple signatures)

Since these atomic signature engines examine single packets, they do not need to maintain state. Therefore, the atomic engines do not store any persistent data across multiple data packets.

Atomic ARP Engine Parameters

Atomic ARP provides the ability to support basic Layer 2 Address Resolution Protocol (ARP) signatures (see RFC 826, "An Ethernet Address Resolution Protocol"). Numerous tools enable an attacker to attack your network at the link layer, including dsniff (http://www.monkey.org/~dugsong/dsniff) and ettercap (http://ettercap.sourceforge.net). The Atomic ARP signature engine enables Cisco IPS to detect the use of these tools on your network. To tune existing Atomic ARP signatures or create custom signatures, you need to understand the parameters shown in Table 6-11.

Table 6-11 *Atomic ARP Engine Parameters*

Parameter Name	Values	Description
ARP Operation	0–255	The ARP operation code that this signature will match on
Mac Flip Times	0–65535	Fires an alert when the Media Access Control (MAC) address for an IP address changes more than this number of times
Request Inbalance	0–65535	Fires an alert when there are this many more ARP requests than replies for an IP address
Type of ARP Sig	Dst Broadcast Same Src and Dst Src Broadcast Src Multicast	Fires an alert when the traffic matches the specified address parameters

The Specify Arp Operation field enables you to create alarms based on a specific ARP operation code. The two normal ARP operations codes are as follows:

- ARP Request (operation code 1)
- ARP Reply (operation code 2)

The Specify Request Inbalance field causes a signature to trigger if more ARP requests than replies are detected for a specific IP address. Normally, the requests and replies are matched up one to one so that an imbalance can indicate malicious activity.

A normal ARP request is sent to the broadcast Ethernet address so that every system on a segment can see the request and potentially respond. A broadcast Ethernet address in any other situation (such as in the Ethernet source address) is an indication of potential intrusive activity and should be investigated. The Specify Type of ARP Sig field enables you to create ARP signatures that look for traffic based on one of the following criteria:

- Destination is broadcast
- Source and destination are the same
- Source is broadcast
- Source is multicast

Atomic IP Engine Parameters

The Atomic IP engine enables you to create specialized atomic signatures based on any IP protocol. Most of your Atomic IP signatures will fall into one of the following protocol categories:

- ICMP (Internet Control Message Protocol)
- TCP
- UDP (User Datagram Protocol)

The Atomic IP signature engine comprises IP-specific fields and the specific fields for the IP protocol that the signature is based on. Table 6-12 identifies the basic IP fields for the Atomic IP signature engine.

IP options provide optional information for the IP datagram. The major options are as follows:

- Security and handling restrictions (IP option 2)
- Record route (IP option 7)
- Timestamp (IP option 4)
- Loose source routing (IP option 3)
- Strict source routing (IP option 9)

Table 6-12 *IP Fields for Atomic IP Signature Engine*

Parameter Name	Values	Description
Fragment Status	Any Fragmented Not Fragmented	Matches all packets Matches only fragmented packets Matches only nonfragmented packets
Layer 4 Protocol	ICMP Protocol Other IP Protocols TCP Protocol UDP Protocol	The Layer 4 protocol that the signature will examine
IP Payload Length	0–65535	The length of the payload to search for
IP Header Length	0–65535	The value for the IP header length to look for
IP Type of Service	0–255	The value for the IP Header type of service (ToS) to match
IP Time-to-Live	0–255	Specifies the value for the Time-to-Live (TTL) field to look for
IP Version	0–16	Specifies the IP version to search for
IP Identifier	0–65535	Specifies the IP identifier to search for
IP Total Length	0–65535	Triggers an alarm if the IP data length exceeds this value
IP Option Inspection Options	IP Option IP Option Abnormal Option	Specifies whether to search for a specific IP option or just abnormal options
IP Option	0-65535	The IP option code to match
IP Option Abnormal Option	Yes No	Specifies whether the signature checks to see if the option list is malformed
IP Address Options	Address with Localhost IP addresses RFC 1918 Addresses Src IP Equal Dst IP	Matches if address is 127.0.0.1 Matches on regular IP addresses Matches on reserved IP address specified by RFC 1918 Both the source IP address and the destination IP address are the same

You can specify an IP option to search for by using the IP Option parameter. The only other option is the IP Option Abnormal Option parameter. By setting this parameter to True, you cause the signature to trigger when a packet with an invalid option is detected.

The IP Address Options field enables you to cause the signature to match based on one of the following IP address types:

- Localhost addresses (127.0.0.1)
- RFC 1918 reserved addresses
- Packets with source equal to destination
- Regular IP addresses

Atomic IP ICMP Parameters

Creating ICMP atomic signatures involves configuring the parameters identified in Table 6-13.

Table 6-13 *ICMP Fields for Atomic IP Signature Engine*

Parameter Name	Values	Description
ICMP Code	0–255	The value to match for the Code field in the ICMP header
ICMP Identifier	0–65535	The value to match for the Identifier field in the ICMP header
ICMP Sequence	0–65535	The value to match for Sequence Number field in the ICMP header
ICMP Type	0–255	The value to match for Type field in the ICMP header
ICMP Total Length	0–65535	The minimum length (of the ICMP header and payload) to match

The ICMP parameters enable you to efficiently detect specific ICMP traffic (see RFC 792) on your network. You can specify single values for the following ICMP header fields:

- Code
- Identifier
- Sequence Number
- Type
- Total Length

Atomic IP TCP Parameters

Creating TCP atomic signatures involves configuring the parameters identified in Table 6-14. These signatures identify traffic based on various TCP fields, such as source and destination ports, or the contents of the packet's data.

Table 6-14 *TCP Fields for Atomic IP Signature Engine*

Parameter Name	Values	Description
Destination Port Range	*port-list*	The destination port range to match (each port can be 0–65535, and the two ports of the range are separated by a hyphen)
Source Port Range	*port-list*	The source port range to match (each port can be 0–65535, and the two ports of the range are separated by a dash)
TCP Flags	FIN SYN RST PSH ACK URG ZERO	The TCP Flags (out of the flags included in the mask) that need to be set for the signature to trigger
TCP Header Length	0–15	(Optional) Indicates the required TCP header length
TCP Mask	FIN SYN RST PSH ACK URG ZERO	The mask used when the TCP Flags This field indicates the TCP flags that you want to include in your checking
TCP Payload Length	0–65535	(Optional) Indicates the length of payload required
TCP Reserved	0–63	(Optional) Indicates the required value for the TCP reserved flags
TCP Urgent Pointer	0–65535	(Optional) Indicates the required urgent field size
TCP Window Size	0–65535	(Optional) Indicates the required window size

When specifying atomic TCP signatures, you must specify the TCP Mask and TCP Flags parameters. The TCP Mask parameter essentially identifies the TCP flags that you are interested in, whereas the TCP Flags parameter indicates which of the TCP flags need to be set. Any TCP flags that you fail to include in the mask cannot impact whether the signature triggers. For instance, assume that you set the TCP Mask parameter to include FIN and ACK, and the TCP Flags parameter to include only FIN. The signature will trigger only based on the values of the FIN and ACK flags in the packets (all of the other TCP flags in the packet will be ignored). Packets will trigger the signature as follows:

- If the ACK and FIN flags are set, the signature will not trigger.
- If the FIN flag is set and the ACK flag is not set, the signature will trigger (regardless of the settings for the other TCP flags).
- If the FIN flag is not set, the signature will not trigger.

Atomic IP UDP Parameters

Creating UDP atomic signatures involves configuring the parameters identified in Table 6-15. These parameters enable you to define UDP signatures. These are Layer 4, or transport layer, signatures.

Table 6-15 *UDP Fields for Atomic IP Signature Engine*

Parameter Name	Values	Description
Destination Port Range	*port-list*	The destination port range to match (each port can be 0–65535, and the two ports of the range are separated by a dash)
UDP Valid Length	0–65535	(Optional) Specifies the required UDP packet length
UDP Length Mismatch	Yes No	(Optional) Causes a match if IP data length is less than the UDP header length
Source Port Range	*port-list*	The source port range to match (each port can be 0–65535, and the two ports of the range are separated by a dash)

This basic engine provides the capability to examine ports and packet lengths. You can search for specific ports by using the Destination Port Range and Source Port Range parameters.

A UDP packet contains two length fields: a length in the IP header that indicates the entire length of the IP packet, and a length in the UDP header that indicates the size of the UDP payload. Using the UDP Length Mismatch parameter, you can create signatures that trigger on packets in which the length in the IP header indicates that the length in the UDP header should be greater than it is.

Atomic IP Payload Parameters

When creating atomic signatures, you can also cause the signature to examine the payload of the packet. The Atomic IP payload parameters are shared by the various types of atomic signatures (including ICMP, TCP, and UDP). Configuring payload inspection involves using the parameters identified in Table 6-16.

Table 6-16 *Payload Inspection Fields for Atomic Signatures*

Parameter Name	Values	Description
Exact Match Offset	0–65535	(Optional) The exact offset at which the string must occur for a match to be valid
Min Match Length	0–65535	(Optional) Requires the string matched to be at least the specified minimum number of bytes
Min Match Offset	1–65535	(Optional) Requires the matched string to occur within the specified number of bytes from the beginning of the packet
Max Match Offset	1–65535	(Optional) Indicates the maximum number of bytes to be inspected during the search for the string match
Regex String	*string*	(Optional) A regular expression to search for in a TCP packet

When inspecting the payload for an atomic signature, you specify a regex string and then refine valid matches by specifying offset and length restrictions. The Min Match Length parameter causes the signature to match only strings that are at least the size specified.

Using the Min Match Offset parameter enables you to force the string to occur within a specified number of bytes from the beginning of the packet. Conversely, Max Match Offset specifies the maximum number of bytes that will be inspected during the search for the string. Finally, you can use the Exact Match Offset parameter to specify the exact location at which the string must occur to be considered a valid match.

Flood Signature Engines

The flood signature engines are shown in Table 6-17.

Table 6-17 *Flood Signature Engines*

Engine	Description
Flood Host	Flood signatures based on ICMP or UDP packets
Flood Net	Flood signatures that use Gap, Peaks, and Rate to trigger a flood of TCP, UDP, and ICMP traffic

The Flood Host signature engine analyzes traffic directed at one specific destination host from many source hosts. It attaches a packets per second (PPS) rate counter to a specific destination address, with the sampling being done on a per-second basis.

The Flood Net signature engine analyzes the aggregate traffic on the entire network segment. The signatures using this engine examine traffic for a specific protocol and generate a PPS counter for a virtual sensor instead of a specific address. Sampling is also done on a per-second basis.

Flood Host Engine Parameters

The Flood Host signature engine analyzes traffic directed at one specific destination host from many source hosts. The signatures using this engine can check for both UDP and ICMP traffic floods. The parameters common to all Flood Host signatures are shown in Table 6-18. For all of the Flood Host signatures, you need to specify the PPS of traffic that should trigger an alert. This maximum rate is specified using the Rate field.

Table 6-18 *Common Fields for Flood Host Signatures*

Parameter Name	Values	Description
Rate	0–65535	Indicates the PPS for the desired traffic that should generate an alert
Protocol	UDP ICMP	The protocol of the traffic the signature will use

Flood Host ICMP Parameters

Using the Flood Host signature engine, you can create signatures that detect ICMP traffic coming from many source hosts to a single destination host. The ICMP-specific parameter is shown in Table 6-19.

Table 6-19 *Flood Host ICMP Engine Parameter*

Parameter Name	Values	Description
ICMP Type	0–255	(Optional) The value to match for the ICMP header TYPE

These signatures identify traffic floods based on either all ICMP traffic (if you do not specify the ICMP Type parameter) or specific ICMP traffic floods based on a specific ICMP type, such as the following common ICMP type codes:

- Echo reply (0)
- Destination unreachable (3)
- Source quench (4)

- Redirect (5)
- Echo request (8)
- Router advertisement (9)
- Router solicitation (10)
- Time exceeded (11)
- Parameter problem (12)
- Timestamp request (13)
- Timestamp reply (14)
- Information request (15)
- Information reply (16)
- Address mask request (17)
- Address mask reply (18)

Flood Host UDP Parameters

The Flood Host signature engine supports signatures that detect floods of UDP traffic to a specific host on your network. The UDP-specific parameters are shown in Table 6-20.

Table 6-20 *Flood Host UDP Engine Parameters*

Parameter Name	Values	Description
Destination Ports	*port-list*	Indicates the destination ports to be included in the flood calculation (separate individual ports with a comma and ranges with a dash)
Source Ports	*port-list*	Indicates the source ports to be included in the flood calculation (separate individual ports with a comma and ranges with a dash)

Flood Net Engine Parameters

The Flood Net signature engine is designed to support flood signatures that are triggered by a flood of traffic against your entire network (as opposed to a single host). The engine-specific parameters are shown in Table 6-21.

Table 6-21 *Flood Net Engine Parameters*

Parameter Name	Values	Description
Gap	0–65535	Defines an interval (in seconds) at which the peak count is reset to 0 if the matched traffic remains below the defined rate
ICMP Type	0–255	(Optional) The value to match for the ICMP header TYPE; this parameter is valid only if the Protocol parameter is set to ICMP
Peaks	0–65535	Defines the maximum period of time (above the specified rate) necessary to trigger the signature
Protocol	ICMP TCP UDP	Protocol for the traffic that the flood signature is looking for
Rate	0–65535	The maximum PPS required to trigger a flood

When defining signatures for this engine, you need to first determine which type of traffic you are going to monitor. You specify the traffic type by using the Protocol parameter. If you set this value to ICMP, you can also specify a type of ICMP traffic by using the ICMP Type parameter.

Next you need to define the following three parameters that specify the amount of traffic that constitutes a flood:

- Gap
- Peaks
- Rate

With the Rate parameter, you specify the maximum time interval during which the monitored traffic is allowed to exceed the specified rate. The Rate parameter works in conjunction with the Peaks parameter. The Peaks parameter defines the maximum period of time in seconds (during a given summary interval) that the monitored traffic must remain above the specified rate to trigger the signature. The final parameter, Gap, indicates how long the monitored traffic must remain below the specified rate before the peak count is reset to 0 (during a summary interval).

When you are setting the parameters for a Flood Net signature, the hardest task is determining the appropriate values for the Rate parameter since it varies from one network to the next. To more accurately calculate the rate, you can run the signature in diagnostic mode or feedback mode.

NOTE Determining the rate at which certain traffic normally occurs on the network can be a challenging task since the rate varies from network to network. By specifying a rate of 0, you can place a Flood Net signature in *diagnostic mode*. In this mode, the signature will trigger informational alarms that indicate the rate of traffic (that matches the signature) that is observed during each summary interval. This information will be provided in the Alarm Details field (as a textual string such as MaxPPS=xyz). By running the signature in diagnostic mode over a period of time, you can determine the normal rate of the traffic for each Flood Net signature. Then you can define a rate that is above the measured normal rate so that the flood signatures will indicate abnormal network activity that needs to be investigated.

Meta Signature Engine

The Meta Signature engine enables you to create signatures that represent a combination of individual signatures. The parameters you use when configuring meta signatures are shown in Table 6-22.

Table 6-22 *Meta Signature Engine Parameters*

Parameter Name	Values	Description
Component Count	1–256	Number of times a specific component signature must trigger for the component entry to generate a match
Component List	*Component_Signatures*	A list of component signatures that comprise the meta signatures
Component List Order	Yes No	Determines whether the individual component signatures must be seen in a specific order
Component Sig ID	1000–50000	ID for a specific component signature
Component SubSig ID	0–128	Subsignature ID of the component signature (default is 0)
Entry Key	*string*	Name of a specific component signature entry
Meta Key	Attacker address Attacker and victim addresses Attacker and victim addresses and ports Victim address	Identifies which addresses are used by the meta signatures when determining matching traffic

continues

Table 6-22 *Meta Signature Engine Parameters (Continued)*

Parameter Name	Values	Description
Meta Reset Interval	0–3600	Defines an interval (in seconds) at which the signature resets the signatures already seen (default is 60 seconds)
Unique Victims	1–256	The number of unique victims needed for the meta signatures to fire (default is 1)

Normalizer Signature Engine

The Normalizer signature engine supports signatures that analyze TCP connection states. Maintaining state on a TCP connection is important to identifying various attacks, such as the following:

- TTL manipulation
- URG pointer manipulation
- Out of order RST or FIN
- Out of order packets
- TCP window size manipulation

The Normalizer engine performs TCP stream reassembly for sensors running in promiscuous mode as well as sensors running in inline mode. With inline mode, however, the Normalizer signatures can actually prevent the various TCP state-based attacks. For instance, to nullify the TTL manipulation attack, the Normalizer engine can force all of the outgoing TCP packets to use the smallest TTL observed during the TCP connection.

Unlike other engines, the Normalizer signature engine does not provide functionality to allow you to create custom signatures. You can, however, configure the existing signatures to fit your network requirements. Most of the signatures enable you to configure only a specific TCP parameter. For instance, signature 1202, "Datagram too long," allows you to configure only the Max Datagram Size parameter.

When your sensor is in inline mode, the Normalizer signatures manipulate TCP sessions in various ways (such as dropping or modifying packets). Many of these signatures, however, do not have the "Produce Alert" signature action. Therefore, when they trigger, they perform their configured actions but provide no indication on your monitoring application. For instance, by default, signature 1330 (subsig 18), "TCP Drop – Segment out of window," only drops the packet (without generating an alert). Another example is signature 1305, "TCP URG flag set." By default, signature 1305 modifies the packet (removing the URG bit) before forwarding the packet (without generating an alert). Usually these default settings are adequate and minimize alert traffic to your monitoring console. However, when debugging network operational problems, you need to understand that your sensor may be modifying or dropping TCP traffic without generating alerts.

Service Signature Engines

The service signature engines analyze traffic above the basic UDP and TCP transport layers. Each of these signature engines has detailed knowledge of the service it examines. This includes decoding application-layer protocols such as remote-procedure call (RPC), Simple Network Management Protocol (SNMP), and Network Time Protocol (NTP). By decoding the traffic payloads similar to the actual applications, the service signatures engines can accurately detect attack traffic while minimizing false positives. The various service signature engines are shown in Table 6-23.

Table 6-23 *Service Signature Engines*

Engine	Description
Service DNS	Examines TCP and UDP DNS packets
Service FTP	Examines FTP port command traffic
Service Generic	Emergency response engine to support rapid signature response
Service H225	Examines voice-over-IP (VoIP) traffic based on the H.225 protocol
Service HTTP	Examines HTTP traffic by using string-based pattern matching
Service Ident	Examines Identification (IDENT) protocol (see RFC 1413) traffic
Service MSRPC	Examines signatures based on the Microsoft RPC service
Service MSSQL	Examines traffic used by the Microsoft SQL server
Service NTP	Examines NTP traffic
Service RPC	Examines RPC traffic
Service SMB	Examines Server Message Block (SMB) traffic
Service SNMP	Examines SNMP traffic
Service SSH	Examines Secure Shell Host (SSH) traffic

Service DNS Engine Parameters

The Service DNS signature engine performs advanced decoding of DNS traffic. This decoding enables detecting various anti-evasion techniques such as following multiple jumps in the DNS payload. The major engine-specific signature parameters for the Service DNS signature engine are shown in Table 6-24.

Table 6-24 *Service DNS Engine Parameters*

Parameter Name	Values	Description
Protocol	TCP UDP	Specifies the protocol to use for the signature
Query Chaos String	*string*	Defines the DNS query class chaos string to match
Query Class	0–65535	Defines the DNS query class 2-byte value to match
Query Invalid Domain Name	Yes No	If Yes, matches when the DNS query length is greater than 255
Query Jump Count Exceeded	Yes No	DNS compression counter
Query Opcode	0–255	Defines the DNS query opcode value
Query Record Data Invalid	Yes No	If Yes, matches when DNS record data is incomplete
Query Record Data Length	0–65535	Determines the DNS-response data length
Query Src Port 53	Yes No	If Yes, matches if the DNS query comes from port 53; if No, matches if the DNS query does not come from port 53
Query Stream Len	0–65535	Matches when the DNS packet length is greater than this value
Query Type	0–65535	Defines the DNS query type to match
Query Value	Yes No	If Yes, matches when the DNS request is a query; if No, matches when the DNS request is a response

The engine-specific parameters for the Service DNS engine enable you to specify values for the following DNS fields:

- Chaos String
- Class
- Opcode
- Type

You can apply your signatures to either DNS response packets or DNS request packets by using the Query Value parameter. If this parameter is set to Yes, the signature will trigger when the traffic is a DNS request. Similarly, you can determine whether a DNS query originates from port 53 by using the Query Src Port 53 parameter.

You can check the size of the domain name by using the Query Invalid Domain Name parameter. If this parameter is set to Yes, the signature will trigger if the domain name is longer than 255 characters. Finally, you can also create DNS signatures that trigger if the DNS packet length is greater than a certain value. You define this value by using the Query Stream Len parameter.

Service FTP Engine Parameters

The String TCP engine is useful for creating many FTP string-based FTP signatures. Certain signatures, however, are not appropriate for the string signature engines. The Service FTP signature fills this gap by providing an engine that supports signatures specifically centered on the FTP port command. This engine decodes FTP port commands and traps invalid port commands or attacks based on the port command. The control traffic is examined only on port 21 traffic since port 20 is used by FTP to transport only data traffic. The major parameters for the Service FTP signature engine are shown in Table 6-25.

Table 6-25 *Service FTP Engine Parameters*

Parameter Name	Values	Description
FTP Inspection Type	Invalid Address in PORT Command Invalid Port in PORT Command PASV Port Spoof	Indicates the type of invalid FTP traffic to search for
Direction	From Service To Service	Determines whether the signature matches on traffic to or from the FTP service port
Service Ports	*port-list*	A comma-separated list of ports or port ranges on which to look for the FTP traffic
Swap Attacker Victim	Yes No	If Yes, the signature switches source and destination Ip addresses in the alarm information

The Service Ports parameter enables you to define which ports the signature engine will analyze. By default this parameter is set to port 21, but you can alter this value if you happen to use other ports for the FTP protocol. In conjunction with this parameter, you can use the Direction parameter to indicate whether the signature will trigger on traffic to the service port or from the service port.

You can specify the following three FTP inspection types that relate to the validity of the actual FTP port commands analyzed by the engine:

- Invalid Address in PORT Command
- Invalid Port in PORT Command
- PASV Port Spoof

Service Generic Engine Parameters

The Service Generic engine is an unusual signature engine. You will not use this engine to create regular custom signatures. Instead, this signature engine is designed as an emergency response engine that supports rapid signature response. The major parameters are shown in Table 6-26.

Table 6-26 *Service Generic Engine Parameters*

Parameter Name	Values	Description
Dst Port	0–65535	Destination port of interest for this signature
Intermediate Instructions	*string*	Assembly or machine code in string form (this field is for expert use only)
IP Protocol	0–255	The IP protocol that applies to this signature
Payload Source	ICMPData L2Header L3Header L4Header TCPData UDPData	Identifies where to begin payload search
Src Port	0–65535	Source port of interest for this signature

The signatures supported by this engine use assembly language and machine code to define how the signatures process different parts of the analyzed packets. These signatures can search various payload sources to locate intrusive activity.

> **CAUTION** Creating signatures by using the Service Generic signature engine requires an expert level of understanding to create the appropriate assembly language instructions and is not intended for use by normal users.

Service H225 Engine Parameters

To improve signature support for VoIP, Cisco IPS version 5.0 includes an H225 signature engine. Table 6-27 shows the parameters for the H225 signature engine.

Table 6-27 *Service H225 Engine Parameters*

Parameter Name	Values	Description
Field Name	*string*	(Optional) Field name to inspect
Invalid Packet Index	0–255	(Optional) Specifies the index of a specific check in a list of built-in checks that validate H225 messages
Message Type	ASN.1-PERS Q.931 SETUP TPKT	H225 message type
Min Match Length	0–2147483647	(Optional) Minimum number of bytes the regex string must match
Policy Type	Field Validation Length Check Presence Regex Value	The policy that the signature will apply to the specified message types
Regex String	*string*	(Optional) The regular expression that the signature searches for in a single packet
Value Range	0–65535	(Optional) Range of values

Using the H225 signature engine, you can easily create signatures that inspect H225 traffic by matching on one or more of the following message types:

- ASN.1-PERS
- Q.931

- SETUP
- TPKT

When processing these message types, you can configure the policy applied to these messages by using one of the following policy types:

- Field Validation
- Length Check
- Presence
- Regex
- Value

For instance, if you have a message type of Q.931, a policy type of Length Check, a Field Name of UserUser, and a Value Range of 10–20, then Q.931 packets where the specified field has a size outside this range will trigger the signature.

Service HTTP Engine Parameters

The Service HTTP signature engine provides regular expression-based pattern inspection specifically designed to analyze HTTP. The major parameters are shown in Table 6-28.

Table 6-28 *Service HTTP Engine Parameters*

Parameter Name	Values	Description
Uri Regex	*string*	(Optional) The regular expression used to search for a pattern in the uniform resource identifier (URI) section of the HTTP request; the URI is after the valid HTTP method and before the first <CR><LF> or argument delimiter (? or &)
Arg Name Regex	*string*	(Optional) The regular expression used to search for a pattern in the Arguments section
Arg Value Regex	*string*	(Optional) The regular expression used to search for a pattern in the Arguments section after the Arg Name regex is matched
Header Regex	*string*	(Optional) The regular expression used to search for a pattern in the Header section
Request Regex	*string*	(Optional) The regular expression used to search for a pattern anywhere in the HTTP request
Max Uri Field Length	0–65535	(Optional) Specifies the maximum URI length considered normal
Max Arg Field Length	0–65535	(Optional) Specifies the maximum Argument field length considered normal

Table 6-28 *Service HTTP Engine Parameters (Continued)*

Parameter Name	Values	Description
Max Header Field Length	0–65535	(Optional) Specifies the maximum Header field length considered normal
Max Request Field Length	0–65535	(Optional) Specifies the maximum HTTP request length considered normal
Deobfuscate	Yes No	Determines whether to perform anti-evasion HTTP deobfuscation before examining the HTTP request (default is Yes)
Service Ports	*port-list*	A comma-separated list of ports or port ranges to search for the HTTP traffic
Min Request Match Length	0–65535	(Optional) The minimum number of bytes that the Uri regex must match

NOTE The <CR><LF> refers to the nonprintable carriage return and line feed characters that are used to delimit command input. Whenever you press **Enter** on your keyboard (while editing a document, for instance) the system inserts a carriage return <CR> character and a line feed <LF> character into the document (even though they are not directly printable). The carriage return character is 13, and the line feed character is 10.

The pattern-matching functionality provided by the Service HTTP signature engine is enabled through the implementation of various regular expression (regex) strings. These regex strings search the following portions of a regular HTTP message:

- Entire HTTP request
- HTTP header
- URI
- Arguments and entity body

Figure 6-1 shows a sample HTTP request that highlights the various HTTP message components.

The URI identifies the file or resource that the HTTP request is attempting to access. The Uri Regex parameter specifies a regular expression that searches this field. The URI begins after the HTTP method (such as GET or POST) and goes up to the first <CR><LF> or argument delimiter (? or &) that is detected.

When you set the Header regex, the HTTP header is searched for the specified pattern. The header section begins after the first <CR><LF> and ends when a double <CR><LF> combination is detected.

Figure 6-1 *Sample HTTP Request*

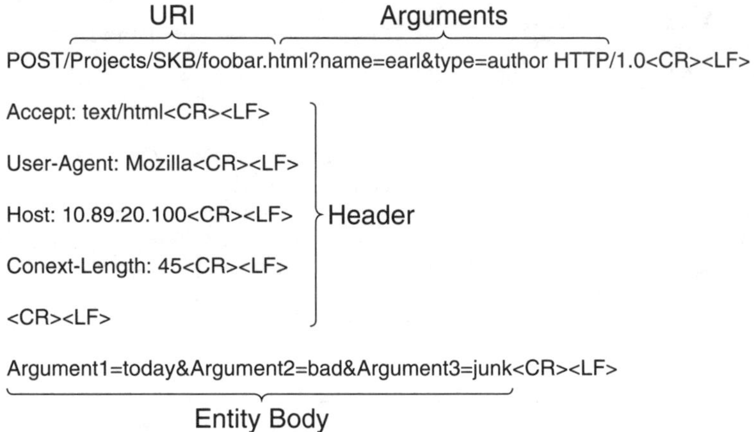

Searching the arguments section involves the following two parameters:

- Arg Name regex
- Arg Value regex

The Arg Name regex is a regular expression that identifies the name of the argument that you are looking for in the HTTP request. If the Arg Name regex is found, the signature uses the Arg Value regex to search for a specific value after the argument that was located. These two regular expressions search for arguments in the following two places (see Figure 6-1):

- After the URI, beginning with the argument delimiter (? or &) and ending at the first <CR><LF>
- The entity body section of the HTTP request

You can also specify the Request Regex parameter. This regular expression identifies a pattern that the signature will search for anywhere in the HTTP request. Sometimes, you may want the signature to trigger if the pattern matched by the Request Regex is larger than a specified size. A large HTTP request can indicate potential buffer overflow attempts. Using the Min Request Match Length parameter, you cause the signature to trigger only if the Request Regex is found and the size of the pattern matched is larger than the value specified by the Min Request Match Length parameter.

> **NOTE** The Min Request Match Length parameter is applicable only when the Request Regex contains an iterator (* or +) that enables the pattern to match on variable length patterns.

Besides pattern matching, you can also specify the following parameters that indicate maximum field values:

- Max Uri Field Length
- Max Arg Field Length
- Max Header Field Length
- Max Request Field Length

If the length of any of these fields exceeds the specified value, the signature will trigger. These parameters enable you to generate alarms if any of these fields are abnormally large in an HTTP request.

The Service Ports parameter enables you to indicate on which ports the signature should look for HTTP traffic. By default, web-servers run on port 80, but many people use various other ports such as 8080. You need to configure this parameter based on your network configuration, indicating all ports that may be used for HTTP traffic.

> **NOTE** Because HTTP pattern matching requires a lot of sensor resources (memory and CPU), if a valid HTTP method (GET, HEAD, or POST) is not detected in the first 20 bytes of the HTTP request, HTTP inspection processing is stopped for the entire data stream.

Service Ident Engine Parameters

The Identification (IDENT) protocol is defined by RFC 1413. Basically, it is a service that enables a remote system to gain information about the user who is attempting to make a TCP connection with it. Numerous security problems have been associated with this protocol, which normally runs on TCP port 113. The parameters for the Service Ident signature engine are shown in Table 6-29.

Table 6-29 *Service Ident Engine Parameters*

Parameter Name	Values	Description
Direction	From Service To Service	Determines whether the signature matches on traffic to the service port or from the service port
Inspection Type	Has Bad Port Has Newline Payload Size	Indicates the type of inspection to be performed

continues

Table 6-29 *Service Ident Engine Parameters (Continued)*

Parameter Name	Values	Description
Max Bytes	0–65535	Defines the maximum number of bytes in the payload that is considered normal (valid only in conjunction with Payload Size inspection type)
Service Ports	*port-list*	A comma-separated list of ports or port ranges on which the service may reside

The Service Ident signature engine performs a basic decode of the IDENT protocol and enables you to look for abnormal IDENT packets. Setting the Inspection Type parameter to Has Bad Port will cause the signature to trigger if the packet contains a bad port number. Similarly, setting the Inspection Type to Has Newline causes the signature to trigger if the packet contains any newline characters besides the one signaling the end of the IDENT request.

As in the Service HTTP engine, you can specify the ports on which the IDENT traffic may be found. The Service Ident signatures will examine all traffic for the ports specified by the Service Ports parameter. Using the Direction parameter, you control whether the signature checks for traffic to the service port or from the service port.

Finally, you can check for buffer overflow attacks by using the Max Bytes parameter (in conjunction with the inspection type of Payload Size). Any IDENT request that is larger than this value will cause your signature to trigger.

Service MSSQL Engine Parameters

The Service MSSQL signature engine inspects the protocol used by the Microsoft SQL (MSSQL) server. The engine-specific parameters are listed in Table 6-30.

Table 6-30 *Service MSSQL Engine Parameters*

Parameter Name	Values	Description
Sql Username	*string*	Determines the username (exact match) to match for a user logging in to the MSSQL service
Password Present	Yes No	If Yes, the signature matches if a password is not provided in the MSSQL login request

Using the Sql Username parameter, you can specify a username that will cause the signature to trigger if the engine detects this username in a login request sent to the SQL server. This parameter is the exact username that will cause the signature to trigger.

You can also use the Password Present parameter to search for login attempts that do not specify a password. If this parameter is set to Yes, the signature will trigger on any login attempts to the SQL server that do not specify a password.

Service NTP Engine Parameters

The Service NTP signature engine inspects NTP traffic. NTP enables systems on your network to synchronize their system clocks. It is defined by RFC 1305. The parameter for this engine is shown in Table 6-31.

Table 6-31 *Service NTP Engine Parameter*

Parameter Name	Values	Description
Inspection Type	Inspect NTP Packets Is Invalid Data Packet Is Non NTP Traffic	Determines the type of NTP traffic inspected

When defining a signature by using the Service NTP engine, you specify only the type of NTP traffic being inspected. You can choose from the following three options:

- Inspect NTP Packets
- Is Invalid Data Packet
- Is Non NTP Traffic

Service RPC Engine Parameters

RPC is a protocol that one program can use to request a specific service from a program located on another computer across the network (see RFC 1057). The major parameters for the Service RPC engine are shown in Table 6-32.

Table 6-32 *Service RPC Engine Parameters*

Parameter Name	Values	Description
Direction	To Service From Service	Specifies whether traffic is matched going to or from the service port (default is To Service)
Port Map Program	0–99999	The program number sent to the portmapper that this signature is interested in

continues

Table 6-32 *Service RPC Engine Parameters (Continued)*

Parameter Name	Values	Description
Protocol	TCP UDP	Specifies the traffic to be examined by the signature
Rpc Max Length	0–99999	Defines the maximum RPC message length that is considered normal
Rpc Procedure	0–65535	The RPC procedure number that this signature will match on
Rpc Program	0–99999	The RPC program number that this signature will match on
Service Ports	*port-list*	A comma-separated list of ports or port ranges on which the service may reside
Is Spool Src	Yes No	If Yes, matches when the source address is 127.0.0.1

RPC has a utility that provides the port numbers for various services that are running on a system. RPC-based signatures typically identify an attacker attempting to bypass the portmapper program and access RPC services directly.

The Port Map Program parameter enables you to create signatures that look for client requests to the portmapper program that are requesting the port for a specific RPC service (identified by a single RPC program number). For instance, if you wanted to create a signature that watches for requests to the ypbind service, you would set the Port Map Program parameter to 100007. Then, any time the sensor detects a client request to the portmapper program with a value of 100007, the signature will trigger an alarm.

You can also create signatures that examine generic RPC traffic. Using the Rpc Program and Rpc Procedure parameters, you can create signatures that decode the RPC header, which enables the signatures to trigger on a specified RPC program number and RPC procedure. For instance, you can create a signature that looks for RPC traffic to a specific procedure within ypbind by creating a custom signature that specifies an Rpc Program value of 100007 (along with defining the value for the RPC procedure that you are interested in).

Service SMB Engine Parameters

The Service SMB signature engine decodes the Server Message Block (SMB) protocol. Using this engine, you can create signatures that detect unwanted SMB traffic. The major parameters for the Service SMB engine are shown in Table 6-33.

Table 6-33 *Service SMB Engine Parameters*

Parameter Name	Values	Description
Allocation Count	0–42949677295	Microsoft RCP (MSRPC) allocation hint
Byte Count	0–65535	(Optional) Specifies a required byte count for the SMB_COM_ TRANSACTION structure
Command	0–255	SMB command
Direction	From Service To Service	Specifies whether the signature looks at traffic to or from the service (default is To Service)
File ID	0–65535	(Optional) Transaction file ID
Function	0–65535	(Optional) Named pipe function
Hit Count	0–65535	(Optional) Threshold number of occurrences in the scan interval to trigger alarms 3302 and 6255
Operation	0–65535	(Optional) MSRPC operation request
Resource	*string*	(Optional) Pipe or SMB filename for signature
Service Ports	*port-list*	A comma-separated list of ports on which to search for traffic (default is 139,445)
Swap Attacker Victim	Yes No	If Yes, the signature will switch source and destination IP addresses in the alarm information (default is Yes)
Scan Interval	1–131071	(Optional) The time interval in seconds that is used to determine alarm rates (for signatures 3302 and 6255 only)
Set Count	0–255	(Optional) Number of setup words
Type	0–255	Type field of MSRPC packet (0, request; 2, response; 11, Bind; 12, Bind Ack)
Word Count	0–255	(Optional) Word count for command parameters

Service SNMP Engine Parameters

The Service SNMP signature engine supports signatures that examine SNMP traffic (see RFC 3412). The major parameters for this engine are shown in Table 6-34.

Table 6-34 *Service SNMP Engine Parameters*

Parameter Name	Values	Description
Community Name	*string*	The SNMP password (community string) that the signature matches on (used with SNMP Inspection inspection type)
Object ID	*string*	The object identifier that the signature will match on (used with SNMP Inspection inspection type)
Brute Force Count	1–65535	Defines the number of unique community names seen between two systems to constitute a brute-force attempt (specified for the Brute Force Inspection inspection type)
Inspection Type	Brute Force Inspection Invalid Packet Inspection Non-SNMP Traffic Inspection SNMP Inspection	Identifies the type of traffic to be inspected

The Service SNMP signature engine has the following inspection types:

- Brute Force Inspection
- Invalid Packet Inspection
- Non-SNMP Traffic Inspection
- SNMP Traffic Inspection

When you set the inspection type to Non-SNMP Traffic Inspection, the signature will trigger when the traffic examined does not represent a valid SNMP packet. Similarly, setting the inspection type to Invalid Packet Inspection causes the signature to trigger when the traffic appears to be an SNMP packet but the data is malformed in some fashion.

You can use the following parameters to check for brute-force attempts to guess a valid community name:

- Brute Force Inspection
- Bruce Force Count

Setting the inspection type to Brute Force Inspection causes the signature to trigger if it detects a single system using more unique community names against a single target system than the value specified by the Brute Force Count parameter. For instance, if the Brute Force Count is set to 4 and the inspection type is Brute Force Inspection, the signature will trigger if host A sends 4 or more SNMP requests (with different community name strings) to host B.

You can also create signatures that search for specific community names or object IDs by setting the Community Name and Object ID parameters and by setting the inspection type to SNMP Inspection.

NOTE The Service SNMP signature engine inspects traffic only for SNMP version 1.

Service SSH Engine Parameters

The Service SSH signature engine supports signatures that examine SSH traffic. Since everything except the initial setup fields are encrypted in an SSH session, these signatures examine only the setup fields. The major parameters for this engine are listed in Table 6-35.

Table 6-35 *Service SSH Engine Parameters*

Parameter Name	Values	Description
Length	0–65535	Defines the RSA key length or user length; the signature triggers when this length is exceeded
Length Type	Key Length User Length	Identifies whether the length being used is the key length or the user length
Packet Depth	0–65535	Defines the number of packets to watch before determining that a session key was missed
Service Ports	*port-list*	A comma-separated list of ports or port ranges at which the SSH service may reside

Using the Service SSH signature engine, you can examine the following setup fields:

- RSA Key Length
- Username Length

State Signature Engine

A state machine consists of a starting state and a list of valid state transitions. Cisco IDS supports the following three state machines:

- Cisco Login
- Line Printer Remote (LPR) Format String
- SMTP

Each of these machines has a set of valid states and configuration parameters. The parameters that are common to all of these state machines are shown in Table 6-36.

Table 6-36 *Common State Signature Engine Parameters*

Parameter Name	Values	Description
Direction	To Service From Service	Indicates whether to inspect traffic to the service (default) or from the service
Exact Match Offset	0–65535	(Optional) The exact offset at which the string must occur for a match to be valid
Min Match Length	0–65535	(Optional) The minimum number of bytes the regex string must match from the beginning to the end of the match
Min Match Offset	0–65535	(Optional) Requires the matched string to occur a minimum number of bytes from the beginning of the packet
Max Match Offset	0–65535	(Optional) Indicates the maximum number of bytes to be inspected during the search for the string match
Regex String	*string*	The regular expression that specifies the pattern to search for

Table 6-36 *Common State Signature Engine Parameters (Continued)*

Parameter Name	Values	Description
Service Ports	*port-list*	A comma-separated list of ports or port ranges at which the SSH service may reside
State Machine	Cisco Login LPR Format String SMTP	Defines the state scenario that the signature applies to
Swap Attacker Victim	Yes No	If Yes, the signature switches source and destination IP addresses in the alarm information (default is Yes)

The State Machine parameter indicates the state machine that will be used to begin searching for the pattern specified by the Regex String parameter. If a match is found in the correct state, the signature triggers.

You can restrict pattern matching by using the Exact Match Offset, Min Match Offset, Max Match Offset, and Min Match Length parameters. The Exact Match Offset parameter limits the searching to a specific location in the packet. The Min Match Offset requires the Regex String parameter match to occur a specified number of bytes from the beginning of the packet, and the Max Match Offset limits the maximum number of bytes in the packet that are inspected during the search for the regex string. The Min Match Length specifies a minimum number of bytes that the Regex String parameter must match in order for the signature to trigger.

Each of the state machines also shares a State Name parameter, but the allowed values vary, depending on the machine chosen.

Cisco Login States

When using the Cisco Login state machine, you can configure your signature to look for one of the following states:

- Cisco Device
- Control C
- Pass Prompt
- Start

Table 6-37 shows the transitions defined for the Cisco Login state machine. These states relate to interactive logins to Cisco devices. You can use these defined transitions (in conjunction with the

State Name parameter) to create signatures that check for specific patterns at different states in the Cisco login process.

Table 6-37 *Cisco Login State Machine Transitions*

Regex String	Required State	Next State	Direction
User[ ]Access[ ]Verification	START	CiscoDevice	FromService
Cisco[ ]Systems[ ]Console	START	CiscoDevice	FromService
assword[:]	CiscoDevice	PassPrompt	FromService
\x03	PassPrompt	ControlC	ToService
(enable)	ControlC	EnableBypass	FromService
\x03[\x00-\xFF]	ControlC	PassPrompt	ToService

NOTE For more information on the format and structure of regex strings, refer to Chapter 7, "Advanced Signature Configuration."

LPR Format String States

When using the LPR Format String state machine, you can configure your signature to look for one of the following states:

- Abort
- Format Char
- Start

NOTE The LPR Format String state engine checks requests being sent to the printer process on UNIX systems and printer devices.

Table 6-38 shows the transitions defined for the LPR Format String state machine.

Table 6-38 *LPR Format String State Machine Transitions*

Regex String	End Offset	Required State	Next State	Direction
[1-9]	1	START	ABORT	ToService
%	n/a	START	FormatChar	ToService
[\x0a\x0d]	n/a	FormatChar	ABORT	ToService

SMTP States

When using the SMTP state machine, you can configure your signature to look for one of the following states:

- Abort
- Mail Body
- Mail Header
- SMTP Commands
- START

Table 6-39 shows the transitions defined for the SMTP state machine. These states relate to SMTP. You can use these transitions (in conjunction with the State Name parameter) to create signatures that check for specific patterns at different states in the SMTP protocol.

Table 6-39 *SMTP State Machine Transitions*

<table>
<tr><th>Regex String</th><th>Required State</th><th>Next State</th><th>Direction</th></tr>
<tr><td>[\r\n]250[ ]</td><td>START</td><td>SmtpCommands</td><td>FromService</td></tr>
<tr><td>250[ ][^\r\n]
[\x7f-\xff]*SNMP</td><td>START</td><td>SmtpCommands</td><td>FromService</td></tr>
<tr><td>(HE|EH)LO</td><td>START</td><td>SmtpCommands</td><td>ToService</td></tr>
<tr><td>[\r\n](235|220.*TLS)</td><td>START</td><td>ABORT</td><td>FromService</td></tr>
<tr><td>[\r\n](235|220.*TLS)</td><td>SmtpCommands</td><td>ABORT</td><td>FromService</td></tr>
<tr><td>[Dd][Aa][Tt][Aa][Bb]
[Dd][Aa][Tt]</td><td>SmtpCommands</td><td>MailHeader</td><td>ToService</td></tr>
<tr><td>[\r\n]354</td><td>SmtpCommands</td><td>MailHeader</td><td>FromService</td></tr>
<tr><td>[\r\n][.][\r\n]</td><td>MailHeader</td><td>SmtpCommands</td><td>ToService</td></tr>
<tr><td>[\r\n][2][0-9][0-9][ ]</td><td>MailHeader</td><td>SmtpCommands</td><td>FromService</td></tr>
<tr><td>([\r\n]|[\n][\r]){2}</td><td>MailHeader</td><td>MailBody</td><td>ToService</td></tr>
<tr><td>[\r\n][.][\r\n]</td><td>MailBody</td><td>SmtpCommands</td><td>ToService</td></tr>
<tr><td>[\r\n][2][0-9][0-9][ ]</td><td>MailBody</td><td>SmtpCommands</td><td>FromService</td></tr>
</table>

String Signature Engines

The String signature engines support regex pattern matching and alarm functionality for the following three protocols: ICMP, UDP, and TCP. Each of these engines shares the common engine-specific parameters shown in Table 6-40.

Table 6-40 *Common String Engine Parameters*

Parameter Name	Values	Description
Direction	To Service From Service	Indicates whether to inspect traffic to the service or from the service
Exact Match Offset	0–65535	The exact stream offset (in bytes) in which the regex string must report a match
Min Match Length	0–65535	The minimum number of bytes the regex string must match from the beginning to the end of the match
Min Match Offset	0–65535	(Optional) Requires the matched string to occur a minimum number of bytes from the beginning of the packet
Max Match Offset	1–65535	(Optional) Indicates the maximum number of bytes to be inspected during the search for the string match
Regex String	*string*	The regular expression that specifies the pattern to search for
Service Ports	*port-list*	A comma-separated list of ports or port ranges at which the service may reside (applies only to TCP and UDP)
Swap Attacker Victim	Yes No	If Yes, the signature switches source and destination IP addresses in the alarm information (default is Yes)

The String signature engines are divided into the following three signature engines:

- String ICMP
- String TCP
- String UDP

Each of the engines supports signatures that search their specific protocol for configured patterns through these common parameters. String ICMP and String TCP also each have a unique engine-specific parameter.

String ICMP Engine Specific Parameters

The unique String ICMP parameter is shown in Table 6-41.

Table 6-41 *String ICMP Unique Engine Parameter*

Parameter Name	Values	Description
ICMP Type	0–18	Indicates the ICMP types in which to search for the string (default is 0–18)

The ICMP Type parameter specifies which ICMP types that the signature will check for the specified string. The following shows some common ICMP type values:

- Echo Reply (0)
- Destination Unreachable (3)
- Source Quench (4)
- Redirect (5)
- Echo Request (8)
- Timestamp (13)
- Timestamp Reply (14)
- Information Request (15)
- Information Reply (16)

String TCP Engine-Specific Parameters

The unique String TCP parameter is shown in Table 6-42.

Table 6-42 *String TCP Unique Engine Parameter*

Parameter Name	Values	Description
StripTelnetOptions	Yes No	If Yes, any Telnet options are stripped off before a regex pattern match is performed on the data (default is No)

Sweep Signature Engines

The Sweep Signature engines identify situations in which one system is making connections to either multiple hosts or multiple ports. The Sweep Signature engines are shown in Table 6-43.

Table 6-43 *Sweep Signature Engines*

Engine	Description
Sweep	Sweeps signatures for ICMP, TCP, and UDP traffic
Sweep Other TCP	Identifies odd sweeps and scans such as nmap

Sweep Signature Engine Parameters

The Sweep Signature engine supports signatures for ICMP, TCP, and UDP sweeps. The parameters that are common to all of these protocols are shown in Table 6-44.

Table 6-44 *Sweep Signature Engine Parameters*

Parameter Name	Values	Description
Port Range	*port-list*	The range of ports that the signature will use when checking for sweep traffic (applicable only to TCP and UDP Sweeps)
Protocol	ICMP TCP UDP	Protocol of the traffic that the sweep signature will detect
Storage Key	Attacker Address Attacker Address and Victim Port Attacker and Victim Addresses	Identifies which addresses determine unique instances of the signature
Swap Attacker Victim	Yes No	If Yes, the signature switches source and destination IP addresses in the alarm information (default is Yes)
Unique	0–65535	Identifies the number of unique connections allowed until the signature fires

Each protocol also has unique parameters that you can configure only for that type of sweep.

Unique ICMP Sweep Parameters

When the protocol selected for the sweep is ICMP, the signature triggers when one host sends ICMP traffic to multiple destination systems. The ICMP-specific parameter is shown in Table 6-45.

Table 6-45 *Unique ICMP Sweep Parameter*

Parameter Name	Values	Description
Icmp Type	0–255	The ICMP type that this signature matches on (default is 0)

You use the Icmp Type parameter to define which type of ICMP traffic you want the signature to trigger on. Then you use the Unique parameter to indicate how many instances of the ICMP traffic are required to trigger the signature.

NOTE If you do not specify a value by using the Icmp Type parameter, the signature examines all ICMP traffic.

Unique TCP Sweep Parameters

When the protocol selected for the sweep is TCP, the signature triggers when one host sends TCP traffic to multiple destination systems (host sweep) or multiple ports on the same systems (port sweep). The TCP-specific parameters are shown in Table 6-46.

Table 6-46 *Unique TCP Sweep Parameters*

Parameter Name	Values	Description
Fragment Status	Any Fragmented Not Fragmented	Identifies whether the fragment status of the packet impacts processing by the signature (default is Any)
Inverted Sweep	Yes No	If Yes, signature uses source port instead of the destination port to count unique connections (default is No)

continues

Table 6-46 *Unique TCP Sweep Parameters (Continued)*

Parameter Name	Values	Description
Mask	FIN SYN RST PSH ACK URG ZERO	The mask used when checking the Tcp Flags This field indicates the TCP flags that you want to include in your checking
Suppress Reverse	Yes No	Do not trigger the signature when a sweep is detected in the reverse direction on this address set (default is No)
TCP Flags	FIN SYN RST PSH ACK URG ZERO	Indicates the TCP flags (out of the flags included in the Mask parameter) that need to be set for the signature to match

Use the following parameters to specify what type of TCP traffic you want the signature to match on:

- Mask
- TCP Flags

The Mask parameter essentially identifies the TCP flags that you are interested in, whereas the TCP Flags parameter indicates which of the TCP flags need to be set. TCP flags that you do not include in the Mask parameter have no impact on whether the signature triggers. For instance, assume that you set the Mask parameter to include FIN and RST and the TCP Flags parameter to include only RST. The signature will trigger based on only the values of the FIN and RST flags in the packets (all of the other TCP flags in the packet are ignored). Packets will trigger the signature as follows:

- If the RST and FIN flags are set, the signature will not trigger.
- If the RST flag is set and the FIN flag is not set, the signature will trigger (regardless of the value for the other TCP flags).
- If the RST flag is not set, the signature will not trigger.

The Unique parameter indicates the number of unique connections required to trigger the signature.

The Sweep signature engine supports detecting both host sweeps and port sweeps. A TCP port sweep is a signature that detects when a single host attempts to connect to multiple TCP ports on the same target system.

As with host sweeps, you need to specify the TCP flags that you want to include in your processing by using the Mask and TCP Flags parameters. TCP Port Sweep signatures, however, also use the following parameters:

- Inverted Sweep
- Suppress Reverse
- Port Range

When you set the Inverted Sweep parameter to Yes, the signature will trigger on the source port instead of the destination port when it is counting unique connections. Similarly, the Suppress Reverse parameter controls whether the signature attempts to automatically trigger in the reverse direction. When the parameter is set to Yes, the reverse direction is not checked.

NOTE When configuring UDP port sweep signatures, you also configure a port range. By default a port range is not specified, so the default signature is a UDP host sweep.

Sweep Other TCP Signature Engine Parameters

The Sweep Other TCP Signature engine supports signatures that trigger when a mixture of TCP packets (with different flags set) is detected on the network. The engine parameters for this engine are shown in Table 6-47.

Table 6-47 *Sweep Other TCP Signature Engine Parameters*

Parameter Name	Values	Description
Port Range	*port-range*	The range of ports that the signature will use when checking for sweep traffic
Set TCP Flags	FIN SYN RST PSH ACK URG ZERO	Identifies a list of TCP flag combinations that cause the signature to fire when packets matching all of the flag combinations (and the other engine parameters) have been detected

The Port Range parameter identifies the ports that are valid for the signature to process. You specify a range of ports by entering the beginning port and the ending port (separated by a dash). For instance, to use ports 1000 through 2000 in your signature, you will use the following port range:

```
1000-2000
```

You can specify a list of TCP flag combinations. Each of the TCP flag combinations that you specify must be detected before the signature triggers. Unlike other TCP-based engines, this engine does not have a Mask parameter. In this situation, the signature looks for only the flags specified in the Set TCP Flags list and ignores any other TCP flags. For instance, suppose you add the following TCP flags combinations to the Set TCP Flags list:

- SYN, FIN
- FIN, RST
- RST, PSH

The signature will not trigger until it sees at least one packet matching each of the following criteria:

- Packet with at least the SYN and FIN flags set
- Packet with at least the FIN and RST flags set
- Packet with at least the RST and PSH flags set

This engine is useful for detecting attacks from various scanning tools (such as Nmap and Queso) that send TCP packets with strange flag combinations in an attempt to identify the target operating system.

Trojan Horse Signature Engines

Attackers can place various backdoor Trojan horse programs on systems in a network to enable them to operate from systems within your network. Cisco IDS has three signature engines specifically designed to detect the presence of Trojan horse programs on your network (see Table 6-48).

Table 6-48 *Trojan Horse Signature Engines*

Engine	Description
Trojan Bo2K	Detects the presence of BO2K by using the TCP protocol
Trojan Tfn2K	Detects the presence of the TFN2K Trojan horse by examining UDP, TCP, and ICMP traffic
Trojan UDP	Detects the presence of BO and BO2K by using the UDP protocol

The only one of these engines that has any user-configurable parameters is the Trojan Horse UDP Signature Engine. With the Trojan horse UDP signature, you can configure the Swap Attacker Victim parameter. Since Trojan horse signature engines are highly specialized, you usually do not create custom signatures for them.

Foundation Summary

Cisco IPS monitors network traffic by using a suite of signature engines. The signature engines fall into the categories shown in Table 6-49.

Table 6-49 *Signature Engine Categories*

Engine Category	Usage
AIC	Used to provide deep-packet inspection from Layer 4 through Layer 7
Atomic	Used for single-packet conditions
Flood	Used to detect denial-of-service (DoS) attempts
Meta	Used to create meta signatures based on multiple individual signatures
Normalizer	Used to normalize fragmented and TCP streams when in inline mode (cannot create custom signatures); also performs stream reassembly for promiscuous mode
Service	Used when services at OSI Layers 5, 6, and 7 require protocol analysis
State	Used when stateful inspection is required
String	Used for string pattern matching
Sweep	Used to detect network reconnaissance scans
Miscellaneous	Includes various signature engines (such as Traffic ICMP and Trojan horse signature engines)

To identify the traffic that a specific signature searches for, you must define signatures by specifying a set of parameters. Each parameter falls into one of the following groups:

- Basic signature fields
- Signature description fields
- Engine-specific fields
- Event counter fields
- Alert frequency fields
- Status fields

Currently, application policy enforcement is available through the following signature engines:

- AIC FTP
- AIC HTTP

Atomic signatures are handled by the following signature engines:

- Atomic ARP
- Atomic IP

Flood signatures are handled by the following signature engines:

- Flood Net
- Flood Host

The various service signature engines are shown in Table 6-50.

Table 6-50 *Service Signature Engines*

Engine	Description
Service DNS	Examines TCP and UDP DNS packets
Service FTP	Examines FTP port command traffic
Service Generic	Emergency response engine to support rapid signature response
Service H225	Examines VoIP traffic based on the H.225 protocol
Service HTTP	Examines HTTP traffic by using string-based pattern matching
Service Ident	Examines IDENT protocol (RFC 1413) traffic
Service MSRPC	Examines Microsoft remote-procedure call (MSRPC) traffic
Service MSSQL	Examines traffic used by the Microsoft SQL (MSSQL) server
Service NTP	Examines Network Time Protocol (NTP) traffic
Service RPC	Examines remote-procedure call (RPC) traffic
Service SMB	Examines Server Message Block (SMB) traffic
Service SNMP	Examines Simple Network Management Protocol (SNMP) traffic
Service SSH	Examines Secure Shell (SSH) traffic

The State Signature engine supports the following three state machines:

- Cisco Login
- Line Printer Remote (LPR) Format String
- Simple Mail Transport Protocol (SMTP)

String signatures are handled by the following three signature engines:

- String ICMP
- String TCP
- String UDP

Sweep signatures are handled by the following two signature engines:

- Sweep
- Sweep Other TCP

The Trojan horse signatures are handled by the signature engines shown in Table 6-51.

Table 6-51 *Trojan Horse Signature Engines*

Engine	Description
Trojan Bo2K	Detects the presence of BO2K by using the TCP protocol
Trojan Tfn2K	Detects the presence of the TFN2K Trojan horse by examining UDP, TCP, and ICMP traffic
Trojan UDP	Detects the presence of BO and BO2K by using the UDP protocol

Q&A

You have two choices for review questions:

- The questions that follow give you a bigger challenge than the exam itself by using an open-ended question format. By reviewing now with this more difficult question format, you can exercise your memory better and prove your conceptual and factual knowledge of this chapter. The answers to these questions are found in the appendix.
- For more practice with exam-like question formats, use the exam engine on the CD-ROM.

1. What are the major groups that signature parameters fall into?
2. What do the Application Inspection and Control (AIC) signature engines provide, and which protocols are currently supported?
3. What signature types can you use for AIC HTTP signatures?
4. What are the atomic signature engines and the types of signatures they support?
5. What is the definition of an atomic signature?
6. What is the difference between the TCP Mask and TCP Flags parameters?
7. Which parameter do you use to specify that a regex string needs to be located at an exact location within the packet or stream?
8. Which Flood Net parameter defines how long the traffic must remain above the configured rate in order to trigger the signature?
9. What is a meta signatures?
10. What are the three inspection types available when you are creating signatures with the Service FTP signature engine?
11. What are the three inspection types available when you are creating signatures with the Service NTP signature engine?
12. What are the four inspection types available when you are creating signatures with the Service SNMP signature engine?
13. Cisco IPS supports what three state machines in the State signature engine?
14. What are the three String signature engines?
15. Which parameter determines how many connections it takes for a sweep signature to trigger?

This chapter covers the following subjects:

- Advanced Signature Configuration
- Meta-Event Generator
- Understanding HTTP and FTP Application Policy Enforcement
- Tuning an Existing Signature
- Creating a Custom Signature

CHAPTER 7

Advanced Signature Configuration

Many Cisco IPS deployments can take advantage of default signature configurations. Sometimes, however, you may need to create a custom signature or tune an existing signature to meet the needs your specific network environment. Cisco IPS provides the capability to tweak existing signatures and to easily create custom signatures based on the various Cisco IPS signature engines.

When default signature configurations do not match your requirements, you can either tune existing signatures to match your requirements or create your own custom signatures. Understanding the various signature fields is vital to your successful completion of either of these operations.

"Do I Know This Already?" Quiz

The purpose of the "Do I Know This Already?" quiz is to help you decide if you really need to read the entire chapter. If you already intend to read the entire chapter, you do not necessarily need to answer these questions now.

The 10-question quiz, derived from the major sections in the "Foundation and Supplemental Topics" portion of the chapter, helps you determine how to spend your limited study time.

Table 7-1 outlines the major topics discussed in this chapter and the "Do I Know This Already?" quiz questions that correspond to those topics.

Table 7-1 *"Do I Know This Already?" Foundation and Supplemental Topics Mapping*

Foundation or Supplemental Topic	Questions Covering This Topic
Advanced Signature Configuration—Regular Expressions String Matching	9
Advanced Signature Configuration—Signature Fields	1, 2
Meta-Event Generator	3, 7
Understanding HTTP and FTP Application Policy Enforcement	8, 10
Tuning an Existing Signature	4, 5
Creating a Custom Signature	6

CAUTION The goal of self-assessment is to gauge your mastery of the topics in this chapter. If you do not know the answer to a question or are only partially sure of the answer, you should mark this question wrong for purposes of the self-assessment. Giving yourself credit for an answer you correctly guess skews your self-assessment results and might provide you with a false sense of security.

1. Which signature field indicates the likelihood that the signature will trigger on attack traffic?
   a. Alert Severity
   b. Signature Fidelity Rating
   c. Target Value Rating
   d. Event Action Override
   e. Alert Notes
2. Which of the following is not a valid value for the Event Count Key field?
   a. Attacker address
   a. Victim address
   b. Attacker and victim addresses
   c. Attacker address and port
   d. Attacker address and victim port
3. To create a signature that generates an alert based on multiple component signatures, which of the following signature engines should you use?
   a. AIC HTTP
   b. Meta
   c. Normalizer
   d. Multi String
   e. Service General
4. Which of the following is considered tuning a signature?
   a. Enabling a signature
   b. Disabling a signature
   c. Changing the Alert Severity level
   d. Changing the signature's engine-specific parameters
   e. Assigning a new signature action

5. Which of the following is not considered tuning a signature?
   a. Changing the signature's engine-specific parameters
   b. Changing the signature's event counter parameters
   c. Assigning a new severity level
   d. Changing the signature's alert frequency parameters
6. What is the first step in creating a custom signature?
   a. Choose a signature engine.
   b. Define event counter parameters.
   c. Test signature effectiveness.
   d. Define alert frequency parameters.
   e. Define basic signature fields.
7. Which of the following is true about meta signatures?
   a. The meta signature can use only component signatures from the same signature engine.
   b. The order of the component signatures can be specified.
   c. The order of the component signatures cannot be specified.
   d. You can configure a reset interval for each component signature.
8. For which protocol is application policy enforcement supported in Cisco IPS version 5.0?
   a. SMTP
   b. NTP
   c. HTTP
   d. ARP
   e. IP
9. Which regex will match one or more As?
   a. [^A]*
   b. [A]+
   c. [A]?
   d. [A]*
   e. [^A]+

10. Which signature engine enables you to detect tunneling of non-HTTP traffic through port 80?

a. Service HTTP

b. Service FTP

c. AIC HTTP

d. AIC FTP

e. Service Generic

The answers to the "Do I Know This Already?" quiz are found in the appendix. The suggested choices for your next step are as follows:

- **8 or less overall score**—Read the entire chapter, including the "Foundation and Supplemental Topics," "Foundation Summary," and Q&A sections.
- **9 or 10 overall score**—If you want more review on these topics, skip to the "Foundation Summary" section and then go to the Q&A section. Otherwise, move to the next chapter.

Foundation and Supplemental Topics

Advanced Signature Configuration

Tuning existing signatures and creating custom signatures is a powerful feature of Cisco IPS. Understanding this functionality enables you to fine-tune your Cisco IPS solution to provide the best protection for your network. This chapter focuses on the following:

- Meta-Event Generator
- Understanding HTTP and FTP application policy enforcement
- Tuning an existing signature
- Creating a custom signature

Before broaching these important topics, however, it is helpful to explain the following topics in more detail:

- Regular expressions string matching
- Signature fields

Regular Expressions String Matching

Many signatures look for intrusive activity by searching for patterns in the analyzed traffic. These patterns are specified as regular expressions (regex). You create regex by using a powerful and flexible notational language that allows you to describe simple as well as complex textual patterns. Using various special characters, you can easily specify succinct expressions that search for almost any arbitrary pattern. The regex syntax options (for Cisco IPS version 5.0) are shown in Table 7-2.

Table 7-2 *Regular Expression Syntax*

Metacharacter	Name	Description
?	Question mark	Repeats 0 or 1 time
*	Star, asterisk	Repeats 0 or more times
+	Plus	Repeats 1 or more times
{x}	Quantifier	Repeats exactly x times
{x,}	Minimum quantifier	Repeats at least x times

continues

Table 7-2 *Regular Expression Syntax (Continued)*

<table>
<tr><th>Metacharacter</th><th>Name</th><th>Description</th></tr>
<tr><td>.</td><td>Dot</td><td>Matches any one character except a new line character (0x0A)</td></tr>
<tr><td>[abc]</td><td>Character class</td><td>Matches any character listed</td></tr>
<tr><td>[^abc]</td><td>Negated character class</td><td>Matches any character not listed</td></tr>
<tr><td>[a-z]</td><td>Character range class</td><td>Matches any character listed in the range (inclusive)</td></tr>
<tr><td>()</td><td>Parenthesis</td><td>Limits the scope of other metacharacters</td></tr>
<tr><td>|</td><td>Alternation, or</td><td>Matches either expression that it separates</td></tr>
<tr><td>^</td><td>Caret</td><td>Forces match to occur at the beginning of a line</td></tr>
<tr><td>\char</td><td>Escaped character</td><td>Matches the literal character (even for metacharacters)</td></tr>
<tr><td>char</td><td>Character</td><td>Matches the literal character (unless character is a metacharacter)</td></tr>
<tr><td>\r</td><td>Carriage return</td><td>Matches the carriage return (0x0D)</td></tr>
<tr><td>\n</td><td>New line</td><td>Matches the new line character (0x0A)</td></tr>
<tr><td>\t</td><td>Tab</td><td>Matches the tab character (0x09)</td></tr>
<tr><td>\f</td><td>Form feed</td><td>Matches the form feed character (0x0C)</td></tr>
<tr><td>\x<i>NN</i></td><td>Escaped hexadecimal character</td><td>Matches character with the hexadecimal value specified by <i>NN</i> (where 0<=<i>N</i><=F)</td></tr>
<tr><td>\<i>NNN</i></td><td>Escaped octal character</td><td>Matches character with the octal value specified by <i>NN</i> (where 0<=<i>N</i><=7)</td></tr>
</table>

Understanding regular expressions can be confusing if you are not familiar with them. To help clarify how regular expressions operate, Table 7-3 outlines numerous regular expressions in conjunction with the patterns that they try to match.

Table 7-3 *Sample Regular Expressions*

Regular Expression	String to Match
Attacker	"Attacker"
[Aa]ttacker	"Attacker" or "attacker"
c(ar)+s	Variations of "cars," "carars," "carararars"
foo.*bar	"foo" and any number of intervening characters (except a new line) between the word "bar"

Table 7-3 *Sample Regular Expressions (Continued)*

<table>
<tr><th>Regular Expression</th><th>String to Match</th></tr>
<tr><td>Earl|Jim</td><td>Either “Earl” or “Jim”</td></tr>
<tr><td>(ball|m)oon</td><td>Either “balloon” or “moon”</td></tr>
<tr><td>\[ABC\]</td><td>“[ABC]”</td></tr>
<tr><td>{XY}3</td><td>“XYXYXY”</td></tr>
</table>

Signature Fields

To understand how to tune existing signatures or create custom signatures, you must understand the various fields that comprise a Cisco IPS signature. The fields fall into the following categories:

- Basic signature fields
- Signature description fields
- Engine-specific fields
- Event counter fields
- Alert frequency fields
- Status fields

Basic Signature Fields

Each signature has the following four basic fields that identify the signature:

- Signature ID
- SubSignature ID
- Signature Fidelity Rating
- Alert Severity

Together, the Signature ID and SubSignature ID uniquely identify the signature. Both fields are numeric. The SubSignature ID enables you to have multiple signatures under a broader signature identified by the Signature ID.

The Signature Fidelity Rating indicates the likelihood that the signature will detect attack traffic (as opposed to normal user traffic) without the sensor having specific knowledge about the target system's operating system or applications. The signature creator assigns a default Signature Fidelity Rating for each signature, but you can change this value if needed. For any custom signatures that you create, you will need to assign an appropriate Signature Fidelity Rating.

To help network security administrators determine the potential severity of a signature, each signature has an associated Alert Severity. The Alert Severity level indicates the relative seriousness of the traffic that has been detected. Each signature has a default Alert Severity, but you can change this value to match your own network environment. The defined severity levels for Cisco IPS signatures, from highest to lowest, are as follows:

- High
- Medium
- Low
- Informational

> **NOTE** When a signature triggers, the event is assigned a Risk Rating based on the combined values of the following items:
>
> - Alert Severity
> - Signature Fidelity Rating
> - Asset Value of Target

Signature Description Fields

Signature description fields define some basic characteristics of a signature. You can use these descriptions to differentiate signatures and textually explain their functionality. Signature descriptions comprise the following five fields:

- Signature Name
- Alert Notes
- User Comments
- Alert Traits
- Release

The signature name provides a textual description for a signature. This name is more meaningful for the security analyst than the basic Signature ID field, which identifies the signature by a numeric value.

The Alert Notes and User Comments fields enable you to record notes about the signature and how it operates on your network. Similarly, the Alert Traits field is a numeric field (0–65535) you can use to develop your own custom categorization scheme.

The Release field indicates the software release at which the signature was introduced into the Cisco IPS software.

Engine-Specific Fields

Engine-specific fields enable you to define fields that determine which type of network traffic the signature will match. Each engine has unique characteristics. Refer to Chapter 6, "Cisco IPS Signature Engines," for more information on engine-specific fields.

Event Counter Fields

By configuring the following event counter fields, you specify how many instances of the signature's traffic are required to cause an alert:

- Event Count
- Event Count Key
- Alert Interval

The Event Count field identifies how many instances of the signature's traffic need to occur before an alert is generated.

The Event Count Key field determines which IP addresses or ports are used when determining unique instances of the signature's traffic. Possible values for the Event Count Key are as follows:

- Attacker address
- Attacker address and victim port
- Attacker and victim addresses
- Attacker and victim addresses and ports
- Victim address

> **NOTE** For most signatures, the attacker address value refers to the source IP address of the offending network traffic, whereas the victim address value refers to the destination IP address of the offending network traffic. If the Swap Attacker Victim signature field is set to **Yes**, then the addresses are reversed, with the attacker address being the destination IP address of the traffic and the victim address being the source address of the traffic.

The final event counter parameter is the Alert Interval. By specifying an Alert Interval, you indicate the time period (in seconds) over which the sensor must see the number of instances of the intrusive traffic equal to the Event Count in order to generate an alert. For instance, if the Alert Interval is set to 60 and the Event Count is 5, then the sensor must see five instances of the signature's traffic in 60 seconds before it generates an alert. At the end of the alert interval, the instance count is reset to 0.

You can also configure a signature without an Alert Interval parameter. In that situation, an alert is generated when the instances of the signature's traffic reach the Event Count, regardless of the time interval.

Alert Frequency Fields

Managing alerts efficiently is vital to the success of your Cisco IPS deployment. To enhance your ability to control the volume of alerts generated by your sensors, Cisco IPS supports several alert modes (including alert summarization). Each of the alert summary modes is designed to assist you in regulating the number of alerts generated by intrusive traffic in different situations. Alert frequency fields are explained in detail in Chapter 5, "Basic Cisco IPS Signature Configuration."

Status Fields

The following status fields indicate whether the signature is enabled and whether the signature has been retired:

- Enabled
- Retired

The valid options for each field are **Yes** and **No**. The main difference between the two options is that disabling a signature only prevents it from generating alerts. Retiring a signature actually removes the signature from the signature engine, thus preventing the signature from having any impact on the sensor's performance.

Meta-Event Generator

A powerful new functionality incorporated into Cisco IPS version 5.0 is the Meta-Event Generator (MEG). The MEG enables you to create compound signatures based on multiple individual signatures. For instance, suppose that a new attack triggers the following five existing signatures:

- 3221
- 3222
- 3223
- 3224
- 3225

By default, these signatures are not enabled. You could enable each of these signatures and have your security analyst try to determine when all of the five signatures trigger within a specific period of time (potentially indicating a new attack). This correlation, however, can become very difficult if some of these signatures are triggering because of other traffic on the network (not related to traffic from your new attack).

Using the MEG, you can easily create a compound signature that triggers only when each of the five individual signatures trigger within a specific time period. When defining a meta signature (a signature based on the meta signature engine), you need to define the following parameters:

- Signatures that comprise the meta signature
- Number of unique victims needed to trigger the meta signature
- IP addresses or ports used to trigger the meta signature
- Order in which signatures need to be detected (optional)

NOTE Besides defining individual signatures based on the meta signature engine, you must also verify that the MEG is enabled (the default) in order to use these signatures. You enable MEG by selecting the **Use Meta Event Generator** check box on the General Settings configuration screen (see Figure 7-1), which you get to by clicking **Event Action Rules > General Settings**.

Figure 7-1 *General Settings Configuration Screen*

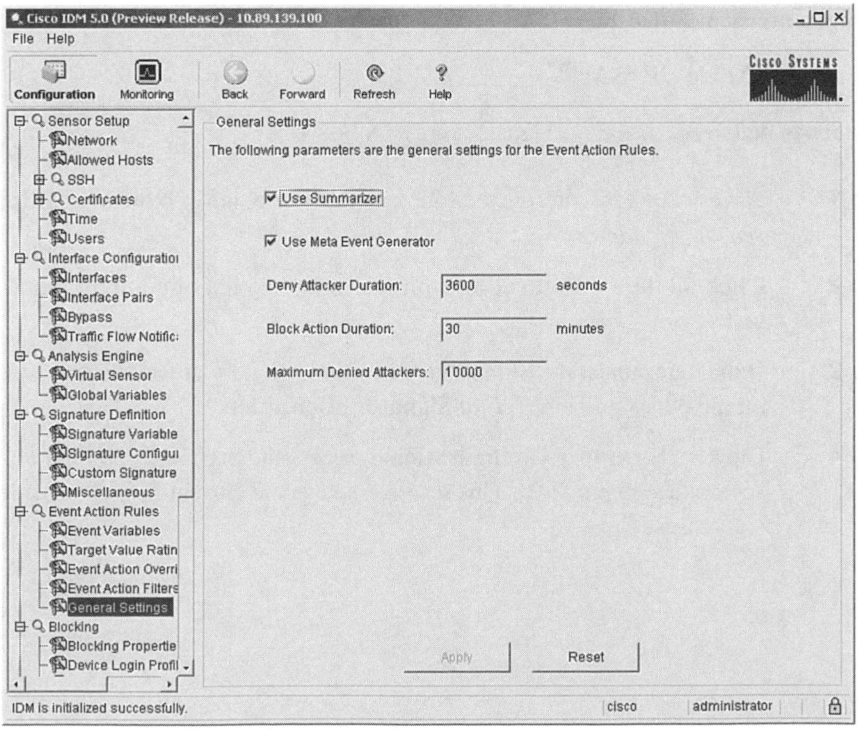

In the ongoing example, suppose that you want to trigger your new meta signature when the five signatures all occur within 90 seconds in the following order:

1. 3225
2. 3222
3. 3224
4. 3223
5. 3221

Furthermore, you want the signature to trigger when all of the signatures originate from a single attacker (or source) IP address. You also want to use the following basic signature parameters:

- Signature ID—61500
- Alert Severity—High
- Signature Fidelity—90
- Event Action—Produce Alert and Deny Attacker Inline
- Signature Name—Custom HTTP Meta Signature
- Summary Mode—Fire All

The steps to define the new meta signature are as follows:

Step 1 Access IDM by entering the following URL in your web browser: **https://** *sensor_ip_address*.

Step 2 Click on the **Configuration** icon to display the list of configuration tasks.

Step 3 If the items under the **Signature Definition** category are not displayed, click on the plus sign to the left of **Signature Definition**.

Step 4 Click on **Signature Configuration** to access the Signature Configuration screen (see Figure 7-2). This screen displays the current list of available signatures.

Figure 7-2 *Signature Configuration Screen*

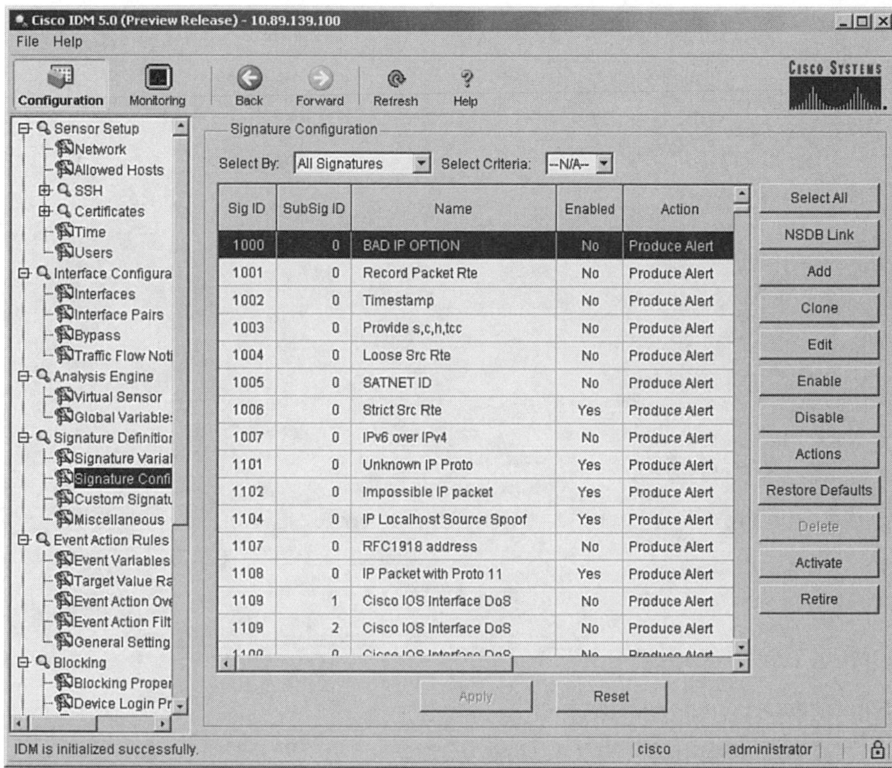

Step 5 Click on **Add** to access the Add Signature popup window (see Figure 7-3).

Step 6 Enter **61500** in the **Signature ID** field.

Step 7 Click on the green square next to **Alert Severity** to override the default Alert Severity value. Then use the pull-down menu to select a severity level of **High**.

Step 8 Click on the green square next to **Signature Fidelity** to override the default Signature Fidelity value. Then enter **90** in the **Signature Fidelity** field.

Step 9 Click on the green square next to **Signature Name** to override the default Signature Name. Then change the Signature Name to **Custom HTTP Meta Signature**.

Step 10 Use the pull-down menu for the **Engine** field to select the **Meta** engine. After you select the Meta engine, the window updates to show the fields available for a meta signature (see Figure 7-4).

Figure 7-3 *Add Signature Popup Window*

Figure 7-4 *Meta Signature Engine Fields*

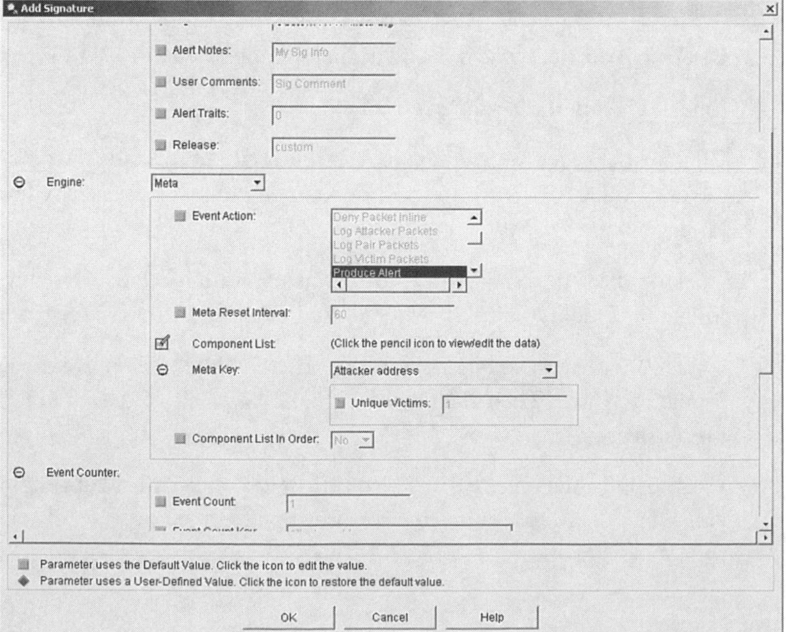

Step 11 Select the square next to **Event Action** to override the default Event Action. Then add the **Deny Attacker Inline** action by holding the **Ctrl** key while clicking on **Deny Attacker Inline** in the pull-down menu (**Produce Alert** is already selected by default).

Step 12 Click on the square next to the **Meta Reset Interval** to override the Meta Reset Interval. Then enter **90**.

Step 13 Next add the signatures that the meta signature will trigger on by clicking on the **Pencil** icon to display the Component List configuration window (see Figure 7-5).

Figure 7-5 *Component List Popup Window*

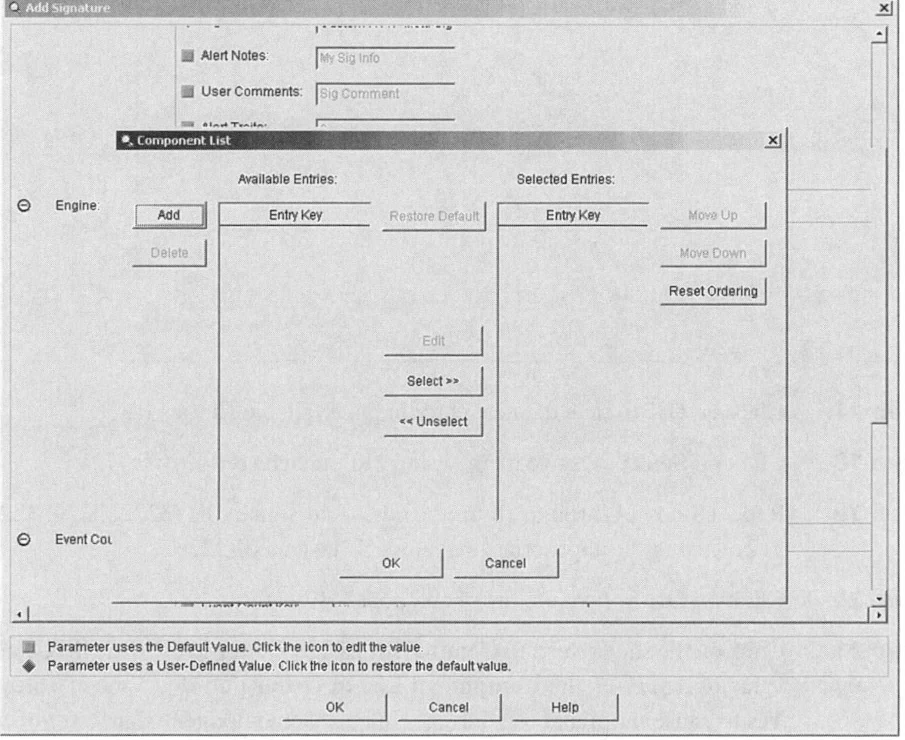

Step 14 Click on **Add** to add a component signature to the meta signature (see Figure 7-6).

Step 15 Enter **3225** in the **Entry Key** field.

Step 16 Enter **3225** in the **Component Sig ID** field.

Figure 7-6 *Add List Entry Popup Window*

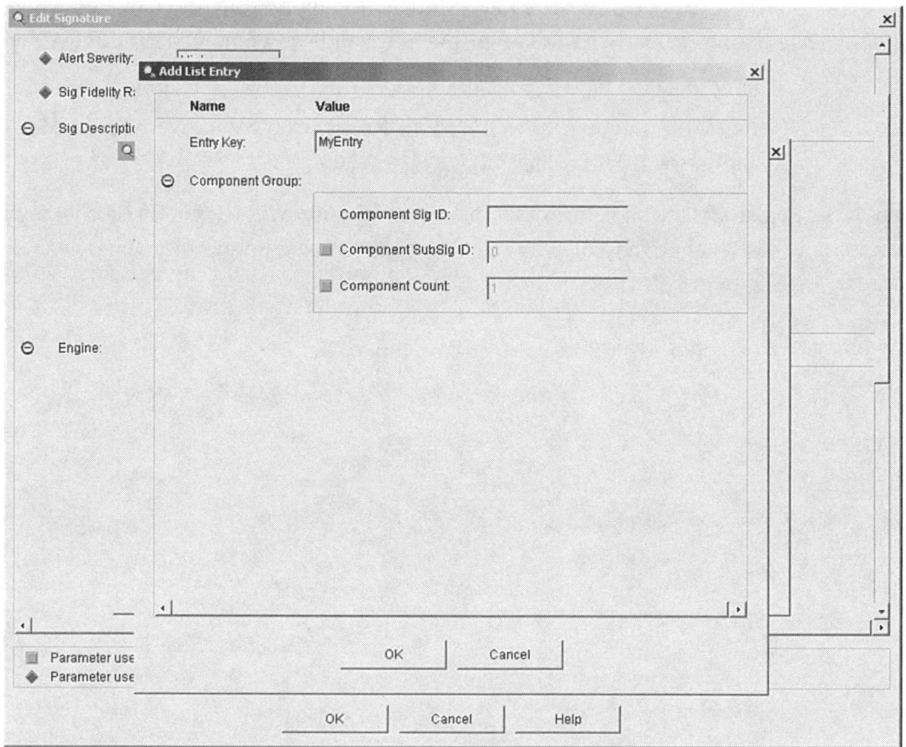

Step 17 Click on **OK** to save the new entry in the Available Entries list.

Step 18 Click on **Select** to move the new entry to the **Selected Entries** list.

Step 19 Repeat Steps 14 through 18 for the other four signatures (3222, 3224, 3223, 3221), using the appropriate signature ID instead of 3225.

Step 20 Click on **OK** to save the list of component signatures.

Step 21 Click on the square next to **Component List in Order** to override the default value of No. From the **Component List in Order** pull-down menu, select **Yes** to cause the signature to trigger only if the component signatures occur in the correct order.

Step 22 Select **Fire All** from the **Summary Mode** pull-down menu.

Step 23 Click on **OK** to save the new signature.

Step 24 Finally, click on **Apply** to save your changes to the sensor's configuration.

Now when your new meta signature generates an alert, you know that all five of the configured signatures have been detected in a specific order within 90 seconds. This automatic correlation performed by the sensor software is much more effective than manually performing the correlation based on the events generated by the individual signatures. Furthermore, using these meta signatures provides you with the ability to create very complex signatures with a minimal amount of effort.

Understanding HTTP and FTP Application Policy Enforcement

HTTP is a protocol that commonly traverses firewalls on many networks. Because of this, many applications (and attackers) have started using this protocol to tunnel non-HTTP traffic through firewalls in an attempt to circumvent the security policies on various networks. Cisco IPS version 5.0 enables you to conduct a more thorough analysis of HTTP and FTP through application policy enforcement. Currently, application policy enforcement is available for both HTTP and FTP. Some HTTP checks include the following:

- Detection of non-HTTP traffic tunneling through port 80
- Ensuring RFC compliance of HTTP methods
- Filtering traffic based on specified Multipurpose Internet Mail Extension (MIME) types
- Control of permitted traffic via user-defined policies

Using a destination port of 80 for traffic that is not related to HTTP is known as *tunneling traffic through port 80*, since port 80 is allowed to provide HTTP access. The easiest way to detect this traffic is to compare traffic going to port 80 against the structure specified in RFC 2616, "Hypertext Transfer Protocol." For instance, a built-in signature that checks for RFC 2616 compliance is signature 12674, "Alarm on non-http traffic." Comparing traffic against the HTTP RFC can also identify malformed requests and illegal HTTP methods.

HTTP traffic can also include traffic encoded using various MIME types. Some of these encodings are commonly used worms and viruses attempting to bypass detection (since the expected content has been encoded in a different form). In other situations your security policy may not allow transferring data using certain transfer encoding mechanisms. You can create signatures using application policy enforcement to filter out unwanted MIME extensions. For instance signature 12090, "Define Transfer-Encoding Gzip," can be enabled to disallow the transfer of gzip-compressed files to port 80.

Finally, you can regulate which HTTP methods are allowed based on your security policy. For instance, your security policy may disallow your internal web servers from enabling certain HTTP methods (such as TRACE and DELETE). You can use the following signatures to enforce these security policy requirements:

- 12079, "Define Request Method DELETE"
- 12085, "Define Request Method TRACE"

The following signature engines provide the HTTP and FTP application policy enforcement functionality:

- AIC FTP
- AIC HTTP

NOTE The Application Inspection and Control (AIC) engines provide deep-packet inspection from Layer 4 through Layer 7, enabling a much more granular verification of your defined security policy.

Tuning an Existing Signature

You can tune the characteristics for all the signatures in Cisco IPS. This tuning capability enables you to customize Cisco IPS to suit many different network environments. Because of the comprehensive list of available built-in signatures, most of your signature configuration will probably involve tuning existing signatures. Furthermore, you can easily restore the default values for any signature field that has been altered simply by clicking on the diamond to the left of the field. Tuning signatures involves performing one or more of the following:

- Changing the signature's engine-specific parameters
- Changing the signature's event counter parameters
- Changing the signature's alert frequency parameters

NOTE The following actions are generally not considered signature tuning:

- Enabling or disabling a signature
- Assigning a severity level
- Assigning a signature action

Basically, tuning a built-in signature involves changing the way it operates to match the needs of your network environment. A simple example of tuning would be to change the Summary mode from Fire Once to one of the alarm summarization modes (such as Global Summarize) to reduce the quantity of alarms that your security operator needs to analyze (especially for certain low-severity signatures).

The basic steps involved in tuning a Cisco IPS signature are as follows:

Step 1 Choose the specific signature that needs tuning.

Step 2 Modify the signature parameters.

Step 3 Save and apply the changes to the sensor's configuration.

Tuning Example

An example may facilitate your understanding of signature tuning. Suppose that the following factors apply to your business:

- You use Cisco IP Phone services.
- Your IP phones are consolidated on a single segment (10.10.20.0/24).
- You have a dedicated TFTP server for the IP phones.
- You want to monitor access to the IP Phone TFTP server from addresses not on the phone segment.
- You want an alert on any attempt to grab a phone configuration file from any network segment besides 10.10.20.0 (the IP phone network segment).
- You want to generate only one alert from a single source IP every five minutes.
- You want to use an inline deny packet to stop the traffic from addresses not on the phone segment.

Examining the signatures provided with Cisco IPS, you see the built-in signature 4612, "Cisco IP Phone TFTP Config Retrieve." This signature is close to what you want, but it requires some tuning since it does not provide the following functionality:

- Generate one alert from a single source IP every five minutes (300 seconds)
- Use the inline deny packet action to prevent matching traffic

The following steps indicate how to use IDM to tune this signature to match your requirements:

Step 1 Access IDM by entering the following URL in your web browser: **https://**_sensor_ip_address_.

Step 2 Click on the **Configuration** icon to display the list of configuration tasks.

Step 3 If the items under the **Signature Definition** category are not displayed, click on the plus sign to the left of **Signature Definition**.

Step 4 Click on **Signature Configuration** to access the Signature Configuration screen (refer to Figure 7-2). This screen displays the current list of available signatures.

Step 5 Use the pull-down menu for the **Select By** field to choose **Sig ID**.

Step 6 Enter **4612** in the **Enter Sig ID** field and then click on **Find**. This displays the signature you want to tune (see Figure 7-7).

Figure 7-7 *Displaying Signature by Signature ID*

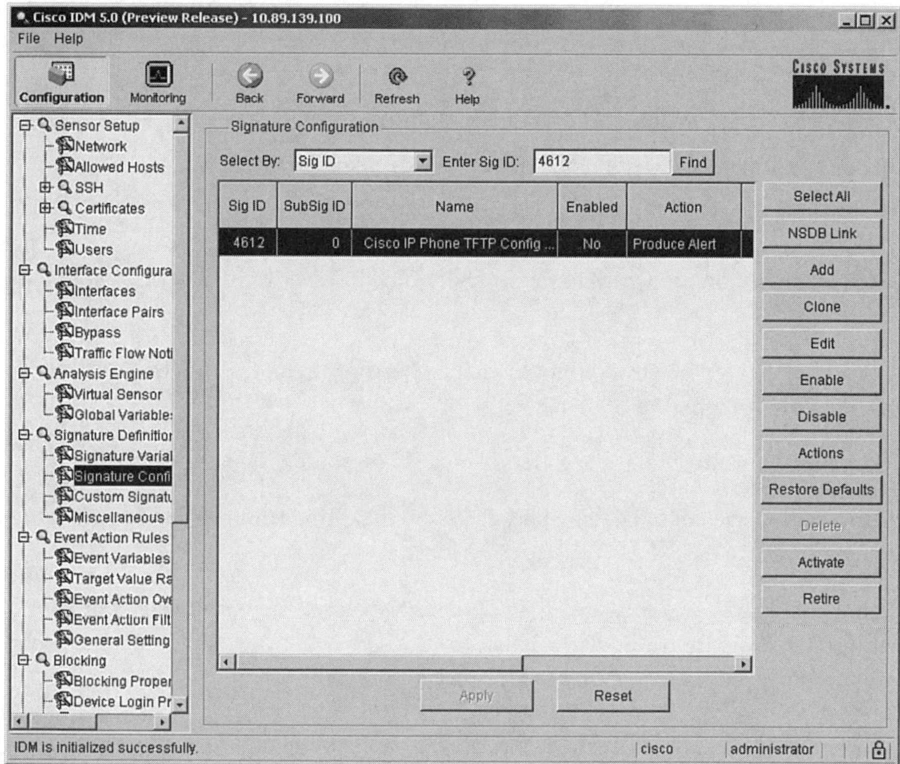

Step 7 Click on **Edit** to access the Edit Signature popup window (see Figure 7-8).

Step 8 Click on the square next to **Event Action** to override the default event action setting (the green square becomes a red diamond).

Step 9 The only action selected by default is **Produce Alert**. You need to add **Deny Packet Inline** by holding the **Ctrl** key while clicking on **Deny Packet Inline** in the **Event Action** scrolling list.

> **NOTE** Just clicking on **Deny Packet Inline** (while holding down the **Ctrl** key) will remove the Produce Alert action that was initially set by default.

Step 10 Click on the square next to **Specify Alert Interval** to override the default setting.

Step 11 Select **Yes** from the **Specify Alert Interval** pull-down menu.

Step 12 Click on the square next to **Alert Interval** to override the default setting.

Step 13 Enter **300** into the **Alert Interval** field.

Figure 7-8 *IDM Edit Signature Popup Window*

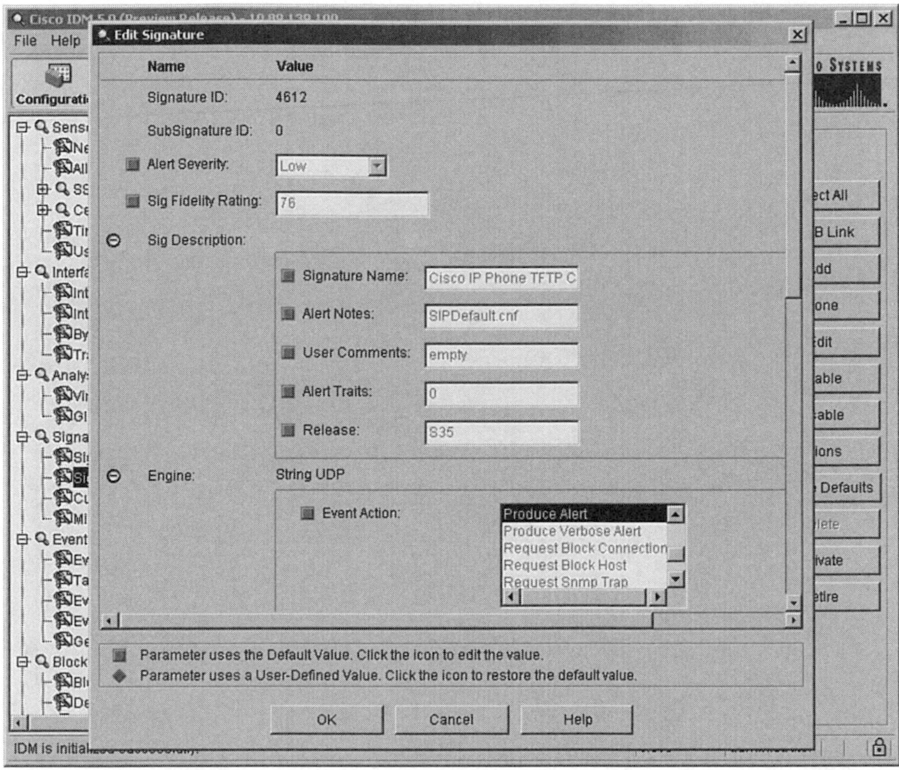

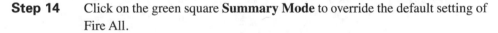

Step 14 Click on the green square **Summary Mode** to override the default setting of Fire All.

Step 15 Select **Fire Once** from the **Summary Mode** pull-down menu.

Step 16 Click on the square next to **Enabled** to override the default setting of No.

Step 17 Select **Yes** from the **Enabled** pull-down menu.

Step 18 Verify that your changes match those in Figure 7-9. Click on **OK** to save your changes.

Step 19 Finally, click on **Apply** to save your changes to the sensor's configuration.

Now that you have tuned the existing signature, there is potentially one more step in this example that is necessary to make the signature effective. In its current state, the signature will work correctly only if your TFTP server is on the IP Phone network segment and the Cisco IPS sensor is operating inline between the IP Phone network segment and the rest of the network. In this configuration, the traffic between the IP phones and the TFTP server (both on the IP Phone network segment) will not be examined by the sensor (so only external traffic is prevented from accessing the TFTP server on the IP Phone network segment).

Figure 7-9 *Tuned Signature 4612*

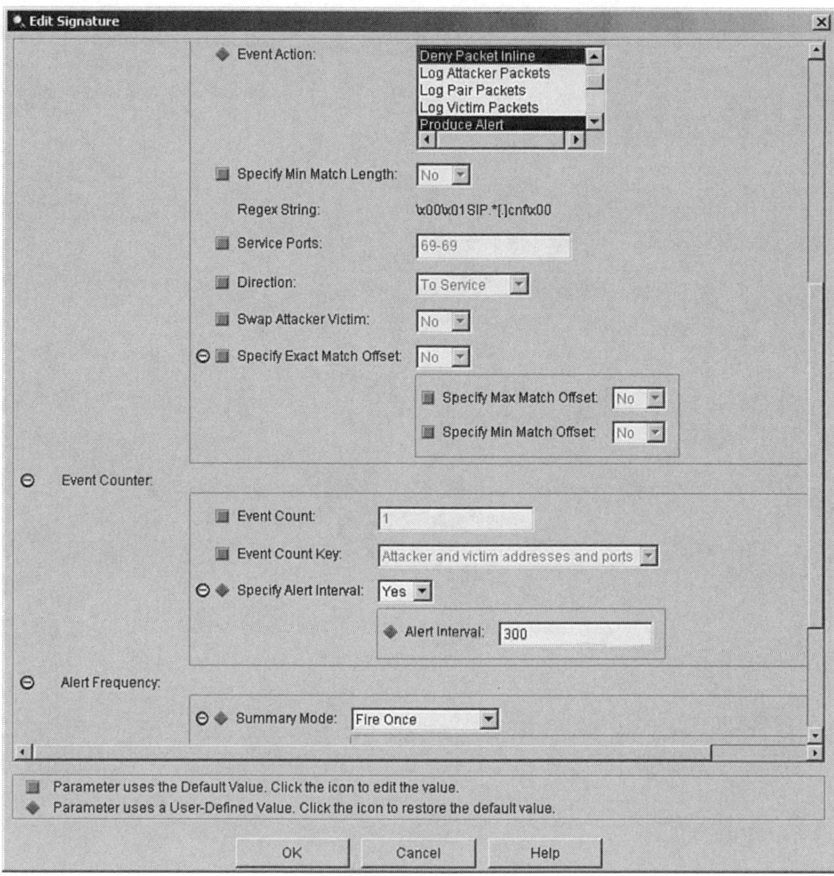

If the sensor is located in a location where it examines TFTP requests generated by your IP phones, then you must also configure an event filter to allow access for the IP phones while allowing the signature to restrict traffic for other systems. Configuring event filters is explained in Chapter 8, "Sensor Tuning."

Creating a Custom Signature

With the wealth of signatures supplied by Cisco IPS, you should rarely need to create custom signatures. You can usually modify or tune existing signatures to meet your intrusion-prevention needs. Sometimes, however, custom signatures are necessary. When creating custom signatures, you need to complete the following tasks:

- Choose a signature engine
- Verify existing functionality

- Define signature parameters
- Test signature effectiveness

Choose a Signature Engine

The various Cisco IPS signatures enable you to create a wide range of custom signatures. When choosing which signature engine to use for a new signature, you need to consider several factors about the traffic being detected, such as the following:

- Network protocol
- Target address
- Target port
- Attack type
- Inspection criteria

Network Protocol

Before creating a new signature, you must first determine the network protocol that needs to be examined to locate the intrusive traffic. Normally, for instance, the protocol for your signatures is fixed based on the signature engine selected. Sometimes you may need to use a signature engine that enables you to specify the protocol to look for. For instance, suppose you want to create an Enhanced Interior Gateway Routing Protocol (EIGRP) signature. This signature requires a signature engine that enables you to specify the IP protocol number because EIGRP uses IP protocol 88.

A quick examination of the signature engines reveals that the Atomic IP engine provides the capability to specify the IP protocol number by using the Specify Layer 4 Protocol parameter. Therefore, this engine is a probably a good candidate engine for your new signature.

Target Address

Attacks are directed at specific systems on your network. Some attacks target a specific host whereas others target many hosts on the network. For instance, if you are creating a signature to detect an attack that floods your network with Internet Control Message Protocol (ICMP) traffic, you will probably use a Flood signature engine. If the target is a single host, then you will use the Flood Host signature engine. If, on the other hand, you are concerned about a flood of traffic against your network, you will use the Flood Net signature engine.

Target Port

Determine the anticipated port or ports that the attack traffic will be sent to. For instance, the Sweep signature engine enables you to detect User Datagram Protocol (UDP) connections to a single UDP port or multiple UDP ports.

Attack Type

Sometimes the type of attack that you want to detect will lead you toward the appropriate signature engine. Flood signature engines, for instance, are almost always used to detect denial-of-service (DoS) attacks. Similarly, sweep signature engines are usually used to detect reconnaissance attacks against your network.

> **NOTE** Although the various engines were designed to detect specific types of attacks, their detection abilities are not limited to those attacks. For instance, some DoS attacks are detected by using atomic signature engines.

Inspection Criteria

Some signatures detect specific packet characteristics such as IP addresses and ports or header length fields. Other signatures require the signature engine to analyze the payload of a packet for a specific string pattern. Many signature engines enable you to specify a string pattern that the signature will trigger on when it is detected in network traffic. The string signature engines enable you to search for a specific pattern in various types of network traffic.

Verify Existing Functionality

After you have determined the signature engine that provides the functionality your custom signature needs, you need to verify that an existing signature does not already perform the functionality you desire. You can do this by examining all of the signatures supported by the chosen engine to determine if any of them already do what you want your new signature to accomplish. In some situations, you may be able to easily tune an existing signature to gain the new functionality you desire.

> **NOTE** Besides examining all of the signatures for a specific engine, you may also view the available signatures based on another characteristic (such as L2/L3/L4 protocol or attack), looking for signatures that use the signature engine that you are interested in. This will narrow the list of available signatures that you need to analyze.

Define Signature Parameters

After selecting a signature engine, you need to decide which values you will use for all of the required parameters as well as determine which optional parameters you need to configure to match the intrusive traffic that you want to detect. When defining parameters, try to consider situations in which the new signature may accidentally alarm on normal user activity. For instance, suppose that you create a signature to detect spam e-mail messages by looking for e-mail messages addressed to a large number of recipients. Certain mailing list programs generate mail messages that have many recipients as well; these messages should not be considered spam. Minimizing false positives is a key consideration when you develop custom signatures.

> **NOTE** *Spam* refers to unsolicited e-mail messages (all having essentially the same content) that are sent to a large number of recipients, usually to promote products or services.

Test Signature Effectiveness

Once you have created a custom signature, you need to test the signature on your live network. First verify that the signature detects the intrusive traffic that you built it to detect. (You might observe that the new signature alarms on traffic that you did not consider.) You should also make sure that your new signature does not significantly impact the performance of your senor.

Custom Signature Scenario

Suppose that your web server contains sensitive files that are located in a directory called Corporate Reports. You might want to create a custom signature that alarms when HTTP requests access this directory.

> **NOTE** To minimize false positives, you will also probably want to establish signature filters that prevent the signature from triggering when the Corporate Reports directory is accessed from legitimate systems or networks.

To define your custom signature, you need to first choose the signature engine that best fits the functionality required. In this situation, you need to search for HTTP requests that access a specific directory on your web server. The Service HTTP signature engine contains a parameter named URI Regex that enables you to define a search pattern that examines the uniform resource identifier (URI) portion of an HTTP request. That is exactly the functionality you need. Besides the default values, your custom signature will use the following parameters:

- Signature ID—64000
- Signature Name—CorporateReports
- Alert Severity—High
- Signature Fidelity—85
- Signature Engine—Service HTTP
- URI Regex—[/\\][Cc][Oo][Rr][Pp][Oo][Rr][Aa][Tt][Ee][Rr][Ee][Pp][Oo][Rr][Tt][Ss]
- Summary Mode—Summary

Creating Custom Signatures Using IDM

One way to create a custom signature in IDM is by using the **Add** button from the signature configuration screen. Creating your custom HTTP signature by using this approach involves the following steps:

Step 1 Access IDM by entering the following URL in your web browser: **https://***sensor_ip_address*.

Step 2 Click on the **Configuration** icon to display the list of configuration tasks.

Step 3 If the items under the **Signature Definition** category are not displayed, click on the plus sign to the left of **Signature Definition**.

Step 4 Click on **Signature Configuration** to access the Signature Configuration screen. This screen displays currently defined signatures based on various search criteria.

Step 5 Click on **Add** to add a new signature to the sensor through the Add Signature popup window (see Figure 7-10).

Figure 7-10 *IDM Add Signature Popup Window*

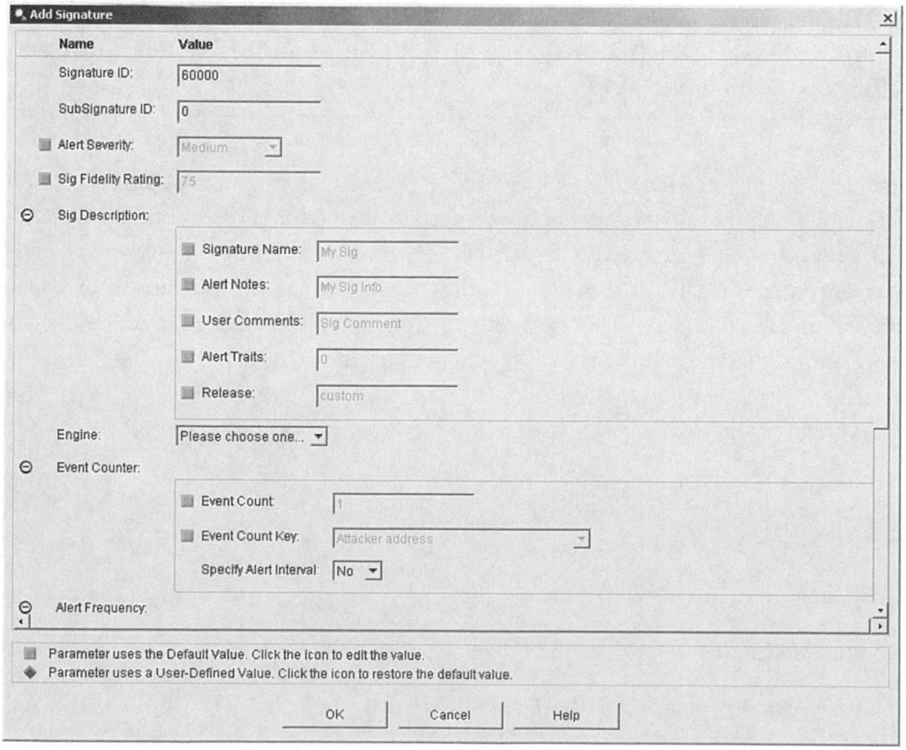

Step 6 Enter **64000** in the **Signature ID** field.

Step 7 Click on the square next to the **Alert Severity** field to override the default value of Medium. Then select **High** from the pull-down menu.

Step 8 Click on the square next to **Signature Fidelity** to override the default value of 75. Then enter **85** in the **Signature Fidelity** field.

Step 9 Click on the square next to **Signature Name** to override the default value of My Sig. Then enter **CorporateReports** into the **Signature Name** field.

Step 10 Select the **Service HTTP** engine from the **Engine** pull-down menu. After you select the engine, the fields for the Service HTTP engine are shown (see Figure 7-11).

Figure 7-11 *IDM Service HTTP Fields*

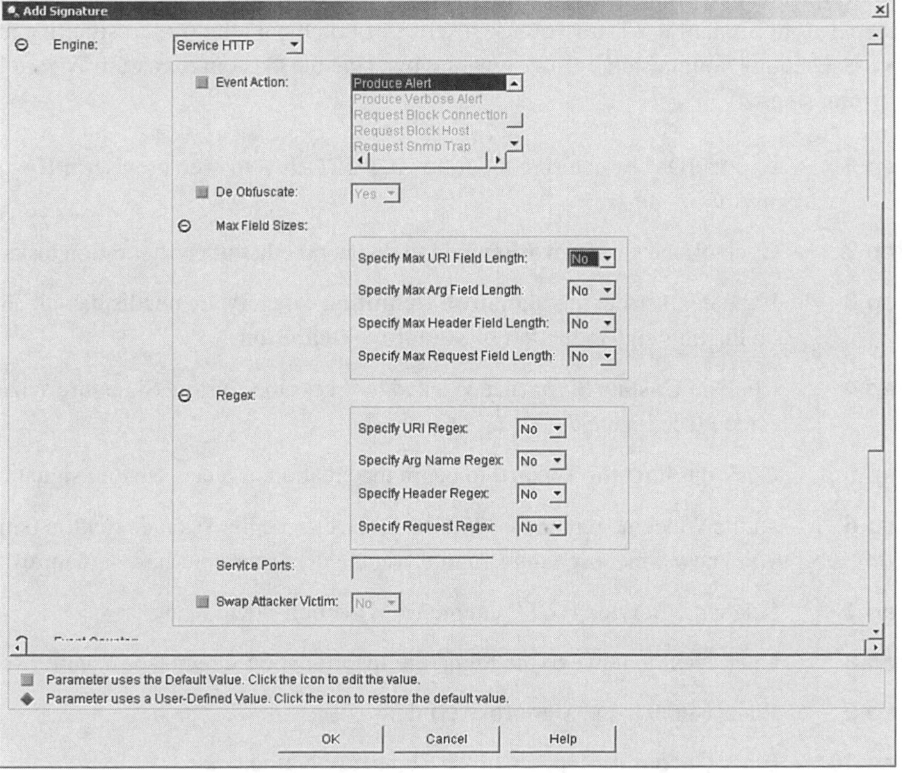

Step 11 Change the **Specify URI Regex** from the default of No to **Yes** by using the pull-down menu. Once you select **Yes**, the **URI Regex** field is displayed.

Step 12 Enter **[/\][Cc][Oo][Rr][Pp][Oo][Rr][Aa][Tt][Ee][Rr][Ee][Pp][Oo][Rr][Tt][Ss]** in the **URI Regex** field.

Step 13 Enter **80** in the **Service Ports** field to apply the signature to traffic to destination port 80.

Step 14 Click on **OK** to save the new signature.

Step 15 Click on **Apply** to apply the changes to the sensor's configuration.

NOTE By default, the De Obfuscate parameter is set to **Yes**. This causes the signature engine to convert different representations (such as Unicode characters) before examining the HTTP request. That should enable your signature to match on various encodings for the CorporateReports directory using the single regex.

Using IDM Custom Signature Wizard

In addition to using the **Add** button from the signature configuration screen, you can also create custom signatures by using the Custom Signature Wizard. Unlike using the basic Add functionality, in the Custom Signature Wizard you use a series of graphical windows to simplify the creation process. Creating your custom HTTP signature by using the Custom Signature Wizard involves the following steps:

Step 1 Access IDM by entering the following URL in your web browser: **https://** *sensor_ip_address*.

Step 2 Click on the **Configuration** icon to display the list of configuration tasks.

Step 3 If the items under the **Signature Definition** category are not displayed, click on the plus sign to the left of **Signature Definition**.

Step 4 Click on **Custom Signature Wizard** to access the Custom Signature Wizard screen (see Figure 7-12).

Step 5 Click on **Start the Wizard** to begin the creation of a new custom signature.

Step 6 At the Welcome screen (see Figure 7-13), choose the **Yes** radio button (since you know which signature engine you are using for your new signature).

Step 7 Select the **Service HTTP** engine from the pull-down menu.

Step 8 Click **Next** to move to the Signature Identification screen (see Figure 7-14).

Step 9 Enter **64000** in the **Signature ID** field.

Step 10 Enter **CorporateReports** in the **Signature Name** field.

Step 11 Click **Next** to move to the Engine-Specific Parameters screen (see Figure 7-15).

Step 12 Change the **Specify URI Regex** from the default of No to **Yes** by using the pull-down menu. Once you select **Yes**, the **URI Regex** field is displayed.

Figure 7-12 *IDM HTTP Custom Signature Wizard Screen*

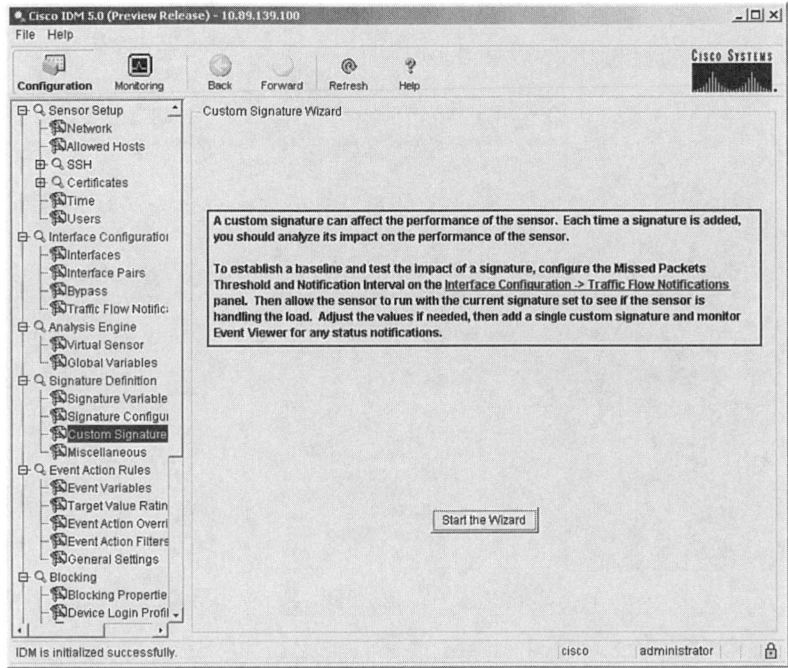

Figure 7-13 *Custom Signature Wizard Welcome Screen*

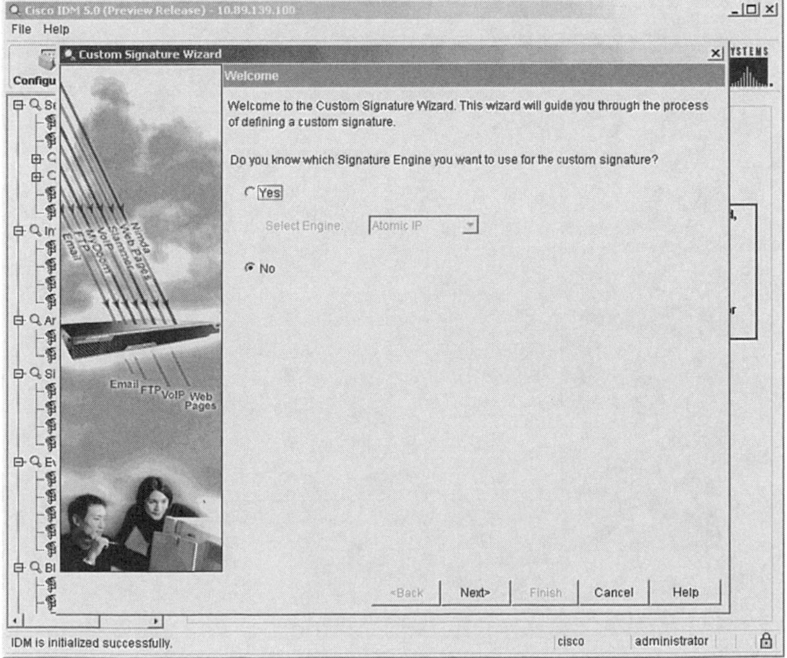

Figure 7-14 *Custom Signature Wizard Signature Identification Screen*

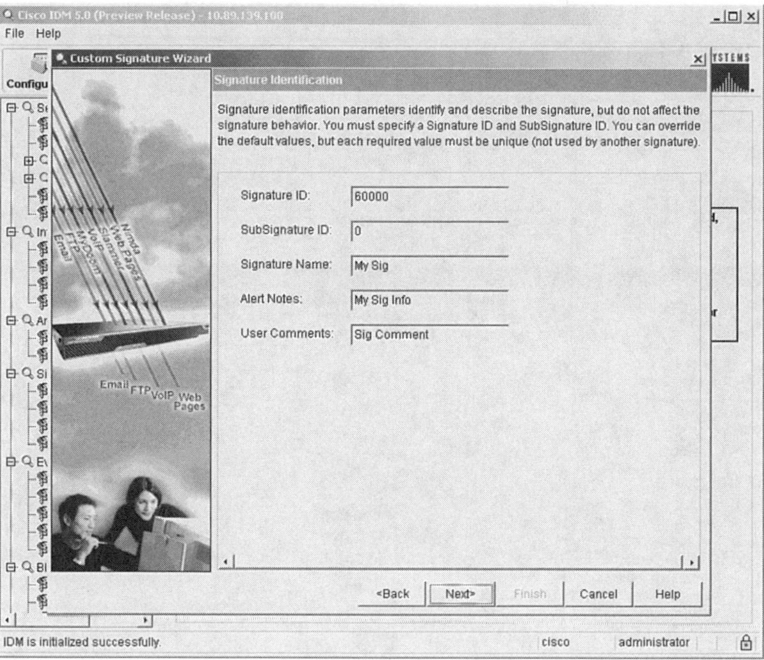

Figure 7-15 *Custom Signature Wizard Engine-Specific Parameters Screen*

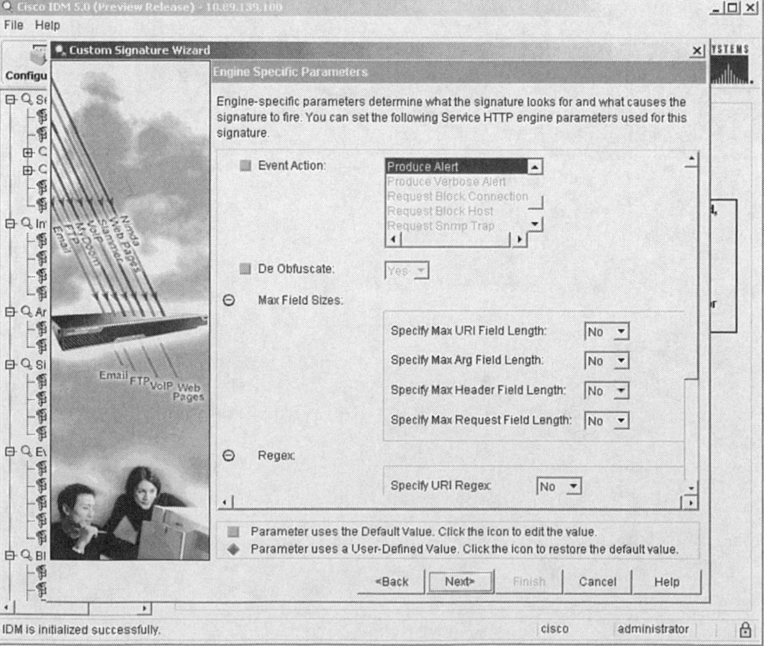

Step 13 Enter **[/\\][Cc][Oo][Rr][Pp][Oo][Rr][Aa][Tt][Ee][Rr][Ee][Pp][Oo][Rr][Tt][Ss]** in the **URI Regex** field.

Step 14 Enter **80** in the **Service Ports** field to apply the signature to traffic to destination port 80.

Step 15 Click **Next** to move to the Alert Response screen (see Figure 7-16).

Figure 7-16 *Custom Signature Wizard Alert Response Screen*

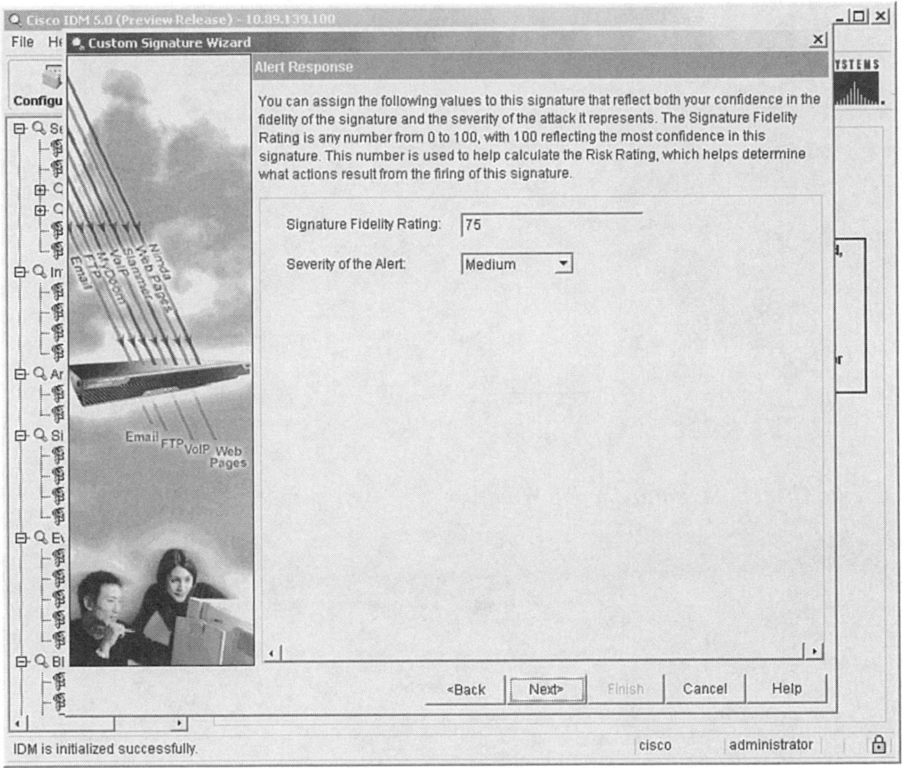

Step 16 Enter **85** in the **Signature Fidelity Rating** field.

Step 17 Change the severity to **High** by using the pull-down menu for the **Severity of the Alert** field.

Step 18 Click **Next** to move to the Alert Behavior screen (see Figure 7-17).

Step 19 Because the default alert behavior matches the new signature (it uses the Summary mode already), you can click on **Finish** to save the new signature.

Step 20 Click **Yes** at the Create Custom Signature popup window (see Figure 7-18) to save the new signature.

Figure 7-17 *Custom Signature Wizard Alert Behavior Screen*

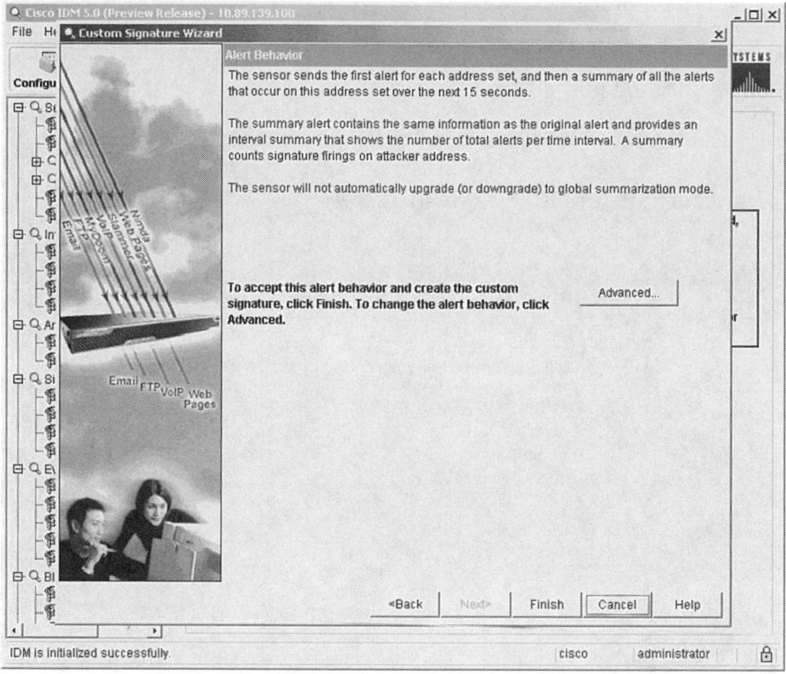

Figure 7-18 *Create Custom Signature Popup Window*

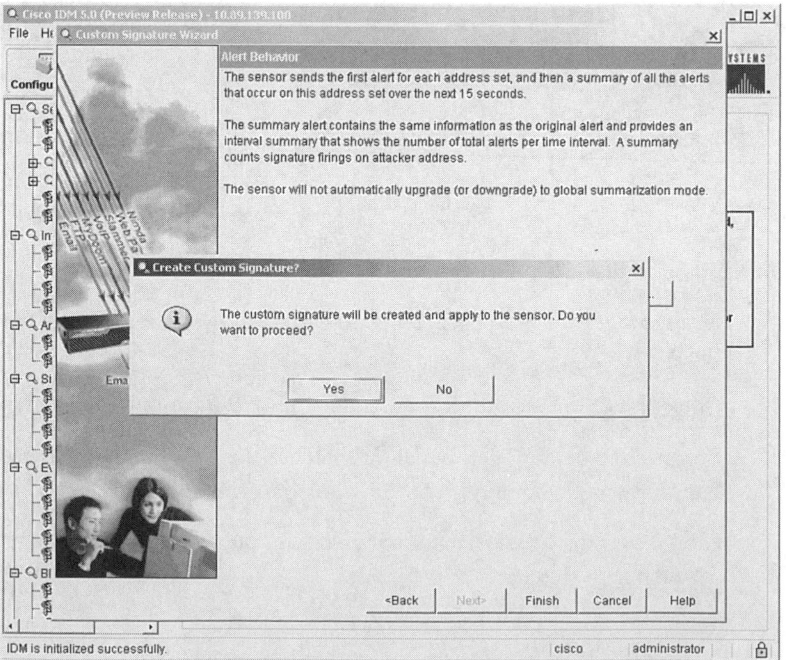

Cloning an Existing Signature

Sometimes you need to create a new signature that closely matches an existing signature. Instead of using the **Add** button on the Signature Configuration screen, you can use the **Clone** button. When you use **Clone** instead of **Add**, most of the signature fields are already populated with the values of the signature being cloned (the highlighted signature). Other field values are changed. For example, a new Signature ID is assigned, and the Signature Name field is assigned the original signature's name with the word Clone appended to it. Other than having some of the fields already populated, the process for adding a signature by using Clone is identical to the process for adding a signature using Add.

Foundation Summary

Tuning existing signatures and creating custom signatures is a powerful feature of Cisco IPS. Understanding this functionality enables you to fine-tune your Cisco IPS solution to provide the best protection for your network.

Each signature is composed of fields in the following categories:

- Basic signature fields
- Signature description fields
- Engine-specific fields
- Event counter fields
- Alert frequency fields
- Status fields

Each signature has the following four basic fields that identify the signature:

- Signature ID
- SubSignature ID
- Alert Severity
- Signature Fidelity Rating

The signature description fields are composed of the following five fields:

- Signature Name
- Alert Notes
- User Comments
- Alarm Traits
- Release

By configuring the following event counter fields, you determine how many instances of the attack traffic are required to cause the signature to generate an alert:

- Event Count
- Event Count Key
- Alert Interval

The possible values for the Event Count Key are as follows:

- Attacker address
- Attacker address and victim port
- Attacker and victim addresses
- Attacker and victim addresses and ports
- Victim address

A powerful new functionality in Cisco IPS version 5.0 is the Meta-Event Generator (MEG). The MEG enables you to create compound signatures based on multiple individual signatures. When defining a meta signature, you need to define the following parameters:

- Signatures that comprise the meta signature
- Number of unique victims needed to trigger the meta signature
- IP addresses or ports used to trigger the meta signature
- Order in which signatures need to be detected (optional)

Cisco IPS version 5.0 enables you to conduct a more thorough analysis of HTTP and FTP by using application policy enforcement. The following signature engines provide the HTTP and FTP application policy enforcement functionality by providing deep-packet inspection for Layer 4 through Layer 7:

- AIC FTP
- AIC HTTP

Tuning signatures involves performing one or more of the following:

- Changing the signature's engine parameters
- Changing the signature's event counter parameters
- Changing the signature's alert frequency parameters

The following tasks are usually not considered tuning a signature:

- Enabling or disabling a signature
- Assigning a severity level
- Assigning a signature action

When creating custom signatures, you need to complete the following tasks:

1. Choose a signature engine.
2. Verify existing functionality.
3. Define signature parameters.
4. Test signature effectiveness.

When choosing which signature engine to use for a new signature, you need to consider several factors about the traffic being detected, such as the following:

- Network protocol
- Target address
- Target port
- Attack type
- Inspection criteria

Q&A

You have two choices for review questions:

- The questions that follow give you a bigger challenge than the exam itself by using an open-ended question format. By reviewing now with this more difficult question format, you can exercise your memory better and prove your conceptual and factual knowledge of this chapter. The answers to these questions are found in the appendix.
- For more practice with exam-like question formats, use the exam engine on the CD-ROM.

1. Which two fields uniquely identify a signature?
2. What does the Signature Fidelity Rating indicate?
3. What does the Alert Severity level indicate?
4. What values can you assign to the Event Count Key field?
5. What does the Event Count Key specify?
6. What is the Meta Event Generator?
7. When configuring a signature with the Meta signature engine, which engine-specific parameters do you need to specify?
8. Explain Application Policy Enforcement and identify which signature engines support this capability.
9. What are some of the checks provided by the AIC HTTP signature engine?
10. Signature tuning involves changing which signature parameters?
11. Signature tuning does not usually involve changing which signature parameters?
12. What are the four high-level steps involved in creating a custom signature?
13. What are the factors that you need to consider when choosing a signature engine for a new signature?
14. What is the difference between adding a new signature and creating a new signature by using the cloning functionality?
15. What regex matches the following patterns: ABXDF, ABXXDF, and ABD?

This chapter covers the following subjects:

- IDS Evasion Techniques
- Tuning the Sensor
- Event Configuration

CHAPTER 8

Sensor Tuning

Attackers are continually trying to find ways to bypass the protection barriers in security mechanisms. Understanding these IDS evasion techniques is important to effectively protect your network using Cisco IPS. Tuning your sensor helps customize its operation to your unique network environment.

Tuning your sensor, a key step to configuring your Cisco IPS, involves several phases. Understanding the global sensor configuration tasks that impact the operation of the sensor enables you to customize the operation of the Cisco IPS software. Configuring the sensor's reassembly options helps minimize the effectiveness of various IDS evasion techniques against systems on your network.

"Do I Know This Already?" Quiz

The purpose of the "Do I Know This Already?" quiz is to help you decide if you really need to read the entire chapter. If you already intend to read the entire chapter, you do not necessarily need to answer these questions now.

The 10-question quiz, derived from the major sections in the "Foundation and Supplemental Topics" portion of the chapter, helps you determine how to spend your limited study time.

Table 8-1 outlines the major topics discussed in this chapter and the "Do I Know This Already?" quiz questions that correspond to those topics.

Table 8-1 *"Do I Know This Already?" Foundation and Supplemental Topics Mapping*

Foundation or Supplemental Topic	Questions Covering This Topic
IDS Evasion Techniques	1, 2
Tuning the Sensor	3–7
Event Configuration	8–10

> **CAUTION** The goal of self-assessment is to gauge your mastery of the topics in this chapter. If you do not know the answer to a question or are only partially sure of the answer, you should mark this question wrong for purposes of the self-assessment. Giving yourself credit for an answer you correctly guess skews your self-assessment results and might provide you with a false sense of security.

1. Which of the following is not an example of an IDS evasion technique?
   a. Sending overlapping fragments
   b. Generating a flood of alarms
   c. Manipulating packet TTL values
   d. Sending attack traffic in an SSH session
   e. Sending attack traffic in a Telnet session

2. Which of the following is not an obfuscation method?
   a. Using control characters
   b. Using hex characters
   c. Using Unicode characters
   d. Using ASCII characters

3. Which of the following parameters is not a global sensor IP log parameter?
   a. Max IP Log Packets
   b. Log Attacker Packets
   c. IP Log Time
   d. Max IP Log Bytes

4. Which of the following values for the Max IP Log Packets field configures your sensor to capture an unlimited number of IP log packets?
   a. 1
   b. –1
   c. 0
   d. 100
   e. You cannot capture an unlimited number of IP log packets

5. Which of the following operating system is not a valid option for the IP Reassemble Mode parameter?
   a. NT
   b. Linux
   c. BSD
   d. Slackware
   e. Solaris

6. Which TCP stream reassembly mode enables the sensor to maintain state even if the sensor captures only half of the TCP stream?
   a. Strict
   b. Asymmetric
   c. Loose
   d. Partial

7. Which TCP stream reassembly parameter is not configured via a specific Normalizer signature?
   a. TCP Session Timeout
   b. TCP Inactive Timeout
   c. TCP Established Timeout
   d. TCP Reassembly Mode

8. Which event parameter is used to calculate the Risk Rating?
   a. Target Value Rating
   b. Event action override
   c. Signature fidelity
   d. Alert severity
   e. Event action

9. Which of the following is not a parameter that you can specify when defining an event action filter?
   a. Risk Rating
   b. Target Value Rating
   c. Actions to Subtract
   d. Stop on Match
   e. Signature Fidelity Rating

10. Which of the following is not a criterion that determines which events an event action filter matches?

    a. Alert severity

    b. Risk Rating

    c. Victim address

    d. Victim port

    e. Attacker address

The answers to the "Do I Know This Already?" quiz are found in the appendix. The suggested choices for your next step are as follows:

- **8 or less overall score**—Read the entire chapter. This includes the "Foundation and Supplemental Topics" and "Foundation Summary" sections and the Q&A section.
- **9 or 10 overall score**—If you want more review on these topics, skip to the "Foundation Summary" section and then go to the Q&A section. Otherwise, move to the next chapter.

Foundation and Supplemental Topics

IDS Evasion Techniques

Attackers are continually trying to find ways to bypass the protection barriers in security mechanisms. Bank robbers are constantly searching for ways to bypass traditional burglar alarms so that they can steal money without being detected. In the same way, attackers are continually trying to find ways to attack your network without being detected. Understanding the following common evasion techniques helps you ensure that these avenues do not create weaknesses in your overall security posture:

- Flooding
- Fragmentation
- Encryption
- Obfuscation
- TTL manipulation

Flooding

One way attackers attempt to bypass your IPS is by flooding the network with intrusive activity. The goal of this flood is to generate thousands of alarms on your IPS console. Then in the middle of this overwhelming volume of alarm traffic, the attacker conducts the real attack. Attackers hope that you will not be able to detect the real attack in the middle of all the bogus attack traffic, or respond to it in a timely manner. Unless your IPS has an efficient mechanism for consolidating this flood of alarm traffic, looking for the real intrusive activity can be similar to looking for a needle in a haystack.

Generating a flood of alarm traffic can also wreak havoc on your sensor's resources. Depending on the attack traffic being flooded, an attacker may attempt to consume all of the memory or CPU processing power on your sensor. If an attacker can consume a large amount of the resources on your sensor with bogus attacks, the sensor may not have enough resources left to detect the actual attack against your network.

Fragmentation

When network packets exceed the maximum size (known as the maximum transmission unit [MTU]), they must be cut into multiple packets in a process known as fragmentation. When the receiving host gets the fragmented packets, it must reassemble the data. Not all hosts perform the reassembly process in the same order. Some operating systems start with the last fragment and work toward the first. Others start at the first fragment and work toward the last. For normal network traffic, the reassembly order does not matter, because the fragments do not overlap. Fragments that do overlap (known as *overwriting fragments*) have different contents and therefore provide varying results depending on the reassembly process used. Attackers can send attacks inside overwriting fragments to try to circumvent network-based IPSs. For example, assume that a packet is divided into the three fragments shown in Figure 8-1. If the fragments are reassembled from first to last, the assembly order is fragment A, fragment B, and fragment C. In this reassembled packet, the last 25 bytes of fragment B are overwritten by the first 25 bytes of fragment C. On the other hand, assembling the packet from last to first results in the last 25 bytes of fragment B overwriting the first 25 bytes of fragment C. This area of overlap is where an attacker will attempt to hide attack traffic. To completely analyze fragmented packets, a network sensor must reassemble the fragments in both orders. Another way to handle this problem is to generate an alarm when overwriting fragments are detected, because overwriting fragments should not occur in normal traffic.

Figure 8-1 *Overlapping Fragments*

Fragment A

Offset: 0	Length: 50
AAAAAAAAAAAAAAAA ... AAAAAAAAAAAAAAAA	

Fragment B

Offset: 50	Length: 50
BBBBBBBBBBBBBBBBB ... BBBBBBBBBBBBBBBBB	

Fragment C

Offset: 75	Length: 100
CCCCCCCCCCCCCCCCC ... CCCCCCCCCCCCCCCCC	

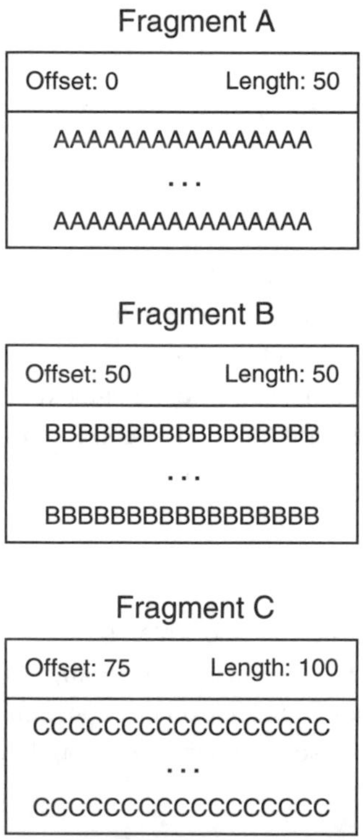

NOTE When two fragments contain data for the same portion of a packet, they are known as *overlapping fragments* because the two segments overlap each other. If the data in the overlapping sections is not the same, the fragments are known as *overwriting fragments*. With overlapping fragments, the reassembly of the packet always produces the same result. With overwriting fragments, however, the reassembly order determines the final contents of the packet.

Reassembling fragmented traffic also requires your sensor to store all the individual fragments. This storage consumes memory resources on your IPS sensors. An attacker may send a flood of incomplete fragmented traffic to cause your sensor to consume memory, hoping to launch the real attack after the sensor is low on system resources.

Encryption

One of the drawbacks of a network-based IPS is that it relies on traffic being sent across the network in clear text. If the data traversing the network is encrypted, your network-based IPS is not capable of examining that data. To protect user credentials and other sensitive information, users and network designers increasingly rely on encrypted sessions. Common examples of encrypted sessions include the following:

- Secure Socket Layer (SSL) connections to secure websites
- Secure Shell Host (SSH) connections to SSH servers
- Site-to-site Virtual Private Network (VPN) tunnels
- Client-to-LAN VPN tunnels

An attacker who establishes an SSL connection to your web server may then attempt to launch an attack against the website through the established secure connection. Since the traffic is encrypted, your network-based IPS will not be able to detect it. A host-based IPS, however, should still be able to detect this attack.

Obfuscation

Most attackers want to be able to attack your network without being detected. To get past your IPS undetected, many attackers attempt to disguise their attack traffic. One way to accomplish this is through obfuscation. The following list shows some of the major obfuscation techniques attackers can use:

- Control characters
- Hex representation
- Unicode representation

Using Control Characters

Control characters have special meaning when processed by the destination host. An example of this is "../" when used in a URL. When translated by the destination server, these characters will cause the server to use the previous directory level in the URL. For instance, suppose you specify the URL http://webserver/the/the/../attack/file.html. The web server will process this URL as if you had typed http://webserver/the/attack/file.html. Your IPS must be able to process control characters to effectively locate attacks that have been obscured with various control characters. Processing the data stream without also processing the control characters will lead to missed attacks and false negatives.

> **NOTE** When your IPS fails to detect an attack that it is programmed to identify, this failure is called a *false negative*. Most signatures are designed to minimize the chances of false negatives since false negatives represent actual attacks against your network that go undetected.

A common attack uses directory traversal to try to break out of the allowed directory tree. Suppose for instance that the web server allows requests only for the web directory beginning with "TopDir," as in http://webserver/TopDir. An attacker may want to retrieve a file outside of this directory tree. Suppose that the attacker sends the following request:

```
http://webserver/TopDir/junk/../../etc/shadow
```

The request appears to be in the approved directory tree, but the request actually becomes http://webserver/etc/shadow after the "../" entries have been processed. Depending on when and how the validity checks are performed on the web server, this request may be able to retrieve the requested file (even though the file is outside of the allowed directory tree).

Using Hex Representation

Most people are familiar with the normal ASCII representation for characters. Another way to represent characters is to use hexadecimal (hex) values. For example, the normal space character can be represented by the hex value 0x20. Many text-based protocols understand either of these ways of representing characters. Your IPS must also understand these multiple representations. Otherwise, your IPS will not be able to effectively analyze data streams when looking for attack traffic.

For instance, the directory "/etc" can be represented in the following two ways (both of which are valid):

- /etc (ASCII)
- 0x2f 0x65 0x74 0x63 (hex)

Using Unicode Representation

Originally, computers used the ASCII character set to represent characters. This encoding scheme, however, allows for only 256 different characters (since each character is represented by a single byte). As computers became more prevalent, 256 characters were insufficient to provide a unique character for every character needed in every platform, program, or language. To overcome this limitation, another encoding mechanism was developed. This mechanism was known as *Unicode*.

Because Unicode uses multiple bytes to represent a single character, it enables a much larger character set than ASCII. This encoding scheme, however, also includes multiple representations for each normal ASCII character (potentially thousands of representations for common characters such as the letter A). Because the destination host interprets each of these representations as the same character, an attacker can send his attack using many different representations in an attempt to sneak the attack past your IPS. If your IPS does not check for these multiple character representations when performing pattern matching, the attacker's traffic can go across your network undetected.

NOTE The Unicode encoding mechanism is documented by RFC 2279, "UTF-8, a transformation format of ISO 10646." This encoding mechanism basically uses multiple bytes to represent each character, whereas ASCII uses a single byte for each character. Different versions of Unicode use a different number of bytes to represent a single character. Across these multiple versions, you end up with potentially thousands of different representations for common characters (such as the letter A). Although each of the representations is different, the destination host will process them all as the letter A. Besides referring to the RFC, you can also find more information on Unicode at http://www.unicode.org.

Sometimes, attackers will also use double encoding to try to evade detection. In this situation, the information is encoded twice. If the IPS does not also decode the information twice, an attacker may be able to avoid detection. Double encoding is probably best explained with an example. Suppose you want to double encode the "?" character. The first encoding simply produces the hexadecimal representation, which is 0x3F. In a URL, hexadecimal values are preceded by a "%", so the first encoding produces "%3F". Now for the second encoding, you simply encode each of the characters again. The "%" produces 0x25. The "3" produces 0x33. The "F" produces 0x46. Adding the "%" before each hexadecimal value produces the final result of %25%33%46.

TTL Manipulation

When traffic traverses your network, each hop (routing device) decreases a packet's Time to Live (TTL) value. If this value reaches 0 before the packet reaches its destination, the packet is discarded, and an Internet Control Message Protocol (ICMP) error message is sent to the originating host.

An attacker can launch an attack that includes bogus packets with smaller TTL values than the packets that make up the real attack. If your network-based sensor sees all of the packets but the target host only sees the actual attack packets, the attacker has managed to distort the information that the sensor uses, causing the sensor to potentially miss the attack (since the bogus packets distort the information being processed by the sensor). Figure 8-2 illustrates this attack. The bogus packets start with a TTL of 3, whereas the real attack packets start with a TTL of 7. The sensor sees both sets of packets, but the target host sees only the real attack packets.

Figure 8-2 *Variable TTL Attack*

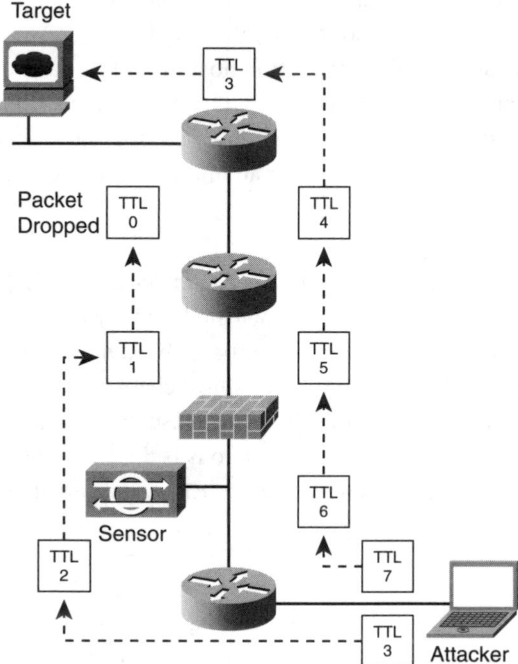

Although this attack is possible, it is very difficult to execute because it requires a detailed understanding of the network topology and location of IPS sensors. Furthermore, many network devices (such as firewalls and inline IP sensors) prevent these types of attacks by normalizing the TCP streams running through them. For instance, the Cisco IPS sensors (running 5.0 software) can monitor a TCP stream (when running in inline mode) and then rewrite the outgoing TTL values to match the lowest TTL value seen on the TCP stream. This prevents an attacker from executing a TTL manipulation attack since either all of the packets will reach the target or none of the packets will (since they all leave the sensor with the same TTL, regardless of what the TTL is on the inbound packet).

Tuning the Sensor

To optimize the effectiveness of your IPS sensors, you need to understand how you can tune the operation of your sensors. Signature tuning impacts the operation of a specific signature, but some tuning operations impact the functionality of the entire sensor. When tuning your sensor, you need to consider the following factors:

- Network topology
- Network address space being monitored
- Statically assigned server addresses

- Dynamic Host Configuration Protocol (DHCP)-assigned addresses
- Operating systems running on your servers
- Applications running on your servers
- Security policy

The location of your sensors determines which traffic they will be monitoring as well as how they can interact with your defined security policy. Tasks involved in tuning your sensors fall into the following three phases based on the length of time that your IPS has been in operation.

- Deployment phase
- Tuning phase
- Maintenance phase

The most drastic changes occur during the deployment phase as you customize the IPS to your unique network environment. Some of the changes that you will likely perform on your sensors during this time include the following:

- Enabling and disabling signatures
- Adjusting alert severities
- Creating basic event action filters

After the initial deployment phase, you can begin more advanced tuning such as changing the sensor's global sensor characteristics. Your tasks for tuning your sensor's global settings fall into the following categories:

- Configuring IP log settings
- Configuring application policy settings
- Configuring reassembly options
- Configuring event processing

After you complete the tuning phase, the maintenance phase involves continually tweaking your IPS to match your ever-changing network environment.

Configuring IP Log Settings

IP logging enables you to capture the actual packets that an attacking host sends to your network. You can then analyze these packets by using a packet analysis tool, such as Ethereal or tcpdump, to determine exactly what an attacker is doing.

You can capture traffic by using IP logging in response to both a signature configured with the IP logging action as well as manually initiated IP logging requests. When logging an attacker's activity, you have the following three options:

- Log attacker packets
- Log pair packets
- Log victim packets

All of these logging options rely on your sensor's IP log settings. These parameters regulate how much information is logged when IP logging is used. You can configure the following IP log settings for your sensor:

- Max IP Log Packets
- IP Log Time
- Max IP Log Bytes

The Max IP Log Packets field indicates the maximum number of packets that your sensor will log in response to a logging action. The default is 0, which allows the sensor to capture an unlimited number of packets for an IP logging action.

The IP Log Time indicates the time period for which traffic will be logged in response to an IP logging action. The default is 30 seconds. You can specify a value from 30 to 300 seconds.

The Max IP Log Bytes limits the maximum number of bytes that an IP logging response will capture. The default is 0 (unlimited). You can specify values from 0 through 2147483647 bytes.

Configuring the sensor's IP log settings by using IDM involves the following steps:

Step 1 Access IDM by entering the following URL in your web browser: **https://***sensor_ip_address*.

Step 2 Click on the **Configuration** icon to display the list of configuration tasks.

Step 3 If the items under the **Signature Definition** category are not displayed, click on the plus sign to the left of **Signature Definition**.

Step 4 Click on **Miscellaneous** to access the Miscellaneous configuration screen. (See Figure 8-3.)

Figure 8-3 *Signature Definition>Miscellaneous Configuration Screen*

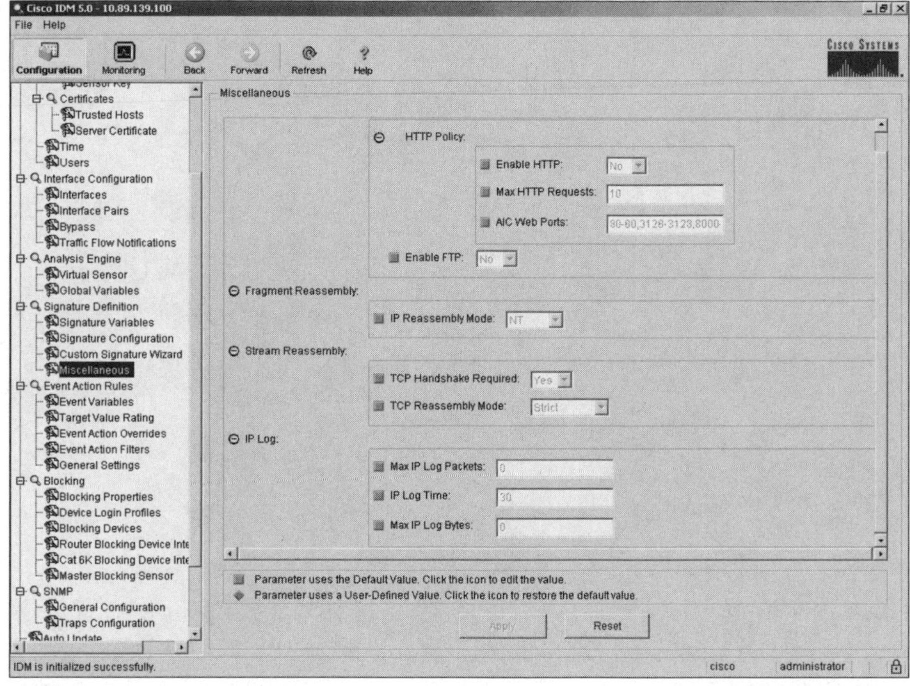

Step 5 (Optional) Click on the square next to **Max IP Log Packets** to override the default value of 0. Then enter the maximum number of packets that you want to capture in conjunction with an IP logging response.

Step 6 (Optional) Click on the square next to **IP Log Time** to override the default value of 30 seconds. Then enter the maximum length of time (in seconds) that you want to capture packets in conjunction with an IP logging response.

Step 7 (Optional) Click on the square next to **Max IP Bytes** to override the default value of 0. Then enter the maximum number of bytes that you want to capture in conjunction with an IP logging response.

Step 8 Click on **Apply** to apply the changes to the sensor's configuration.

> **NOTE** You can also configure the maximum number of IP log files that can be open at any time. This parameter is available on the Analysis Engine>Global Variables configuration screen. (See Figure 8-4.) The default is 20.

Figure 8-4 *Analysis Engine>Global Variables Configuration Screen*

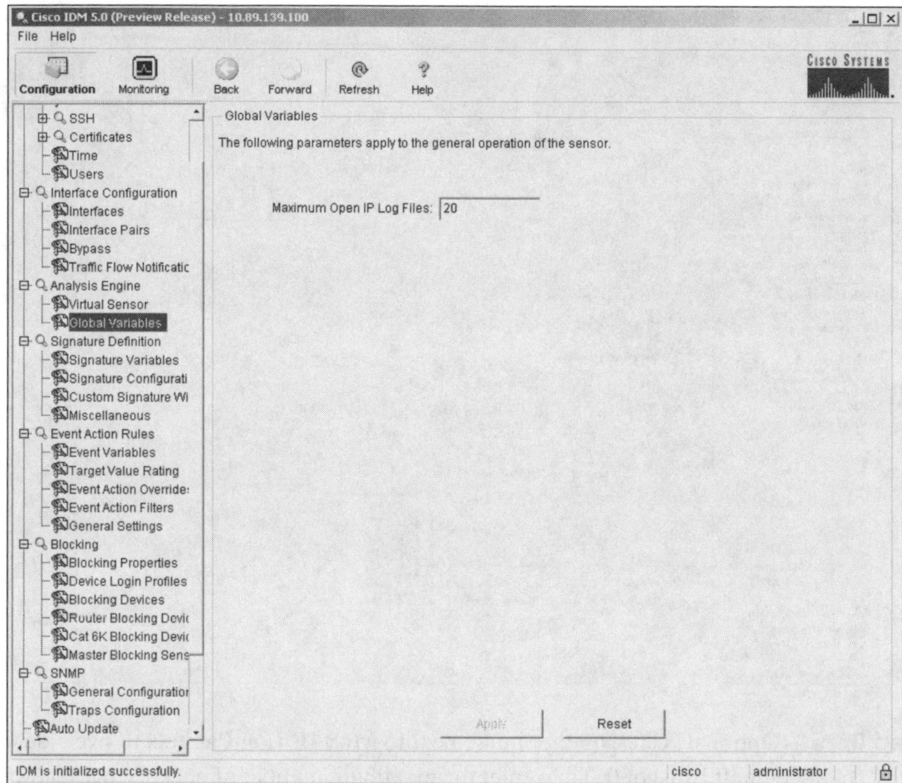

Configuring Application Policy Settings

Cisco IPS 5.0 provides the capability to perform application policy enforcement for both HTTP and FTP. This functionality is provided by the following two signature engines:

- AIC HTTP
- AIC FTP

NOTE The Application Inspection and Control (AIC) engines provide deep-packet inspection from Layer 4 through Layer 7, enabling a much more granular verification of your defined security policy.

To use this functionality, however, you must enable it on your sensor (by default it is disabled). Table 8-2 lists the application policy fields that you can configure on your sensor.

Table 8-2 *Application Policy Sensor Parameters*

Parameter	Description
Enable HTTP	Used to enable and disable the application policy enforcement for HTTP on the sensor (default is No)
Max HTTP Requests	Specifies the maximum number of HTTP requests allowed for each connection (default is 10)
AIC Web Ports	Specifies the destination ports of traffic that you want the sensor to perform HTTP policy inspection on
Enable FTP	Used to enable and disable the application policy enforcement for FTP on the sensor (default is No)

To configure the application policy sensor parameters using IDM, access the Signature Definition>Miscellaneous configuration screen. (See Figure 8-5.) After changing any of the parameters listed in Table 8-2, you simply click on **Apply** to save the changes to the sensor's configuration.

Figure 8-5 *Configuring Application Policy Parameters*

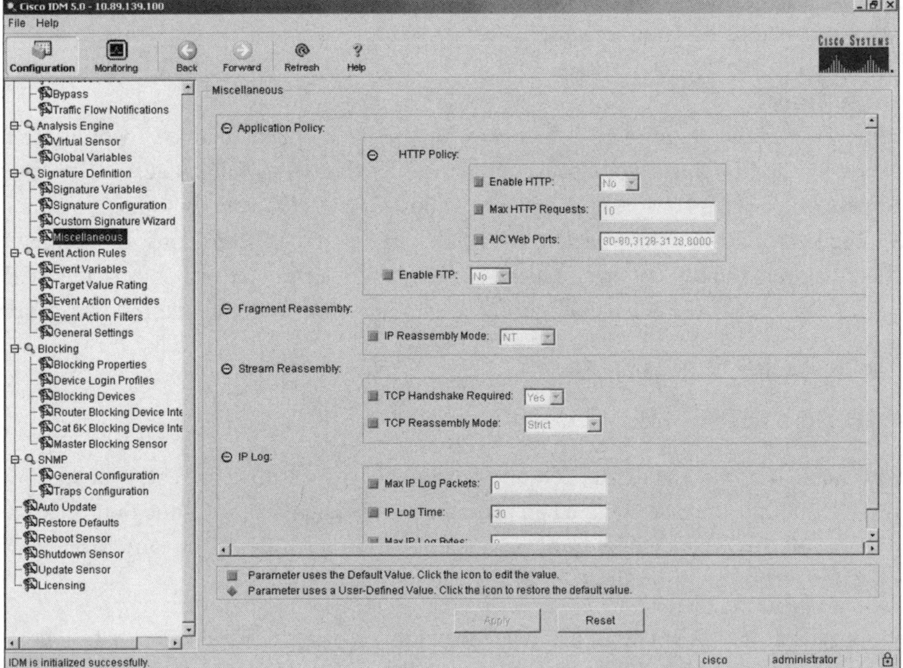

Configuring Reassembly Options

Since many attacks involve fragmented traffic, Cisco IPS provides various reassembly options that impact the manner in which your sensor reassembles traffic when analyzing network traffic. Reassembly options fall into the following two categories:

- Fragment reassembly
- Stream reassembly

Fragment Reassembly

Different operating systems reassemble IP fragmented packets in slightly different ways. You can use the IP Reassemble Mode parameter to configure your sensor to reassemble IP fragmented traffic the same way as one of the following operating systems:

- NT (default)
- Solaris
- Linux
- BSD

When you configure this parameter, it applies to all of the packets processed by your sensor. Therefore, you probably want to set it to an operating system that is representative of the greatest number of systems on your network.

Stream Reassembly

Normal TCP traffic begins with a three-way handshake and ends with a FIN or an RST packet (a packet with the FIN flag set or a packet with the RST flag set). Many attackers, however, will flood your network with traffic that appears to be valid TCP attack traffic, with the intent to cause your IPS to generate alarms. This attack traffic is not part of valid TCP sessions. By tuning your sensor's TCP stream reassembly options, you can control how your sensor responds to the TCP traffic that traverses your network. When configuring stream reassembly, define the following parameters:

- TCP Handshake Required
- TCP Reassemble Mode

If you enable the TCP Handshake Required parameter (by setting it to Yes), your sensor will analyze only TCP streams that start with a complete three-way handshake. Although this can reduce the number of alarms generated by traffic that is not part of a valid TCP stream, it can also potentially cause your sensor to miss valid attacks against your network.

Each IP packet in a TCP stream has sequence numbers that enable the destination host to put the packets into the correct order and identify missing packets. You can choose one of the following three TCP reassembly modes, depending on your network environment:

- Strict
- Loose
- Asymmetric

The *strict* TCP stream reassembly causes your sensor to ignore streams that are missing packets (based on the sequence numbers). Once a gap (a missing packet in the sequence) in a TCP session is detected, the sensor stops processing data for the TCP stream. Strict reassembly mode is the most accurate configuration since the analysis is performed only on complete TCP streams. The drawback is that if the sensor drops any packets in the stream, none of the traffic (for that TCP connection) after the dropped packet is analyzed. This can happen if the traffic load on the sensor exceeds its maximum processing capacity, such as in a burst of traffic.

The *loose* TCP stream reassembly attempts to place the packets collected during a specific period of time in the correct sequence, but it still processes the packets if missing packets never arrive. Since it allows gaps in the sequence numbers received for the TCP session, this option can lead to false positives since the TCP stream is incomplete. This option, however, guarantees that the sensor will attempt to analyze all the traffic that it captures for a TCP connection, regardless of any dropped packets within the TCP session.

Asymmetric mode is useful for situations in which your sensor does not have access to all the traffic for the TCP connections because of asymmetric routing on your network. Asymmetric stream reassembly mode enables your sensor to maintain state for the signatures that do not require the traffic going in both directions to operate effectively. Asymmetric mode, however, is weaker from a security perspective because it examines only the traffic flowing in one direction on a TCP stream. Only by examining both sides of the TCP conversation can you perform a thorough security analysis on the TCP stream.

NOTE Most of the TCP timeout parameters and other TCP stream reassembly settings are handled by the Normalizer engine in Cisco IPS version 5.0. So to change parameters such as the following, you need to change the corresponding signature that enforces the parameter using the Normalizer signature engine:

- TCP Established Timeout
- TCP Embryonic Timeout
- TCP Max Queue Size

Furthermore, some of Normalizer-based signatures have default mandatory behaviors that will occur even if the signature is disabled, such as in "TCP Drop – Segment out of window" (SigID 1330, Sub SigID 18). This signature will enforce a default TCP Embryonic Timeout of 30 even when the signature is disabled. Another thing to watch for is that some of the Normalizer signatures have a default action of Deny (when running inline mode), but they are not configured to generate an alert. This can cause packets to be dropped without an alert, making debugging more difficult.

CAUTION If you deploy a sensor in inline mode in an environment with asymmetric routing, the mandatory behaviors defined in the Normalizer signatures will break the operation of the network.

NOTE Asymmetric routing happens when traffic going between two systems takes multiple paths to reach the systems. When monitoring traffic between systems in an asymmetric routing environment, the monitoring system sees only the traffic flowing in one direction (between the two systems being monitored). Capturing traffic flowing in only one direction (on the TCP stream) makes regular TCP stream reassembly impossible.

Configuring Reassembly Options

To configure reassembly options using IDM, you need to perform the following steps:

Step 1 Access IDM by entering the following URL in your web browser: **https://***sensor_ip_address*.

Step 2 Click on the **Configuration** icon to display the list of configuration tasks.

Step 3 If the items under the **Signature Definition** category are not displayed, click on the plus sign to the left of **Signature Definition**.

Step 4 Click on **Miscellaneous** to access the Miscellaneous configuration screen.

Step 5 Configure the fragment reassembly parameters.

Step 6 Configure the stream reassembly parameters.

Step 7 Click on **Apply** to apply the changes to the sensor's configuration.

NOTE The parameters accessible via the Miscellaneous configuration screen represent the fragment and TCP stream reassembly parameters that you can control globally. The other parameters related to fragment and TCP stream reassembly are specified by certain signatures that use the Normalizer signature engine. These parameters must be configured by editing the appropriate signature.

Event Configuration

Whenever a signature triggers, your sensor generates an event. In addition to configuring signature parameters, you can also configure event parameters on your sensor. These event parameters fall into the following categories:

- Event variables
- Target Value Rating

- Event action override
- Event action filters

Event Variables

Sometimes, you may want to use the same value (such as an address range) in multiple event filters. Event variables enable you to configure values that are used in multiple event filters. The advantage of using event variables instead of typing the actual values is that you can change the settings of the event variables so that all the filters that use those settings are automatically changed.

Suppose that you have an engineering network segment (10.20.10.0/24) that contains only Linux-based systems. To reduce your monitoring duties, you may not want to see alerts based on Microsoft Windows-based attacks against these engineering systems. By configuring an event variable that defines this address range, you can use this variable in multiple event filters to eliminate Windows-based alerts against systems in this IP address range.

Although this approach reduces your monitoring duties, it prevents you from detecting valid attacks if someone happens to place a Windows system on the network (either temporarily or permanently). Therefore, before filtering alerts for a specific operating system, you need to carefully analyze your current network configuration and the likelihood that the operating systems in use will change.

You use the following steps to configure an event variable named ENG-NETWORK that identifies the 10.20.10.0/24 network segment using IDM:

Step 1 Access IDM by entering the following URL in your web browser: **https://***sensor_ip_address*.

Step 2 Click on the **Configuration** icon to display the list of configuration tasks.

Step 3 If the items under the **Event Action Rules** category are not displayed, click on the plus sign to the left of **Event Action Rules**.

Step 4 Click on **Event Variables** to access the Event Variables screen. (See Figure 8-6.) This screen displays the currently configured event variables.

Step 5 Click on **Add** to access the Add Event Variable popup window. (See Figure 8-7.)

Figure 8-6 *Event Variables Configuration Screen*

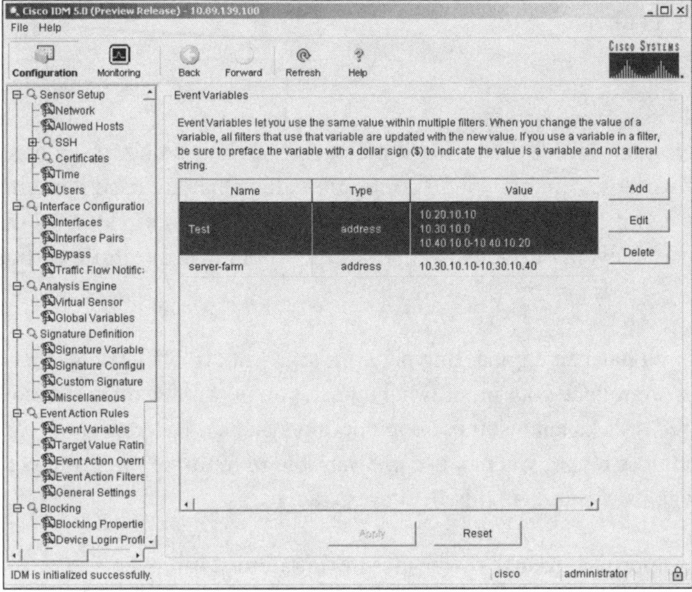

Figure 8-7 *Add Event Variable Popup Window*

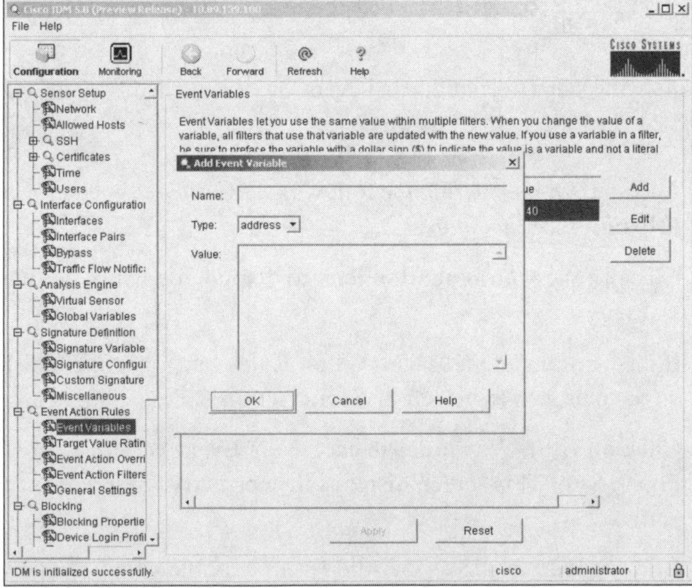

Step 6 Enter **ENG-NETWORK** in the **Name** field.

Step 7 Enter **10.20.10.0-10.20.10.255** in the **Value** field.

Step 8 Click on **OK** to save the new event variable.

Step 9 Click on **Apply** to save your changes to the sensor's configuration.

> **NOTE** When defining the addresses for an event variable, you can separate individual addresses with commas, or you can specify address ranges by separating the starting address and ending address with a hyphen.

Target Value Rating

The Target Value Rating enables you to assign an asset value rating to specific IP addresses on your network. This rating is used to calculate the Risk Rating for attacks against those systems. The target values that you can assign to an IP address or range of IP addresses are as follows:

- Mission Critical
- High
- Medium
- Low
- No Value

The process of assigning values to systems is subjective; the important factor to remember is that the asset values enable you prioritize the devices on your network based on their perceived value. For instance, you may use the following classification model:

- Mission Critical—Server systems
- High—Infrastructure systems
- Medium—IP Phones
- Low—Desktops and laptops
- No Value—Printers

Event Action Override

Besides the actions you can configure a signature to perform, you can also configure an event action override for each Cisco IPS response action. This override causes actions to be added to signatures if the Risk Rating of the event matches the override definition. Each override defines a minimum and maximum Risk Rating. If a signature generates an alert that falls within the defined Risk Rating range, the specific response action is added to the alert event.

For instance, suppose you want the sensor to use the Deny Connection Inline action whenever a signature generates an event with a Risk Rating greater than 90. The following steps define the event action override for the specified action:

Step 1 Access IDM by entering the following URL in your web browser: **https://***sensor_ip_address*.

Step 2 Click on the **Configuration** icon to display the list of configuration tasks.

Step 3 If the items under the **Event Action Rules** category are not displayed, click on the plus sign to the left of **Event Action Rules**.

Step 4 Click on **Event Action Override** to access the Event Action Overrides screen. (See Figure 8-8.) This screen displays the currently configured action overrides.

Figure 8-8 *Event Action Overrides Configuration Screen*

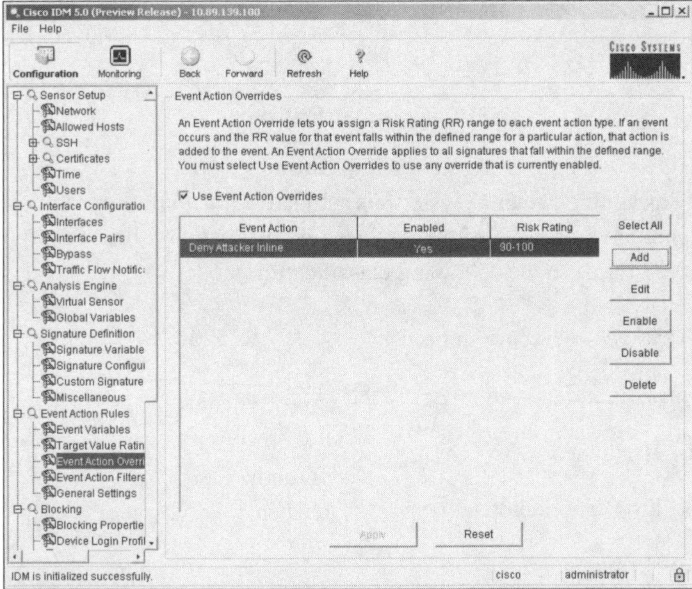

Step 5 Click on **Add** to access the Add Event Action Override popup window. (See Figure 8-9.)

Step 6 Select the **Deny Connection Inline** action from the **Event Action** pull-down menu.

Step 7 Verify that the **Enabled** radio box is selected.

Figure 8-9 *Add Event Action Override Popup Window*

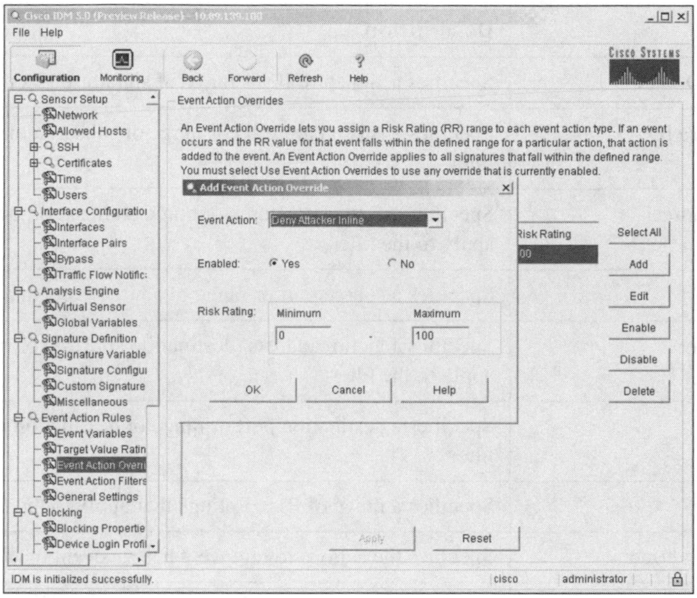

Step 8 Enter **90** for the **Minimum Risk Rating**.

Step 9 Verify that the **Maximum Risk Rating** is set to **100**.

Step 10 Click on **OK** to save the action override.

Step 11 Click on **Apply** to save your changes to the sensor's configuration.

Event Action Filters

Event action filters enable you to configure your sensor to remove actions from events based on one or more of the criteria shown in Table 8-3. Event filter tasks can be very simple, such as removing the alert action for events based on a single signature ID and victim address. They can also be very complex, such as removing the Request SNMP Trap action when an event matches the following criteria:

- Attacker address is 10.89.10.102
- Attacker port is 200
- Victim address is 10.10.200.10
- Victim port is 53
- Event Risk Rating is between 50 and 75

Table 8-3 *Event Action Filter Criteria*

Parameter	Description
Signature ID	Specifies a signature ID or range of signature IDs that apply to the filter
SubSignature ID	Specifies a subsignature ID or range of subsignature IDs that apply to the filter
Attacker Address	Specifies an attacker address (source address) or range of addresses that apply to the filter
Attacker Port	Specifies a source port or range of source ports that apply to the filter
Victim Address	Specifies a victim address (destination address) or range of addresses that apply to the filter
Victim Port	Specifies a destination port or range of destination ports that apply to the filter
Risk Rating	Specifies a range of Risk Ratings that apply to the filter
Actions to Subtract	Specifies the actions to remove when an event matches the event filter
Stop on Match	Specifies whether other event filters are processed after an event filter matches an event False: Continue processing event filters True: Stop processing when a match is found

Configuring event action filters is better understood by going through an actual example. Suppose that you have tuned the built-in signature 4612, "Cisco IP Phone TFTP Config Retrieve," so that besides generating an alert, it also drops the offending traffic by using the inline deny packet action. This modification prevents systems from retrieving IP phone configuration files from your TFTP server. Your IP phones, however, still need to download configuration files from the TFTP server. Therefore, you should implement an event action filter to remove the inline packet deny action when the traffic comes from your IP phone network segment. Assuming that the IP phone segment is 10.10.20.0/24, the steps to configure the appropriate event action filter are as follows:

Step 1 Access IDM by entering the following URL in your web browser: **https://***sensor_ip_address*.

Step 2 Click on the **Configuration** icon to display the list of configuration tasks.

Step 3 If the items under the **Event Action Rules** category are not displayed, click on the plus sign to the left of **Event Action Rules**.

Step 4 Click on **Event Action Filters** to access the Event Action Filters configuration screen. (See Figure 8-10.) This screen displays the currently configured event action filters.

Figure 8-10 *Event Action Filters Configuration Screen*

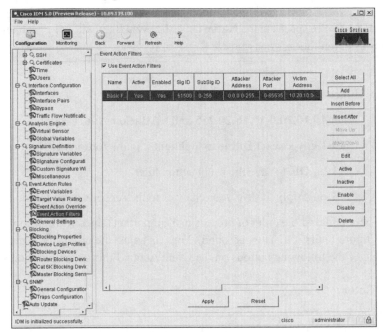

Step 5 Click on **Add** to access the Add Event Action Filter popup window to add a new event action filter. (See Figure 8-11.)

Figure 8-11 *Add Event Action Filter Popup Window*

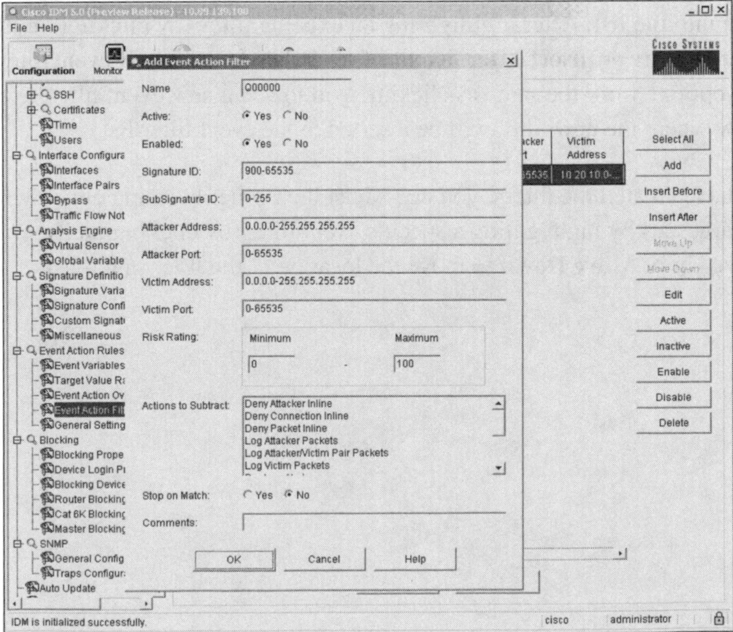

Step 6 Enter **PhoneConfigTFTP** in the **Name** field.

> **NOTE** If you place spaces in the **Name** field, the event filter will have problems being added to the sensor's configuration when you click on **Apply**.

Step 7 Enter **4612** in the **Signature ID** field.

Step 8 Enter **10.10.20.0-10.10.20.255** in the **Attacker Address** field.

Step 9 Click **Deny Packet Inline** to highlight it in the **Actions to Subtract** field.

Step 10 Click on **OK** to save the event action filter.

Step 11 Click on **Apply** to save your changes to the sensor's configuration.

With event action filters, the order of processing is important (since you can configure a filter to stop processing future filters if a match is found). You can adjust the order of the event action filters by using one of the following buttons on the Event Action Filters configuration screen:

- Insert Before
- Insert After
- Move Down
- Move Up

Using either **Insert Before** or **Insert After** enables you to decide where new event action filters will be inserted into the list. After highlighting an existing filter (by clicking on it), you can click on either **Insert Before** or **Insert After** to indicate exactly where the new event filter should be inserted. These two options work the same as clicking **Add** to add a new event filter, except that they can also specify where the new filter will be inserted in the event filter list.

Once you have created the filters, you can adjust their order by using either **Move Up** or **Move Down**. Again, start by highlighting a specific event filter (by clicking on it). Then you can click on either **Move Up** or **Move Down** to move the location of the filter in the list.

Foundation Summary

Attackers are continually trying to find ways to bypass the protection barriers in security mechanisms. Understanding the following common IDS evasion techniques helps you ensure that these avenues do not create weaknesses in your overall security posture:

- Flooding
- Fragmentation
- Encryption
- Obfuscation
- TTL manipulation

The following list shows some of the major obfuscation techniques:

- Using control characters
- Using hex representation
- Using Unicode representation

To optimize the effectiveness of your IPS sensors, you need to understand how you can tune the operation of your sensors. When tuning your sensor, you need to consider the following factors:

- Network topology
- Network address space being monitored
- Statically assigned server addresses
- DHCP-assigned addresses
- Operating systems running on your servers
- Applications running on your servers
- Security policy

Tasks involved in tuning your sensors fall into the following three phases based on the length of time that your IPS has been in operation.

- Deployment phase
- Tuning phase
- Maintenance phase

Some of the changes you will likely perform during the deployment phase include the following:

- Enabling and disabling signatures
- Adjusting alert severities
- Creating basic event action filters

Tasks involved in tuning your sensor's global settings fall into the following categories:

- Configuring IP log settings
- Configuring application policy settings
- Configuring reassembly options
- Configuring event processing

You can configure the following IP log settings for your sensor:

- Max IP Log Packets
- IP Log Time
- Max IP Log Bytes
- Maximum Open IP Log Files

Cisco IPS 5.0 provides the capability to perform application policy enforcement for both HTTP and FTP. This functionality is provided by the following two signature engines:

- AIC HTTP
- AIC FTP

To use this functionality, however, you must enable it on your sensor (by default it is disabled).

Reassembly options fall into the following two categories:

- Fragment reassembly
- Stream reassembly

When configuring stream reassembly, you define the following parameters:

- TCP Handshake Required
- TCP Reassemble Mode

Whenever a signature triggers, your sensor generates an alert and, potentially, an event. Besides configuring your signature parameters, you can also configure event parameters on your sensor. These event parameters fall into the following categories:

- Event variables
- Target Value Rating
- Event action override
- Event action filters

The Target Value Rating enables you to assign an asset value rating to specific IP addresses on your network. The target values that you can assign to an IP address or range of IP addresses are as follows:

- Mission Critical
- High
- Medium
- Low
- No Value

In addition to configuring signature actions, you can configure an event action override for each Cisco IPS response action. This override causes actions to be added to signatures if the Risk Rating of the event matches the override definition.

Event action filters enable you to configure your sensor to remove actions from events based on one or more of the following criteria:

- Signature ID
- Subsignature ID
- Attacker address
- Attacker port
- Victim address
- Victim port
- Risk Rating

Q&A

You have two choices for review questions:

- The questions that follow give you a bigger challenge than the exam itself by using an open-ended question format. By reviewing now with this more difficult question format, you can exercise your memory better and prove your conceptual and factual knowledge of this chapter. The answers to these questions are found in the appendix.
- For more practice with exam-like question formats, use the exam engine on the CD-ROM.

1. What are the IDS evasion techniques?
2. What is the Target Value Rating?
3. What is event action override?
4. How can fragmentation be used to evade detection?
5. Which common obfuscation techniques are used by attackers?
6. What are some of the factors to consider when tuning your IPS sensors?
7. What are the global IP log sensor parameters?
8. What does it mean when the Max IP Log Bytes is configured to 0?
9. What must you do to use the signatures that are based on the AIC HTTP signature engine?
10. When configuring fragment reassembly on your sensor, which operating systems can you use when specifying the IP reassembly mode?
11. What is the difference between strict stream reassembly and loose stream reassembly?
12. What is an event action filter?
13. Which parameters can you specify when defining an event action filter?
14. What is the purpose of the Stop on Match parameter in the context of configuring an event action filter?
15. Why is the order of event action filters important?

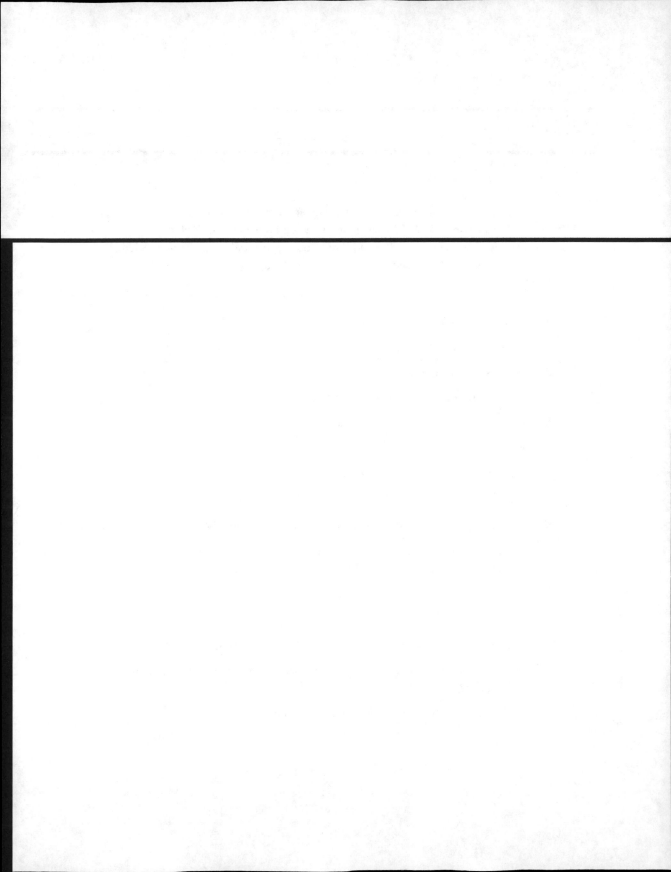

Part III: Cisco IPS Response Configuration

This chapter covers the following subjects:

- Cisco IPS response overview
- Inline actions
- Logging actions
- IP blocking
- Configuring IP blocking
- Manual blocking
- TCP reset

CHAPTER 9

Cisco IPS Response Configuration

The heart of the Cisco IPS is the signatures that the sensor uses to identify intrusive traffic on your network. Each signature can be configured to perform numerous actions whenever the signature fires. Configuring signature responses is vital to efficiently using your Cisco IPS sensors to protect your network.

Besides detecting specific traffic on your network, you can configure numerous actions that the sensor will perform when a signature triggers. These actions vary from simply generating an alert to logging network traffic to denying traffic from a specific IP address for a configured period of time. To effectively protect your network, you need to customize the signature actions to your specific network environment.

"Do I Know This Already?" Quiz

The purpose of the "Do I Know This Already?" quiz is to help you decide if you need to read the entire chapter. If you already intend to read the entire chapter, you do not necessarily need to answer these questions now.

The 10-question quiz, derived from the major sections in the "Foundation and Supplemental Topics" portion of the chapter, helps you determine how to spend your limited study time.

Table 9-1 outlines the major topics discussed in this chapter and the "Do I Know This Already?" quiz questions that correspond to those topics.

Table 9-1 *"Do I Know This Already?" Foundation and Supplemental Topics Mapping*

Foundation or Supplemental Topic	Questions Covering This Topic
Cisco IPS Response Overview	3
Inline Actions	1, 7
Logging Actions	2, 6
IP Blocking	4, 5, 9

continues

Table 9-1 *"Do I Know This Already?" Foundation and Supplemental Topics Mapping (Continued)*

Foundation or Supplemental Topic	Questions Covering This Topic
Configuring IP Blocking	8, 10
Manual Blocking	-
TCP Reset	-

CAUTION The goal of self-assessment is to gauge your mastery of the topics in this chapter. If you do not know the answer to a question or are only partially sure of the answer, you should mark this question wrong for purposes of the self-assessment. Giving yourself credit for an answer you correctly guess skews your self-assessment results and might provide you with a false sense of security.

1. The Deny Connection Inline action stops traffic that matches which of the following descriptions (where "source" and "destination" refer to the traffic that caused the signature to trigger)?
   a. Source IP address and destination port
   b. Source IP address and destination IP address
   c. Source IP address, destination IP addresses, source port, and destination port
   d. Source IP address, destination IP address, and destination port
2. When you manually configure IP logging, which parameter is not a valid parameter that you can configure with IDM?
   a. Maximum Number of Packets
   b. Duration (in seconds)
   c. Maximum Number of Bytes
   d. All of these answers are valid parameters
3. Which of the following is not a valid Cisco IPS response action?
   a. Request SNMP Trap
   b. Produce Verbose Alert
   c. Modify Packet Inline
   d. Deny Packet Inline
   e. Request Block Packet

4. What is a major difference between Access Control Lists (ACLs) and VLAN Access Control Lists (VACLs)?

a. ACLs are available only on routers.

b. ACLs apply to traffic either entering or leaving an interface.

c. ACLs are directionless.

d. VACLs are directionless.

e. VACLs apply to traffic either entering or leaving an interface.

5. When is a Master Blocking Sensor necessary?

a. When your managed devices are PIX™ Firewalls

b. When one sensor manages multiple managed devices

c. When multiple sensors are configured for IP blocking

d. When one sensor manages both PIX Firewalls and Cisco IOS® routers

6. What is the default logging duration when you manually configure IP logging?

a. 10 minutes

b. 15 minutes

c. 20 minutes

d. 30 minutes

e. 60 minutes

7. Which of the following is true about the Deny Attacker Duration parameter?

a. It is measured in minutes.

b. The default is 90 minutes.

c. The default is 3600 seconds.

d. It is measured in minutes, and the default is 90 minutes.

8. By default, which of the following is true about configuring never-block addresses?

a. You must configure a never-block address to prevent the sensor from being blocked.

b. The sensor can never block itself.

c. By default, the sensor will not block its own address.

9. Which of the following is not a consideration for implementing IP blocking?
   a. Antispoofing mechanisms
   b. Critical hosts
   c. Blocking duration
   d. Interface ACL requirements
   e. Frequency of attack traffic
10. By default, what is the maximum number of entries allowed in the blocking ACL?
   a. 100
   b. 200
   c. 250
   d. 500
   e. 1000

The answers to the "Do I Know This Already?" quiz are found in the appendix. The suggested choices for your next step are as follows:

- **8 or less overall score**—Read the entire chapter, including the "Foundation and Supplemental Topics," "Foundation Summary," and Q&A sections.
- **9 or 10 overall score**—If you want more review on these topics, skip to the "Foundation Summary" section and then go to the Q&A section. Otherwise, move to the next chapter.

Foundation and Supplemental Topics

Cisco IPS Response Overview

Beginning with Cisco IPS version 5.0, your signature response options increased because of the inline response options. Now when you configure your signatures, you can choose one or more of the following responses for a triggered signature:

- Deny Attacker Inline
- Deny Connection Inline
- Deny Packet Inline
- Log Attacker Packets
- Log Pair Packets
- Log Victim Packets
- Modify Packet Inline
- Produce Alert
- Produce Verbose Alert
- Request Block Connection
- Request Block Host
- Request SNMP Trap
- Reset TCP Connection

NOTE The Modify Packet Inline action was added to support the Normalizer signature engine. For more information on using the Normalizer signature engine, refer to Chapter 6, "Cisco IPS Signature Engines."

The standard response to a triggered signature is the generation of an alert (alarm). This chapter focuses on other actions that your IPS signatures can invoke.

Inline Actions

By adding inline functionality, Cisco IPS was able to incorporate the following signature actions:

- Deny Packet Inline
- Deny Connection Inline
- Deny Attacker Inline

These actions impact even the initial traffic from an attacking system. Therefore, they can be used to prevent attack traffic from reaching the target system or network. To use these actions, however, you must configure your sensor using inline mode.

Deny Packet Inline

Configuring a signature with the Deny Packet Inline action causes your sensor to drop any packets that match the signature's parameters. This action is useful for preventing specific attack traffic while allowing all other traffic to continue to travel through the network.

Deny Connection Inline

In some situations, you need to deny all of the traffic for an entire connection (not just the initial attack traffic). Configuring a signature with the Deny Connection Inline action causes the sensor to drop all traffic for the connection that triggered the signature. A connection is defined as all traffic in which the following fields match the traffic that triggered the signature:

- Source IP Address
- Source Port
- Destination IP Address
- Destination Port

The traffic for the connection is denied for the length of time specified by the Deny Attacker Duration parameter. After the configured amount of time has passed, the traffic matching the connection's parameters is no longer denied.

Deny Attacker Inline

Configuring a signature with the Deny Attacker Inline action causes the sensor to drop all packets from the attacker's IP address. This action prevents the entry of all traffic originating from the attacker's IP address, not just traffic that matches the initial connection that triggered the signature. Again, the Deny Attacker Duration parameter determines for how long the traffic from the attacker's IP address is denied.

Configuring Deny Attacker Duration Parameter

When using inline actions, you need to define the length of time that the sensor continues to deny the traffic. This length of time (measured in seconds) is defined by the Deny Attacker Duration parameter. You can also configure the maximum number of attackers that the sensor will deny at one time by using the Maximum Denied Attackers field.

To configure both of these parameters, perform the following steps:

Step 1 Access IPS Device Manager (IDM) by entering the following URL in your web browser: **https://***sensor_ip_address*.

Step 2 Click on the **Configuration** icon to display the list of configuration tasks.

Step 3 If the items under the **Event Action Rules** category are not displayed, click on the plus sign to the left of **Event Action Rules**.

Step 4 Click on **General Settings** to access the General Settings configuration screen. (See Figure 9-1.)

Figure 9-1 *IDM General Settings Configuration Screen*

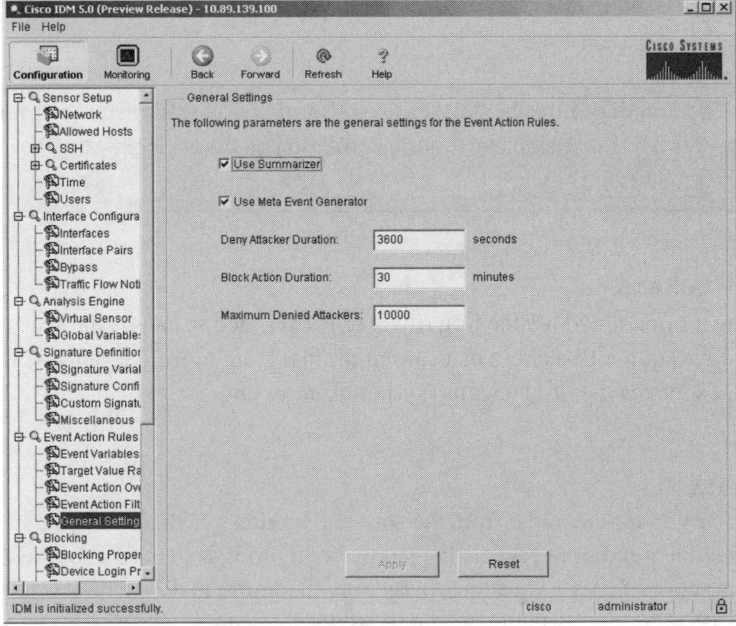

Step 5 Enter the length of time (in seconds) that the denied action will remain active by entering a value in the **Deny Attacker Duration** field. (The default is 3600 seconds, or 1 hour.)

Step 6 Enter the maximum number of attackers that the sensor will attempt to deny by entering a value in the **Maximum Denied Attackers** field. (The default is 10,000.)

Step 7 Click on **Apply** to apply the changes to the sensor's configuration.

Logging Actions

IP logging enables you to capture the actual packets that an attacking host is sending to your network. These packets are stored on the sensor, either on the hard drive or in memory (for sensors without hard drives). You can then analyze these packets by using a packet analysis tool, such as Ethereal, to determine exactly what an attacker is doing.

You can capture traffic by using IP logging in response to both a signature configured with the IP logging action as well as a manually initiated IP logging request. When logging an attacker's activity, you have the following three options:

- Log Attacker Packets
- Log Pair Packets
- Log Victim Packets

> **NOTE** The length of time that the sensor logs traffic after a signature is triggered depends on the values of the IP Log parameters. For information on how to configure these parameters, refer to Chapter 8, "Sensor Tuning."

Log Attacker Packets

Configuring a signature to use the Log Attacker Packets action causes the sensor to log (or capture) traffic from the source IP address that caused the signature to trigger. This will show you all the systems and services that the attacking system is accessing.

Log Pair Packets

Instead of logging all the traffic from the source IP address of the traffic that triggers a signature, you can limit the number of packets logged by configuring a signature for the Log Pair Packets action. This action causes a signature to log only the traffic that matches both the source and destination IP addresses that initially triggered the signature.

Log Victim Packets

The third logging option is Log Victim Packets. This action causes the sensor to log all the packets going to the victim (destination) IP address. This option is useful for monitoring the target system in situations where the attack may be coming from multiple IP addresses. By logging traffic to the target system, you can identify all the traffic going to the victim machine.

Manual IP Logging

Sometimes you may want to capture the traffic from a specific source address. When initiating manual logging, you can specify the amount of traffic to capture by using one of the following characteristics:

- Duration (in minutes)
- Number of packets
- Number of bytes

To manually initiate IP logging using IDM, perform the following steps:

Step 1 Access IDM by entering the following URL in your web browser: **https://** *sensor_ip_address*.

Step 2 Click on the **Monitoring** icon to display the list of monitoring tasks.

Step 3 Click on **IP Logging** to access the IP Logging monitoring screen. (See Figure 9-2.) This screen displays the current list of systems being logged.

Figure 9-2 *IDM IP Logging Monitoring Screen*

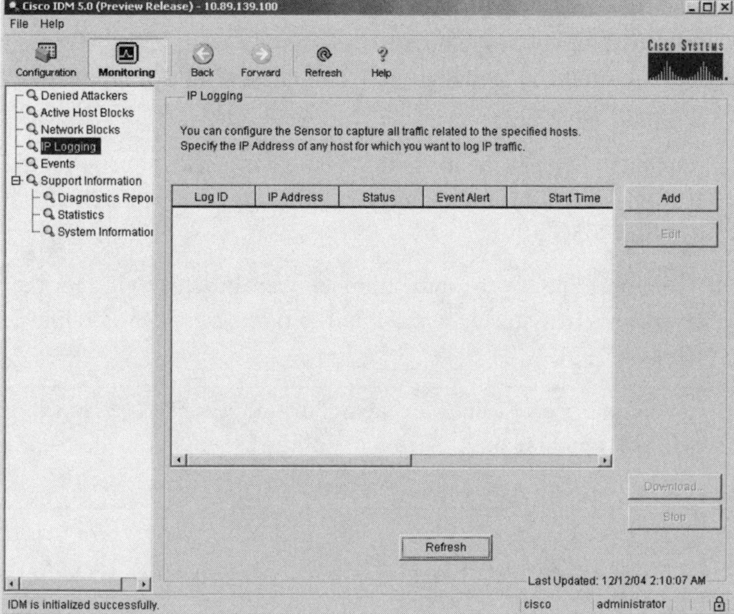

Step 4 Click on **Add** to manually add an IP address to the list of systems being logged. This displays the Add IP Logging popup window. (See Figure 9-3.)

Figure 9-3 *Add IP Logging Popup Window*

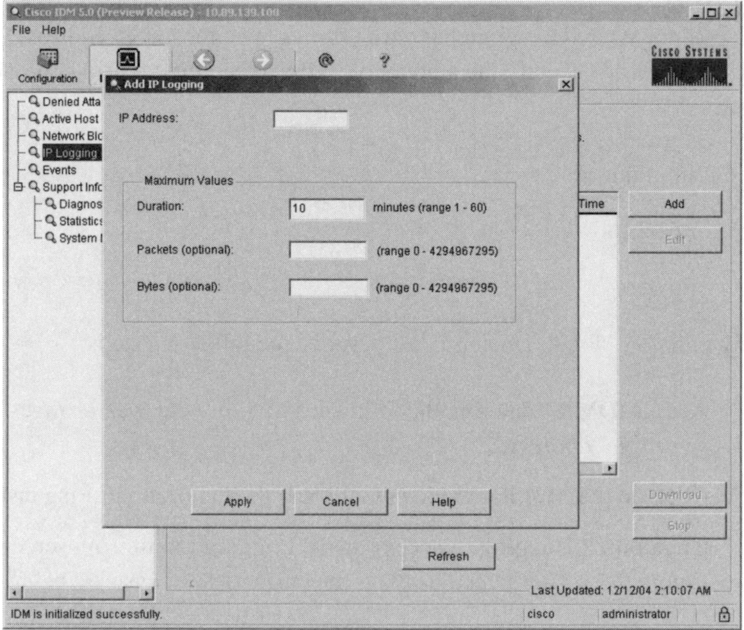

Step 5 Enter the IP address of the host to log in the **IP Address** field.

Step 6 Enter the length of the duration in minutes by entering a value in the Duration field. (The default is 10 minutes, with the valid range being 1 through 60).

Step 7 (Optional) Specify the maximum number of packets to log for the specified IP address by entering a value in the Packets field (valid range 0 to 4294967295).

Step 8 (Optional) Specify the maximum number of bytes to log for the specified IP address by entering a value in the Bytes field (valid range 0 to 4294967295).

> **NOTE** If you do not specify values for the optional fields (**Packets** and **Bytes**), the manually initiated logging will continue until the amount of time specified by the Duration parameter is reached.

Step 9 Click on **Apply** to start logging traffic for the specified IP address.

IP Blocking

IP blocking enables you to halt future traffic from an attacking host for a specified period of time, thereby limiting the attacker's access to your network. You have the following two options with respect to IP blocking:

- Request Block Host
- Request Block Connection

The Request Block Host action causes the sensor to block all traffic from the host that triggered the signature. This is very effective at protecting your network because all the traffic from the attacking system is prevented from entering your network. The drawback is that if the alarm is a false positive, you will cause a denial of service (DoS) attack until you have time to analyze the situation and remove the block (or until it expires automatically). The same situation applies if the attacker is able to spoof the source address in the attack traffic, such as with User Datagram Protocol (UDP) traffic since it is connectionless. In that case, the attack traffic can be used to arbitrarily block access to various systems by spoofing their IP addresses.

The Request Block Connection action, however, blocks only traffic (from the host that triggered the signature) to the destination port of the traffic that triggered the signature. If an attacker targets a specific service on systems across your network, Request Block Connection would prevent the attack from proceeding. The attacker would still be able to send traffic to other services or ports (any destination port except the destination port that originally triggered the alarm). In a false positive situation, you deny only a single service (port number) on the normal user's system. This is still a DoS situation but is not as severe as denying all traffic from the user.

You configure IP blocking on an individual-signature basis. This section focuses on explaining the following topics:

- IP blocking devices
- Blocking guidelines
- Blocking process
- Access Control List (ACL) considerations

Before broaching these topics, you may benefit from reviewing some of the terminology used in conjunction with IP blocking.

IP Blocking Definitions

Table 9-2 lists the terms commonly used in conjunction with IP blocking.

Table 9-2 *IP Blocking Common Terms*

Term	Definition
Active ACL	The dynamically created Access Control Lists (ACL) that the sensor applies to the managed device.
Blocking sensor	A sensor that you have configured to control one or more managed devices.
Device management	The capability of a sensor to interact with certain Cisco devices and dynamically reconfigure them to block the source of an attack by using an ACL, a VACL, or the **shun** command on the PIX Firewall.
IP blocking	A feature of Cisco IPS that enables your sensor to block traffic from an attacking system that has triggered a signature that is configured for blocking.
Interface/direction	The combination of the interface and direction on the interface (in or out) determines where a blocking ACL is applied on your managed device. You can configure the Network Access Controller (NAC) to block a total of ten interface/direction combinations (across all devices on the sensor).
Managed device	The Cisco device that blocks the source of an attack after being reconfigured by the blocking sensor.
Managed interface	The interface on the managed device on which the sensor applies the dynamically created ACL. This is also known as the *blocking interface*.

IP Blocking Devices

You can configure your sensor to perform device management on a variety of Cisco devices. You can use the following types of devices as managed devices:

- Cisco routers
- Cisco Catalyst 6000 switches
- Cisco PIX Firewalls or Adaptive Security Appliances (ASAs)

Cisco Routers

The following Cisco routers have been tested and approved to serve as blocking devices:

- Cisco routers running IOS 11.2 or later
- Catalyst 5000 switches with a Remote Switch Module (RSM)
- Catalyst 6000 with an Multilayer Switch Feature Card (MSFC)

The Network Access Controller (NAC) on a single sensor can control up to ten interfaces on any of the supported devices.

When using IP blocking, your sensor must be able to communicate with the managed device in order to reconfigure the device to block the traffic from the attacking system. Your sensor logs in to the managed device and dynamically applies an ACL. The sensor also removes the block after a configured amount of time. To manipulate the ACLs on the managed device, configure the following on your managed routers:

- VTY access—Enabled
- Line password—Assigned to VTY
- Telnet or Secure Shell (SSH) access—Allowed from sensor
- Router's enable password—Assigned

NOTE Although Telnet is available, SSH access to your IOS router is preferred because the communication with the router is encrypted (preventing someone on the network from sniffing your login credentials).

Cisco Catalyst 6000 Switches

Some Catalyst 6000 switches do not support ACLs (for example, those without an MSFC). You can still use these devices to perform device management by using VLAN Access Control Lists (VACLs) if you have a Policy Feature Card (PFC) and you are running CatOS.

NOTE To support ACLs on your Catalyst 6000 switch, you must have an MSFC installed on the switch. If your supervisor module contains a PFC, your Catalyst 6000 switch supports VACLs. If you have neither a PFC nor an MSFC, your Catalyst 6000 switch supports neither VACLs nor ACLs, and it cannot be used for IP blocking.

To manipulate the VACLs on the Catalyst 6000 switch device, you must configure the following on your Catalyst switch:

- Telnet Access (VTY)—Enabled
- Line password—Assigned to VTY
- Telnet Access or SSH access—Allowed from sensor
- Switch's enable password—Assigned

NOTE If your Catalyst 6000 switch has an MSFC and you are running CatOS on your switch, you have the option of using ACLs or VACLs when implementing IP blocking.

NOTE Although Telnet is available, SSH access to your Catalyst 6000 switch is preferred because the communication with the switch is encrypted (preventing someone on the network from sniffing your login credentials).

Cisco PIX Firewalls

In addition to Cisco routers and Catalyst 6000 switches, you can also use Cisco PIX Firewalls (and ASAs) to serve as managed devices. Instead of updating an ACL on the router, however, the sensor uses the PIX Firewall's **shun** command to block the traffic from the attacking system. Since the **shun** command was introduced in version 6.0 of the PIX operating system, any of the following PIX models running version 6.0 or higher can serve as a managed device:

- 501
- 506E
- 515E
- 525
- 535

Just as with the Cisco routers that serve as blocking devices, your sensor must be able to communicate with the PIX Firewalls being used as blocking devices. To communicate with the PIX Firewall, you must enable one of the following communication protocols:

- Telnet
- SSH

NOTE Although Telnet is available, SSH access to your PIX Firewall is preferred because the communication with the firewall is encrypted (preventing someone on the network from sniffing your login credentials). This is especially important for access to your PIX Firewall because it is installed to protect your network.

No matter which of these communication protocols you decide to use, you must assign an enable password to your PIX Firewall.

Blocking Guidelines

The IP blocking functionality in Cisco IPS provides a powerful tool to protect your network. If IP blocking is used incorrectly, however, a knowledgeable attacker can use the error against your network in a DoS attack.

The IP blocking feature generates ACLs that are based solely on IP addresses. The sensor has no mechanism to determine whether the address being blocked is a critical server on your network or the address of a legitimate attacker. Therefore, implementing IP blocking requires careful planning and analysis. Some of the important considerations in designing and implementing IP blocking are as follows:

- Antispoofing mechanisms
- Critical hosts
- Network topology
- Entry points
- Signature selection
- Blocking duration
- Device login information
- Interface ACL requirements

Antispoofing Mechanisms

Attackers will usually forge packets with IP addresses that are either private addresses (refer to RFC 1918) or addresses of your internal network. The attacker's goal is to have Cisco Secure IPS block valid IP addresses, thus causing a DoS. When you properly implement an antispoofing mechanism, Cisco Secure IPS will not block these valid addresses.

An excellent reference on IP address filtering is RFC 2827, "Network Ingress Filtering: Defeating Denial of Service Attacks Which Employ IP Source Address Spoofing." This reference explains how you can apply basic filtering to your router interfaces. Although these recommendations are not foolproof, they significantly help reduce the IP spoofing attacks against your network.

Basically, you want to make sure that all of the traffic leaving your protected network comes from a source IP address that is a valid address on your protected network. Consequently, for traffic entering your protected network, you need to make sure that the source IP address is not one of your valid internal addresses. Addresses that violate these criteria are probably spoofed and need to be dropped by your router.

Critical Hosts

Many hosts on your network perform critical tasks. To prevent any possible disruption of the operation of your network, these systems should not be blocked. Critical components that should not be blocked include the following:

- Cisco IDS sensors
- AAA server
- Perimeter firewall
- DNS servers

By establishing never-block addresses (see "Defining Addresses Never to Block" later in the chapter) for these critical systems, you can prevent IP blocking from disrupting the operation of these important systems (either accidentally or during a deliberate attack).

Network Topology

Your network topology impacts the implementation of IP blocking. You will have sensors deployed throughout your network, but a single blocking device can be controlled by only one sensor. You need to decide which sensors will control which managed devices. Furthermore, a single sensor can perform IP blocking only on a maximum of ten interfaces across one or more managed devices.

Entry Points

Many networks have multiple entry points to provide redundancy and reliability. These entry points provide multiple avenues for an attacker to access your network. You need to decide if all of these entry points need to participate in IP blocking. Furthermore, you need to make sure that when IP blocking is initiated on one entry point, an attacker cannot bypass the block by using another entry point. If multiple sensors perform blocking on your network, you will need to configure Master Blocking Sensors to coordinate blocking between these various sensors.

Signature Selection

Cisco IPS supports hundreds of signatures. It is not feasible or manageable to perform IP blocking on all of these signatures. Some signatures are more susceptible to spoofing than others. If you implement IP blocking on a UDP signature, for instance, an attacker may be able to impersonate one of your business partners, causing you to generate a DoS attack against your own network.

Other signatures are prone to false positives. Implementing IP blocking on these signatures can disrupt normal user traffic since the sensor has no way of distinguishing a false positive from a real attack.

Deciding which signatures you want to perform IP blocking and whether the blocking will be for the destination port only (Request Block Connection) or all traffic (Request Block Host) is one of the major configuration tasks in implementing IP blocking on your network.

Blocking Duration

The default blocking duration is 30 minutes for signatures configured to perform IP blocking. You need to decide whether this value is appropriate for your network environment. IP blocking is designed to stop traffic from an attacking host to enable you to analyze what is happening and give you time to take more long-term blocking actions, if appropriate.

> **NOTE** For manually initiated IP blocking, the default duration is 60 minutes.

If your blocking duration is too short, the attacker will regain access to your network before you have had a chance to fully examine the extent of the attack and to take appropriate actions. If the initial attack compromises a system, the subsequent access (after the blocking duration expires) might appear to be normal user traffic and might not trigger any of your IPS signatures. So it is important to thoroughly analyze the attack before the attacker can regain access to your network.

Setting your blocking duration too high, however, also has its drawbacks. A very large duration value creates a DoS situation when the block occurs because of a false positive. Since the block duration is long, it will impact the normal user for a longer period of time (usually until you have analyzed the circumstances and determined that the alarm was a false positive). You must carefully consider the appropriate blocking duration for your network environment.

Device Login Information

When implementing IP blocking, your sensor must be able to log in to the managed device and dynamically apply an ACL (or other IP blocking feature). Therefore, your sensor needs to have privileged login credentials to this device. Some devices support SSH, whereas others may support only Telnet. When you connect via Telnet, the connection needs to traverse a secure network (to protect login credentials), whereas SSH access has somewhat more flexibility because the traffic is encrypted.

Interface ACL Requirements

An interface/direction on your managed device can have only one ACL applied to it. If you already have existing ACL entries on a given interface/direction (besides the block entries generated by the NAC), you need to configure these entries in either a Pre-Block ACL or Post-Block ACL (or both) on your managed device.

When the NAC generates a blocking ACL for a device, it first includes all of the entries from the Pre-Block ACL. Then it adds the block entries that it dynamically creates. Finally, it adds the entries from the Post-Block ACL. This is the complete ACL that is applied to the managed device.

Blocking Process

Blocking is initiated when a signature configured for IP blocking triggers an alarm or when a manual blocking event is generated. This causes the NAC to create the appropriate blocking ACLs (or sets of configurations) and to send this information to all of the managed devices that it controls. At the same time, an alarm is sent to the Event Store. When the block duration expires, the NAC updates the ACLs (or configurations) to remove the block from each controlled device.

The NAC is the sensor service that controls starting and stopping blocks on routers, switches, and PIX Firewalls (and ASAs). A block is initiated when one of the following two events occurs:

- A signature configured with the block action triggers
- You manually initiate a block (from a management interface such as the Command Line Interface [CLI] or IDM)

NOTE Usually, blocks expire after a configured amount of time. You can also configure the NAC to initiate a permanent block that does not expire until you remove it. These permanent blocks will initiate a persistent connection with your managed device until you remove the block.

The blocking process involves the following sequence of operations:

1. An event or action configured for blocking occurs.
2. The NAC sends a new set of configurations or ACLs (one for each interface/direction) to each controlled device. It applies the block to each interface/direction on all the devices that the sensor is configured to control.
3. For alarm events, the alarm is sent to the Event Store at the same time that the block is applied. These events happen independently of each other.
4. When the configured block duration expires, the NAC updates the configurations or ACLs to remove the block.

ACL Placement Considerations

When applying ACLs on your network, consider your operational requirements and network topology. You have several options when applying ACLs to one of your network devices. The ACL might be applied on either the external or internal interface of the router. It can also be configured for inbound or outbound traffic on each of these two interfaces (when using ACLs). Although you can choose inbound or outbound traffic (with respect to the router interface, not your network) on each physical interface, the most ACL placements are illustrated in Figure 9-4.

Figure 9-4 *ACL Placement*

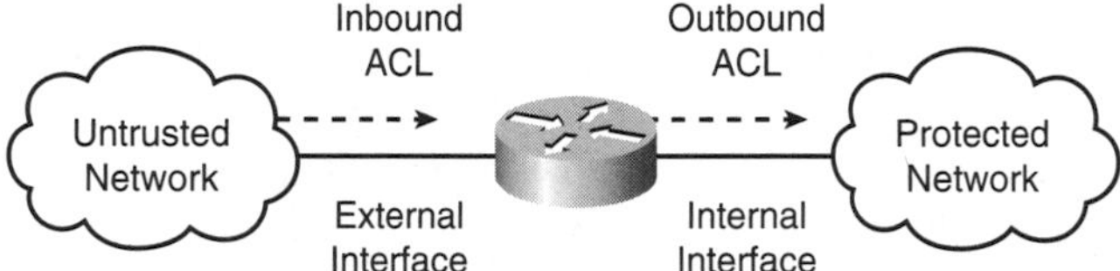

When deciding where to apply your ACLs, you need to understand the various options available to you. These options are as follows:

- Traffic direction
- External interface or internal interface

> **NOTE** VACLs do not have a concept of traffic direction. If you use VACLs, you must limit traffic without regard to the traffic's direction.

The *traffic direction* option specifies whether the ACL is applied to traffic entering the interface or to traffic leaving the interface. You can allow certain traffic into an interface while denying this same traffic from leaving the interface. You must apply a traffic direction when creating an ACL for a given interface on your network.

The *external interface* is located on the unprotected side of your network device (see Figure 9-4). Applying your ACL to your external interface for inbound traffic provides the best protection since the traffic is denied before it enters the router.

The *internal interface* resides on the protected side of your network device (see Figure 9-4). Applying your ACL to your internal interface for inbound traffic does not block traffic from reaching the router itself and prevents you from accidentally blocking traffic that your router needs.

External Versus Internal

Applying the ACL to the external interface in the inward direction denies a host access before the router processes the packets. If the attacker is generating a large amount of traffic (common for DoS attacks), this reduces the performance impact on your router.

Applying the ACL to the internal interface in the outbound direction denies traffic from a host to the devices on your protected network but allows the packets to be processed by the router. This scenario is less desirable, but it has the benefit of preventing you from accidentally denying traffic that the router needs, such as routing updates.

Each network configuration has its own requirements. You must decide, based on your unique network architecture, which configuration meets your needs for security and user functionality.

ACLs Versus VACLs

In most situations, you are limited to using either ACLs or VACLs. But if you have an MSFC and a Catalyst 6000 running CatOS, you can choose to use either VACLs or ACLs. Therefore, it is helpful to understand the benefits of each of these access-control mechanisms.

VACLs are directionless. You can't specify a direction as you can when defining ACLs. This means that if direction is important to you when blocking the traffic, using an ACL is the only choice.

ACLs are applied to the MSFC on the switch. The MSFC is essentially a headless router, and any ACLs that you define on the MSFC are used to restrict only the flow of traffic between different VLANs or broadcast domains. ACLs can't be used to restrict traffic between systems on the same network segment (since the traffic is transmitted at the link layer). A VACL, however, is applied at the link layer on the switch (which is one of the reasons why VACLs are directionless). This means that VACLs can restrict traffic between systems that are on the same network segment or VLAN.

Using Existing ACLs

In some situations, you may need to configure an IP block on an interface/direction on which you already have an ACL. If you simply configure your sensor to generate blocks for an interface/direction on the managed device, your existing ACL entries will be lost because the blocking sensor will take control of the interface and apply its own ACL. Therefore, to use blocking on an interface/direction that has an existing ACL, you need to define the following extra ACLs:

- Pre-Block ACL
- Post-Block ACL

When you configure a sensor as a blocking sensor, it takes control of the ACL for the specified interface and traffic direction on the managed device. If you configure either a Pre-Block or Post-Block ACL, the sensor applies these entries to the managed device by creating a single ACL composed of the Pre-Block and Post-Block entries. When a blocking event occurs, the NAC creates a new single ACL to perform the blocking. This ACL begins with the Pre-Block ACL entries following by the dynamically created block entries and ending with the Post-Block entries.

NOTE Consider carefully which entries you place in your Pre-Block ACL. The addresses allowed by the Pre-Block ACL will come before the dynamically created block entries (in the ACL that is applied to the managed device). That means that these entries can't be blocked by the block entries because the router looks for only the first match in the ACL.

Master Blocking Sensor

Depending on your network configuration, you may have multiple entry points into your network. When one of your sensors initiates a blocking event, it prevents further intrusive traffic from entering your network from that source address. If more than one of your sensors is configured for IP blocking, you probably need these sensors to coordinate their blocking actions with each other so that all entry points into you network are blocked when an attack is noticed by any of your sensors. A Master Blocking Sensor can handle this coordination.

It is, perhaps, easiest to explain the Master Blocking Sensor through an example. Figure 9-5 illustrates a scenario in which a network is connected to the Internet through multiple Internet service providers (ISPs). A Cisco Secure IPS sensor monitors each of the entry points into this network. Furthermore, each of the sensors is configured to perform device management on its associated border or perimeter router.

Figure 9-5 *Master Blocking Sensor Scenario*

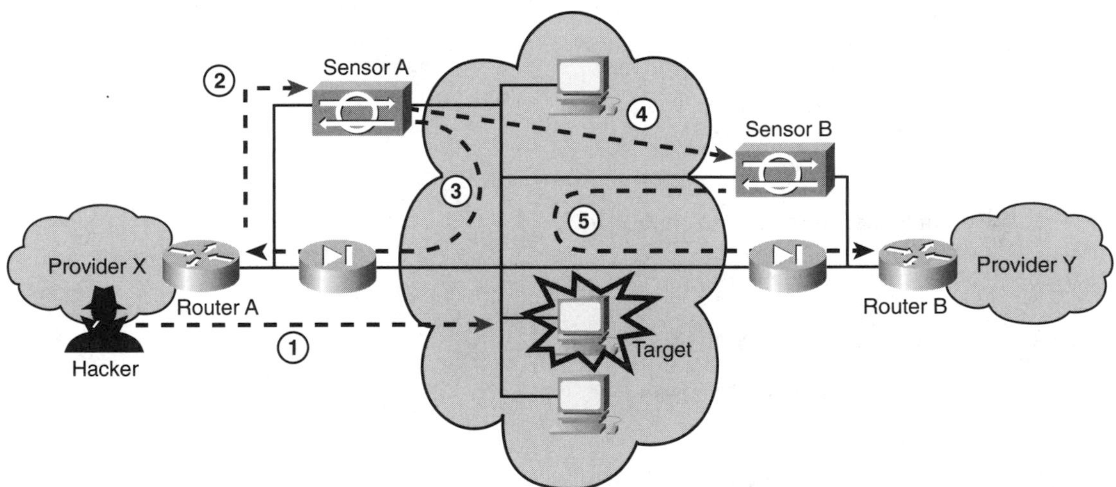

An attacker attempts to compromise a host on the protected network (Step 1 in Figure 9-5). This usually involves the attacker launching an exploit against the target machine.

When Sensor A detects the attack, it fires one of the signatures in its database (Step 2 in Figure 9-5). Because the signature is configured for blocking, Sensor A telnets (or uses SSH) into Router A and updates the ACL to block the traffic from the attacker's host. At the same time, the sensor performs other signature actions such as generating the alert event (Step 3 in Figure 9-5).

The ACL on Router A will prevent the attacker from sending any traffic into the network through Provider X's network (see Figure 9-5). Because there are two entry points into the network, however, the attacker can reroute his traffic through Provider Y's network because it is still allowing traffic from the attacker's host. Therefore, to completely protect the network from the attacker, Sensor B is configured as a Master Blocking Sensor.

After blocking the attacker's traffic at Router A, Sensor A then tells Sensor B to also block the attacker's traffic. Since Sensor B is configured as the Master Blocking Sensor (for Sensor A), Sensor B accepts Sensor A's request and telnets (or uses SSH) into Router B to update the ACL to also block the attacker's traffic. At this point, both entry points into the network are now protected from the attacker.

NOTE A savvy network security administrator will configure Sensor A to command Sensor B to block traffic from Provider Y's router. This will protect the network from attacks initiated through Provider X's network. Then to complete the security configuration, the administrator also needs to configure Sensor A as the Master Blocking Sensor for Sensor B. Therefore, whether an attack comes from Provider X or Provider Y's network, both entry points are protected.

Configuring IP Blocking

When configuring IP blocking, you need to perform numerous configuration operations. These operations fall into the following categories:

- Assigning a block action
- Setting blocking properties
- Defining addresses never to block
- Setting up logical devices
- Defining blocking devices
- Defining Master Blocking Sensors

Assigning a Blocking Action

Before your sensor will initiate IP blocking, configure one or more of your Cisco IPS signatures with a blocking action. In IDM version 5.0, you can configure the actions for a signature by performing the following steps:

Step 1 Access IDM by entering the following URL in your web browser: **https://** *sensor_ip_address*.

Step 2 Click on the **Configuration** icon to display the list of configuration tasks.

Step 3 If the items under the **Signature Definition** category are not displayed, click on the plus sign to the left of **Signature Definition**.

Step 4 Select **Signature Configuration** from the IDM configuration options to access the Signature Configuration screen.

Step 5 Click on **Actions** to access the Assign Actions popup window (see Figure 9-6).

Figure 9-6 *Assign Actions Popup*

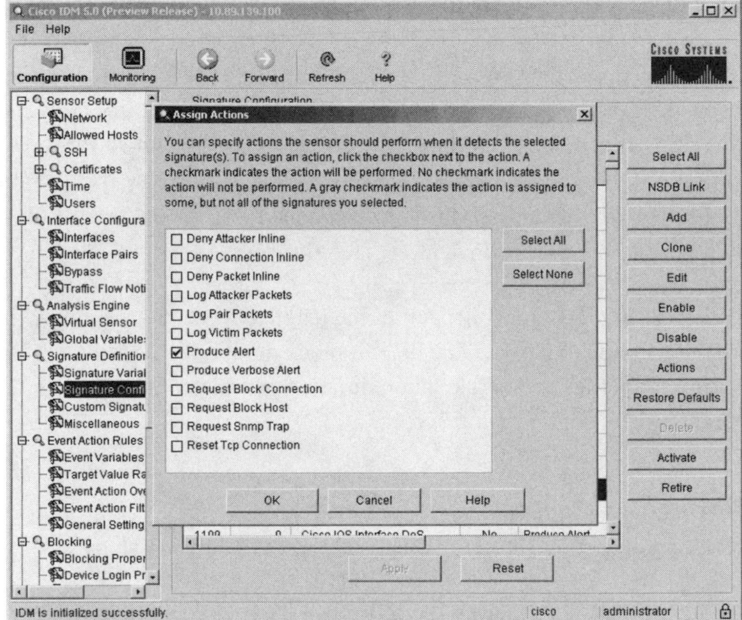

Step 6 Assign the desired actions by clicking on the box next to the action until a check mark appears. (Clicking on a box with a check mark removes the check mark.)

Step 7 Click on **OK** to accept the action changes for the highlighted signature.

Step 8 Click on **Apply** to save the configuration information to the sensor.

> **NOTE** You can also configure the actions for a signature by editing the **Event Action** field for the signature. Configuring signatures is explained in detail in Chapter 5, "Basic Cisco IPS Signature Configuration," and Chapter 7, "Advanced Signature Configuration."

Setting Blocking Properties

Certain blocking properties apply to all of the signatures that are configured with the block action. The following blocking parameters apply to all automatic blocks that the NAC initiates:

- Maximum block entries
- Allow the sensor IP address to be blocked
- Block duration

The *maximum block entries* parameter specifies the maximum number of dynamically created block entries that the blocking sensor can place into the ACL to block attacking hosts. This value prevents the sensor from generating an ACL that contains an abnormally large number of entries, which could impact the performance of the managed device. The default value is 250 entries.

The blocking properties screen contains a check box that is labeled with something similar to "Allow the sensor IP address to be blocked" (phrasing varies slightly between management systems). Checking this box causes the sensor to place a permit entry for the sensor's IP address at the beginning of the dynamically created block entries. Because this permit statement is processed before any deny entries, traffic to the sensor's IP address can't be blocked by the blocking ACL.

The *block action duration* parameter specifies the length of time that your blocking sensor will wait before removing the blocking ACL. The default block duration is 30 minutes. Unlike the other two general blocking properties, the block action duration parameter is located on the Event Action Rules>General Settings configuration screen.

Setting Blocking Properties via IDM

To set the blocking properties through IDM, perform the following steps:

Step 1 Access IDM by entering the following URL in your web browser: **https://** *sensor_ip_address*.

Step 2 Click on the **Configuration** icon to display the list of configuration tasks.

Step 3 If the items under the **Blocking** category are not displayed, click on the plus sign to the left of **Blocking**.

Step 4 Click on **Blocking Properties** to access the Blocking Properties configuration screen. (See Figure 9-7.)

Step 5 Enter the maximum number of entries allowed in the blocking ACL by entering a value in the **Maximum Block Entries** field. (The default is 250.)

Step 6 Make sure the check box next to **Enable blocking** is checked. (This is the default.)

Step 7 Make sure that the check box next to **Allow the sensor IP address to be blocked** is not selected. (This is the default, to prevent the sensor from blocking its own IP address.)

Step 8 Click on **Apply** to apply the changes to the sensor's configuration.

Figure 9-7 *IDM Blocking Properties Configuration Screen*

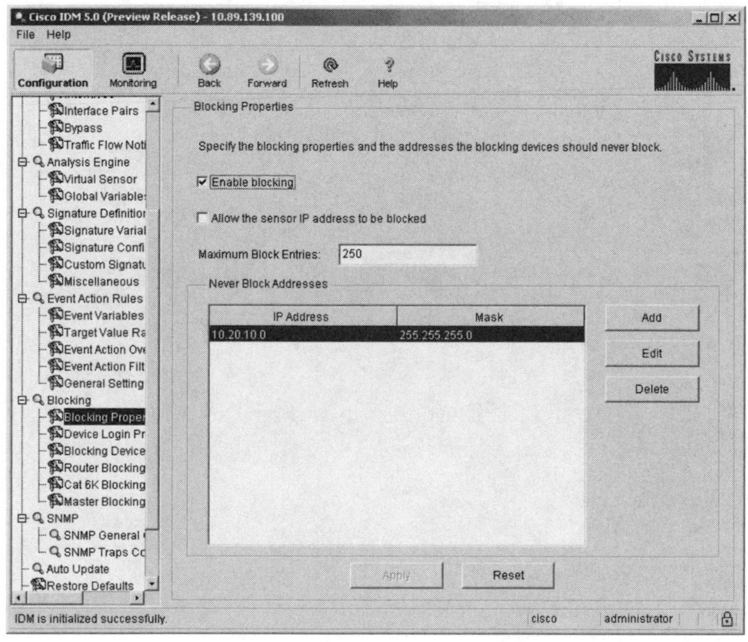

Defining Addresses Never to Block

To prevent your blocking sensor from blocking traffic to critical systems on your network (either accidentally or because of a deliberate attack), you can configure which IP addresses your blocking device should never block.

> **NOTE** The never-block entries are added (as permit statements) before the dynamically created blocking entries that are generated by the sensor. Since these entries come before any blocking entries, these addresses can't be blocked by the blocking ACL.

To configure which addresses can't be blocked by the blocking ACL generated by your blocking sensor when using IDM, perform the following steps:

Step 1 Access IDM by entering the following URL in your web browser: **https://** *sensor_ip_address*.

Step 2 Click on the **Configuration** icon to display the list of configuration tasks.

Step 3 If the items under the **Blocking** category are not displayed, click on the plus sign to the left of **Blocking**.

Step 4 Click on **Blocking Properties** to access the Blocking Properties configuration screen. (See Figure 9-8.)

Figure 9-8 *Configuring Never Block Addresses in IDM*

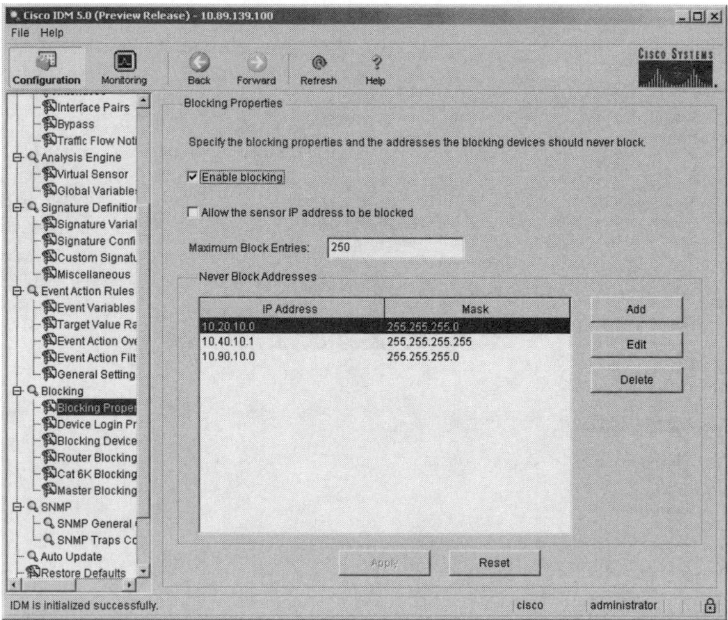

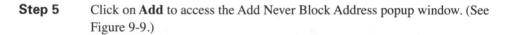

Step 5 Click on **Add** to access the Add Never Block Address popup window. (See Figure 9-9.)

Figure 9-9 *Never Block Address Popup Window*

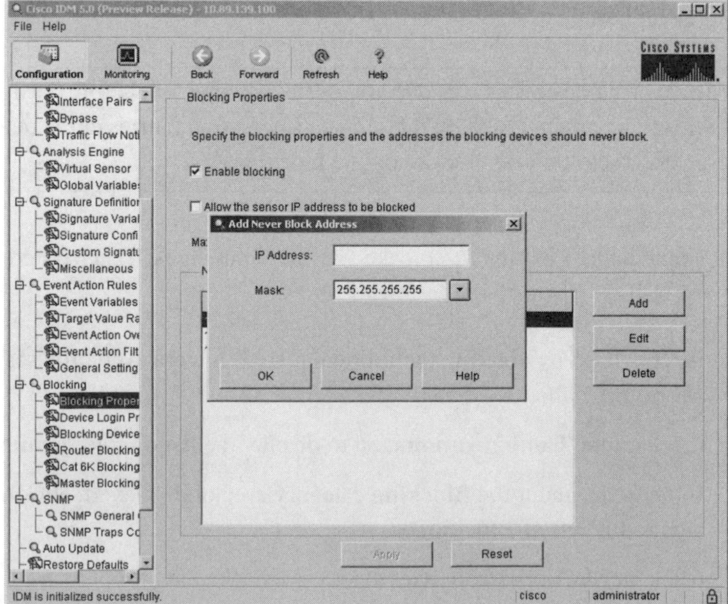

Step 6 In the **IP Address** field, enter the IP address (or network address) that should not be blocked.

Step 7 Use the pull-down menu for the **Mask** field to define the network mask associated with the IP address that you entered (the default is the single host network mask [255.255.255.255]).

Step 8 Click on **OK** to save the never-block address that you specified.

Step 9 Click on **Apply** to apply the changes to the sensor's configuration.

NOTE From the Never Block Addresses screen, you can manipulate existing entries by highlighting the entry that you want to modify and then clicking on either **Edit** or **Delete**.

Setting Up Logical Devices

If you use IDM to manage your sensors, you can configure Device Login Profiles to identify the following authentication parameters for a blocking device:

- Username
- Password
- Enable Password

When you create a blocking device, you associate the appropriate login profile with it. A single login profile can be associated with multiple blocking devices.

To configure a device login profile in IDM, perform the following steps:

Step 1 Access IDM by entering the following URL in your web browser: **https://***sensor_ip_address*.

Step 2 Click on the **Configuration** icon to display the list of configuration tasks.

Step 3 If the items under the **Blocking** category are not displayed, click on the plus sign to the left of **Blocking**.

Step 4 Click on **Device Login Profiles** to access the Device Login Profiles configuration screen. (See Figure 9-10.)

Step 5 Click on **Add** to access the Add Device Login Profile popup window. (See Figure 9-11.)

Step 6 Enter the name of the new profile in the Profile Name field.

Step 7 Enter the desired username in the Username field.

Figure 9-10 *IDM Device Login Profiles Configuration Screen*

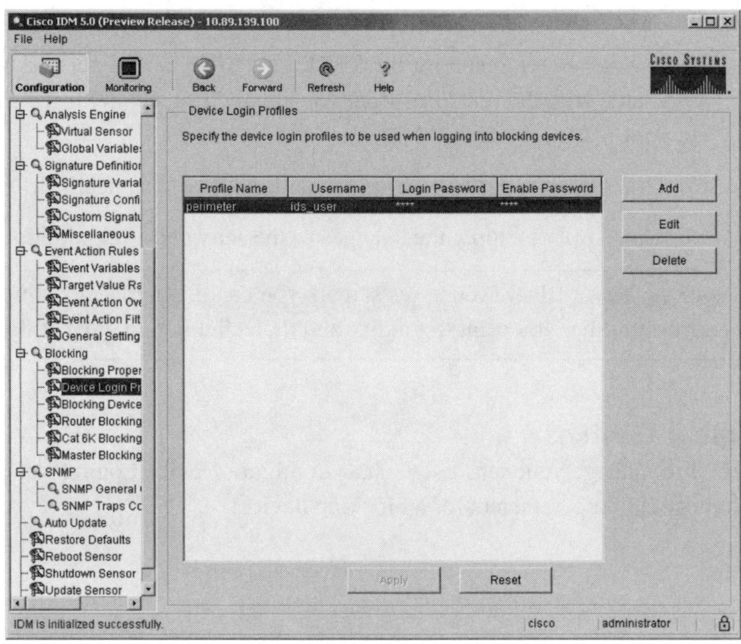

Figure 9-11 *IDM Add Device Login Profile Popup Window*

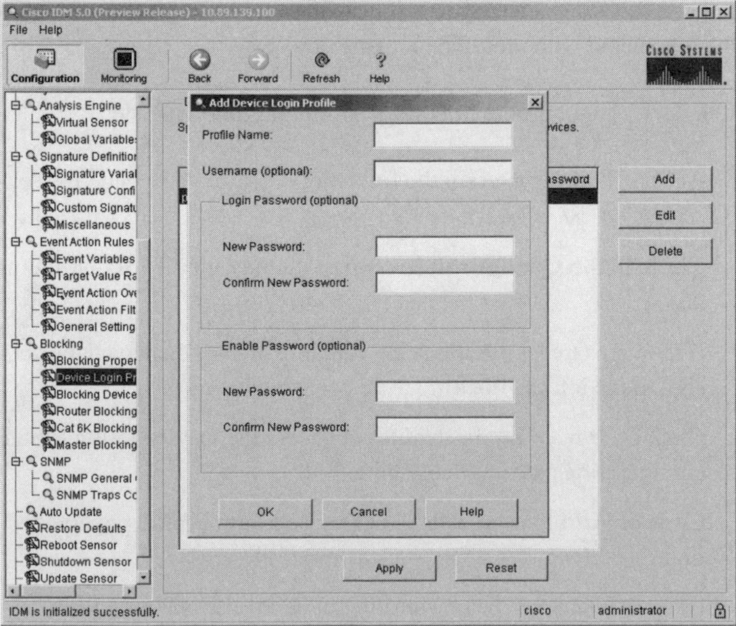

Step 8 (Optional) Enter the login password in the Login Password New Password and Confirm New Password fields.

Step 9 (Optional) Enter the enable password in the Enable Password New Password and Confirm New Password fields.

Step 10 Click on **OK** to save the device login profile.

Step 11 Click on **Apply** to apply the changes to the sensor's configuration.

Defining Blocking Devices

Cisco IPS supports the following three types of blocking devices:

- IOS routers
- Catalyst 6000 switches with a PFC (running CatOS)
- PIX Firewalls (and ASAs)

Each of these blocking devices uses a slightly different mechanism to block traffic on the network. The routers use ACLs to restrict traffic flow. The Catalyst switch uses VACLs to restrict traffic, and the PIX Firewalls use the **shun** command to restrict traffic. Therefore, the processes for configuring each of these types of blocking devices differ slightly.

NOTE It is important to choose the correct device type when defining a blocking device. The sensor creates the commands to initiate blocking based on this device type. Using the wrong device type (especially with respect to the operating system running on the Catalyst switch) will prevent blocking from operating correctly.

Defining Blocking Devices Using IDM

When you use IDM, defining a blocking device is a two-step process. You must first define the blocking device. Then you define one of the following interfaces that you associate with the blocking device:

- Router Blocking Device interface
- Cat6K Blocking Device interface

NOTE You do not need to create an interface when you are using a PIX Firewall as your blocking device. The PIX Firewall performs the blocking via its **shun** command, so you do not need to specify an interface. So with PIX-managed devices, you need to define only the blocking device itself.

You define blocking devices through IDM by defining the fields shown in Table 9-3.

Table 9-3 *IDM Blocking Device Fields*

Field	Description
IP Address	The IP address that the sensor will use to communicate with the blocking device.
Sensor's NAT Address	(Optional) The NAT address of the blocking device.
Device Login Profile	Pull-down menu that allows you to select a device that logically defines the login credentials for the blocking device.
Device Type	Pull-down menu that allows you to select the blocking device type. Valid options are **Cisco Router**, **Catalyst 6000 VACL**, and **PIX**.
Communication	Pull-down menu that allows you to select the communication vehicle that you plan to use to communicate with the blocking device. Valid options are **SSH DES**, **SSH 3DES**, and **Telnet**.

NOTE If you choose **SSH DES** or **SSH 3DES**, you need to use the CLI command **ssh host-key** to add the router to the list of valid SSH servers before the sensor will be able to successfully communicate with your blocking device. For more information on adding a host key, refer to the section titled "Adding a Known SSH Host" in Chapter 2.

To add a blocking device by using the IDM interface, you perform the following steps:

Step 1 Access IDM by entering the following URL in your web browser: **https://***sensor_ip_address*.

Step 2 Click on the **Configuration** icon to display the list of configuration tasks.

Step 3 If the items under the **Blocking** category are not displayed, click on the plus sign to the left of **Blocking**.

Step 4 Click on **Blocking** to access the Blocking Devices configuration screen. (See Figure 9-12.)

Step 5 Click on **Add** to access the Add Blocking Device popup window. (See Figure 9-13.)

Step 6 Define the blocking device by entering the correct values for the blocking device fields specified in Table 9-3.

Figure 9-12 *IDM Blocking Devices Configuration Screen*

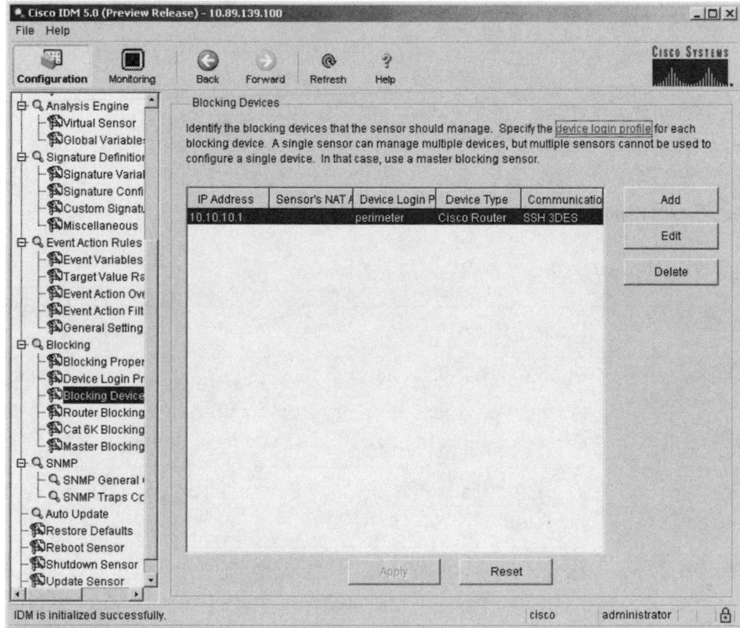

Figure 9-13 *IDM Add Blocking Device Popup Window*

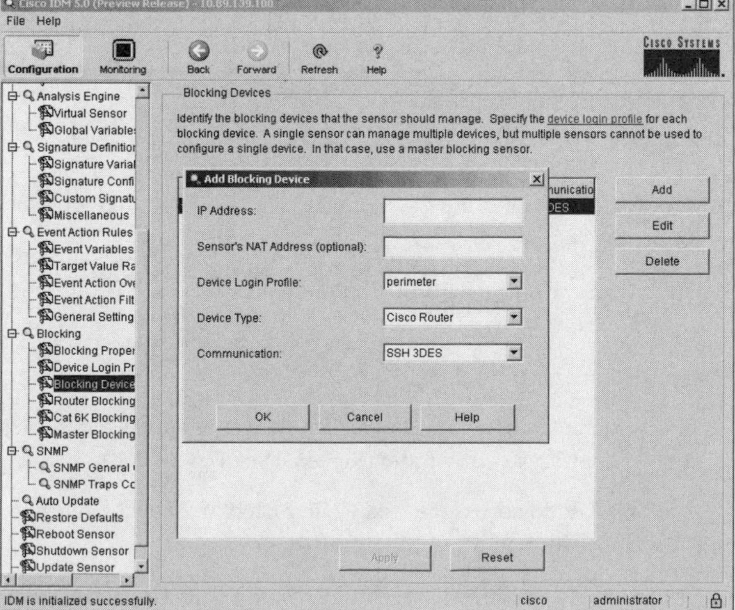

Step 7 Click on **OK** to save the new blocking device entry.

Step 8 Click on **Apply** to apply the changes to the sensor's configuration.

Defining Router Blocking Devices Interfaces Using IDM

Your blocking sensor needs to know which interface on your router you want to apply the blocking ACL to. You configure this information by defining a router-blocking device interface entry using the fields listed in Table 9-4.

Table 9-4 *IDM Router Blocking Device Interface Fields*

Field	Description
IP Address	The IP address that the sensor will use to communicate with the blocking device. You select this entry from a pull-down menu that lists the addresses of the router-blocking devices that you have defined.
Blocking Interface	The interface on the blocking device where the blocking sensor will apply the blocking ACL.
Blocking Direction	Determines whether the blocking ACL will be applied on inbound or outbound traffic on the blocking interface. You select either **In** or **Out** from the pull-down menu.
Pre-Block ACL Name	(Optional) Name of the ACL (on the blocking device) whose entries will be inserted at the beginning of the blocking ACL.
Post-Block ACL Name	(Optional) Name of the ACL (on the blocking device) whose entries will be placed at the end of the blocking ACL.

To add a router interface in the IDM interface, perform the following steps:

Step 1 Access IDM by entering the following URL in your web browser: **https://** *sensor_ip_address*.

Step 2 Click on the **Configuration** icon to display the list of configuration tasks.

Step 3 If the items under the **Blocking** category are not displayed, click on the plus sign to the left of **Blocking**.

Step 4 Click on **Router Blocking Device Interfaces** to access the Router Blocking Device Interfaces configuration screen. (See Figure 9-14.)

Step 5 Click on **Add** to access the Add Router Blocking Device Interface screen. (See Figure 9-15.)

Step 6 Define the router blocking device interface by entering the correct values for the router blocking device interface fields specified in Table 9-4.

Figure 9-14 *IDM Router Blocking Device Interfaces Configuration Screen*

Figure 9-15 *IDM Add Router Blocking Device Interfaces Screen*

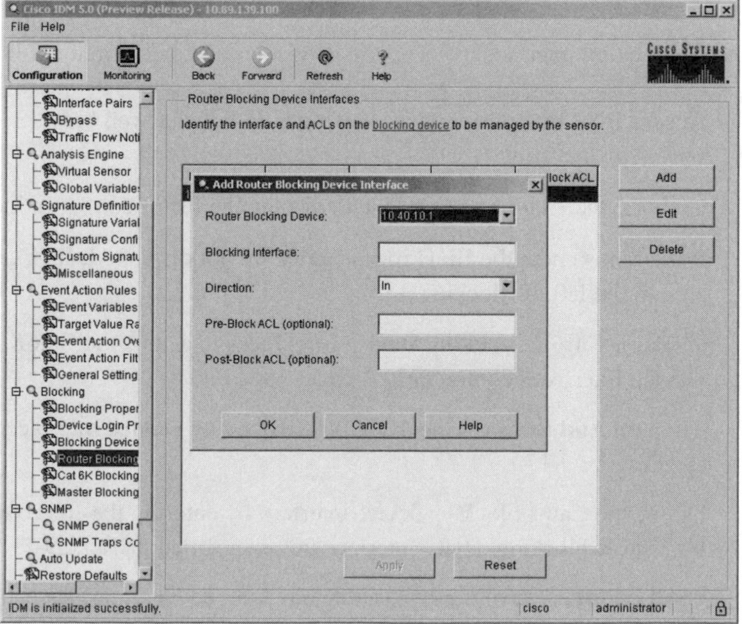

Step 7 Click on **OK** to save the new router blocking device interface entry.

Step 8 Click on **Apply** to apply the changes to the sensor's configuration.

Defining Cat6K Blocking Device Interfaces Using IDM

Your blocking sensor needs to know which VLAN on your Catalyst 6000 switch you want to apply the blocking VACL to, along with your Pre-Block and Post-Block information. You configure this information by defining the fields listed in Table 9-5.

Table 9-5 *IDM Cat6K Blocking Device Interface Fields*

Field	Description
IP Address	The IP address that the sensor will use to communicate with the blocking device. You select this entry from a pull-down menu that lists the addresses of the Cat6K blocking devices that you have defined.
VLAN Number	The VLAN on the blocking device where the blocking sensor will apply the blocking VACL.
Pre-Block VACL Name	The name of the VACL (on the blocking device) whose entries will be inserted at the beginning of the blocking ACL.
Post-Block VACL Name	The name of the VACL (on the blocking device) whose entries will be placed at the end of the blocking ACL.

To add a Cat6K blocking interface by using the IDM interface, perform the following steps:

Step 1 Access IDM by entering the following URL in your web browser: **https://** *sensor_ip_address*.

Step 2 Click on the **Configuration** icon to display the list of configuration tasks.

Step 3 If the items under the **Blocking** category are not displayed, click on the plus sign to the left of Blocking.

Step 4 Click on **Cat6K Blocking Device Interfaces** to access the Cat6K Blocking Device Interfaces configuration screen. (See Figure 9-16.)

Step 5 Click on **Add** to access the Add Cat6K Blocking Device Interface screen. (See Figure 9-17.)

Step 6 Define the Cat6k blocking device interface by entering the correct values for the Cat6K blocking device interface fields specified in Table 9-5.

Step 7 Click on **OK** to save the new Cat6K blocking device interface entry.

Step 8 Click on **Apply** to apply the changes to the sensor's configuration.

Figure 9-16 *IDM Cat6K Blocking Device Interfaces Configuration Screen*

Figure 9-17 *IDM Add Cat6K Blocking Device Interfaces Screen*

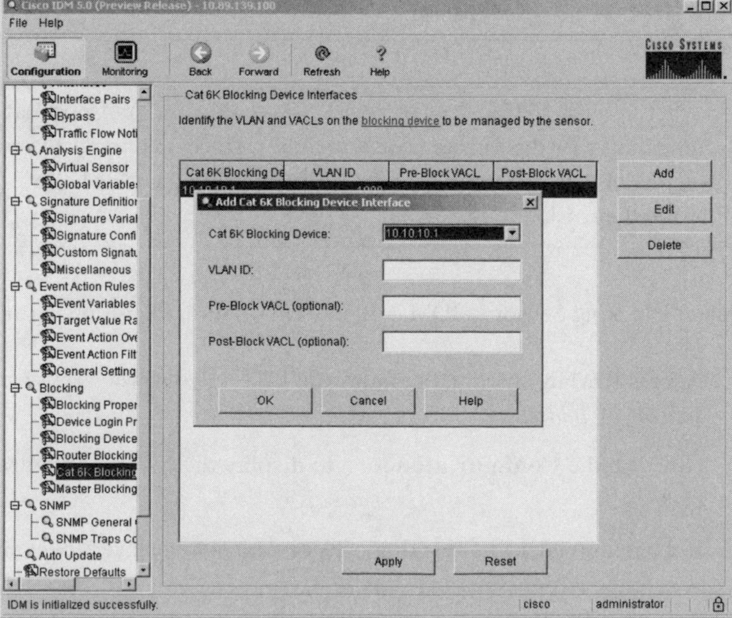

Defining Master Blocking Sensors

One sensor can initiate blocking on multiple managed devices on your network. Only one sensor, however, can initiate blocking on a specific managed device. If you use multiple sensors to perform IP blocking on your network, you will need to define Master Blocking Sensors to coordinate your blocking so that all entrances into your network are protected.

Configuring a Master Blocking Sensor in IDM

When defining a Master Blocking Sensor in IDM, you need to specify the parameters listed in Table 9-6.

Table 9-6 *IDM Master Blocking Sensor Fields*

Field	Description
IP Address	Specifies the IP address of the sensor that will apply the blocking requests to the managed device
Port	Indicates the port that the sensor will connect to when communicating with the Master Blocking Sensor
Username	Username of the account that the sensor will use when connecting to the Master Blocking Sensor
Password	Password of the account that the sensor will use when connecting to the Master Blocking Sensor
Use TLS	Check box indicating whether the communication with the Master Blocking Sensor is over an encrypted channel

NOTE As when you use SSH instead of Telnet, you should use Transport Layer Security (TLS) when communicating with the Master Blocking Sensor since it encrypts the communication session, preventing an attacker from viewing the information (such as login credentials) exchanged during the session.

To add a Master Blocking Sensor in IDM, you need to perform the following steps:

Step 1 Access IDM by entering the following URL in your web browser: **https://***sensor_ip_address*.

Step 2 Click on the **Configuration** icon to display the list of configuration tasks.

Step 3 If the items under the **Blocking** category are not displayed, click on the plus sign to the left of **Blocking**.

Step 4 Click on **Master Blocking Sensor** to access the Master Blocking Sensor configuration screen. (See Figure 9-18.)

Figure 9-18 *IDM Master Blocking Sensor Configuration Screen*

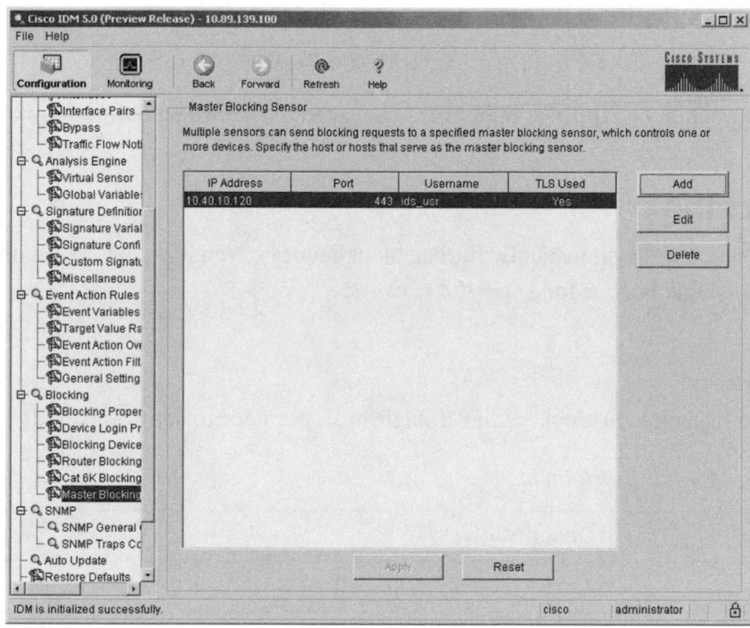

Step 5 Click on **Add** to access the Add Master Blocking Sensor popup window. (See Figure 9-19.)

Figure 9-19 *IDM Add Master Blocking Sensor Popup Window*

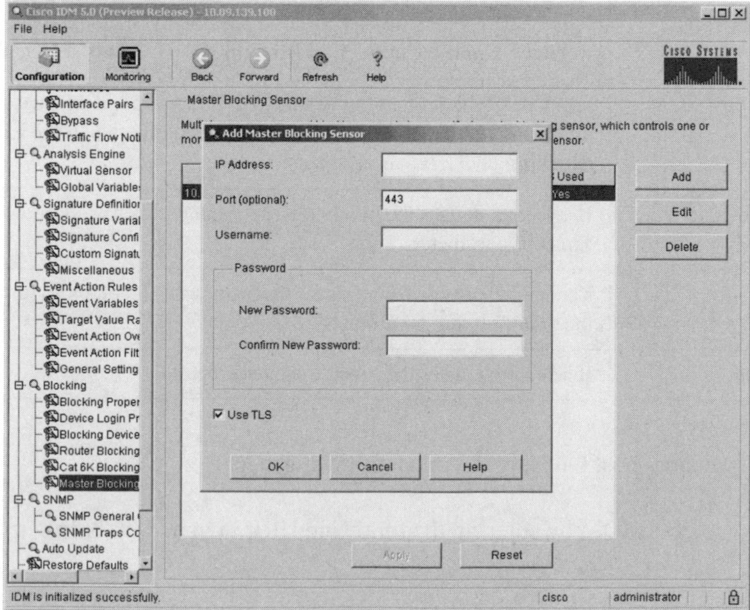

Step 6 Define the Master Blocking Sensor by entering the correct values for the Master Blocking Sensor fields specified in Table 9-6.

Step 7 Click on **OK** to save the new Master Blocking Sensor entry.

Step 8 Click on **Apply** to apply the changes to the sensor's configuration.

Manual Blocking

Using IDM, you can also manually initiate block requests. You have the option of initiating manual blocks for a single host or for a specific network.

Blocking Hosts

When defining a manual block against a single host, you need to define the fields shown in Table 9-7.

Table 9-7 *IDM Host Manual Block Fields*

Field	**Description**
Source IP	The source address that will be blocked by the block request.
Enable Connection Blocking	Check box that enables blocking of connections (source IP combined with destination IP and possibly destination port) instead of just all traffic from the source host.
Destination IP	The destination address of the traffic to be blocked (required when the **Enable Connection Blocking** check box is selected.
Destination Port	(Optional) The destination port of the traffic to be blocked (can be specified only when the **Enable Connection Blocking** check box is selected).
Protocol	(Optional) The protocol to be blocked. Valid options are **any**, **tcp**, and **udp**, with **any** being the default (these can be specified only when the **Enable Connection Blocking** check box is selected).
Enable Timeout	If selected, causes the block to last for the number of minutes specified by the Timeout parameter.
Timeout	The length of time (in minutes) that you want the block to remain in effect, with the default being 60 minutes.
No Timeout	If selected, causes the block to never time out.

To initiate a manual host block, perform the following steps:

Step 1 Access IDM by entering the following URL in your web browser: **https://***sensor_ip_address*.

Step 2 Click on the **Monitoring** icon to display the list of monitoring tasks.

Step 3 Click on **Active Host Blocks** to access the Active Host Blocks monitoring screen. (See Figure 9-20.)

Figure 9-20 *IDM Active Host Blocks Monitoring Screen*

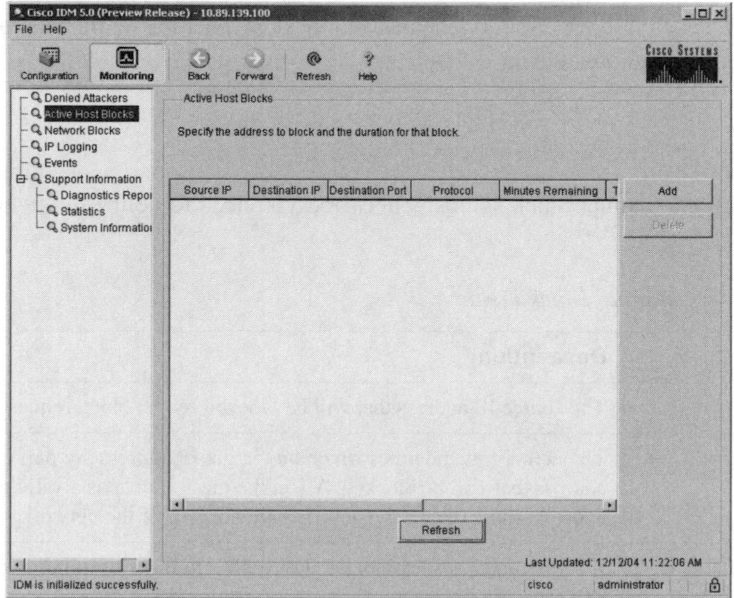

Step 4 Click on **Add** to access the Add Active Host Block popup window. (See Figure 9-21.)

Figure 9-21 *IDM Add Active Host Block Popup Window*

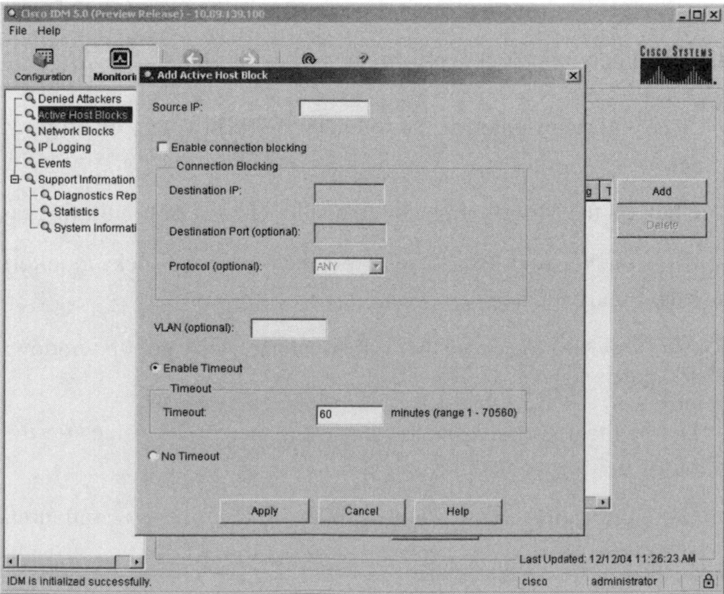

Step 5 Define the host to block by entering the correct values for the host block fields specified in Table 9-7.

Step 6 Click on **Apply** to apply the host block to the sensor's configuration.

> **NOTE** You can remove current manual host blocks by clicking on the host block entry to highlight it and then by clicking on **Delete**.

Blocking Networks

When defining a manual block against a network, you need to define the fields shown in Table 9-8.

Table 9-8 *IDM Network Manual Block Fields*

Field	Description
Source IP	The source IP address that will be blocked by the block request.
Netmask	The netmask that defines which bits in the IP address are part of the network address that will be blocked. A 1 in the mask indicates a valid part of the network address, and a 0 indicates bits that are not part of the network.
Enable Timeout	If selected, causes the block to last for the number of minutes specified by the Timeout parameter.
Timeout	The length of time (in minutes) that you want the block to remain in effect, with the default being 60 minutes.
No Timeout	If selected, causes the block to never time out.

To initiate a manual network block, perform the following steps:

Step 1 Access IDM by entering the following URL in your web browser: **https://** *sensor_ip_address*.

Step 2 Click on the **Monitoring** icon to display the list of monitoring tasks.

Step 3 Click on **Network Blocks** to access the Network Blocks monitoring screen. (See Figure 9-22.)

Step 4 Click on **Add** to access the Add Network Block popup window. (See Figure 9-23.)

Step 5 Define the network to block by entering the correct values for the network block fields specified in Table 9-8.

Step 6 Click on **Apply** to apply the host block to the sensor's configuration.

Figure 9-22 *IDM Network Blocks Monitoring Screen*

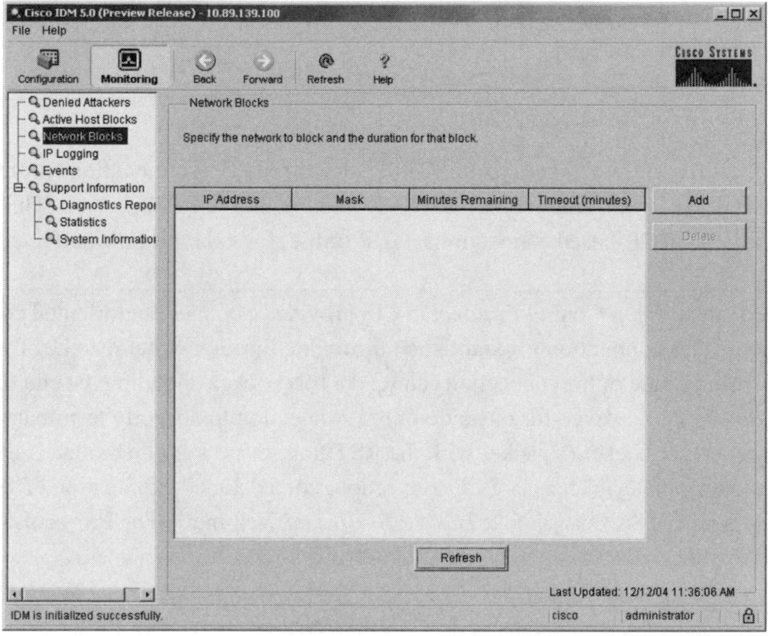

Figure 9-23 *IDM Add Network Block Popup Window*

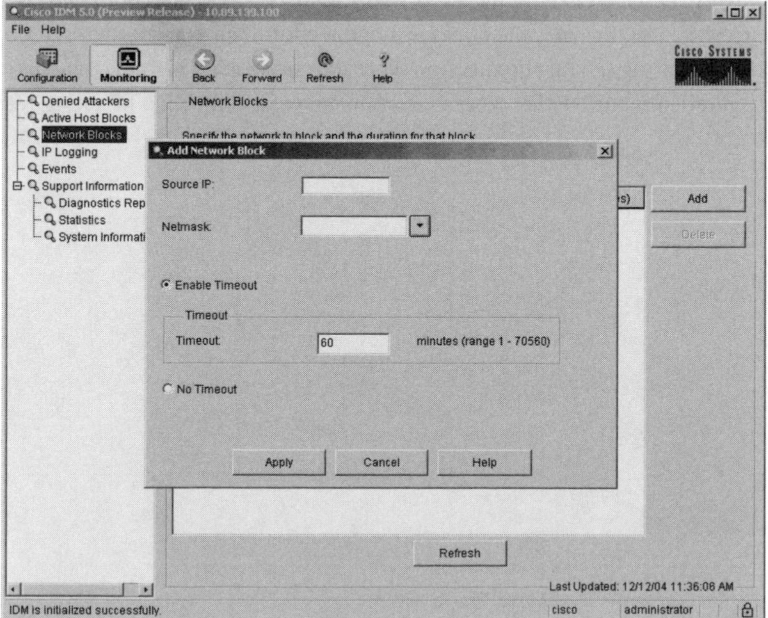

NOTE You can remove the current manual network block entry by first selecting the network block entry and then clicking on **Delete**.

TCP Reset

The TCP reset response action essentially kills the current TCP connection from the attacker by sending a TCP reset packet to both systems involved in the TCP connection. This response is effective only for TCP-based connections. UDP traffic, for example, is unaffected by TCP resets.

NOTE Transmission Control Protocol (TCP) provides a connection-oriented communication mechanism. The connection is established through a three-way handshake. To terminate a connection, each side of the connection can send a FIN packet, signaling the end of the connection. It is also possible, however, for one side of the connection to abruptly terminate the connection by sending a reset packet (a packet with the RST flag set) to the other side. The sensor uses this approach to terminate an attacker TCP connection. For a detailed explanation of TCP/IP protocols, refer to W. Richard Stevens's book, *TCP/IP Illustrated,* Volume 1: The Protocols, published by Addison-Wesley.

To configure a (TCP-based) signature to perform the TCP reset response action, you only need to configure the **Reset TCP Connection** action for the signature. Then, when a specific TCP connection triggers the signature, the sensor will send TCP resets to both ends of the connection to terminate it. Although this ends the attacker's connection with your network, it does not prevent the attacker from initiating another connection with your network. This new connection will work until another triggered signature either resets the connection or initiates a blocking response.

Foundation Summary

Beginning with Cisco IPS version 5.0, you can configure your sensor to perform one or more of the following responses when a specific signature triggers:

- Deny Attacker Inline
- Deny Connection Inline
- Deny Packet Inline
- Log Attacker Packets
- Log Pair Packets
- Log Victim Packets
- Modify Packet Inline
- Produce Alert
- Produce Verbose Alert
- Request Block Connection
- Request Block Host
- Request SNMP Trap
- Reset TCP Connection

Configuring a signature with the Deny Packet Inline action causes your sensor to drop any packets that match the signature's parameters. The Deny Connection Inline action causes the sensor to drop all traffic for the connection (same source and destination IP address and source and destination ports) of the traffic that triggered the signature. Finally, the Deny Attacker Inline action causes the sensor to drop all packets from the attacker's IP address.

Cisco IPS version 5.0 provides the following logging actions:

- Log Attacker Packets
- Log Pair Packets
- Log Victim Packets

Besides logging traffic when a specific signature triggers, you can also manually log traffic in IDM.

IP blocking enables you to halt future traffic from an attacking host for a specified period of time by using one of the following two actions:

- Request Block Host
- Request Block Connection

Table 9-9 lists the terms commonly used in conjunction with IP blocking.

Table 9-9 *IP Blocking Common Terms*

Term	Definition
Active ACL	The dynamically created ACL that the sensor applies to the managed device.
Blocking Sensor	A sensor that you have configured to control one or more managed devices.
Device Management	The ability of a sensor to interact with certain Cisco devices and dynamically reconfigure them to block the source of an attack by using an ACL, VACL, or the **shun** command on the PIX Firewall.
IP Blocking	A feature of Cisco IPS that enables your sensor to block traffic from an attacking system that has triggered a signature that is configured for blocking.
Interface/Direction	The combination of the interface and direction on the interface (in or out) determines where a blocking ACL is applied on your managed device. You can configure the NAC to block a total of ten interface/direction combinations (across all devices on the sensor).
Managed Device	The Cisco device that blocks the source of an attack after being reconfigured by the blocking sensor.
Managed Interface	The interface on the managed device on which the sensor applies the dynamically created ACL (also known as the blocking interface).

You can use the following types of devices to serve as managed devices (for IP blocking):

- Cisco routers
- Cisco Catalyst 6000 switches
- Cisco PIX Firewalls or Adaptive Security Appliances (ASAs)

To manipulate the ACLs on a managed device, you must configure the following on your managed devices:

- Telnet Access (VTY)—Enabled

- Line password—Assigned to VTY
- Telnet or SSH access—Allowed from sensor
- Device's enable password—Assigned

IP blocking requires careful planning and analysis. Some of the important items that you need to consider when designing and implementing IP blocking are as follows:

- Antispoofing mechanisms
- Critical hosts
- Network topology
- Entry points
- Signature selection
- Blocking duration
- Device login information
- Interface ACL requirements

A block action is initiated when one of the following two events occurs:

- A signature configured with the block action triggers
- You manually initiate a block (from a management interface such as the CLI or IDM)

The blocking process involves the following sequence of operations:

1. An event or action configured for blocking occurs.
2. The NAC sends a new set of configurations or ACLs (one for each interface/direction) to each controlled device. It applies the block to each interface/direction on all of the devices that the sensor is configured to control.
3. For alarm events, the alarm is sent to the Event Store at the same time that the block is applied. Each of these events happens independently of the other.
4. When the configured block duration expires, the NAC updates the configurations or ACLs to remove the block.

When applying ACLs on your network, consider your operational requirements and network topology. You have several options when applying ACLs to one of your network devices. The ACL might be applied on either the external or internal interface of the router. It can also be configured for inbound or outbound traffic on each of these two interfaces (when using ACLs).

To use IP blocking on an interface/direction that has an existing ACL, you need to define the following additional ACLs:

- Pre-Block ACL
- Post-Block ACL

If more than one of your sensors is configured for IP blocking, you need these sensors to coordinate their blocking actions with each other so that all entry points into you network are blocked when an attack is noticed by any of your sensors. This coordination is handled by configuring a Master Blocking Sensor.

When configuring IP blocking, you need to perform numerous configuration operations. These operations fall into the following categories:

- Assigning the block action
- Setting blocking properties
- Defining addresses never to block
- Setting up logical devices
- Defining blocking devices
- Defining Master Blocking Sensors

The following blocking parameters apply to all automatic blocks that the NAC initiates:

- Maximum block entries
- Allow the sensor IP address to be blocked
- Block action duration

To prevent your blocking sensor from blocking traffic to critical systems on your network (either accidentally or because of a deliberate attack), you can configure which IP addresses your blocking device should never block.

Using IDM, you can manually initiate block requests. You have the option of initiating manual blocks for a single host or for a specific network.

The TCP reset response action essentially kills the current TCP connection from the attacker by sending a TCP reset packet to both systems involved in the TCP connection.

Q&A

You have two choices for review questions:

- The questions that follow give you a bigger challenge than the exam itself by using an open-ended question format. By reviewing now with this more difficult question format, you can exercise your memory better and prove your conceptual and factual knowledge of this chapter. The answers to these questions are found in the appendix.
- For more practice with exam-like question formats, use the exam engine on the CD-ROM.

1. What are the three inline response actions?
2. What traffic does the Deny Connection Inline response action prevent?
3. What are the three logging options available in Cisco IPS version 5.0?
4. What two blocking actions can you configure to occur when a signature triggers?
5. What types of devices can Cisco IPS sensors use as managed devices?
6. What must you configure when implementing IP blocking on an interface that already has an ACL applied to it?
7. When do you need to configure a Master Blocking Sensor?
8. How many sensors can initiate IP blocking on a single managed device?
9. How can you protect the traffic from critical systems from accidentally being blocked by the IP blocking functionality?
10. What are the two steps for defining a router blocking device in IDM?
11. Which response actions can be manually configured via the IDM interface?
12. What response action uses the Simple Network Management Protocol (SNMP)?
13. How long does the Deny Attacker Inline action block traffic from the attacker's IP address?
14. Which parameter determines how long IP blocking actions remain in effect?
15. Which blocking mechanism enables you to restrict traffic between systems on the same network segment?

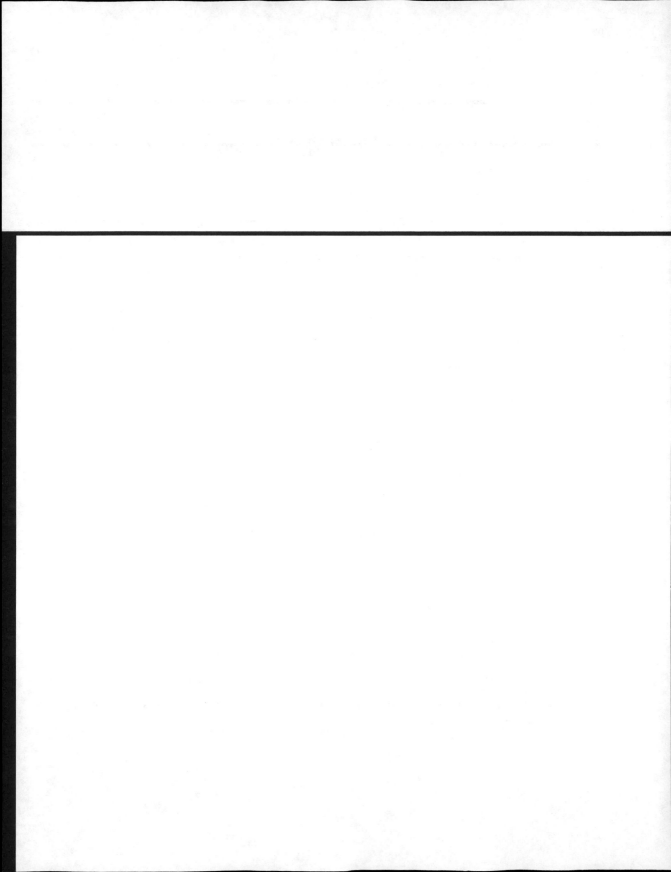

Part IV: Cisco IPS Event Monitoring

This chapter covers the following subjects:

- CiscoWorks 2000
- Security Monitor
- Installing Security Monitor
- Security Monitor Configuration
- Security Monitor Event Viewer
- Security Monitor Administration
- Security Monitor Reports

CHAPTER 10

Alarm Monitoring and Management

When deploying a large number of Cisco IPS sensors, you need an efficient way to monitor the alerts from these devices. Security Monitor (a component of the CiscoWorks VPN/Security Management Solution [VMS] product) provides this functionality. Using Security Monitor, you can correlate and analyze events from multiple sensors deployed throughout your network through a graphical interface. Configuring Security Monitor correctly is crucial to efficiently identifying intrusive activity on your network.

"Do I Know This Already?" Quiz

The purpose of the "Do I Know This Already?" quiz is to help you decide if you really need to read the entire chapter. If you already intend to read the entire chapter, you do not necessarily need to answer these questions now.

The 10-question quiz, derived from the major sections in the "Foundation and Supplemental Topics" portion of the chapter, helps you determine how to spend your limited study time.

Table 10-1 outlines the major topics discussed in this chapter and the "Do I Know This Already?" quiz questions that correspond to those topics.

Table 10-1 *"Do I Know This Already?" Foundation and Supplemental Topics Mapping*

Foundation or Supplemental Topic	Questions Covering This Topic
CiscoWorks 2000	-
Security Monitor	-
Installing Security Monitor	1, 2, 3
Security Monitor Configuration	4, 5, 6
Security Monitor Event Viewer	7, 8
Security Monitor Administration	10
Security Monitor Reports	9

> **CAUTION** The goal of self-assessment is to gauge your mastery of the topics in this chapter. If you do not know the answer to a question or are only partially sure of the answer, you should mark this question wrong for purposes of the self-assessment. Giving yourself credit for an answer you correctly guess skews your self-assessment results and might provide you with a false sense of security.

1. What is the minimum recommended amount of RAM for the Security Monitor server?
   a. 2 GB
   b. 1 GB
   c. 512 MB
   d. 256 MB
   e. 1.5 GB

2. What is the minimum recommended amount of RAM for the client systems that access Security Monitor?
   a. 2 GB
   b. 1 GB
   c. 512 MB
   d. 256 MB
   e. 1.5 GB

3. What part of the Security Monitor interface provides a visual road map indicating where you are?
   a. Path bar
   b. Options bar
   c. Instruction box
   d. Content area
   e. Road map

4. When you add a monitored device to Security Monitor, which of the following devices does not allow you to specify the protocol that the device uses to communicate with Security Monitor?
   a. RDEP device
   b. PostOffice device
   c. IPS 5.0 sensor

- **d.** PIX Firewall
- **e.** IDS 4.0 sensor

5. Which of the following is not a characteristic that you can specify when configuring an event rule?

- **a.** Originating device
- **b.** Signature name
- **c.** Attacker port
- **d.** Severity
- **e.** Victim address

6. Which of the following is not a category whose statistics you can view using Security Monitor?

- **a.** Network Access Controller
- **b.** Analysis Server
- **c.** Transaction Server
- **d.** Event Server
- **e.** Analysis Engine

7. Which of the following items is not configurable when you change the Event Viewer display preferences?

- **a.** Columns displayed
- **b.** Event severity indicator type
- **c.** Default expansion boundary
- **d.** Time for Security Monitor-initiated blocks
- **e.** Maximum events per grid

8. Which color is the background of the count field for medium-severity events?

- **a.** Red
- **b.** Orange
- **c.** Yellow
- **d.** Green
- **e.** White

9. Which of the following is not a parameter that you can configure when customizing a report template?
   a. Source IP address
   b. Destination direction
   c. IDS devices
   d. IDS signatures
   e. Risk Rating

10. Which of the following is not a parameter that you can configure when defining a database rule?
   a. Total IDS events in database exceed
   b. Total audit log events in database exceed
   c. Total PIX events in database exceed
   d. Database free space less than (megabytes)
   e. Repeat every

The answers to the "Do I Know This Already?" quiz are found in the appendix. The suggested choices for your next step are as follows:

- **8 or less overall score**—Read the entire chapter. This includes the "Foundation and Supplemental Topics" and "Foundation Summary" sections and the Q&A section.
- **9 or 10 overall score**—If you want more review on these topics, skip to the "Foundation Summary" section and then go to the Q&A section. Otherwise, move to the next chapter.

Foundation and Supplemental Topics

CiscoWorks 2000

CiscoWorks 2000 is the heart of the Cisco family of comprehensive network management tools that allow you to easily access and manage the advanced capabilities of the Cisco Architecture for Voice, Video, and Integrated Data (AVVID). It provides the foundation that Intrusion Detection System Management Center (IDS MC) is built upon. IDS MC is a component of the CiscoWorks VMS bundle.

Before you can access the IDS MC application, you must first log in to CiscoWorks 2000. CiscoWorks 2000 also manages access to all of the applications in the VMS bundle. To use IDS MC, you need to understand the following CiscoWorks 2000 components:

- Login process
- Authorization roles
- Adding users

Login Process

To access the applications supported by CiscoWorks, such as IDS MC and the Security Monitor, you must first log in to the CiscoWorks server desktop. The CiscoWorks server desktop is the interface used for CiscoWorks network management applications such as IDS MC.

To log in to CiscoWorks, you connect to the CiscoWorks desktop via your web browser. The web server is listening on port 1741. Therefore, if your CiscoWorks desktop is on a machine named CW2000 with an IP address of 10.89.139.71, you could connect to it by entering either of the following URLs:

- http://CW2000:1741/
- http://10.89.139.71:1741/

NOTE If you are on the CiscoWorks server, you can also access CiscoWorks through the localhost host address by using the following URL: http://127.0.0.1:1741/

> **NOTE** If you configure CiscoWorks to Secure HTTP (HTTPS), you access the CiscoWorks server by using port 1742. For HTTPS access, the example URLs become the following:
>
> - https://CW2000:1742/
> - https://10.89.139.71:1742/

At the initial CiscoWorks screen, you log in to CiscoWorks by entering a valid username and password (see Figure 10-1).

> **NOTE** Initially, you can log in by using the administrator account created during installation. The default value is **admin** for both the username and the password (unless you changed these values during the installation process). For security reasons, you should change these values.

Figure 10-1 *CiscoWorks Login Screen*

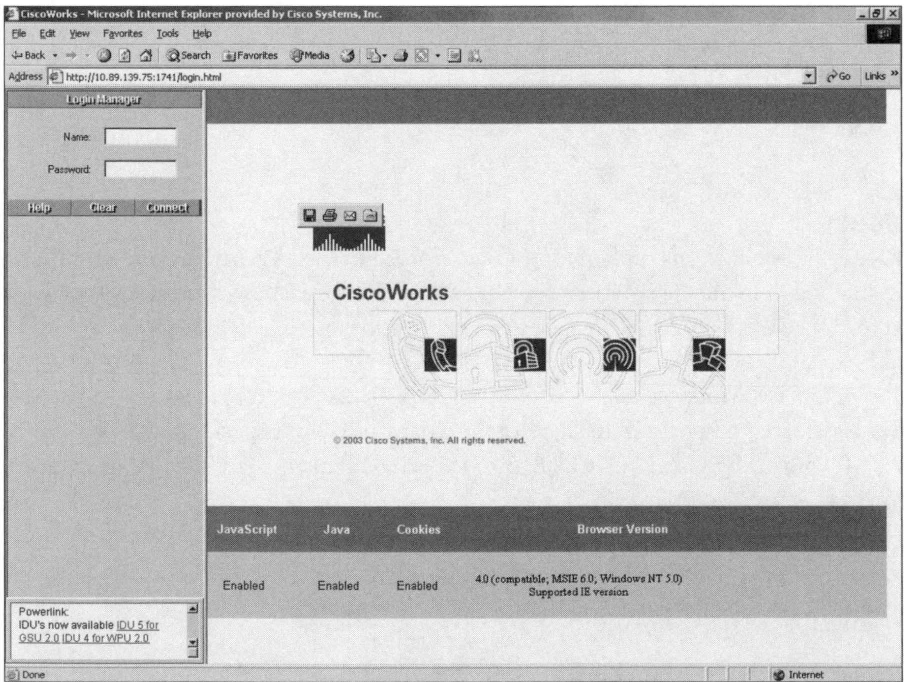

Authorization Roles

Like IDM, CiscoWorks enables you to define different roles for different users. These roles enable the user to perform specific operations when using CiscoWorks and any of the applications that are built upon CiscoWorks (like IDS MC and Security Monitor). CiscoWorks supports five user roles that are relevant to IDS MC and Security Monitor operations (see in Table 10-2).

Table 10-2 *CiscoWorks User Roles*

User Role	Description
Help Desk	Read-only for the entire CiscoWorks system
Approver	Read-only for entire CiscoWorks system; includes the configuration approval privileges
Network Operator	Read-only for the entire CiscoWorks system; generates reports and includes configuration-deployment privileges
Network Administrator	Read-only for the entire CiscoWorks system; includes privileges to edit devices and device groups
System Administrator	Performs all operations

NOTE You can assign each user multiple authorization roles (depending on their responsibilities). CiscoWorks 2000 also supports two other roles: Export Data and Developer. These roles are not relevant to the IDS MC or Security Monitor operations.

Adding Users

As part of your IDS MC and Security Monitor configuration, you need to configure accounts for the various users who need to access these applications. The CiscoWorks 2000 Add User screen enables you to create new accounts that have access to the CiscoWorks 2000 applications. To create a new account in CiscoWorks 2000, perform the following steps:

Step 1 Log in to the CiscoWorks 2000 desktop.

Step 2 Choose **Server Configuration > Setup > Security > Add Users**. The Add User window appears. (See Figure 10-2.)

Step 3 Enter values for the new user (Table 10-3 describes these various fields).

Step 4 In the **Roles** section of the Add User window, select the role(s) associated with the user's responsibilities. You can assign multiple roles to a single user.

Step 5 Click on **Add** to complete the addition of the user to the CiscoWorks 2000 database.

Figure 10-2 *CiscoWorks Add User Window*

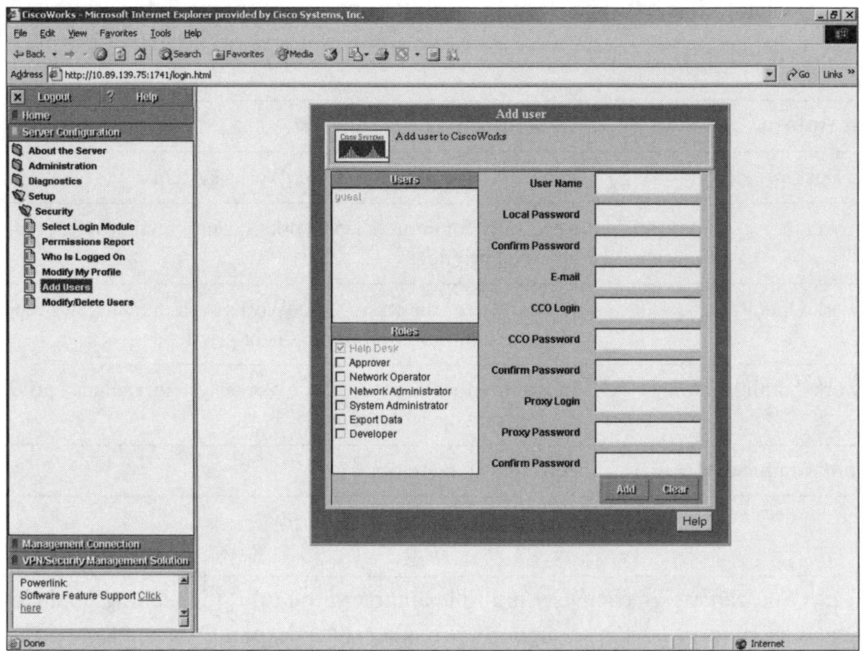

Table 10-3 *CiscoWorks Add User Fields*

Field	**Description**
User Name	Username of the user being added
Local Password	Password for the new user
Confirm Password	Confirmation of the user's password
E-Mail	(Optional) User's e-mail address
CCO Login	(Optional) User's Cisco.com login name (used for downloading software updates from the Cisco website)
CCO Password	User's Cisco.com password (required only if CCO Login is specified)
Confirm Password	Confirmation of user's Cisco.com password (required only if CCO Password is entered)
Proxy Login	(Optional) Enter the user's proxy login (required if your network requires use of a proxy server)
Proxy Password	User's proxy password (required only if Proxy Login is specified)
Confirm Password	Confirmation of user's proxy login (required only if Proxy Login is specified)

Security Monitor

Security Monitor is a component of the CiscoWorks VMS product. VMS integrates into a single solution numerous security applications, such as the following:

- CiscoWorks
- Security Monitor
- VPN Monitor
- VMS Common Services

Security Monitor provides numerous features such as the following:

- Device monitoring
- Web-based monitoring
- Custom reporting

Using Security Monitor, you can monitor IPS/IDS events from up to 300 Cisco IPS-capable devices, such as the following:

- Sensor appliances
- IDS modules
- Router modules
- IOS routers
- PIX Firewalls

Using a compatible web browser, you can access the Security Monitor to administer and monitor the alerts from your IDS devices. Furthermore, you can easily use an extensive list of common reports to support your reporting requirements.

Installing Security Monitor

You can install Security Monitor on the following two platforms:

- Windows 2000
- Solaris

For more information on the Solaris requirements, refer to Cisco documentation.

Windows Installation

When installing Security Monitor, you need to understand the hardware and software requirements for the different components. The major components involved in a Security Monitor Windows installation are as follows:

- CiscoWorks 2000 server
- Client systems
- Sensors

Since the sensors are appliances, the software and hardware are fairly fixed. The other two components, however, are built on your own machines. To ensure an operable installation, these systems must match some minimum requirements.

Server Requirements

To support all of the functionality provided by Security Monitor and the underlying CiscoWorks 2000 foundation, your CiscoWorks 2000 server needs to match the following requirements:

- IDM PC-compatible computer
- 1 GHz (or faster) processor
- Color monitor with video card capable of viewing 16-bit color
- CD-ROM drive
- 10BASE-T (or faster) network connection
- Minimum of 1 GB of RAM
- 2 GB of virtual memory
- Minimum of 9 GB free hard drive space (formatted using NT Files System [NTFS])
- Windows 2000 Professional, Server or Advanced Server, with Service Pack 4 (and Terminal Services turned off)

Client Requirements

Your users access Security Monitor via a browser on their system. These user systems should meet certain minimum requirements to ensure successful system operation. Your client systems should meet the following requirements:

- IBM PC-compatible
- 300 MHz (or faster) processor

- Minimum 256 MB RAM
- 400 MB virtual memory (free space on hard drive for Windows)

In addition to meeting these requirements, your clients need to be running one of the following operating systems:

- Windows 2000 Professional with Service Pack 3
- Windows 2000 Server with Service Pack 3
- Windows XP with Service Pack 1 with Microsoft Virtual Machine

One final requirement is that your client systems need to use one of the following web browsers and have the Java plug-in version 1.41_02:

- Internet Explorer 6.0 with Service Pack 1
- Netscape Navigator 7.1

Security Monitor User Interface

Although the Security Monitor user interface is graphical and easy to use, it is helpful to understand how the interface is structured. The Security Monitor user interface is composed of the following major sections (see Figure 10-3):

- Configuration tabs
- Options bar
- Table of contents (TOC)
- Path bar
- Instruction box
- Content area
- Tools bar

Configuration Tabs

The configuration tasks are divided into the following five major categories:

- Devices—Enables you to perform initial setup of devices to be monitored by Security Monitor
- Configuration—Enables you to configure event rules for Security Monitor

Figure 10-3 *Security User Interface*

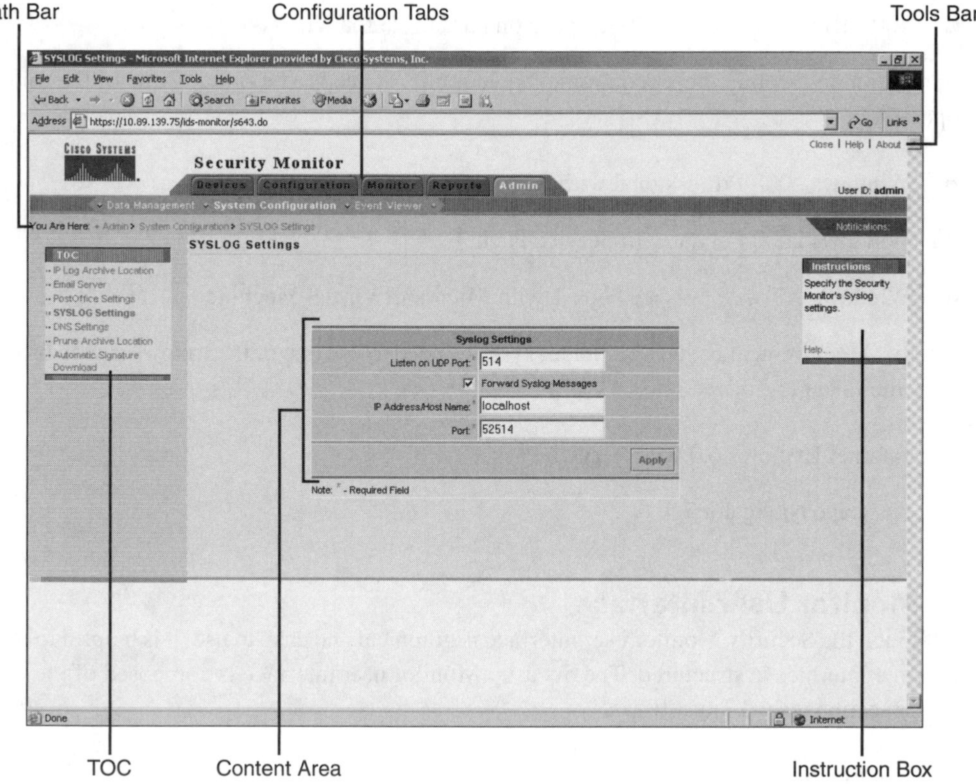

- Monitor—Enables you to monitor information about your devices and launch the Event Viewer
- Reports—Enables you to generate reports, view scheduled reports, and view reports
- Admin—Enables you to administer system and database settings

To access one of the categories, click on the tab labeled with the appropriate name. These tabs are located across the top of the Security Monitor display.

Options Bar

After you click on one of the major configuration tabs, the options for that selection are displayed in a list located on the screen just below the configuration tabs. Figure 10-3 shows a screen in which the user has clicked on the **Admin** tab. The options associated with the **Admin** tab are as follows:

- Data Management
- System Configuration
- Event Viewer

Clicking on any of these options causes a menu of available choices to be displayed on the left side of the Security Monitor interface (known as the TOC).

TOC

The TOC is a menu of choices that is displayed down the left side of the Security Monitor interface. It represents the list of suboptions that you can select (based on the option chosen). In Figure 10-3, you can see that the **Admin > System Configuration** option provides the following selections:

- IP Log Archive Location
- E-Mail Server
- PostOffice Settings
- SYSLOG Settings
- DNS Settings
- Prune Archive Location
- Automatic Signature Download

Path Bar

The path bar provides a visual road map indicating where you are with respect to the Security Monitor interface. It is located above the TOC and below the options bar and begins with the text "You Are Here."

Figure 10-3 shows a situation in which the path bar's value is **Admin > System Configuration > SYSLOG Settings**. This indicates that you performed the following steps to reach the current screen:

Step 1 Clicked on the **Admin** tab.

Step 2 Selected **System Configuration** from the options bar.

Step 3 Selected **SYSLOG Settings** from the TOC.

Instruction Box

Some pages provide you with an instructions box on the right side of the Security Monitor display. This box (when displayed) provides you with a brief overview of the page you have selected. This information is a quick summary of information provided through the Help option on the tools bar.

Content Area

The content area displays information associated with the selection you click on the TOC menu. Sometimes the option selected from the options bar has no TOC options. In this situation, you can click on the option from the options bar to directly display information in the content area. An example of this is **Configuration > Event Rules**.

Tools Bar

The tools bar is located at the upper right of the Security Monitor interface. From the tools bar you can access the following items:

- Close
- Help
- About

Close enables you to close the Security Monitor program. The Help option displays Security Monitor's help information in a separate browser window. Finally, the About option displays the Security Monitor software version.

Security Monitor Configuration

Before you can use Security Monitor to analyze the events from your IPS devices, you must add the IPS devices to Security Monitor. You can configure the rules that Security Monitor uses to access events from the devices being monitored. For Remote Data Exchange Protocol (RDEP) devices, you can also monitor connection and statistical information. This section will focus on the following Security Monitor configuration operations:

- Adding devices
- Importing devices
- Event notification
- Monitoring devices

Adding Devices

Security Monitor enables you to view events from various Cisco IPS devices deployed throughout your network. Before you can monitor these devices, however, you must add them to Security Monitor. The Devices window (see Figure 10-4) shows you the devices that you have already added to Security Monitor and enables you to add or import new devices as well as perform the following operations on existing devices:

- Edit

- Delete
- View

Figure 10-4 *Devices Window in Security Monitor*

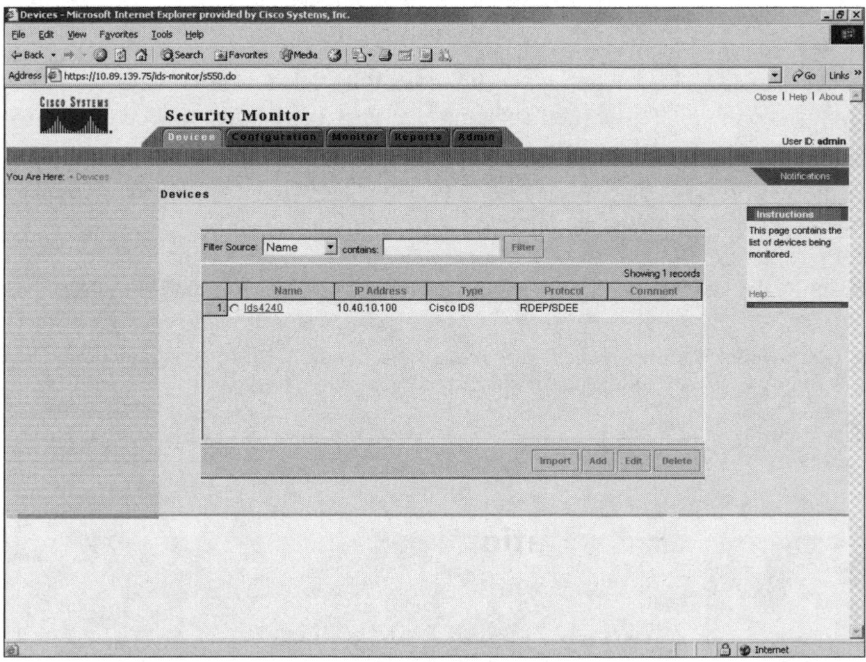

Security Monitor monitors the following types of devices:

- Cisco IDS
- Cisco IOS IDS/IPS
- Cisco PIX/FWSM
- Cisco Security Agent MC
- Remote Cisco Security Monitor

Adding RDEP Devices

Security Monitor uses RDEP to communicate with your Cisco IPS version 5.0 sensors. When adding an RDEP device to Security Monitor, you must specify the following information about the device:

- IP Address
- Device Name

- Web Server Port
- Username
- Password
- Minimum Event Level

The **IP Address**, **Device Name**, and **Web Server Port** fields identify the device so that Security Monitor can communicate it. The **Username** and **Password** fields provide the login credentials necessary to access the RDEP device. Finally, the **Minimum Event Level** field sets the minimum alert level for the events that Security Monitor will retrieve from the device. By default, only events of medium severity or higher are retrieved.

To add an RDEP device to Security Monitor, you need to perform the following steps:

Step 1 Click on the **Devices** tab on the main Security Monitor screen. The Devices window will appear in the content area.

Step 2 Click on the **Add** button. The Add Device window appears (see Figure 10-5).

Figure 10-5 *Security Monitor Add Device Window*

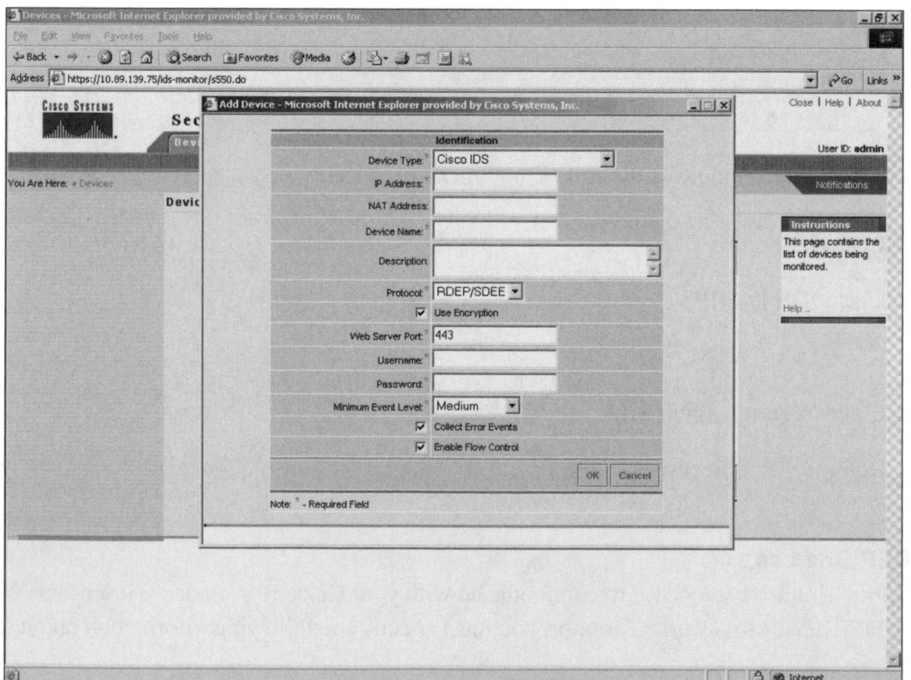

Step 3 Select the correct device being added by using the pull-down menu for the **Device Type** field. In this situation, you should select **Cisco IDS** (the default).

Step 4 In the **IP Address** field, enter the IP address of the sensor.

Step 5 In the **Device Name** field, enter the name of the sensor.

Step 6 In the **Username** field, enter the username that Security Monitor will use to communicate with the sensor.

Step 7 In the **Password** field, enter the password for the account that Security Monitor will use to communicate with the sensor.

Step 8 Select the minimum level of events that you want Security Monitor to retrieve. Choices include **High**, **Medium**, **Low**, and **Informational** (the default is **Medium**).

Step 9 Click on **OK** to add the new device to Security Monitor.

Adding PostOffice Devices

Security Monitor can receive events from Cisco IDS version 3.x sensors. You can add these devices by selecting **Postoffice** as the protocol. When adding a version 3.x sensor, you must specify the following fields (see Figure 10-6):

- IP Address
- Device Name
- Host ID
- Org Name
- Org ID
- Port
- Heartbeat

NOTE The PostOffice protocol is a proprietary protocol used to communicate with Cisco IDS version 3.x sensors. This protocol should not be confused with the Post Office Protocol (POP) specified in RFC 1939 (http://www.faqs.org/rfcs/rfc1939.html), which is a mail-distribution protocol.

Figure 10-6 *Adding a PostOffice Device*

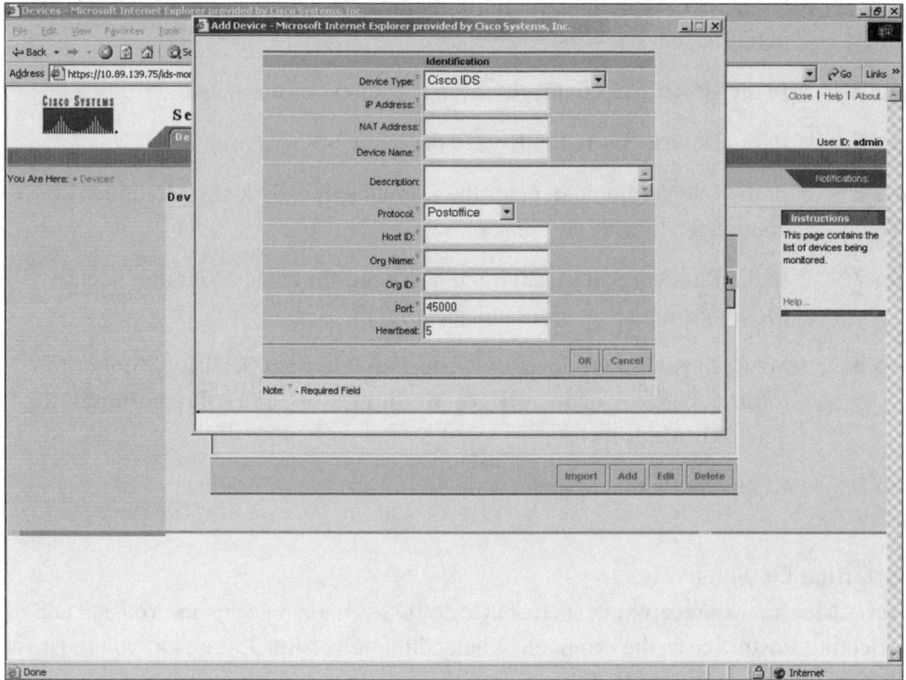

Adding IOS Devices

Besides receiving events from Cisco IPS sensors, Security Monitor can also receive events from other Cisco IDS devices (such as IOS routers and PIX Firewalls). You can add IOS devices by selecting **IOS IDS/IPS** in the **Device Type** field. When adding an IOS IDS device, you must specify the following fields:

- IP Address
- Device Name
- Web Server Port
- Protocol
- Username
- Password
- Minimum Event Level

Some IOS devices can run the PostOffice protocol. If you want Security Monitor to communicate with the IOS device using PostOffice, you need to select **Postoffice** in the **Protocol** field. This will enable you to enter the following PostOffice parameters:

- Host ID
- Org Name
- Org ID
- Port
- Heartbeat

Adding PIX Devices

Similar to IOS IDS devices, Security Monitor can be configured to receive events from PIX Firewalls. You must specify the following fields to add PIX Firewall devices.

- IP Address
- Device Name

Since the PIX Firewalls can communicate only via syslog (UDP port 514), you are not allowed to specify the protocol for PIX devices.

Importing Devices

Instead of adding new devices by specifying all of the information necessary for Security Monitor to communicate with them, you can import devices from an instance of IDS MC that is already monitoring the devices that you wish to add. To import a device from IDS MC into Security Monitor, perform the following steps:

Step 1 Click on the **Devices** tab on the main Security Monitor screen. The Devices window will appear in the content area.

Step 2 Click on the **Import** button. The Enter IDS MC Server Information window will appear in the content area. (See Figure 10-7.)

Step 3 Enter the IP address (or hostname) of the IDS MC server from which you want to import devices.

Step 4 Enter the username and password required to log in to the IDS MC server.

Step 5 Click on the **Next** button to continue. The Select Devices window will appear in the content area. (See Figure 10-8.) It shows all of the devices that the IDS MC server is managing.

Figure 10-7 *Enter IDS MC Server Information Window*

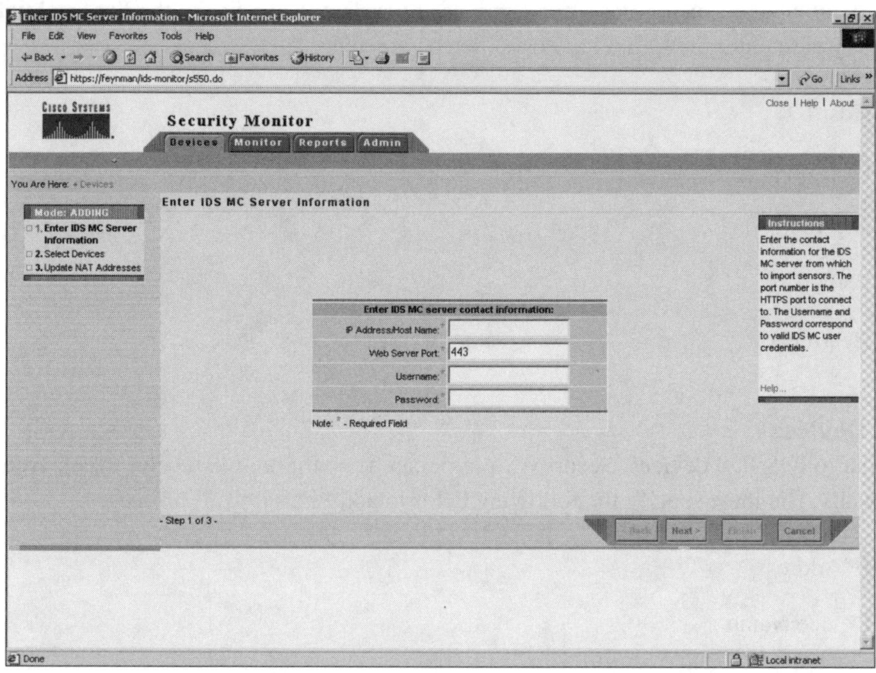

Figure 10-8 *Select Devices Window*

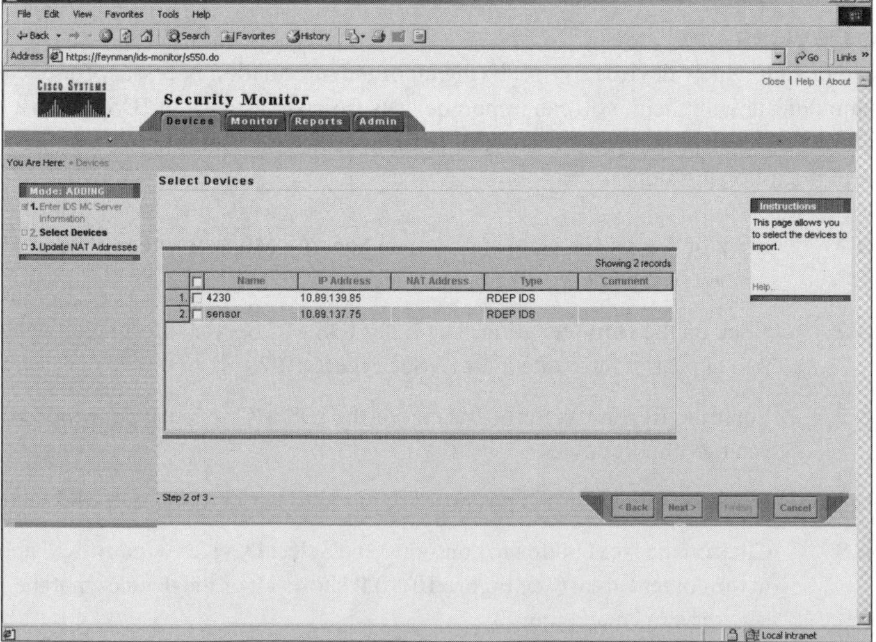

Step 6 Click on the check box next to each sensor that you want to import.

Step 7 Click on the **Finish** button to import the selected sensors. A Summary window will be displayed in the content area. It indicates which sensors you imported.

Event Notification

When multiple security devices are deployed throughout your network, they can generate a large number of events. Analyzing every one of these events by using the Event Viewer can be very time-consuming. Furthermore, it may be impossible to monitor the Event Viewer 24 hours a day. You can define event rules that perform specific actions when the Security Monitor receives traffic matching specific properties. You could use this functionality, for instance, to cause Security Monitor to e-mail you when certain traffic is detected on your network.

When defining an event rule, you can identify traffic based on the alert characteristics shown in Table 10-4.

Table 10-4 *Event Rule Characteristics*

Characteristic	Description
Originating Device	Enables you to specify a monitor device
Originating Device Address	Enables you to specify the originating address of the device
Attacker Address	Enables you to filter based on the IP address of the attacker
Victim Address	Enables you to filter based on the IP address of the victim or system being attacked
Signature Name	Enables you to filter based on the name of a signature
Signature ID	Enables you to filter based on the ID of a signature
Severity	Enables you to filter based on the severity of the alarm received (Informational, Low, Medium, or High)

For each characteristic, you specify a value and one of the following operators to equate the characteristic to the value:

- < (Less than)
- <= (Less than or equal)
- = (Equal)
- != (Not equal)
- >= (Greater than or equal)
- > (Greater than)

> **NOTE** Not all of these operators are valid for each characteristic. For some of the characteristics (such as Originating Device), only "equal" and "not equal" are valid.

Each characteristic plus a value is known as a clause. You combine multiple clauses for a single rule by specifying one of the following Boolean operators:

- AND
- OR
- NOT

After entering your clauses that define which traffic the event rule applies to, you need to define the action that you want Security Monitor to perform for traffic that actually matches the rule. Each rule can perform one or more of the following actions:

- Notify via e-mail
- Log a console notification event
- Execute a shell script

> **NOTE** Each event rule you define can have up to five clauses. Furthermore, you can define up to 10 event rules that you can have active at one time.

Adding Event Rules

Event rules specify the criteria that an event must match in order to cause a specific action. When adding event rules, you need to perform the following four tasks:

- Assign a name to the event rule
- Define the event filter criteria
- Assign the event rule action
- Define the event rule threshold and interval

Complete the following steps to add an event rule:

Step 1 Click on the **Configuration** tab on the main Security Monitor screen.

Step 2 Select **Event Rules** from the options bar (or from the content area). The Event Rules window appears in the content area. (See Figure 10-9.)

Step 3 Click on the **Add** button. The Identify the Rule window will appear in the content area. (See Figure 10-10.)

Figure 10-9 *Event Rules Window*

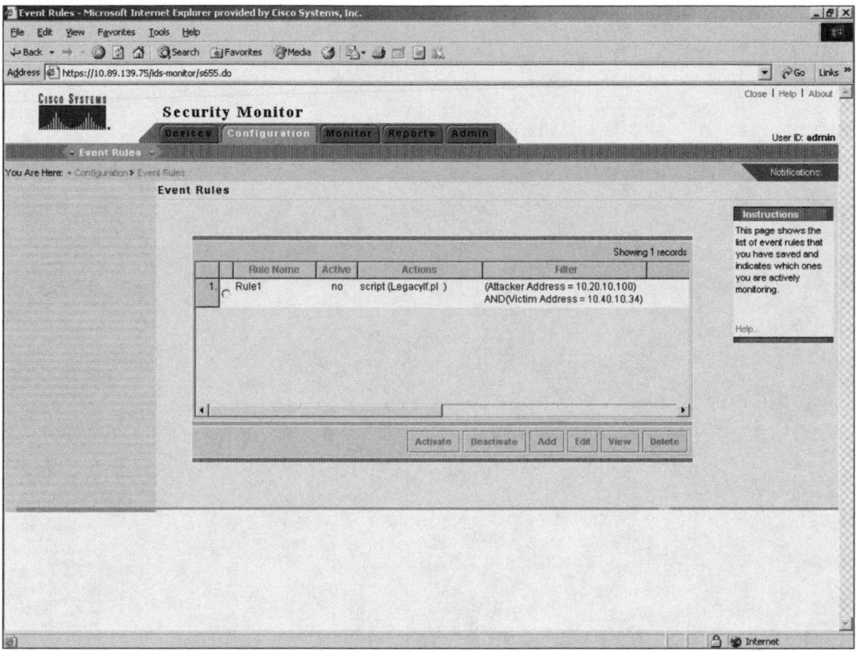

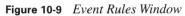

Figure 10-10 *Identify the Rule Window*

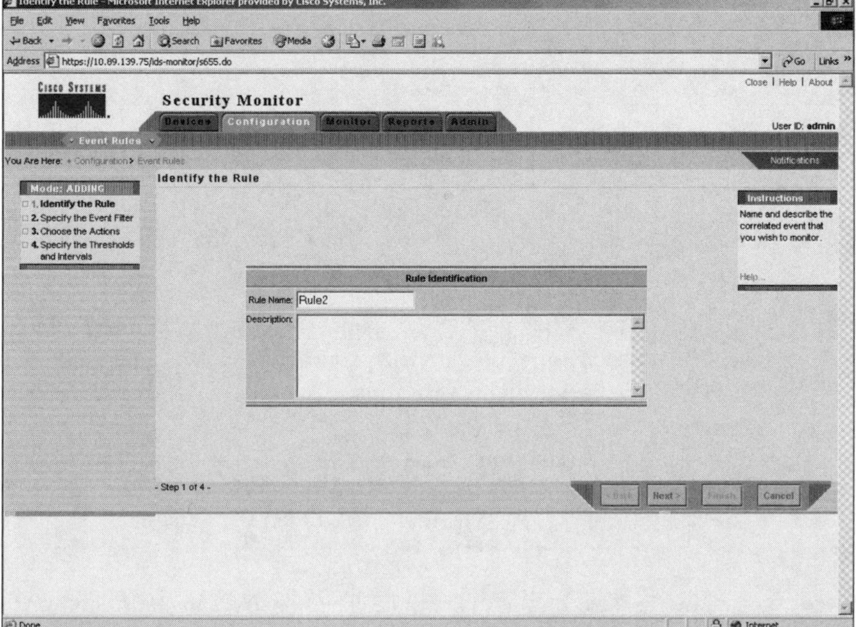

Step 4 Enter a name for the rule in the **Rule Name** field.

Step 5 Enter a textual description for the rule.

Step 6 Click on the **Next** button. The Specify the Event Filter window will appear in the content area. (See Figure 10-11.)

Figure 10-11 *Specify the Event Filter Window*

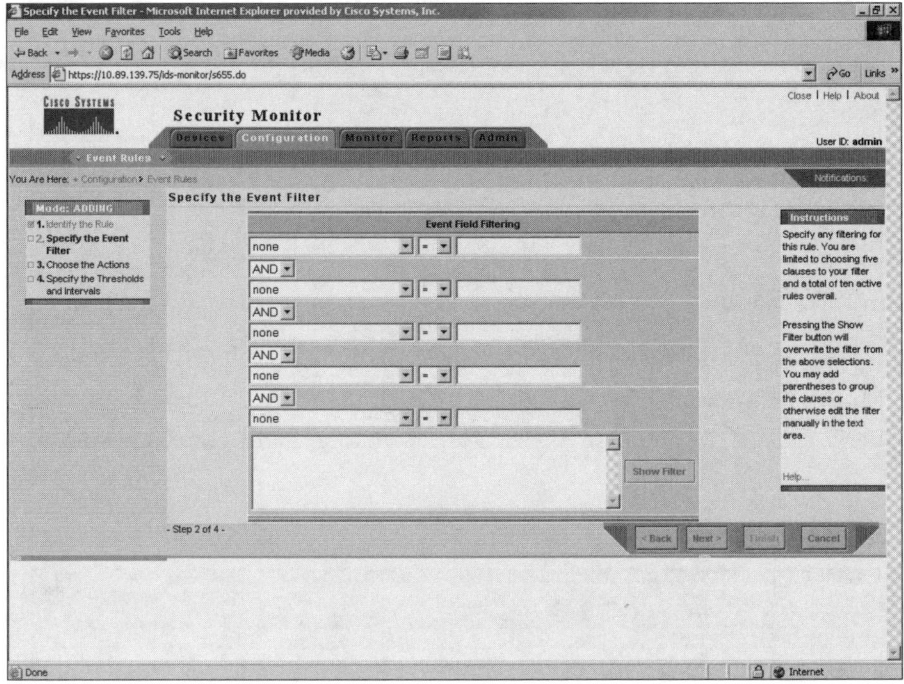

Step 7 Define the clauses that make up the event rule and the associations between clauses.

Step 8 Click on the **Next** button to continue. The Choose the Actions window will appear in the content area. (See Figure 10-12.)

Step 9 Click on the check box next to the action(s) that you want assigned to this event rule. Specify any rule-specific parameters (such as an e-mail address for the Notify via E-Mail option). You can assign one or more actions to each event rule.

> **NOTE** If you have not configured an e-mail server by following **Admin > System Configuration > E-Mail Server**, the e-mail option will not be available.

Step 10 Click on the **Next** button to continue. The Specify Thresholds and Intervals window will appear in the content area. (See Figure 10-13.)

Figure 10-12 *Choose the Actions Window*

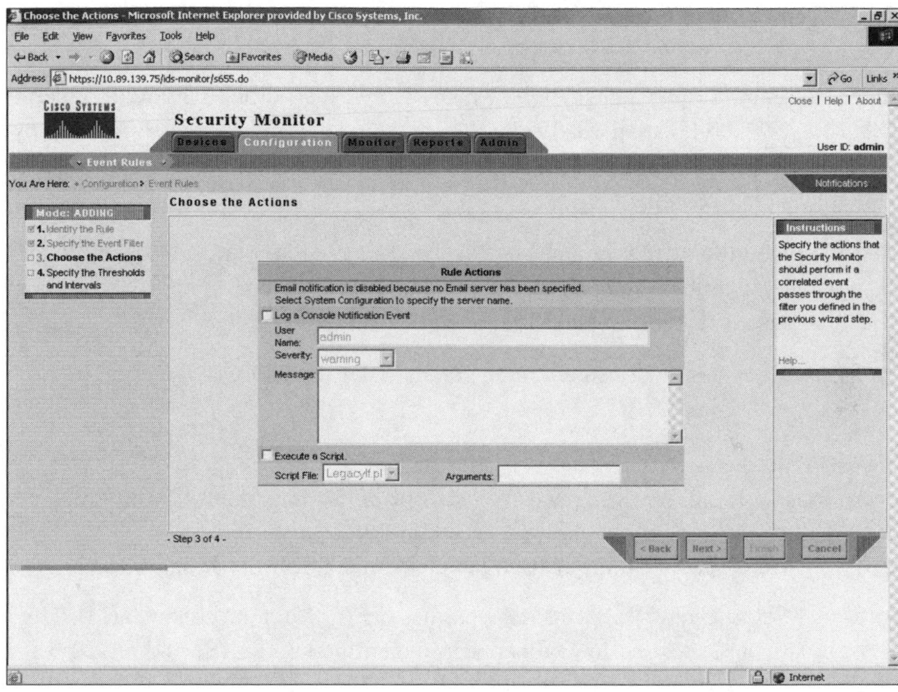

Figure 10-13 *Specify the Thresholds and Intervals Window*

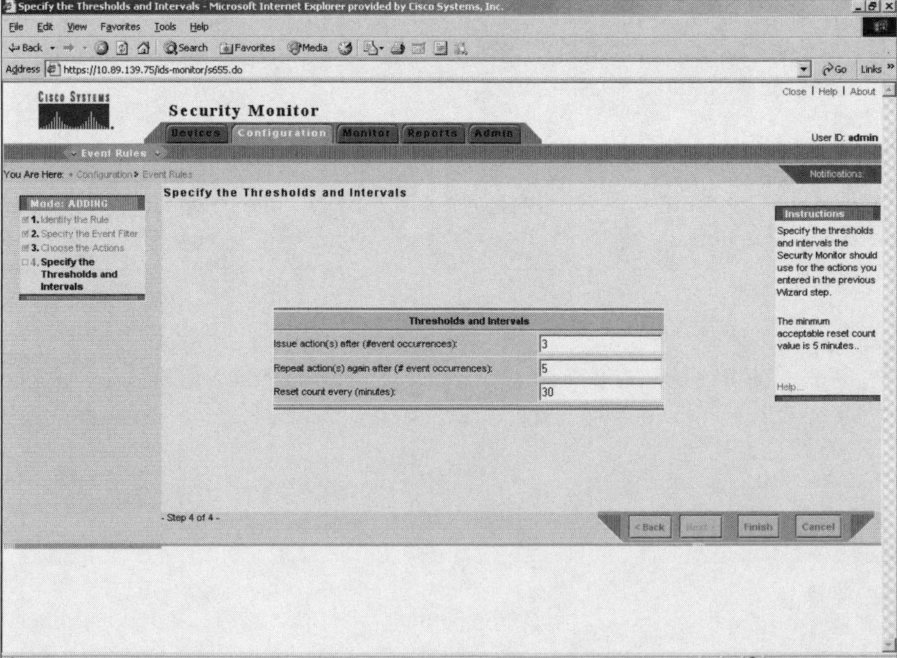

Step 11 Enter a value for how many event occurrences are needed to trigger the rule's action(s) by entering a number into the **Issue action(s) after (#event occurrences)** field (the default is 3).

Step 12 Enter a value indicating how many more events (after the initial triggering of the rule) are needed before the action(s) are triggered again; do this by entering a number in the **Repeat action(s) again after (#event occurrences)** field (the default is 5).

Step 13 Define how many minutes must elapse before the count value is reset; do this by entering a value in the **Reset count every (minutes)** field. The minimum reset value is 5 minutes (the default is 30).

Step 14 Click on the **Finish** button to complete the definition of the event rule.

Activating Event Rules

After defining an event rule, you must activate it by performing the following steps:

Step 1 Click on the **Configuration** tab on the main Security Monitor screen.

Step 2 Select **Event Rules** from the options bar (or from the content area). The Event Rules window will appear in the content area. (See Figure 10-9.)

Step 3 Click on the radio button next to the rule that you want to activate.

NOTE You can know which event rules are active by examining the **Active** field. If a rule is active, this field has a value of **yes**. Rules that have not been activated have a value of **no** in this field.

Step 4 Click on the **Activate** button.

NOTE You can deactivate event rules by following this same procedure but clicking on the **Deactivate** button instead of the **Activate** button.

Monitoring Devices

You can monitor information about the devices that you have added to Security Monitor. This information falls into the following three categories:

- Connections
- Statistics
- Events

Monitoring Connections

Security Monitor needs to communicate with all of the devices from which it receives information. With RDEP devices, Security Monitor actually connects to the sensor and retrieves the alerts. PostOffice devices send the information directly to Security Monitor. You can check the status of RDEP and PostOffice devices by using the Connections window. (See Figure 10-14.)

Figure 10-14 *The Connections Window*

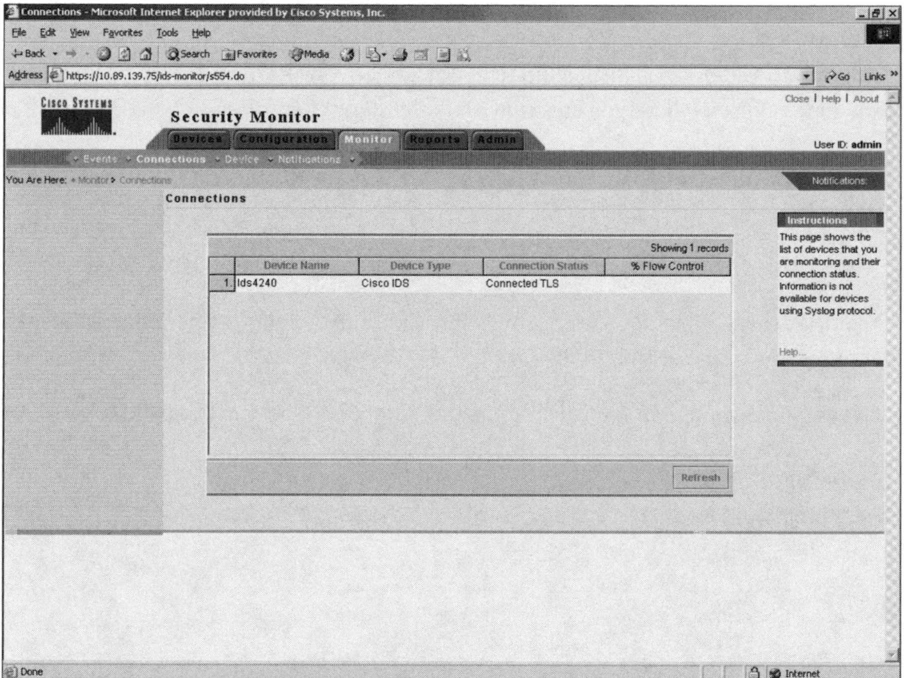

If the Connection status is either "Connected" or "Connected TLS," Security Monitor is receiving events from the device correctly. A Connection status of "Not Connected" represents a problem and can indicate one of the following conditions:

- The device has been added to Security Monitor, but it is not yet configured to send event data. This situation commonly arises if you add devices to Security Monitor before you have actually deployed them on your network.
- The device is configured incorrectly. For PostOffice devices, verify that the device is sending events to the correct IP address (for Security Monitor) on the correct port.
- Security Monitor is configured incorrectly. Verify the settings for the device in Security Monitor to make sure that the PostOffice communication parameters match the actual device parameters or that the RDEP logging credentials and IP address are valid.

- Network connectivity between Security Monitor and the device has been lost. Try to ping the device from the underlying CiscoWorks software on the Security Monitor server.

NOTE IOS IDS devices (those not using PostOffice or RDEP) and PIX Firewalls do not show up in the connection list, since they send information to the Security Monitor in a connectionless fashion by using syslog messages.

Monitoring Statistics

You can view a wealth of statistical information about your RDEP devices. Using the Statistics window (see Figure 10-15), you can view statistics about the following items:

- **Analysis Engine**—MAC, virtual sensor, TCP Stream Reassembly, and signature database statistics
- **Authentication**—Successful and failed login attempts to the RDEP device
- **Event Server**—General and specific subscription information about the devices that have connections to the server
- **Event Store**—General information on and number of specific events that have occurred

Figure 10-15 *Statistics Window*

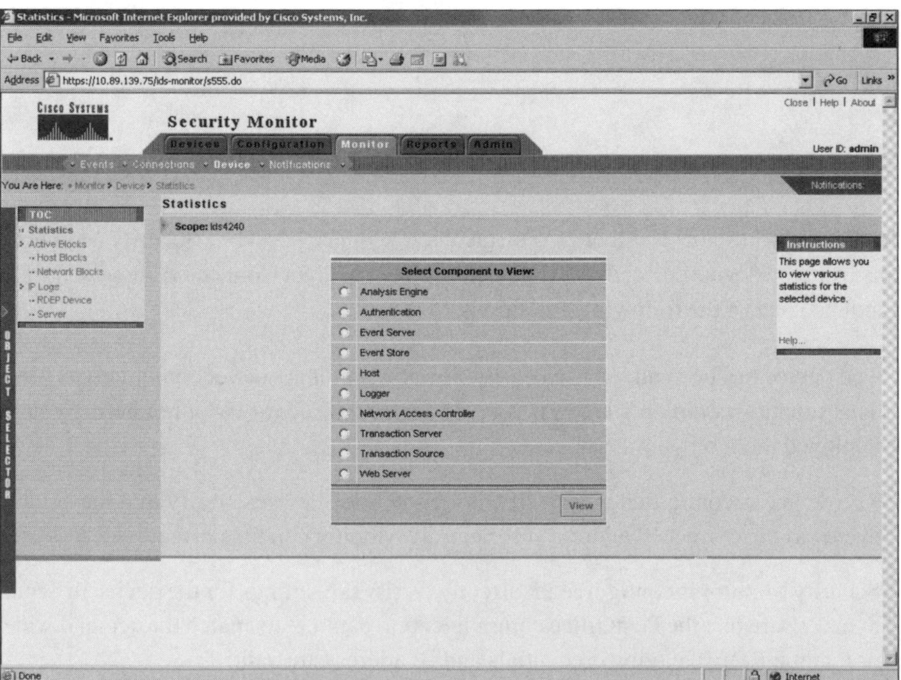

- **Host**—Network statistics, memory usage, and swap-file usage
- **Logger**—Number of events and log messages written by the logger process
- **Network Access Controller**—Information about the sensor's current shunning (blocking) configuration
- **Transaction Server**—Counts indicating the failed and total number of control transactions for the server
- **Transaction Source**—Counts indicating the failed and total number of source control transactions
- **Web Server**—Configuration information for the device web server and statistics for connections to the web server

To view any of these statistics, follow these steps:

Step 1 Click on the **Monitor** tab on the main Security Monitor screen.

Step 2 Select **Device** from the options bar (or the content area). This displays the Monitor Device window. (See Figure 10-16.)

Figure 10-16 *Monitor Device Window*

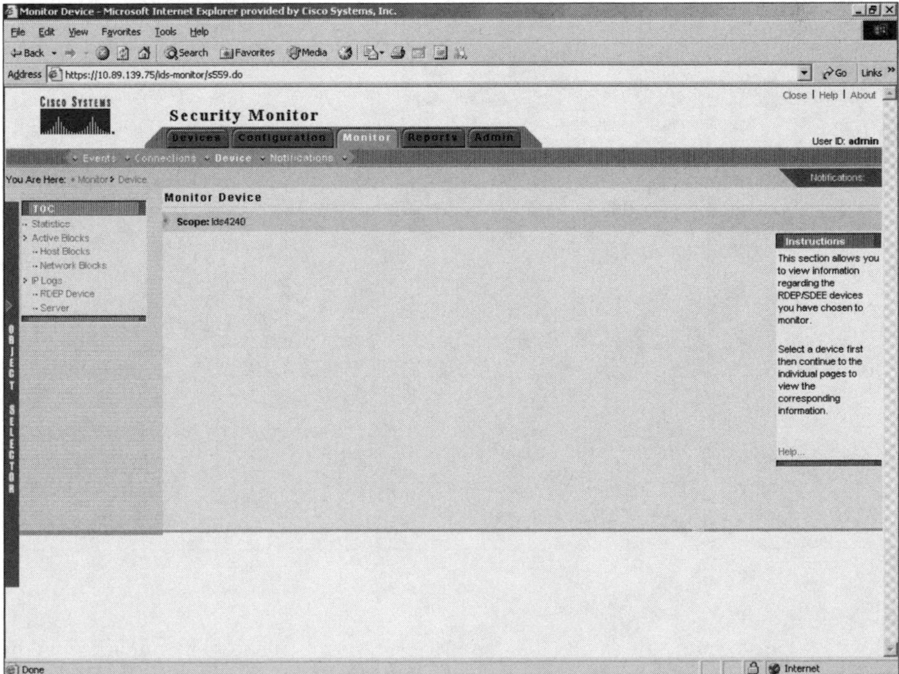

Step 3 Select the device on which you want to view statistics by using the object selector. In this example, the device selected is Ids4240.

Step 4 Select **Statistics** from the TOC. This displays the Statistics window in the content area. (See Figure 10-15.)

Step 5 Select which statistical information you want to view by using the radio button next to one of the displayed categories. In this example, the **Event Store** category is selected.

Step 6 Click on the **View** button to view the selected information. The information is displayed in a separate browser window (see Figure 10-17).

Figure 10-17 *EventStore Statistics for Device Ids4240*

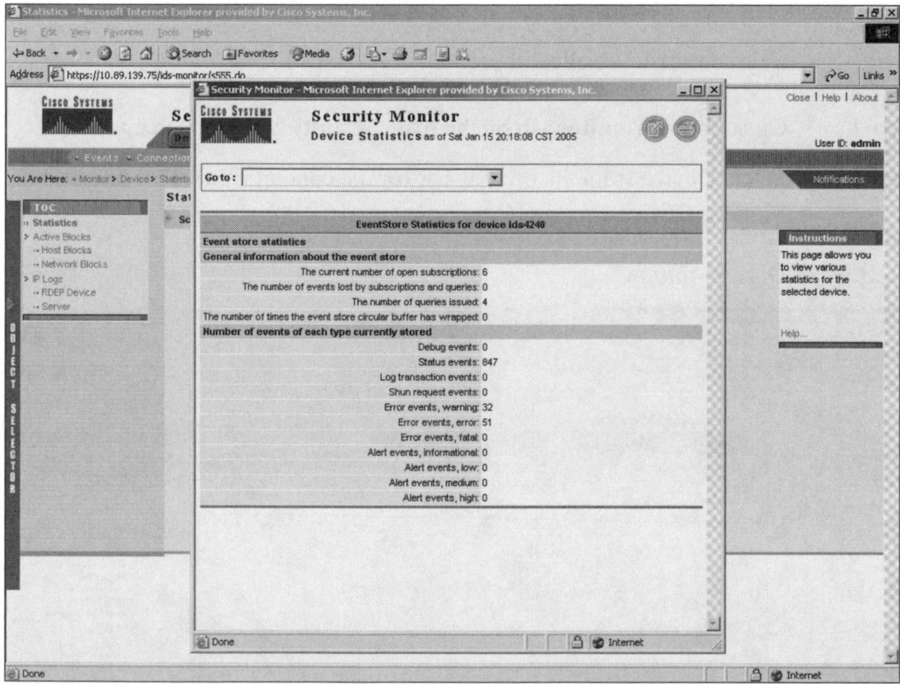

> **NOTE** You can view multiple statistical reports (one at a time) since each of the reports is displayed in a new browser window. These reports are a snapshot of the information from the device and are not updated. To get updated information, you must generate another report.

Monitoring Events

Finally, you can monitor the events that Security Monitor is receiving from all of the monitored devices. This is probably the most important feature of Security Monitor since it enables you to identify attacks against your network. You view the events that Security Monitor has collected through the Security Monitor Event Viewer, which is accessed by choosing **Monitor > Events**. Before the event viewer is launched, you need to specify the criteria on which events should be included in the display (see Figure 10-18).

Figure 10-18 *Launch Event Viewer Window*

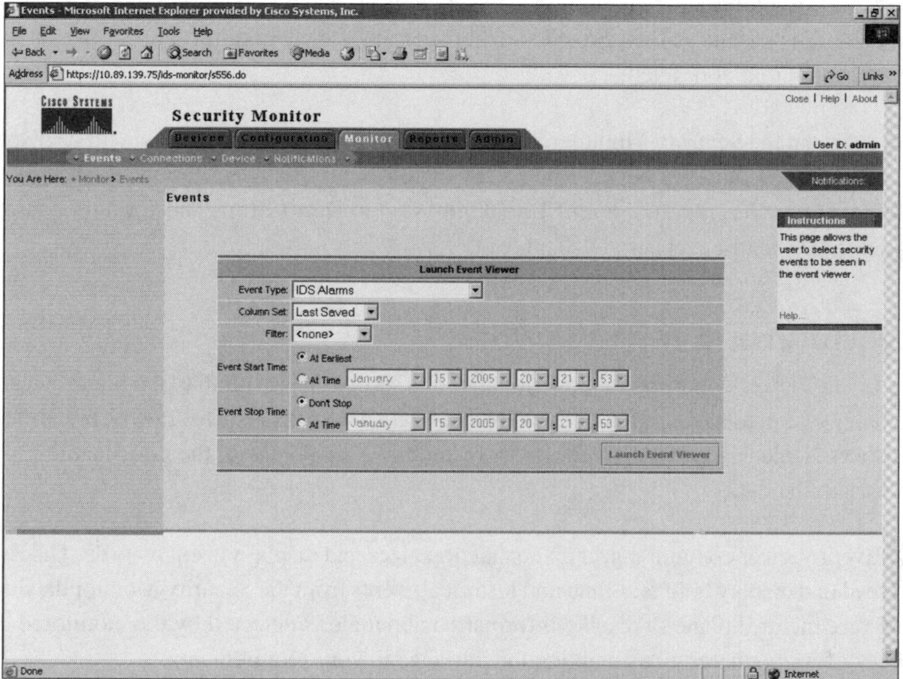

You basically specify a time window and event type for the information that you want included in the Event Viewer display by configuring the following parameters:

- Event Type
- Column Set
- Filter
- Event Start Time
- Event End Time

You can specify numerous options for the **Event Type** field by using the Event Type pull-down menu. Some of the options that you can choose from are as follows:

- All IDS Alarms
- CSA Alarms

- PIX Security Summaries
- PIX Deny Inbound
- Audit Log

The **Column Set** parameter determines the column set that will be used when the Event Viewer is launched. The default is **Last Saved** so that the Event Viewer columns appear the same as the last configuration that you saved.

Any events in the Security Monitor database that match the specified criteria will be displayed in the Event Viewer display. By default, the **Event Type** is set to **All IDS Alarms**, the **Event Start Time** is set to **At Earliest**, and the **Event End Time** is set to **Don't Stop**. These values cause all of the available IDS alarm events to be displayed.

Security Monitor Event Viewer

The Event Viewer combines the functionality of a spreadsheet with that of a hierarchical, drilldown directory to create a collection of event records called a drillsheet (drilldown spreadsheet). The drillsheet displays groups of similar event records on a single row of the grid, enabling you to detect patterns in the data.

The Event Viewer contains a grid plane that organizes and displays event records. The Event Viewer can read and display both real-time and historical events from the Security Monitor database. You can configure the grid plane to display information about alerts detected by the monitored devices in a variety of ways, thereby customizing the interface to your requirements.

Configuring the Event Viewer involves understanding the following options:

- Moving columns
- Deleting rows and columns
- Collapsing rows
- Expanding rows
- Suspending and resuming new events
- Changing display preferences
- Creating graphs
- Using the **Tools** pull-down menu options
- Resolving host names

Moving Columns

The default order of fields within an alarm entry may not suit your operational environment. You can change the order in which the columns are displayed in the Event Viewer. To move a column, click and drag the column header of the column to the new position where you want it to be.

> **NOTE** This change will persist only if you save the changes by choosing **Columns > Save Column Set**.

Deleting Rows and Columns

When an alarm has been acknowledged, dealt with, or both, you may want to remove it from the Event Viewer grid or from the actual Security Monitor database. At other times, you may want to remove certain columns from the Event Viewer display to make the display easier to work with. You can delete both rows and columns from the Event Viewer display. You access the delete options by right-clicking on a specific alert entry to display a popup window with various options. (See Figure 10-19.)

Figure 10-19 *Row and Column Deletion Options*

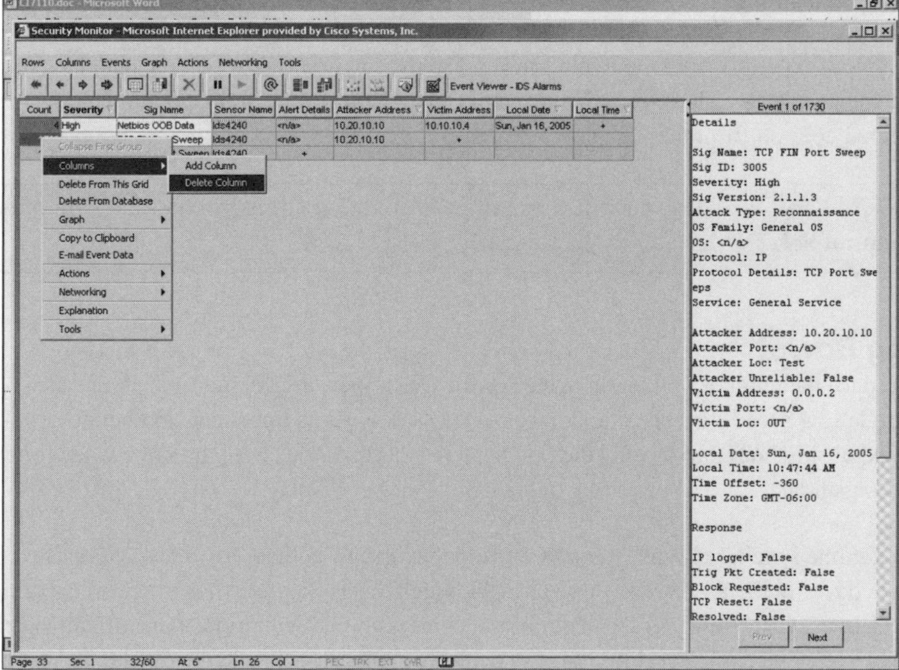

You have three deletion options to choose from:

- Delete From This Grid
- Delete From Database
- Delete Column

Delete from This Grid

To remove a row from the Event Viewer display, you right-click on a field in the row to be deleted. Then you select **Delete From This Grid** to delete the selected alert from the Event Viewer where the action is being performed. This procedure will not delete alerts from other Event Viewer instances or the Security Monitor database.

> **NOTE** This change is not persistent. If you open another instance of the Event Viewer, the original rows will be restored.

Delete from Database

To remove a row from the Security Monitor database, you right-click on a field in the row to be deleted. Then you select **Delete From Database** to delete the selected alert from all of the open Event Viewers as well as the Security Monitor database. If you use this option, the alert is completely gone, and you cannot display it in the Event Viewer again, even if you open another Event Viewer instance.

Delete Column

To remove columns from the Event Viewer display, you first right-click on a field in the column that you want to delete. Then select **Columns > Delete Column** from the popup window to remove the selected column from the Event Viewer display.

> **NOTE** This change is persistent only if you save the changes by choosing **Columns > Save Column Set**.

Collapsing Rows

To reduce the number of lines displayed on the Event Viewer grid, multiple alarms are collapsed into a single row based on a specific number of fields (known as the expansion boundary). By default, the expansion boundary is only the first field. All alarm entries with the same value for the first field are consolidated into a single row on the Event Viewer display.

To examine specific alarms, you may expand the display so that only a few alarms are consolidated on each row in the Event Viewer display. Although this is helpful when you are analyzing a specific attack, the Event Viewer grid can quickly become cluttered with more alarms than you can manage. When your Event Viewer display is too cluttered, you can collapse the display so that multiple alarms are consolidated onto a single line. From the **Rows** pull-down menu, you have the following collapse options to consolidate rows in the Event Viewer:

- **Collapse > First Group**
- **Collapse > All Rows**

> **NOTE** Besides using the **Rows** pull-down menu, you can also collapse columns by using the arrow icons pointing to the left (see Figure 10-20). The single left arrow icon performs the same operation as **Collapse > First Group**, and the double left arrow icon performs the same operation as **Collapse > All Rows**.

Figure 10-20 *Event Viewer Window*

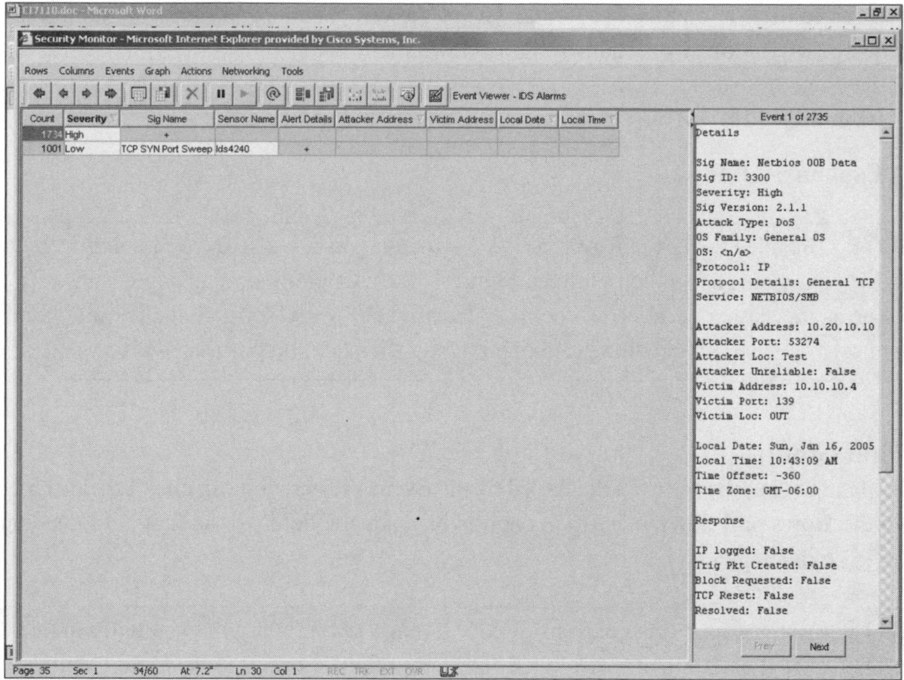

Collapse > First Group

Using the **Collapse > First Group** option from the **Rows** pull-down menu, you can quickly collapse a selected row to the first row that causes some consolidation (a reduction in the number of lines displayed in the Event Viewer).

> **NOTE** Collapsed rows are not a persistent change. This means that closing the Event Viewer and re-opening it will bring back the default settings and expansion boundary.

Collapse > All Rows

The **Collapse > All Rows** option from the **Rows** pull-down menu enables you to consolidate all of the alarm entries based on the first column in the Event Viewer display. Using this feature, you can quickly collapse all of the rows without having to collapse them one group at a time.

> **NOTE** Collapsed rows are not a persistent change. This means that closing the Event Viewer and re-opening it will bring back the default settings and expansion boundary.

Expanding Rows

Besides collapsing the entries on the display, you may frequently need to expand the amount of alarm detail shown on the Event Viewer grid. Expanding columns provides more information and causes more rows to be displayed in the Event Viewer. When expanding columns, you have the following two options from the **Rows** pull-down menu:

- **Expand > First Group**
- **Expand > All Rows**

> **NOTE** Besides using the **Rows** pull-down menu, you can also expand columns by using the arrow icons pointing to the right (see Figure 10-20). Clicking on the single right-arrow icon performs the same operation as choosing **Expand > First Group**, and clicking on the double right-arrow icon performs the same operation as choosing **Expand > All Rows**.

Expand > First Group

To expand the number of rows displayed by the Event Viewer, you can click **Expand > First Group** from the **Rows** pull-down menu. This option expands the fields to the first field that causes more rows to be displayed.

> **NOTE** When expanding columns in your Event Viewer, you will eventually increase the number of row entries being displayed. The count field shows you how many entries are consolidated into a single row in the Event Viewer. This consolidation is based on the columns that are currently expanded. As you expand fields, fewer of the alarm entries will have the same values for all of the expanded columns. When you expand all of the columns, each row will probably represent only one alarm entry (count equal to 1) since it is unlikely that two separate alarm entries will have the exact same values for every column.

> **NOTE** Expanded rows are not a persistent change. This means that closing the Event Viewer and re-opening it will bring back the default settings and expansion boundary.

Expand > All Rows

Expanding an alarm entry one group at a time can be tedious, especially if the column that you are interested in is many fields away. In one click you can expand all of the fields for the currently selected row. To expand all of the columns for the current alarm entry, select **Expand > All Columns** from the **Rows** pull-down menu.

> **NOTE** Expanded rows are not a persistent change. This means that closing the Event Viewer and re-opening it will bring back the default settings and expansion boundary.

Suspending and Resuming New Events

Sometimes you may want to freeze the Event Viewer display and temporarily display no more alarms. This might happen during a flood of alarms. If alarms keep updating the Event Viewer, you may have difficulty analyzing what is happening. At that point, it is nice to freeze your Event Viewer window so that you can investigate the alarms that you already have in your window.

Security Monitor provides you the capability to suspend the Event Viewer from displaying new alarms. To suspend the Event Viewer, choose **Suspend New Events** from the **Events** pull-down menu. (See Figure 10-21.) To resume alarms, choose **Resume New Events** from the **Events** pull-down menu. Only one of the options is available at a time. For instance, when you have suspended alarms, the resume option becomes available (it is no longer grayed out). Furthermore, suspending alarms does not prevent new alarms from being added to the Security Monitor database; it only prevents them from being displayed in your current Event Viewer.

Figure 10-21 *Events Pull-Down Menu*

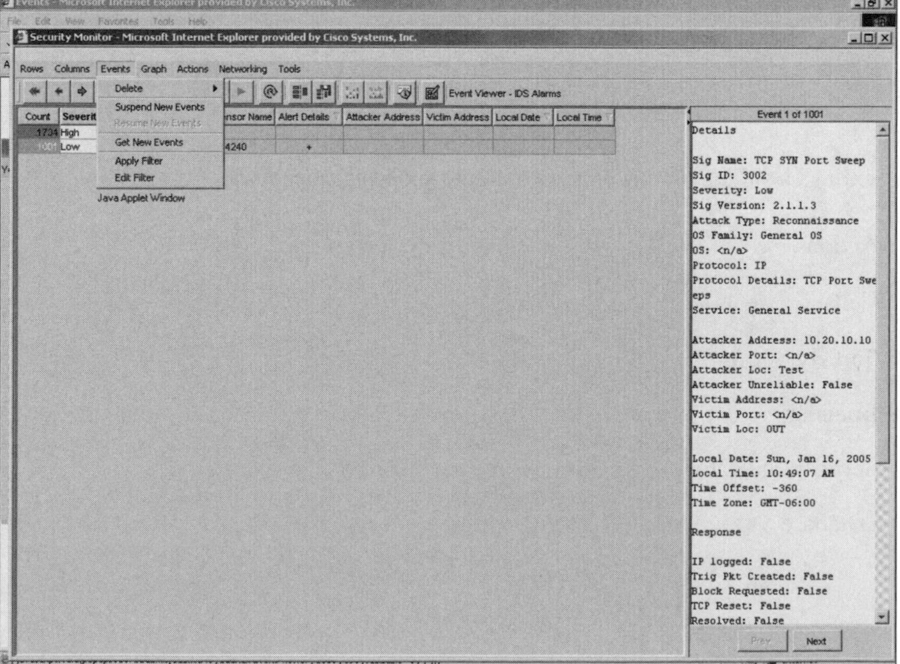

Changing Display Preferences

This section describes the different preference settings that you can use to customize the Event Viewer. To access the Preferences window, choose **Tools > Options**. This will display the Preferences window. (See Figure 10-22.)

Figure 10-22 *Event Viewer Preferences Window*

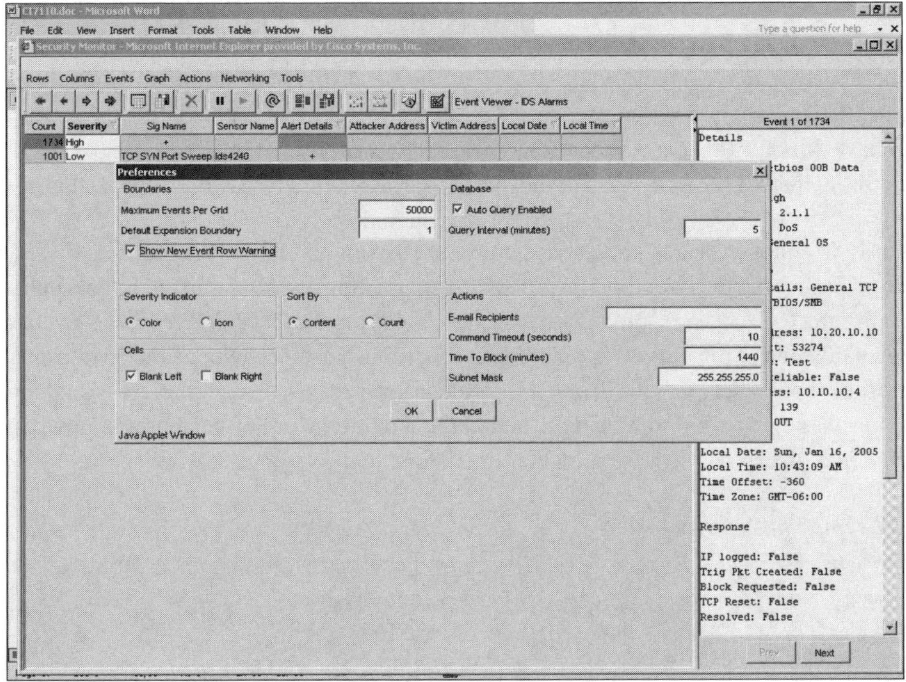

The settings available in this window fall into six basic categories:

- Actions
- Cells
- Sort By
- Boundaries
- Severity Indicator
- Database

Actions

The Actions group box in the Preferences window (see Figure 10-22) allows you to set the following parameters:

- E-Mail Recipients
- Command Timeout
- Time To Block
- Subnet Mask

The Command Timeout value determines how long (in seconds) the Event Viewer will wait for a response from the sensor before it concludes that it has lost communication with the sensor. In most cases, you will not need to modify this value. If you find that you are experiencing frequent command timeout errors, you might consider increasing the Command Timeout value or diagnosing the reason your Event Viewer is experiencing such a slow response time.

The Command Timeout value applies to all functions that require communication through the PostOffice infrastructure. For example, functions such as retrieving sensor statistics, viewing sensor block lists, and requesting that the sensor block a particular IP address all must be completed during the specified Command Timeout period. This timeout value is not used for non-PostOffice functions, such as DNS queries. The default value is 10 seconds, with an allowable range between 1 and 3600 seconds (one hour).

The Time To Block value specifies how long (in minutes) the sensor blocks traffic from the specified source when you issue a Block command from the Event Viewer. The block duration value that can be specified for the sensor in the Network Topology tree (NTT) applies only to blocks that are generated automatically by that sensor. The Time To Block value in the Preferences dialog box applies only to manually generated blocks from the Event Viewer. The default value is 1440 minutes (one day). The allowable range is from 1 to 525,600 minutes (one year).

The Subnet Mask value is used to define the network portion of the IP address that will be used to block a range of addresses. Your sensors use this information when they publish a blocking rule to the blocking devices on your network. The Subnet Mask is applied only to the **Block > Network** and **Remove Block > Network** options from the Event Viewer. The default value is 255.255.255.0 and represents a class C address range.

Cells

The **Blank Left** and **Blank Right** check boxes in the Cells section of the Preferences window enable you to specify whether certain cells will be blank or filled in (see Figure 10-22).

When you choose the **Blank Left** check box, you can control whether values that are suggested by a cell above a row are filled in on following rows in the Event Viewer. For example, consider the following alarms triggered by the same source IP address of 172.30.4.150: WWW perl interpreter attack, WWW IIS view source attack, and WWW IIS newdsn attack. If the **Blank Left** box is selected, the grid appears as follows:

172.30.4.150	WWW perl interpreter attack
<blank>	WWW IIS view source attack
<blank>	WWW IIS newdsn attack

If the **Blank Left** box is not selected, the grid appears as follows:

172.30.4.150	WWW perl interpreter attack
172.30.4.150	WWW IIS view source attack
172.30.4.150	WWW IIS newdsn attack

When you choose **Blank Right**, you can control how the collapsed cells are displayed in the Event Viewer. When cells are collapsed their background color is gray. If the collapsed values are different, a plus sign is displayed. When **Blank Right** is selected, a plus sign is displayed in a collapsed cell regardless of whether or not the cell values are different.

The default setting is for **Blank Right** to be unselected. In this state, a plus sign is displayed in collapsed cells only if the values in the cells differ. If the values in the collapsed cell are the same, the actual value is displayed in the Event Viewer.

Sort By

The Sort By group box in the Preferences window (see Figure 10-22) enables you to specify how the events are sorted in the Event Viewer. You can choose from the following two options:

- Count
- Content

When you choose to sort by count, the entries in the Event Viewer are sorted by the count of alarms listed in the first column of each row. If you sort by content, the entries in the Event Viewer are sorted alphabetically by the first field that is unique (starting with the far left field and moving to the right until a differing field value is found).

Boundaries

The Boundaries group box in the Preferences window (see Figure 10-22) enables you to set the following values:

- Default Expansion Boundary
- Maximum Events Per Grid
- Show New Event Row Warning

The Default Expansion Boundary value specifies the default number of columns in which the cells of a new event are expanded. By default, only the first field of an event is expanded.

NOTE The *expansion boundary* is the block of columns that will be automatically expanded when a new alarm entry comes into the table. The block of columns is contiguous and starts at the first column in the Event Viewer. By default the expansion boundary expands the first field of an alarm entry. When setting a new expansion boundary, you have to specify only the number of columns to be expanded. All columns from the first column to the column count that you specify will be expanded for new alarm entries.

The Maximum Events per Grid defines the maximum number of alarms that can be displayed in a single Event Viewer. When the maximum value is reached, an error message is displayed. The default value is 50,000 alarms.

Severity Indicator

There are two event Severity Indicator options that you can select from (see Figure 10-22):

- Color
- Icon

The default setting uses colors to indicate severity in the Event Viewer. The color affects the background of the Count field. The following colors are used to indicate alarm severity:

- Red—High severity
- Yellow—Medium severity
- Green—Low severity

Besides the default color severity indicator, you can also choose to display the severity of your alarms by using icons. The icons used to display alarm severity are the following:

- Red exclamation point—High severity

- Yellow flag—Medium severity
- No icon—Low severity

Database

The Database group box in the Preferences window (see Figure 10-22) enables you configure whether the Event Viewer automatically retrieves new events from the Security Monitor database. If you check the **Auto Query Enabled** check box, you can configure how often the Event Viewer automatically retrieves events from the Security Monitor database.

> **NOTE** You can manually retrieve new events from the Security Monitor database by selecting **Get New Events** from the **Events** pull-down menu.

Creating Graphs

You can create graphs of the data, or a subset of the data, shown in Event Viewer. These graphs represent a static snapshot of the information and are not updated dynamically. You can choose from the following two types of graphs on the **Graphs** pull-down menu (see Figure 10-23):

- By Child
- By Time

Figure 10-23 *Event Viewer Graph Options*

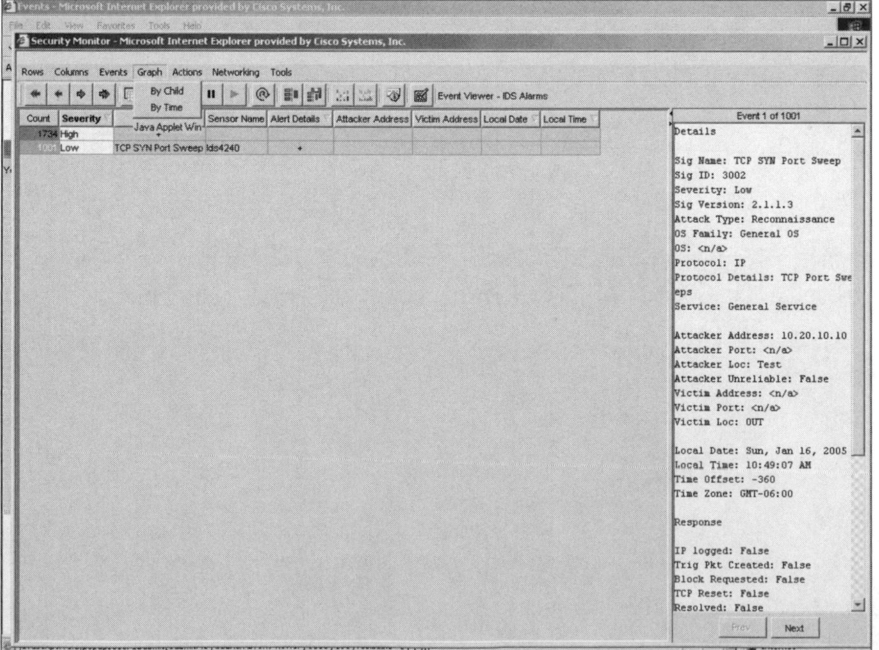

By Child

To see the distribution of children events, select **By Child** from the **Graphs** pull-down menu. The graph displays the children events (the events in the column to the right of the selected node) across the X-axis and the number of occurrences along the Y-axis. Event severity is indicated by the color of the bar.

By Time

To see how the selected events are distributed over time, select **By Time** from the **Graphs** pull-down menu. The graph displays along the X-axis the range of time over which the event occurred and along the Y-axis the number of occurrences. Event severity is indicated by the color of the bar.

Tools Pull-Down Menu Options

Selecting the **Tools** pull-down menu in the Event Viewer enables you to access the following items:

- Explanation
- Trigger Packet
- IP Logs
- Statistics
- Options

Explanation

Selecting **Explanation** from the **Tools** pull-down menu displays the Network Security Database (NSDB) entry for the highlighted alert. The NSDB is the Cisco HTML-based encyclopedia of network-vulnerability information. You can examine the NSDB for information on a specific alarm. The Cisco Secure Encyclopedia (CSEC) is the online equivalent of the NSDB.

> **NOTE** Unlike IPS Device Manager (IDM), which requires Internet access to retrieve NSDB information, the CiscoWorks VPN/Security Management Solution (VMS) provides the NSDB information as part of the software package. Therefore, NSDB information can be viewed without Internet access.

CSEC has been developed as a central warehouse of security knowledge to provide Cisco security professionals with an interactive database of security vulnerability information. CSEC contains detailed information about security vulnerabilities such as countermeasures, affected systems and software, and Cisco Secure products that can help you test for vulnerabilities or detect when malicious users attempt to exploit your systems. The CSEC can be found at http://www.cisco.com/go/csec.

Trigger Packet

For many signatures it is helpful to capture the initial traffic that caused the signature to fire. Cisco IPS enables signatures to capture the actual trigger packet for its signatures. Selecting **Trigger Packet** from the **Tools** pull-down menu displays the trigger packet for the signature (if the signature is configured to capture it).

IP Logs

One of the actions that a signature can initiate is IP logging. This action captures raw packets for a connection so that you can analyze them. To view the IP log information using Security Monitor, you highlight the alarm that contains the IP log information and then select **IP Log** from the **Tools** pull-down menu.

Statistics

You can view event statistics for a row in Event Viewer. The statistics include the following information:

- Severity level for the row
- Number of child nodes for the row
- Number of events represented by the row
- Percentage of the total events (based on the events currently displayed by the Event Viewer) that the selected row represents

To access the statistics for a specific row, you select the row by clicking on a field in the row. Then you click on **Statistics** from the **Tools** pull-down menu. A pop-up window appears in the content area, indicating the statistics (see Figure 10-24).

Options

Selecting **Options** from the **Tools** pull-down menu enables you to configure preference settings that you can use to customize the Event Viewer. Configuring these options has already been explained in the "Changing Display Preferences" section earlier in the chapter.

Resolving Host Names

By default, the alerts stored by the Event Viewer indicate the IP addresses of the systems involved in the event. Using the **Resolve** option from the **Actions** pull-down menu, you can cause the Event Viewer to attempt to resolve the host names for the IP addresses in the selected alerts.

> **NOTE** Since a single row can represent multiple alarms, it may take the Event Viewer a significant amount of time to resolve all of the IP addresses. If you attempt to resolve a large number of alerts, a warning pop-up window will appear in the content area, indicating that your request could take several minutes to complete.

Figure 10-24 *Event Statistics Popup Window*

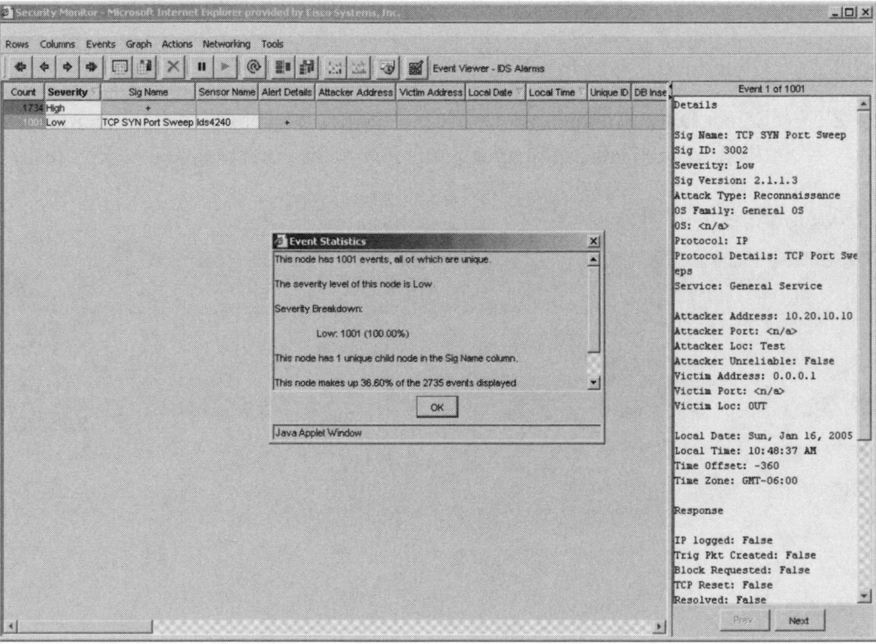

Security Monitor Administration

Although a large percentage of your time will be spent using the Event Viewer functionality of Security Monitor, there are also various tasks that you may need to perform to administer and maintain your Security Monitor software. Security Monitor server administration and maintenance tasks fall into the following categories:

- Data management
- System configuration settings
- Defining Event Viewer preferences

Data Management

When the Security Monitor database becomes large, system performance may begin to degrade. How large the database can become depends upon many factors, including system specifications and the number and types of applications running on the system. Using database rules, you can automatically manage the size of your database, send e-mail notifications, log a console notification event, or execute a script when specific thresholds or intervals are met. Database thresholds may be reached, for example, if the database exceeds a certain size or if the database receives more than a defined number of events.

By defining custom database rules, you can keep your Security Monitor database working at its peak efficiency. To add your own custom database rule, perform the following steps:

Step 1 Click on the **Admin** tab on the main Security Monitor screen.

Step 2 Select **Data Management** from the options bar (or the content area). This displays the Data Management window in the content area (see Figure 10-25).

Figure 10-25 *Data Management Window*

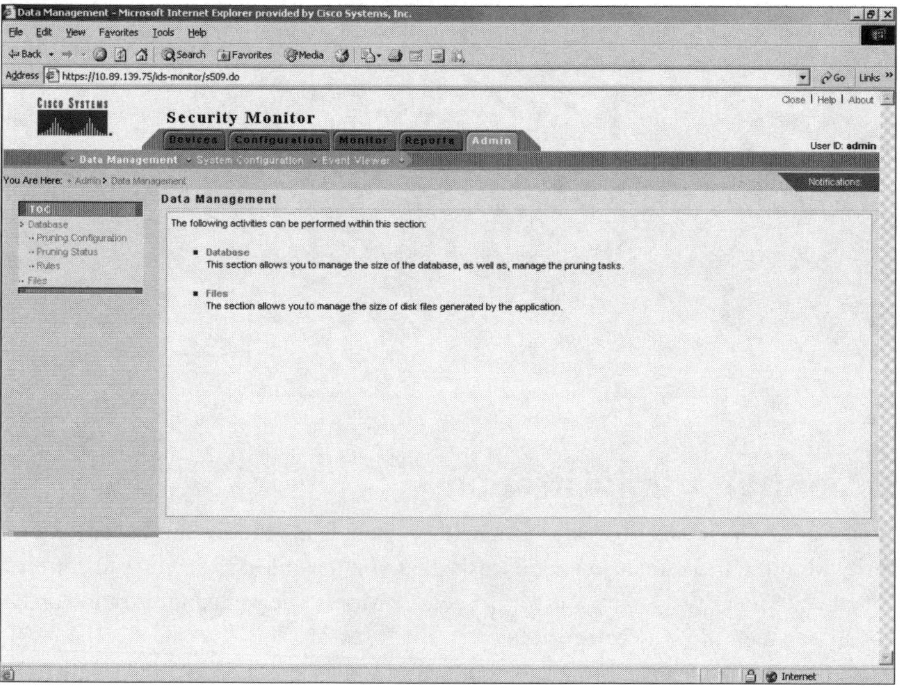

Step 3 Select **Database > Rules** from the TOC. This displays the Database Rules window in the content area (see Figure 10-26).

Step 4 Click on the **Add** button. The Enter Rule Name window appears in the content area.

Step 5 In the **Rule Name** field, enter the name of the database rule being created.

Step 6 In the **Comment** field, enter a textual description of the rule.

Step 7 Click on **Next**. The Choose the Actions window appears in the content area (see Figure 10-27).

Step 8 Choose the actions that the rule will initiate by selecting the check boxes next to the available actions.

Figure 10-26 *Database Rules Window*

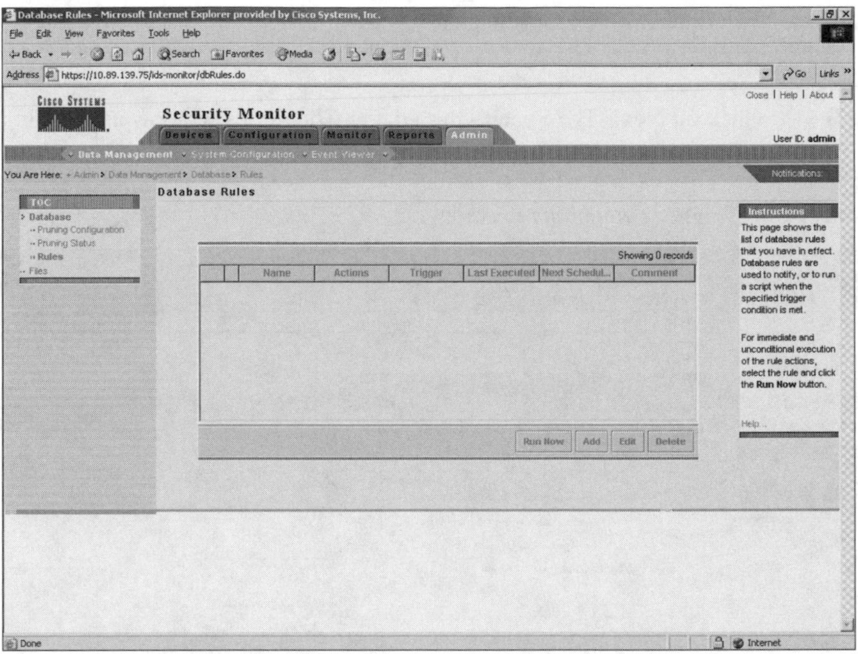

Figure 10-27 *Choosing Actions for Database Rules*

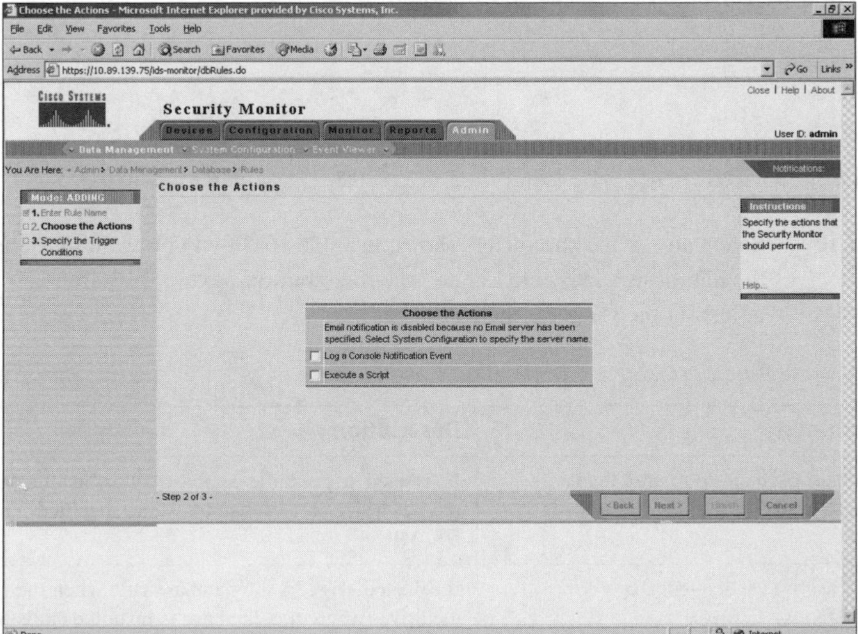

NOTE These actions are the same as those that you specify for event rules (see the "Event Notification" section earlier in this chapter).

Step 9 Click on **Next**. The Specify the Trigger Conditions window appears in the content area (see Figure 10-28).

Figure 10-28 *Specify the Trigger Conditions Window*

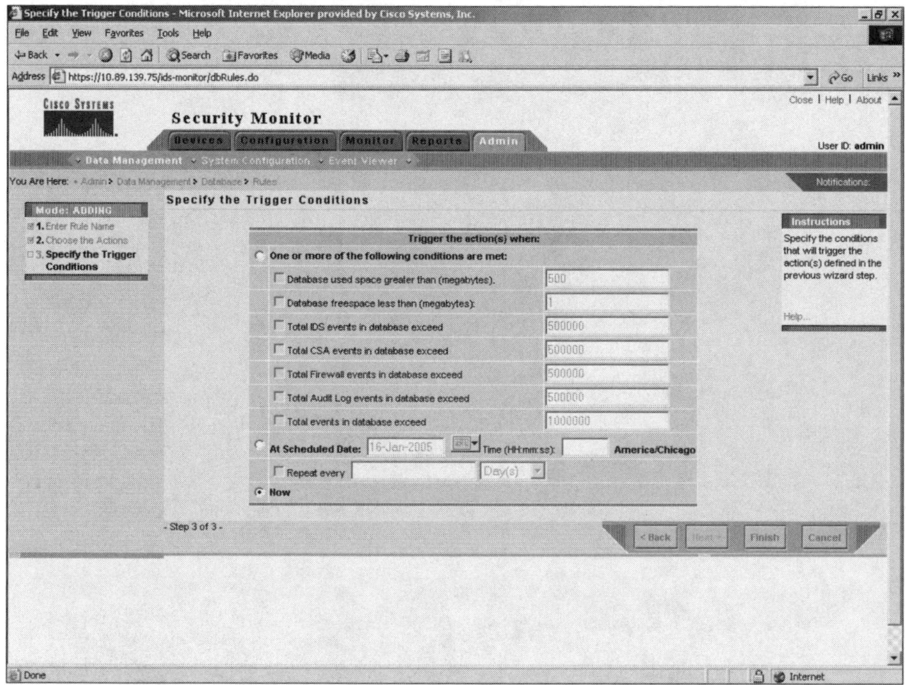

Step 10 Select any of the parameters shown in Table 10-5 that you want to use in the database rule by clicking on the radio button next to the parameter and adjusting the value for the parameter.

Table 10-5 *Database Rule Parameters*

Parameter	Description
Database used space greater than (megabytes)	If selected, triggers the database rule when the database reaches a size greater than the value specified. The default is 500 MB.
Database free space less than (megabytes)	If selected, triggers the database rule when the free space on the drive (where the database is installed) falls below the specified size. The default is 1.

Table 10-5 *Database Rule Parameters (Continued)*

Parameter	Description
Total IDS events in database exceed	If selected, triggers the database rule when the total number of IDS events is more than the specified value. The default is 500,000.
Total CSA events in database exceed	If selected, triggers the database rule when the total number of CSA events is more than the specified value. The default is 500,000.
Total firewall events in database exceed	If selected, triggers the database rule when the total number of firewall events is greater than the specified value. The default is 500,000.
Total Audit Log events in database exceed	If selected, triggers the database rule when the total number of Audit Log events is greater than the specified value. The default is 500,000.
Total events in database exceed	If selected, triggers the database rule when the total number of all events is more than the specified value. The default is 1,000,000.
At scheduled date	If selected, allows the database rule to be triggered at the specified date and time. The default is set to the current date, and the time is left blank.
Repeat every	If selected, causes the rule to trigger again at the specified number of days, weeks, or months. (This is valid only in conjunction with the **At scheduled date** parameter).

Step 11 Click on the **Finish** button to complete the addition of the new database rule.

System Configuration Settings

Selecting **Admin > System Configuration** enables you to configure the following communication properties:

- IP Log Archive Location
- E-Mail Server
- PostOffice Settings
- Syslog Settings
- DNS Settings

- Prune Archive Location
- Automatic Signature Download

The IP Log Archive Location enables you to specify the location on the system where the IP log information for the alerts will be stored. For Windows, the default location is C:\PROGRA~1\CSCOpx\MDC\secmon\iplogs.

The E-mail Server enables you to configure its properties and to specify the e-mail server that Security Monitor uses for event notifications. PostOffice Settings enables you to specify the settings used to establish the communication infrastructure between Security Monitor and Cisco IDS version 3.x IDS devices. Syslog Settings enables you to specify the port that Security Monitor uses to monitor syslog messages along with the IP address and port that it will send syslog messages to if you choose to forward syslog messages.

The DNS Settings option enables you to configure whether DNS lookups are performed in the following two situations:

- When generating firewall reports
- When decoding IP log and trigger packets

When the database is pruned, the information is archived on the hard disk of the system. The Prune Archive Location option enables you to specify the location at which this pruned database information will be stored. In Windows, the default location is C:\PROGRA~1\CSCOpx\MDC\secmon\AlertPruneData.

Attackers are continually developing new attacks to launch against your network. Therefore, it is important that you keep your signature definitions as current as possible. Using the Automatic Signature Download option, you can configure how often Security Monitor checks for new signature updates from either Cisco.com or your own local server.

> **NOTE** Although the option is titled "Automatic Signature Download," it can be used to retrieve signature updates as well as service packs for your sensors.

Defining Event Viewer Preferences

When working in the Event Viewer, you can configure your Event Viewer preferences (see the "Changing Display Preferences" section earlier in this chapter). Some of the changes, however, such as setting the default expansion boundary, are not persistent and are lost whenever you close the Event Viewer. If you want your preferences to be applied every time you open the Event Viewer, you need to change the Event Viewer preferences by using the administration options. Administratively, you can configure your Event Viewer preferences by using the following three options:

- Your Preferences

- Default Preferences
- Users

After choosing **Your Preferences**, you can configure you own personal display preferences. These changes will apply only to the user account in which you are currently logged in to Security Monitor. These options enable you to customize the Event Viewer to your personal preferences.

The **Default Preferences** option, on the other hand, changes the default display settings for all users. You can use this option to establish display preferences from which all users will benefit.

After choosing **Users**, you can view the list of users who have event-viewing preferences stored in the database.

Security Monitor Reports

Security Monitor enables you to generate reports based on the audit and alarm information collected by Security Monitor. These reports can be generated immediately, or you can schedule them to be generated later. Although you can create your own custom report templates, Security Monitor provides the following predefined report templates for IDS alarms:

- **IDS Summary Report**—Provides a summary of event information for an organization during a specified time period. It is filterable by Date/Time, Organization, Source Direction, Destination Direction, Signature or Signature Category, and Event Level.
- **IDS Top Sources Report**—Reports the specified number of source IP addresses that have generated the most events during a specified time period. It is filterable by Date/Time, Top *n* (where *n* is the number of sources), Destination Direction, Destination IP Address, Signature or Signature Category, Sensor, and Event Level.
- **IDS Top Destinations Report**—Reports the specified number of destination IP addresses that have been targeted for attack during a specified time period. It is filterable by Date/Time, Top *n* (where *n* is the number of destinations), Source Direction, Source Address, Signature or Signature Category, Sensor, and Event Level.
- **IDS Top Alarms Report**—Reports the specified number of top alarms (by signature name) that have been generated during a specified time period. It is filterable by Date/Time, Top *n* (where *n* is the number of alarms), Source Direction, Destination Direction, Source Address, Destination Address, Signature or Signature Category, Sensor, and Event Level.
- **IDS Top Source/Destination Pairs Report**—Reports the specified number of source/destination pairs (that is, connections or sessions) that have generated the most alarms during a specified time period. It is filterable by Date/Time, Top *n* (where *n* is the number of source/destination pairs), Signature or Signature Category, Sensor, Event Level, Source Direction, Destination Direction, Source Address, and Destination Address.

- **IDS Alarm Source Report**—Reports alarms based on the source IP address that generated the alarm. It is filterable by Date/Time, Destination Direction, Destination Address, Signature or Signature Category, Sensor, Event Level, Alarm Count, Source Direction, and Source Address.
- **IDS Alarm Destination Report**—Reports alarms based on the destination IP address that generated the alarm. It is filterable by Date/Time, Source Direction, Source Address, Signature or Signature Category, Sensor, Event Level, Event Count, Destination Direction, and Destination Address.
- **IDS Alarm Report**—Reports logged alarms based on signature names. It is filterable by Date/Time, Source Direction, Destination Direction, Source Address, Destination Address, Sensor, Event Level, Event Count, and Signature or Signature Category.
- **IDS Alarm Source/Destination Pair Report**—Reports logged alarms based on source/destination IP address pairs (that is, connections or sessions). It is filterable by Date/Time, Signature or Signature Category, Sensor, Event Level, Alarm Count, Source Direction, Destination Direction, Source Address, and Destination Address.
- **IDS Alarms by Hour Report**—Reports alarms in one-hour intervals over the time specified by the user. It is filterable by Date/Time, Source Direction, Destination Direction, Source Address, Destination Address, Signature or Signature Category, Sensor, Event Level, and Event Count.
- **IDS Alarms by Day Report**—Reports alarms in one-day intervals over the time specified by the user. It is filterable by Date/Time, Source Direction, Destination Direction, Source Address, Destination Address, Signature or Signature Category, Sensor, Event Level, and Event Count.
- **IDS Alarms by Sensor Report**—Reports logged alarms based on the sensor (host ID) that detected the event. It is filterable by Date/Time, Source Direction, Destination Direction, Source Address, Destination Address, Signature or Signature Category, Sensor, Event Level, and Event Count.
- **24-Hour Metrics Report**—Reports all alarm traffic from the most recent 24 hours in 15-minute intervals. There are no filters for this report.
- **Daily Metrics Report**—Reports event traffic totals (by day) from the selected date until the current date. Reporting occurs in 24-hour intervals, starting at midnight. The report shows events by platform (PIX, IOS, Sensor, RDEP) and event type (IDS or Security).

Creating a report using Security Monitor involves the following tasks:

- Defining the report
- Running the report
- Viewing the report

Defining the Report

When creating an IDS report using Security Monitor, you can either create a custom report template (from scratch or by modifying an existing report template) or use one of the predefined report templates. When modifying an existing report template, you can specify the following filtering parameters (see Figure 10-29) to customize the template to your IPS/IDS reporting requirements:

- Report Template
- Event Level
- Event Count
- Date and Time Characteristics
- Source Direction
- Source IP Address
- Destination Direction
- Destination IP Address
- IDS Devices

Figure 10-29 *Report Filtering Window*

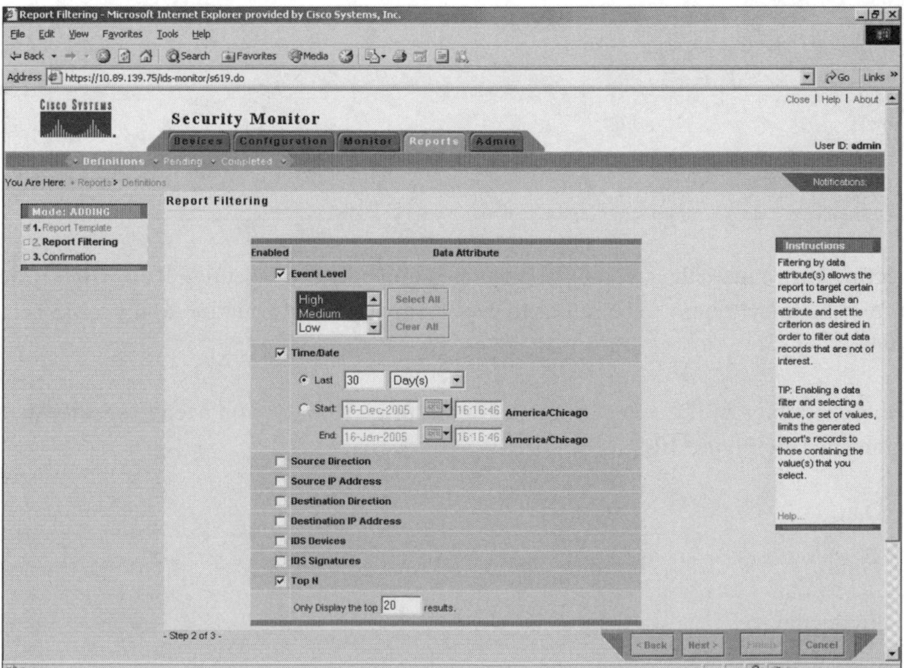

Running the Report

When you want to generate a report, you can run the report by using one of the following two options (see Figure 10-30):

- Run
- Run with Options

Figure 10-30 *Defined Reports Window*

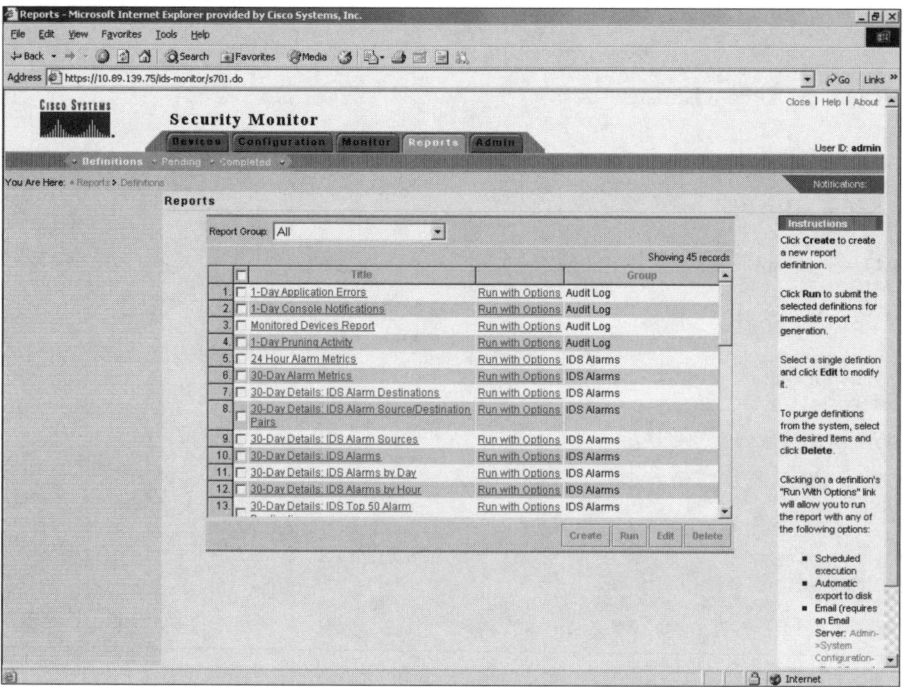

Selecting **Run** causes the report to be generated immediately. Selecting **Run with Options** enables you to schedule a report to be run or to export the report information to the VMS server (see Figure 10-31).

When scheduling an IDS report to run using Security Monitor, you need to specify the following parameters (see Figure 10-32):

- Date
- Time
- Frequency

Figure 10-31 *Run with Options Window*

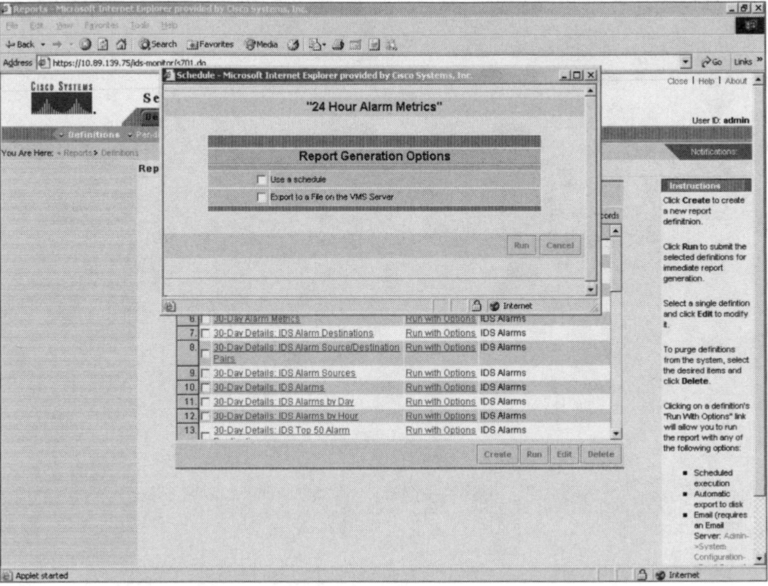

Figure 10-32 *Schedule Report Window*

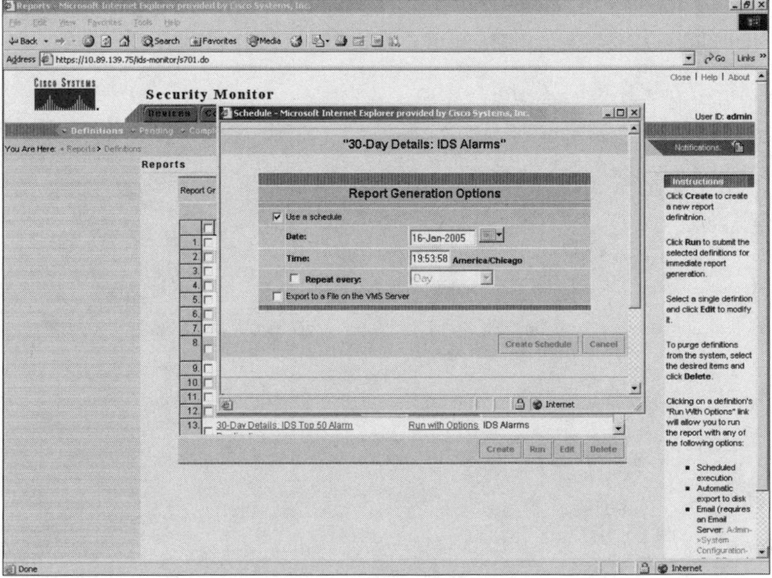

Viewing the Report

After generating your reports, you can view them by choosing **Reports > Completed**. This displays the Choose Completed Report window in the content area (see Figure 10-33).

Figure 10-33 *Choose Completed Report Window*

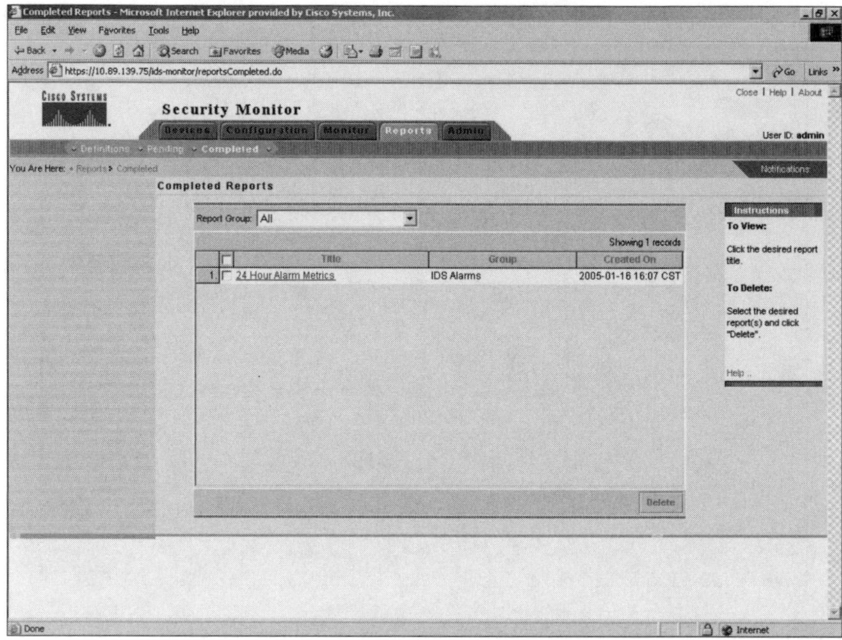

To view a report that you have generated, click on the name of the report that you want to view. The report is then displayed in a new browser window (see Figure 10-34).

Figure 10-34 *24-Hour Alarm Metrics Report*

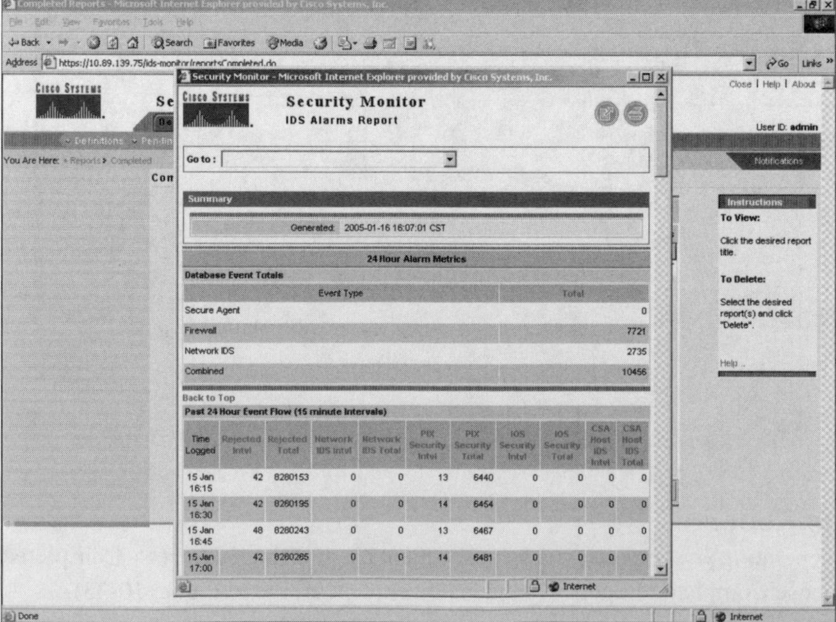

Foundation Summary

CiscoWorks 2000 is the heart of the Cisco family of comprehensive network management tools. It provides the foundation that Intrusion Detection System Management Center (IDS MC) is built upon. IDS MC is a component of the CiscoWorks VMS bundle. CiscoWorks supports five different user roles that are relevant to IDS MC operations. These roles are described in Table 10-6.

Table 10-6 *CiscoWorks User Roles*

User Role	Description
Help Desk	Read-only for the entire system
Approver	Read-only for entire system; includes the configuration approval privileges
Network Operator	Read-only for the entire system; generates reports and includes configuration-deployment privileges
Network Administrator	Read-only for the entire system; includes privileges to edit devices and device groups
System Administrator	Performs all operations

Security Monitor is a component of the CiscoWorks VMS product. VMS integrates into a single solution numerous security applications, such as the following:

- CiscoWorks
- Security Monitor
- VPN Monitor
- VMS Common Services

Security Monitor provides numerous features, such as the following:

- Device monitoring
- Web-based monitoring platform
- Custom reporting capability

Using Security Monitor, you can receive IPS/IDS events from up to 300 Cisco IPS-capable devices, such as the following:

- Sensor appliances
- IDS modules

- Router modules
- IOS routers
- PIX Firewalls

You can install Security Monitor on the following two platforms:

- Windows 2000
- Solaris

The minimum requirements for the Security Monitor server include the following:

- IBM PC-compatible computer
- 1 GHz (or faster) processor
- Color monitor with video card capable of viewing 16-bit color
- CD-ROM drive
- 10BASE-T (or faster) network connection
- Minimum of 1 GB of RAM
- 2 GB of virtual memory
- Minimum of 9 GB free hard drive space (NTFS)
- Windows 2000 Professional, Server or Advanced Server, with Service Pack 4 (and Terminal Services turned off)

Your client systems that access Security Monitor should meet the following hardware requirements:

- IBM PC-compatible
- 300 MHz (or faster) processor
- Minimum 256 MB RAM
- 400 MB virtual memory (free space on hard drive for Windows)

Your client systems need to be running one of the following operating systems:

- Windows 2000 Professional with Service Pack 3
- Windows 2000 Server with Service Pack 3
- Windows XP with Service Pack 1 with Microsoft Virtual Machine

One final requirement is that your client systems need to use one of the following web browsers to access Security Monitor:

- Internet Explorer 6.0 with Service Pack 1
- Netscape Navigator 7.1

The Security Monitor user interface is composed of the following major sections:

- Configuration tabs
- Options bar
- TOC
- Path bar
- Instruction box
- Content area
- Tools bar

Security Monitor monitors the following types of devices:

- Cisco IDS
- Cisco IOS IDS/IPS
- Cisco PIX/FWSM
- Cisco Security Agent MC
- Remote Cisco Security Monitor

When adding RDEP devices and IOS IPS devices to Security Monitor, you must specify the following information about the devices:

- IP address
- Device name
- Web server port
- Protocol
- Username
- Password
- Minimum event level

When using the PostOffice protocol to add devices that communicate with Security Monitor, you need to specify the following information about the devices:

- IP address
- Device name
- Host ID
- Org Name
- Org ID
- Port
- Heartbeat

You specify the following fields only when adding PIX/FWSM devices since they use syslog to communicate with Security Monitor:

- IP Address
- Device Name

You can define event rules that perform specific actions when the Security Monitor receives traffic matching specific properties. When defining an event rule, you can identify traffic based on the alert characteristics shown in Table 10-7.

Table 10-7 *Event Rule Characteristics*

Characteristic	Description
Originating Device	Enables you to specify a monitor device
Originating Device Address	Enables you to specify the originating address of the device
Attacker Address	Enables you to filter based on the IP address of the attacker
Victim Address	Enables you to filter based on the IP address of the victim or system being attacked
Signature Name	Enables you to filter based on the name of a signature
Signature ID	Enables you to filter based on the ID of a signature
Severity	Enables you to filter based on the severity of the alarm received (Informational, Low, Medium, or High)

When adding event rules, you need to perform the following four tasks:

Step 1 Assign a name to the event rule

Step 2 Define the event filter criteria

Step 3 Assign the event rule action

Step 4 Define the event rule threshold and interval

You can monitor the following information about the devices that you have added to Security Monitor:

- Connections
- Statistics
- Events

You can view statistics about the following items:

- **Analysis Engine**—MAC, virtual sensor, TCP Stream Reassembly, and signature database statistics
- **Authentication**—Successful and failed login attempts to the RDEP device
- **Event Server**—General and specific subscription information about the devices that have connections to the server
- **Event Store**—General information on and number of specific events that have occurred
- **Host**—Network statistics, memory usage, and swap-file usage
- **Logger**—Number of events and log messages written by the logger process
- **Network Access Control**—Information about the sensor's current shunning (blocking) configuration
- **Transaction Server**—Counts indicating the failed and total number of control transactions for the server
- **Transaction Source**—Counts indicating the failed and total number of source control transactions
- **Web Server**—Configuration information for the device web server and statistics for connections to the web server

Using the Event Viewer, you can monitor the events that Security Monitor is receiving from all of the monitored devices. When launching the Event Viewer, you need to specify the following information:

- Event Type
- Column Set
- Filter
- Event Start Time
- Event End Time

Configuring the Event Viewer involves understanding the following options:

- Moving columns
- Deleting rows and columns
- Collapsing rows
- Expanding rows
- Suspending and resuming new events
- Changing display preferences
- Creating graphs
- Using the **Tools** pull-down menu options
- Resolving host names

You can create the following two types of graphs based on the data, or a subset of the data, shown in Event Viewer:

- By Child
- By Time

Security Monitor server administration and maintenance tasks fall into the following categories:

- Data management
- System configuration
- Event viewer

Defining database rules involves specifying the parameters shown in Table 10-8.

Table 10-8 *Database Rule Parameters*

Parameter	Description
Database used space greater than (megabytes)	If selected, triggers the database rule when the database reaches a size greater than the value specified. The default is 500 MB.
Database free space less than (megabytes)	If selected, triggers the database rule when the free space on the drive (where the database is installed) falls below the specified size. The default is 1.
Total IDS events in database exceed	If selected, triggers the database rule when the total number of IDS events is more than the specified value. The default is 500,000.
Total CSA events in database exceed	If selected, triggers the database rule when the total number of CSA events is more than the specified value. The default is 500,000.
Total firewall events in database exceed	If selected, triggers the database rule when the total number of firewall events is more than the specified value. The default is 500,000.
Total Audit Log events in database exceed	If selected, triggers the database rule when the total number of Audit Log events is more than the specified value. The default is 500,000.
Total events in database exceed	If selected, triggers the database rule when the total number of all events is more than the specified value. The default is 1,000,000.
At scheduled date	If selected, allows the database rule to be triggered at the specified date and time. The default is set to the current date, and the time is left blank.
Repeat every	If selected, causes the rule to trigger again at the specified number of days, weeks, or months (valid only in conjunction with **At scheduled date** parameter).

System configuration tasks involve configuring the following communication properties:

- IP Log Archive Location
- E-Mail Server
- PostOffice Settings
- Syslog Settings

- DNS Settings
- Prune Archive Location
- Automatic Signature Download

Security Monitor enables you to generate reports based on the audit and alarm information collected by Security Monitor. These reports can be generated immediately, or you can schedule them to be generated at a later time. The predefined IDS alarm report templates include the following:

- IDS Summary Report
- IDS Top Sources Report
- IDS Top Destinations Report
- IDS Top Alarms Report
- IDS Top Source/Destination Pairs Report
- IDS Alarm Source Report
- IDS Alarm Destination Report
- IDS Alarm Report
- IDS Alarm Source/Destination Pair Report
- IDS Alarms by Hour Report
- IDS Alarms by Day Report
- IDS Alarms by Sensor Report
- 24-Hour Metrics Report
- Daily Metrics Report

Creating a report using Security Monitor involves the following tasks:

- Defining the report
- Running the report
- Viewing the report

Q&A

You have two choices for review questions:

- The questions that follow give you a bigger challenge than the exam itself by using an open-ended question format. By reviewing now with this more difficult question format, you can exercise your memory better and prove your conceptual and factual knowledge of this chapter. The answers to these questions are found in the appendix.
- For more practice with exam-like question formats, use the exam engine on the CD-ROM.

1. What are the five CiscoWorks user roles that are relevant to IDS MC and Security Monitor operations?
2. What is the minimum amount of RAM and virtual memory recommended for a Windows server running Security Monitor?
3. What is the minimum amount of RAM and virtual memory recommended for a Windows client system used to connect to Security Monitor?
4. Which two browsers are supported for use by the Windows-based Security Monitor client systems?
5. What types of devices can you monitor with Security Monitor?
6. What are the two major protocols used to communicate between Security Monitor and IDS/IPS devices?
7. Which parameters can you use to configure event rules?
8. What actions can an event rule initiate?
9. What are the four tasks that you need to perform when adding an event rule?
10. What device statistical categories can you view using Security Monitor?
11. What are your two options when deleting rows from the Event Viewer, and how are they different?
12. What is the default expansion boundary?
13. Which report template would you use to find out which systems have launched the most attacks against your network in a specified time period?
14. What icons are used to indicate alarm severity?
15. What does the Blank Left check box do when configured as your cell preference?

Part V: Cisco IPS Maintenance and Tuning

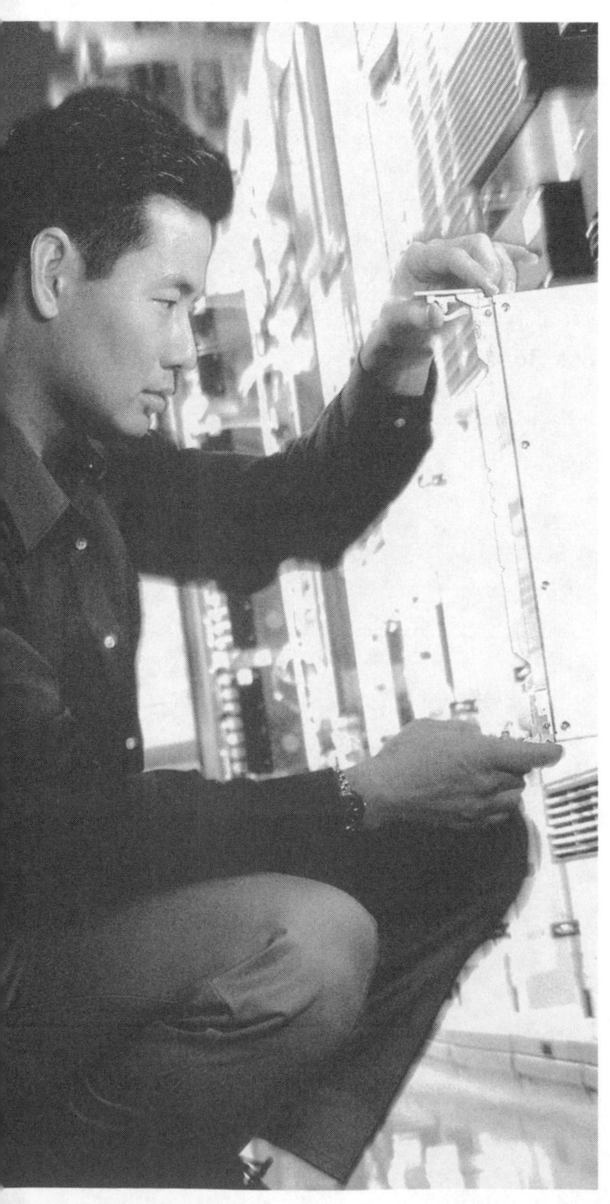

This chapter covers the following subjects:

- Sensor Maintenance
- Software Updates
- Upgrading Sensor Software
- Updating the Sensor's License
- Image Recovery
- Restoring Default Sensor Configuration
- Resetting and Powering Down the Sensor

CHAPTER 11

Sensor Maintenance

To keep your IPS operating effectively and efficiently, you need to maintain the software versions on your IPS devices. Cisco IPS software is continually being improved. Maintaining current software versions ensures that you have the latest functionality available in your Cisco IPS.

Updating the software on your Cisco IPS devices is vital to effectively protecting your network from attack. Cisco IPS is continually evolving, with new signatures and IPS functionality. Updating your IPS software regularly guarantees that your IPS has the latest signatures and IPS functionality.

"Do I Know This Already?" Quiz

The purpose of the "Do I Know This Already?" quiz is to help you decide if you really need to read the entire chapter. If you already intend to read the entire chapter, you do not necessarily need to answer these questions now.

The 10-question quiz, derived from the major sections in the "Foundation and Supplemental Topics" portion of the chapter, helps you determine how to spend your limited study time.

Table 11-1 outlines the major topics discussed in this chapter and the "Do I Know This Already?" quiz questions that correspond to those topics.

Table 11-1 *"Do I Know This Already?" Foundation and Supplemental Topics Mapping*

Foundation or Supplemental Topic	Questions Covering This Topic
Software Updates	1, 3
Upgrading Sensor Software	4, 8, 9
Updating the Sensor's License	5
Image Recovery	2
Restoring Default Sensor Configuration	7, 10
Resetting and Powering Down the Sensor	6

> **CAUTION** The goal of self-assessment is to gauge your mastery of the topics in this chapter. If you do not know the answer to a question or are only partially sure of the answer, you should mark this question wrong for purposes of the self-assessment. Giving yourself credit for an answer you correctly guess skews your self-assessment results and might provide you with a false sense of security.

1. Which of the following is not a component of the Cisco IPS software filename?
   a. IPS version
   b. Service pack level
   c. Update type
   d. Signature version
   e. Software type

2. Which command enables you to fix a corrupted image on your sensor?
   a. **repair**
   b. **downgrade**
   c. **restore**
   d. **recover**
   e. **update**

3. If the filename of a software version is IDS-K9-sp-5.1-3-S36.rpm.pkg, what signature release is included in the software release?
   a. 36
   b. 5.1
   c. 3
   d. 1
   e. 1-3

4. When you are upgrading sensor images by using the CLI, which of the following is not a valid file transfer protocol?
   a. FTP
   b. HTTP
   c. HTTPS
   d. SCP
   e. TFTP

5. Which of the following is true if a Cisco IPS sensor running 5.0 software has an invalid license key?
   a. The sensor will not perform inline functionality.
   b. The sensor will not accept signature updates.
   c. The sensor will not operate in promiscuous mode.
   d. The sensor will not operate in promiscuous or inline mode.

6. When rebooting the sensor via the sensor's CLI, which command do you use?
   a. **reboot**
   b. **reload**
   c. **shutdown**
   d. **reset**
   e. **restart**

7. Which of the following sensor CLI commands is not valid?
   a. **default service analysis-engine**
   b. **default service logger**
   c. **default service ssh-certificates**
   d. **default service trusted-certificates**
   e. **default service web-server**

8. When configuring daily automatic updates via IDM, which of the following is not a valid configuration?
   a. Check for updates every 3 hours, beginning at 2 seconds after 12:00
   b. Check for updates every 20 minutes, beginning at 6:00
   c. Check for updates every 60 minutes, beginning at 10 seconds after 6:00
   d. Check for updates every 120 minutes, beginning at 5 seconds after 19:00

9. Which sensor CLI command enables you to return to a previous sensor software image?
   a. **downgrade**
   b. **restore**
   c. **recover**
   d. **revert**

10. Which of the following is true?

   a. You can only use the sensor CLI to restore the sensor's default configuration.

   b. You can only use IDM to restore the sensor's default configuration.

   c. You can selectively restore the sensor's default configuration by using IDM.

   d. You can selectively restore the sensor's default configuration by using the sensor CLI.

The answers to the "Do I Know This Already?" quiz are found in the appendix. The suggested choices for your next step are as follows:

- **8 or less overall score**—Read the entire chapter. This includes the "Foundation and Supplemental Topics" and "Foundation Summary" sections and the Q&A section.
- **9 or 10 overall score**—If you want more review on these topics, skip to the "Foundation Summary" section and then go to the Q&A section. Otherwise, move to the next chapter.

Foundation and Supplemental Topics

Sensor Maintenance

New vulnerabilities that pose a threat to networks and hosts are discovered every day. Cisco regularly releases signature updates to enhance the capability of your sensors to detect these new attacks by adding new attack signatures to the sensor's database. Cisco also releases service packs to improve the sensor's intrusion-prevention capabilities.

You can install these software updates either automatically or manually (using the sensor's command-line interface [CLI] or the IPS Device Manager [IDM]). Besides installing software updates, you may periodically need to troubleshoot the operation of your sensor. The sensor's CLI provides several commands that inform you about the operation of your sensor and enable you to perform some basic troubleshooting on your sensor.

Software Updates

Cisco is continually enhancing the capabilities of its IPS software. New signatures are being added to address new attacks as they are discovered. These improvements are deployed via the following two types of software releases:

- Service packs
- Signature updates

The file format of new software releases indicates the type of software update along with its version information. In addition, you have several ways in which you can retrieve and install the updates on your sensors.

IPS Software File Format

The Cisco IPS software releases have a filename that comprises the following components (see Figure 11-1):

- Software type
- Cisco IPS version
- Service pack level
- Signature version
- Extension

Figure 11-1 *Cisco IPS Software File Naming Convention*

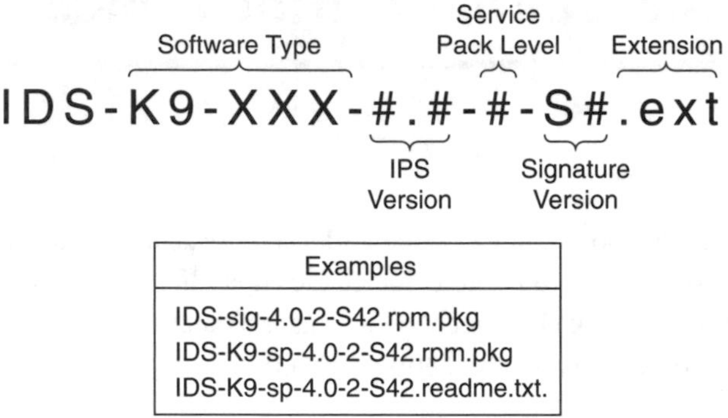

Software Type

Cisco releases the following two types of software updates:

- Service packs
- Signature updates

Service packs are updates to the actual sensor software, enhancing the functionality of your sensor with new capabilities. A service pack is recognizable by the keyword *sp* in the filename.

> **NOTE** You may also encounter a minor version update. This file is indicated by the *min* keyword in the filename (instead of the *sp* keyword). A minor update typically includes only small enhancements to the sensor's functionality (along with bug fixes), whereas a major update usually includes significant changes to the sensor's functionality along with bug fixes.

Unlike service packs, signature updates do not add new features to your sensor's software. They are released to add new signatures to your sensor. Since Cisco IPS uses multiple signature engines, it is easy to add new signatures without actually changing the software that the sensor is running. A signature update is recognizable by the keyword *sig* in the filename.

Cisco IPS Version

The Cisco IPS version comprises the following two numbers:

- Major version
- Minor version

The major version is listed first and is followed by the minor version. The two numeric values are separated by a decimal. For instance, if the Cisco IPS version is 4.1, the major version is 4 and the minor version is 1.

Service Pack Level

Between major and minor software releases, Cisco releases service packs. Service packs are usually released to patch the Cisco IPS software. These updates are incremental improvements to the Cisco IPS software. For instance, 4.0-2 indicates that there have been two service packs for the 4.0 software release.

Signature Version

As signatures are added to Cisco IPS, it is important to know which signatures are included in which software versions. Therefore, the software updates include a signature version that indicates which signatures are included in the update. The signature version is a number, such as 42, preceded by an S.

Extension

The extension can be one of the following values:

- *rpm.pkg*
- *readme* or *readme.txt*
- *zip*

The *rpm.pkg* extension contains an executable file that contains either a signature update or a new service pack.

The *readme* (or *readme.txt*) extension is a text file that provides you with relevant information about a specific service pack or signature update. Reading this information before you update your sensor is important to maintaining the correct operation of your Cisco IPS since it indicates any problems associated with the new software. The readme files also indicate any hardware requirements as well.

The *zip* extension (indicating standard zip compression format) is used by the updates that you need to apply to IDS MC so that it can understand the new signatures that are added to a sensor. IDS MC needs this information because it maintains a copy of the sensor's configuration that it enables the user to modify.

Software Update Guidelines

To ensure the correct operation of your Cisco IPS sensors, you need to follow several guidelines when updating you sensor software. The guidelines are divided into the following tasks:

- Read the release notes
- Download the appropriate updates to your server
- Install the software update on the sensor

An important step in updating your sensors is to read the release notes. These documents contain important caveats and known issues that apply to the software update. By understanding these issues beforehand, you can make an informed decision as to whether these factors impact the installation of the new software on your sensors.

> **NOTE** Service pack updates must be applied in order since they are incremental updates to the sensor software. For instance, to go from 3.1-0 to 3.1-2, you must first apply 3.1-1 and then apply 3.1-2. Signature updates are cumulative and do not have the same restriction.

Upgrading Sensor Software

You can upgrade your sensor software through the following two mechanisms:

- Sensor's CLI
- IDM

Saving Current Configuration

When you upgrade your sensor software, it automatically preserves your current configuration information. Backing up the current configuration before you perform the upgrade, however, is a good safety measure in case the image becomes corrupted during the upgrade. To back up the current configuration to a remote system using the sensor's CLI, use the following command:

```
copy current-config destination-url
```

When you specify the destination URL, you use one of the following protocols (for more information on specifying URLs refer to the following section, "Software Installation via CLI"):

- FTP
- HTTP/HTTPS
- Secure Copy (SCP)

You can also maintain a backup of the current configuration on the sensor by using the following command:

```
copy current-config backup-config
```

> **NOTE** Regularly saving a copy of your sensor's configuration is useful in case you ever have to re-image your sensor. When you re-image your sensor, you lose most of your configuration information. Having a backup of the configuration enables you to easily restore the original configuration.

Software Installation via CLI

To upgrade the sensor software from the sensor's CLI, you first need to have access to the update file. Using the CLI, you can use the following methods to access the update file:

- FTP
- HTTP/HTTPS
- SCP

Next you need to log in to the sensor with an account that has been assigned the Administrator role, since running the **upgrade** command requires administrative privileges. The syntax of the **upgrade** command is as follows:

```
upgrade source-URL-of-update
```

Using this single command, you can apply both service packs as well as signature updates. The source URL indicates where the update file is stored. The URL syntax varies slightly, depending on the type of server where the update resides. Use the following guidelines when designating the source of the update file:

- **ftp:**//*username*@*ipaddress*/*RelativeDirectory*/*filename*
- **ftp:**//*username*@*ipaddress*//*AbsoluteDirectory*/*filename*
- **https:**//*username*@*ipaddress*/*directory*/*filename*
- **http:**//*username*@*ipaddress*/*directory*/*filename*
- **scp:**//*username*@*ipaddress*/*RelativeDirectory*/*filename*
- **scp:**//*username*@*ipaddress*//*AbsoluteDirectory*/*filename*

NOTE The sensor cannot download signature updates and service packs directly from Cisco.com. You must download the signature update or service pack from Cisco.com to your FTP server and then configure the sensor to download it from your FTP server.

The **upgrade** command prompts you for the password that is required to authenticate the file transfer. Instead of specifying all of the parameters, you can also just supply the server type, as in the following example:

```
upgrade ftp:
```

When you just specify the server type, you will be prompted for the rest of the fields as in the command sequence in Example 11-1.

Example 11-1 *Upgrading Sensor Software via the Sensor CLI*

```
sensor(config)# upgrade ftp:
User: stat
Server's IP Address: 10.89.152.40
Port[21]:
File name: /tftpboot/IDS/IDS-K9-min-4.1-0.2-S42-0.2-.rpm.pkg
Password: *****
Warning: Executing this command will apply a minor version upgrade to the
 application partition. The system may be rebooted to complete the upgrade.
Continue with upgrade? : yes
```

Software Installation Using IDM

Instead of using the sensor's CLI, you can also use the IDM interface to apply service packs and signature updates to your sensor. Again, you need to first download the update to your own server. Then you need to perform the following steps (when using IDM to apply software updates to your sensor):

Step 1 Access IDM by entering the following URL in your web browser: **https://** *sensor_ip_address*.

Step 2 Click on the **Configuration** icon to display the list of configuration tasks.

Step 3 Click on **Update Sensor** to access the Update Sensor configuration screen (see Figure 11-2).

Figure 11-2 *Update Sensor Configuration Screen*

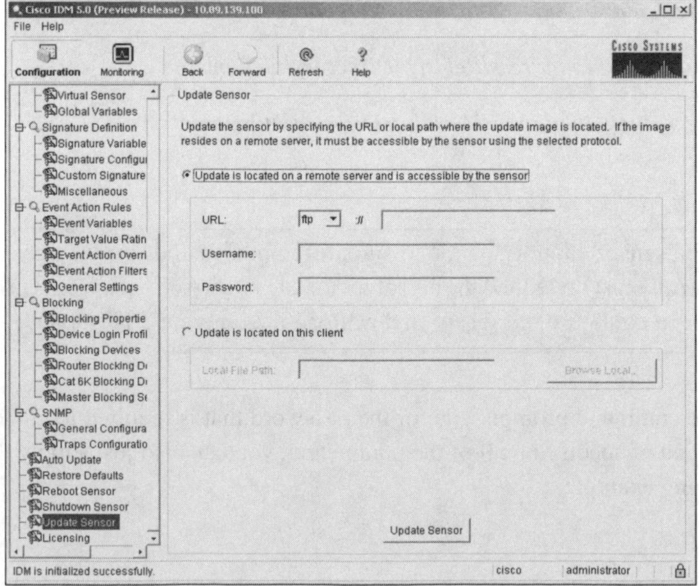

Step 4 Using the pull-down menu for the **URL** field, select the transport protocol (The default is **ftp**).

Step 5 In the second half of the **URL** field, enter the location of the update file.

Step 6 Enter the username to access the update file in the **Username** field.

Step 7 Enter the password needed for the account specified in the **Username** field in the **Password** field.

Step 8 Click on **Update Sensor** to apply the update to the sensor.

Configuring Automatic Software Updates Using IDM

Using IDM, you can configure the sensor to automatically update the software on your sensor. You basically configure your sensor to regularly check a specific server (controlled by your organization) for software updates by using one of the following intervals:

- Hourly
- Daily

> **NOTE** You can also configure your sensor to automatically update the software on your sensor from the sensor CLI by using the **auto-upgrade-option** command that is available in the "service host" configuration mode.

If you choose to update hourly, you must specify a frequency (in hours) at which the sensor will check for new software updates. Your other option is to specify a day of the week on which to check for new software updates. For both of these options, you must also specify the time of day on which you want the actual update to be performed. When a new software update is found on the server, the sensor will wait to apply the software update until the time of day that you have specified.

To use the automatic update mechanism available via IDM, you need to perform the following steps:

Step 1 Access IDM by entering the following URL in your web browser: **https://***sensor_ip_address*.

Step 2 Click on the **Configuration** icon to display the list of configuration tasks.

Step 3 Click on **Auto Update** to access the Auto Update configuration screen (see Figure 11-3).

Step 4 Click on the **Enable Auto Update** check box to enable the automatic update feature.

Figure 11-3 *Auto Update Configuration Screen*

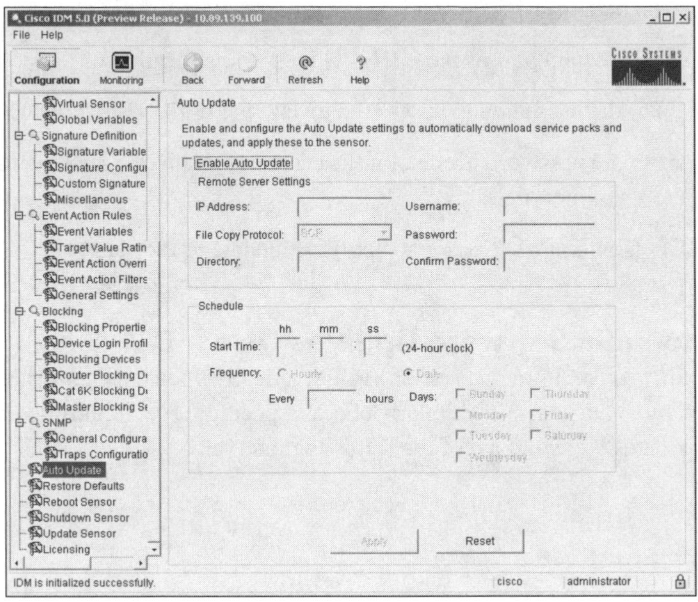

Step 5 Enter the IP address of the server where the updates can be retrieved.

Step 6 Enter the directory where the updates will be located.

Step 7 Specify the username and password to be used to access the server and retrieve the updates.

Step 8 Confirm the password entry by re-entering the password in the **Confirm Password** field.

Step 9 Choose the retrieval method by using the **File Copy Protocol** pull-down menu (you can choose either **FTP** or **SCP** as the value).

Step 10 Choose to check for new updates either hourly or on a specific day of the week by selecting either the **Hourly** or the **Daily** radio button.

Step 11 If you choose **Hourly**, specify the start time and the frequency (number of hours between checks). You can specify a number between 1 and 8670 for the frequency.

Step 12 If you choose **Daily**, specify the start time and the day of the week on which you want to check for new software updates.

Step 13 Click on **Apply** to save the changes to the sensor's configuration.

Downgrading an Image

In some situations, you may need to return to a previous sensor software version. This capability enables you to test a new software release on your sensor but provides protection in that you can always revert to your previous sensor software version if you have any problems. The **downgrade** sensor CLI command provides this functionality. The syntax for this command is as follows:

```
downgrade
```

When you run the **downgrade** command, you remove the software installed by the most recent use of the **upgrade** command. Using the **downgrade** command, you can restore only the sensor software image that the sensor was running before the last upgrade. The sensor software has no visibility past the previous image running on the sensor, so you cannot run the **downgrade** command multiple times to return to images prior to the previous image that was running on the sensor.

> **NOTE** You can determine which software the **downgrade** command will remove by running the **show version** command on the sensor's CLI and examining the Upgrade History section.

Updating the Sensor's License

Your Cisco IPS version 5.0 sensor software will function without a valid license key. To install software updates, however, you will need to configure your sensor with a valid license key. You can configure you sensor with a license key from the Cisco.com licensing server, or you can specify a license file on your local system.

> **NOTE** When requesting a license key from Cisco.com (http://www.cisco.com/go/license), you will need to provide the serial number for the sensor. You can obtain the serial number by using the **show version** sensor CLI command. The serial number is also displayed on the IDM Licensing configuration screen.

To update your sensor license by using IDM, perform the following steps:

Step 1 Access IDM by entering the following URL in your web browser: **https://** *sensor_ip_address*.

Step 2 Click on the **Configuration** icon to display the list of configuration tasks.

Step 3 Click on **Licensing** to access the IDM Licensing configuration screen (see Figure 11-4). This screen displays the license currently in use.

Step 4 Select the location to retrieve the license from by selecting the radio button next to either **Cisco Connection Online** or **License File**.

Figure 11-4 *IDM Licensing Configuration Screen*

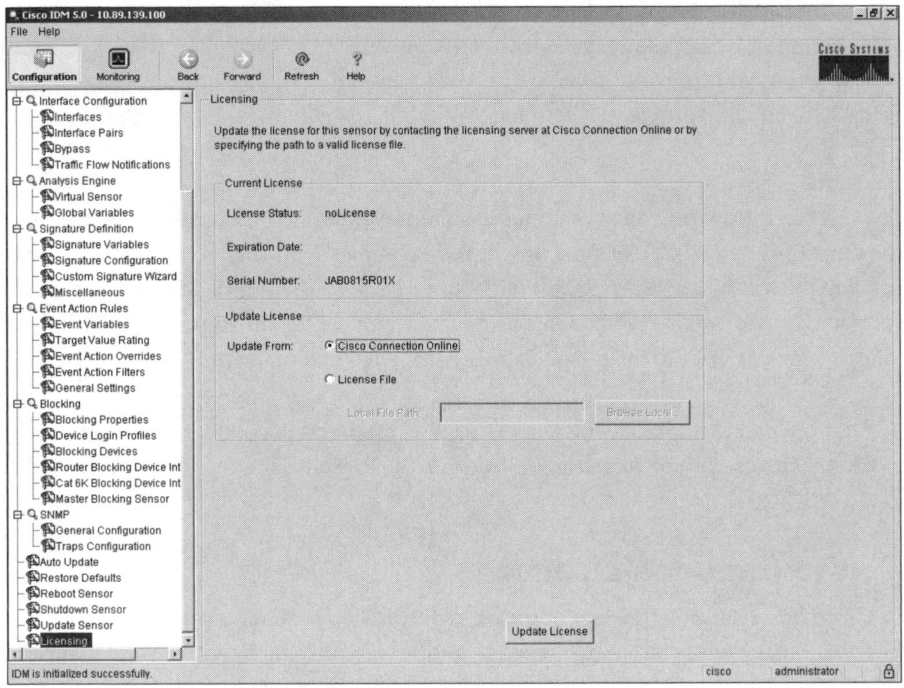

Step 5 If you selected **License File**, you need to also specify the name of the license file by typing it in or clicking on the **Browse Local** button to use a file browser to specify the license file.

Step 6 Click on **Update License** to update the license file that the sensor is using.

Image Recovery

If your sensor's software becomes corrupted, you will need to re-image your sensor to restore its software to the correct operational condition. When you re-image a sensor, all accounts are removed and the default Cisco account is reset to the default password (cisco). You must also initialize the sensor again by running the **setup** command.

> **NOTE** Before re-imaging your sensor, you should back up the current configuration. You can use the CLI command **copy current-config** *destination-URL*.

When using the **recover application-partition** CLI command, you replace all the applications on your sensor with copies of these programs stored on the recovery partition. After using the **recover application-partition** command, all of your configuration information on the sensor is removed except for the network parameters, such as the IP address.

> **NOTE** Signature updates and service packs are not automatically applied to the recovery partition. Therefore, you need to keep your recovery partition updated with signatures and service packs. Otherwise, you will need to use the **upgrade** command (after using the **recover** command) to reapply the signature updates and service packs. You can update the recovery partition by using the **upgrade** command with an image specifically created for the recovery partition. These images contain an *r* in their name, as in IPS-K9-r-1.1-a-5.0-0.30.pkg.

Restoring Default Sensor Configuration

Sometimes you may want to remove all of the changes that you have performed to a sensor's configuration. This option is helpful if you want to reconfigure a sensor and guarantee that you are starting at the initial default settings. You may do this when you are initially deploying sensors on your network and run into a problem with the configuration or when you are moving a sensor from one location in the network to another and want to reconfigure the sensor from its default configuration.

Restoring Default Configuration Using the CLI

To return a sensor to all of the default settings, you use the **default service** command. This command allows you to selectively reset portions of the sensor configuration to their default settings by specifying one of the service keywords shown in Table 11-2.

> **NOTE** The service keywords correspond to the same keywords you use when configuring the sensor with the **service** command whose syntax is as follows:
>
> **service** *service-keyword*

Table 11-2 **default service** *Command Keywords*

Keyword	Description
analysis-engine	Resets the sensor's analysis engine options to their default values
authentication	Resets the sensor's authentication options to their default settings
event-action-rules	Resets the sensor's event action rules to their default settings
host	Resets the sensor's host parameters to their default settings
interface	Resets the sensor's interface configuration parameters to their default settings
logger	Resets the sensor's debug logger parameters to their default settings
network-access	Resets the sensor's Network Access Controller (NAC) parameters to their default settings
notification	Resets the sensor's notification application parameters to their default settings

continues

Table 11-2 **default service** *Command Keywords (Continued)*

Keyword	Description
signature-definition	Resets the sensor's signature definition settings to their default settings
ssh-known-hosts	Resets the sensor's Secure Shell (SSH) known host settings to their default settings
trusted-certificates	Resets the sensor's trusted certificate parameters to their default settings
web-server	Resets the sensor's web server parameters to their default settings

Restoring Default Configuration Using IDM

When using IDM to restore the default sensor configuration, you do not have the option of selectively clearing portions of the sensor's configuration. Instead, all of the default parameters for the sensor's configuration are restored. Restoring the default sensor configuration by using IDM involves the following steps:

Step 1 Access IDM by entering the following URL in your web browser: **https://** *sensor_ip_address*.

Step 2 Click on the **Configuration** icon to display the list of configuration tasks.

Step 3 Click on **Restore Defaults** to access the Restore Defaults configuration screen (see Figure 11-5).

Figure 11-5 *Restore Defaults Configuration Screen*

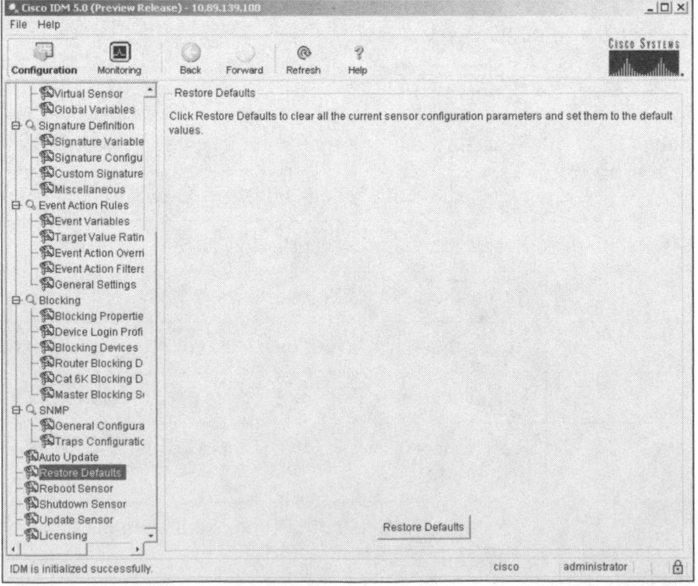

Step 4 Click on **Restore Defaults** to restore the sensor's default configuration.

Step 5 Click on **OK** to confirm the restoration of the sensor's default settings.

Resetting and Powering Down the Sensor

When operating your Cisco IPS, you will occasionally need to either reset or power down your Cisco IPS devices. You can perform both of these operations at the sensor CLI and through the IDM graphical interface.

Resetting the Sensor Using the Sensor CLI

From the sensor CLI, you can reset or power down the sensor by using the **reset** command. The syntax for the **reset** command is as follows:

```
reset [powerdown]
```

Using the **reset** command without any command line options causes the sensor to reboot. Before rebooting the sensor, however, you must confirm the operation by entering **yes** in response to the following prompt:

```
Ids4240# reset
Warning: Executing this command will stop all applications and reboot the node.
Continue with reset? []:
```

Adding the **powerdown** option causes the **reset** command to shut down the sensor instead of rebooting the sensor.

NOTE To execute the **reset** command, your account must be assigned the Administrator role.

Resetting the Sensor Using IDM

From the IDM graphical interface, you can also reset or power down the sensor. To reset the sensor from IDM, perform the following steps:

Step 1 Access IDM by entering the following URL in your web browser: **https://** *sensor_ip_address*.

Step 2 Click on the **Configuration** icon to display the list of configuration tasks.

Step 3 Click on **Reboot Sensor** to access the Reboot Sensor configuration screen (see Figure 11-6).

Step 4 Click on **Reboot Sensor** to reboot the sensor.

Step 5 Click on **OK** on the Reboot Sensor confirmation popup window (see Figure 11-7).

Figure 11-6 *Reboot Sensor Configuration Screen*

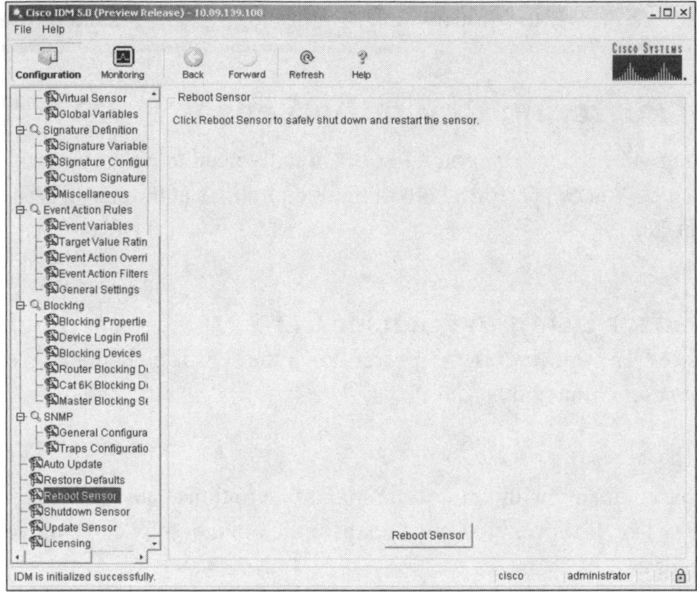

Figure 11-7 *Reboot Sensor Confirmation Popup Window*

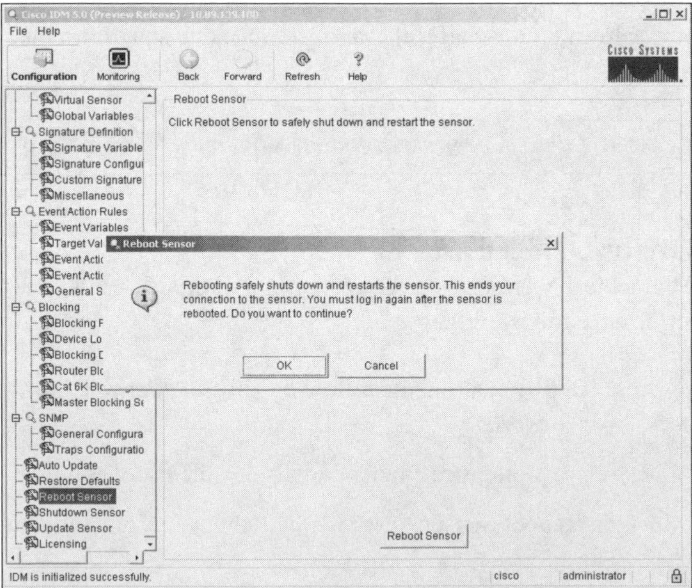

NOTE The process for shutting down the sensor is similar to the process for rebooting the sensor, except that you click on **Shutdown Sensor** instead of **Reboot Sensor**.

Foundation Summary

Cisco is continually enhancing the capabilities of its IPS software. New signatures are being added to address new attacks as they are discovered. These improvements are deployed via the following two types of software releases:

- Service packs
- Signature updates

The Cisco IPS software releases have a filename that comprises the following components:

- Software type
- Cisco IPS version
- Service pack level
- Signature version
- Extension

To ensure the correct operation of your Cisco IPS sensors, you need to follow several guidelines when updating you sensor software. The guidelines are divided into the following tasks:

- Read the release notes
- Download the appropriate updates to your server
- Install the software update on the sensor

Using the **upgrade** CLI command, you can use the following methods to access the software update files:

- FTP
- HTTP/HTTPS
- SCP

To install signature updates on your 5.0 sensor, your sensor needs to have a valid license key installed.

You can configure your sensor to automatically check a specific server on a regular basis to look for new software updates at one of the following intervals:

- Hourly
- Daily

The **downgrade** sensor CLI command enables you to revert your sensor to the previous software image. You can re-image the sensor software by using the **recover application-partition** CLI command. After you use the **recover application-partition** command, all of your configuration information on the sensor is removed except for the network parameters, such as the IP address.

To return a sensor to all of the default settings by using the CLI, you use the **default service** command in conjunction with one of the following keywords:

- **analysis-engine**
- **authentication**
- **event-action-rules**
- **host**
- **interface**
- **logger**
- **network-access**
- **notification**
- **signature-definition**
- **ssh-known-hosts**
- **trusted-certificates**
- **web-server**

To return a sensor to its default settings using IDM, your only option is to reset all parameters to their default settings.

From the sensor CLI, you can reset or power down the sensor by using the **reset** command.

Q&A

You have two choices for review questions:

- The questions that follow give you a bigger challenge than the exam itself by using an open-ended question format. By reviewing now with this more difficult question format, you can exercise your memory better and prove your conceptual and factual knowledge of this chapter. The answers to these questions are found in the appendix.
- For more practice with exam-like question formats, use the exam engine on the CD-ROM.

1. What two types of software releases does Cisco IPS provide?
2. What are the major components identified in a Cisco IPS software filename?
3. What are the common extensions for Cisco IPS software files?
4. Which sensor CLI command enables you to update the software on your sensor?
5. When updating the sensor software via the CLI, which file transfer protocols can you use?
6. What are the two basic intervals for performing automatic software updates?
7. Which sensor CLI command enables you to revert to a previous sensor software image?
8. Which sensor CLI command enables you to re-image the sensor from the recovery partition?
9. What CLI command enables you to reset your sensor configuration to its default settings?
10. What is the difference between restoring the default configuration by using the CLI and restoring it by using IDM?
11. Which sensor CLI command enables you to reboot the sensor, and which keyword causes it to shut down instead of reboot?
12. Which keywords can you specify in conjunction with the **default service** CLI command?

This chapter covers the following subjects:

- Verifying System Configuration
- Viewing Sensor Configuration
- Viewing Sensor Statistics
- Viewing Sensor Events
- Debugging Sensor Operation
- Sensor SNMP Access

CHAPTER 12

Verifying System Configuration

The sensor's command-line interface (CLI) provides numerous commands to verify the operation of your IPS sensor. You can also check the status of your sensor through IDM. Being able to verify that your sensor is operating correctly and running the latest Cisco IPS software is vital to maintaining your Cisco IPS solution.

Checking the status and operation of your IPS sensors is important to maintaining a strong IPS solution. Verifying that your sensors have the latest signature releases and service packs ensures that your sensors have the latest signatures and IPS functionality. Understanding the sensor CLI commands enables you to efficiently check the status of your IPS sensors. Some functions can also be performed via IDM.

"Do I Know This Already?" Quiz

The purpose of the "Do I Know This Already?" quiz is to help you decide if you really need to read the entire chapter. If you already intend to read the entire chapter, you do not necessarily need to answer these questions now.

The 10-question quiz, derived from the major sections in the "Foundation and Supplemental Topics" portion of the chapter, helps you determine how to spend your limited study time.

Table 12-1 outlines the major topics discussed in this chapter and the "Do I Know This Already?" quiz questions that correspond to those topics.

Table 12-1 *"Do I Know This Already?" Foundation and Supplemental Topics Mapping*

Foundation or Supplemental Topic	Questions Covering This Topic
Viewing Sensor Configuration	1, 2
Viewing Sensor Statistics	4
Viewing Sensor Events	3, 5, 6
Debugging Sensor Operation	7, 8, 9
Sensor SNMP Access	10

CAUTION The goal of self-assessment is to gauge your mastery of the topics in this chapter. If you do not know the answer to a question or are only partially sure of the answer, you should mark this question wrong for purposes of the self-assessment. Giving yourself credit for an answer you correctly guess skews your self-assessment results and might provide you with a false sense of security.

1. Which of the following is not provided in the output of the **show version** sensor CLI command?
   a. Sensor uptime
   b. Recovery partition software version
   c. Sensor host name
   d. Current sensor software version
   e. Previous sensor software version

2. Which of the following is not one of the sections of the sensor configuration output?
   a. event-action-rules
   b. signature-definition
   c. network-access
   d. trusted-certificates
   e. alarm-channel-configuration

3. Which of the following is not a valid event type for the **show events** CLI command?
   a. **error**
   b. **debug**
   c. **nac**
   d. **status**
   e. **log**

4. Which of the following is true about viewing sensor statistics?
   a. You can only use the sensor CLI to view sensor statistics.
   b. You can use the sensor CLI to selectively view statistics based on various categories.
   c. You can only use IDM to view sensor statistics.
   d. You can use IDM to selectively view statistics based on various categories.

5. Which of the following is not a keyword used with the "|" symbol to limit the output of various sensor CLI commands?
   a. **start**
   b. **begin**
   c. **include**
   d. **exclude**

6. When you are choosing events to display through IDM, which of the following is not a configuration option?
   a. Selecting all events in the Event Store
   b. Selecting all high-severity alerts that happened in the last 2 hours
   c. Selecting all informational alerts that happened between January 12, 2005, and January 14, 2005.
   d. Selecting all NAC events that happened in the last 30 minutes
   e. Selecting all log events that happened in the last 2 hours

7. Which sensor CLI command captures traffic for the GigabitEthernet0/0 interface and saves it to a file?
   a. **packet display GigabitEthernet0/0**
   b. **display packet GigabitEthernet0/0**
   c. **capture packet GigabitEthernet0/0**
   d. **packet capture GigabitEthernet0/0**

8. What does the **password** keyword do when added to the **show tech-support** CLI command?
   a. **password** is not a valid option for the **show tech-support** command.
   b. It removes sensitive information, such as passwords, from the tech-support output.
   c. It includes sensitive information, such as passwords, in the tech-support output.
   d. It is used with the **destination** keyword to specify login credentials for the destination system.

9. What is the tech-support output called in IDM?
   a. Tech-support report
   b. System report
   c. Operational report
   d. Diagnostic report
   e. IDM does not provide tech-support output

10. Which sensor CLI command would you use to configure SNMP parameters on your sensor?

    a. **service snmp**

    b. **service notification**

    c. **service host**

    d. **service logger**

    e. **service network-access**

The answers to the "Do I Know This Already?" quiz are found in the appendix. The suggested choices for your next step are as follows:

- **8 or less overall score**—Read the entire chapter. This includes the "Foundation and Supplemental Topics" and "Foundation Summary" sections and the Q&A section.
- **9 or 10 overall score**—If you want more review on these topics, skip to the "Foundation Summary" section and then go to the Q&A section. Otherwise, move to the next chapter.

Foundation and Supplemental Topics

Verifying System Configuration

Besides configuring your Cisco IPS to protect your network, you also need to periodically check the operation of your IPS sensors. This may be as simple as verifying the software version running on your sensor or manually capturing network packets on a specific sensor interface. This chapter focuses on the following:

- Viewing Sensor Configuration
- Viewing Sensor Statistics
- Viewing Sensor Events
- Debugging Sensor Operation
- Sensor SNMP Access

Viewing Sensor Configuration

Using the sensor's CLI, you can view various sensor configuration parameters as well as the software version currently installed on the sensor. You will periodically perform the following tasks:

- Display software version
- Display sensor configuration
- Display sensor Product Evolution Program (PEP) inventory

NOTE The *Product Evolution Program* (PEP) provides a consistent mechanism to identify hardware characteristics for Cisco products (including a unique identifier for each device). This information provides customers with the ability to more effectively integrate and manage evolving Cisco hardware products in their network and business operations.

Displaying Software Version

Maintaining the latest Cisco IPS software version is important to maintaining an effective security posture. Knowing which software version is running on your sensors enables you to identify which sensors need to be upgraded and which sensors have already been upgraded when new software, such as signature releases, becomes available.

To display the version of software running on a sensor, you use the **show version** sensor CLI command. This command displays various characteristics about the sensor, such as the following:

- Sensor uptime
- Recovery partition software version
- Current sensor software version
- Previous sensor software version

The output in Example 12-1 shows the information provided by the **show version** command.

Example 12-1 *Displaying the Sensor's System Information*

```
Ids4240# show version
Application Partition:

Cisco Intrusion Prevention System, Version 5.0(0.21)S129.0

OS Version 2.4.26-IDS-smp-bigphys
Platform: IPS-4240-K9
Serial Number: JAB0815R01X
No license present
Sensor up-time is 19 days.
Using 354369536 out of 1984704512 bytes of available memory (17% usage)
system is using 17.3M out of 29.0M bytes of available disk space (59% usage)
application-data is using 39.0M out of 166.8M bytes of available disk space
  (25% usage)
boot is using 35.5M out of 68.6M bytes of available disk space (55% usage)


MainApp          2004_Dec_13_03.00   (Release)   2004-12-13T03:19:10-0600
  Running
AnalysisEngine   2004_Dec_13_03.00   (Release)   2004-12-13T03:19:10-0600
  Running
CLI              2004_Dec_13_03.00   (Release)   2004-12-13T03:19:10-0600

Upgrade History:

  IDS-K9-maj-5.0-0.21-S91-0.21-.pkg   09:00:00 UTC Fri Dec 10 2004

Recovery Partition Version 1.1 - 5.0(0.21)S91(0.21)

Ids4240#
```

Displaying Sensor Configuration

After configuring your sensor, you will want to save the sensor's configuration in case you need to re-image the sensor. The **show configuration** sensor CLI command displays the current configuration of the sensor. The configuration is divided into the following service categories that correspond to the global configuration **service** CLI command:

- **analysis-engine**
- **authentication**
- **event-action-rules**
- **host**
- **interface**
- **logger**
- **network-access**
- **notification**
- **signature-definition**
- **ssh-known-hosts**
- **trusted-certificates**
- **web-server**

The partial output in Example 12-2 shows the initial information from the **show configuration** CLI command.

Example 12-2 *Viewing the Sensor's Configuration*

```
Ids4240# show configuration
! ------------------------------
! Version 5.0(0.21)
! Current configuration last modified Tue Dec 14 13:49:43 2004
! ------------------------------
service analysis-engine
exit
! ------------------------------
service authentication
exit
! ------------------------------
service event-action-rules rules0
variables server-farm address 10.30.10.10-10.30.10.40
variables Test address 10.20.10.10,10.30.10.0,10.40.10.0-10.40.10.20
overrides deny-attacker-inline
override-item-status Enabled
risk-rating-range 90-100
exit
```

continues

Example 12-2 *Viewing the Sensor's Configuration (Continued)*

```
filters edit NewFilter
signature-id-range 61500
attacker-address-range 10.200.10.0-10.200.10.255
risk-rating-range 50-100
actions-to-remove request-snmp-trap
exit
filters edit PhoneConfigTFTP
signature-id-range 6412
attacker-address-range 10.10.20.0-10.10.20.255
actions-to-remove deny-packet-inline
filter-item-status Disabled
exit
filters edit TestFilter
actions-to-remove reset-tcp-connection
exit
filters move TestFilter begin
filters move PhoneConfigTFTP after TestFilter
filters move NewFilter after PhoneConfigTFTP
exit
! ------------------------------
service host
network-settings
host-ip 10.40.10.100/24,10.40.10.1
host-name Ids4240
telnet-option disabled
access-list 10.10.10.0/24
access-list 10.0.0.0/8
access-list 64.101.0.0/16
exit
time-zone-settings
offset -360
standard-time-zone-name GMT-06:00
exit
exit
! ------------------------------
```

Displaying Sensor PEP Inventory

Sometimes you may need to display the PEP inventory information for your sensor. The PEP information includes information such as the following:

- Orderable Product ID (PID)
- Version ID (VID)
- Serial Number (SN)

The PEP information is provided by the **show inventory** sensor CLI command. Sample output from the **show inventory** command is displayed in Example 12-3.

Example 12-3 *Displaying the Sensor's Inventory Information*

```
Ids4240# show inventory

Name: "Chassis", DESCR: "IPS 4240 Intrusion Prevention Sensor"
PID: IPS-4240-K9, VID: V01 , SN: JAB0815R01X

Name: "Power Supply", DESCR: ""
PID: ASA-180W-PWR-AC, VID: V01 , SN: DTH0822000F
Ids4240#
```

Viewing Sensor Statistics

To check the operation of your sensors, you can view operational statistics from the sensor. The operational statistics fall into the following categories (keywords for the **show statistics** CLI command):

- **analysis-engine**
- **authentication**
- **denied-attackers**
- **event-server**
- **event-store**
- **host**
- **logger**
- **network-access**
- **notification**
- **sdee-server**
- **transaction-server**
- **transaction-source**
- **virtual-sensor**
- **web-server**

You can view this information by using the **show statistics** CLI command. You must also supply the statistics category that you want to view. For instance, suppose that you want to view the host statistics on the sensor. To view this information, you use the CLI command in Example 12-4.

Example 12-4 *Viewing the Sensor's Host Statistics Information*

```
Ids4240# show statistics host
General Statistics
   Last Change To Host Config (UTC) = 23:01:54  Sun Jan 02 2005
   Command Control Port Device = Management0/0
Network Statistics
   ma0_0     Link encap:Ethernet  HWaddr 00:0F:F7:75:4A:94
             inet addr:10.40.10.100  Bcast:10.40.10.255  Mask:255.255.255.0
             UP BROADCAST RUNNING MULTICAST  MTU:1500  Metric:1
             RX packets:47451 errors:0 dropped:0 overruns:0 frame:0
             TX packets:75437 errors:0 dropped:0 overruns:0 carrier:0
             collisions:0 txqueuelen:1000
             RX bytes:3371163 (3.2 MiB)  TX bytes:84409951 (80.4 MiB)
             Interrupt:16 Base address:0x9c00 Memory:f8300000-f8300038
NTP Statistics
   status = Not applicable
Memory Usage
   usedBytes = 354967552
   freeBytes = 1629736960
   totalBytes = 1984704512
Swap Usage
   Used Bytes = 0
   Free Bytes = 0

   Total Bytes = 0
CPU Statistics
   Usage over last 5 seconds = 0
   Usage over last minute = 1
   Usage over last 5 minutes = 0
Memory Statistics
   Memory usage (bytes) = 354873344
   Memory free (bytes) = 1629831168
Auto Update Statistics
   lastDirectoryReadAttempt = N/A
   lastDownloadAttempt = N/A
   lastInstallAttempt = N/A
   nextAttempt = N/A
Ids4240#
```

Instead of viewing the statistics for each of the categories individually via the CLI, you can also use IDM to view all of the statistics categories. Viewing the statistics information via IDM involves the following steps:

Step 1 Access IDM by entering the following URL in your web browser: **https://***sensor_ip_address*.

Step 2 Click on the **Monitoring** icon to display the list of monitoring tasks.

Step 3 If the items under **Support Information** are not displayed, click on the plus sign to the left of **Support Information**.

Step 4 Click on **Statistics** to view the statistics for all of the categories (see Figure 12-1).

Figure 12-1 *IDM Statistics Screen*

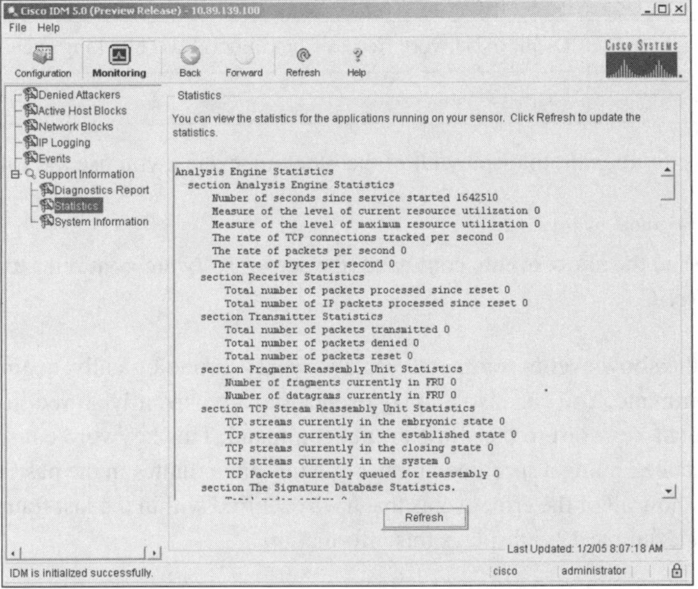

> **NOTE** To update the statistics information displayed on the IDM Statistics screen, you can click on **Refresh**.

Viewing Sensor Events

To monitor the attacks against your network, you monitor events from your sensors by using a monitoring application such as Security Monitor (http://www.cisco.com/go/ids). Sometimes, however, you may want to check the sensor events to verify that the sensor is operating correctly. In these situations, you can use both the sensor CLI and the IDM to view events on the sensor.

Viewing Events Using the CLI

Through the CLI, you can view events generated on the sensor by using the **show events** command. This command enables you to selectively display events based on the keywords shown in Table 12-2.

Table 12-2 **show events** *Command Keywords*

Keyword	Description
alert	Displays local system alerts
error	Displays error events
log	Displays log events
nac	Displays Network Access Controller (NAC) blocking events
status	Displays status events

For instance, if you want to display all of the blocking events, you use the following command:

```
Sensor# show events nac
```

When you issue the **show events** command, the sensor software continues to display events until you press **Ctrl-C**.

By default, the **show events** command displays events chronologically, beginning from when you issue the command. You can also display events that are currently stored in the Event Store by adding the **past** keyword to the **show events** command. This keyword causes the command to display events beginning a specified number of hours and minutes in the past. For instance, suppose you want to show all of the error events that have occurred within the last four and a half hours. The command in Example 12-5 displays this information.

Example 12-5 *Viewing Sensor Events Using the CLI*

```
Ids4240# show events error past 4:30

evError: eventId=1103038377039120319 severity=warning vendor=Cisco
  originator:
    hostId: Ids4240
    appName: cidwebserver
    appInstanceId: 1046
  time: 2005/01/02 23:14:51 2005/01/02 17:14:51 GMT-06:00
  errorMessage: name=errTransport while sending a TLS warning alert close_notify,
      the following error occurred: socket error [3,32]


Ids4240#
```

NOTE When specifying a time value, you can also specify a number of seconds, but the number of seconds is optional.

Sometimes you may want to limit the events generated by the **show events** command. Appending the | character (known as a *pipe* in UNIX terminology) to the command (and other CLI commands) enables you to limit the output by using one of the keywords shown in Table 12-3.

Table 12-3 **show events** *Output Keywords*

Keyword	Description
begin	Begins displaying events with a line that matches the specified criteria
include	Includes only events that match the specified criteria
exclude	Excludes any events that match the specified criteria

Suppose that you want to display all of the events from the cidwebserver application that have occurred in the past two hours. The command to retrieve those events is displayed in Example 12-6.

Example 12-6 *Filtering Sensor Events Displayed Using the CLI*

```
Ids4240# show events past 02:00 | include cidwebserver

evStatus: eventId=1103038377039120318 vendor=Cisco
  originator:
    hostId: Ids4240
    appName: cidwebserver
    appInstanceId: 261
  time: 2005/01/02 23:14:26 2005/01/02 17:14:26 GMT-06:00
  loginAction: action=loggedIn
    description: User logged into HTTP server
    userName: cisco
    userAddress: port=4083 10.66.254.58


evError: eventId=1103038377039120319 severity=warning vendor=Cisco
  originator:
    hostId: Ids4240
    appName: cidwebserver
    appInstanceId: 1046
  time: 2005/01/02 23:14:51 2005/01/02 17:14:51 GMT-06:00
  errorMessage: name=errTransport while sending a TLS warning alert close_notify,
     the following error occurred: socket error [3,32]
```

Viewing Events Using IDM

IDM also enables you to display various events by using the events monitoring screen (see Figure 12-2).

Figure 12-2 *IDM Events Monitoring Screen*

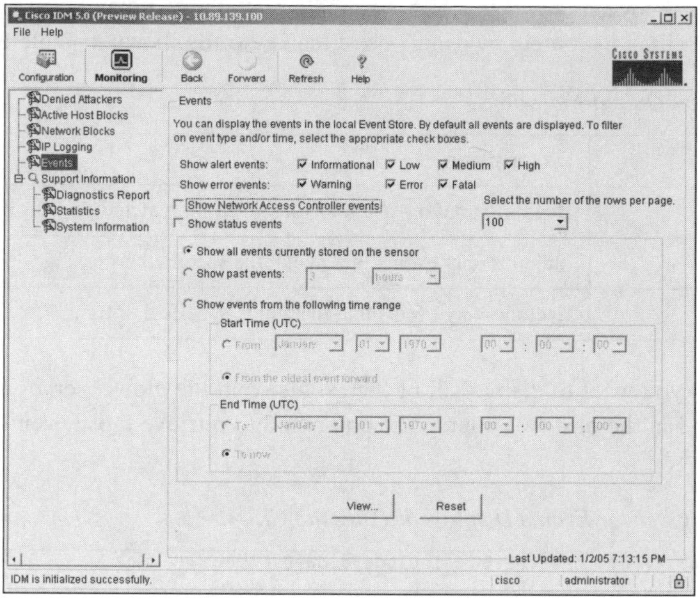

When displaying events by using IDM, you need to select the event types to display along with the time frame in which the events occurred.

Selecting Event Types

When displaying events by using IDM, you specify the types of events to display by selecting check boxes next to specific event types.

For alert events you can select the following event types (enabled by default):

- Informational
- Low
- Medium
- High

For error events you can select the following event types (enabled by default):

- Warning

- Error
- Fatal

You can also choose whether or not to display status events and Network Access Controller (NAC) events by selecting the appropriate check boxes (both disabled by default).

Selecting Time Frame for Events

When choosing the time frame for events, you can choose one of the following options:

- All events in the Event Store
- Events a specified number of hours or minutes in the past
- Events in a specified date and time range

Using the IDM Event Viewer

When you view events using IDM, they are displayed in the IDM Event Viewer (Figure 12-3). If the number of events selected by your criteria exceeds a single page, you can move through the events by clicking on the **Back** or **Next** buttons. You can also display the details for an event by first highlighting the event (clicking on it) and then clicking on **Details**. This will display the details for the highlighted event in a separate window (Figure 12-4).

Figure 12-3 *IDM Event Viewer Screen*

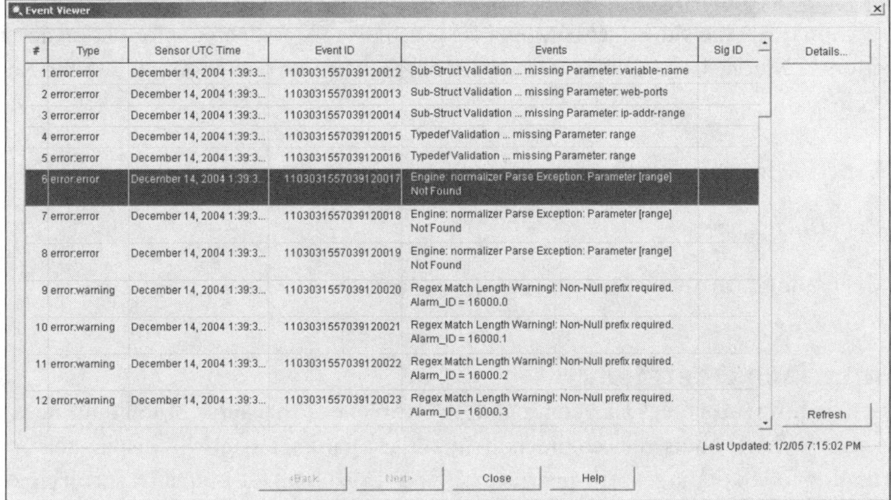

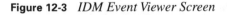

Figure 12-4 *IDM Event Details Screen*

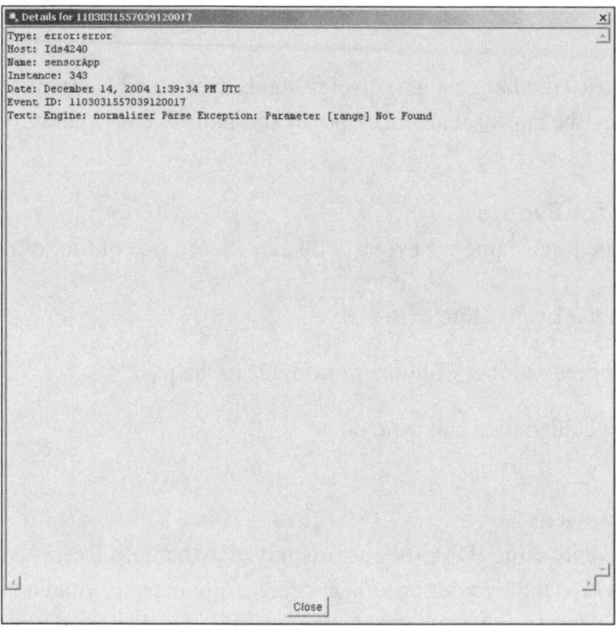

Debugging Sensor Operation

Besides viewing the sensor configuration and the statistics on various sensor parameters, it is important to be able to verify that the sensor is capturing network traffic. Generating debugging information using the **show tech-support** CLI also provides valuable information about the operation of your sensor. Tasks involved in debugging sensor operation fall into the following categories:

- Verifying interface operation
- Capturing packets
- Generating tech-support output

Verifying Interface Operation

Using the **show interfaces** CLI command, you can check the status of the interfaces on your IPS sensor. When you use this command without any parameters, it will display the operational information for all of the sensor's interfaces. You can also limit the output by specifying an interface (such as GigabitEthernet0/0). Table 12-4 shows the keywords that you can specify with the **show interfaces** command.

Table 12-4 **show interfaces** *Keywords*

Keyword	Description
FastEthernet	Displays the operational information for all of the Fast Ethernet ports
FastEthernet*card/port*	Displays the operational information for the Fast Ethernet interface specified
GigabitEthernet	Displays the operational information for all of the Gigabit Ethernet ports
GigabitEthernet*card/port*	Displays the operational information for the Gigabit Ethernet interface specified
Management	Displays the operational information for all of the management ports
Management*card/port*	Displays the operational information for the management interface specified

NOTE Not all interface types are available on every sensor. Using the **show interfaces ?** CLI command will display the available interfaces for your specific sensor.

The output in Example 12-7 shows the interface statistics for the management interface.

Example 12-7 *Displaying the Statistics for the Management Interface*

```
Ids4240# show interfaces Management0/0
MAC statistics from interface Management0/0
   Media Type = TX
   Link Status = Up
   Link Speed = Auto_100
   Link Duplex = Auto_Full
   Total Packets Received = 54299
   Total Bytes Received = 3865128
   Total Multicast Packets Received = 0
   Total Receive Errors = 0
   Total Receive FIFO Overruns = 0
   Total Packets Transmitted = 85959
   Total Bytes Transmitted = 95837551
   Total Transmit Errors = 0
   Total Transmit FIFO Overruns = 0
Ids4240#
```

To clear the operational statistics for the sensor interface, you add the **clear** keyword to the **show interfaces** command, as shown in the following command:

```
show interfaces clear
```

This command displays the interface statistics and then clears all of the parameters. Clearing the statistics is useful when you want to start from known values and then observe how the parameters are changing.

Appending the | character to the command enables you to limit the output when you use one of the following keywords:

- **begin**
- **include**
- **exclude**

Using **begin** causes the output to start at the first instance of the text you specify after the **begin** keyword. For instance specifying | **begin interface** will cause the output to start at the first instance of the word *interface* in the output. The **include** keyword causes the output to only show lines that include the specified text, while the **exclude** keyword causes the output to show only the lines that do not include the specified text.

Capturing Packets

Besides viewing the statistics for the interfaces on the sensor, sometimes you may want to view the actual packets being received on an interface. The **packet capture** CLI command enables you to capture packets for a specific interface. The packets are saved to a file in tcpdump format. Packets are captured until you press **Ctrl-C**. The following command captures traffic from GigabitEthernet0/0:

```
packet capture GigabitEthernet0/0
```

> **NOTE** You can limit the traffic captured by the **packet capture** command by specifying the **expression** keyword followed by a tcpdump filter expression. For more information on tcpdump filter expressions, refer to the documentation for tcpdump.

The packets from the **packet capture** command are stored in a file named packet-file. You can view the packets by using the **packet display** command, as shown in Example 12-8.

Example 12-8 *Displaying Captured Packets Stored in packet-file*

```
Ids4240# packet display packet-file
reading from file /usr/cids/idsRoot/var/packet-file, link-type EN10MB (Ethernet)
09:45:11.922176 00:01:c9:6d:64:fa > 01:00:0c:cc:cc:cc snap ui/C len=35
09:45:11.922180 00:01:c9:6d:64:fa > 01:00:0c:00:00:00 snap ui/C len=65
09:45:12.922078 00:01:c9:6d:64:fa > 01:00:0c:cc:cc:cc snap ui/C len=35
09:45:12.922080 00:01:c9:6d:64:fa > 01:00:0c:00:00:00 snap ui/C len=65
```

Example 12-8 *Displaying Captured Packets Stored in packet-file (Continued)*

```
09:45:13.975583 CDPv2, ttl: 180s, Device-ID 'stat-6000', length 424
09:45:13.977456 CDPv2, ttl: 180s, Device-ID 'stat-6000', length 424
09:45:13.979205 CDPv2, ttl: 180s, Device-ID 'stat-6000', length 424
09:45:15.562836 802.1d config 8410.00:d0:00:2e:dc:00.806b root
    8410.00:d0:00:2e:dc:00 pathcost 0 age
 0 max 20 hello 2 fdelay 15
09:45:17.563393 802.1d config 8410.00:d0:00:2e:dc:00.806b root
    8410.00:d0:00:2e:dc:00 pathcost 0 age
 0 max 20 hello 2 fdelay 15
Ids4240#
```

You can also display packets without saving them to a file by using the **packet display** command and specifying the interface on which you want to see the traffic. The output in Example 12-9 shows traffic captured from GigabitEthernet 0/0 using the **packet display** command.

Example 12-9 *Displaying Captured Packets for GigabitEthernet0/0*

```
Ids4240# packet display GigabitEthernet0/0
Warning: This command will cause significant performance degradation
tcpdump: WARNING: ge0_0: no IPv4 address assigned
tcpdump: verbose output suppressed, use -v or -vv for full protocol decode
listening on ge0_0, link-type EN10MB (Ethernet), capture size 65535 bytes
09:46:34.796832 00:01:c9:6d:64:fa > 01:00:0c:cc:cc:cc snap ui/C len=35
09:46:34.796835 00:01:c9:6d:64:fa > 01:00:0c:00:00:00 snap ui/C len=65
09:46:35.796987 00:01:c9:6d:64:fa > 01:00:0c:cc:cc:cc snap ui/C len=35
09:46:35.796990 00:01:c9:6d:64:fa > 01:00:0c:00:00:00 snap ui/C len=65
09:46:36.850740 CDPv2, ttl: 180s, Device-ID 'stat-6000', length 424
09:46:36.852612 CDPv2, ttl: 180s, Device-ID 'stat-6000', length 424
09:46:36.854361 CDPv2, ttl: 180s, Device-ID 'stat-6000', length 424
09:46:37.590140 802.1d config 8410.00:d0:00:2e:dc:00.806b root 8410.00:d0:00:2e:dc:00
pathcost 0 age
 0 max 20 hello 2 fdelay 15
8 packets captured
8 packets received by filter
0 packets dropped by kernel
Ids4240#
```

NOTE You can also transfer files from your sensor to other systems to view the captured information by using freely available tools, such as Ethereal (http://www.ethereal.com). To copy the packet-capture file from the sensor, use the **copy** command, as in the following example that uses Secure Copy (SCP):

```
copy packet-file scp:
```

Generating Tech-Support Output

Using the **show tech-support** command, you can display a comprehensive list of status and system information about your sensor. This command consolidates the output from the following commands and other data sources:

- **show configuration**
- **show version**
- Debug logs
- XML configuration files

The Technical Assistance Center (TAC) frequently uses the output from this command to debug problems with the operation of your sensor. The syntax for the **show tech-support** command is as follows:

```
show tech-support [page][password][destination destination-url]
```

Table 12-5 explains the parameters for the **show tech-support** command.

Table 12-5 **show tech-support** *Parameters*

Parameter	Description
page	(Optional) Causes the output to display one page of information at a time. You can display the next line of output by using the **Enter** key or page through the information with the **Spacebar**.
password	(Optional) Leaves password and other security information in the output. If **password** is not used, passwords and other sensitive security information in the output are replaced with the label <removed>. The default is to not include password and security information in the output.
destination	(Optional) Tag indicating that the information should be formatted as HTML and sent to the destination following the tag.
destination-url	Indicates the destination for the HTML-formatted output. (Required if the **destination** parameter is specified.)

When specifying a destination for the **show tech-support** command output, you can choose one of the following destination formats:

- **ftp:**//*username*@*ip_address*/*RelativeDirectory*/*filename*
- **ftp:**//*username*@*ip_address*//*AbsoluteDirectory*/*filename*

- **scp://***username@ip_address/RelativeDirectory/filename*
- **scp://***username@ip_address//AbsoluteDirectory/filename*

> **NOTE** Using SCP protects the tech-support output from being viewed since the information is encrypted before it is transmitted across the network. Attackers will try to obtain this information to better understand how security protection is configured so that they can bypass it.

Instead of specifying all of the options on the command line, you can specify just the server type. In this situation, you are prompted for the individual parameters, as in the sample output in Example 12-10.

Example 12-10 *Displaying tech-support Information Using Sensor CLI*

```
sensor# show tech-support destination scp:
User: root
Server's IP Address: 10.89.156.78
Port[22]:
File name: Sensor4230.out
Password: ********
```

Since this command has the capability to display passwords and other sensitive information, you can execute this command only using an account that has been assigned the Administrator role. You can also use IDM to generate the tech-support output. The steps to generate the tech-support output using IDM are as follows:

Step 1 Access IDM by entering the following URL in your web browser: **https://***sensor_ip_address.*

Step 2 Click on the **Monitoring** icon to display the list of monitoring tasks.

Step 3 If the items under **Support Information** are not displayed, click on the plus sign to the left of **Support Information**.

Step 4 Click on **Diagnostic Report** to view the Diagnostic Report screen (see Figure 12-5).

Step 5 Click on **Generate Report** to generate the diagnostic report information (see Figure 12-6).

> **NOTE** If you have already generated a diagnostic report during an IDM session, you will see the information from the previously generated report when you access the Diagnostic Report screen. You can view that information or refresh the information by clicking on **Generate Report**.

Figure 12-5 *IDM Diagnostic Report Screen*

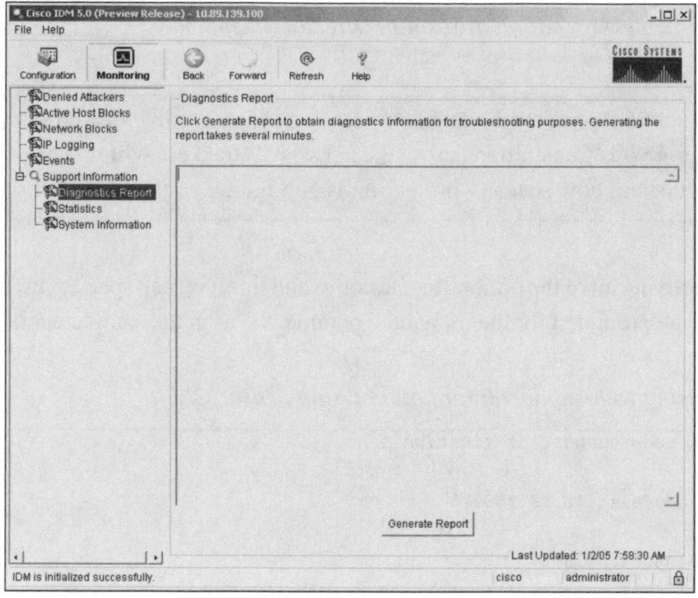

Figure 12-6 *IDM Diagnostic Report Information*

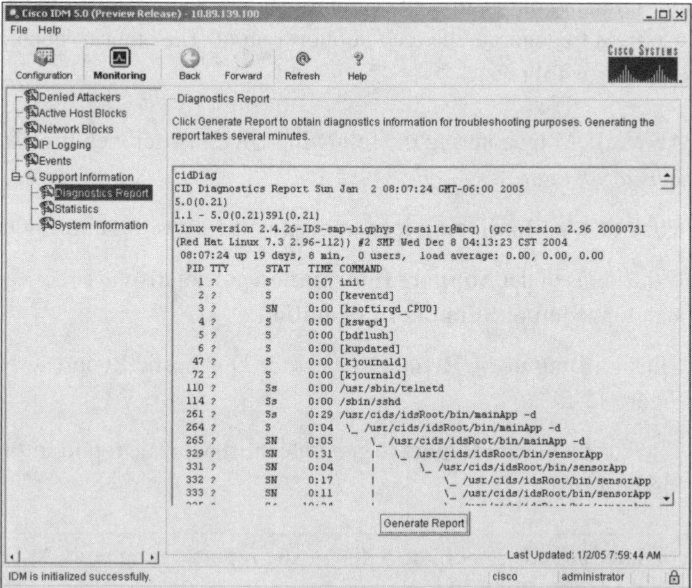

Sensor SNMP Access

Besides using the sensor CLI and IDM to view the operation of your sensor, you can also access your sensor via Simple Network Management Protocol (SNMP). SNMP access to your sensor is configured using the **service notification** sensor CLI global configuration command. Using SNMP traps facilitates management in large deployments since the sensors can generate traps when a problem arises instead of having your management software continually poll all of your IPS devices.

After issuing the **service notification** CLI command, you have the options listed in Table 12-6.

Table 12-6 **service notification** *Configuration Parameters*

Keyword	Description
enable-detail-traps	Removes the size limits on traps sent, as opposed to those in sparse mode (fewer than 484 bytes)
enable-notifications	Enables (or disables) SNMP event notifications
enable-set-get	Enables (or disables) the ability of your management software to use SNMP sets and gets
error-filter	Enables you to determine which errors generate SNMP traps (options are **warning**, **error**, and **fatal**)
read-only-community	Sets the read-only community name string
read-write-community	Sets the read-write community name string
snmp-agent-port	Sets the port at which the SNMP agent will listen for requests from your management software
snmp-agent-protocol	Determines whether SNMP requests use TCP or User Datagram Protocol (UDP)
system-contact	Identifies the contact information for the sensor
system-location	Identifies the location of the sensor
trap-community-name	Specifies the name used when sending traps if no name is specified when defining trap destinations
trap-destinations	IP address to receive generated traps

Enabling SNMP Traps by Using the Sensor CLI

Normally, your management console issues an SNMP request for information from your sensor. If the request is valid, the sensor replies with the requested information. This is referred to as polling (since the management device initiates the SNMP request to each of the sensors to check their status). Polling can become very cumbersome if you are managing a large number of sensors.

When you enable SNMP traps (using the **enable-notifications** command), your sensor will automatically send SNMP messages to the IP addresses defined by the **trap-destinations** command. The trap destinations identify which systems are your SNMP management consoles. Whenever a relevant event happens on the sensor, the sensor automatically sends an unsolicited SNMP message to the specified management consoles. Since each sensor sends SNMP traps only when relevant events happen, the workload on your management consoles is reduced.

Example 12-11 shows the commands needed to enable SNMP traps and define 10.20.10.10 as your SNMP management console. The example also defines the trap community name (for 10.20.10.10) as F$1%g.

Example 12-11 *Enabling SNMP Traps via the Sensor CLI*

```
Ids4240# configure terminal
Ids4240(config)# service notification
Ids4240(config-not)# enable-notifications true
Ids4240(config-not)# trap-destinations 10.20.10.10
Ids4240(config-not-tra)# trap-community-name F$1%g
Ids4240(config-not-tra)# exit
Ids4240(config-not)# exit
Apply Changes:?[yes]:
Ids4240(config)#
```

Enabling SNMP Traps Using IDM

Instead of using the sensor CLI, you can also enable traps using IDM. To enable traps and assign the SNMP community name of F$1%g to your management console located at 10.20.10.10, perform the following steps:

Step 1 Access IDM by entering the following URL in your web browser: **https://***sensor_ip_address.*

Step 2 Click on the **Configuration** icon to display the list of monitoring tasks.

Step 3 If the items under **SNMP** are not displayed, click on the plus sign to the left of **SNMP**.

Step 4 Click on **Traps Configuration** to view the Traps Configuration screen (see Figure 12-7).

Step 5 Click on the check box next to **Enable SNMP Traps**.

Figure 12-7 *IDM Traps Configuration Screen*

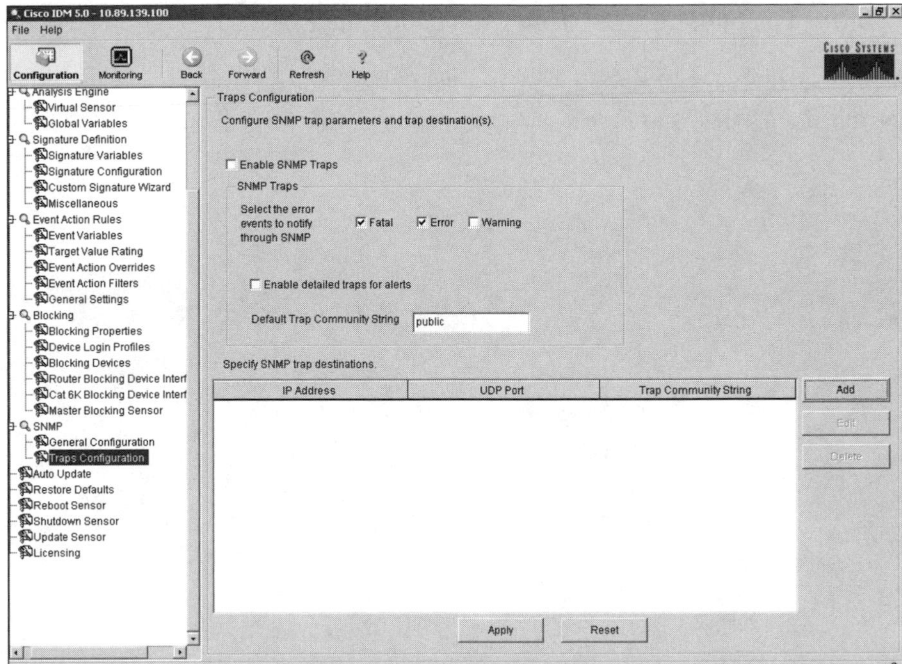

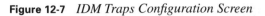

Step 6 Click on **Add** to add a new SNMP trap destination (SNMP management console). This will display the Add SNMP Trap Destination popup window (see Figure 12-8).

Figure 12-8 *Add SNMP Trap Destination Popup Window*

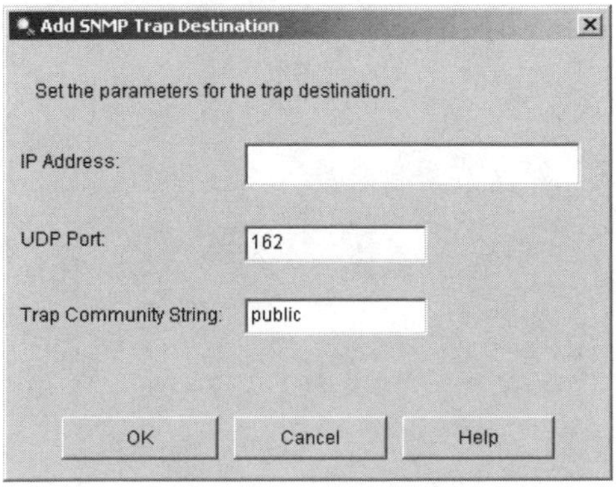

Step 7 Enter **10.20.10.10** in the **IP Address** field.

Step 8 Enter **F$1%g** in the **Trap Community Name** field.

Step 9 Click on **OK** to save the new trap destination.

Step 10 Click on **Apply** to save the configuration changes to the sensor.

Foundation Summary

Maintaining the latest Cisco IPS software version is important to maintaining an effective security posture. To display the version of software running on a sensor, you use the **show version** sensor CLI command. This command displays various characteristics about the sensor, such as the following:

- Sensor uptime
- Recovery partition software version
- Current sensor software version
- Previous sensor software version

The **show configuration** sensor CLI command displays the current configuration of the sensor. The configuration is divided into the following service categories that correspond to the global configuration **service** CLI command:

- **analysis engine**
- **authentication**
- **event-action-rules**
- **host**
- **interface**
- **logger**
- **network-access**
- **notification**
- **signature-definition**
- **ssh-known-hosts**
- **trusted-certificates**
- **web-server**

The **show inventory** command shows the Product Evolution Program (PEP) information, such as the following:

- Orderable Product ID (PID)
- Version ID (VID)
- Serial Number (SN)

The operational statistics fall into the following categories (specified as keywords on the **show statistics** command):

- **analysis-engine**
- **authentication**
- **denied-attackers**
- **event-server**
- **event-store**
- **host**
- **logger**
- **network-access**
- **notification**
- **sdee-server**
- **transaction-server**
- **transaction-source**
- **virtual-sensor**
- **web-server**

You can view this information by using the **show statistics** CLI command.

Through the CLI, you can view events generated on the sensor by using the **show events** command. This command enables you to selectively display events based on the keywords shown in Table 12-7.

Table 12-7 **show events** *Command Keywords*

Keyword	Description
alert	Displays local system alerts
error	Displays error events
log	Displays log events
nac	Displays Network Access Controller (NAC) blocking events
status	Displays status events

Appending the | character (known as a *pipe* in UNIX terminology) to many CLI commands enables you to limit the output when you use one of the keywords shown in Table 12-8.

Table 12-8 **show events** *Output Keywords*

Keyword	Description
begin	Begins displaying events with a line that matches the specified criteria
include	Includes only events that match the specified criteria
exclude	Excludes any events that match the specified criteria

Besides using the CLI, you can use IDM to display sensor events. When choosing the time frame for events in IDM, you can choose one of the following options:

- All events in the Event Store
- Events a specified number of hours or minutes in the past
- Events in a specified date and time range

Using the **show interfaces** CLI command, you can check the status of the interfaces on your IPS sensor. The **packet capture** and **packet display** CLI commands enable you to capture packets on specific sensor interfaces.

Using the **show tech-support** command, you can display a comprehensive list of status and system information about your sensor. This command consolidates the output from the following commands and other data sources:

- **show configuration**
- **show version**

- Debug logs
- XML configuration files

The IDM diagnostic report provides the same information as the **show tech-support** CLI command.

You can configure SNMP access to your sensor by using the **service notification** sensor CLI global configuration command, which has the options listed in Table 12-9.

Table 12-9 **service notification** *Configuration Parameters*

Keyword	Description
enable-detail-traps	Removes the size limits on traps sent, as opposed to those in sparse mode (fewer than 484 bytes)
enable-notifications	Enables (or disables) SNMP event notifications
enable-set-get	Enables (or disables) the ability of your management software to use SNMP sets and gets
error-filter	Enables you to determine which errors generate SNMP traps (options are **warning**, **error**, and **fatal**)
read-only-community	Sets the read-only community name string
read-write-community	Sets the read-write community name string
snmp-agent-port	Sets the port at which the SNMP agent will listen for requests from your management software
snmp-agent-protocol	Determines whether SNMP requests use TCP or UDP
system-contact	Identifies the contact information for the sensor
system-location	Identifies the location of the sensor
trap-community-name	Specifies the name used when sending traps if no name is specified when defining trap destinations
trap-destinations	IP address to receive generated traps

Q&A

You have two choices for review questions:

- The questions that follow give you a bigger challenge than the exam itself by using an open-ended question format. By reviewing now with this more difficult question format, you can exercise your memory better and prove your conceptual and factual knowledge of this chapter. The answers to these questions are found in the appendix.
- For more practice with exam-like question formats, use the exam engine on the CD-ROM.

1. Which sensor CLI command would you use to display the sensor uptime and previous sensor software version?
2. What are the sections of the sensor configuration file output?
3. What do the different sections of the sensor configuration file correspond to?
4. Which sensor CLI command displays the Product Evolution Program (PEP) information for your sensor?
5. What is the main difference between displaying sensor statistics via the CLI and displaying sensor statistics by using IDM?
6. In the sensor CLI, which command displays events, and which types of events can you display?
7. What are the three ways to specify the time frame for events when you use IDM to display events?
8. Which sensor CLI command enables you to view the operational status of the interfaces on the sensor?
9. Which CLI command captures network traffic to a tcpdump capture file?
10. Which CLI command captures network traffic and displays it in the screen for all Gigabit Ethernet interfaces?
11. Which sensor CLI command displays a comprehensive list of status and system information about your sensor?
12. What does the diagnostic report in IDM provide?
13. Which **service notification** option removes the size limit on SNMP traps?
14. What does the **error-filter** option of the **service notification** command do?

This chapter covers the following subjects:

- Cisco IDS Module
- IDSM-2 Configuration
- IDSM-2 Ports
- Catalyst 6500 Switch Configuration
- IDSM-2 Administrative Tasks
- Troubleshooting the IDSM-2

CHAPTER 13

Cisco IDS Module (IDSM)

One of the advantages of Cisco IPS is the multiple locations at which you can deploy sensors throughout your network. The Cisco IDS Module (IDSM) enables you to deploy your sensor directly into your Catalyst 6500 switch via a switch-line card.

Besides tuning Cisco IPS to match your unique network requirements, you must also thoroughly understand the various locations throughout your network at which you can deploy IPS sensors. A key traffic-crossing point is your Catalyst 6500 family switches. Deploying an Intrusion Detection System Module 2 (IDSM-2) in your Catalyst 6500 switch enables you to efficiently and effectively monitor traffic traversing your network. Understanding the benefits and limitations of the IDSM-2 is crucial to monitoring a key location in your network infrastructure.

"Do I Know This Already?" Quiz

The purpose of the "Do I Know This Already?" quiz is to help you decide if you really need to read the entire chapter. If you already intend to read the entire chapter, you do not necessarily need to answer these questions now.

The 10-question quiz, derived from the major sections in the "Foundation and Supplemental Topics" portion of the chapter, helps you determine how to spend your limited study time.

Table 13-1 outlines the major topics discussed in this chapter and the "Do I Know This Already?" quiz questions that correspond to those topics.

Table 13-1 *"Do I Know This Already?" Foundation and Supplemental Topics Mapping*

Foundation or Supplemental Topic	Questions Covering This Topic
Cisco IDS Module	1, 2
IDSM-2 Configuration	5
IDSM-2 Ports	3, 4, 8
Catalyst 6500 Switch Configuration	9
IDSM-2 Administrative Tasks	10
Troubleshooting the IDSM-2	6, 7

CAUTION The goal of self-assessment is to gauge your mastery of the topics in this chapter. If you do not know the answer to a question or are only partially sure of the answer, you should mark this question wrong for purposes of the self-assessment. Giving yourself credit for an answer you correctly guess skews your self-assessment results and might provide you with a false sense of security.

1. What is the maximum amount of traffic that the IDSM-2 can monitor?
   a. 500 Mbps
   b. 450 Mbps
   c. 600 Mbps
   d. 250 Mbps
   e. 1000 Mbps

2. Which of the following is false about the IDSM-2?
   a. It has the ability to monitor multiple VLANs.
   b. It impacts the switch performance.
   c. It runs the same code base as the appliance sensor.
   d. It supports improved management techniques (such as IDM).

3. Which port on IDSM-2 is the command and control port?
   a. Port 1
   b. Port 7
   c. Port 8
   d. Port 2

4. Which port on IDSM-2 is the TCP reset port?
   a. Port 1
   b. Port 2
   c. Port 7
   d. Port 8

5. Which of the following IOS commands accesses an IDSM-2 located in slot 7?
   a. **session 7**
   b. **telnet 2089**
   c. **session slot 7 processor 1**
   d. **session slot 7 processor 0**

6. Which switch command can you use to check the status of the IDSM-2 in slot 5?
   a. **show slot 5**
   b. **show module 5**
   c. **show idsm status**
   d. **show card 5**

7. What does a red status light-emitting diode (LED) on the front of the IDSM-2 indicate?
   a. The IDSM-2 is running through its boot and self-test diagnostic sequence.
   b. The IDSM-2 is disabled.
   c. A diagnostic other than an individual port test has failed.
   d. The IDSM-2 is in the shutdown state.
   e. The IDSM-2 is operational.

8. Which of the following ports is an IDSM-2 monitoring port?
   a. 1
   b. 4
   c. 2
   d. 7
   e. 3

9. Which IOS command changes the VLAN for a specific port on the switch?
   a. **switchport access vlan**
   b. **set vlan**
   c. **set port**
   d. **set interface vlan**

10. Which command do you use from the IDSM-2 CLI to shut down the device?
    a. **shutdown module**
    b. **reset powerdown**
    c. **reload module**
    d. **reboot module**

The answers to the "Do I Know This Already?" quiz are found in the appendix. The suggested choices for your next step are as follows:

- **8 or less overall score**—Read the entire chapter. This includes the "Foundation and Supplemental Topics" and "Foundation Summary" sections and the Q&A section.
- **9 or 10 overall score**—If you want more review on these topics, skip to the "Foundation Summary" section and then go to the Q&A section. Otherwise, move to the next chapter.

Foundation and Supplemental Topics

Cisco IDS Module

The Cisco IDS Module (IDSM) integrates Cisco IPS functionality directly into your Catalyst 6000 family switch. This line card captures traffic directly off of the switch's backplane. Beginning with Cisco IDS version 4.0, Cisco introduced the second-generation IDSM, called the IDSM-2. This new module runs the same code base as the appliance sensor. Therefore, both platforms now support the same functionality.

IDSM-2 Technical Specifications

In deploying IDSM-2 throughout your network, it is helpful to understand its capabilities and requirements. The specifications for deploying IDSM-2 fall into the following two categories:

- Performance capabilities
- Catalyst 6500 requirements

Performance Capabilities

The IDSM-2 is a single-slot switch card that provides the following enhanced capabilities:

- Performance—600 Mbps
- Monitoring interfaces—Gigabit
- Command and control interface—Gigabit
- TCP reset interface—Gigabit
- Optional interface—No
- Performance upgrade—No

Catalyst 6500 Requirements

Unlike the appliance sensor, the IDSM-2 is a switch card. Therefore, to deploy the IDSM-2 you must have a Catalyst 6500 family switch. Furthermore, to successfully use your IDSM-2 as another component in your overall Cisco IPS solution, your switch operating system must fulfill one of the following requirements:

- Catalyst OS 7.5(1) or later (on supervisor engine)
- Cisco IOS Release 12.1(19)E or later

If you have Catalyst OS 7.5(1) or later, you also need to have one of the following supervisor engines:

- Supervisor Engine 1A
- Supervisor Engine 1A/Policy Feature Card 2 (PFC2)
- Supervisor Engine 1A/Multilayer Switch Feature Card 1 (MSFC1)
- Supervisor Engine 1A/MSFC2
- Supervisor Engine 2
- Supervisor Engine 2/MSFC2

If you have IOS Release 12.1(19)E or later, you also need to have one of the following supervisor engines:

- Supervisor Engine 1a with MSFC2
- Supervisor Engine 2 with MSFC2

NOTE Cisco IOS Software Release 12.2(14)SY requires Supervisor Engine 2 and MSFC2, and Cisco IOS Software Release 12.2(14)SX1 requires Supervisor Engine 720.

Although meeting the operating system version on your supervisor engine enables you to install and use the IDSM-2 on your switch, there are a few other requirements, depending on the features that you plan to use in conjunction with the IDSM-2.

You have several traffic-capture options on your Catalyst switch. The most common is probably the Switched Port Analyzer (SPAN) feature. If you plan to capture traffic using VLAN Access Control Lists (VACLs), however, you also need to have a Policy Feature Card (PFC).

Your IDSM-2 also supports device management. This means that it can dynamically restrict network traffic by updating access controls on various network devices, such as the following:

- Cisco IOS routers
- Catalyst 6000 switches
- PIX Firewalls

Key Features

Originally, the IDSM incorporated IDS functionality directly into your switch infrastructure. This original switch sensor included the following functionalities:

- Merged switching and security into a single chassis
- Provided ability to monitor multiple VLANs
- Did not impact switch performance

This first-generation switch sensor, however, did not provide all of the functionality of the appliance sensors. To enhance the capability of the switch sensor, the IDSM-2 provides more capabilities than the original IDSM. Besides increasing the bandwidth capacity of the IDSM-2, it provides the following capabilities or features:

- Merges switching and security into a single chassis
- Provides ability to monitor multiple VLANs
- Does not impact switch performance
- Supports attacks and signatures equal to appliance sensor
- Uses the same code base as the appliance sensor
- Supports improved management techniques (such as IDM)

IDSM-2 Traffic Flow

Unlike traffic flow to the network appliance, the traffic flow to the IDSM-2 line card requires a little more explanation (see Figure 13-1). Furthermore, understanding this traffic flow is an important aspect of effectively using your IDSM-2 to capture and analyze network traffic. Although the IDSM-2 receives traffic directly from your switch's backplane, your Catalyst 6500 family switch must be configured to enable traffic to flow to and from the various ports on the IDSM-2 line card.

Figure 13-1 *IDSM-2 Traffic Flow*

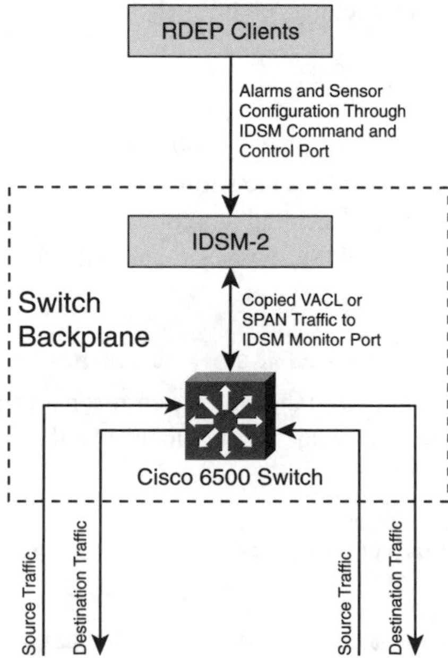

Traffic that enters the Catalyst 6500 switch is destined for a host or network. After passing through the switch, a copy of this traffic is diverted through the switch backplane to your IDSM-2 for intrusion-detection analysis. As in the appliance sensors, alerts are stored in the Event Store until your monitoring application retrieves these alarms via the command and control interface by using the Remote Data Exchange Protocol (RDEP).

IDSM-2 Configuration

Since the IDSM-2 has the same code base as the appliance sensor, the initialization steps performed on the appliance sensor also apply to the IDSM-2. The major difference between the appliance sensor and the IDSM-2 is that you need to configure the capture ports on the IDSM-2, and you need to initially access the command-line interface (CLI) through the switch. The IDSM-2 capture ports are internally connected to the switch's backplane; this structure differs from that of the appliance sensor, where you physically connect the monitoring ports to your switch (or other network device) via Ethernet cables.

To enable your IDSM-2 to become a functional component of your Cisco IPS, perform the following basic initialization tasks:

- Verify IDSM-2 status
- Initialize the IDSM-2
- Configure the command and control port
- Configure the traffic capture settings on the switch

Verifying IDSM-2 Status

After installing the IDSM-2 on your Catalyst 6500 family switch, you can verify that the switch has recognized the IDSM-2 line card via the **show module** switch command (see "Catalyst 6500 Commands" later in this chapter). Executing this command provides detailed information about the line cards in your switch. You should see a line similar to the following for your IDSM-2 line card (if using CatOS):

```
8   8   8     Intrusion Detection Syste WS-SVC-IDSM2        yes ok
```

The "ok" indicates that the card is working, and the correct name indicates that the switch correctly recognizes the line card. The similar line for IOS looks like the following:

```
Mod Ports Card Type                               Model              Serial No.
--- ----- -------------------------------------- ------------------ -----------
  9    2  Intrusion Detection System              WS-X6381-IDS       SAD05050GDY

Mod MAC addresses                       Hw     Fw           Sw           Status
--- ---------------------------------- ------ ------------ ------------ -------
  9  0003.3282.ee0a to 0003.3282.ee0b  1.1    4B4LZ0XA     3.0(5)S23    Ok
```

NOTE It is normal for the **show module** command to display a status of "other" instead of "ok" when IDSM is first installed. When the IDSM-2 completes its diagnostic routines and comes online, the status will change to "ok," but this can take up to 5 minutes.

Initializing the IDSM-2

The basic initialization tasks for the IDSM-2 are the same as for the appliance sensor. (See Chapter 2, "IPS Command-Line Interface.") These tasks include the following:

- Accessing the IDSM-2 CLI
- Logging in to the IDSM-2
- Running the **setup** command
- Configuring trusted hosts
- Entering the network communication parameters

Other tasks that you might need to perform during initialization include the following:

- Changing your password
- Adding and removing users
- Adding known Secure Shell (SSH) hosts

One of the benefits of having the same code base on both the appliance sensor and the IDSM-2 is that the configuration tasks are very similar, which reduces the total amount of knowledge needed to install both types of sensors.

Although the sensor appliance can be configured to use either its internal clock or Network Time Protocol (NTP), the IDSM-2 can only be configured to use either the switch's time or NTP. The IDSM-2 cannot be configured to use an internal clock. Therefore, there is no option to set the clock time in the IDSM-2 CLI.

By default, the IDSM-2 is configured to use the switch's time. The switch converts its local time into the Coordinated Universal Time (UTC) that is used by the sensor to time-stamp its events. Because the sensor's time zone is also configurable, the sensor uses its time zone and summer time settings to convert the UTC to local time. The sensor uses both its local time and UTC time settings for time-stamping events, as well as for other time functions. For this reason, it is important to ensure that the time zone and summer time settings are correct on both the switch and the IDSM-2, and to set the clock on the switch to the correct time.

> **NOTE** The switch only sends a UTC time to the IDSM-2. Therefore, the IDSM-2 can not convert the time using the switch's time zone and summer time settings, because these settings are not reported to the module.

Accessing the IDSM-2 CLI

You initially access the IDSM-2 from the switch console. When using CatOS, the **session** switch command gives you access to the IDSM-2 CLI. The syntax for the Catalyst operating system **session** command is as follows:

```
session mod
```

The term *mod* indicates the slot where the IDSM-2 is located.

When using IOS, you access the IDSM-2 CLI by using the **session slot** switch command. The syntax for the IOS **session slot** command is as follows:

```
session slot mod {processor processor-id}
```

Suppose that your IDSM-2 is in slot 5. The IOS command to access the IDSM-2 CLI would be as follows:

```
Switch# session slot 5 processor 1
```

> **NOTE** Currently, the only processor ID supported by the IDSM-2 is 1.

Logging in to the IDSM-2

As with the appliance sensors, you initially log in to the IDSM-2 with a username and password of "cisco." After logging in, you must immediately change the password to this account for security reasons.

Configuring the Command and Control Port

To enable your monitoring applications and management software (such as IDM and Security Monitor) to communicate with your IDSM-2, you need to configure the command and control port on the IDSM-2. This includes assigning the command and control port an IP address, configuring the default gateway for the IDSM-2 command and control port, and assigning the command and control port to the correct management VLAN.

Configuring the Switch Traffic Capture Settings

Besides establishing management access, you need to configure the capture ports on your IDSM-2 so that your switch sensor can analyze your network traffic. Capturing important network traffic (while not exceeding the IDSM-2's 600-Mbps capacity) is the key to successfully deploying the IDSM-2 on your network.

IDSM-2 Ports

To perform its operation, the IDSM-2 uses four internal ports that fall into the following three functional categories:

- TCP reset port
- Command and control port
- Monitoring ports

> **NOTE** The ports on the IDSM-2 are not physical ports that you can see. Instead, they are directly connected into the switch's backplane.

TCP Reset Port

The initial version of IDSM did not provide the capability to initiate TCP resets in response to attack traffic. This limitation has been overcome in IDSM-2 by the inclusion of a port specifically for generating TCP resets. A TCP reset port was necessary because the two monitoring ports on the IDSM-2 cannot transmit the TCP reset packets. Plus this enables the monitoring ports to focus strictly on capturing traffic.

Port 1 on the IDSM-2 is used for TCP reset traffic. You need to configure port 1 with the same settings (with respect to VLANs) as your promiscuous monitoring ports. It will not be monitoring any traffic, but it needs to be able to generate a TCP reset for any connection that your IDSM-2 promiscuous monitoring ports can analyze.

Command and Control Port

Your management application needs to be able to communicate with the IDSM-2 to change its configuration and operating characteristics. Your monitoring application needs to access the IDSM-2 to retrieve alerts. Both of these operations are conducted through the command and control interface.

Port 2 on the IDSM-2 is the command and control interface. You will configure an actual IP address for this port (and assign the appropriate VLAN on your switch) to make your IDSM-2 accessible from the network.

Monitoring Ports

The last two ports on the IDSM-2 are the monitoring ports. Your IDSM-2 receives all of the network traffic that it analyzes through these two monitoring ports.

Ports 7 and 8 are the monitoring ports on the IDSM-2. You can use either or both of these ports to monitor your network traffic. Because of processor limitations, the IDSM-2 is capable of processing only 600 Mbps of network traffic. The two monitoring interfaces are easily capable of exceeding the 600-Mbps limitation, so you must be careful to not overload your IDSM-2 with too much traffic.

> **NOTE** The reason that the IDSM-2 has two monitoring ports is that it uses the same accelerator card that is used by the IDS-4250 appliance sensor.

Catalyst 6500 Switch Configuration

A significant portion of the initial setup of your IDSM-2 involves configuring the switch to send traffic to your IDSM-2 monitoring ports and enabling external applications to access the IDSM-2 via the command and control port.

Configuring the Command and Control Port

Your management and monitoring applications (such as IDM and Security Monitor) access the IDSM-2 through the command and control interface. When initially configuring the IDSM-2 through its CLI, you assign the command and control interface an IP address and default gateway. To complete the configuration of the command and control port, however, you must also assign the correct VLAN to the command and control port on the Catalyst 6500 switch.

Setting VLANs by Using IOS

If your switch is running IOS, you can assign a VLAN to the command and control port by using the **switchport access vlan** interface configuration command.

Setting VLANs by Using CatOS

To define a VLAN for a port on your Catalyst 6500 switch (running CatOS), use the **set vlan** command. This command groups one or more switch ports into a single VLAN. You can also use this command to set the private VLAN type or unmap VLANs. These extra features are explained in the Catalyst switch documentation. The syntax for the basic **set vlan** command is as follows:

```
set vlan vlan_num mod/ports
```

The parameters for the **set vlan** command are explained in Table 13-2.

Table 13-2 **set vlan** *Parameters*

Parameter	Description
vlan_num	Number identifying the VLAN
mod/ports	Number of the module and ports on the module that you want to add to the specifying VLAN

NOTE The IDSM-2 command and control port (port 2) must be assigned to a VLAN that can communicate with your management and monitoring applications. Otherwise, you will not be able to configure the IDSM-2 or retrieve alarm information.

To assign ports 4 through 8 on module 3 to VLAN 120 (using CatOS), use the following command:

```
Console> (enable) set vlan 120 3/4-8
VLAN 120 modified.
VLAN  Mod/Ports
---- -----------------
120   3/4-8
Console> (enable)
```

NOTE If your switch is running IOS, you can assign a VLAN to the command and control port by using the **switchport access vlan** interface configuration command.

Monitored Traffic

The IDSM-2 has the processing power to capture and analyze approximately 600 Mbps of network traffic. This traffic is captured directly off of the switch's backplane.

To analyze traffic, your IDSM-2 must receive traffic on its monitoring ports (port 7 and port 8). You need to configure your Catalyst switch to copy selected traffic to the monitoring ports on your IDSM-2 line card. You can use the following three mechanisms to capture your network traffic:

- Remote Switched Port Analyzer (RSPAN) feature
- SPAN feature
- VACL capture feature

Each of these options is explained in detail in Chapter 15, "Capturing Network Traffic."

IDSM-2 Administrative Tasks

When using your IDSM-2, besides configuring the normal operational characteristics, you may also need to perform the following two administrative tasks:

- Enable full memory test
- Stop the IDSM

Enabling Full Memory Test

By default, the IDSM-2 performs a partial memory test when it boots. In some troubleshooting situations, you may need to run a complete memory test. If your switch is running CatOS, you can configure your IDSM-2 to run a complete memory test by using the **set boot device** switch command. (Refer to the Cisco documentation for detailed information on this command.)

CAUTION A full memory test will take significantly more time (up to 12 minutes) than a partial memory test. This will considerably increase the time that it takes your IDSM-2 to come online.

Stopping the IDS Module

To prevent corruption of the IDSM-2, you must shut it down properly. To properly shut down the IDSM-2, you need to log in to the IDSM-2 and execute the **reset** command. The **reset** command on the IDSM-2 CLI enables you to reboot and power down the IDSM-2. The syntax for this command is as follows:

```
reset [powerdown]
```

The **reset** command without any options will cause the IDSM-2 to perform an orderly reboot. If you add the **powerdown** option, the IDSM-2 will perform an orderly shutdown and will either power off the device or place it in a state where it can be powered off.

NOTE Do not remove the IDSM-2 line card from the switch until the module has shut down completely. Removing the module without going through the shutdown procedure can damage the module.

Troubleshooting the IDSM-2

You may need to troubleshoot the operation of your IDSM-2. Besides running various commands on your Catalyst 6500 switch, you can examine the status LED on the IDSM-2 itself.

IDSM-2 Status LED

The front panel of the IDSM-2 contains a single LED. This LED provides you with a visual indication of the state of the IDSM-2 line card. This LED can be in one of the states listed in Table 13-3.

Table 13-3 *IDSM-2 Status LED*

Color	Description
Green	All diagnostics tests have passed—IDSM is operational.
Red	A diagnostic other than an individual port test failed.

Table 13-3 *IDSM-2 Status LED (Continued)*

Color	Description
Amber	The IDSM is • Running through its boot and self-test diagnostic sequence. • Disabled. • In the shutdown state.
Off	The IDSM power is off.

Catalyst 6500 Commands

Since the IDSM-2 is a line card in your Catalyst switch, you can use several switch commands to examine its operation. The following three commands provide detailed information on your IDSM-2 line card and its ports:

- **show module**
- **show port**
- **show trunk**

show module Command

The **show module** CatOS switch command enables you to display information about the line cards that you have installed in your Catalyst 6500 switch. The syntax for the **show module** command is as follows:

```
show module [mod]
```

The only parameter, *mod,* indicates the module number that the card is in. For instance, on a 6509 you have nine slots, so the module numbers are numbered from one to nine. If your IDSM-2 line card is in slot 8, you could view its information with the **show module** command in Example 13-1.

Example 13-1 *Viewing the Status of the IDSM-2 Module in Slot 8*

```
Cat6k> show module 8
Mod Slot Ports Module-Type               Model              Sub Status
--- ---- ----- ------------------------- ------------------ --- --------
8   8    8     Intrusion Detection Syste WS-SVC-IDSM2       yes ok

Mod Module-Name          Serial-Num
--- -------------------- -----------
8                        SAD062004LV
```

continues

Example 13-1 *Viewing the Status of the IDSM-2 Module in Slot 8 (Continued)*

```
Mod MAC-Address(es)                        Hw     Fw         Sw
--- -------------------------------------- ------ ---------- ----------------
8   00-e0-b0-ff-3b-80 to 00-e0-b0-ff-3b-87 0.102  7.2(0.67)  4.1(0.3)S42(0.3

Mod Sub-Type                Sub-Model          Sub-Serial  Sub-Hw Sub-Sw
--- ----------------------- ------------------ ----------- ------ ------
8   IDS 2 accelerator board WS-SVC-IDSUPG      .           2.0
Cat6k>
```

You can also specify the **show module** CatOS command without any parameters to obtain some basic information about all the line cards in your switch, as displayed in Example 13-2.

Example 13-2 *Viewing the Status for All of the Modules in a Catalyst 6500 Switch*

```
Cat6k> show module
Mod Slot Ports Module-Type               Model               Sub Status
--- ---- ----- ------------------------- ------------------- --- --------
1   1    2     1000BaseX Supervisor      WS-X6K-SUP1A-2GE    yes ok
15  1    1     Multilayer Switch Feature WS-F6K-MSFC         no  ok
3   3    48    10/100BaseTX Ethernet     WS-X6548-RJ-45      no  ok
4   4    8     1000BaseX Ethernet        WS-X6408-GBIC       no  ok
6   6    8     Intrusion Detection Syste WS-SVC-IDSM2        yes ok
8   8    8     Intrusion Detection Syste WS-SVC-IDSM2        yes ok
9   9    16    10/100/1000BaseT Ethernet WS-X6516-GE-TX      no  ok

Mod Module-Name          Serial-Num
--- -------------------- -----------
1                        SAD04200CUH
15                       SAD04190BS5
3                        SAD0612021X
4                        JAB04040859
6                        SAD0625018D
8                        SAD062004LV
9                        SAL06365QSP

Mod MAC-Address(es)                        Hw     Fw         Sw
--- -------------------------------------- ------ ---------- ----------------
1   00-30-7b-95-26-86 to 00-30-7b-95-26-87 3.2    5.3(1)     7.6(1)
    00-30-7b-95-26-84 to 00-30-7b-95-26-85
    00-09-44-89-90-00 to 00-09-44-89-93-ff
15  00-30-7b-95-00-3c to 00-30-7b-95-00-7b 1.4    12.1(13)E3 12.1(13)E3
3   00-01-63-d7-5a-ca to 00-01-63-d7-5a-f9 4.2    6.3(1)     7.6(1)
4   00-30-a3-38-9a-30 to 00-30-a3-38-9a-37 2.3    4.2(0.24)V 7.6(1)
6   00-10-7b-00-0e-e8 to 00-10-7b-00-0e-ef 0.102  7.2(1)     4.1(0.3)S42(0.3
8   00-e0-b0-ff-3b-80 to 00-e0-b0-ff-3b-87 0.102  7.2(0.67)  4.1(0.3)S42(0.3
9   00-09-11-e4-89-c4 to 00-09-11-e4-89-d3 2.2    6.3(1)     7.6(1)
```

Example 13-2 *Viewing the Status for All of the Modules in a Catalyst 6500 Switch (Continued)*

```
Mod Sub-Type                Sub-Model          Sub-Serial  Sub-Hw Sub-Sw
--- ----------------------- ------------------ ----------- ------ ------
1   L3 Switching Engine     WS-F6K-PFC         SAD04200DP9 1.1
6   IDS 2 accelerator board WS-SVC-IDSUPG      .           2.0
8   IDS 2 accelerator board WS-SVC-IDSUPG      .           2.0
Cat6k>
```

IOS also provides a **show module** command to display the status of the line cards. This output is similar to the CatOS output but is slightly different. Specifying the **show module** IOS command without any parameters generates output similar to that in Example 13-3.

Example 13-3 *Showing Module Status When Running IOS*

```
Cat6500#show module
Mod Ports Card Type                              Model              Serial No.
--- ----- -------------------------------------- ------------------ -----------
  1    2  Catalyst 6000 supervisor 2 (Active)    WS-X6K-SUP2-2GE    SAL0605HFH7
  2   48  48 port 10/100 mb RJ-45 ethernet       WS-X6248-RJ-45     SAD050504C1
  4   48  48 port 10/100 mb RJ45                 WS-X6348-RJ-45     SAD041606Y5
  5    6  Firewall Module                        WS-SVC-FWM-1       SAD060300N9
  6    6  Firewall Module                        WS-SVC-FWM-1       SAD0707016K
  8    2  Intrusion Detection System             WS-X6381-IDS       SAD03403897
  9    2  Intrusion Detection System             WS-X6381-IDS       SAD05050GDY

Mod MAC addresses                       Hw     Fw           Sw           Status
--- ---------------------------------- ------ ------------ ------------ -------
  1  0006.d65a.9694 to 0006.d65a.9695   3.5   6.1(3)       7.5(0.6)HUB2 Ok
  2  0001.c96d.64d0 to 0001.c96d.64ff   1.4   5.4(2)       7.5(0.6)HUB2 Ok
  4  00d0.c0cd.86c8 to 00d0.c0cd.86f7   1.1   5.3(1)       7.5(0.6)HUB2 Ok
  5  00e0.b0ff.3438 to 00e0.b0ff.343f   0.201 7.2(1)       2.3(0)60     Ok
  6  0002.7ee4.f610 to 0002.7ee4.f617   1.1   7.2(1)       2.3(0)60     Ok
  8  00e0.140e.f7ec to 00e0.140e.f7ed   0.201 4B4LZ0XA     7.5(0.6)HUB2 PwrDown
  9  0003.3282.ee0a to 0003.3282.ee0b   1.1   4B4LZ0XA     3.0(5)S23    Ok

Mod Sub-Module                  Model           Serial          Hw     Status
--- --------------------------- --------------- --------------- ------- -------
  1 Policy Feature Card 2       WS-F6K-PFC2     SAL06100RH2     3.2    Ok
  1 Cat6k MSFC 2 daughterboard  WS-F6K-MSFC2    SAL06090F5F     2.2    Ok
  4 Inline Power Module         WS-F6K-PWR                      1.0    Ok

Mod Online Diag Status
--- -------------------
  1 Pass
  2 Pass
  4 Pass
  5 Pass
```

continues

Example 13-3 *Showing Module Status When Running IOS (Continued)*

```
  6 Pass
  8 Unknown
  9 Not Supported
Cat6500#
```

show port Command

You can use the **show port** (CatOS) command to examine the different ports on your switch. While debugging, you might want to see the packet statistics and error information for the monitoring ports on your IDSM-2. If your IDSM-2 line card is in slot 8, you can examine the first monitoring port with the **show port** command in Example 13-4.

Example 13-4 *Showing Port Status When Running CatOS*

```
Cat6k> show port 8/7
* = Configured MAC Address

Port  Name                 Status     Vlan       Duplex Speed Type
----- -------------------- ---------- ---------- ------ ----- ------------
 8/7                       connected  trunk        full  1000 Intrusion De


Port     Broadcast-Limit Multicast Unicast Total-Drop          Action
-------- --------------- --------- ------- -------------------- -----------
 8/7                   -         -       -                    0 drop-packets

Port  Status      ErrDisable Reason    Port ErrDisableTimeout  Action on Timeout
----  ----------  ------------------   --------------------    ----------------
 8/7  connected                    -   Enable                  No Change

Port  Align-Err  FCS-Err    Xmit-Err   Rcv-Err    UnderSize
----- ---------- ---------- ---------- ---------- ---------
 8/7          0          0          0          0         0

Port  Single-Col Multi-Coll Late-Coll  Excess-Col Carri-Sen Runts     Giants
----- ---------- ---------- ---------- ---------- --------- --------- ---------
 8/7          0          0          0          0         0         0         -

Port  Last-Time-Cleared
----- --------------------------
 8/7  Fri May 16 2003, 16:50:42

Idle Detection
--------------
   --
Cat6k>
```

show trunk Command

The VLANs that the monitoring ports on your IDSM-2 are trunking determine what traffic is actually received by your IDSM-2. Initially, the monitoring ports are configured to trunk all of the VLANs on your switch, but you may need to change this configuration to support multiple IDSM-2 line cards and limit broadcast traffic to the IDSM-2. To examine which trunks a specific port is trunking, use the **show trunk** (CatOS) switch command. If your IDSM-2 line card is in slot 8, you can examine the trunks supported by the second monitoring port with the **show trunk** command, as in Example 13-5.

Example 13-5 *Showing Trunk Port Status When Running CatOS*

```
cat6k> (enable) show trunk 8/8
* - indicates vtp domain mismatch
Port      Mode         Encapsulation  Status        Native vlan
--------  -----------  -------------  ------------  -----------
 8/8      auto         negotiate      not-trunking  140

Port      Vlans allowed on trunk
--------  ---------------------------------------------------------------------
 8/8      1-1005,1025-4094

Port      Vlans allowed and active in management domain
--------  ---------------------------------------------------------------------
 8/8      140

Port      Vlans in spanning tree forwarding state and not pruned
--------  ---------------------------------------------------------------------
 8/8
cat6k> (enable)
```

Foundation Summary

The Cisco IDSM integrates Cisco IPS functionality directly into your Catalyst 6000 family switch.

The IDSM-2 is a single-slot switch card that provides the following enhanced capabilities:

- Performance—600 Mbps
- Monitoring interfaces—Gigabit
- Command and control interface—Gigabit
- TCP reset interface—Gigabit
- Optional interface—No
- Performance upgrade—No

Your switch operating system must match one of the following requirements:

- Catalyst OS 7.5(1) or later (on supervisor engine)
- Cisco IOS Release 12.1(19)E or later

If you have Catalyst OS 7.5(1) or later, you also must have one of the following supervisor engines:

- Supervisor Engine 1A
- Supervisor Engine 1A/Policy Feature Card 2 (PFC2)
- Supervisor Engine 1A/MSFC1
- Supervisor Engine 1A/MSFC2
- Supervisor Engine 2
- Supervisor Engine 2/MSFC2

If you have IOS Release 12.1(19)E or later, you also must have one of the following supervisor engines:

- Supervisor Engine 1a with MSFC2
- Supervisor Engine 2 with MSFC2

Besides increasing the bandwidth capacity of the IDSM-2 (compared to the original IDSM), the IDSM-2 provides the following capabilities or features:

- Merges switching and security into a single chassis
- Provides ability to monitor multiple VLANs
- Does not impact switch performance
- Supports attacks and signatures equal to appliance sensor
- Uses the same code base as the appliance sensor
- Supports improved management techniques (such as IDM)

To enable your IDSM-2 to become a functional component of your Cisco IPS, you need to perform the following basic initialization tasks:

- Verify IDSM-2 status
- Initialize the IDSM-2
- Configure the command and control port
- Configure the switch traffic capture settings

The basic initialization tasks for the IDSM-2 are the same as those for the appliance sensor. These tasks include the following:

- Accessing the IDSM-2 CLI
- Logging in to the IDSM-2
- Running the **setup** command
- Configuring trusted hosts
- Entering the network communication parameters

To perform its operation, the IDSM-2 uses several internal ports that fall into the following three functional categories:

- TCP reset port (port 1)
- Command and control port (port 2)
- Monitoring ports (ports 7 and 8)

To prevent corruption of the IDSM-2, you must shut it down properly. To properly shut down the IDSM-2, you need to log in to the IDSM-2 and execute the **reset** command.

The front panel of the IDSM-2 contains a single-status light-emitting diode (LED) that can be in one of the states listed in Table 13-4.

Table 13-4 *IDSM-2 Status LED*

Color	Description
Green	All diagnostics tests have passed—IDSM is operational.
Red	A diagnostic other than an individual port test has failed.
Amber	The IDSM is • Running through its boot and self-test diagnostic sequence. • Disabled. • In the shutdown state.
Off	The IDSM power is off.

The **show module** switch command enables you to display information about the line cards that you have installed in your Catalyst 6500 switch.

When using CatOS, you can use the **show port** and **show trunk** commands to view the status of your switch ports.

Q&A

You have two choices for review questions:

- The questions that follow give you a bigger challenge than the exam itself by using an open-ended question format. By reviewing now with this more difficult question format, you can exercise your memory better and prove your conceptual and factual knowledge of this chapter. The answers to these questions are found in the appendix.
- For more practice with exam-like question formats, use the exam engine on the CD-ROM.

1. What is the maximum amount of traffic that the IDSM-2 can monitor?
2. How many interfaces does the IDSM-2 have, and what are their functions?
3. What version of CatOS must you run to use IDSM-2?
4. What version of IOS must you run to use IDSM-2?
5. How does the operation of the IDSM-2 impact the switch's performance?
6. Which switch command do you use to verify the IDSM-2 status?
7. Which two time-configuration options do you have for the IDSM-2?
8. If your IDSM-2 is in slot 6, what IOS switch command enables you to access the IDSM-2 CLI?
9. Which ports are monitoring ports on the IDSM-2?
10. Which port is the command and control port on the IDSM-2?
11. Which port is the TCP reset port on the IDSM-2?
12. What does a red status LED on the IDSM-2 indicate?
13. What does an amber status LED on the IDSM-2 indicate?

This chapter covers the following subjects:

- NM-CIDS Overview
- NM-CIDS Hardware Architecture
- Traffic Capture for NM-CIDS
- NM-CIDS Installation and Configuration Tasks
- NM-CIDS Maintenance Tasks
- Recovering the NM-CIDS Software Image

CHAPTER 14

Cisco IDS Network Module for Access Routers

Flexibility of deployment options is a strength of the Cisco IPS solution. Besides deploying appliance sensors, you can also deploy sensors in your Catalyst 6500 switches via the IDSM-2. A final deployment location is your access routers. Deploying IPS sensors in your access routers enables you to incorporate intrusion prevention by using your existing network infrastructure devices.

NOTE Access routers are the network devices you use to connect your internal network with remote sites (via private lines or public carriers).

Understanding the various deployment options is vital to effectively deploying a Cisco IPS solution that is customized to your network environment. Although the Cisco IDS Network Module (NM-CIDS) for access routers is a full-featured IPS sensor, there are unique configuration and operational tasks associated with this device. Understanding these unique tasks will assist you in incorporating the network module into your Cisco IPS solution.

"Do I Know This Already?" Quiz

The purpose of the "Do I Know This Already?" quiz is to help you decide if you really need to read the entire chapter. If you already intend to read the entire chapter, you do not necessarily need to answer these questions now.

The 10-question quiz, derived from the major sections in the "Foundation and Supplemental Topics" portion of the chapter, helps you determine how to spend your limited study time.

Table 14-1 outlines the major topics discussed in this chapter and the "Do I Know This Already?" quiz questions that correspond to those topics.

Table 14-1 *"Do I Know This Already?" Foundation and Supplemental Topics Mapping*

Foundation or Supplemental Topic	Questions Covering This Topic
NM-CIDS Overview	1, 2, 3
NM-CIDS Hardware Architecture	-
Traffic Capture for NM-CIDS	4, 5
NM-CIDS Installation and Configuration Tasks	6, 7
NM-CIDS Maintenance Tasks	8, 9
Recovering the NM-CIDS Software Image	10

CAUTION The goal of self-assessment is to gauge your mastery of the topics in this chapter. If you do not know the answer to a question or are only partially sure of the answer, you should mark this question wrong for purposes of the self-assessment. Giving yourself credit for an answer you correctly guess skews your self-assessment results and might provide you with a false sense of security.

1. What is the maximum amount of traffic that the network module can examine?
   a. 85 Mbps
   b. 45 Mbps
   c. 60 Mbps
   d. 100 Mbps
   e. 150 Mbps

2. How many external interfaces are on the network module?
   a. No external ports
   b. 1 Ethernet port
   c. 1 Ethernet port and 1 console port
   d. 1 console port

3. Which router platform is not a supported router platform for the network module?
   a. 3700 Series
   b. 3660
   c. 2691
   d. 2600XM Series
   e. 800 Series

4. Which of the following are true about packets being forwarded to the NM-CIDS? (Choose two.)
   a. Packets dropped by an input ACL are forwarded.
   b. Packets dropped by an output ACL are not forwarded.
   c. Packets dropped by an input ACL are not forwarded.
   d. Packets dropped by an output ACL are forwarded.

5. Which of the following packets would be forwarded to NM-CIDS?
   a. ARP packet
   b. Packet with a bad IP version
   c. Packet whose length is 18 bytes
   d. Packet with a TTL of 1
   e. Packet with an incorrect header length

6. Which name does the router assign to the NM-CIDS?
   a. network-module
   b. ids-module
   c. ids-sensor
   d. sensor-module
   e. ids-device

7. Which port would you use to access the NM-CIDS in slot 2 via Telnet?
   a. 2001
   b. 2033
   c. 2010
   d. 2065
   e. 2045

8. Which command performs a hardware reboot of the NM-CIDS?
   a. **service-module ids-sensor 1/0 reload**
   b. **service-module ids-sensor 1/0 reset**
   c. **service-module ids-sensor 1/0 reboot**
   d. **service-module ids-sensor 1/0 restart**

9. Which command (if used incorrectly) can cause you to lose data on your NM-CIDS hard disk?
   a. **service-module ids-sensor 1/0 reload**
   b. **service-module ids-sensor 1/0 shutdown**
   c. **service-module ids-sensor 1/0 restart**
   d. **service-module ids-sensor 1/0 reset**
   e. **service-module ids-sensor 1/0 reboot**

10. Which of the following is not a valid file transfer protocol to use when you re-image the application image via the boot helper?
   a. FTP
   b. SCP
   c. TFTP

The answers to the "Do I Know This Already?" quiz are found in the appendix. The suggested choices for your next step are as follows:

- **8 or less overall score**—Read the entire chapter. This includes the "Foundation and Supplemental Topics" and "Foundation Summary" sections and the Q&A section.
- **9 or 10 overall score**—If you want more review on these topics, skip to the "Foundation Summary" section and then go to the Q&A section. Otherwise, move to the next chapter.

Foundation and Supplemental Topics

NM-CIDS Overview

NM-CIDS for access routers is a full-featured IPS sensor that provides the ability to inspect all traffic traversing a router. Figure 14-1 shows an NM-CIDS. It is factory-loaded with the latest Cisco IPS sensor software and is at feature and function parity (with the except of inline mode) with the other implementations of Cisco IPS, such as the sensor appliance and the Intrusion Detection System Module 2 (IDSM-2); therefore, the NM-CIDS can be managed and monitored with the same applications as the other Cisco IPS sensor devices.

Figure 14-1 *NM-CIDS*

This chapter focuses on the following aspects of the NM-CIDS:

- Key features
- Specifications
- Configuration
- Image recovery

NM-CIDS Key Features

The NM-CIDS can monitor traffic from all interfaces on the router, including inside and outside interfaces. Through collaboration with the Cisco IOS software, NM-CIDS can monitor IP Security

(IPSec) Virtual Private Network (VPN) and generic routing encapsulation (GRE) traffic in decrypted form when these tunnels terminate on the router, providing inspection at the first point of entry into the network. This capability is an industry first.

> **NOTE** The NM-CIDS can monitor traffic from all the interfaces on the router except for the console and auxiliary ports because these are not regular network interfaces.

The NM-CIDS fits into a single network module slot on the Cisco 2600XM Series 2691, 3660, 3725, and 3745 routers. Only one NM-CIDS is supported in a given router, but it is not restricted to a specific network module slot within the router.

By integrating IPS and branch-office routing, the NM-CIDS reduces the complexity of securing WAN links while offering reduced operating costs. The NM-CIDS also simplifies power management by using the power options on the router.

The NM-CIDS uses a separate processor and memory to maximize performance. This design frees the router CPU from any processor-intensive IPS tasks.

NM-CIDS Specifications

Besides understanding the key features of the NM-CIDS, you must also understand its specifications (such as bandwidth capacity) so that you can effectively use this device in your overall Cisco IPS solution. The specifications for the NM-CIDS are as follows:

- Performance—45 Mbps
- Monitoring interface—Internal 100 Mbps
- Command and control interface—External 100 Mbps
- Supported routers—Cisco 2600XM Series 2691, 3660, 3725, and 3745
- Cisco IOS software—12.2(15)ZJ or later
- IPS sensor software—Cisco IPS version 4.1 or later

> **NOTE** To use NM-CIDS on 2691 and 3700 Series routers, your ROM version must be 12.2(8r)T2 or later.

NM-CIDS Front Panel

Although NM-CIDS is a line card that you insert into your router, it does have some indicators on its front panel that indicate its current operational status. (See Figure 14-2.) The external Fast

Ethernet interface for command and control is also located on the front panel of NM-CIDS. The status LEDs available on the front panel of NM-CIDS are as follows:

- ACT—Displays activity on the Fast Ethernet connection
- DISK—Displays activity on the IPS hard-disk drive
- EN—Indicates that the NM-CIDS has passed the self-test and is available to the router
- LINK—Indicates that the Fast Ethernet connection is available to the NM-CIDS
- PWR—Indicates that power is available to the NM-CIDS

Figure 14-2 *NM-CIDS Front Panel*

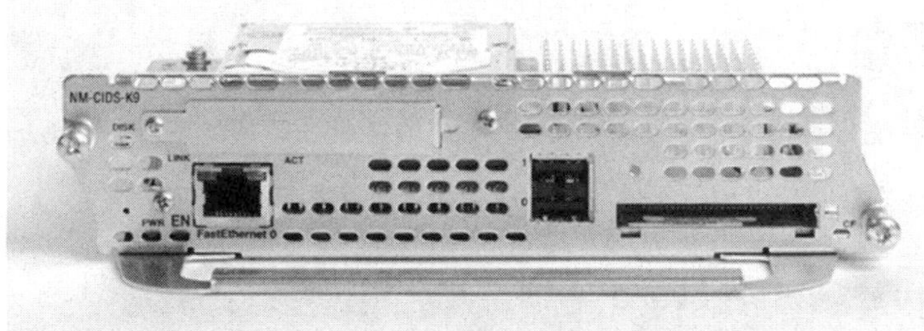

Traditional Appliance Sensor Network Architecture

Before the introduction of NM-CIDS, the traditional network architecture for a branch office includes two devices, the router and a dedicated Cisco IPS sensor. (See Figure 14-3.) This solution typically consists of a Cisco 26xx, 36xx, or 37xx branch-office router connected to a sensor. The Cisco IPS sensor portfolio for the branch office consists of the Cisco IPS 4210 and 4215 and the 4235 platforms. Each sensor functions as an external appliance that typically has two Fast Ethernet interfaces: one for packet monitoring and the other for command and control.

Little to no configuration is required on the branch router, and the branch router's CPU is affected only to the extent that it processes WAN traffic to the correct LAN interface. This process should not tax the router, so the CPU utilization should remain low.

The Cisco IPS sensors run their own Cisco IPS software. The router's Cisco IOS software is not affected when a signature file needs to be updated. Since the router is not actively participating in the IPS inspection, the level of performance that can be inspected within a network increases dramatically. For example, the IPS 4215 can inspect up to 80 Mbps, and the IPS 4235 can inspect up to 250 Mbps.

There are some disadvantages to using this two-box solution. The Cisco IPS appliance solution is a two-box solution that affects the real estate needs within your branch office and adds complexity to your network management solution, as compared to a one-box solution.

Figure 14-3 *Traditional Appliance Sensor Network Architecture*

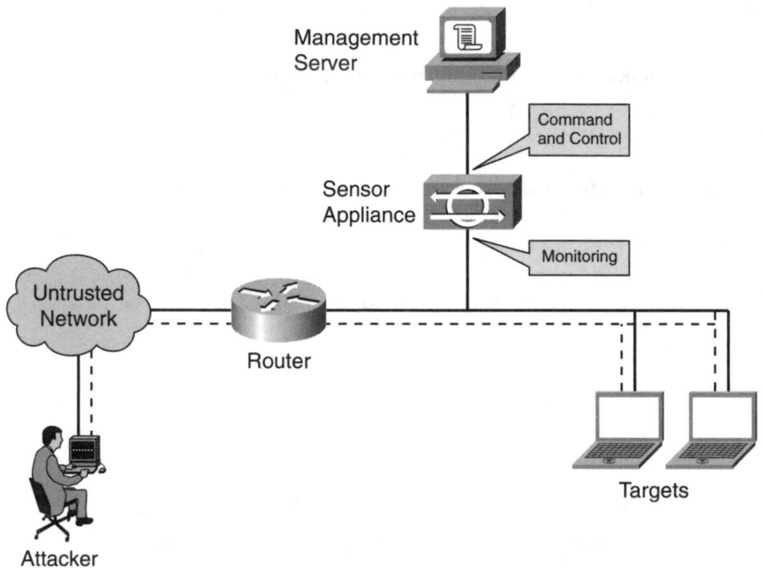

NM-CIDS Network Architecture

The scenario illustrated in Figure 14-4 is similar to that of the appliance sensor network architecture; however, in this scenario the network architecture includes the NM-CIDS. The NM-CIDS integrates the functionality of the Cisco IPS sensor into the branch router. The NM-CIDS is physically installed in a network module slot inside a Cisco 2600XM, 2691, 3660, 3725, or 3745 router. This provides a one-box IPS solution and the ability to monitor all the router's interfaces.

Figure 14-4 *NM-CIDS Network Architecture*

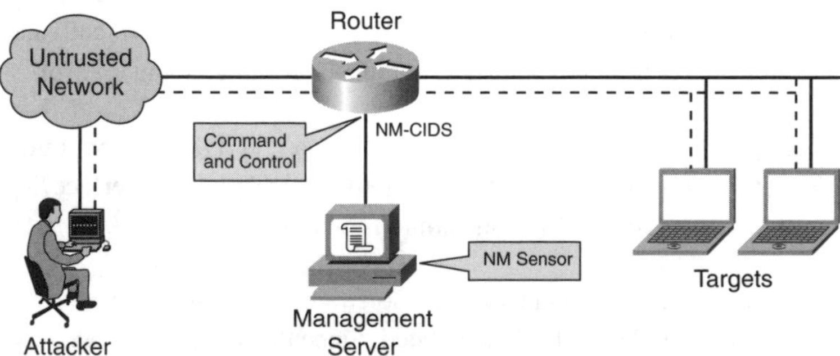

The NM-CIDS is directly connected to the router's backplane via an internal Fast Ethernet interface onboard the NM-CIDS. This internal interface serves as a monitoring port for traffic. Traffic entering the branch office from the WAN interface no longer needs to be ported to the LAN interface as is required for the sensor appliance solution; rather, the data is copied across the backplane to the internal Fast Ethernet monitoring port of the NM-CIDS.

As with Cisco IOS-IDS, WAN interface traffic can be inspected without having to be routed to a LAN interface. However, the NM-CIDS has an advantage over the Cisco IOS-IDS solution because it runs the same Cisco IPS sensor software as the appliance sensor. This feature allows support for a greater number of signatures and ease of signature update.

The disadvantage to this solution is that it impacts the performance of the router. Although the actual packet inspection function is offloaded to the NM-CIDS module, the router must copy packets to the module, which places an additional load on the router's processor.

NM-CIDS Hardware Architecture

The NM-CIDS provides interface-level packet monitoring capability. You can select one or more router interfaces or subinterfaces for IPS monitoring. The following are the hardware components of the router and NM-CIDS that enable this functionality (see Figure 14-5):

- NM-CIDS internal Fast Ethernet interface
- NM-CIDS external Fast Ethernet interface
- Internal Universal Asynchronous Receiver/Transmitter (UART) interface
- NM-CIDS disk, Flash, and memory

Figure 14-5 *NM-CIDS Hardware Architecture*

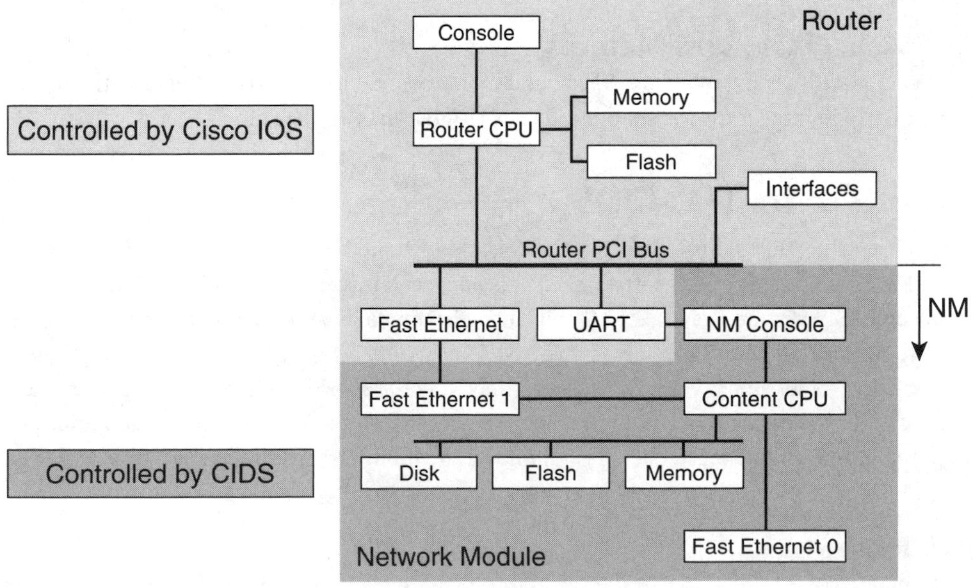

NM-CIDS Internal Fast Ethernet Interface

The NM-CIDS internal Fast Ethernet interface connects to the internal protocol control information (PCI) bus on the router's backplane to provide monitoring capability. This internal Fast Ethernet interface provides a 100-Mbps full-duplex interface between the router and the NM-CIDS. The router sends a copy of each packet to be inspected from its PCI bus to this internal Fast Ethernet interface. The packets are passed through the internal monitoring interface for classification and processing. The router-side interface for the internal Ethernet segment is known as interface ids–sensor in the Cisco IOS software. This interface is the only interface associated with the IPS that is visible in the output of the **show interfaces** sensing command. The router-side internal interface is connected to the router PCI backplane.

NM-CIDS External Fast Ethernet Interface

The NM-CIDS external Fast Ethernet interface is used as the command and control port. This interface can be connected to a switch, to a hub, or directly to a workstation that has IPS management software.

Internal Universal Asynchronous Receiver/Transmitter Interface

The Internal Universal Asynchronous Receiver/Transmitter (UART) provides a virtual console access to the NM-CIDS from the backplane of the router. The NM-CIDS differs from a standalone IPS appliance in that it does not have an external console port. The internal UART interface is used to provide the console access. Console access to the NM-CIDS is enabled when you issue a **service-module ids-sensor** *slot*/**0 session** command from the Cisco IOS command line interface (CLI).

NM-CIDS Disk, Flash, and Memory

The NM-CIDS has its own disk, Flash, and memory and does not share those of the router. This minimizes the impact that the operation of NM-CIDS has on the router.

Traffic Capture for NM-CIDS

The forwarding of packets to the NM-CIDS is implemented in the Cisco Express Forwarding (CEF) switching path of Cisco IOS software. CEF is advanced Layer 3 IP switching technology supported in Cisco IOS Software Releases 12.0 and later. CEF mode must be enabled at the router CLI in order for the router to forward packets to the NM-CIDS. Several Cisco IOS forwarding features and services are implemented within the CEF architecture. Based on which feature or service is configured, these features are processed in a sequence. The content of packets may be altered after processing certain features, and altered packets can impact the monitoring done by the NM-CIDS.

Cisco IOS Features

The contents of a packet may be altered after processing certain Cisco IOS forwarding features such as Network Address Translation (NAT). The following is a list of the features whose processing can impact the operations of the NM-CIDS:

- Access Control Lists (ACLs)
- Encryption
- Network Address Translation (NAT)
- IP multicast
- UDP flooding
- IP broadcast
- GRE tunnels

Access Control Lists and NM-CIDS

The Cisco IOS-IDS implementation checks for certain signatures before an input ACL filters the packet. The purpose is to look for any possible attacks that were destined for the network before they were dropped by the router.

Such an approach is difficult to implement with the NM-CIDS. The router sends a copy of the packet to the NM-CIDS, and it is desirable to send only one copy of the packet. If the packet is forwarded to the NM-CIDS even before it is dropped, the router has to send another copy of the packet after the packet is decrypted (if encryption is enabled) or when the IP address is changed because of NAT. To avoid sending multiple copies of packets to the NM-CIDS, the router does not forward any packet that should be dropped according to an input ACL. However, the Cisco IOS software performs an output-ACL check after the packet is forwarded to the NM-CIDS, so the packet is forwarded to the NM-CIDS even if the output ACL drops the packet.

Encryption and NM-CIDS

If an IPSec tunnel is terminated at the router, the router decrypts incoming packets before passing them to the NM-CIDS. It encrypts outgoing packets after copying them to the NM-CIDS. Therefore, the NM-CIDS can fully analyze those packets. However, if encrypted traffic is merely passed through the router, the router does not decrypt it but passes the packets to the NM-CIDS in the encrypted state. The NM-CIDS cannot analyze those encrypted packets.

Inside NAT and NM-CIDS

Network Address Translation (NAT) is a common router feature that can be configured to change the source or destination address of a packet. The IPS signature engines maintain the TCP session states for all TCP sessions they monitor. The engines need to analyze packets in both directions in order to adequately analyze TCP sessions. The source and destination IP addresses of the bidirectional packets must be consistent. NAT can impact the ability of the sensor to determine a true source or destination address.

In Figure 14-6, Interfaces A and B are configured on the router. Interface A is on the inside of the NAT domain, whereas B is on the outside. The packet entering Interface A has a source address of 10.1.1.10 and a destination address of 100.20.10.10. The router processes the packet and sends it to the outbound interface, changing the source address of the outbound packet to 150.1.1.10. The outside domain sees this address as the IP address of the host inside the NAT domain.

Figure 14-6 *Inside NAT and NM-CIDS*

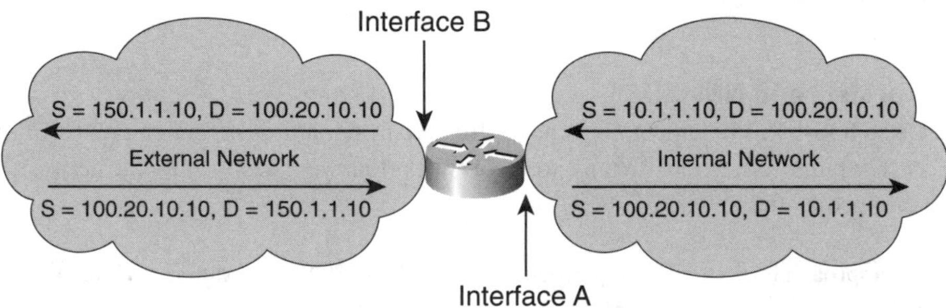

When the return packet arrives on Interface B, the source IP address is 100.20.10.10, whereas the destination IP address is 150.1.1.10. The router translates the destination address to 10.1.1.10 and sends the packet out Interface A.

If a 10.1.1.10 address is recorded by the NM-CIDS as the source address for packets moving from Interface A to Interface B, but a 150.1.1.10 address is recorded as the destination in the return packet moving from Interface B to Interface A, the NM-CIDS is unable to maintain a consistent session state. In order for a session state to be accurately maintained, either the 10.1.1.10 address or the 150.1.1.10 address must be recorded.

The outside, or global, IP addresses are often dynamically assigned and shared. If outside IP addresses were sent to the NM-CIDS, it would be difficult to identify which of the hosts on the inside network was attacked. Therefore, the router sends only the inside IP addresses to the NM-CIDS. In the scenario in the figure, only the 10.0.1.12 address is sent.

Outside NAT and NM-CIDS

With inside NAT, an inside local address is translated to an outside global address. Figure 14-7 shows the router's behavior in relation to the NM-CIDS when outside NAT, or outside-local to outside-global translation, is configured. The global address 10.1.1.10 is seen as 150.1.1.10 by the inside network. The inside address 100.20.10.10 is passed without translation by the router. The NM-CIDS analyzes the packet with the 150.1.1.10 address. When an attack is detected, the alarm contains information about the 150.1.1.10 address, and the attacker's actual address, 10.1.1.10, is not displayed. This means that the attack source may not be easily traced.

Figure 14-7 *Outside NAT Example*

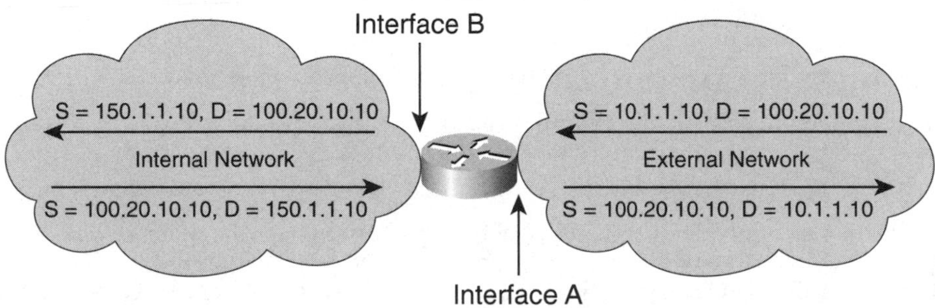

IP Multicast, IP Broadcast, and UDP Flooding and NM-CIDS

When the router receives IP multicast traffic, UDP traffic, or IP broadcast traffic, the packets received on an input interface are forwarded on one or more output interfaces. In this situation, if the input interface is configured for IPS monitoring, the packet is sent to the NM-CIDS. However, if only the output interfaces are configured for monitoring, the packet is not forwarded to the NM-CIDS.

GRE Tunnels and NM-CIDS

The NM-CIDS does not analyze GRE-encapsulated packets. If a GRE packet is received and the incoming interface is enabled for IPS monitoring, the packet is not forwarded to the NM-CIDS for monitoring. However, if the router encapsulates a packet in a GRE tunnel and the incoming interface is enabled for IPS monitoring, the packet is sent to the NM-CIDS before encapsulation.

Packets Not Forwarded to NM-CIDS

There are other cases in which the packet is not inspected by the NM-CIDS. For example, Address Resolution Protocol (ARP) packets are not forwarded to the NM-CIDS. Therefore, ARP-based signatures are missed by the NM-CIDS. In addition, Cisco IOS software examines the IP header of all packets and drops any packet that contains an error, such as an irregularity in a field. Possible irregularities include the following:

- Bad IP version
- Incorrect IP option field
- Bad header length

- Total packet length greater than 8192 bytes or less than 20 bytes
- IP cyclic redundancy check (CRC) failure
- Time to Live (TTL) less than 1

NM-CIDS Installation and Configuration Tasks

The configuration tasks for the NM-CIDS are similar to those of the IPS sensor appliance, with the following exceptions:

- The initial configuration requires establishing a session from the router console.
- The NM-CIDS clock cannot be set directly. It must use the router's clock or a Network Time Protocol (NTP) server as a reference clock.

Installing and configuring the NM-CIDS involves the following tasks:

Step 1 Installing the NM-CIDS

Step 2 Configuring the internal ids-sensor interface

Step 3 Assigning the clock settings

Step 4 Setting up packet monitoring

Step 5 Accessing the NM-CIDS console

Step 6 Performing initial sensor configuration

After completing your configuration, you should verify that the NM-CIDS is analyzing traffic, and you should back up the configuration when it is functioning properly.

Installing the NM-CIDS

Installing the NM-CIDS into your router involves performing the following tasks:

Step 1 Insert the NM-CIDS into a router.

Step 2 Connect the NM-CIDS to the network.

Step 3 Verify that the router recognizes the NM-CIDS.

Step 4 Verify that Cisco IOS-IDS is not running.

Inserting the NM-CIDS into a Router

When installing the NM-CIDS into your router, you need to follow a few guidelines. First, you need to power down your router if it is a 2600XM Series router or a 2691 router. This step is not necessary if you are installing the NM-CIDS into a 3660, 3725, or 3745 router since each of these allows online insertion and removal (OIR) of network cards (hot swapping the network module into the router's chassis).

You can install only one NM-CIDS into a router. Furthermore, you cannot operate Cisco IOS-IDS and NM-CIDS on the same router since the combination will adversely impact the performance of the router.

Connecting the NM-CIDS to the Network

To connect the NM-CIDS to the network, use a straight-through two-pair Category 5 unshielded twisted-pair (UTP) cable. Connect the RJ-45 port to the NM-CIDS Fast Ethernet 0 port, which is the command and control interface (the only external interface available). Connect the other end to a switch, hub, repeater, server, or other network device.

Verifying That the Router Recognizes the NM-CIDS

Make sure the router recognizes the NM-CIDS by using the **show running-config** command at the router console prompt. If the router recognizes the NM-CIDS, you should see the following line in the command output:

```
interface IDS-sensor1/0
```

You can also use the **show version** command for the same purpose. If the router recognizes the NM-CIDS, the **show version** output contains the following line:

```
1 cisco ids sensor(s),ids monitoring on slot 1
```

If the router does not recognize the presence of the NM-CIDS, verify that you are using the correct Cisco IOS version—12.2(15)ZJ or later—and that the NM-CIDS is firmly seated in the router.

Verifying That Cisco IOS-IDS is Not Running

Running Cisco IOS-IDS while the NM-CIDS is present is not recommended because doing so significantly reduces router performance. The easiest way to determine whether Cisco IOS-IDS is enabled is to use the **show ip audit interface** command. If Cisco IOS-IDS is not running, the output of this command should be blank.

Configuring the Internal ids-sensor Interface

The router-side internal Fast Ethernet interface is known as interface ids-sensor. It can be seen in the Cisco IOS **show interface** and **show controller** command output. An IP address must be assigned to this interface in order to obtain console access to the NM-CIDS. However, if this IP address is advertised via routing updates, the monitoring interface itself can become vulnerable to attacks. Therefore, it is highly recommended that you assign a loopback address to this interface (since the loopback address is not advertised). To assign a loopback address to this interface, complete the following tasks:

Step 1 Verify the NM-CIDS slot number.

Step 2 Enable CEF.

Step 3 Configure the interface.

Verifying the NM-CIDS Slot Number

Use the **show interfaces ids-sensor** command to confirm the NM-CIDS slot number in your router. Cisco IOS software gives the NM-CIDS the name "ids-sensor." Assuming that you put your NM-CIDS into slot 1, the appropriate **show interfaces** command output is as displayed in Example 14-1.

Example 14-1 *Viewing NM-CIDS Interface Information Using the* **show interfaces** *Command*

```
router# show interfaces ids-sensor 1/0
IDS-Sensor1/0 is up, line protocol is up
  Hardware is I82559FE, address is 000d.bc3a.d090 (bia 000d.bc3a.d090)
  Interface is unnumbered. Using address of Loopback0 (1.2.3.4)
  MTU 1500 bytes, BW 100000 Kbit, DLY 100 usec,
     reliability 255/255, txload 1/255, rxload 1/255
  Encapsulation ARPA, loopback not set
  Keepalive set (10 sec)
  ARP type: ARPA, ARP Timeout 04:00:00
  Last input 00:00:17, output 00:00:00, output hang never
```

NOTE The port number for the **show interfaces** command is always 0 since there is only one port on the NM-CIDS.

To display the contents of the currently running configuration file or the configuration for a specific interface, use the **show running-config** command in Privileged Exec mode, as displayed in Example 14-2. The **show running-config** command without any arguments or keywords displays the entire contents of the running configuration file.

Example 14-2 *Viewing NM-CIDS Interface Information Using the* **show running-config** *Command*

```
router# show running-config

!*** Configuration content abbreviated for clarity ***

interface FastEthernet0/1
 ip address 172.30.2.2 255.255.255.0
 duplex auto
 speed auto
!
```

Example 14-2 *Viewing NM-CIDS Interface Information Using the* **show running-config** *Command (Continued)*

```
interface IDS-Sensor1/0
 ip unnumbered Loopback0
 hold-queue 60 out
```

Enabling CEF

Use the **ip cef** command to enable the CEF switching path. This must be done in order for the router to forward packets to the NM-CIDS.

Configuring the Interface

The **session** command used to access the NM-CIDS console starts a reverse Telnet connection using the IP address of the ids-sensor interface. The ids-sensor interface is between the NM-CIDS and the router. You must assign an IP address to the ids-sensor interface before invoking the session command. However, assigning a routable IP address can make the ids-sensor interface itself vulnerable to attacks. To counter that vulnerability, you can assign a loopback IP address to the ids-sensor interface.

NOTE Usually, when using Telnet, you connect the client system to the server system. With reverse Telnet, the connection is reversed in that the server initiates the connection to the client when you invoke the **session** command to a specific port on the router.

Configuring a loopback interface for the ids-sensor interface involves choosing a loopback number and assigning an IP address to that loopback number. Example 14-3 assigns loopback 0 to the IP address 10.1.1.1.

Example 14-3 *Assigning an IP Address to the Loopback Interface*

```
Router# conf t
Router(config)# interface loopback 0
Router(config-if)# ip address 10.1.1.1 255.255.255.255
```

After you create the loopback interface and assign an IP address to it, you must map the loopback interface to the ids-sensor interface. Example 14-4 maps the loopback interface to the ids-sensor interface in slot 1.

Example 14-4 *Assigning a Loopback Interface to the ids-sensor Interface*

```
Router# conf t
Router(config)# interface ids-sensor 1/0
Router(config-if)# ip unnumbered loopback 0
Router(config-if)# no shutdown
Router(config-if)# end
Router# write memory
```

After completing the configuration of the ids-sensor interface, execute the **show interfaces ids-sensor** command to view the configuration. The output should be similar to that in Example 14-5.

Example 14-5 *Verifying a Loopback Address Using the* **show interfaces** *Command*

```
Router# show interfaces ids-sensor 1/0
IDS-Sensor1/0 is up, line protocol is up
  Hardware is I82559FE, address is 000d.bc3a.d090 (bia 000d.bc3a.d090)
  Interface is unnumbered. Using address of Loopback0 (10.1.1.1)
  MTU 1500 bytes, BW 100000 Kbit, DLY 100 usec,
     reliability 255/255, txload 1/255, rxload 1/255
  Encapsulation ARPA, loopback not set
  Keepalive set (10 sec)
  ARP type: ARPA, ARP Timeout 04:00:00
  Last input 00:00:17, output 00:00:00, output hang never
  Last clearing of "show interface" counters never
  Input queue: 0/75/0/0 (size/max/drops/flushes); Total output drops: 0
  Queueing strategy: fifo
  Output queue: 0/60 (size/max)
  5 minute input rate 0 bits/sec, 0 packets/sec
  5 minute output rate 1000 bits/sec, 2 packets/sec
     3042 packets input, 185400 bytes, 0 no buffer
     Received 0 broadcasts, 0 runts, 0 giants, 0 throttles
     0 input errors, 0 CRC, 0 frame, 0 overrun, 0 ignored
     0 input packets with dribble condition detected
     63975 packets output, 6750422 bytes, 0 underruns
     0 output errors, 0 collisions, 2 interface resets
     0 babbles, 0 late collision, 0 deferred
     0 lost carrier, 0 no carrier
     0 output buffer failures, 0 output buffers swapped out
```

Assigning the Clock Settings

The NM-CIDS clock cannot be set directly. It must use the router's clock or an NTP server as a reference clock. By default, the NM-CIDS automatically synchronizes its clock with the router time.

If you use the default setting, Greenwich Mean Time (GMT) is synchronized between the router and the NM-CIDS. The time zone and summer time settings are not synchronized between the router and the NM-CIDS. Therefore, be sure to set the time zone and summer time settings on both the router and the NM-CIDS to ensure that the GMT time settings are correct.

It is recommended that you use an NTP time synchronization source. NTP uses an authoritative time source to set the time on your NM-CIDS.

The following are clock recommendations, listed in order from the best choice to the worst choice:

1. Use NTP mode on the NM-CIDS.

2. Run an NTP client on the router, and use Cisco IOS clock mode on the NM-CIDS.
3. Run Cisco IOS clock mode on the NM-CIDS, and set the Cisco IOS time zone to UTC.
4. Run Cisco IOS clock mode on the NM-CIDS, and set the Cisco IOS time zone to the local time zone.

NOTE The NM-CIDS alarm time stamps indicate both UTC and local time.

Using the Router Time Source

When using Cisco IOS clock mode, accurate NM-CIDS time depends on the following:

- Router's local time
- Router's time zone offset
- Router's summer time mode and offset
- NM-CIDS's time zone offset
- NM-CIDS's summer time mode and offset

When you use the router's clock, several factors impact the time values that your NM-CIDS uses to time-stamp events. Understanding the factors is crucial to effectively using the router's time for NM-CIDS.

Coordinated Universal Time (UTC) sent to the NM-CIDS is calculated by the router based on its local time, time zone, and summer time settings. If the router's time zone settings are incorrect, the UTC time sent to the NM-CIDS will also be incorrect. Therefore, you should configure the router clock to UTC to minimize configuration mistakes.

Whenever the router is rebooted, the router's clock setting is also reset. This can cause inconsistency in time stamps if the clock is not set correctly after each reboot.

NOTE Transport Layer Security (TLS) certificates expire based on current time. If the router time is accidentally set to a time before the certificates were issued or a time after they expire, those certificates will not work.

Using an NTP Time Source

When you are using NTP mode, accurate NM-CIDS time depends on the following:

- NTP server's clock reference, which is configured in the router's Cisco IOS software
- NM-CIDS's NTP configuration

- NM-CIDS's time zone offset
- NM-CIDS's summer time mode and offset

Configuring NM-CIDS Clock Mode

To configure NTP mode, first specify the NTP server's IP address by using the **ntp server** command. The syntax for the **ntp server** command is as follows:

```
ntp server ip-address [version-number] [key keyid] [source-interface] [prefer]
```

Table 14-2 explains the parameters for the **ntp server** command.

Table 14-2 **ntp server** *Command Parameters*

Parameter	Description
ip-address	IP address of the time server providing the clock synchronization.
version-number	(Optional) Defines the NTP version number. Valid values are 1 through 3.
key *keyid*	(Optional) Keyword that indicates that the next value (*keyid*) is the number of the authentication key to use when sending packets to this peer.
source-interface	(Optional) Name of the interface from which to pick the IP source address.
prefer	(Optional) Keyword that specifies that the server referenced in this command is preferred over other configured NTP servers.

To complete the task of configuring your NM-CIDS to use NTP, define an authentication key for NTP by using the **ntp authentication-key** command. The authentication key consists of a key ID, which is a unique numeric identifier, and a key value, which is the authentication key. When this command is written to nonvolatile RAM (NVRAM), the key is encrypted so that it is not displayed when the configuration is viewed.

The syntax for the **ntp authentication-key** command is as follows:

```
ntp authentication-key number md5 value
```

Table 14-3 explains the parameters for the **ntp authentication-key** command.

Table 14-3 **ntp authentication-key** *Command Parameters*

Parameter	Description
number	The unique numeric value identifying this authentication key entry
md5	Keyword indicating the type of message hashing to use
value	A string of characters specifying the key value

Setting Up Packet Monitoring

To configure packet monitoring, enter configuration mode for the interface you want the NM-CIDS to monitor. Then use the **ids-service-module monitoring** command to specify that all packets sent and received on this interface are sent to the NM-CIDS for inspection.

> **NOTE** You must configure each interface and subinterface that you want the NM-CIDS to monitor.

Suppose that you want to monitor traffic on FastEthernet 1/0 with NM-CIDS. To set up packet monitoring on this interface, perform the configuration commands in Example 14-6.

Example 14-6 *Setting Up Packet Monitoring on FastEthernet 1/0*

```
Router# configure terminal
Router(config)# interface FastEthernet1/0
Router(config-if)# ids-service-module monitoring
Router(config-if)# end
Router# write memory
```

Logging In to NM-CIDS Console

Unlike the IPS appliances, the NM-CIDS does not have its own console port. Internal UARTs provide console access to the NM-CIDS through the Cisco IOS software. The Cisco IOS software performs a reverse Telnet that enables you to access the NM-CIDS console. The reverse Telnet to the NM-CIDS console can be invoked indirectly by the **service-module** command or directly by using Telnet.

Accessing NM-CIDS via a Session

You can access NM-CIDS by using the **service-module** command. The syntax for this command is as follows:

```
service-module ids-sensor slot-number/port-number session
```

For instance, to session in to the NM-CIDS located in slot 1 on your router, you would use the following command:

```
Router# service-module ids-sensor 1/0 session
```

Accessing NM-CIDS via Telnet

Another method to access the NM-CIDS console is by using direct Telnet. You can open a Telnet session by using the IP address of any interface on the router and a special port number. This actually opens a connection to the console via the internal UART, just like the session command from the router console.

The formula for calculating the port number is (32 * *slot number*) + 2001. For example, the port number for slot 1 would be 2033, and the port number for slot 2 would be 2065.

> **NOTE** For Telnet access to work, you must also configure the vty port to support Telnet. For information on configuring VTY ports, refer to the Cisco IOS documentation.

NM-CIDS Login

Like the sensor appliances, the NM-CIDS is configured with a default Administrator account with a username and password of "cisco."

You can use this account to initially log in to the NM-CIDS. However, the default "cisco" password is temporary and expires upon initial login. When prompted, you must change the password for this default account to a string that is not a dictionary word and is at least eight alphanumeric characters long. Special characters are not supported. After logging in, you are presented with the privileged EXEC sensor prompt. You can then perform the initial NM-CIDS configuration as you would for any other sensor by using the **setup** command.

Performing Initial Sensor Configuration

After accessing the NM-CIDS CLI, you can perform the initial sensor configuration as you would for any other appliance sensor. This includes running the **setup** command. Chapter 2, "IPS Command-Line Interface," provides more information on the initial sensor configuration tasks.

NM-CIDS Maintenance Tasks

Besides the normal maintenance operations available to a sensor, with the NM-CIDS, you can perform some maintenance operations from the router CLI. The **service-module ids-sensor** command enables you to perform the following tasks from the router CLI:

- Reload the NM-CIDS
- Reset the NM-CIDS
- Establish a session to the NM-CIDS
- Shut down the NM-CIDS
- View the status of the NM-CIDS

The syntax for the **service-module ids-sensor** command is as follows:

```
service-module ids-sensor slot number/port number {reload | reset |
    session | shutdown | status}
```

Reloading the NM-CIDS

To reload the NM-CIDS from the router CLI, use the **reload** keyword for the **service-module ids-sensor** command. This command initiates a software reboot on the NM-CIDS that stops and then reloads the IPS sensor software. Example 14-7 illustrates reloading the NM-CIDS located in slot 1.

Example 14-7 *Reloading the NM-CIDS*

```
Router# service-module ids-sensor 1/0 reload
Do you want to proceed with the reload? [confirm] y
Trying to reload Service Module IDS-Sensor1/0
```

Resetting the NM-CIDS

To reset the NM-CIDS from the router CLI, you use the **reset** keyword for the **service-module ids-sensor** command. This command initiates a hardware reboot of the NM-CIDS. Example 14-8 illustrates resetting the NM-CIDS located in slot 1.

Example 14-8 *Resetting the NM-CIDS*

```
Router# service-module ids-sensor 1/0 reset
Use reset only to recover from shutdown or failed state
Warning: May lose data on the hard disc!
Do you want to reset? [confirm] y
```

WARNING You should reset an NM-CIDS only to recover from a failed state. Resetting an operational NM-CIDS should be a last resort since it may cause you to lose all the data on the NM-CIDS hard disk.

NOTE After you shut down the NM-CIDS, you will need to reset the NM-CIDS (or reboot the router) to return the NM-CIDS to operational status if you do not remove the module from the router.

Shutting Down the NM-CIDS

To shut down the NM-CIDS from the router CLI, use the **shutdown** keyword for the **service-module ids-sensor** command. This command gracefully halts the Linux operating system on the NM-CIDS. You typically use this command before removing the NM-CIDS from the router to avoid potentially corrupting the data on the NM-CIDS hard disk. Example 14-9 illustrates shutting down the NM-CIDS located in slot 1.

Example 14-9 *Shutting Down the NM-CIDS*

```
Router# service-module ids-sensor 1/0 shutdown
Do you want to proceed with the reload? [confirm] y
Use service module reset command to recover from shutdown
Router#
Dec 12 18:30:13.715: %SERVICEMODULE-5-SHUTDOWN2: Service module
    IDS-Sensor1/0 shutdown complete
```

NOTE After removing the NM-CIDS, you should install a blank panel to cover the open slot if you do not reinsert a NM-CIDS or other router module.

Viewing the NM-CIDS Status

To view the status of the NM-CIDS from the router CLI, you use the **status** keyword for the **service-module ids-sensor** command. This command displays the status of the NM-CIDS software. If the NM-CIDS is operational, the following line is displayed in the output:

```
Service Module is in Steady state
```

Example 14-10 illustrates viewing the status of the NM-CIDS located in slot 1.

Example 14-10 *Viewing NM-CIDS Status Using the* **service-module** *Command*

```
Router# service-module ids-sensor 1/0 status
Service Module is Cisco IDS-Sensor1/0
Service Module supports session via TTY line 33
Service Module is in Steady state
Getting status from the Service Module, please wait...
Cisco Systems Intrusion Detection System Network Module
  Software version:  4.1(1)S47
  Model:NM-CIDS
  Memory:254676 KB
sensor#
```

Recovering the NM-CIDS Software Image

In the following situations, you might need to recover the NM-CIDS software image:

- You cannot access the NM-CIDS, because of a lost password
- NM-CIDS operating system becomes corrupt
- NM-CIDS hard drive becomes corrupt

After you finish the recovery procedure, all NM-CIDS configuration settings are reset to the defaults. You must either use a backed-up configuration to restore your custom settings or re-enter them manually.

To recover the NM-CIDS software image, you need the following:

- Application image
- Helper image
- Latest signature and service pack updates
- Backup configuration file

> **NOTE** A helper image is an image used only for installing the application image. It is stored on a network TFTP server and downloaded by the NM-CIDS each time the helper image is booted.

Image recovery involves the following tasks:

Step 1 Configure the boot loader.

Step 2 Boot the helper image.

Step 3 Select the file-transfer method.

Step 4 Install the application image.

Step 5 Boot the application image.

Step 6 Configure the IPS application.

Configuring the Boot Loader

To configure the boot loader, you must first download the helper file from Cisco.com to a TFTP server on your network and copy the helper image to the /tftpboot directory on your TFTP server. Then access the boot loader prompt. The following steps show how to access the boot loader prompt for an NM-CIDS in slot 1:

Step 1 Establish a session in to the NM-CIDS (**service-module ids-sensor 1/0 session**).

Step 2 Suspend the session by pressing **Ctrl-Shift-6** and then **x**. You should see the *router#* prompt.

Step 3 Reset the NM-CIDS (**service-module ids-sensor 1/0 reset**).

Step 4 Resume the suspended session by pressing **ENTER**.

> **NOTE** After displaying its version, the boot loader displays the following prompt for 15 seconds:
>
> ```
> Please enter '***' to change boot configuration
> ```

Step 5 Enter *** (at the prompt). If you type *** during the 15-second delay or if there is no default boot device configured, the device enters the boot loader CLI.

Step 6 At the boot loader CLI prompt, enter **config** to begin configuring the boot loader network parameters (ServicesEngine boot-loader>**config**).

Step 7 Set up the boot loader network parameters shown in Table 14-4.

Table 14-4 *Boot Loader Network Parameters*

Parameter	Description
IP address	Address of the external Fast Ethernet port on the NM-CIDS. This address must be a real IP address on your network.
Subnet mask	Subnet mask corresponding to the IP address provided.
TFTP server	IP address of your TFTP server that contains the helper image and IPS software images.
Gateway IP address	Default gateway address through which the NM-CIDS will route traffic.
Default helper file	Name of the boot helper file.
Ethernet interface	Specifies the interface through which to send and receive traffic. Options are **internal** and **external**.
Default boot device	Device that NM-CIDS should use to boot the system (options are **none**, **helper**, and **disk**). After the application image is installed, this must be set to **disk** to enable NM-CIDS to boot from a disk.

Booting the Helper Image

To boot the helper image, enter **boot helper** at the **ServicesEngine boot-loader>** prompt as shown in the following command line:

```
ServicesEngine boot-loader> boot helper
```

The boot loader brings up the external interface and locates the TFTP server host. When the TFTP load actually begins, a spinning character is displayed to indicate packets arriving from the TFTP server. When the load completes, a message indicates that the helper is valid, and the helper utility is launched, as shown in the output in Example 14-11.

Example 14-11 *Boot Helper Menu Options*

```
Image signature verified successfully.

Cisco Systems, Inc.
Services engine helper utility for NM-CIDS
Version 1.0(1) [200305011547]
---
Main menu
1 - Download application image and write to HDD
2 - Download bootloader and write to flash
3 - Display software version on HDD
4 - Display total RAM size
5 - Change file transfer method (currently secure shell)
r - Exit and reset Services Engine
h - Exit and shutdown Services Engine
Selection [12345rh]:
```

Selecting the File Transfer Method

From the helper image, you select **5** to choose the file transfer method to be used for downloading the application image. This controls the protocol used for downloading application and boot-loader image files only. The boot loader always uses TFTP when downloading the helper image. The command sequence in Example 14-12 selects Secure Shell (SSH) to retrieve the image files.

Example 14-12 *Selecting SSH for Boot Helper File Transfer*

```
Selection [12345rh]: 5
Change file transfer method menu
The current file transfer method is secure shell.
1 - Change to secure shell
2 - Change to tftp
r - return to main menu
1
```

Installing the Application Image

To begin re-imaging the hard disk, enter **1** at the **Selection [12345rh]:** prompt. Then you need to complete the following steps:

Step 1 Enter the SSH server username.

Step 2 Enter the SSH server IP address.

Step 3 Enter the full path name of the recovery image.

Step 4 Enter **y** when asked if you are sure you are ready to begin.

Step 5 Enter **yes** when asked if you are sure you want to continue connecting.

Step 6 Enter the SSH server password.

If the restore is successful, you receive the message in Example 14-13 and are then returned to the main menu with the **Selection [12345rh]:** prompt.

Example 14-13 *Boot Helper Successful Restore Message*

```
Disk restore was successful
The operation was successful
```

Booting the Application Image

After downloading and installing the application image, reboot the NM-CIDS by entering **r** at the **Selection [12345rh]:** prompt, as shown in the command output in Example 14-14.

Example 14-14 *Rebooting the NM-CIDS by Using the Boot Helper*

```
Selection [12345rh]: r
About to exit and reset Services Engine
Are you sure? [y/n] y
```

After the reboot, you must initialize your NM-CIDS by logging in to the NM-CIDS and running the **setup** command. After running **setup**, you will also need to restore the NM-CIDS original configuration or reconfigure it manually.

Configuring the IPS Application

The same software revision upgrades, service packs, and signature updates that you use for any Cisco IPS sensor also apply to the NM-CIDS. After installing the application image, you need to use the **upgrade** CLI command to restore the NM-CIDS software to the correct service pack level and signature release. The upgrade process is the same as for other Cisco IPS sensors.

Foundation Summary

The Cisco IDS Network Module (NM-CIDS) for access routers is a full-featured IPS sensor that provides the ability to inspect all traffic traversing a router.

The specifications for the NM-CIDS are as follows:

- Performance—45 Mbps
- Monitoring interface—Internal 100 Mbps
- Command and control interface—External 100 Mbps
- Supported routers—Cisco 2600XM Series 2691, 3660, 3725, and 3745 routers
- Cisco IOS software—12.2(15)ZJ or later
- IDS sensor software—Cisco IPS version 4.1 or later

The status light-emitting diodes (LEDs) available on the front panel of NM-CIDS are as follows:

- ACT—Displays activity on the Fast Ethernet connection
- DISK—Displays activity on the IPS hard-disk drive
- EN—Indicates that the NM-CIDS has passed the self-test and is available to the router
- LINK—Indicates that the Fast Ethernet connection is available to the NM-CIDS
- PWR—Indicates that power is available to the NM-CIDS

The following is a list of the features whose processing can impact the operations of the NM-CIDS:

- Access Control Lists (ACLs)
- Encryption
- Network Address Translation (NAT)
- IP multicast
- UDP flooding
- IP broadcast
- GRE tunnels

Cisco IOS software examines the IP header of all packets and drops any packet that contains an error, such as an irregularity in a field. Possible irregularities include the following:

- Bad IP version
- Incorrect IP option field
- Bad header length
- Total packet length greater than 8192 bytes or less than 20 bytes
- IP cyclic redundancy check (CRC) failure
- Time to Live (TTL) less than 1

Installing and configuring the NM-CIDS involves the following tasks:

Step 1 Installing the NM-CIDS

Step 2 Configuring the internal ids-sensor interface

Step 3 Assigning the clock settings

Step 4 Setting up packet monitoring

Step 5 Accessing the NM-CIDS console

Step 6 Performing initial sensor configuration

Installing the NM-CIDS into your router involves performing the following tasks:

Step 1 Insert the NM-CIDS into a router.

Step 2 Connect the NM-CIDS to the network.

Step 3 Verify that the router recognizes the NM-CIDS.

Step 4 Verify that Cisco IOS-IDS is not running.

When using Cisco IOS clock mode, accurate NM-CIDS time depends on the following:

- Router's local time
- Router's time zone offset
- Router's summer time mode and offset
- NM-CIDS's time zone offset
- NM-CIDS's summer time mode and offset

When you are using Network Time Protocol (NTP) mode, accurate NM-CIDS time depends on the following:

- NTP server's clock reference, which is configured in the router's Cisco IOS software
- NM-CIDS's NTP configuration
- NM-CIDS's time zone offset
- NM-CIDS's summer time mode and offset

The following are NM-CIDS clock recommendations, listed in order from the best choice to the worst choice:

1. Use NTP mode on the NM-CIDS.
2. Run an NTP client on the router, and use Cisco IOS clock mode on the NM-CIDS.
3. Run Cisco IOS clock mode on the NM-CIDS, and set the Cisco IOS time zone to UTC.
4. Run Cisco IOS clock mode on the NM-CIDS, and set the Cisco IOS time zone to the local time zone.

Unlike the IPS appliances, the NM-CIDS has no console port of its own. Internal Universal Asynchronous Receiver/Transmitters (UARTs) provide console access to the NM-CIDS through the Cisco IOS software. The Cisco IOS software performs a reverse Telnet that enables you to access the NM-CIDS console. The reverse Telnet to the NM-CIDS console can be indirectly invoked by the **service-module** command or directly invoked by using Telnet.

The **service-module ids-sensor** command enables you to perform the following tasks from the router CLI:

- Reload the NM-CIDS
- Reset the NM-CIDS
- Establish a session to the NM-CIDS
- Shut down the NM-CIDS
- View the status of the NM-CIDS

NM-CIDS image recovery involves the following tasks:

Step 1 Configure the boot loader.

Step 2 Boot the helper image.

Step 3 Select the file-transfer method.

Step 4 Install the application image.

Step 5 Boot the application image.

Step 6 Configure the IPS application.

Q&A

You have two choices for review questions:

- The questions that follow give you a bigger challenge than the exam itself by using an open-ended question format. By reviewing now with this more difficult question format, you can exercise your memory better and prove your conceptual and factual knowledge of this chapter. The answers to these questions are found in the appendix.
- For more practice with exam-like question formats, use the exam engine on the CD-ROM.

1. How many NM-CIDS devices can you have in a single access router?
2. How much traffic can an NM-CIDS monitor?
3. NM-CIDS is supported on which router platforms?
4. What does the "EN" LED on the NM-CIDS front panel indicate?
5. Which IOS forwarding features impact the operations of the NM-CIDS?
6. Are packets dropped by ACLs forwarded to NM-CIDS for examination?
7. Which type of encrypted traffic can NM-CIDS analyze?
8. When you use inside NAT, which IP addresses are forwarded to NM-CIDS?
9. Which types of packets are not forwarded to NM-CIDS for analysis?
10. Should you run Cisco IOS-IDS in conjunction with NM-CIDS?
11. What is the preferred clock configuration on NM-CIDS?
12. What is the least-preferred clock configuration on NM-CIDS?
13. When you are using Cisco IOS clock mode, accurate NM-CIDS time depends on what factors?
14. What are the two methods for accessing the console on the NM-CIDS?
15. What is the formula for calculating the port number to Telnet to when you are accessing NM-CIDS via Telnet?
16. Which command enables you to shut down the NM-CIDS from the router CLI?

This chapter covers the following subjects:

- Capturing Network Traffic
- Capturing Traffic for Inline Mode
- Capturing Traffic for Promiscuous Mode
- Configuring SPAN for Catalyst 4500 and 6500 Traffic Capture
- Configuring RSPAN for Catalyst 4500 and 6500 Traffic Capture
- Configuring VACLs for Catalyst 6500 Traffic Capture
- Configuring VACLs for Traffic Capture With Cisco Catalyst 6500 IOS Firewall
- Advanced Catalyst 6500 Traffic Capture

CHAPTER 15

Capturing Network Traffic

Effectively using either the IPS or IDS functionality of your Cisco IPS involves making sure that the traffic to be monitored reaches your IPS sensors. This configuration varies depending on whether your sensors are configured for inline processing or promiscuous traffic processing. You can even configure a single sensor to perform inline processing in conjunction with promiscuous processing.

Using inline processing involves bridging traffic through the sensor between two separate VLANs. Each VLAN is connected to a separate sensor interface. With promiscuous processing, a single sensor interface passively collects network traffic. Configuring your system for both of these methods is vital to effectively protecting your network with Cisco IPS.

"Do I Know This Already?" Quiz

The purpose of the "Do I Know This Already?" quiz is to help you decide if you really need to read the entire chapter. If you already intend to read the entire chapter, you do not necessarily need to answer these questions now.

The 10-question quiz, derived from the major sections in the "Foundation and Supplemental Topics" portion of the chapter, helps you determine how to spend your limited study time.

Table 15-1 outlines the major topics discussed in this chapter and the "Do I Know This Already?" quiz questions that correspond to those topics.

Table 15-1 *"Do I Know This Already?" Foundation and Supplemental Topics Mapping*

Foundation or Supplemental Topic	Questions Covering This Topic
Capturing Traffic for Inline Mode	1, 8
Capturing Traffic for Promiscuous Mode	2, 3, 9
Configuring SPAN for Catalyst 4500 and 6500 Traffic Capture	5
Configuring RSPAN for Catalyst 4500 and 6500 Traffic Capture	-

continues

Table 15-1 *"Do I Know This Already?" Foundation and Supplemental Topics Mapping (Continued)*

Foundation or Supplemental Topic	Questions Covering This Topic
Configuring VACLs for Catalyst 6500 Traffic Capture	6, 10
Configuring VACLs for Traffic Capture With Cisco Catalyst 6500 IOS Firewall	4, 7
Advanced Catalyst 6500 Traffic Capture	-

CAUTION The goal of self-assessment is to gauge your mastery of the topics in this chapter. If you do not know the answer to a question or are only partially sure of the answer, you should mark this question wrong for purposes of the self-assessment. Giving yourself credit for an answer you correctly guess skews your self-assessment results and might provide you with a false sense of security.

1. Operating in inline mode requires how many sensor interfaces?
   a. Two
   b. One
   c. Three
   d. One or two
   e. None of the above

2. Which infrastructure device(s) enables your sensor to capture traffic by default?
   a. Switch
   b. Router
   c. Hub
   d. Firewall
   e. Switch and hub

3. Which switch capture mechanism enables you to capture traffic from multiple Cisco switches?
   a. SPAN
   b. RSPAN
   c. Network tap
   d. VACLs

4. Which switch capture mechanism requires special consideration when you use IOS Firewall functionality?

   a. VACLs
   b. SPAN
   c. RSPAN
   d. SPAN and RSPAN
   e. VACLs, SPAN, and RSPAN

5. Which IOS command enables you to configure SPAN to capture network traffic?

   a. **set span**
   b. **monitor session**
   c. **switchport trunk**
   d. **switchport span**
   e. **monitor span**

6. Which of the following is not a step in creating VACLs for IOS?

   a. Configure an ACL
   b. Commit VACL to memory
   c. Create a VLAN access map
   d. Configure capture ports
   e. Apply the access map to VLANs

7. Which of the following is not a step in creating VACLs when you use IOS Firewall?

   a. Configure the extended ACL
   b. Assign the capture port
   c. Apply ACL to an interface or VLAN
   d. Apply the access map to VLANs

8. Where do you need to create an artificial VLAN boundary to use inline mode?

   a. Between devices with virtual switch ports
   b. Between a router and a firewall
   c. Between a switch and a router
   d. Between a switch and a firewall
   e. Between two routers

9. Which switch traffic capture mechanism uses ACLs to specify interesting traffic?
   a. SPAN
   b. RSPAN
   c. VACL
   d. SPAN and VACL
   e. SPAN, RSPAN, and VACL

10. Which IOS command specifies the interface to receive the traffic from the VACL?
   a. **switchport trunk**
   b. **switchport capture**
   c. **set security acl**
   d. **switchport acl**
   e. **set security capture**

The answers to the "Do I Know This Already?" quiz are found in the appendix. The suggested choices for your next step are as follows:

- **8 or less overall score**—Read the entire chapter. This includes the "Foundation and Supplemental Topics" and "Foundation Summary" sections and the Q&A section.
- **9 or 10 overall score**—If you want more review on these topics, skip to the "Foundation Summary" section and then go to the Q&A section. Otherwise, move to the next chapter.

Foundation and Supplemental Topics

Capturing Network Traffic

Your IPS sensors can process only traffic that they receive on one of their interfaces. Inline processing mode uses pairs of sensor interfaces, whereas promiscuous mode requires only a single sensor interface. This chapter focuses on the following methods of traffic capture:

- Capturing traffic for inline mode
- Capturing traffic for promiscuous mode

It also provides the following detailed sections to explain how the different traffic capture methods can be applied to the Catalyst 4500 and 6500 switches:

- Configuring Switched Port Analyzer (SPAN) for Catalyst 4500 and 6500 Traffic Capture
- Configuring Remote Switched Port Analyzer (RSPAN) for Catalyst 4500 and 6500 Traffic Capture
- Configuring VACLs for Catalyst 6500 Traffic Capture
- Configuring VACLs for Traffic Capture With Cisco Catalyst 6500 IOS Firewall
- Advanced Catalyst 6500 Traffic Capture

Capturing Traffic for Inline Mode

Running a sensor in inline mode requires using a pair of sensor interfaces to bridge the traffic between two VLANs. A basic inline configuration is shown in Figure 15-1. The interface from each router is connected to a different sensor interface. The only way traffic passes from one router to the other is if the IPS sensor allows the traffic to pass by taking traffic it receives on one of its interfaces and bridging it to the other interface.

Figure 15-1 *Basic Inline Configuration*

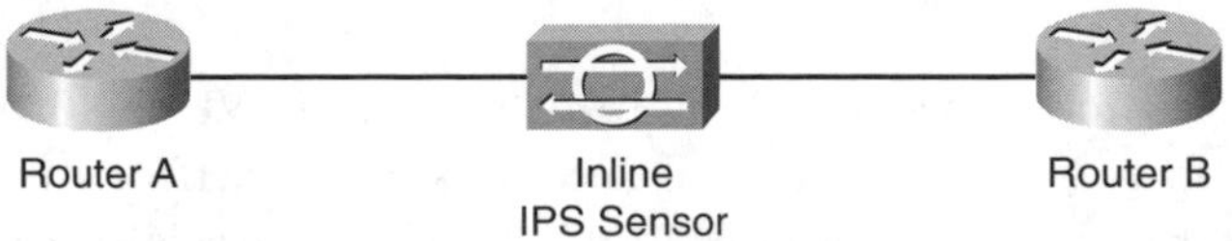

> **NOTE** To bridge traffic means to pass Ethernet traffic (in the link layer) between two interfaces that are on different VLANs.

Some common locations for deploying inline IPS include the following:

- Between two routers
- Between a firewall and a router
- Between a switch and a router
- Between a switch and a firewall

Basically, you can easily deploy inline IPS between any two physical interfaces. The configuration becomes more difficult, however, with a device such as a switch, in which the router is integrated into the switch's backplane via virtual interfaces (the router does not have physical interfaces). The same situation arises with line cards like the IDSM-2, which are also directly connected to the switch's backplane and do not have physical interfaces.

When dealing with devices (such as the Multilayer Switch Feature Card [MSFC] and IDSM-2) that are connected to your switch via virtual ports, you must artificially create a VLAN boundary at which you can deploy your inline IPS sensor.

Assume that you want to place inline IPS between the user systems on VLAN 1020 and the Internet. (See Figure 15-2.)

Figure 15-2 *Basic Network Configuration*

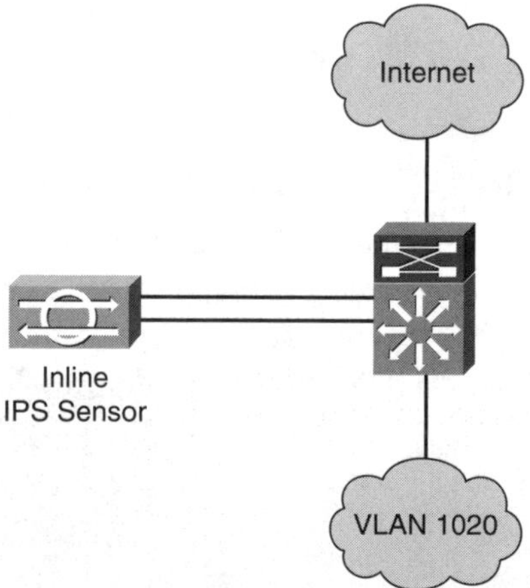

Initially, traffic goes from systems on VLAN 1020 directly to the VLAN 1020 interface, allowing the MSFC to route it to the Internet. You cannot connect the sensor's interface to the MSFC since it has only virtual ports, but you can create an artificial VLAN boundary by placing the MSFC on another VLAN (for instance, VLAN 1030) and then using the sensor to bridge traffic from VLAN 1020 to VLAN 1030. The following are the steps required to create this artificial VLAN boundary on your switch:

Step 1 Shut down the VLAN interface for VLAN 1020.

Step 2 Create another VLAN interface for VLAN 1030 and assign it the original MSFC IP address for VLAN 1020.

Step 3 Enable the new VLAN 1030 interface.

Step 4 Configure a switch port to be in VLAN 1020.

Step 5 Configure a switch port to be in VLAN 1030.

Step 6 Connect one sensor inline interface (of the inline interface pair) to the switch port in VLAN 1020.

Step 7 Connect the second sensor inline interface (of the inline interface pair) to the switch port in VLAN 1030.

After you create the artificial VLAN boundary, the systems on VLAN 1020 can no longer communicate with the MSFC (since the VLAN 1020 interface is shut down). Now the systems must rely on the sensor to bridge the traffic (destined for the Internet) to VLAN 1030. Once the traffic reaches VLAN 1030, the MSFC can route the traffic to the Internet. The same situation also applies to traffic coming from the Internet to systems on VLAN 1020.

Capturing Traffic for Promiscuous Mode

At the network level, your Cisco IPS sensors are the eyes of your intrusion prevention system. But to detect intrusive activity, sensors running in promiscuous mode must be able to view the traffic that is traversing your network. Via its monitoring interface, each promiscuous sensor examines the network traffic that it sees. Unless the monitoring interface is plugged into a hub, you must configure your infrastructure devices to pass specified network traffic to your sensor's monitoring interface. Besides identifying the infrastructure devices that you can use to pass network traffic to your sensors, this section will also examine the following three mechanisms that you can use to configure Cisco switches to mirror traffic to your sensor's promiscuous interface:

- Switched Port Analyzer (SPAN)
- Remote Switched Port Analyzer (RSPAN)
- VLAN Access Control List (VACL)

Traffic Capture Devices

For your sensors running in promiscuous mode to detect intrusive activity, they must be able to view the traffic that is traversing your network. Your sensor's monitoring interface is directly connected to an infrastructure device that mirrors specified network traffic to your sensor for analysis. You can use the following three link-layer network devices to pass traffic to your sensors:

- Hubs
- Network taps
- Switches

Hub Traffic Flow

A hub is a very simple link-layer device. Whenever a device connected to the hub generates network packets, the hub passes that traffic to all of the other ports on the hub. Figure 15-3 shows that when Host A sends traffic to Host C, all of the other devices connected to the hub also receive a copy of the traffic. The other devices connected to the hub simply ignore the traffic that does not match their Ethernet Media Access Control (MAC) address.

Figure 15-3 *Hub Traffic Flow*

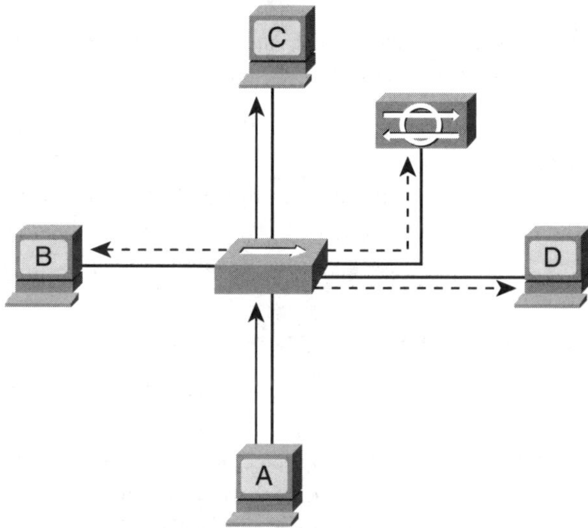

> **NOTE** Just as a host is identified by its IP address at the IP layer, each host also has an address, known as the Ethernet MAC address, at the link layer. This address is a 12-byte value that indicates the link-layer address that other devices on the same network segment use to send traffic to it. Your network card has a default Ethernet address assigned by the manufacturer, but most systems allow you to change the value.

If the network segment that you want to monitor with your Cisco IDS sensor uses a hub, your sensor can access the network traffic simply by connecting its monitoring interface into a port on the hub. Unlike other devices that ignore the traffic that does not match their Ethernet MAC address, your sensor puts its interface in promiscuous mode so that it accepts all packets that its network interface card receives.

Network Tap Traffic Flow

Sometimes, you may need to monitor a network segment between two infrastructure devices that are connected without an intervening switch or hub. In this situation you can use a network tap to capture the traffic traversing the segment. A network tap is a device that enables you to split a full-duplex connection into two traffic flows (each flow representing the traffic originating from one of the two devices). The separate traffic flows can then be redirected to an aggregation switch and eventually to your sensor.

NOTE An aggregation switch is simply a switch that you use to combine multiple traffic flows and pass the traffic to your sensor. When aggregating flows through the switch, however, you must be careful not to exceed the capacity of your sensor. For instance, if your sensor is an IDS-4215 appliance sensor, aggregating two 100-Mbps traffic flows can overwhelm the sensor's capabilities since the sensor is not rated at 200 Mbps (the maximum capacity of the combined two flows).

Figure 15-4 shows a situation in which you want to monitor the network traffic traversing between a Cisco router and a PIX Firewall. Initially, these devices are connected to each other directly. To monitor this traffic, you can install a network tap between these devices. The network tap continues to pass the traffic between the router and the firewall, but it also sends a copy of this traffic (via the two specific flows) to your aggregation switch.

Figure 15-4 *Network Tap Traffic Flow*

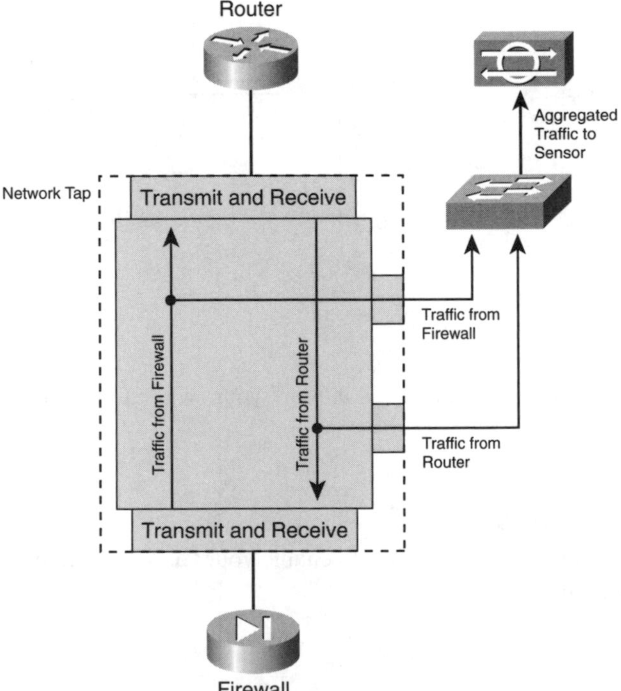

NOTE With inline functionality, you can also simply connect your sensor in line between two infrastructure devices (instead of using a network tap).

Switch Traffic Flow

The most common link-layer device on your network is probably a switch. Unlike a hub, a switch is selective as to the ports through which it passes network traffic. The switch maintains a content-addressable memory (CAM) table that maintains a mapping between Ethernet MAC addresses and the port on which that traffic was observed. When the switch receives traffic for an Ethernet MAC address that is not in its CAM table, it floods the packet out all of the ports (on the same VLAN) similar to a hub. Once the destination host replies, the CAM table is updated. Now when Host A sends traffic to Host C (see Figure 15-5), the traffic is sent only to Host C (instead of every device connected to the switch). In this scenario, your IDS sensor will not be able to monitor your network for intrusive activity since the monitoring interface on your sensor does not receive all the traffic traversing your network.

Figure 15-5 *Switch Traffic Flow*

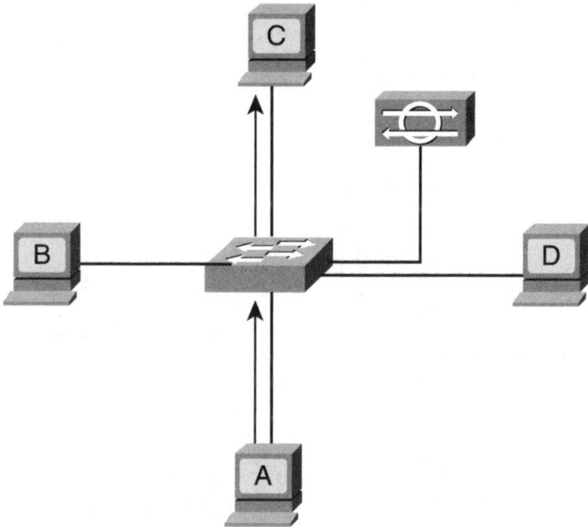

To overcome this problem, you need to configure your switch to mirror specific network traffic to your IDS sensor.

Switch Capture Mechanisms

You can use the following three features to enable your Cisco switch to mirror traffic to your IDS sensor's monitoring interface:

- SPAN
- RSPAN
- VACL

NOTE Not all of the switch-traffic capture features are available on every Cisco switch platform, but all Cisco switches support some form of the SPAN feature.

Switched Port Analyzer

The Switched Port Analyzer (SPAN) feature enables you to select traffic for analysis by a network analyzer. People refer to SPAN ports by various names, such as "port mirroring" or "port monitoring." Regardless of the name used, the SPAN feature enables you to cause your Cisco switch to pass selected traffic to your IDS sensor's monitoring interface for analysis.

NOTE A network analyzer is a device that examines network traffic and provides you with statistics or information about your network traffic. Many network analyzers identify the different types of traffic and their frequency on your network. Using these statistics, you can tune your network to optimize its performance. Your IDS sensor also analyzes the traffic on your network when watching for intrusive activity.

NOTE When you use SPAN (or RSPAN) to capture traffic for a specific VLAN, there is a chance that the same traffic can be captured twice. For instance, traffic from two systems on the same VLAN will be captured twice (if you use SPAN to monitor the VLAN in both directions). This occurs because the packets are first captured coming from the originating system and then a second time when the packet goes to the target system. This can cause multiple alerts because the packets are duplicated.

Remote Switched Port Analyzer

Sometimes, you may want to capture traffic from ports that are located on multiple switches. To accomplish this, you can use the Remote Switched Port Analyzer (RSPAN) feature that is available on certain Cisco switches.

RSPAN allows you to monitor source ports spread all over your switched network. This functionality works similarly to normal SPAN functionality, except that instead of traffic being mirrored to a specific destination port, the monitored traffic is flooded to a special RSPAN VLAN. (See Figure 15-6.) The destination port(s) can be located on any switch that has access to this RSPAN VLAN.

If you configure RSPAN to monitor traffic sent by Host A (see Figure 15-6), whenever Host A generates a packet to Host B, a copy of the packet is passed by an application-specific integrated circuit (ASIC) of the Catalyst 6000 Policy Feature Card (PFC) into the predefined RSPAN VLAN. From there, the packet is flooded to all of the ports belonging to the RSPAN VLAN. All of the interswitch links shown in Figure 15-6 are trunks. RSPAN uses these trunks to support the traversal of the RSPAN VLAN traffic. The only access points to the RSPAN-captured traffic are the defined destination ports (where you would locate you IDS sensors).

Figure 15-6 *RSPAN Traffic Flow*

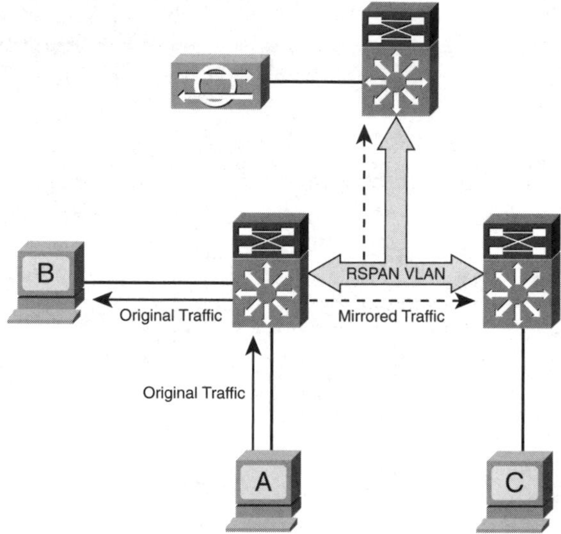

> **NOTE** The RSPAN feature is not available on all Cisco switches. Usually, RSPAN is available only on the high-end switches, such as the Catalyst 4000 and 6500. You also need to have a fairly new operating system version. Refer to the online Cisco documentation to determine whether your switch supports this feature.

VLAN Access Control Lists

A VLAN Access Control List (VACL) access-controls all packets on your Catalyst 6500 switch through the PFC. VACLs are strictly for security packet filtering and redirecting traffic to specific physical switch ports. Unlike IOS ACLs, VACLs are not defined by the direction of the traffic (inbound or outbound).

VACLs are mainly provided to filter traffic on the switch. The **capture** keyword enables you to use a VACL to mirror matched traffic to a designated capture port. This capture option specifies that packets that match the specified *flows* are switched normally as well as being captured and transmitted to the configured capture port. Only permitted traffic is sent to the capture port. VACLs enable you to use a fine degree of granularity when specifying which traffic you want to capture. You can use VACLs to capture traffic for both IDS Modules (IDSMs) and appliance sensors.

> **NOTE** A flow comprises a traffic stream between a source and destination IP address, a source port and destination port, or a combination of source IP address and source port in conjunction with a destination IP address and destination port. Your VACLs essentially define the flows that represent the interesting traffic on which you want your sensor to perform intrusion-detection analysis. Furthermore, your MSFC uses flows to effectively send packets between different VLANs by crossing the switch's backplane only once.

TCP Resets and Switches

One of the actions that your sensor can take in response to detecting a TCP-based attack is to reset the TCP connection. The sensor resets the TCP connection by sending out TCP packets with the RST flag set to both the source and destination of the TCP connection via its monitoring interface.

Not all switches allow a port that is configured as the SPAN destination port to receive incoming traffic. Since the sensor's monitoring interface is usually a SPAN port on a Cisco switch, this presents a problem. If the switch does not enable the SPAN destination port to receive incoming traffic, the TCP RST packets will not be accepted, thus preventing the sensor from resetting the TCP connection. Therefore, if you are using a SPAN port to capture your network traffic and plan to use the TCP reset capability, you need to verify that your switch supports the capability to receive incoming traffic on the SPAN destination port.

> **NOTE** A switch learns the Ethernet MAC addresses that it sees coming from a specific port so that the switch can direct traffic to that port in the future. To prevent the sensor's Ethernet MAC address from being learned by the switch (enabling an attacker to potentially identify the location of the sensor and attack it), your Cisco IDS sensor uses a randomly-generated Ethernet MAC address when it creates its TCP reset packets.

Configuring SPAN for Catalyst 4500 and 6500 Traffic Capture

The SPAN functionality on Catalyst 4000 and 6500 switches provides more functionality than the SPAN functionality provided on the Catalyst 2900XL/3500Xl switches. For instance, on the Catalyst 4000 and 6500 switches, you can typically configure four to six SPAN sessions, compared with one or two on the Catalyst 2900XL/3500Xl switches. Plus your destination port can be configured to accept incoming traffic (useful for TCP reset functionality).

The monitor session Command

To capture traffic by using the SPAN feature on a Catalyst 4000 or 6500 (running IOS), you need to use the **monitor session** command. This command enables you to specify whether you want to capture all the traffic to the monitored ports or just the received or sent traffic. The syntax for the **monitor session** command is as follows:

```
monitor session {session} {source {interface port(s)} [rx|tx|both]}
monitor session {session} {source vlan vlan_id [rx]}
monitor session {session} {destination {interface port}}
```

Unlike the **port monitor** command, the **monitor session** command requires you to explicitly specify the source and destination ports by using two different forms of the command. Table 15-2 describes the parameters for the **monitor session** global configuration command.

Table 15-2 monitor session *Parameters*

Parameter	Description
session	Number of the SPAN session. The only valid value is usually 1, but some switches support more than one SPAN session.
source	Keyword indicating that you are specifying a source port (the port to be monitored).
source vlan	Keyword indicating that you are specifying a source VLAN (to be monitored).
destination	Keyword indicating that you are specifying a destination port for the SPAN session.
interface	Keyword indicating that you are specifying a port.
port(s)	The port to be configured as either a source or destination. The port includes the interface type, module, and port, such as FastEthernet 0/10. For source ports, you can specify a comma-delimited list or a range of ports (such as "10-20").
rx	Keyword indicating that you want to capture only the traffic received by the source port(s) (ingress traffic).
tx	Keyword indicating that you want to capture only the traffic transmitted by the source port(s) (egress traffic).
both	Keyword indicating that you want to capture all traffic on the source port(s).
vlan	Keyword indicating that you are specifying a VLAN to be monitored.
vlan-id	ID of the VLAN to be monitored. Valid IDs are in the range from 1 to 1005. You do not need to enter the leading zeros for the VLAN ID.

Using the **monitor session** command, you need to define both the source port(s) and the destination port, since this command is entered in the global configuration mode.

If you want to configure SPAN so that traffic transmitted and received on FastEthernet ports 3/9 and 3/12 (SPAN source ports) is mirrored on FastEthernet port 3/4 (SPAN destination), you use the following command:

```
Console(config)# monitor session 1 source interface fa3/9 , fa3/12 both
Console(config)# monitor session 1 destination fa3/4
```

Configuring RSPAN for Catalyst 4500 and 6500 Traffic Capture

To use the RSPAN functionality on your Catalyst 4500 and 6500 switches (running IOS), you must define a VLAN to be used for RSPAN by using the **remote-span** command in the VLAN subconfiguration command. You must also perform other configuration tasks, such as defining the trunks to carry the RSPAN VLAN traffic. For information on these other configuration tasks, refer to the SPAN and RSPAN documentation available on Cisco.com.

NOTE To remove an existing RSPAN association, you need to use the **no remote-span** command in the VLAN subconfiguration command mode for the current RSPAN VLAN.

Suppose that you want to configure VLAN 1040 as your RSPAN VLAN. The following commands make VLAN 1040 your RSPAN VLAN:

```
Cat6# configure terminal
Cat6(config)# vlan 1040
Cat6(config-vlan)# remote-span
```

NOTE You will need to configure the RSPAN VLAN on each switch, along with establishing trunks between the various switches.

Configuring VACLs for Catalyst 6500 Traffic Capture

When configuring a VACL on Cisco IOS, you need to go through the following steps:

Step 1 Configure an Access Control List (ACL).

Step 2 Create a VLAN access map.

Step 3 Match the ACL to the access map.

Step 4 Define an action for the access map.

Step 5 Apply the access map to the VLANs.

Step 6 Configure capture ports.

You also need to configure the TCP reset port to complete the configuration. This is not part of configuring your VACL, but it is necessary to ensure that the TCP reset traffic can reach the hosts for which it is intended.

Configure an ACL

With IOS, you specify the interesting traffic that you want to monitor using an ACL. Therefore, the first step in setting up a VACL is to create your ACL. Suppose, for example, that you are using the IDSM-2 to protect a web server farm and that the subnet for the web servers is 172.12.31.0. You may create an ACL similar to the following to allow any hosts to connect to port 80 on any system on the server farm subnet:

```
Router(Config)# access-list 110 permit tcp any 172.12.31.0 0.0.0.255 eq 80
```

NOTE In many situations, you may be able to use ACLs that you have already constructed to restrict traffic into your network.

Create a VLAN Access Map

You begin to configure the VACL by establishing a VLAN access map by using the **vlan access-map** command. After creating a VLAN access map, you must match it to an ACL and define its actions by using the following two subcommands:

- **match**
- **action**

The **vlan access-map** command basically creates the access map and enables you to assign a name to it. The following command creates an access map named "my_map":

```
Router(config)# vlan access-map my_map
```

Match ACL to Access Map

To specify which traffic the VLAN access map applies to, you need to associate the VLAN access map with an ACL on the router. You do this via the **match** subcommand. In our example, the ACL is 110, so the commands would be as follows:

```
Router(config)# vlan access-map my_map
Router(config-access-map)# match ip address 110
Router(Config-access-map)#
```

Define Action for Access Map

Besides specifying the interesting traffic by associating an ACL to the VLAN access map, you must also specify an action to be performed on the traffic that the ACL matches. You accomplish this by using the **action** subcommand. For our example, the action is to forward and capture the traffic, so the commands would be as follows:

```
Router(config)# vlan access-map my_map
Router(config-access-map)# action forward capture
Router(Config-access-map)#
```

NOTE Although you are interested in capturing the traffic, you must also specify the forward action. Otherwise, the traffic matched by the VLAN access map will not be sent by the switch functionality to its destination, which is similar to denying the traffic with an ACL deny statement.

Apply Access Map to VLANs

Now you need to decide which VLANs on your router you are going to apply to your VLAN access map. You accomplish this with the **vlan filter** command. For our example, you would use the following command:

```
Router(config)# vlan filter my_map 10-12,15
```

Configure Capture Ports

Finally, you need to configure which port on your router will receive the captured traffic. You accomplish this with the **switchport capture** command. For our example, the commands would be as follows:

```
Router(config)# interface fa 5/7
Router(config-if) switchport capture allowed vlan 10-12,15
```

The **allowed** keyword enables you to limit the traffic sent to the capture port. Any VLANs that are not included in the allowed list will not be sent to the capture port. Using this option enables you to separate captured traffic between multiple capture ports (such as when you have multiple IDSM-2 blades in the same chassis). The VACL captures all of the interesting traffic. Then you limit which traffic is actually sent to each capture port.

Configuring VACLs for Traffic Capture With Cisco Catalyst 6500 IOS Firewall

When using the Cisco IOS Firewall on your Multilayer Switch Feature Card (MSFC), you may be unable to directly configure VACLs to capture network traffic for your sensor. If you apply the **ip inspect** IOS Firewall command on a specific VLAN interface, you cannot create a VACL for that same VLAN at the switch level. These two features are mutually incompatible. To overcome this limitation, you can use the **mls ip ids** MSFC router command to designate which packets will be captured by your security ACL.

With normal VACLs, the VACL establishes a security ACL that actually determines which traffic is allowed through the switch. With the **mls ip ids** command, however, you will be defining an extended ACL (on your MSFC) to designate which traffic will be captured. A copy of any traffic that is permitted by the extended ACL will be passed to your capture port, but the extended ACL will not prevent this traffic from reaching its intended destination.

When using the **mls ip ids** command, you need to go through the following steps to configure a VACL:

Step 1 Configure the extended ACL.

Step 2 Apply the ACL to an interface or VLAN.

Step 3 Assign the capture port.

Configure the Extended ACL

Just as in regular VACL configuration, your first step in creating an IOS Firewall VACL is to define the interesting traffic. In this situation, the interesting traffic is determined by an extended ACL that you create on your MSFC. The command to create the extended ACL is **ip access-list** and its syntax is as follows:

```
ip access-list extended access-list-number {deny|permit} protocol source_IP
    source_wild-card destination_IP destination_wild-card [log|log-input]
```

Table 15-3 describes the major parameters for the **ip access-list** router configuration command.

Table 15-3 **ip access-list** *Parameters*

Parameter	Description
access-list-number	Number identifying the ACL being created. Valid values are between 100 and 199, and 2000 and 2699.
deny	Keyword indicating that the traffic being specified should be dropped by the ACL.
permit	Keyword indicating that the traffic should be allowed by the ACL.
protocol	Name or number of an IP protocol that defines the traffic that you are interested in. Some common keywords are **tcp**, **udp**, **icmp**, and **eigrp**.
source_IP	The source host or network IP address of packets that you are interested in.
source_wildcard	A mask that indicates which bits in the *source_IP* address are used for comparison. Each zero bit in the mask indicates bits in the *source_IP* address that must exactly match the address of the packet being checked. Bits set to 1 are automatically matched.
destination_IP	The destination host or network IP address of packets that you are interested in.
destination_wildcard	A mask that indicates which bits in the *destination_IP* are used for comparison. Each zero bit in the mask indicates bits in the *destination_IP* address that must exactly match the address of the packet being checked. Bits set to 1 are automatically matched.
log	(Optional) Causes an informational logging message to be sent to the console when packets are matched to the ACL.
log-input	(Optional) Includes the input interface and source Ethernet MAC address in logging output.

The **ip access-list** command is executed on your MSFC, not on your Catalyst switch console. Suppose that you want to define an ACL (150) that permits User Datagram Protocol (UDP) traffic from 10.20.30.1 to 10.30.30.1. To accomplish this, you enter the following commands on your router console:

```
MSFC# configure terminal
MSFC(config)# ip access-list extended 150 permit tcp 10.20.30.1 0.0.0.0
     10.30.30.1 0.0.0.0
MSFC(config)#
```

Apply ACL to an Interface or VLAN

Next you need to apply the extended ACL to a VLAN interface on the MSFC. You use the **interface vlan** command to enter the configuration mode for a specific interface. Then you use the **mls ip ids** command to apply the extended ACL to that interface.

The syntax for the **interface vlan** command is as follows:

```
interface vlan vlan_number
```

The syntax for the **mls ip ids** command is as follows:

```
mls ip ids acl_number
```

To continue with our example, you would enter the following commands on your router to apply ACL 150 to VLAN 40.

```
MSFC# configure terminal
MSFC(config)# interface vlan 40
MSFC(config-if)# mls ip ids 150
```

Assign the Capture Port

Finally, you need to assign the capture port to receive the traffic that is captured (permitted) by your extended ACL. You need to use the **switchport capture** command to define your capture ports. This command is executed on your switch console.

> **NOTE** If your switch is running CatOS instead of IOS, you would use the **set security acl** command to define your capture ports. For more information on this command, refer to the Cisco documentation.

The syntax for the **switchport capture** command is as follows:

```
switchport capture
```

In our ongoing example, you would need to enter the following command on your switch console to establish port 5 on module 3 as you capture port:

```
Cat6# configure terminal
Cat6(config)# interface fastethernet 3/5
Cat6(config-if)# switchport capture
```

> **NOTE** If you want to limit the traffic to a capture port, you can use the **switchport capture allowed vlan** command to restrict the traffic sent to a specific capture port based on the traffic's VLAN. By dividing the traffic to the capture ports based on the traffic's VLAN, you can limit the amount of traffic being sent to the single capture port. When deploying multiple IDSM-2 modules in a single switch, you need to use the **switchport capture allowed vlan** command to divide your captured traffic across multiple capture ports (since each IDSM-2 can process a maximum of 600 Mbps).

Advanced Catalyst 6500 Traffic Capture

So far our examination has focused on the ways that you can use your Cisco switch to capture network traffic for analysis by your sensor. The next step involves configuring the port on the switch through which your sensor receives its captured traffic.

By default your appliance sensors are usually connected to your switch via a standard access port. Since this port is usually not configured as a trunk, your sensor will receive only traffic that belongs to the same VLAN as the VLAN assigned to the switch port.

The monitoring port on your IDSM, however, is configured as a trunk port by default and accepts all of the traffic that it receives. You might not want the IDSM's monitoring port analyzing traffic from every VLAN on the switch.

In both of these situations, you need to understand how to configure the trunking properties of the ports on your switch so that you can limit the acceptable traffic to only those VLANs that you consider interesting.

> **NOTE** The examples here use IOS command examples. For information on how to perform these operations using CatOS, refer to the Cisco documentation.

When configuring a trunk port on your switch, you will need to perform various tasks to change the port's characteristics. You use specific switch commands to change your port's properties, but you will essentially also need to perform the following high-level tasks:

Step 1 Configure a destination port.

Step 2 Define trunks to capture.

Step 3 Assign switch ports to a VLAN.

Step 4 Create a VACL.

Configure Destination Port

The first task you need to perform to configure a trunk port on your switch is to convert your destination port (the port through which your sensor's monitoring interface is connected to the switch) to a trunk port instead of to a regular access port.

> **NOTE** The monitoring port on your IDSM is configured as a trunk port by default. Therefore, this step is not necessary if you are configuring multiple VLANs for your IDSM's monitoring port.

To change the basic characteristics of a switch port so that it becomes a trunk port, use the **switchport trunk** IOS command. This command is executed from the interface configuration mode.

If your destination port is port 5 on module 3, you need to enter the following command on your switch to enable trunking on that port:

```
Cat6# configure terminal
Cat6(config)# interface fastethernet 3/5
Cat6(config-if)# switchport trunk encapsulation dot1q
```

Define Trunks to Capture

At this point, your destination port is configured as a trunk port. Now you need to define the VLANs that you want the destination port to accept. The **switchport trunk** IOS command also enables you to define which VLANs an existing trunk port is allowed to process.

If your destination port is port 5 on module 3 and you want to trunk VLANs 30, 40, and 50, you need to enter the following commands on your switch to define the allowed VLANs on the destination port:

```
Cat6# configure terminal
Cat6(config)# interface fastethernet 3/5
Cat6(config-if)# switchport trunk allowed vlan 30,40,50
```

Assign Switch Ports to VLANs

Besides configuring the VLANs that your destination port will accept, you also need to know how to assign ports on your switch to various VLANs. You do this with the **switchport access** IOS command.

> **NOTE** Before you can use the **switchport access** command, you must make sure that the port is configured as a switch port by using the **switchport** IOS command.

Suppose that you want to place port 3 on module 2 into VLAN 10 and port 4 on module 4 into VLAN 8. The switch commands to accomplish this are displayed in Example 15-1.

Example 15-1 *Configuring Switch Ports Using IOS*

```
Cat6# configure terminal
Cat6(config) interface fastethernet 3/2
Cat6(config-if)# switchport
Cat6(config-if)# switchport access vlan 10
Cat6(config-if)# exit
Cat6(conf)# interface fastethernet 4/4
Cat6(config-if)# switchport
Cat6(config-if)# switchport access vlan 8
```

Create the VACL

You have now configured the characteristics of your trunk port that represents the connection to the monitoring interface on your sensor. You still need to go through the various tasks (explained earlier in this chapter) to create your VACL. Then you need to assign that VACL to the trunk port that you configured as its capture port.

Foundation Summary

Your IPS sensors can process only traffic that they receive on one of their interfaces. There are two methods for traffic capture:

- Capturing traffic for inline mode
- Capturing traffic for promiscuous mode

Some common locations for deploying inline IPS include the following:

- Between two routers
- Between a firewall and a router
- Between a switch and a router
- Between a switch and a firewall

In promiscuous mode, you can use the following infrastructure devices to capture network traffic:

- Hubs
- Network taps
- Switches

When using switches, you can use the following three mechanisms to configure Cisco switches to mirror traffic to you sensor's promiscuous interface:

- Switched Port Analyzer (SPAN)
- Remote Switched Port Analyzer (RSPAN)
- VLAN Access Control List (VACL)

To capture traffic by using the SPAN feature on a Catalyst 4000 or 6500 (running IOS), you need to use the **monitor session** command.

When configuring a VACL on Cisco IOS, you need to go through the following tasks:

Step 1 Configure an ACL.

Step 2 Create a VLAN access map.

Step 3 Match the Access Control List (ACL) to the access map.

Step 4 Define action for the access map.

Step 5 Apply the access map to VLANs.

Step 6 Configure capture ports.

When using the IOS Firewall (**mls ip ids** command), you need to go through the following steps to configure a VACL:

Step 1 Create the extended ACL.

Step 2 Apply the ACL to an interface or VLAN.

Step 3 Assign the capture port.

Q&A

You have two choices for review questions:

- The questions that follow give you a bigger challenge than the exam itself by using an open-ended question format. By reviewing now with this more difficult question format, you can exercise your memory better and prove your conceptual and factual knowledge of this chapter. The answers to these questions are found in the appendix.
- For more practice with exam-like question formats, use the exam engine on the CD-ROM.

1. What are the common locations to deploy inline IPS?
2. When do you need to construct an artificial VLAN boundary to use inline IPS?
3. What are the three network devices commonly used to capture network traffic for processing by your sensor?
4. Which three switch mechanisms can you use to mirror traffic to your IPS sensors?
5. How is SPAN different from RSPAN?
6. Which IOS command is used to configure SPAN on your Catalyst 4500 and 6500 switches?
7. What are the steps involved in configuring a VACL on IOS?
8. Which command may impact your ability to capture traffic by using VACLs?
9. When do you need to use the **mls ip ids** IOS command?
10. What steps are involved in using VACLs when you have the IOS Firewall on your Catalyst 6500 switch?
11. Which IOS command do you use to enable trunking on a switch port?
12. Which IOS command enables you to create a VLAN access map?
13. Which action must you specify (when using VLAN access maps) to enable the traffic to pass to the destination hosts and not be denied?

APPENDIX

Answers to the "Do I Know This Already?" Quizzes and Q&A Questions

Chapter 1

"Do I Know This Already?" Quiz

1. B
2. C
3. D
4. B
5. A
6. C
7. A
8. C
9. B
10. A

Q&A

1. *What is a false positive?*

   Answer: A false positive happens when a signature triggers incorrectly during normal user traffic instead of attack traffic.

2. *What is a true positive?*

   Answer: A true positive happens when a signature correctly identifies an attack launched against the network.

3. *If your sensor has only two monitoring interfaces, can you operate in promiscuous and inline modes simultaneously?*

   Answer: No, because running inline requires a pair of sensor interfaces. If you have only two interfaces, you can run either a single interface pair (in inline mode) or two interfaces (in promiscuous mode).

4. *What factors are use to calculate the risk rating?*

   Answer: The risk rating is based on the event severity, the signature fidelity, and the target's asset value.

5. *How is the asset value of a target configured?*

   Answer: You configure the asset value of a target by assigning one of the following values to an IP address or range of address: low, medium, high, mission critical, or no value.

6. *Which appliance sensors support the inline mode of operation?*

   Answer: Inline mode is supported on the following appliance sensors: IDS 4215, IDS 4235, IDS 4240, IDS 4250, and IDS 4255.

7. *Which appliance sensors are diskless?*

   Answer: The IDS 4240 and IDS 4255 appliance sensors are diskless.

8. *Which appliance sensor comes with dual 1 Gb monitoring interfaces?*

   Answer: The IDS 4250XL comes with dual 1 Gb monitoring interfaces.

9. *What are the three modes that you can configure for software bypass when using inline mode?*

   Answer: When using inline mode, you can configure software bypass to one of the following modes: auto, off, or on.

10. *If you want the sensor to fail close when operating in inline mode, what software bypass mode would you use?*

    Answer: To cause a sensor running in inline mode to fail close, you need to configure the software bypass to off.

11. *What are the four network boundaries that you need to consider when deploying sensors on your network?*

    Answer: When deploying sensors on your network, you need to consider the following network boundaries: Internet, intranets, extranets, and remote access.

12. *What factors (besides network boundaries) must you consider when deploying your sensors?*

    Answer: When deploying your sensors, you must consider the following factors: sensor placement, sensor management and monitoring, number of sensors, and external sensor communications.

13. *Which XML-based protocol does your sensor use to transfer event messages to other Cisco IPS devices?*

    Answer: Your sensor uses RDEP to transfer event messages to other Cisco IPS devices.

14. *Which standard provides a product-independent standard for communicating security device events?*

    Answer: SDEE defines a product-independent standard for communicating security events.

15. *What is a true negative?*

    Answer: A true negative is a situation in which a signature does not fire during normal user traffic on the network.

16. *What is the Meta-Event Generator (MEG)?*

    Answer: The MEG is a signature engine that enables you to construct meta signatures that are based on correlating distinct individual signatures. Using the MEG, you can construct signatures that trigger only when specific individual signatures all trigger within a specific time period.

17. *What is the main difference between intrusion detection and intrusion prevention?*

    Answer: Intrusion detection passively captures traffic looking for intrusive activity. Intrusion prevention operates in inline mode when examining network traffic, enabling intrusion prevention to actively drop intrusive activity.

Chapter 2

"Do I Know This Already?" Quiz

1. C
2. A
3. D
4. E

5. B
6. D
7. B
8. C
9. D
10. B, D

Q&A

1. *What character do you use to obtain help via the appliance CLI, and what are the two ways you can use it to obtain help?*

   Answer: To obtain help, you type the **?** character. This character will show you all of the valid options when used by itself or all of the options that match your partial specification.

2. *What command enables you to allow a host or all of the hosts on a network to connect to the sensor?*

   Answer: The **service host > network-settings** command enables you to allow a host or network to access the sensor.

3. *How many different user roles are available to assign to accounts on your sensor?*

   Answer: The sensor software provides four different user roles: Administrator, Operator, Viewer, and Service.

4. *What is the most privileged user role that you can assign to a CLI user?*

   Answer: The Administrator role is the most privileged user role for the CLI. It provides access to all CLI operations.

5. *Which user role provides the user with the ability to examine the sensor's events and configuration but does not allow the user to change the configuration?*

   Answer: The Viewer role provides the user with the ability to look at the configuration of the sensor and monitor events but not to change the configuration.

6. *What parameters can you configure by using the **setup** CLI command?*

   Answer: When you run the **setup** command, you can configure the basic sensor characteristics, including the host name, IP address, network mask, default gateway, access list entries, time settings, Telnet enablement, and web server port.

7. *What is the purpose of the Service user role?*

   Answer: The Service user role enables you to configure an account that bypasses the CLI. This account assists the TAC in troubleshooting problems with your sensor.

8. *What command do you use on the CLI to enter Global Configuration mode?*

   Answer: As in IOS, you enter the command **configure terminal** to enter Global Configuration mode.

9. *How many Service accounts can you have on your sensor?*

   Answer: You can assign the Service role to just one account on you sensor.

10. *What user role would you usually assign to the account that you use to enable your monitoring applications to retrieve information from your sensor?*

    Answer: You would normally assign the Viewer role to your monitoring application since it only needs to be able to retrieve information from the sensor, not to change the configuration.

11. *What character do you use on the CLI to cause your sensor to automatically expand the rest of a command for you?*

    Answer: When you press the **Tab** key after entering a command at the CLI, the system will automatically expand the command if only one command matches the partial command that you entered. Otherwise, all of the commands that could match your entry are shown, and your partial command is redisplayed.

12. *When a CLI command's output extends beyond a single screen, what character do you use to show the next screen of information?*

    Answer: When the output of a CLI command extends beyond a single screen, the output stops at one screen's worth and displays the *–more–* prompt. To show the next screen of information, press the **Space** key.

13. *When a CLI command's output extends beyond a single screen, what character do you use to see just the next line of output?*

    Answer: When the output of a CLI command extends beyond a single screen, the output stops at one screen's worth and displays the *–more–* prompt. To scroll the output by a single line, press the **Enter** key.

14. *Which sensors cannot be upgraded with a recovery CD and why?*

    Answer: The diskless sensors (IDS 4215, 4240, and 4255) cannot be upgraded with a recovery CD since they do not come with a CD-ROM drive.

15. *What are the transfer options available for upgrading appliance sensors through the network?*

    Answer: To upgrade diskless appliance sensors, you can use SCP, FTP, HTTP, or HTTPS to retrieve the new software image.

16. *Before you can use SCP to retrieve a new image file or signature update, what must you do on the sensor?*

    Answer: Before you retrieve a new image file or signature update via SCP, you must first add the SSH server key for the system where the software is located (using the **ssh host** global configuration command).

Chapter 3

"Do I Know This Already?" Quiz

1. A
2. A
3. D
4. C
5. C
6. A
7. A
8. E
9. A
10. D

Q&A

1. *Which Windows operating systems are supported for accessing IDM?*

   Answer: Both Windows 2000 and Windows XP are supported operating systems for accessing IDM.

2. *What is the minimum amount of RAM that is recommended for systems to run IDM?*

   Answer: The minimum recommended RAM is 256 MB for systems that run IDM.

3. *Which fields can you configure when you choose the **Sensor Setup>Network** option?*

   Answer: When configuring sensor communication parameters (via **Sensor Setup>Network**), you can configure the host name, IP address, network mask, default route, and port for secure web access.

4. *What SNMP functionality is available for Cisco IPS version 5.0?*

   Answer: Beginning with Cisco IPS version 5.0, you can manage your sensors via SNMP and configure your sensors to generate SNMP traps.

5. *Which web browsers are supported for IDM use on systems running Windows operating systems?*

   Answer: For systems running Windows operating systems, both Internet Explorer 6.0 and Netscape 7.1 are supported web browsers for accessing IDM.

6. *Which web browser is supported for accessing IDM from both Solaris and Linux operating systems?*

   Answer: Mozilla 1.7 is the supported web browser for accessing IDM from both Solaris and Linux.

7. *Is Telnet access to the sensor enabled by default?*

   Answer: No, Telnet access to the sensor is disabled by default.

8. *What two blocking actions can you configure on the sensor?*

   Answer: You can configure a host block and a connection block.

9. *What versions of Solaris are supported for access to IDM?*

   Answer: Both Solaris versions 2.8 and 2.9 are supported operating systems for accessing IDM.

10. *What is the purpose of the* ***Back*** *icon?*

    Answer: As you navigate to different configuration screens inside IDM the software keeps a list of these screens. Clicking on the **Back** icon enables you to move backward through the list of screens visited (similar to how your browser's **Back** button scrolls through previously visited web pages).

11. *What are the main categories of configuration options available to a user with Administrator privileges?*

    Answer: The main categories of configuration options available to a user with Administrator privileges are Sensor Setup, Interface Configuration, Analysis Engine, Signature Definition, Event Action Rules, Blocking, and SNMP.

12. *Is SSH access to the sensor enabled by default?*

    Answer: Yes, SSH access to the sensor is enabled by default, but the only systems that access the sensor (by default) are systems that are located on the class C subnet 10.1.9.0.

Chapter 4

"Do I Know This Already?" Quiz

1. A
2. E
3. B
4. D
5. C
6. B
7. C
8. A
9. B
10. C

Q&A

1. *What must you do before you can manage or configure your sensor across the network?*

   Answer: Before you can manage or configure your sensor across the network, you must configure which hosts are allowed to access the sensor.

2. *What roles can you assign to a user account on your sensor?*

   Answer: When creating user accounts on your sensor, you can assign one of the following roles: Administrator, Operator, Viewer, or Service.

3. *Which user role can be assigned to only a single user account?*

   Answer: The Service role can be assigned to only a single user account on your sensor.

4. *What are the two ways that you can configure time on your sensor?*

   Answer: You can configure time manually on your sensor, or you can configure the sensor to retrieve time automatically via an NTP server.

5. *When configuring your summertime settings, what are the two date formats that you can use?*

   Answer: When configuring the summertime settings on your sensor, you can enter specific dates or specify recurring dates.

6. *What fields should you use to specify recurring dates?*

   Answer: Recurring time-change dates are specified using the fields for the month, day of the month, and week of the month.

7. *What must you do before your sensor can initiate blocking via your infrastructure devices?*

   Answer: Before your sensor can initiate blocking via your infrastructure devices, you must add the SSH public keys for those infrastructure devices.

8. *When editing a monitoring interface's parameters by using IDM, what parameters can you alter?*

   Answer: When editing the characteristics of a monitoring interface by using IDM, you can alter the following parameters: interface description, interface speed, interface duplex, enabled status, and alternate TCP-reset interface.

9. *What are the three options for configuring inline software bypass?*

   Answer: When configuring inline software bypass, you can choose Auto, On, or Off.

10. *How does the Auto software bypass mode work?*

    Answer: Auto software bypass mode causes the sensor to bypass inspection when the analysis engine is stopped, thus preventing a network disruption.

11. *What is the Missed Packet Threshold?*

    Answer: The Missed Packet Threshold specifies the percentage of packets that must be missed during the notification interval before a notification event is generated.

12. *How does the Off software bypass mode work?*

    Answer: The Off software bypass mode causes the sensor to pass traffic only after it has been inspected by the analysis engine. If the analysis engine is stopped, traffic is not allowed to pass.

13. *Can you configure inline interface pairs and promiscuous interfaces to the same virtual sensor?*

    Answer: Yes, you can assign inline interface pairs and promiscuous interfaces to the same virtual sensor.

Chapter 5

"Do I Know This Already?" Quiz

1. E
2. A
3. C
4. E
5. B
6. D
7. E
8. A
9. B
10. D

Q&A

1. *In IDM, which signature groups can you use to view signatures?*

   Answer: Using IDM, you can view signatures by using the following nine signature groups: Attack, L2/L3/L4 Protocol, Operating System, Signature Release, Service, Signature ID, Signature Name, Signature Action, and Signature Engine.

2. *In IDM, which types of attacks can you view signatures by?*

   Answer: When using IDM, you can view signatures by the following types of attacks: DoS, File Access, General Attack, IDS Evasion, Informational, Policy Violation, Reconnaissance, and Viruses/Trojans/Worms.

3. *In IDM, what field is searched when you display signatures by signature name?*

   Answer: When displaying signatures by signature name, IDM searches for matches (of the text string that you entered) in the signature name field.

4. *What summary-key values can you specify for a signature?*

   Answer: The summary-key values are attacker address, victim address, attacker and victim addresses, attacker address and victim port, attacker and victim addresses and ports.

5. *What is the difference between Fire All and Fire Once alarm summary modes?*

   Answer: Fire All generates an alarm for every occurrence of traffic that triggers a specific signature, whereas Fire Once generates an alarm for the first occurrence of traffic that triggers a specific signature during a specific summary interval.

6. *What is the difference between Summary and Global Summary alarm summary modes?*

   Answer: Summary mode summarizes alerts based on the specified summary key, whereas Global Summary mode summarizes alerts based on all address and port combinations.

7. *What does the Benign Trigger(s) field on the NSDB signature page provide?*

   Answer: The NSDB Benign Trigger(s) field indicates situations in which normal user traffic may cause a signature to fire.

8. *What are the two methods (via IDM) that you can use to create new custom signatures?*

   Answer: When creating new custom signatures (via IDM), you can use Clone or Add. Clone enables you to start with the parameters of an existing signature and customize it to your environment. Add lets you build a signature from scratch.

9. *Using IDM, how can you remove a signature from a signature engine?*

   Answer: To remove a signature from a signature engine, you use the Retire functionality.

10. *What signature responses (actions) are unique to inline mode?*

    Answer: The signature responses unique to inline mode are Deny Attacker Inline, Deny Connection Inline, and Deny Packet Inline.

11. *Which signature response (action) uses SNMP?*

    Answer: The Request SNMP Trap response (action) generates an SNMP trap when the signature fires.

12. *Besides using the **Select All** button, how can you select multiple signatures on the Signature Configuration screen?*

    Answer: You can select multiple signatures on the Signature Configuration screen by holding down either the **Shift** or **Ctrl** key when highlighting signatures.

Chapter 6

"Do I Know This Already?" Quiz

1. A
2. D
3. B
4. C
5. A
6. D
7. E
8. B
9. E
10. C

Q&A

1. *What are the major groups that signature parameters fall into?*

   Answer: The signature parameters fall into the following groups: basic signature fields, signature description fields, engine-specific fields, event counter fields, alert frequency fields, and status fields.

2. *What do the Application Inspection and Control (AIC) signature engines provide, and which protocols are currently supported?*

   Answer: The AIC signature engines support signatures that provide deep-packet inspection from Layer 4 through Layer 7. The two protocols currently supported are HTTP and FTP.

3. *What signature types can you use for AIC HTTP signatures?*

   Answer: The signature types available for AIC HTTP signatures are Content Types, Define Web Traffic Policy, Max Outstanding Requests Overrun, Msg Body Pattern, Request Methods, and Transfer Encodings.

4. *What are the atomic signature engines and the types of signatures they support?*

   Answer: The Atomic ARP signature engine supports ARP signatures, and the Atomic IP signature engine supports ICMP, TCP, and UDP atomic signatures.

5. *What is the definition of an atomic signature?*

   Answer: An *atomic signature* means that everything needed to check for a signature match is available in a single packet. These signatures do not require any state information to be saved.

6. *What is the difference between the TCP Mask and TCP Flags parameters?*

   Answer: The TCP Flags parameter determines which flags you want set, and the TCP Mask parameter indicates the flags that you are interested in. Flags not included in the TCP Mask cannot impact whether the signature triggers.

7. *Which parameter do you use to specify that a regex string needs to be located at an exact location within the packet or stream?*

   Answer: The Exact Match Offset parameter indicates that the regex string needs to occur at exactly the specified number of bytes from the beginning of the packet or stream.

8. *Which Flood Net parameter defines how long the traffic must remain above the configured rate in order to trigger the signature?*

   Answer: The Peaks Flood Net parameter defines how long the traffic flood must remain above the configured rate in order to trigger the flood signature.

9. *What is a meta signature?*

   Answer: A meta signature is a signature that is composed of multiple individual signatures. After each of the component signatures trigger (within a specified time), the meta signature triggers.

10. *What are the three inspection types available when you are creating signatures with the Service FTP signature engine?*

    Answer: When creating signatures with the Service FTP signature engine, you can create signatures using the following inspection types: Invalid Address in PORT Command, Invalid Port in PORT Command, and PASV Port Spoof.

11. *What are the three inspection types available when you are creating signatures with the Service NTP signature engine?*

    Answer: When creating signatures with the Service NTP signature engine, you can create signatures using the following inspection types: Inspect NTP Packets, Is Invalid Data Packet, and Is Non NTP Traffic.

12. *What are the four inspection types available when you are creating signatures with the Service SNMP signature engine?*

    Answer: When creating signatures with the Service SNMP signature engine, you can create signatures using the following inspection types: Brute Force Inspection, Invalid Packet Inspection, Non-SNMP Traffic Inspection, and SNMP Traffic Inspection.

13. *Cisco IPS supports what three state machines in the State signature engine?*

    Answer: The State signature engine supports the following three state machines: Cisco Login, LPR Format String, and SMTP.

14. *What are the three String signature engines?*

    Answer: The three String signature engines are String ICMP, String TCP, and String UDP.

15. *Which parameter determines how many connections it takes for a sweep signature to trigger?*

    Answer: The Unique parameter determines how many connections it takes to trigger a sweep signature.

Chapter 7

"Do I Know This Already?" Quiz

1. B
2. D
3. B
4. D
5. C
6. A
7. B
8. C
9. B
10. C

Q&A

1. *Which two fields uniquely identify a signature?*

    Answer: Together, the Signature ID and SubSignature ID uniquely identify a signature.

2. *What does the Signature Fidelity Rating indicate?*

   Answer: The Signature Fidelity Rating indicates the likelihood that a signature will detect actual attack traffic without the sensor having specific knowledge about the target system's operating system and applications.

3. *What does the Alert Severity level indicate?*

   Answer: The Alert Severity level indicates the relative seriousness of the traffic that the signature is designed to detect.

4. *What values can you assign to the Event Count Key field?*

   Answer: You can assign the following values to the Event Count Key field: attacker address, attacker address and victim port, attacker and victim addresses, attacker and victim addresses and ports, or victim address.

5. *What does the Event Count Key specify?*

   Answer: The Event Count Key specifies which IP address and or ports are used when determining unique instances of a signature's traffic.

6. *What is the Meta Event Generator?*

   Answer: The Meta Event Generator enables you to create compound (meta) signatures based on multiple individual component signatures.

7. *When configuring a signature with the Meta signature engine, which engine-specific parameters do you need to specify?*

   Answer: When defining a signature with the Meta signature engine, you need to define the signatures that comprise the meta signature, the number of unique victims needed to trigger the signature, the IP addresses or ports used to determine unique signature instances, and potentially whether the order of the component signatures is important.

8. *Explain Application Policy Enforcement and identify which signature engines support this capability.*

   Answer: Application Policy Enforcement refers to the capability to provide deep-packet inspection for Layer 4 through Layer 7 for specific protocols, enabling a much more granular verification of your defined security policy. This functionality is provided by the AIC HTTP and AIC FTP signature engines.

9. *What are some of the checks provided by the AIC HTTP signature engine?*

   Answer: The AIC HTTP signature engine provides functionality such as detection of covert tunneling through port 80, ensuring RFC compliance of HTTP methods, filtering traffic based on specified MIME types, and controlling permitted traffic based on user-defined policies.

10. *Signature tuning involves changing which signature parameters?*

    Answer: Signature tuning involves changing the following signature parameters: engine-specific fields, event counter fields, and alert frequency fields.

11. *Signature tuning does not usually involve changing which signature parameters?*

    Answer: Signature tuning does not usually involve enabling or disabling a signature, changing the alert severity, or assigning a signature action.

12. *What are the four high-level steps involved in creating a custom signature?*

    Answer: When creating a custom signature, you need to perform the following tasks: choose a signature engine, verify existing functionality, define the signature parameters, and test the new signature's effectiveness.

13. *What are the factors that you need to consider when choosing a signature engine for a new signature?*

    Answer: When choosing a signature engine for a new signature, you need to consider the following factors about the traffic being detected: network protocol, target address, target port, attack type, inspection criteria.

14. *What is the difference between adding a new signature and creating a new signature by using the cloning functionality?*

    Answer: Using the cloning functionality enables you to initially populate a new signature with the values for an existing signature. This can save time when you are creating a new signature based on an existing signature.

15. *What regex matches the following patterns: ABXDF, ABXXDF,* and *ABD?*

    Answer: A regex that detects ABXDF, ABXXF, and ABD is AB[X]*D[F]*. The asterisk (*) enables those patterns to occur 0 or more times. With the patterns specified, you could have also specified [D]+ to allow one or more Ds, since it is not clear from the patterns if more than one D is allowed.

Chapter 8

"Do I Know This Already?" Quiz

1. E
2. D
3. B
4. C
5. D
6. B
7. D
8. A
9. B
10. A

Q&A

1. *What are the IDS evasion techniques?*

   Answer: The IDS evasion techniques are flooding, fragmentation, encryption, obfuscation, and TTL manipulation.

2. *What is the Target Value Rating?*

   Answer: The Target Value Rating enables you to assign an asset value rating to specific IP addresses on your network. This value is used when calculating the Risk Rating for a signature.

3. *What is event action override?*

   Answer: An event action override enables you to define specific actions that will be added to events when the Risk Rating for the event matches the values specified by the event action override. Each action can have its own event action override specification.

4. *How can fragmentation be used to evade detection?*

   Answer: By sending the attack traffic in overwriting fragments, an attacker can avoid detection if the IPS reassembles the traffic in the wrong order. However, overwriting fragments by themselves will usually generate an alert as well.

5. *Which common obfuscation techniques are used by attackers?*

   Answer: To avoid detection, attackers employ the following obfuscation techniques: using control characters, using the hex representation of characters, and using the Unicode representation of characters.

6. *What are some of the factors to consider when tuning your IPS sensors?*

   Answer: When tuning your IPS sensors, you need to consider factors such as the following: network topology, address range being monitored, statically configured IP addresses, DHCP address space, operating systems and applications running on your servers, and your security policy.

7. *What are the global IP log sensor parameters?*

   Answer: The global IP log sensor parameters are Max IP Log Packets, IP Log Time, Max IP Log Bytes, and the Maximum Open IP Log Files.

8. *What does it mean when the Max IP Log Bytes is configured to 0?*

   Answer: Configuring the Max IP Log Bytes parameter to 0 causes the sensor to capture IP log information without enforcing a maximum byte limit.

9. *What must you do to use the signatures that are based on the AIC HTTP signature engine?*

   Answer: To use the signatures that are based on the AIC HTTP signature engine, you must enable application policy enforcement for HTTP.

10. *When configuring fragment reassembly on your sensor, which operating systems can you use when specifying the IP reassembly mode?*

    Answer: When configuring the IP reassembly mode, you can choose one of the following operating systems: NT, Solaris, Linux, or BSD.

11. *What is the difference between strict stream reassembly and loose stream reassembly?*

    Answer: With loose stream reassembly, the sensor attempts to place the received packets in order (processing the packets even with gaps after a timeout period). For strict stream reassembly, however, the sensor does not process packet data after gaps (based on sequence number).

12. *What is an event action filter?*

    Answer: Event action filters enable you to configure your sensor to remove actions from events based on one or more criteria.

13. *Which parameters can you specify when defining an event action filter?*

    Answer: When defining an event action filter, you can specify the following parameters: Signature ID, SubSignature ID, Attacker Address, Attacker Port, Victim Address, Victim Port, Risk Rating, Actions to Subtract, and Stop on Match.

14. *What is the purpose of the Stop on Match parameter in the context of configuring an event action filter?*

    Answer: The Stop on Match parameter causes an event action filter to stop processing any other event filters when a match is found.

15. *Why is the order of event action filters important?*

    Answer: The order of event action filters is important because you can configure an event action filter to stop further processing of filters (using the Stop on Match parameter). Therefore, placing filters in the incorrect order may cause them to be skipped.

Chapter 9

"Do I Know This Already?" Quiz

1. C
2. B
3. E
4. D
5. C
6. A
7. C
8. C
9. E
10. C

Q&A

1. *What are the three inline response actions?*

   Answer: The three inline response actions are Deny Packet Inline, Deny Connection Inline, and Deny Attacker Inline.

2. *What traffic does the Deny Connection Inline response action prevent?*

   Answer: The Deny Connection Inline response action prevents traffic that matches the source IP address, source port, destination IP address, and destination port for the traffic that matches the traffic that triggered the signature.

3. *What are the three logging options available in Cisco IPS version 5.0?*

   Answer: Cisco IPS version 5.0 provides the following three logging actions: Log Attacker Packets, Log Pair Packets, and Log Victim Packets.

4. *What two blocking actions can you configure to occur when a signature triggers?*

   Answer: You can configure the following two blocking actions for signatures: Request Block Host and Request Block Connection.

5. *What types of devices can Cisco IPS sensors use as managed devices?*

   Answer: Cisco IPS sensors can use IOS routers, Catalyst 6000 switches, and PIX Firewalls (and ASAs) as managed devices.

6. *What must you configure when implementing IP blocking on an interface that already has an ACL applied to it?*

   Answer: To implement IP blocking on an interface that already has an ACL applied to it, you must configure a Pre-Block or Post-Block ACL (or both).

7. *When do you need to configure a Master Blocking Sensor?*

   Answer: When configuring multiple sensors to perform IP blocking, you need to configure a Master Blocking Sensor to coordinate IP blocking between the multiple sensors.

8. *How many sensors can initiate IP blocking on a single managed device?*

   Answer: Only one sensor can initiate IP blocking on a single managed device.

9. *How can you protect the traffic from critical systems from accidentally being blocked by the IP blocking functionality?*

   Answer: To prevent IP blocking from impacting traffic from critical systems, you can configure a never-block address for the critical system.

10. *What are the two steps for defining a router blocking device in IDM?*

    Answer: When defining a router blocking device using IDM, you need to first define the blocking device and then define and associate an interface to be used by the blocking device.

11. *Which response actions can be manually configured via the IDM interface?*

    Answer: Using the IDM interface, you can manually configure IP logging, host blocks, and network blocks.

12. *What response action uses the Simple Network Management Protocol (SNMP)?*

    Answer: The Request SNMP Trap action uses SNMP traps to indicate when a signature triggers.

13. *How long does the Deny Attacker Inline action block traffic from the attacker's IP address?*

    Answer: The Deny Attacker Inline action remains in effect for the length of time specified by the Deny Attacker Duration parameter.

14. *Which parameter determines how long IP blocking actions remain in effect?*

    Answer: The block action duration parameter specifies the length of time that IP blocking actions remain in effect.

15. *Which blocking mechanism enables you to restrict traffic between systems on the same network segment?*

    Answer: VACLs enable you to restrict traffic between systems on the same network segment.

Chapter 10

"Do I Know This Already?" Quiz

1. B
2. D
3. A
4. D
5. C
6. B
7. A
8. C
9. E
10. C

Q&A

1. *What are the five CiscoWorks user roles that are relevant to IDS MC and Security Monitor operations?*

   Answer: The CiscoWorks user roles that are relevant to IDS MC and Security Monitor are Help Desk, Approver, Network Operator, Network Administrator, and System Administrator.

2. *What is the minimum amount of RAM and virtual memory recommended for a Windows server running Security Monitor?*

   Answer: The minimum amount of RAM recommended for the Security Monitor server is 1 GB, and the recommended minimum amount of virtual memory is 2 GB.

3. *What is the minimum amount of RAM and virtual memory recommended for a Windows client system used to connect to Security Monitor?*

   Answer: The minimum amount of RAM recommended for a Security Monitor client is 256 MB, and the recommended minimum amount of virtual memory is 400 MB.

4. *Which two browsers are supported for use by the Windows-based Security Monitor client systems?*

   Answer: The supported browsers for Windows-based Security Monitor client systems are Internet Explorer 6.0 with Service Pack 1 and Netscape Navigator 7.1.

5. *What types of devices can you monitor with Security Monitor?*

   Answer: You can monitor the following devices with Security Monitor: Cisco IDS devices, Cisco IOS IDS/IPS devices, Cisco PIX/FWSM devices, Cisco Security Agent Management Centers, and Remote Cisco Security Monitors.

6. *What are the two major protocols used to communicate between Security Monitor and IDS/IPS devices?*

   Answer: To communicate with IDS/IPS devices, Security Monitor uses both RDEP and PostOffice protocols.

7. *Which parameters can you use to configure event rules?*

   Answer: When defining event rules, you can specify the following parameters: Originating Device, Originating Device Address, Attacker Address, Victim Address, Signature Name, Signature ID, and Severity.

8. *What actions can an event rule initiate?*

   Answer: An event rule can initiate any of the following actions: send a notification via e-mail, log a console notification event, and execute a script.

9. *What are the four tasks that you need to perform when adding an event rule?*

   Answer: When adding an event rule, you need assign a name to the event rule, define the event filter criteria, assign the event rule action, and define the event rule threshold and interval.

10. *What device statistical categories can you view using Security Monitor?*

    Answer: Using Security Monitor, you can view the following device statistical categories: Analysis Engine, Authentication, Event Server, Event Store, Host, Logger, Network Access Controller, Transaction Server, Transaction Source, and Web Server.

11. *What are your two options when deleting rows from the Event Viewer, and how are they different?*

    Answer: When deleting rows from the Event Viewer, you can choose Delete From This Grid (which removes the rows from only the current Event Viewer) or Delete From Database (which removes the events from all instances of the Event Viewer, both current and future).

12. *What is the default expansion boundary?*

    Answer: The default expansion boundary specifies the default number of columns in which the cells of a new event are expanded. By default, only the first field of an event is expanded.

13. *Which report template would you use to find out which systems have launched the most attacks against your network in a specified time period?*

    Answer: To identify the systems that have launched the most attacks against your network in a specified time period, you would use the IDS Top Sources Report template.

14. *What icons are used to indicate alarm severity?*

    Answer: The icons used to display alarm severity are a red exclamation point for high severity alerts, a yellow flag for medium severity alerts, and no icon for low severity alerts.

15. *What does the Blank Left check box do when configured as your cell preference?*

    Answer: The Blank Left check box causes the Event Viewer display to show blank columns (after the first row) in which multiple rows have the same value for that column.

Chapter 11

"Do I Know This Already?" Quiz

1. C
2. D
3. A
4. E
5. B
6. D
7. C
8. B
9. A
10. D

Q&A

1. *What two types of software releases does Cisco IPS provide?*

   Answer: Cisco IPS provides both service packs and signature updates.

2. *What are the major components identified in a Cisco IPS software filename?*

   Answer: Cisco IPS software filenames identify the following components: software type, Cisco IPS version, service pack level, signature version, and extension.

3. *What are the common extensions for Cisco IPS software files?*

   Answer: The common extensions for Cisco IPS software filenames are *rpm.pkg*, *readme* or *readme.txt*, and *zip*.

4. *Which sensor CLI command enables you to update the software on your sensor?*

   Answer: The **upgrade** CLI command enables you to update or upgrade the sensor software.

5. *When updating the sensor software via the CLI, which file transfer protocols can you use?*

   Answer: When upgrading sensor software via the CLI, you can use FTP, HTTP, HTTPS, and SCP.

6. *What are the two basic intervals for performing automatic software updates?*

   Answer: The two basic intervals for performing automatic software updates are hourly and weekly.

7. *Which sensor CLI command enables you to revert to a previous sensor software image?*

   Answer: The **downgrade** sensor CLI command causes the sensor to return to the previous software version.

8. *Which sensor CLI command enables you to re-image the sensor from the recovery partition?*

   Answer: The **recover application-partition** sensor CLI command enables you to re-image the sensor software from the recovery partition.

9. *What CLI command enables you to reset your sensor configuration to its default settings?*

   Answer: The **default service** sensor CLI command enables you to selectively reset portions of the sensor's configuration based on the service keyword you specify.

10. *What is the difference between restoring the default configuration by using the CLI and restoring it by using IDM?*

    Answer: When restoring the default configuration by using IDM, your only option is to restore all of the default settings. With the CLI, you can reset portions of the configuration individually based on a service keyword.

11. *Which sensor CLI command enables you to reboot the sensor, and which keyword causes it to shut down instead of reboot?*

    Answer: The **reset** command enables you to reboot the sensor. Adding the **powerdown** keyword to the **reset** command causes the sensor to shut down instead of reboot.

12. *Which keywords can you specify in conjunction with the **default service** CLI command?*

    Answer: The **default service** CLI command accepts the following keywords: **analysis-engine**, **authentication**, **event-action-rules**, **host**, **interface**, **logger**, **network-access**, **notification**, **signature-definition**, **ssh-known-hosts**, **trusted-certificates**, and **web-server**.

Chapter 12

"Do I Know This Already?" Quiz

1. C
2. E

3. B
4. B
5. A
6. E
7. D
8. C
9. D
10. B

Q&A

1. *Which sensor CLI command would you use to display the sensor uptime and previous sensor software version?*

   Answer: The **show version** sensor CLI command displays information such as the sensor uptime, current and previous software versions, and recovery partition software version.

2. *What are the sections of the sensor configuration file output?*

   Answer: The sensor configuration file output is divided into the following sections: analysis-engine, authentication, event-action-rules, host, interface, logger, network-access, notification, signature-definition, ssh-known-hosts, trusted-certificates, and web-server.

3. *What do the different sections of the sensor configuration file correspond to?*

   Answer: The different sections of the configuration file correspond to the options available for the sensor **service** CLI configuration command.

4. *Which sensor CLI command displays the Product Evolution Program (PEP) information for your sensor?*

   Answer: The **show inventory** sensor CLI command displays the PEP inventory information.

5. *What is the main difference between displaying sensor statistics via the CLI and displaying sensor statistics by using IDM?*

   Answer: In IDM a single command displays all of the sensor statistics, whereas in the CLI you can choose one of 14 statistical categories, which allows you to display only a limited amount of statistical information.

6. *In the sensor CLI, which command displays events, and which types of events can you display?*

   Answer: Using the **show events** CLI command, you can display alert, error, log, NAC, and status events.

7. *What are the three ways to specify the time frame for events when you use IDM to display events?*

   Answer: When using IDM to display events, you can specify the time frame for events by a number of minutes or hours in the past, events within a date range, and all events in the Event Store.

8. *Which sensor CLI command enables you to view the operational status of the interfaces on the sensor?*

   Answer: The **show interfaces** CLI command enables you to view the operational status of interfaces on the sensor.

9. *Which CLI command captures network traffic to a tcpdump capture file?*

   Answer: The **packet capture** CLI command captures network traffic to a tcpdump capture file.

10. *Which CLI command captures network traffic and displays it in the screen for all Gigabit Ethernet interfaces?*

    Answer: The **packet display GigabitEthernet** command displays capture traffic from all of the Gigabit Ethernet interfaces on the sensor.

11. *Which sensor CLI command displays a comprehensive list of status and system information about your sensor?*

    Answer: The **show tech-support** CLI command displays a comprehensive list of status and system information about your sensor.

12. *What does the diagnostic report in IDM provide?*

    Answer: The diagnostic report in IDM provides a comprehensive list of status and system information about your sensor. This is the same information as the CLI command **show tech-support**.

13. *Which* ***service notification*** *option removes the size limit on SNMP traps?*

    Answer: The **enable-detail-traps** option removes the size limits on traps sent, as opposed to those in sparse mode (fewer than 484 bytes).

14. *What does the* ***error-filter*** *option of the* ***service notification*** *command do?*

    Answer: The **error-filter** option of the **service notification** command enables you to determine which errors generate SNMP traps (options are **warning**, **error**, and **fatal**).

Chapter 13

"Do I Know This Already?" Quiz

1. C
2. B
3. D
4. A
5. C
6. B
7. C
8. D
9. A
10. B

Q&A

1. *What is the maximum amount of traffic that the IDSM-2 can monitor?*

   Answer: The IDSM-2 can monitor a maximum of 600 Mbps.

2. *How many interfaces does the IDSM-2 have, and what are their functions?*

   Answer: The IDSM-2 has four interfaces: two monitoring ports, one command and control port, and one TCP reset port.

3. *What version of CatOS must you run to use IDSM-2?*

   Answer: To use IDSM-2, you must use Catalyst OS 7.5(1) or later.

4. *What version of IOS must you run to use IDSM-2?*

   Answer: To use IDSM-2, you must use Cisco IOS Release 12.1(19)E or later.

5. *How does the operation of the IDSM-2 impact the switch's performance?*

   Answer: Since the IDSM-2 receives traffic directly from your switch's backplane, it does not impact the performance of the Catalyst switch.

6. *Which switch command do you use to verify the IDSM-2 status?*

   Answer: The **show module** switch command enables you to verify the status of the IDSM-2.

7. *Which two time-configuration options do you have for the IDSM-2?*

   Answer: The IDSM-2 can be configured to either use the switch's time or get time from an NTP server.

8. *If your IDSM-2 is in slot 6, what IOS switch command enables you to access the IDSM-2 CLI?*

   Answer: The **session slot 6 processor 1** command enables you to access the IDSM-2 in slot 6 on a switch running IOS.

9. *Which ports are monitoring ports on the IDSM-2?*

   Answer: Ports 7 and 8 are monitoring ports on the IDSM-2.

10. *Which port is the command and control port on the IDSM-2?*

    Answer: Port 2 is the command and control port on the IDSM-2.

11. *Which port is the TCP reset port on the IDSM-2?*

    Answer: Port 1 is the TCP reset port on the IDSM-2.

12. *What does a red status LED on the IDSM-2 indicate?*

    Answer: A red status LED on the IDSM-2 indicates that a diagnostic other than an individual port test has failed.

13. *What does an amber status LED on the IDSM-2 indicate?*

    Answer: An amber status LED on the IDSM-2 indicates that the IDSM is running through its boot and self-test diagnostic sequence, it is disabled, or it is shut down.

Chapter 14

"Do I Know This Already?" Quiz

1. B
2. B
3. E

4. C, D
5. D
6. C
7. D
8. B
9. D
10. A

Q&A

1. *How many NM-CIDS devices can you have in a single access router?*

   Answer: You can have only one NM-CIDS installed in each access router.

2. *How much traffic can an NM-CIDS monitor?*

   Answer: An NM-CIDS can examine a maximum of 45 Mbps of traffic.

3. *NM-CIDS is supported on which router platforms?*

   Answer: The NM-CIDS is supported on the following router platforms: 2600XM Series 2691, 3660, 3725, and 3745.

4. *What does the "EN" LED on the NM-CIDS front panel indicate?*

   Answer: The "EN" LED on the NM-CIDS front panel indicates that the NM-CIDS has passed the self-test and is available to the router.

5. *Which IOS forwarding features impact the operations of the NM-CIDS?*

   Answer: The following IOS forwarding features impact the operation of the NM-IDS: Access Control Lists (ACLs), encryption, Network Address Translation (NAT), IP multicast, UDP flooding, IP broadcast, and GRE tunnels.

6. *Are packets dropped by ACLs forwarded to NM-CIDS for examination?*

   Answer: Packets dropped by input ACLs are not forwarded to NM-CIDS (to avoid duplicate packets), but packets dropped by output ACLs are forwarded to NM-CIDS for examination.

7. *Which type of encrypted traffic can NM-CIDS analyze?*

   Answer: NM-CIDS can examine encrypted traffic for IPSec tunnels terminated on the router, but it cannot analyze encrypted traffic passing through the router.

8. *When you use inside NAT, which IP addresses are forwarded to NM-CIDS?*

Answer: With inside NAT, only the inside IP addresses are sent to the NM-CIDS.

9. *Which types of packets are not forwarded to NM-CIDS for analysis?*

Answer: Address Resolution Protocol (ARP) packets are not forwarded to NM-CIDS for examination. Packets in which an IP header field contains an error, such as an irregularity in a field, are not forwarded to NM-CIDS for examination.

10. *Should you run Cisco IOS-IDS in conjunction with NM-CIDS?*

Answer: No. Running Cisco IOS-IDS in conjunction with NM-CIDS can adversely impact the operation of your access router.

11. *What is the preferred clock configuration on NM-CIDS?*

Answer: The preferred clock configuration for NM-CIDS is to use NTP mode on the NM-CIDS.

12. *What is the least-preferred clock configuration on NM-CIDS?*

Answer: The least-preferred clock configuration on NM-CIDS is to run Cisco IOS clock mode on the NM-CIDS and set the Cisco IOS time zone to the local time zone.

13. *When you are using Cisco IOS clock mode, accurate NM-CIDS time depends on what factors?*

Answer: When you are using Cisco IOS clock mode, accurate NM-CIDS time depends on the router's local time, the router's time zone offset, and the router's summer time mode and offset, as well as the NM-CIDS's time zone offset and the NM-CIDS's summer time mode and offset.

14. *What are the two methods for accessing the console on the NM-CIDS?*

Answer: The Cisco IOS software performs a reverse Telnet that enables you to access the NM-CIDS console via Telnet or the **service-module** command.

15. *What is the formula for calculating the port number to Telnet to when you are accessing NM-CIDS via Telnet?*

Answer: The formula for calculating the Telnet port is (32 × *slot number*) + 2001.

16. *Which command enables you to shut down the NM-CIDS from the router CLI?*

Answer: The command to shut down the NM-CIDS from the router CLI is **service-module ids-sensor** *slot*/**0 shutdown**.

Chapter 15

"Do I Know This Already?" Quiz

1. A
2. C
3. B
4. A
5. B
6. B
7. D
8. A
9. C
10. B

Q&A

1. *What are the common locations to deploy inline IPS?*

   Answer: Some common locations at which to deploy inline IPS include between two routers, between a firewall and a router, between a switch and a router, and between a firewall and a router.

2. *When do you need to construct an artificial VLAN boundary to use inline IPS?*

   Answer: When dealing with devices (such as the MSFC and IDSM-2) that have virtual ports connected to your switch, you need to construct an artificial VLAN boundary to force traffic to go through the sensor for inline IPS to work correctly.

3. *What are the three network devices commonly used to capture network traffic for processing by your sensor?*

   Answer: The three devices commonly used to capture network traffic for processing by your sensor include hubs, network taps, and switches.

4. *Which three switch mechanisms can you use to mirror traffic to your IPS sensors?*

   Answer: To mirror traffic to your IPS sensors, you can use Switched Port Analyzer (SPAN), Remote Switched Port Analyzer (RSPAN), and VLAN Access Control Lists (VACLs).

5. *How is SPAN different from RSPAN?*

Answer: RSPAN enables you to capture traffic from ports that are located on multiple switches.

6. *Which IOS command is used to configure SPAN on your Catalyst 4500 and 6500 switches?*

Answer: Configuring SPAN (for IOS) involves using the **monitor session** command.

7. *What are the steps involved in configuring a VACL on IOS?*

Answer: The steps involved in configuring a VACL when running IOS are (1) configure the ACL, (2) create a VLAN access map, (3) match the ACL to the access map, (4) define the action for the access map, (5) apply the access map to VLANs, and (6) configure capture ports.

8. *Which command may impact your ability to capture traffic by using VACLs?*

Answer: If you apply the **ip inspect** IOS Firewall command on a specific VLAN interface, you cannot create a VACL for the same VLAN at the switch level.

9. *When do you need to use the **mls ip ids** IOS command?*

Answer: When you apply the **ip inspect** IOS Firewall command on a specific VLAN interface, you need to use the **mls ip ids** command to designate which traffic will be captured for your VACL.

10. *What steps are involved in using VACLs when you have the IOS Firewall on your Catalyst 6500 switch?*

Answer: The steps involved in using VACLs when you have the IOS Firewall on the Catalyst 6500 switch are (1) configure the extended ACL, (2) apply the ACL to an interface or VLAN, and (3) assign the capture port.

11. *Which IOS command do you use to enable trunking on a switch port?*

Answer: To enable trunking on a switch port (for IOS), you use the **switchport trunk encapsulation dot1q** interface configuration command.

12. *Which IOS command enables you to create a VLAN access map?*

Answer: To create a VLAN access map (when using IOS), you use the **vlan access-map** global configuration command.

13. *Which action must you specify (when using VLAN access maps) to enable the traffic to pass to the destination hosts and not be denied?*

Answer: When specifying actions for the VLAN access map, you must specify the **forward** keyword to enable the packets that match the access map to be passed to the destination hosts.

Index

A

B

D

E

F

G - H

I

K - L

M

N

O

P

R

S

T

U

V

W - Z

Cisco Press
Learning is serious business.
Invest wisely.

ciscopress.com

Cisco Press

FUNDAMENTALS SERIES

ESSENTIAL EXPLANATIONS AND SOLUTIONS

1-57870-168-6

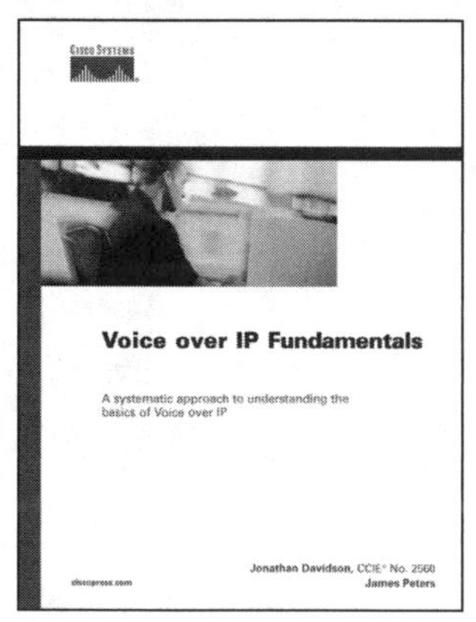

When you need an authoritative introduction to a key networking topic, **reach for a Cisco Press Fundamentals book**. Learn about network topologies, deployment concepts, protocols, and management techniques and **master essential networking concepts and solutions.**

Look for Fundamentals titles at your favorite bookseller

802.11 Wireless LAN Fundamentals
ISBN: 1-58705-077-3

Cisco CallManager Fundamentals: A Cisco AVVID Solution
ISBN: 1-58705-008-0

Cisco LAN Switching Fundamentals
ISBN: 1-58705-089-7

Cisco Unity Fundamentals
ISBN: 1-58705-098-6

Data Center Fundamentals
ISBN: 1-58705-023-4

IP Addressing Fundamentals
ISBN: 1-58705-067-6

IP Routing Fundamentals
ISBN: 1-57870-071-X

Network Security Fundamentals
ISBN: 1-58705-167-2

Storage Networking Fundamentals
ISBN: 1-58705-162-1

Voice over IP Fundamentals
ISBN: 1-57870-168-6

Coming in Fall 2005

Cisco CallManager Fundamentals: A Cisco AVVID Solution, Second Edition
ISBN: 1-58705-192-3

Visit **www.ciscopress.com/series** for details about the Fundamentals series and a complete list of titles.

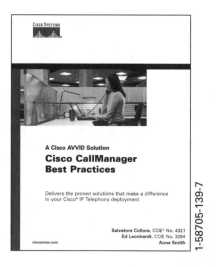

Cisco Press

NETWORK BUSINESS SERIES

JUSTIFY YOUR NETWORK INVESTMENT

Understand the business case for technologies with Network Business books from Cisco Press. Designed to support anyone **searching for optimal network systems,** Network Business titles help you justify your network investments.

1-58720-121-6

Look for Network Business titles at your favorite bookseller

The Business Case for E-Learning
Kelly / Nanjiani • ISBN: 1-58720-086-4

The Business Case for Network Security
Paquet / Saxe • ISBN: 1-58720-121-6

The Business Case for Storage Networks
Williams • ISBN: 1-58720-118-6

The Case for Virtual Business Processes
Young / Jude • ISBN: 1-58720-087-2

IP Telephony Unveiled
Brown • ISBN: 1-58720-075-9

Power Up Your Small-Medium Business
Aber • ISBN: 1-58705-135-4

The Road to IP Telephony
Carhee • ISBN: 1-58720-088-0

Taking Charge of Your VoIP Project
Walker / Hicks • ISBN: 1-58720-092-9

Coming in Fall 2005

The Business Case for Enterprise-Class Wireless LANs
Castaneda / Alasdair / Vinckier • ISBN: 1-58720-125-9

MPLS for Decision Makers
Sayeed / Morrow • ISBN: 1-58720-120-8

Network Business Series. **Justify Your Network Investment.**

Visit **www.ciscopress.com/netbus** for details about the Network Business series and a complete list of titles.

Learning is serious business. **Invest wisely.**

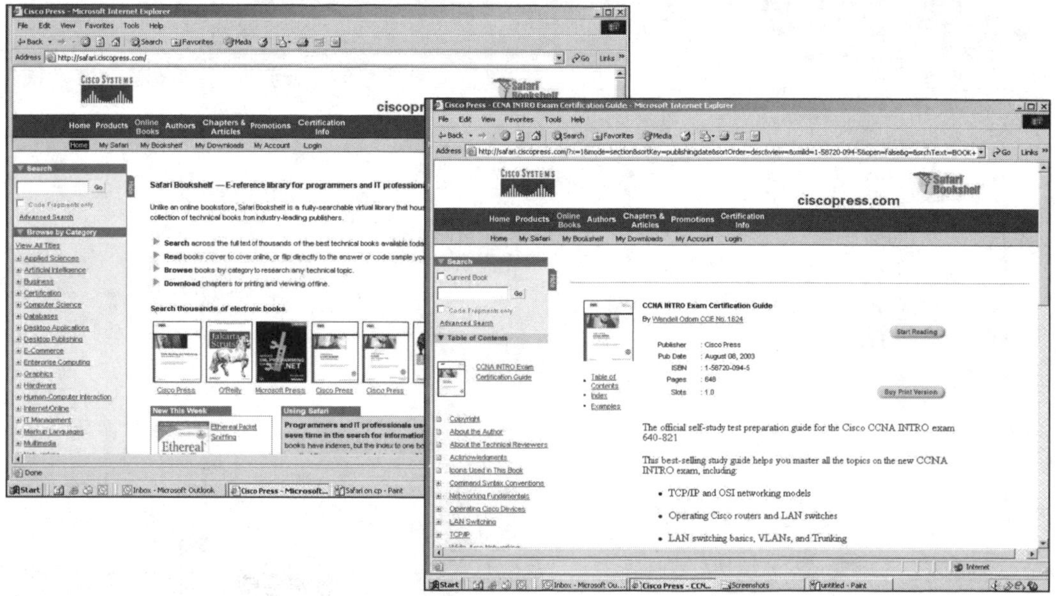